Public Records Online

The National Guide to Private & Government Online Sources of Public Records

Public Records Online

The National Guide to Private & Government Online Sources of Public Records

©1999 By Facts on Demand Press
4653 South Lakeshore Drive, Suite 3
Tempe, AZ 85282
(800) 929-3811

ISBN 1-889150-10-X
Cover Design by Robin Fox & Associates
Edited by Michael L. Sankey and James R. Flowers Jr.

Cataloging-in-Publication Data

350.714   **Sankey, Michael Lawrence, 1949, July 13-**
PUB   Public Records Online : the national guide to private &
              government online sources of public records / editors
              Michael L. Sankey and James R. Flowers Jr. – 2nd ed.
              Tempe, Ariz : Facts on Demand Press, ©1999.

              480 p. ; 7 x 10 in. – (Online ease)

              Summary: A national directory to government agencies
              and private companies that furnish online automated public
              record information, maintain proprietary public record
              databases, and offer CD-ROMs.

                  ISBN: 1-889150-10-X

                  1. Public records – Directories   2. Online catalogs –
              Directories I. Sankey, Michael Lawrence, 1949- II.
              Flowers, Jr., James Robert 1973-

                                        350.714_dc20

Contents

Forward

"Public Records" often conveys an image of a complex, almost mysterious source of information that is inaccessible, difficult to find, and likely to be of interest only to private investigators and reporters. This view could not be further from the *truth*!

Indeed, the use of public records is one of the fundamental principles of our democratic society.

Have you ever—

☑   obtained a driver's license?

☑   applied for a voter registration card?

☑   borrowed money for your business?

☑   set up a corporation?

☑   purchased a home or a vehicle?

☑   been involved in a court matter?

If so, you have not only become involved in the "public record information trail," but probably left an online trace.

The Doorway to Online Public Records

Today, there are literally thousands of public records and public information sources accessible by anyone with a computer and a modem. With this rapid growth, it becomes necessary for online users to understand what information is available and what information is not, to know how the information is gathered and stored, and to know who "has" the information and where it is located.

This book is your key to opening the door to online public records information. Whether you surf the World Wide Web, connect via modem to a court's computer system or utilize a company's dial-up system, *Public Records Online* is your gateway to the world of online records research.

The information you desire is probably out there somewhere. You need only find its particular "trail." To that end, this book has been designed to be your tour guide when traveling the trail of online information. With this book in hand, you've made the first step on your trip. Now, we suggest that you read the beginning chapters to fully prepare you for your journey. Once you're familiar with the cyber scenery, you'll need only to scan the chapters and sources to find the right "trail" to take.

Our goal is to provide you with a complete primer—so you can understand what you need, where it might be, and how to access that information like a pro.

Equipped with the information contained in these pages, you can find the facts, gain access to the information you need and even track your own "trail."

Good hunting!

A Public Records Primer

■■■ The Information Trail

Modern society has become extremely dependent on information. Information is, indeed, the life load of most business and personal interaction. Government and private industry require record keeping to regulate, license, and hire or fire. Individuals need public information for managing personal affairs and meeting one's responsibilities as citizens.

Nearly all individuals and business entities create a trail of information that is a history of daily life. You could say that the trail starts with a birth certificate, a Social Security Number or articles of incorporation. The trail extends past the death certificate or record of dissolution into, virtually, infinite time. These many records—some accessible, some accessible with restrictions, and some inaccessible—create and embellish an identity. Finding and staying "on the trail" of accurate discovery takes knowledge and persistence. Thankfully, computers and the Internet now allow us to examine these trails where they exist online.

Whether you are new at searching public records or not, there are a myriad of issues that must be considered and questions that must be answered if you are to become an effective, efficient user of the online tools now available.

Finding information is not an easy process; *Public Records Online* aims to make it so. *Public Records Online* reveals where records are kept, outlines access requirements and gives searching hints so that you can explore the depths of the public record industry.

■■■ Information – Public or Private?

Let's define the types of records held by government or by private industry from the viewpoint of a professional record searcher.

Definition of Public Records

Public records are records of **incidents** or **actions** filed or recorded with a government agency for the purpose of notifying others—the "public"—about the matter. These incidents can be court actions, filings at a county recorder's office, or marriages. The strict **definition** of **public records** is—

> *"Those records maintained by government agencies that are open without restriction to public inspection, either by statute or by tradition."*

The **deed** to your house recorded at the county recorder's office is a public record. It is a legal requirement that you "record it" with the county recorder. Anyone requiring details about your property may review or copy the documents. According to the above definition, if access to a record held by a government agency is restricted in some way, or if a private company holds the record, it is not a public record.

However, this does not take into consideration the **accessibility paradox**. For example, in some states access to a specific category of records is severely restricted, and consequently records are not public, while the very same category of records may be 100% open in other states. Among these categories are criminal histories, motor vehicle records, and worker's compensation records.

Just because records are maintained in a certain way in your state or county, do not assume that any other county or state does things the same way that you are used to.

Public Information

Your **telephone listing** in the phone book is an example of public information; it is not public record information. Public information is furnished freely by people and businesses. The use of public information contributes to the flow of commercial and private communications. While this is an important distinction, it is important to keep in mind certain pieces of information can appear both in public records and public information. **Therefore, this book makes an effort to cover many sources of public information as well as public records.**

Personal Information

Any information about a person or business that the person or business might consider private and confidential in nature, such as your **Social Security Number**, is personal information. Such information will remain private to a limited extent unless you disclose it to some outside entity that could make it public. **Often, personal information may be found in either public records or in public information.**

Many people confuse these three categories, lump them into one, and wonder how "Big Brother" accumulated so much information about them. The distinctions are important. Consider as fact that much of this information is given **willingly**.

There are two ways that personal information can enter the public domain— voluntary and statutory. In a **voluntary** transaction, you **share** personal information of your own free will. In a **statutory** transaction, you **disclose** personal information because the law **requires** it.

The increasing conflict between privacy advocates and commercial interests is driving legislation that would apply more and more **restrictions** on the **dissemination of personal information**—the same personal information which, in fact, is willingly shared by most people and companies in order to participate in our market economy. To view some excellent web sites dealing with privacy issues, turn to page 477-478..

The Benefits of Public Records

Public records are meant to be used for the benefit of society. Whether you are a business owner, a reporter, an investigator, or even a father trying to check on your daughter's first date, you can access public records to meet your needs. As a member of the public, you or someone in authority is entitled to review the public records held and established by government agencies.

Here are a few basic examples of the benefits of public records and public record searching:

For your family & friends
- learn whether your child's teacher is also a child molester;
- determine if your spouse is hiding assets;
- discover whether a long lost friend is alive and well.

For your business
- find out if a prospective employee is falsifying a resume;
- ascertain whether a potential business partner is legitimate;
- determine if a new client is a risk or is likely to pay promptly.

For your community
- learn if a bus driver has one or more DUIs;
- find out if a public official is also a convicted felon;
- determine whether 911 and the fire department know where you live.

Where to Obtain Public Records

There are two places you can find public records—

♦ at a **government agency**

♦ within the database of a **private company**

Government agencies keep or maintain records in a variety of ways. While many state agencies and highly populated county agencies are computerized, many still use microfiche, microfilm, and paper storage of files and indexes. Agencies that have converted to computer have not necessarily placed complete file records on their system; they are more apt to include only an index, pointer, or summary data to the computerized files. Again, be aware that certain records may be available without restriction in one state or county, yet be restricted in another.

Private enterprises develop their databases in one of two ways: they buy the records in bulk from government agencies, or they send personnel to the agencies to compile this information by using a copy machine or keying into a laptop computer. The database is then available for internal use, for resale online, or is accessible in some other form. This book contains profiles of the nation's elite private vendors of public record information.

Public records purchased and/or compiled by private companies for resale purposes must follow the same access and restriction regulations as the related government jurisdiction.

How to Obtain Public Records

Whether it is a public record or not, there are two ways to obtain a piece of information:

♦   Look it up or obtain it yourself;

♦   Have someone else look it up for you.

In the world of public records and public information, you may be able to look it up - or "do the search" - yourself under these circumstances:

1. The information is available in your own geographic area, and you can retrieve it in-person;

2. The information is available by written request;

3. The information can be obtained over the telephone;

4. **The information is available online or on CD-ROM.**

The purpose of this book is to examine #4 above. These pages reflect which government agencies offer online access to their public record databases, and which elite private companies compile and maintain their own proprietary databases of public record information.

Fees & Charges for Accessing Public Records

Public records are not necessarily free of charge—certainly not if they are maintained by private industry. Remember, public records are records of incidents or transactions. Among these incidents can be civil or criminal court actions, recordings, filings or occurrences such as speeding tickets or accidents. **It costs money** (time, salaries, supplies, etc.) **to record and track these events**. Common charges found at the government level for non-online access include copy fees (to make copies of the document), search fees (for clerical personnel to search for the record), and certification fees (to certify the document as being accurate and coming from the particular agency). These fees can vary from $.10 per page for copies to a $15.00 or more search fee for court personnel to do the actual look-up. Some government agencies will allow you to walk in and view records at no charge, many times from a "counter terminal." Yet fewer will release information over the phone without a fee.

Online access of government-held records usually costs less money on a per record basis than non-online. A key to purchasing public records online direct from some government agencies is the **frequency of usage requirements**. Many agencies require a minimum amount of requests per month or per session. Certainly, it does not make economic sense to spend a lot of money on programming and set-up fees if you intend on ordering only five records per month. You would be better off to do the search by more conventional methods (mail, visit in person) or hire a search vendor. Going direct online to the source is not always the least expensive option!

When private enterprise is in the business of maintaining a public records database, it generally does so to offer these records for resale based on volume of usage. However, government agencies have one price per category, regardless of the number of requests. One exception is when government agencies sell database lists in bulk, in which case prices are on a "per thousand records" basis.

Finding Online Sources of Public Records

Over the past twenty years, public record information has been compiled into vast computer databases. As mentioned previously, these databases are being compiled by the government and by private enterprise. Searching online for what you need is a challenge; you must utilize the appropriate online resource, gather the information you want, and use it effectively.

Government Online Sources

For the purposes of this book, the term "government" refers to every level of government from city/township through county/parish and state, up to and including the federal level. All levels collect data and, provided the law allows, will provide you with access.

Some agencies provide a higher degree of online access than others. Typical state government agencies offer extensive online access include secretary of state offices (corporate records, Uniform Commercial Code records) and department of motor vehicle offices (driver and vehicle records). Federal court records are virtually all online. However, finding real estate, assessor, civil and criminal information online directly from a local or state government agency can be difficult. A few states, among them Alabama, Maryland, Oregon, Utah, and Washington, provide their court records online to the public from a statewide system. A few scattered county courts that have implemented their own local remote online systems. And, the Internet is not a major component (see below).

Private Online Sources

Private companies have been more aggressive than government agencies in making this computerized information available online. By buying or collecting indexes from government agencies, private companies combine data in ways that are generally more useful to the public. For a fee, these companies make their information available to individuals and other companies through an **online** connection or on **CD-ROM**. Chances are if the information you seek is not available online from the government, it may be obtained from a private company.

There are over 150 private companies offering online access to their proprietary database(s) of public record information. The competition is overlapping due to an enormous amount of sharing and wholesaling of data between vendors and resellers.

The next chapter reviews 23 categories of public records and public information. The index pages found at the beginning of the Private Company Sources Section is a good place to start to find a particular company for a specific type or category of public record.

Searching on the Internet

Fact: there are less 1% of the 55 government locations in the US that offer free access to the public record and public information categories reviewed in this publication. But the good news is that there's a definite trend for more government sites to be placed on the 'Net. This is especially true for the records held by the secretary of state offices, and by the county recorder and assessor offices.

Needless to say, there are plenty of great government web sites offering valuable information, forms, explanations of policies and procedures, lists of locations of offices and personnel, etc. The Government Sources Section includes web addresses with the profiled agencies, when appropriate.

Probably the best trend involving the Internet and public record access is that the Internet is replacing many of the costly dial-up access systems. When fees or subscriptions are required to obtain a record, the switchover to the Internet has helped reduce or do away with the access fee charges

Also, the Web Section found on pages 460-478 presents over 100 very useful web sites oriented to finding information on people and businesses. For those interested in more details on the Internet, Facts on Demand Press's *Find It Online* is a recommended resource of not only 1,200 web sites, but also it is an in-depth Internet research guide.

Other Searching Methods

When all methods of online access fail for a particular record search, it may be necessary to physically retrieve the records you want. In such cases, utilizing a public record retriever, someone who is in the business of retrieving records and providing copies for a fee, is probably the most efficient method. In the event of such a necessity, refer to the Public Record Retriever Network (PRRN) found at www.brbpub.com. This web site lists reputable retrieval firms and contact information by state, county and type of record.

Online Information Categories

The following pages examine the 23 general categories of records considered either public record, public information or restricted information (such as credit reports). Although there are more general ways to categorize this information, such as court records instead of civil or criminal records, such generalizations tend to mask important variations in how certain type of records are subject to access restrictions.

In considering these alphabetically-listed summaries, keep the following points in mind:

- Very little of what you may perceive as government record information is truly open to the general public. Even the seemingly most harmless information is subject to restrictions somewhere in the US. On the other hand, what you may think of as highly confidential information is likely public information somewhere.

- Simply because your state or county has certain rules, regulations and practices regarding the accessibility and content of public records, does not mean that another state or county adheres to the same rules.

Addresses & Telephone Numbers

Basic locator information about a person or organization

This category of online information may be obtained from either government or private sources.

As the most elementary of public information categories, addresses and telephone numbers are no longer considered restricted information by most people. Even though you have an unlisted telephone number, it still can be found if you have listed that number on, for example, a voter registration card or magazine subscription form.

 To access this type of information from government agencies beyond a single look-up, you must normally purchase the data on magnetic tapes, disks, or cartridges, but rarely will you find it available online.

Some government agencies offer customized lists for sale. Typical types of agencies include those holding motor vehicle, voter registration, corporation filings, or business license records.

Private companies develop databases of addresses and telephone numbers in two ways. They may do this in the normal course of business, such as phone companies, credit card companies, or credit bureaus. Or, they may purchase and merge government and/or private company databases to create their own database. They then sell this "new database" online in a batch format, perhaps on CD-ROM. These companies must be careful to follow any restrictions that government agencies may place on the release of the data. For example, Experian collects information about vehicle owners to supply vehicle manufacturers with address and telephone data for vehicle recalls. Experian also sells information from that same database for direct marketing purposes, but only if state regulations permit.

The Internet is filled with people-finder sites, most search engines have one, which is an excellent way to do a national white-pages search.

Bankruptcy

Case information about people and businesses that have filed for protection under the bankruptcy laws of the United States.

Only federal courts handle bankruptcy cases.

The federal government offers online access to bankruptcy records through its PACER system. Turn to page 29 for details on this relatively inexpensive access mode.

Several private companies compile their own bankruptcy databases with names and dates - and make this information available online.

Corporate & Trade Names

Registration information about corporations and other business entities

Each state maintains basic information about businesses that register with them for the purpose of making their business name public and protecting its uniqueness. A number of states offer this information online. In fact, there is a trend for state agencies to use the **Internet** as a means to provide this information. BRB Publication's web site at www.brbpub.com is an excellent source to check for new sites.

As in many other categories, private companies purchase and/or compile a database for resale via online. Fees are based on volume.

The amount of business information collected by government agencies varies widely from state to state. Much, but not all, of the information collected by government agencies is open to public inspection. For example, annual reports are not available in some states, yet may be available for a fee in others.

Credit Information

Records derived from financial transactions of people or businesses

Private companies *maintain* this information; government agencies only *regulate* access.

Availability of certain credit information about individuals is restricted by law, such as the federal Fair Credit Reporting Act. Even more restrictive laws apply in many states. Major credit companies prefer to sell credit information online. High volume, ongoing requesters pay in the $2.00 per record range for credit reports.

Keep in mind that a business' credit information is not restricted by law and is fully open to anyone who requests (pays for) it.

Criminal History

Information about criminal activities, taken primarily from court records, are often combined into a central state database and always available from local courts

Criminal history information has probably the most diverse treatment of all categories of public record. All states maintain some type of central database of information about arrest and criminal court activity. 17 states consider this information open public record, while 6 states consider it closed. The remaining 28 states impose various types of restrictions on access to criminal information. In most states, criminal court information is openly accessible from the local court where the arraignments, preliminary hearings and/or trials took place. One open source of information about criminal activities is the newspaper, freely and openly accessible in any public library and searchable online through various services.

Two states (Colorado & Texas) offer the public online access to a central criminal record repository. However, a number of states maintain a central repository of court records open to online access, as you will find in the Government Sources Section.

Another source of criminal record information is from state corrections (prison) agencies. However, this information is not available online, and can be incomplete. The only truly national criminal database is the FBI's NCIC file, but it is not open to the public.

Very few private companies purchase local records to create databases for resale. Their "online access" of criminal record information usually involves 24-48 hour service, unless they are connected to one of the state court systems, such as in Washington or Maryland.

Driver & Vehicle Information

Information about licensed drivers and registered motor vehicles of all types

All states maintain records of drivers, vehicle registrations, and vehicle owners. Some private companies buy records from permitting states and offer commercial access to name, address and vehicle data.

Driver history, accident reports, and vehicle information, which traditionally have been open public record in most states, are (for now) subject to federal legislation. The Drivers' Privacy Protection Act (DPPA) required each state to impose at least a minimum set of restrictions on access to that information.

All states offer an electronic means to obtain some type of motor vehicle information, usually by online access or magnetic tape. 36 states offer online retrieval to approved accounts. Access is not always immediate; some states require a wait of up to four hours before retrieving the data. In many instances, a minimum order requirement must be agreed to before an online access account is permitted.

Driver history (MVR) information can be ordered online from many search firms throughout the country. However, only a handful of companies have the ability to directly access multiple state DMVs. Most public record search firms and specialty firms buy MVRs from one of these companies and then resell them to clients.

Vessel title and registration information is usually maintained by the same state agency responsible for vehicle records, but not as often is it found online. Some of these state agencies also hold lien information on vessels, but usually lien records should be searched where Uniform Commercial Code recordings are maintained. **Aviation** records must be searched at the federal level or through private companies.

Education & Employment

Information about an individual's schooling, training, education, and jobs

Learning institutions maintain their own records of attendance, completion, and degree/certification granted. Employers will confirm certain information about former employees.

Education and employment information is an example of private information that becomes public by voluntary disclosure. As part of your credit record, this information would be considered restricted. However if, for example, you disclose this information to *Who's Who*, it becomes public information.

Environmental

Information about hazards to the environment

There is little tradition and less consistency in laws regarding how open or restricted information is at the state and local (recorder's office) levels.

Most information about hazardous materials, soil composition, and even OSHA inspection reports is, in fact, public record.

Finding online access to this type of information at the government level is difficult. However, a few private companies compile and maintain databases of environmental information.

Legislation & Regulations

Laws and regulations at all levels of government

This information is always open public record.

Each state's legislative branch make this information available, although records older than 2 years are harder to find. This category of information is increasingly finding its way onto **Internet** sites maintained by the state legislatures.

A number of private companies market a customized search-and-retrieval product of pending legislation and regulatory information. Access includes online and CD-ROM products.

Licenses, Registrations & Permits

Registration of individuals and businesses with government agencies related to specific professions, businesses, or activities

Basic information about registrants, including address and status, is generally public record from state agencies and licensing boards. Some boards consider that their data should not be open to public inspection. Others boards will sell their entire database to commercial marketing vendors.

Also, there is significant variation in the extent of information that each state or local agency will disclose from a particular record. Some will release addresses, phone numbers, present place of employment, and current status. Other agencies will only give you "yes or no" responses.

To find this information online or on CD-ROM, you must turn to the private sector. A good example of a vendor with this type of information available is Merlin Information Systems or BRB Publication's *The Sourcebook of State Public Records* (call 800-929-3811 for information) wherein over 5,000 state agencies are listed.

Litigation & Civil Judgments

Information about civil litigation in municipal, state, or federal courts

Actions under federal laws are found at US District Courts. Actions under state laws are found within the state court system at the county level. Municipalities also have courts where information may be kept. Litigation and judgment information is often collected by commercial database vendors.

The traditional general rule says that what goes on in a courtroom is public record. However, some types of court proceedings, such as juvenile cases, are closed. Judges may close or seal any portion of any case record at their discretion.

As with criminal information, there are a few state court systems and some local courts that offer online access. There are a number of private companies who create databases of this information for online access by their clients. These companies have the option of purchasing a tape from the government agency or sending personnel with laptop computers to manually gather case information at the court house.

Medical

Information about an individual's medical status and history

Medical records are summarized in various repositories that are accessible only to authorized insurance, legal, and other private company personnel.

Medical information is neither public information nor closed record. Like credit information, it is not meant to be shared with anyone, unless you give authorization. Only those who have the proper authority are able to access the information online.

Military Service

Information about individuals who are or were in military service

Each military branch maintains its own records. Much of this, such as years of service and rank, is open public record. However, some details in the file of an individual may be subject to access restrictions—approval by the subject may be required. For further information regarding this subject, the *Armed Forces Locator Guide* by MIE Publishing (800-937-2133) is recommended.

Real Estate & Assessor

Information about the ownership, transfer, value and mortgaging of real property

The county (or parish) recorder's office is the legal source. Traditionally, real estate records are public so that everyone can know who owns any given property. Liens on real estate must be public record so potential buyers know all the facts about whether the title is clear.

The real estate industry needs quick access to this information. Most communities have a local multiple listing service (MLS) showing records of sales. This is generally available online. Many title companies and abstract companies will buy a "plant" from the local recorder's office. This is usually in a microfiche or microfilm format and is updated on a regular basis.

A number of private companies purchase entire county record files and create their own database for commercial purposes. This information is generally sold online or in some form of bulk medium such as magnetic tape.

SEC & Other Financial Data

Information on publicly and privately held businesses

The Securities and Exchange Commission is the public repository for information about publicly held companies, which are required to share their material facts with existing and prospective stockholders. The common online access mode is through the government's EDGAR system (see page 40 for further details).

Non-publicly held companies, on the other hand, are not required to be "open" to public scrutiny, so their financial information is public information only to the extent that the company itself decides to disclose it.

There are private companies who compile this information and make it available online, on CD-ROM, or in book format.

Social Security Numbers

The most extensively used individual identifier in the US

There is a persistent myth that a Social Security Number (SSN) is private information. The truth is that individuals gave up the privacy of that number by writing it on a voter registration form, using it on a driver's license number (in eight states), or by any of a myriad of other voluntary disclosures made over the years. It is probable that one can find the Social Security Number of anyone (along with at least an approximate birth date) with ease.

SSNs find their way into many databases maintained by private sources, including credit bureaus, marketing list compilers, voter registration list compilers, and some motor vehicle record compilers.

Finding this data online is not a problem although some privacy advocates would have us turn back the clock to 1936 by deleting SSN information from the public record. The fact is, right or wrong, that the SSN is a common identifier and found in many public accessible records.

Tax & Other Involuntary Liens

Liens filed by the government and others against individuals and businesses without their consent

Liens are filed, according to a state's law, either at a state agency or county recorder's office. Some states require filing at both locations.

Mortgages and UCC liens are voluntary liens accepted by a borrower in order to obtain financing. Involuntary liens, on the other hand, arise by action of law against a person or business owing a debt that would otherwise be unsecured. The federal and state governments file tax liens when there is a failure to pay income or withholding taxes. Another example: a contractor can file a mechanic's lien to be first in line to receive payment for materials used on a job.

States that offer online access to corporate records generally make their lien records available online also. While there is less likelihood of finding this information online at the local government level, a limited number of local recorder offices make the information available online.

Liens are a very competitive arena for private companies offering online access. There are several nationwide databases available as well as a number of strong regionally-oriented companies who offer this information online to their clientele.

Tenant

History information about people who rent

This, like credit history, is another example of a combination of public and proprietary information collected by private businesses for the purpose of tracking an element of personal life important to an industry—in this case the housing rental industry.

These records are often shared within the industry on a restricted online basis according to disclosure rules set by the companies themselves.

Trademarks, Patents & Copyrights

Protection of intellectual property and proprietary ideas

The state agency controlling trademarks and service marks is generally at the same location as corporate records. The Lanham Act provides for a trademark registration system mandated by the federal government. The federal government controls copyrights and patents. Several private companies maintain online searchable databases of trademarks, service marks, and patents.

The filing for public review of trademarks and patents is designed to protect these assets from copying.

Uniform Commercial Code

Transactions that are secured by personal property

As with tax liens, Uniform Commercial Code (UCC) recordings are filed either at the state or county level, according to each state's law. Some states require dual filing.

UCC filings are to personal property what mortgages are to real property. They are in the category of financial records that must be fully open to public scrutiny so potential lenders are given notice about which assets of the borrower have been pledged.

UCC filings can be found online from a number of state agencies, and access via the Internet is increasing.

A number of private companies have created their own databases for commercial resale. As with tax liens, this is a very competitive arena. There are nationwide database companies available as well as a number of strong, regionally-oriented companies who offer this information online to their clientele.

Vital Records

Birth, death, marriage, and divorce information

Most states have central repositories for each of these four types of vital records. In some states divorce records are maintained at the county level, but the state maintains a searchable index.

State regulations vary regarding which of these four types of records are public and which are subject to restrictions. States impose approval or use restrictions similar to those imposed by schools with regard to access to student transcript information.

Finding online access to vital records from either government agencies or private companies is rare. Some agencies do offer access to an index, but the documents themselves are not available online.

Voter Registration

Information on the application to become a registered voter

Voter registration applications are maintained at the local level. Generally, they are a public record accessible by anyone. This makes them an important source, for instance, of the real signature of a person or of an **unlisted** telephone number. At the state level, many states aggregate the local information into a central database.

Access to many state-held databases is restricted to non-commercial use. However, one third of the states have set no restrictions on the use of voter registration records, including information gathered that otherwise would be considered private such as a Social Security Number or unlisted telephone number.

Several privates companies purchase databases from states wherein voter registration information is "open," and make that data available online. Profiles of these companies are included in this book.

Workers' Compensation Records

Work related injury claims and case history

Each state has a board or commission responsible for these records.

Access to this information is generally restricted to those who have a direct interest in the case. Due to federal legislation, only seven states now consider their Workers Compensation records to be unrestricted open public record. Few offer the information online.

Several companies purchase and combine entire state databases to create a proprietary database for resale, which may be available online.

Searching Hints—Court Records

What You Will Find in the Courthouse

Before signing up for every court online access available, you should be familiar with certain court basics! Whether it is filed in federal, state, or municipal court, each case is subject to a similar processing. Determining the exact location of case records depends upon: (1) the county where the subject is located; (2) the specific court structure of that state or district; and (3) the types of cases.

Criminal

In **criminal cases**, the plaintiff is a government jurisdiction, which brings the action against the defendant under one of its statutes. Criminal cases are categorized as *felonies* or *misdemeanors*. A general rule to distinguish these is: usually a felony may involve a jail term of one year or more, whereas a misdemeanor may only involve a monetary fine and/or short jail terms.

Civil

A **civil case** usually commences when plaintiffs file a *complaint* against defendants with a court. The defendants respond to the complaint with an *answer*. After this initial round, literally hundreds of activities may occur before the court issues a judgment. These activities can include revised complaints and their answers, motions of various kinds, and discovery proceedings including depositions to establish the documentation and facts involved in the case. All of these activities are listed on a **docket sheet**.

Civil cases are categorized as *tort*, *contract*, and *real property* rights. Torts include but are not limited to *automobile accidents, medical malpractice and product liability* cases. Actions for small money damages, typically under $3,000, are known as *small claims*.

Other

Other types of cases that frequently are handled by separate courts or divisions of courts include *juvenile*, *domestic relations*, and *probate* (wills and estates).

In **bankruptcy cases**, there is neither defendant nor plaintiff. Instead, the debtor files voluntarily for bankruptcy protection against creditors, or the creditors file against the debtor in order to force that debtor into involuntary bankruptcy.

State Court Structure

The vast majority of court cases in the United States are filed within the state court system at the county level. The secret to determining where a state court case and its records are located is to understand how the court system is structured within each state. The general structure of all states' court systems has four levels:

- Limited Jurisdiction Courts
- General Jurisdiction Courts
- Intermediate Appellate Courts
- Appellate Courts

Most cases originate in general or limited jurisdiction courts. General jurisdiction courts usually handle a full range of civil and criminal litigation. These courts usually handle felonies and larger civil cases.

Limited Jurisdiction courts come in two varieties. First, many limited jurisdiction courts handle smaller civil claims (usually $10,000 or less), misdemeanors, and pretrial hearing for felonies. Second, some of these courts, sometimes called special jurisdiction courts, are limited to one type of litigation, such as Court of Claims in New York, which only handles liability cases against the state.

The two highest court levels hear cases on appeal from the trial courts only. Opinions of these appellate courts are of interest primarily to attorneys who need legal precedent information for new cases. Once a lower court issues a judgment, either party may appeal the ruling to an appellate division or court. In the case of a monetary decision or award, the winning side can usually file the judgment as a lien with the county recorder. The appellate division usually deals only with the legal issues and not with the facts of the case.

Some states, Iowa for instance, have consolidated their general and limited jurisdiction court structure into one combined court system. In other states, there is a further distinction between state-supported courts and municipal courts. In New York, for example, nearly 15,000 justice courts handle local ordinance and traffic violations, including DWI cases.

Searching State Courts Online

Online searching is generally limited to a copy of the courts' docket sheets. The docket sheet contains the basics of the case: name of court, including location (division) and the judge assigned; case number and case name; names of all plaintiffs and defendants/debtors; names and addresses of attorneys; and nature and cause of action. Information from cover sheets and from documents filed as a case goes forward is also recorded on the docket sheet. While docket sheets differ somewhat in format, basic information contained on a docket sheet is consistent from court to court. Docket sheets are used in both the state court systems and the federal court system.

Most courts are computerized in-house, which means that the docket sheet data is entered into a computer system of the courthouse itself. Checking a courthouse's computer index is the quickest way to find if case records exist online.

Not a large number of state courts provide electronic access to their records. In Alabama, Maryland, Oregon, and Washington where "statewide" online systems are available, you still need to understand (1) the court structure in that state, (2) which particular courts are included in their online system, and (3) what types of cases are included. Without proper consideration of these variables, these online systems are subject to misuse, which can lead to disastrous consequences like failing to discover that an applicant for a security guard position is a convicted burglar.

Maryland has a two-tiered structure with higher courts named "Circuit Courts" and the lower courts called "District Courts," but their online system includes the District Courts and *only 3 Circuit Courts*. Since the courts with online records do handle most preliminary hearing and some felony cases, it has been suggested that a name search in the online system is adequate to discover all criminal cases. However, it is possible for a felony case to be brought before a higher court only. A full criminal search of courts in Maryland would require manual searches of all the Circuit Courts as well as through the District Court online system.

If Records Are Not Available Online

If you need copies of case records, court personnel may make copies for you for a fee, or you may be able to make copies yourself if the court allows. Also, court personnel may certify the document for you for a fee. Perhaps due to a shortage of staff or fear of litigation, some courts that previously would conduct searches of criminal records on behalf of the public are no longer making that service available. Typically, these courts do one of two things. In some states, such as Kentucky, the courts refer the searcher to a state agency that maintains a database combining individual court records (which may not be very current). In other states, such as Nebraska, the courts simply refuse to conduct searches, leaving the searcher with no choice but to use a local retrieval firm or other individual to conduct the search on his or her behalf.

Internet Access to State Court Systems

Although there are a handful of state (local county) courts profiled in this book that provide Internet access to case index information, most sites charge fees. However, there is a growing wealth of information available on the Internet about state court structure and rules, as well as higher court opinions. A good place to start is www.ncsc.dni.us/court/sites/courts.htm. This site is maintained by the National Center for State Courts (NCSC) and includes Internet addresses for state-level information and for many local court locations as well. NCSC publications are the definitive source of information about the structure of state court systems and for state court statistics.

A second locator site is the Villanova Center for Information Law and Technology at `http://ming.law.vill.edu/State-Ct/index.html`.

There is an excellent list available of courts with records accessible via the Internet. This list is maintained on a web page found at `www.brbpub.com`.

Federal Court Structure

The Federal Court system includes three levels of courts, plus some special courts, described as follows—

Supreme Court of the United States

The Supreme Court of the United States is the court of last resort in the United States. It is located in Washington, DC, where it hears appeals from the United States Courts of Appeals and from the highest courts of each state.

United States Court of Appeals

The United States Court of Appeals consists of thirteen appellate courts which hear appeals of verdicts from the courts of general jurisdiction. They are designated as follows:

The Federal Circuit Court of Appeals hears appeals from the US Claims Court and the US Court of International Trade. It is located in Washington, DC.

The District of Columbia Circuit Court of Appeals hears appeals from the district courts in Washington, DC as well as from the Tax Court.

Eleven geographic **Courts of Appeals**—each of these appeal courts covers a designated number of states and territories. The chart on the pages 31-32 lists the circuit numbers (1 through 11) and location of the Court of Appeals for each state.

United States District Courts

The United States District Courts are the courts of general jurisdiction, or trial courts, and are subdivided into two categories—

The District Courts are courts of general jurisdiction, or trial courts, for federal matters, excluding bankruptcy. Essentially, this means they hear cases involving federal law and cases where there is diversity of citizenship. Both **civil** and **criminal** cases come before these courts.

The Bankruptcy Courts generally follow the same geographic boundaries as the US District Courts. There is at least one bankruptcy court for each state; within a state there may be one or more judicial districts and within a judicial district there may be more than one location (division) where the courts hear cases. While civil lawsuits may be filed in either state or federal courts depending upon the applicable law, all bankruptcy actions are filed with the US Bankruptcy Courts.

Special Courts/Separate Courts

The Special Courts/Separate Courts have been created to hear cases or appeals for certain areas of litigation demanding special expertise. Examples include the US Tax Court, the Court of International Trade and the US Claims Court.

How Federal Trial Courts are Organized

At the federal level, all cases involve federal or US constitutional law or interstate commerce. The task of locating the right court is seemingly simplified by the nature of the federal system—

- ◆ All court locations are based upon the plaintiff's county of domicile.

- ◆ All civil and criminal cases go to the US District Courts.

- ◆ All bankruptcy cases go to the US Bankruptcy Courts.

However, a plaintiff or defendant may have cases in any of the 500 court locations, so it is really not all that simple to find them.

There is at least one District and one Bankruptcy Court in each state. In many states there is more than one court, often divided further into judicial districts— e.g., the State of New York consists of four judicial districts, the Northern, Southern, Eastern and Western. Further, many judicial districts contain more than one court location (usually called a division).

The Bankruptcy Courts generally use the same hearing locations as the District Courts. If court locations differ, the usual variance is to have fewer Bankruptcy Court locations.

▬▬▬ How Federal Trial Courts are Organized

Case Numbering

When a case is filed with a federal court, a case number is assigned. This is the primary indexing method. Therefore, in searching for case records, you will need to know or find the applicable case number. If you have the number in good form already, your search should be fast and reasonably inexpensive.

You should be aware that case numbering procedures are not consistent throughout the Federal Court system: one judicial district may assign numbers by district while another may assign numbers by location (division) within the judicial district or by judge. Remember that case numbers appearing in legal text citations may not be adequate for searching unless they appear in the proper form for the particular court.

All the basic civil case information that is entered onto docket sheets, and into computerized systems like PACER (see on next page), starts with standard form JS-44, the Civil Cover Sheet, or the equivalent.

Docket Sheet

As in the state court system, information from cover sheets, and from documents filed as a case goes forward, is recorded on the **docket sheet**, which then contains the case history from initial filing to its current status. While docket sheets differ somewhat in format, the basic information contained on a docket sheet is consistent from court to court. As noted earlier in the state court section, all docket sheets contain:

- ♦ Name of court, including location (division) and the judge assigned;

- ♦ Case number and case name;

- ♦ Names of all plaintiffs and defendants/debtors;

- ♦ Names and addresses of attorneys for the plaintiff or debtor;

- ♦ Nature and cause (e.g., US civil statute) of action;

- ♦ Listing of documents filed in the case, including docket entry number, the date and a short description (e.g., 12-2-92, #1, Complaint).

Assignment of Cases

Traditionally, cases were assigned within a district by county. Although this is still true in most states, the introduction of computer systems to track dockets has led to a more flexible approach to case assignment, as is the case in Minnesota and Connecticut. Rather than blindly assigning all cases from a county to one judge, their districts are using random numbers and other logical methods to balance caseloads among their judges.

This trend may appear to confuse the case search process. Actually, the only problem that the searcher may face is to figure out where the case records themselves are located. Finding cases has become significantly easier with the wide availability of PACER from remote access and on-site terminals in each court location with the same district-wide information base.

Computerization

Traditionally, cases were assigned within a district by county. Although this is still true in most states, the introduction of computer systems to track dockets has led to a more flexible approach to case assignment, as is the case in Minnesota and Connecticut. Rather than blindly assigning all cases from a county to one judge, their districts are using random numbers and other logical methods to balance caseloads among their judges.

This trend may appear to confuse the case search process. Actually, the only problem that the searcher may face is to figure out where the case records themselves are located. Finding cases has become significantly easier with the wide availability of PACER from remote access and on-site terminals in each court location with the same district-wide information base.

Computerized Indexes are Available

Computerized courts generally index each case record by the names of some or all the parties to the case—the plaintiffs and defendants (debtors and creditors in Bankruptcy Court) as well as by case number. Therefore, when you search by name you will first receive a listing of all cases in which the name appears, both as plaintiff and defendant.

Nationwide Programs for Electronic Access to Federal Courts

Numerous programs have been developed for electronic access to Federal Court records. In recent years the Administrative Office of the United States Courts in Washington, DC has developed three innovative public access programs: VCIS, PACER, and ABBS. The most useful program for online searching is PACER.

PACER

PACER, the acronym for **P**ublic **A**ccess to **E**lectronic **C**ourt **R**ecords, provides docket information online for open cases at **all US Bankruptcy courts** and **most US District courts**. Cases for the US Court of Federal Claims are also available. The user fee is $.60 per minute. Each court controls its own computer system and case information database; therefore, there are some variations among jurisdictions as to the information offered.

A new PACER service is being developed. PACER-Net is designed as a PACER access mode on the Internet. User fees still apply. At press time, PACER-Net is a pilot project with less than 1% of the courts involved.

A continuing problem with PACER is that each court determines when records will be purged and how records will be indexed, leaving you to guess how a name is spelled or abbreviated and how much information about closed cases your search will uncover. A PACER search for anything but open cases **cannot** take the place of a full seven-year search of the federal court records available by written request from the court itself or through a local document retrieval company. Many districts report that they have closed records back a number of years, but at the same time indicate they purge docket items every six months.

Sign-up and technical support is handled at the PACER Service Center in San Antonio, Texas (800) 676-6856. You can sign up for all or multiple districts at once. In many judicial districts, when you sign up for PACER access, you will receive a PACER Primer that has been customized for each district. The primer contains a summary of how to access PACER, how to select cases, how to read case numbers and docket sheets, some searching tips, who to call for problem resolution, and district specific program variations.

Other Online Systems

Before the ascendancy of PACER, some courts had developed their own electronic access systems. They have names like NIBS, JAMS and BANCAP. All but a few of these are now available for sign-up at the PACER Center in San Antonio.

A new trend for some federal courts is to place case index information on the Internet for no charge. The seven courts listed below are examples:

♦ AZ - Bankruptcy Court (limited data) - http://ecf.azb.uscourts.gov

♦   CA - Southern District - www.casd.uscourts.gov/html/fileroom.htm

♦   GA - Northern District -http://ecf.ganb.uscourts.gov

♦   ID - District and Bankruptcy - www.id.uscourts.gov/doc.htm

♦   NY - Bankruptcy, Southern District - www.nysb.uscourts.gov

♦   OH - Northern District -www.ohnd.uscourts.gov

♦   VA - Eastern District - http://ecf.vaeb.uscourts.gov

Another system worth mentioning is **VCIS** (Voice Case Information System). Nearly all of the US Bankruptcy Court judicial districts provide **VCIS**, a means of accessing information regarding open bankruptcy cases by merely using a touch-tone telephone. There is no charge. Individual names are entered last name first with as much of the first name as you wish to include. For example, Carl R. Ernst could be entered as ERNSTC or ERNSTCARL. Do not enter the middle initial. Business names are entered as they are written, without blanks. BRB Publications has books available with all the VCIS numbers listed (800-929-3811).

Federal Records Centers and the National Archives

After a federal case is closed, the documents are held by Federal Courts themselves for a number of years, then stored at a designated Federal Records Center (FRC). After 20 to 30 years, the records are then transferred from the FRC to the regional archives offices of the National Archives and Records Administration (NARA). The length of time between a case being closed and its being moved to an FRC varies widely by district. Each court has its own transfer cycle and determines access procedures to its case records, even after they have been sent to the FRC.

When case records are sent to an FRC, the boxes of records are assigned accession, location and box numbers. These numbers, which are called case locator information, **must be obtained from the originating court in order to retrieve**

documents from the FRC. Some courts will provide such information over the telephone, but others require a written request. This information is now available on PACER in certain judicial districts. The Federal Records Center for each state is listed as follows:

State	Circuit	Appeals Court	Federal Records Center
AK	9	San Francisco, CA	Anchorage (Some temporary storage in Seattle)
AL	11	Atlanta, GA	Atlanta
AR	8	St. Louis, MO	Fort Worth
AZ	9	San Francisco, CA	Los Angeles
CA	9	San Francisco, CA	Los Angeles (Central & Southern) San Francisco (Eastern & Northern)
CO	10	Denver, CO	Denver
CT	2	New York, NY	Boston
DC		Washington, DC	Washington, DC
DE	3	Philadelphia, PA	Philadelphia
FL	11	Atlanta, GA	Atlanta
GA	11	Atlanta, GA	Atlanta
GU	9	San Francisco, CA	San Francisco
HI	9	San Francisco, CA	San Francisco
IA	8	St. Louis, MO	Kansas City, MO
ID	9	San Francisco, CA	Seattle
IL	7	Chicago, IL	Chicago
IN	7	Chicago, IL	Chicago
KS	10	Denver, CO	Kansas City, MO
KY	6	Cincinnati, OH	Atlanta
LA	5	New Orleans, LA	Fort Worth
MA	1	Boston, MA	Boston
MD	4	Richmond, VA	Philadelphia
ME	1	Boston, MA	Boston
MI	6	Cincinnati, OH	Chicago
MN	8	St. Louis, MO	Chicago
MO	8	St. Louis, MO	Kansas City, MO
MS	5	New Orleans, LA	Atlanta

State	Circuit	Appeals Court	Federal Records Center
MT	9	San Francisco, CA	Denver
NC	4	Richmond, VA	Atlanta
ND	8	St. Louis, MO	Denver
NE	8	St. Louis, MO	Kansas City, MO
NH	1	Boston, MA	Boston
NJ	3	Philadelphia, PA	New York
NM	10	Denver, CO	Denver
NV	9	San Francisco, CA	Los Angeles (Clark County) San Francisco (Other counties)
NY	2	New York, NY	New York
OH	6	Cincinnati, OH	Chicago, Dayton (Some bankruptcy)
OK	10	Denver, CO	Fort Worth
OR	9	San Francisco, CA	Seattle
PA	3	Philadelphia, PA	Philadelphia
PR	1	Boston, MA	New York
RI	1	Boston, MA	Boston
SC	4	Richmond, VA	Atlanta
SD	8	St. Louis, MO	Denver
TN	6	Cincinnati, OH	Atlanta
TX	5	New Orleans, LA	Fort Worth
UT	10	Denver, CO	Denver
VA	4	Richmond, VA	Philadelphia
VI	3	Philadelphia, PA	New York
VT	2	New York, NY	Boston
WA	9	San Francisco, CA	Seattle
WI	7	Chicago, IL	Chicago
WV	4	Richmond, VA	Philadelphia
WY	10	Denver, CO	Denver

GU is Guam, PR is Puerto Rico, and VI is the Virgin Islands.

According to some odd logic, the following Federal Records Centers are located somewhere else:

Atlanta—East Point, GA;   Boston—Waltham, MA;   Los Angeles—Laguna Niguel, CA; New York—Bayonne, NJ; San Francisco—San Bruno, CA

Searching Hints — Recorded Documents at County Agencies

Types of Records Available

A multitude of information can be found at the county, parish or city recorders' offices. Recorded documents include:

- ♦ Real Estate Transactions

- ♦ Uniform Commercial Code (UCC) Filings

- ♦ All liens, including State and Federal Tax Liens

Descriptions of these categories of records appear on pages in the previous chapter.

The County Rule

The County Courts and Recording Offices section in each state chapter presents detailed instructions and searching hints. Where to search for **recorded documents** usually isn't a difficult problem to overcome in everyday practice. In most states, these transactions are recorded at one designated recording office in the county where the property is located.

We call this the "**County Rule**." It applies to types of public records such as real estate recordings, tax liens, Uniform Commercial Code (UCC) filings, vital records, and voter registration records. However, as with most government rules, there are a variety of exceptions which are summarized here.

The Exceptions

The five categories of exceptions to the County Rule (or Parish Rule, if searching in Louisiana) are listed below (the details are listed in the chart to follow)—

♦ Special Recording Districts (AK, HI)

♦ Multiple Recording Offices (AL, AR, IA, KY, ME, MA, MS, TN)

♦ Independent Cities (MD, MO, NV, VA)

♦ Recording at the Municipal Level (CT, RI, VT)

♦ Identical Names—Different Place (CT, IL, MA, NE, NH, PA, RI, VT, VA)

The Personal Property Problem and the Fifth Exception

The real estate recording system in the US is self-auditing to the extent that you generally cannot record a document in the wrong recording office. However, many documents are rejected for recording because they are submitted to the wrong recording office. There are a number of reasons why this occurs, one of which is the overlap of filing locations for real estate and UCC.

Finding the right location of a related UCC filing is a different and much more difficult problem from finding a real estate recording. In the majority of states, the usual place to file a UCC financing statement is at the Secretary of States office—these are called **central filing states**. In the **dual** and **local filing** states, the place to file, in addition to the central filing office, is **usually** at the same office where your real estate documents are recorded. However, where there are identical place names referring to two different places, it becomes quite confusing, so hence, the fifth exemption.

▬▬ The County Rule—Exceptions Chart

Each of these five categories of recording exceptions is summarized below by state.

AL	Four counties contain two separate recording offices. They are Barbour, Coffee, Jefferson, and St. Clair.
AK	The 23 Alaskan counties are called boroughs. However, real estate recording is done under a system that was established at the time of the Gold Rush (whenever that was) of **34 Recording Districts**. Some of the Districts are identical in geography to boroughs, such as the Aleutian Islands, but other boroughs and districts overlap. Therefore, you need to know which recording district any given town or city is located in.
AR	Ten counties contain two separate recording offices. They are Arkansas, Carroll, Clay, Craighead, Franklin, Logan, Mississippi, Prairie, Sebastian, and Yell.
CT	There is **no county recording** in this state. All recording is done at the city/town level. Lenders persist in attempting to record or file documents in the counties of Fairfield, Hartford, Litchfield, New Haven, New London, Tolland, and Windham related to property located in other cities/towns because each of these cities/towns bears the same name as a Connecticut county.
HI	All recording is done at one central office.
IL	Cook County has separate offices for real estate recording and UCC filing.
IA	Lee county has two recording offices.

KY	Kenton County has two recording offices. Jefferson County has a separate office for UCC filing.
LA	Louisiana counties are called **Parishes**. One parish, St. Martin, has two non-contiguous segments.
ME	Aroostock and Oxford counties have two separate recording offices.
MD	The City of Baltimore has its own separate recording office.
MA	Berkshire and Bristol counties each has three recording offices. Essex, Middlesex and Worcester counties each has two recording offices. Cities/towns bearing the same name as a county are Barnstable, Essex, Franklin, Hampden, Nantucket, Norfolk, Plymouth, and Worcester. UCC financing statements on personal property collateral are submitted to cities/towns, while real estate recording is handled by the counties.
MS	Ten counties contain two separate recording offices. They are Bolivar, Carroll, Chickasaw, Harrison, Hinds, Jasper, Jones, Panola, Tallahatchie, and Yalobusha.
MO	The City of St. Louis has its own recording office.
NE	Fifteen counties have separate offices for real estate recording and for UCC filing.
NH	Cities/towns bearing the same name as a county are Carroll, Grafton, Hillsborough, Merrimack, Strafford, and Sullivan. UCC financing statements on personal property collateral are submitted to cities/towns, while real estate recording is handled by the counties.
NV	Carson City has its own recording office.
PA	Each county has a separate recording office and prothonotary office. UCC financing statements on personal property are submitted to the prothonotary, and real estate documents are submitted to the recorder.
RI	There is **no county recording** in this state. All recording is done at the city/town level. Lenders persist in attempting to record or file documents in the counties of Bristol, Newport, and Providence related to property located in other cities/ towns because each of these cities/towns bears the same name as a Rhode Island county.
TN	Sullivan County has two separate recording offices.
VT	There is **no county recording** in this state. All recording is done at the city/town level. Lenders persist in attempting to record or file documents in the counties of Addison, Bennington, Chittenden, Essex, Franklin, Grand Isle, Orange, Rutland, Washington, Windham, and Windsor related to property located in other cities/towns because each of these cities/towns bears the same name as a Vermont county. Adding to the confusion, there are four place names in the state that refer to both a city and a town: Barre, Newport, Rutland, and St. Albans.

| VA | There are 41 independent cities in Virginia. Twenty-seven have separate recording offices. The following 15 share their filing offices with the surrounding county: |

INDEPENDENT CITY	*FILE IN*
Bedford	Bedford County
Covington	Alleghany County
Emporia	Greenville County
Fairfax	Fairfax County
Falls Church	Arlington or Fairfax County
Franklin	Southhampton County
Galax	Carroll County
Harrisonburg	Rockingham County
Lexington	Rockbridge County
Manassas	Prince William County
Manassas Park	Prince William County
Norton	Wise County
Poquoson	York County
South Boston	Halifax County
Williamsburg	James City County

Online Searching For Asset/Lien Records

A relatively few number of county government jurisdictions provide online access to recorded documents and they can be found in the Government Sources Section. Most are fee sites, but there is a growing number of free sites available via the Internet.

Keep in mind there are a number of private companies who compile and maintain these records and offer them for resale, and they offer the most comprehensive source. Look for a list of these companies in the Index portion of the Private Company Sources Section.

Also, the BRB Publications site at www.brbpub.com has an updated list of county agencies offering free access to records over the Internet.

Searching Hints — State Agencies

Types of Records Available

Each state has government agencies that maintain records in each of the following 18 categories—

Criminal Records	Sales Tax Registrations
Corporation Records	Workers' Compensation Records
Limited Partnership Records	Marriage Records
Limited Liability Company Records	Divorce Records
Trademark, Trade Name	Birth Records
Fictitious or Assumed Names	Death Records
Uniform Commercial Code Filings	Driver Records
Federal Tax Liens	Vehicle & Ownership Records
State Tax Liens	State Investigated Accident Reports

Certain of these categories are more apt to offer online access, and some rarely do. For definitions, descriptions and comments about online accessibility of these categories starting on page 13.

Each state chapter in the Government Sources Section begins with a heading of the address and phone number of the following offices: Governor, Attorney General, State Archives, and the State Court Administrator's Office. Also included is the official main web site for each state. This is an excellent starting point to answer questions about topics or agencies not covered in this book.

State Public Records Restrictions Table

On the following pages, the **State Agency Public Record Restrictions Table** is an excellent state-by-state access summary to seven categories of records.

This table shows the wide disparity of access and restriction guidelines between similar agencies from different states.

State Agency Public Record Restrictions Table

Codes

O   Open to Public
R   Some Access Restrictions (Requesters Screened)
N/A   Not Available to the Public
F   Special Form Needed
S   Severe Access Restrictions (Signed Authorization, etc.)
L   Available only at Local Level

State	Criminal Records	UCC Records	Worker's Comp	Driving Record [2]	Vehicle Records	Vessel Records	Voter Reg. [3]
Alabama	S	O,F	S	R	S	O	L
Alaska	R	O,F	R	S	R	N/A	L
Arizona	R	O,F	S	S	S	R	L
Arkansas	S	O,F	O	S	R	O	L
California	N/A,L	O,F	R	S	S	S	L
Colorado	O	O,F	S	R	R	O	O
Connecticut	O	O,F	S	S	S	O	L
Delaware	S	O,F	S	R	R	R	O
Dist. of Columbia	S,F	O,F	S	S	S	S	O
Florida	O	O,F	S	R	R	R	L
Georgia	S	L,F₁	S	S	S	O	O
Hawaii	O	O,F	S	R	N/A	R	L
Idaho	S	O,F	S	R	R	S	L
Illinois	S,F	O,F	O	S	R	O	L
Indiana	R,F	O,F	S	R	R	R	L
Iowa	O	O,F	O	R	R	L	O
Kansas	O,F	O,F	R	R	R	R	L
Kentucky	R	O,F	R	R	R	O	O
Louisiana	S	L,F₁	R	R	R	O	L
Maine	O	O,F	R	R	R	O	L
Maryland	S	O,F	O	R	R	O	L
Massachusetts	R,F	O,F	R	R	R	O	L
Michigan	O	O,F	R	R	R	R	L
Minnesota	R	O,F	S	R	R	O	L
Mississippi	N/A,L	O,F	R	R	R	O	L
Missouri	O	O,F	R	R	R	R	L
Montana	O	O,F	R	R	R	R	O
Nebraska	O	O,F	R	R	R	L	L
Nevada	S	O,F	S	R	R	O	L
New Hampshire	S	O,F	S	R	S	S	L

State	Criminal Records	UCC Records	Worker's Comp	Driving Record [2]	Vehicle Records	Vessel Records	Voter Reg. [3]
New Jersey	R	O,F	O,F	S	S	S	L
New Mexico	S	O,F	S	S	S	S	L
New York	L	O,F	S	R	R	R	L
North Carolina	N/A,L	O,F	R	R	R	O	L
North Dakota	S	O,F	S	R	R,F	O	L
Ohio	S,F	O,F	O	R	R	O	O&L
Oklahoma	O	O,F	O	R	O	R	O&L
Oregon	O	O,F	S	R	R	O	L
Pennsylvania	R,F	O,F	S	S	S	N/A	L
Rhode Island	S,L	O,F	S	R	S	R	L
South Carolina	O	O,F	S	R	R	O	O
South Dakota	S,F	O,F	S	R	R	R	L
Tennessee	N/A,L	O,F	S	R	R	O	L
Texas	O	O,F	S,F	R	R	R	L
Utah	N/A,L	O,F	S	R	R	R	L
Vermont	N/A,L	O,F	S	R	R	R	L
Virginia	S,F	O,F	R	S	S	R	L
Washington	O	O,F	S	S	S	S	L
West Virginia	S,F	O,F	S	R	R	R	L
Wisconsin	O	O,F	S	R	R	O	L
Wyoming	S,F	O,F	S	R	R	O	L

[1] = Georgia and Louisiana UCCs are filed locally, but a state central index is available.

[2] = This category, Driving, indicates restriction codes based on the assumption the requester is the general public. In general, these records are open ("O") to employers and their agents.

[3] = This category, Voter Registration, indicates most record searching requires going to the local county or municipality. However, many state election agencies will sell customized voter lists statewide or for multiple counties.

Searching Hints — Other Federal Agencies

EDGAR

EDGAR, the Electronic Data Gathering Analysis, and Retrieval system was established by the Securities and exchange Commission (SEC) to allow companies to make required filing to the SEC by direct transmission. As of May 6, 1996, all public domestic companies are required to make their filings on EDGAR, except for filings made to the Commission's regional offices and those filings made on paper due to a hardship exemption.

EDGAR is an extensive repository of US corporation information and it is available online.

What is Found on EDGAR?

Companies must file the following reports with the SEC:

◆ 10-K, an annual financial report, which includes audited year-end financial statements.

◆ 10-Q, a quarterly report, unaudited.

◆ 8K - a report detailing significant or unscheduled corporate changes or events.

◆ Securities offering and trading registrations and the final prospectus.

The list above is not conclusive. There are other miscellaneous reports filed, including those dealing with security holdings by institutions and insiders. Access to these documents provides a wealth on information.

How to Access EDGAR Online

EDGAR is searchable online at: www.sec.gov/edgarhp.htm. LEXIS/NEXIS (see page 393) acts as the data wholesaler or distributor on behalf of the government. LEXIS/NEXIS sells data to information retailers, including it's own NEXIS service.

There is an additional number of companies found in the Company Information Category Index (see page 299) that may very well offer online access to EDGAR.

Many of these companies have compiled data prior to May 1996 and offer proprietary databases of SEC and other company documents.

Aviation Records

The Federal Aviation Association (FAA) is the US government agency with the responsibility of all matters related to the safety of civil aviation. The FAA, among other functions, provides the system that registers aircraft, and documents showing title or interest in aircraft. Their web site, at www.faa.gov, is the ultimate source of aviation records, airports and facilities, safety regulations, and civil research and engineering.

The Aircraft Owners and Pilots Association is the largest organization of its kind with a 340,000 members. Their web site is www.aopa.org and is an excellent source of information regarding the aviation industry.

Two other excellent sources are *Jane's World Airlines* at www.janes.com and the Insured Aircraft Title Service at 800-654-4882 or its web site at www.insured.aircraft.com

Military Records

This topic is so broad that there can be a book written about it, and in fact there is! *The Armed Forces Locator Directory* from MIE Publishing (800-937-2133) is an excellent source. The author, Lt. Col. Richard S Johnson, covers every conceivable topic regarding military records.

The Privacy Act of 1974 (5 U.S.C. 552a) and the Department of Defense directives require a written request, signed and dated, to access military personnel records. For further details, visit the NPRC site listed below.

Internet Sources

There are a number of great Internet sites that provide valuable information on obtaining military and military personnel records as follows:

www.nara.gov/regional/mpr.html This is the National Personnel Records Center (NPRC), maintained by the National Archives and Records Administration. This site is full of useful information and links.

www.army.mil	The official site of the US Army
www.af.mil	The official site of the US Air Force
www.navy.mil	The official site of the US Navy
www.usmc.mil	The official site of the US Marine Corps
www.ngb.dtic.mil	The official site of the National Guard (Army & Air Force)
www.uscg.mil	The official site of the US Coast Guard

Searching Hints — Using a Private Vendor

Hiring Someone to Obtain the Record Online

There are five main categories of public record professionals: distributors and gateways; search firms; local document retrievers; investigative firms; and information brokers. Pages 312-457 contain profiles of 415 distributors and search firms who offer or utilize record information online or via CD-ROM.

In the interest of presenting an all-encompassing overview, the five categories are described below—

Distributors and Gateways (Proprietary Database Vendors)

Distributors are automated public record firms who combine public sources of bulk data and/or online access to develop their own database product(s). Primary Distributors include companies that collect or buy public record information from its source and reformat the information in some useful way. They tend to focus on one or a limited number of types of information, although a few firms have branched into multiple information categories.

Gateways are companies that either compile data from or provide an automated gateway to Primary Distributors. Gateways thus provide "one-stop shopping" for multiple geographic areas and/or categories of information.

Companies can be both Primary Distributors and Gateways. For example, a number of online database companies are both primary distributors of corporate information and also gateways to real estate information from other Primary Distributors

Search Firms

Search firms are companies that furnish public record search and document retrieval services through outside online services and/or through a network of specialists, including their own employees or correspondents (see Retrievers below). There are three types of Search Firms.

Search Generalists offer a full range of search capabilities in many public record categories over a wide geographic region. They may rely on gateways, primary distributors and/or networks of retrievers. They combine online proficiency with document retrieval expertise.

Search Specialists focus either on one geographic region—like Ohio—or on one specific type of public record information—like driver/vehicle records.

Application Specialists focus on one or two types of services geared to specific needs. In this category are pre-employment screening firms and tenant screening firms. Like investigators, they search many of the categories of public records in order to prepare an overall report about a person or business.

Local Document Retrievers

Local document retrievers use their own personnel to search specific requested categories of public records usually in order to obtain documentation for legal compliance (e.g., incorporations), for lending, and for litigation. They do not usually review or interpret the results or issue reports in the sense that investigators do, but rather return documents with the results of searches. They tend to be localized, but there are companies that offer a national network of retrievers and/or correspondents. The retriever or his/her personnel goes directly to the agency to look up the information. A retriever may be relied upon for strong knowledge in a local area, whereas a search generalist has a breadth of knowledge and experience in a wider geographic range.

The 650+ members of the **Public Record Retriever Network (PRRN)** can be found, by state and counties served, at www.brbpub.com. This organization has set industry standards for the retrieval of public record documents and operates under a Code of Professional Conduct. Using one of these record retrievers is an excellent way to access records in those jurisdictions that do not offer online access.

Private Investigation Firms

Investigators use public records as tools rather than as ends in themselves, in order to create an overall, comprehensive "picture" of an individual or company for a particular purpose. They interpret the information they have gathered in order to identify further investigation tracks. They summarize their results in a report compiled from all the sources used.

Many investigators also act as Search Firms, especially as tenant or pre-employment screeners, but this is a different role from the role of Investigator per se, and screening firms act very much like investigators in their approach to a project. In addition, an investigator may be licensed, and may perform the types of services traditionally thought of as detective work, such as surveillance.

Information Brokers

There is one additional type of firm that occasionally utilizes public records. **Information Brokers** (IB) gather information that will help their clients make informed business decisions. Their work is usually done on a custom basis with each project being unique. IB's are extremely knowledgeable in online research of full text databases and most specialize in a particular subject area, such as patent searching or competitive intelligence. The Association of Independent Information Professionals (AIIP), at www.aiip.org, has over 750 experienced professional information specialist members from 21 countries. *The Burwell World Directory of Information Brokers,* found in print and CD-ROM (972-732-0160) is an excellent source of IB's in over 48 countries.

━━━ Which Type of Vendor is Right for You?

With all the variations of vendors and the categories of information, the obvious question is; "How do I find the right vendor to go to for the public record information I need?" Before you start calling every interesting online vendor that catches your eye, you need to narrow your search to the **type** of vendor for your needs. To do this, ask yourself the following questions—

What is the Frequency of Usage?

If you have on-going, recurring requests for a particular type of information, it is probably best to choose a different vendor then if you have infrequent requests. Setting up an account with a primary distributor, such as Metromail, will give you an inexpensive per search fee, but the monthly minimum requirements will be prohibitive to the casual requester, who would be better off finding a vendor who accesses or is a gateway to Metromail. (See page 400)

What is the Complexity of the Search?

The importance of hiring a vendor who understands and can interpret the information in the final format increase with the complexity of the search. Pulling a driving record in Maryland is not difficult, but doing an online criminal record search in Maryland, when only a portion of the felony records are online, is not so easy.

Thus, part of the answer to determining which vendor or type of vendor to use is to become conversant with what is (and is not) available from government agencies. Without knowing what is available (and what restrictions apply), you cannot guide the search process effectively. Once you are comfortable knowing the kinds of information available in the public record, you are in a position to find the best method to access needed information.

What are the Geographic Boundaries of the Search?

A search of local records close to you may require little assistance, but a search of records nationally or in a state 2,000 miles away will require seeking a vendor who covers the area you need to search. Many national primary distributors and gateways combine various local and state databases into one large comprehensive system available for searching. However, if your record searching is narrowed by a region or locality, an online source that specializes in a specific geographic region, like Superior Information Services in NJ, may be an alternative to a national vendor. Keep in mind that many national firms allow you to order a search online, even though results cannot be delivered immediately and some hands-on local searching is required.

Of course, you may want to use the government agency online system if available for the kind of information you need.

Eleven Questions to Ask an Online Vendor

(Or a Vendor Who Uses Online Sources)

The following discussion focuses specifically on automated sources of information because many valuable types of public records have been entered into a computer and, therefore, require a computer search to obtain reliable results. The original version of this article was authored by **Mr. Leroy Cook**, Director of ION and The Investigators Anywhere Resource Line (see page 386). Mr. Cook has graciously allowed us to edit the article and reprint it for our readers.

1. Where does he or she get the information?

You may feel awkward asking a vendor where he or she obtained the information you are purchasing. The fake Rolex watch is a reminder that even buying physical things based on looks alone—without knowing where they come from—is dangerous.

Reliable information vendors *will* provide verification material such as the name of the database or service accessed, when it was last updated, and how complete it is.

It is important that you know the gathering process in order to better judge the reliability of the information being purchased. There *are* certain investigative sources that a vendor will not be willing to disclose to a you. However, that type of source should not be confused with the information that is being sold item by item. Information technology has changed so rapidly that some information brokers may still confuse "items of information" with "investigative reports." Items of information sold as units are *not* investigative reports. The professional reputation of an information vendor is a guaranty of sorts. Still, because information as a commodity is so new, there is little in the way of an implied warranty of fitness.

2. How often is the information database source updated?

Any answer *except* a clear, concise date and time or the vendor's personal knowledge of an ongoing system's methods of maintaining information currency is a reason to keep probing. Ideally, the mechanism by which you purchase items of information *should* include an update or statement of accuracy—as a part of the reply—*without* having to ask.

3. How long does it take for the new information or changes to get into the system?

In view of the preceding question, this one might seem repetitive, but it *really* is a different issue. Microfiche or a database of records may have been updated last week at a courthouse or a DMV, but the department's computer section may also be working with a three-month backlog. In this case, a critical incident occurring one month ago would *not* show up in the information updated last week. The importance of timeliness is a variable to be determined by you, but to be truly informed you need to know how "fresh" the information is.

4. What are the searchable fields? Which fields are mandatory?

If your knowledge of "fields" and "records" is limited to the places where cattle graze and those flat, round things that play music, you *could* have a problem telling a good database from a bad one. An MVR vendor, for example, should be able to tell you that a subject's middle initial is critical when pulling an Arizona driving record. You don't have to become a programmer to use a computer and you needn't know a database management language to benefit from databases, *but* it is very helpful to understand how databases are constructed and (*at the least*) what fields, records, and indexing procedures are used.

As a general rule, the computerized, public-record information world is not standardized from county to county or from state to state; in the same way, there is little standardization within or between information vendors. Look at the system documentation from the vendor. The manual should include this sort of information.

5. How much latitude is there for error (misspellings or inappropriate punctuation) in a data request?

If the vendor's requirements for search data appear to be concise and meticulous, then you're probably on the right track. Some computer systems will tell (or "flag") an operator when they make a mistake such as omitting important punctuation or using an unnecessary comma. Other systems allow you to make inquiries by whatever means or in whatever format you like—and then tell you the requested information has *not* been found. In this instance, the desired information may *actually* be there, but the computer didn't understand the question because of the way in which it was asked. It is easy to misinterpret "no record found" as "there is no record." Please take note that the meanings of these two phrases are quite different.

6. What method is used to place the information in the repository and what error control or edit process is used?

In some databases, information may be scanned in or may be entered by a single operator as it is received and, in others, information may be entered *twice* to allow the computer to catch input errors by searching for non-duplicate entries. You don't have to know *everything* about all the options, but the vendor selling information in quantity *should*.

7. How many different databases or sources does the vendor access *and* how often?

The chance of obtaining an accurate search of a database increases with the frequency of access and the vendor's/searcher's level of knowledge. If he or she only makes inquiries once a month—and the results are important—you may need to find someone who sells data at higher volume. The point here is that it is usually better to find someone who specializes in the type of information you are seeking than it is to utilize a vendor who *can* get the information, but actually specializes in another type of data.

8. Does the price include assistance in interpreting the data received?

A report that includes coding and ambiguous abbreviations may look impressive in your file, but may not be too meaningful. For all reports, except those you deal with regularly, interpretation assistance can be *very* important. Some information vendors offer searches for information they really don't know much about through sources that they only use occasionally. Professional pride sometimes prohibits them from disclosing their limitations—until *you* ask the right questions.

9. Do vendors "keep track" of requesters and the information they seek (usage records)?

This may not seem like a serious concern when you are requesting information you're legally entitled to; however, there *is* a possibility that your usage records could be made available to a competitor. Most probably, the information itself is *already* being (or will be) sold to someone else, but you may not necessarily want *everyone* to know what you are requesting and how often. If the vendor keeps records of who-asks-what, the confidentiality of that information should be addressed in your agreement with the vendor.

10. Will the subject of the inquiry be notified of the request?

If your inquiry is sub rosa or if the subject's discovery of the search could lead to embarrassment, double check! There are laws that mandate the notification of subjects when certain types of inquires are made into their files. If notification is required, the way in which it is accomplished could be critical.

11. Is the turnaround time and cost of the search made clear at the outset?

You should be crystal clear about what you expect and/or need; the vendor should be succinct when conveying exactly what will be provided and how much it will cost. Failure to address these issues can lead to disputes and hard feelings.

These are excellent questions and concepts to keep in mind when reviewing the vendor profiles found in the Private Company Sources Section.

Government Sources

How to Read the State Chapters

Each State Chapter Contains:

- ◆ Addresses and phone numbers of the Governor, Attorney General, State Archives, and State Legislation.

- ◆ Useful state **facts**, including the official state Internet site.

- ◆ Detailed **examinations** of **state level agencies** that offer online access to their records.

- ◆ Profiles of the federal **Bankruptcy and US District Courts,** including the a breakdown of which counties are assigned to which geographic district. Special attention is given to PACER.

- ◆ Analysis of the **structure and organization** of all of the county courts and the county recording offices, including **search hints** and typical costs of record searching.

- ◆ **Profiles** of the **county level courts and recording offices** that do offer online access.

Alabama

Governor's Office
PO Box 302751   334-242-7100
Montgomery, AL 36130-2751   Fax 334-242-4541
www.state.al.us/govoff.html

Attorney General's Office
State House   334-242-7300
11 S. Union Street   Fax 334-242-7458
Montgomery, AL 36130   8AM-5PM
www.e-pages.com/aag

State Archives
Archives & History Dept   334-242-4435
Reference Room,   Fax 334-240-3433
PO Box 300100   8AM-5PM T-F
Montgomery, AL 36130-0100   9AM-5PM SA
www.asc.edu/archives/agis.html

Capital:	Montgomery
	Montgomery County
Time Zone:	CST
Number of Counties:	67
Population:	4,319,154
Web Site:	www.state.al.us

State Court Administrator
Director of Courts   334-242-0300
300 Dexter Ave   Fax 334-242-2099
Montgomery, AL 36104   8AM-5PM

State Agencies Online

Criminal Records
State Court Administrator, Director of Courts, 300 Dexter Ave, Montgomery, AL 36104; 334-242-0300, 334-242-2099 (Fax), 8AM-5PM.

Online search: The State Court Administration has an online system (SJIS) containing criminal records from all 75 county courthouses in the state. There is a $100 setup fee, $35 per month fee, and $.35 per minute charge. The system is open 24 hours a day, but interruptions in service can occur after 7 PM. All modem speeds work. Call (800) 392-8077 for more information

Corporation Records
Limited Partnership Records
Limited Liability Company Records
Limited Liability Partnerships
www.alalinc.net/alsecst

Secretary of State, Corporations Division, PO Box 5616, Montgomery, AL 36103-5616; (Courier: 11 S Union St, Ste 207, Montgomery, AL 36104); 334-242-5324, 334-242-5325 (Trademarks), 334-240-3138 (Fax).

General Information: Records are available for all corporations, active or inactive. All information here on file is considered public information. Formal registration of trademarks and service marks was codified in 1981, and trade name registration in 1989. It takes 1 month before new records are available for inquiries. The office for trademarks, trade names, and service marks is located in Room 127.

Online search: The online access is available for free from 7 AM to 12 PM for corporation and UCC records. Contact Robina Wilson at (334) 242-7200 to sign up.

Uniform Commercial Code
Federal Tax Liens
State Tax Liens
www.alalinc.net/alsecst

UCC Division, Secretary of State, PO Box 5616, Montgomery, AL 36103-5616; (Courier: 11 South Union St, Suite 207, Montgomery, AL 36104); 334-242-5231, 8AM-5PM.

General Information: The search includes tax liens. Federal and state tax liens on individuals may also be filed at the county level. All tax liens on businesses are filed here. Include debtor name in your request.

Online search: There is no charge for their dial-up access system. The system is open from 7 AM to 12 PM. Corporation data is also available. Call Jim Brasher at (334) 242-7000 for more information

Driver Records

Department of Public Safety, Central Records, PO Box 1471, Montgomery, AL 36102-1471; (Courier: 500 Dexter Ave, Montgomery, AL 36104); 334-242-4400, 334-242-4639 (Fax), 8AM-5PM.

General Information: Records are available for convictions in last five years for moving violations, surrendered licenses, DWI and suspensions. It takes 2 weeks before new records are available for inquiries. Addresses are shown unless subject opted out. Some juvenile records are considered confidential and are not released.

Online search: Alabama offers real time batch processing access via the AAMVAnet 3270 Terminal Connection. The fee is $5.75 per record. There is a minimum order requirement of 500 requests per month.

Requesters must provide their own connection device and terminal emulation software. Generally, requests are available 30 minutes after request transmission.

Legislation-Current/Pending
Legislation-Passed
www.legislature.state.al.us

Alabama Legislature, State House, 11 S Union St, Montgomery, AL 36130-4600; 334-242-7826 (Senate), 334-242-7637 (House), 334-242-8819 (Fax), 8:30AM-4:30PM.

General Information: Records are available from 1995-present on computer and from 1819 in journal books.

Online search: The online access system is called "ALIS" and provides state code, bill text, bill status, voting history, statutory retrieval, and boards/commission information. The initial fee is $400 plus $100 per month. You must sign up for 12 months. The fees entitle you to 30 hours of usage per month. The system is open 24 hours a day, 7 days a week. For details, call Angela Sayers at 334-242-7482.

Information About County Agencies

Court Structure

The Circuit and District Courts are combined in all but eight larger counties. Barbour, Coffee, Jefferson, St. Clair, Talladega, and Tallapoosa Counties have two court locations within the county.

Jefferson County (Birmingham), Madison (Huntsville), Marshall, and Tuscaloosa Counties have separate criminal divisions for Circuit and/or District Courts. Misdemeanors committed with felonies are tried with the felony. The Circuit Courts are appeals courts for misdemeanors. District Courts can receive guilty pleas in felony cases. All counties have separate probate courts.

About the County Courts

Online Access

Remote, online computer access is available through the Remote Access system of the State Judicial Information System (SJIS). Remote Access is designed to provide "off-site" users with a means to retrieve basic case information and to allow a user access to any criminal, civil, or traffic record in the state. The SJIS system is available 24 hours per day. To participate in Remote Access, a user must possess: a PC that is XT equivalent, a modem and modem software that allows VT-100 simulation ("Crosstalk" is recommended). There is a $100 setup fee, and the monthly charge is $35 plus $0.35 per minute connect time. Call Mike Carroll or Cheryl Lenoir (334-242-0300 or 800-392-8077) for additional information.

Searching Hints

Although in most counties Circuit and District courts are combined, each index may be separate. Therefore, when you request a search of both courts, be sure to state that the search is to cover "both the Circuit and District Court records." Several offices do not perform searches. Some offices do not have public access computer terminals.

- - - - - - - - - - - - - - - - -

About the Recorder's Office

Organization

67 counties, 71 recording offices. The recording officer is Judge of Probate. Four counties have two recording offices— Barbour, Coffee, Jefferson, and St. Clair. See the notes under each county regarding how to determine which office is appropriate to search. The entire state is in the Central Time Zone.

Real Estate Records

Most counties do not perform real estate searches. Copy fees vary. Certification fees vary. Tax records are located at the Assessor's Office.

UCC Records

Financing statements are filed at the state level, except for consumer goods, farm collateral and real estate related collateral, which are filed with the county Judge of Probate. Only one-third of counties will perform UCC searches. Use search request form UCC-11. Search fees vary from $5.00 to $12.00 per debtor name. Copies usually cost $1.00 per page.

Other Lien Records

Federal and state tax liens on personal property of businesses are filed with the Secretary of State. Other federal and state tax liens are filed with the county Judge of Probate. Counties do **not** perform separate tax lien searches although the liens are usually filed in the same index with UCC financing statements. Other liens are: mechanics, judgment, lis pendens, hospital, vendor.

County Courts & Recording Offices Online

There is a statewide program available through the Remote Access system of the State Judicial Information System (SJIS). Remote Access is designed to provide "off-site" users with a means to retrieve basic case information and to allow a user access to any criminal, civil, or traffic record in the state. The SJIS system is available 24 hours per day. To participate in Remote Access, a user must possess: a PC that is XT equivalent, a modem and modem software that allows VT-100 simulation ("Crosstalk" is recommended). There is a $100 setup fee, and the monthly charge is $35 plus $0.35 per minute connect time. Call Mike Carroll or Cheryl Lenoir (334-242-0300 or 800-392-8077) for additional information for online access to Civil, Criminal and Traffic records.

No remote online access is available from real estate recorder's office in Alabama.

Federal Courts Online

County-to-Court Cross Reference (Bankruptcy Court locations in Parenthesis if different)

County	District	Court
Autauga	Middle	Montgomery
Baldwin	Southern	Mobile
Barbour	Middle	Montgomery
Bibb	Northern	Birmingham (Tuscaloosa)
Blount	Northern	Birmingham
Bullock	Middle	Montgomery
Butler	Middle	Montgomery
Calhoun	Northern	Birmingham (Anniston)
Chambers	Middle	Opelika (Montgomery)
Cherokee	Northern	Gadsden (Anniston)
Chilton	Middle	Montgomery
Choctaw	Southern	Mobile
Clarke	Southern	Mobile
Clay	Northern	Birmingham (Anniston)
Cleburne	Northern	Birmingham (Anniston)
Coffee	Middle	Dothan (Montgomery)
Colbert	Northern	Florence (Decatur)
Conecuh	Southern	Mobile
Coosa	Middle	Montgomery
Covington	Middle	Montgomery
Crenshaw	Middle	Montgomery
Cullman	Northern	Huntsville (Decatur)
Dale	Middle	Dothan (Montgomery)
Dallas	Southern	Selma (Mobile)
De Kalb	Northern	Gadsden (Anniston)
Elmore	Middle	Montgomery
Escambia	Southern	Mobile
Etowah	Northern	Gadsden (Anniston)
Fayette	Northern	Jasper (Tuscaloosa)
Franklin	Northern	Florence (Decatur)
Geneva	Middle	Dothan (Montgomery)
Greene	Northern	Birmingham (Tuscaloosa)
Hale	Southern	Selma (Mobile)
Henry	Middle	Dothan (Montgomery)
Houston	Middle	Dothan (Montgomery)
Jackson	Northern	Huntsville (Decatur)
Jefferson	Northern	Birmingham
Lamar	Northern	Jasper (Tuscaloosa)
Lauderdale	Northern	Florence (Decatur)
Lawrence	Northern	Huntsville (Decatur)
Lee	Middle	Opelika (Montgomery)
Limestone	Northern	Huntsville (Decatur)
Lowndes	Middle	Montgomery
Macon	Middle	Opelika (Montgomery)
Madison	Northern	Huntsville (Decatur)
Marengo	Southern	Selma (Mobile)
Marion	Northern	Jasper (Tuscaloosa)
Marshall	Northern	Gadsden (Anniston)
Mobile	Southern	Mobile
Monroe	Southern	Mobile
Montgomery	Middle	Montgomery
Morgan	Northern	Huntsville (Decatur)
Perry	Southern	Selma (Mobile)
Pickens	Northern	Birmingham (Tuscaloosa)
Pike	Middle	Montgomery
Randolph	Middle	Opelika (Montgomery)
Russell	Middle	Opelika (Montgomery)
Shelby	Northern	Birmingham
St. Clair	Northern	Gadsden (Anniston)
Sumter	Northern	Birmingham (Tuscaloosa)
Talladega	Northern	Birmingham (Anniston)
Tallapoosa	Middle	Opelika (Montgomery)
Tuscaloosa	Northern	Birmingham (Tuscaloosa)
Walker	Northern	Jasper (Tuscaloosa)
Washington	Southern	Mobile
Wilcox	Southern	Selma (Mobile)
Winston	Northern	Jasper (Tuscaloosa)

US District Court
Middle District of Alabama

PACER sign-up number is 800-676-6856. Both civil and criminal case records are available online.

Montgomery Division, Records Search, PO Box 711, Montgomery, AL 36101-0711, 334-223-7308.

Dothan Division, c/o Montgomery Division, PO Box 711, Montgomery, AL 36101, 334-223-7308.

Opelika Division, c/o Montgomery Division, PO Box 711, Montgomery, AL 36101, 334-223-7308.

US Bankruptcy Court
Middle District of Alabama

PACER sign-up number is 800-676-6856.

Montgomery Division, PO Box 1248, Montgomery, AL 36102-1248, 334-206-6300, Fax: 334-206-6374.

US District Court
Northern District of Alabama

PACER sign-up number is 800-676-6856. Both civil and criminal case records are available online.

Birmingham Division, Room 140, US Courthouse, 1729 5th Ave N, Birmingham, AL 35203, 205-731-1700.

Gadsden Division, c/o Birmingham Division, Room 140, US Courthouse, 1729 5th Ave N, Birmingham, AL 35203, 205-731-1700.

Jasper Division, c/o Birmingham Division, Room 140, US Courthouse, 1729 5th Ave N, Birmingham, AL 35203, 205-731-1700.

Florence Division, PO Box 776, Florence, AL 35630, 205-760-5815, Civil Docket Section: 205-760-5722, Criminal Docket Section: 205-760-5725, Fax: 205-760-5727.

Huntsville Division, Clerk's Office, US Post Office & Courthouse, 101 Holmes Ave NE, Huntsville, AL 35801, 205-534-6495.

US Bankruptcy Court
Northern District of Alabama

PACER sign-up number is 800-676-6856.

Anniston Division, Room 103, 12th & Noble Sts, Anniston, AL 36201, 205-237-5631, Fax: 205-237-6547.

Birmingham Division, Room 120, 1800 5th Ave N, Birmingham, AL 35203, 205-714-3830.

Decatur Division, PO Box 1289, Decatur, AL 35602, 205-353-2817, Fax: 205-350-7334.

Tuscaloosa Division, PO Box 3226, Tuscaloosa, AL 35403, 205-752-0426, Record Room: 205-752-0426, Fax: 205-752-6468.

US District Court
Southern District of Alabama

PACER sign-up number is 800-676-6856. Both civil and criminal case records are available online.

Selma Division, c/o Mobile Division, 113 St Joseph St, Mobile, AL 36602, 334-690-2371, Civil Docket Section: 334-690-2371, Criminal Docket Section: 334-690-2371.

Mobile Division, Clerk, 113 St Joseph St, Mobile, AL 36602, 334-690-2371.

US Bankruptcy Court
Southern District of Alabama

PACER sign-up number is 800-676-6856.

Mobile Division, Clerk, 201 St. Louis St, Mobile, AL 36602, 334-441-5391, Fax: 334-441-6286.

Alaska

Governor's Office

PO Box 110001   907-465-3500
Juneau, AK 99811-0001   Fax 907-465-3532
www.gov.state.ak.us/gov/home2.html

Attorney General's Office

Law Department   907-465-3600
PO Box 110300   Fax 907-465-2075
Juneau, AK 99811-0300   8AM-4:30PM
www.law.state.ak.us

State Archives

Department of Education   907-465-2270
Archives Division   Fax 907-465-2465
141 Willoughby Ave   9AM-5PM
Juneau, AK 99801-1720
http:/ccl.alaska.edu/local/archives

Capital:	Juneau
	Juneau Borough
Time Zone:	AK (Alaska Standard Time)*

* Alaska's Aleutian Islands are Hawaii Standard Time)

Number of Counties:	23
Population:	609,311
Web Site:	www.state.ak.us

State Court Administrator

Office of the Admin. Director   907-264-9547
303 K St   Fax 907-264-0881
Anchorage, AK 99501   8AM-4:30PM
www.alaska.net/~akctlib/homepage.htm

State Agencies Online

Corporation Records
Fictitious Name
Assumed Name
Limited Partnership Records
Limited Liability Company Records

commerce.state.ak.us/dced/bsc/search.htm

Department of Commerce, Division of Banking, Securities & Corporations, PO Box 110808, Juneau, AK 99811; (Courier: 333 Willoughby Ave, 9th Floor of the State Office Bldg, Juneau, AK 99811); 907-465-2530, 907-465-3257 (Fax), 8AM-5PM.

General Information: New records are available for inquiry immediately. All information contained is considered public record

Online search: At the web site, one can access status information on corps, LLCs, LLP, LP (all, both foreign and domestic) as well as registered and reserved names. There is no fee. For bulk purchase, the requester must use a third party. Call 907-465-2530 for more information.

Workers' Compensation Records

www.state.ak.us

Workers Compensation, PO Box 25512, Juneau, AK 99802; (1111 W Eighth St, Rm 307, Juneau, AK 99802); 907-465-2790, 907-465-2797 (Fax), 8AM-4:30PM.

General Information: Records are available from 1982 on the computer and prior to 1982 the records are on microfilm and/or microfiche to the 1960s

Online search: Online access is available for pre-approved accounts. Request in writing to the Director.

Driver Records

Division of Motor Vehicles, Driver's Records, PO Box 20020, Juneau, AK 99802-0020; (Courier: 450 Whitter St, Room 105, Juneau, AK 99802); 907-465-4335 (Motor Vehicle Reports Desk), 907-463-5860 (Fax), 8AM-5PM.

General Information: Records are available for minor moving violations and suspensions for three years, major moving violations for five years. Convictions are automatically purged from public record by conviction date. Accidents are reported only if action is taken. Any private company or individual must have a signed release from the licensee or a subpoena. High volume requesters may maintain these forms rather than send in with requests. Casual requesters cannot obtain records

Online search: Online access costs $5.00 per record. Inquiries may be made at any time, 24 hours a day. Batch inquires may call back within thirty minutes for responses. Search by the first four letters of driver's name, license number and date of birth. At present, there is only one phone line available for users; you may experience a busy signal

Legislation-Current/Pending Legislation-Passed
www.legis.state.ak.us

Alaska State Legislature, State Capitol, 130 Seward St, Suite 313, Juneau, AK 99801-1182; 907-465-4648, 907-465-2864 (Fax), 8AM-5PM.

Online search: All information is on the Internet at no fee. State Statues are on the Internet.

Information About County Agencies

Court Structure

Alaska is not organized into counties, but rather into 15 boroughs (3 unified home rule municipalities that are combination borough and city, and 12 boroughs) and 12 home rule cities, which do not directly coincide with the 4 Judicial Districts into which the judicial system is divided, that is, judicial boundaries cross borough boundaries. Probate is handled by the Superior Courts.

Online Access

There is no internal or external online statewide judicial computer system available.

About the County Courts

Searching Hints

Documents may not be filed by fax in any AK court location without prior authorization of a judge.

The fees established by court rules for Alaska courts are: Search Fee — $15.00 per hour or fraction thereof; certification Fee — $5.00 per document and $2.00 per additional copy of the document; copy Fee — $.25 per page.

Magistrate Courts vary widely in how records are maintained and in the hours of operation (some are open only a few hours per week).

About the Recorder's Office

Organization

23 boroughs, 34 recording offices. Recording is done by districts, which overlay the borough system. The recording officer is District Recorder. The entire state except the Aleutian Islands is in the Alaska Time Zone (AK).

Real Estate Records

Districts do not perform real estate searches. Certification fees are usually $5.00 per document.

UCC Records

Financing statements are filed at the state level, except for consumer goods, farm collateral and real estate related collateral, which are filed with the District Recorder. All districts will perform UCC searches at $5.00 per debtor name for information and $15.00 with copies. Use search request form UCC-11. Copies ordered separately usually cost $2.00 per financing statement.

Other Lien Records

All state and federal tax liens are filed with the District Recorder. Districts do not perform separate tax lien searches.

County Courts & Recording Offices Online

There is no online access to county level records available to the public.

No remote online access is available from real estate recorder's office in Alaska.

Federal Courts Online

County-to-Court Cross Reference (Bankruptcy Court locations in Parenthesis if different)

Aleutian Islands, East .... Anchorage

Aleutian Islands, West .... Anchorage

Anchorage Borough .... Anchorage

Bethel .... Fairbanks (Anchorage)

Bristol Bay Borough .... Anchorage

Fairbanks North Star Borough .... Fairbanks (Anchorage)

Haines Borough .... Juneau (Anchorage)

Juneau Borough .... Juneau (Anchorage)

Kenai Peninsula Borough .... Anchorage

Ketchikan Gateway Borough .... Ketchikan (Anchorage)

Kodiak Island Borough .... Anchorage

Matanuska-Susitna Borough .... Anchorage

Nome .... Nome (Anchorage)

North Slope Borough .... Fairbanks (Anchorage)

Northwest Arctic Borough .... Fairbanks (Anchorage)

Prince of Wales-Outer Ketchikan .... Juneau (Anchorage)

Sitka Borough .... Juneau (Anchorage)

Southeast Fairbanks .... Fairbanks (Anchorage)

Valdez-Cordova .... Anchorage

Wade Hampton .... Fairbanks (Anchorage)

Wrangell-Petersburg .... Juneau (Anchorage)

Yakutat .... Juneau (Anchorage)

Yukon-Koyukuk .... Fairbanks (Anchorage)

US District Court
District of Alaska

PACER sign-up number is 800-676-6856. Both civil and criminal case records are available online.

Anchorage Division, Box 4, 222 W 7th Ave, Anchorage, AK 99513-7564, 907-271-5568, Civil Docket Section: 907-271-5574, Criminal Docket Section: 907-271-5661.

Fairbanks Division, Room 332, 101 12th Ave, Fairbanks, AK 99701, 907-451-5791.

Juneau Division, PO Box 020349, Juneau, AK 99802-0349, 907-586-7458.

Ketchikan Division, 648 Mission St, Room 507, Ketchikan, AK 99901, 907-247-7576.

Nome Division, PO Box 1110, Nome, AK 99762, 907-443-5216, Fax: 907-443-2192.

US Bankruptcy Court
District of Alaska

PACER sign-up number is 800-676-6856.

Anchorage Division, Historic Courthouse, Suite 138, 605 W 4th Ave, Anchorage, AK 99501-2296, 907-271-2655.

This Bankruptcy Division services all of Alaska.

Arizona

Governor's Office
State Capitol, W Wing   602-542-4331
1700 W Washington   Fax 602-542-7601
Phoenix, AZ 85007
www.governor.state.az.us

Attorney General's Office
1275 W Washington   602-542-5025
Phoenix, AZ 85007   Fax 602-542-1275
www.attorney_general.state.az.us

Capital:	Phoenix
	Maricopa County
Time Zone:	MST
Number of Counties:	15
Population:	4,554,966
Web Site:	www.state.az.us

State Archives
Library, Archives   602-542-4159
& Public Records Department   Fax 602-542-4402
1700 W Washington, Rm 442   8AM-5PM
Phoenix, AZ 85007
www.dlapr.lib.az.us/archives/index.htm

State Court Administrator
Admin. Offices of the Courts   602-542-9301
Arizona Supreme Court Bldg   8AM-5PM
1501 W Washington
Phoenix, AZ 85007
www.supreme.state.az.us

State Agencies Online

Corporation Records
Limited Liability Company Records
www.cc.state.az.us

Corporation Commission, 1300 W Washington, Phoenix, AZ 85007; 602-542-3026 (Status), 602-542-3285 (Annual Reports), 602-542-3414 (Fax), 8AM-5PM.

General Information: It takes after 2-3 months before new records are available for inquiries. Fictitious Name & Assumed Name records are found at the county level.

Online search: The online system is called STARPAS. It functions 24 hours a day, 7 days a week. The initial set-up fee is $36 and access costs $.30 per minute. Call Ann Shaw at (602) 542-0685 for a sign-up package.

Uniform Commercial Code
Federal Tax Liens
State Tax Liens
www.sosaz.com

UCC Division, Secretary of State, State Capitol, West Wing, 7th Floor, Phoenix, AZ 85007; 602-542-6178, 602-542-7386 (Fax), 8AM - 5PM.

General Information: Records are available from 06/95-present on the Internet. The search includes tax liens recorded here. Please note that tax liens recorded on individuals may be filed at the county level and not here.

Online search: UCC records can be searched over the web site. Searching can be done by debtor, secured party name, or file number. From this site you can also pull down a weekly microfiche file of filings (about 10 megabytes).

Driver Records

Motor Vehicle Division, Record Services Section, PO Box 2100, Mail Drop 539M, Phoenix, AZ 85001; (Courier: Customer Records Services, 1801 W Jefferson, Lobby room 345, Phoenix, AZ 85007); 602-255-8357, 8AM-5PM.

General Information: Records are available for either a thirty-nine month record or for a five-year record. CDL records may be available for ten years. It takes 2 weeks before new records are available for inquiries. Exempt requesters need only supply 2 out of the 3 items required to search. The driver's address is provided as part of the record to exempt requesters.

Online search: Arizona's online system is interactive. This system is primarily for those requesters who are exempt. Fee is $3 per record. For more information call "Third Party Programs" at 602-255-7235.

Vehicle Ownership
Vehicle Identification

Motor Vehicle Division, Record Services Section, PO Box 2100, Mail Drop 504M, Phoenix, AZ 85001; (Courier: Customer Records Services, 1801 W Jefferson, Room 345, Phoenix, AZ 85007); 602-255-8359, 8AM-5PM.

General Information: Records are available for 5 years to present. It takes 2 weeks before new records are available for inquiries

Online search: Online access is offered to permissible users. The system is open 24 hours a day, seven days a week. Fee is $3.00 per record. For more information, call (602) 255-7235.

Legislation-Current/Pending
Legislation-Passed

www.azleg.state.az.us/

Arizona Legislature, State Senate - Room 203, 1700 W Washington, Phoenix, AZ 85007; (Courier: Senate Wing or, House Wing, Phoenix, AZ 85007); 602-542-3559 (Senate Information), 602-542-4221 (House Information), 602-542-3429 (Senate Fax), 602-542-4099 (House Fax), 8AM-5PM.

Online search: Most information, beginning with 1997, is available through the Internet (i.e. bill text, committee minutes, committee assignments, member bios, etc.). There is no fee.

Information About County Agencies

Court Structure

The Superior, Justice, and Municipal courts generally have separate jurisdiction over case types as indicated in the charts. Most courts will search their records by plaintiff or defendant. Estate cases are handled by Superior Court. Fees are the same as for civil and criminal case searching.

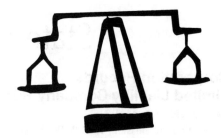

Online Access

A system called ACAP (Arizona Court Automation Project) is implemented in 106 courts. Only Mohave County is not a part of ACAP. ACAP is, fundamentally, a case and cash management information processing system. When fully

About the County Courts

implemented ACAP will provide all participating courts access to all records on the system. Current plans call for public availability in 2000.

The Maricopa and Pima county courts maintain their own systems, but will also, under current planning, be part of ACAP.

Searching Hints

Public access to all Maricopa County court case indexes is available at a central location: 1 W Madison Ave in Phoenix. Copies however must be obtained from the court where the case is heard.

Many offices do not perform searches due to personnel and/or budget constraints. As computerization of record offices increases across the state, more record offices are providing public access computer terminals.

Although Courts may choose to charge no fees, rate card fees across all jurisdictions, as established by the Arizona Supreme Court and State Legislature, are as follows as of January 1, 1998:

Search—Superior Court: $18.00 per name; lower courts: $17.00 per name; Certification—Superior Court: $18.00 per document; lower courts: $17.00 per document; Copies—$.50 per page.

About the Recorder's Office

Organization

15 counties, 16 recording offices. The Navajo Nation is profiled here. The recording officer is County Recorder. Recordings are usually placed in a Grantor/Grantee index. The entire state is in the Mountain Time Zone (MST), and does not change to daylight savings time.

Real Estate Records

Counties do not perform real estate searches. Copy fees are usually $1.00 per page. Certification fees are usually $3.00 per document.

UCC Records

Financing statements are filed at the state level, except for consumer goods, farm collateral, and real estate related collateral, which are filed with the County Recorder. All counties will perform UCC searches. Use search request form UCC-3. Search fees are generally $10.00 per debtor name. Copies usually cost $1.00 per page.

Other Lien Records

Federal and state tax liens on personal property of businesses are filed with the Secretary of State. Other federal and state tax liens are filed with the County Recorder. Counties do not perform separate tax lien searches. Other liens are: executions, judgments, labor.

County Courts & Recording Offices Online

Maricopa County

Felony, Civil Actions Over $5,000, Probate

www.supcourt.maricopa.gov

Superior Court, 201 W Jefferson, Phoenix AZ 85003, 602-506-3360. Fax: 602-506-7619. Hours: 8AM-5PM (MST).

Online search: Online access is available via the Internet at no charge. This system shows the entire case file rather than merely an index. Searching is by name or case number.

Liens, Real Estate

http://recorder.maricopa.gov

County Recorder, 111 S 3rd Av, Phoenix AZ 85003, 602-5063535. Fax: 602-506-3069.

Online search: Access is available by direct dial-up or on the Internet. On the Internet, one may view document images. Official copies can be ordered for $1.00, certified copies are $3.00. Hours are 6AM-12AM M, 6AM-1AM T-F and 8AM-5PM S-S. For online access, there is a one time setup fee of $300, plus $.06 cents per minute. The system operates 8AM-10PM M-F and 8AM-5PM S-S. Records date back to 1983. There are no fees for using the Internet. Baud rates up to 28.8 are supported. One can search by name, Grantee/Grantor and recording number. For additional information, contact Linda Kinclhloe at 602-506-3637.

Pima County

Tax Assessor Records

www.asr.co.pima.az.us

County Assessor's Office, 115 N Church, Tucson AZ 85701, 520-740-8630. Fax: 520-792-9825

Online search: Records are available on the Internet for no fee. One may search by name, parcel and street name and number.

Federal Courts Online

County-to-Court Cross Reference (Bankruptcy Court locations in Parenthesis if different)

Apache ....Prescott (Phoenix)

Cochise ....Tucson

Coconino ....Prescott (Phoenix)

Gila..Phoenix (Tucson)

Graham ....Tucson

Greenlee..Tucson

La Paz...Phoenix (Yuma)

Maricopa..Phoenix

Mohave..Prescott (Yuma)

Navajo...Prescott (Phoenix)

Pima ....Tucson

Pinal ....Phoenix (Tucson)

Santa Cruz...Tucson

Yavapai..Prescott (Phoenix)

Yuma ....Phoenix (Yuma)

US District Court
District of Arizona

PACER sign-up number is 800-676-6856. Both civil and criminal case records are available online.

Phoenix Division, Room 1400, 230 N 1st Ave, Phoenix, AZ 85025-0093, 602-514-7101, Civil Docket Section: 602-514-7102, Criminal Docket Section: 602-514-7103.

Prescott Division, c/o Phoenix Division, Room 1400, 230 N 1st Ave, Phoenix, AZ 85025-0093, 602-514-7101.

Tucson Division, Room 202, 44 E Broadway Blvd, Tucson, AZ 85701-1711, 520-620-7200, Fax: 520-620-7199.

US Bankruptcy Court
District of Arizona

http://ecf.azb.uscouts.gov

Limited documents, searchable by case number and type, are made available to the public for free at the URL listed above.

www.azb.uscourts.gov

PACER sign-up number is 800-676-6856.

Phoenix Division, PO Box 34151, Phoenix, AZ 85067-4151, 602-640-5800

Tucson Division, Suite 8112, 110 S Church Ave, Tucson, AZ 85701-1608, 520-620-7500

Yuma Division, Suite D, 325 W 19th St, Yuma, AZ 85364, 520-783-2288

Arkansas

Governor's Office
State Capitol, Room 250   501-682-2345
Little Rock, AR 72201   Fax 501-682-1382
www.state.ar.us/governor/governor.html

Attorney General's Office
200 Catlett-Prien Tower,
323 Center St   501-682-1323
Little Rock, AR 72201   Fax 501-682-8084
www.ag.state.ar.us/advscripts/front.asp

State Archives
Arkansas History Commission   501-682-6900
State Archives   8AM-4:30PM
One Capitol Mall
Little Rock, AR 72201
www.state.ar.us/ahc/ahc.html

Capital:	Little Rock
	Pulaski County
Time Zone:	CST
Number of Counties:	75
Population:	2,522,819
Web Site:	www.state.ar.us

State Court Administrator
Admin. Office of Courts
625 Marshall Street,   501-682-9400
Justice Bldg   Fax 501-682-9410
Little Rock, AR 72201-1078   8AM-5PM
www.courts.state.ar.us

State Agencies Online

Corporation Records
Fictitious Name
Limited Liability Company Records
Limited Partnerships
sosweb.state.ar.us/corps/incorp/

Secretary of State, Corporation Department-Aegon Bldg, 501 Woodlane, Rm 310, Little Rock, AR 72201-1094; 501-682-3409, 501-682-3437 (Fax), 8AM-4:30PM.

General Information: Corporation records are on computer from 1987 on. Prior records, such as dissolved corporations, may be in paper files. New records are available for inquiry immediately. Franchise tax information is not released.

Online search: The Internet site permits searches, at no fee, of corporation records. You can search by name, registered agent, or filing number.

Trademarks/Servicemarks
www.sosweb.state.ar.us/corps/trademk/

Secretary of State, Trademarks Section, 501 Woodlane, #301, Little Rock, AR 72201; 501-682-3405, 501-682-3437 (Fax), 8AM-5PM.

Online search: Searching is available at no fee over the Internet site.

Driver Records
www.state.ar.us

Department of Driver Services, Driving Records Division, PO Box 1272, Room 127, Little Rock, AR 72203; (Courier: 7th & Wolfe Sts, Ledbetter Bldg, Room 127, Little Rock, AR 72202); 501-682-7207, 501-682-2075 (Fax), 8AM-4:30PM.

General Information: Records are available for 3 years for moving violations, 3 years for employment or insurance purposes and are retained indefinitely for departmental purposes. DWI and suspensions show until all requirements are met. Arkansas requires signed authorization by the driver to obtain a driving record. Volume requesters must have these authorizations on file.

Interstate highway violations not exceeding 75 mph won't show on records requested for insurance purposes.

Online search: Access is available through the Information Network of Arkansas (INA). The system is interactive, fees are $8.00 per record or $11.00 if on a commercial driver. The system is only available to INA subscribers who have statutory rights to the data. For more information, visit the web site at www.ark.org/ina/premium.html or call (501) 324-8900.

Legislation-Current/Pending
Legislation-Passed

www.arkleg.state.ar.us

Arkansas Secretary of State, State Capitol, Room 256, Little Rock, AR 72201; 501-682-1010, 501-682-3408 (Fax), 8AM-5PM.

Online search: This is the best way to search through legislative records. There is no fee.

Information About County Agencies

Court Structure

County Courts are, fundamentally, administrative courts dealing with county fiscal issues. Probate is handled by the Chancery and Probate Courts, or by County Clerk in some counties. Civil limit raised to $5000 as of 8/2/97.

Searching Hints

There is a very limited internal online computer system at the Administrative Office of Courts.

About the
County Courts

Most courts that allow written search requests require a SASE. Fees vary widely across jurisdictions as do prepayment requirements.

About the
Recorder's Office

Organization

75 counties, 85 recording offices. The recording officer is the Clerk of Circuit Court, who is Ex Officio Recorder. Ten counties have two recording offices—Arkansas, Carroll, Clay, Craighead, Franklin, Logan, Mississippi, Prairie, Sebastian, and Yell. See the notes under each county for how to determine which office is appropriate to search. The entire state is in CST.

Real Estate Records

Most counties do not perform real estate searches. Copy fees and certification fees vary.

UCC Records

This is a dual filing state. Financing statements are filed at the state level and with the Circuit Clerk, except for consumer goods, farm and real estate related collateral, which are filed only with the Circuit Clerk. Most counties will perform UCC searches. Use search request form UCC-11. Search fees are usually $6.00 per debtor name. Copy fees vary.

Other Lien Records

Federal tax liens on personal property of businesses are filed with the Secretary of State. Other federal and all state tax liens are filed with the Circuit Clerk. Many counties will perform separate tax lien searches. Search fees are usually $6.00 per name. Other liens are: mechanics, lis pendens, judgments, hospital, child support, materialman.

County Courts & Recording Offices Online

There are no Arkansas County Courts with online access.

No remote online access is available from real estate recorder's offices in Arkansas.

Federal Courts Online

County-to-Court Cross Reference (Bankruptcy Court locations in Parenthesis if different)

Arkansas .... Eastern .... Pine Bluff (Little Rock)
Ashley .... Western (Eastern) ... El Dorado (Little Rock)
Baxter .... Western .... Harrison (Fayetteville)
Benton .... Western .... Fayetteville
Boone .... Western .... Harrison (Fayetteville)
Bradley .... Western (Eastern) ... El Dorado (Little Rock)
Calhoun .... Western (Eastern) ... El Dorado (Little Rock)
Carroll .... Western .... Harrison (Fayetteville)
Chicot .... Eastern .... Pine Bluff (Little Rock)
Clark .... Western (Eastern) ... Hot Springs (Little Rock)
Clay .... Eastern .... Jonesboro (Little Rock)
Cleburne .... Eastern .... Batesville (Little Rock)
Cleveland .... Eastern .... Pine Bluff (Little Rock)
Columbia .... Western (Eastern) ... El Dorado (Little Rock)
Conway .... Eastern .... Little Rock
Craighead .... Eastern .... Jonesboro (Little Rock)
Crawford .... Western .... Fort Smith (Fayetteville)
Crittenden .... Eastern .... Jonesboro (Little Rock)
Cross .... Eastern .... Helena (Little Rock)
Dallas .... Eastern .... Pine Bluff (Little Rock)
Desha .... Eastern .... Pine Bluff (Little Rock)
Drew .... Eastern .... Pine Bluff (Little Rock)
Faulkner .... Eastern .... Little Rock
Franklin .... Western .... Fort Smith (Fayetteville)
Fulton .... Eastern .... Batesville (Little Rock)
Garland .... Western (Eastern) ... Hot Springs (Little Rock)
Grant .... Eastern .... Pine Bluff (Little Rock)
Greene .... Eastern .... Jonesboro (Little Rock)
Hempstead .... Western (Eastern) ... Texarkana (Little Rock)
Hot Spring .... Western (Eastern) ... Hot Springs (Little Rock)
Howard .... Western (Eastern) ... Texarkana (Little Rock)
Independence ... Eastern .... Batesville (Little Rock)
Izard .... Eastern .... Batesville (Little Rock)
Jackson .... Eastern .... Batesville (Little Rock)
Jefferson .... Eastern .... Pine Bluff (Little Rock)
Johnson .... Western .... Fort Smith (Fayetteville)
Lafayette .... Western (Eastern) ... Texarkana (Little Rock)
Lawrence .... Eastern .... Jonesboro (Little Rock)

Lee .... Eastern .... Helena (Little Rock)
Lincoln .... Eastern .... Pine Bluff (Little Rock)
Little River .... Western (Eastern) ... Texarkana (Little Rock)
Logan .... Western .... Fort Smith (Fayetteville)
Lonoke .... Eastern .... Little Rock
Madison .... Western .... Fayetteville
Marion .... Western .... Harrison (Fayetteville)
Miller .... Western (Eastern) ... Texarkana (Little Rock)
Mississippi .... Eastern .... Jonesboro (Little Rock)
Monroe .... Eastern .... Helena (Little Rock)
Montgomery .... Western (Eastern) ... Hot Springs (Little Rock)
Nevada .... Western (Eastern) ... Texarkana (Little Rock)
Newton .... Western .... Harrison (Fayetteville)
Ouachita .... Western (Eastern) ... El Dorado (Little Rock)
Perry .... Eastern .... Little Rock
Phillips .... Eastern .... Helena (Little Rock)
Pike .... Western (Eastern) ... Hot Springs (Little Rock)
Poinsett .... Eastern .... Jonesboro (Little Rock)
Polk .... Western .... Fort Smith (Fayetteville)
Pope .... Eastern .... Little Rock
Prairie .... Eastern .... Little Rock
Pulaski .... Eastern .... Little Rock
Randolph .... Eastern .... Jonesboro (Little Rock)
Saline .... Eastern .... Little Rock
Scott .... Western .... Fort Smith (Fayetteville)
Searcy .... Western .... Harrison (Fayetteville)
Sebastian .... Western .... Fort Smith (Fayetteville)
Sevier .... Western (Eastern) ... Texarkana (Little Rock)
Sharp .... Eastern .... Batesville (Little Rock)
St. Francis .... Eastern .... Helena (Little Rock)
Stone .... Eastern .... Batesville (Little Rock)
Union .... Western (Eastern) ... El Dorado (Little Rock)
Van Buren .... Eastern .... Little Rock
Washington ..... Western .... Fayetteville
White .... Eastern .... Little Rock
Woodruff .... Eastern .... Helena (Little Rock)
Yell .... Eastern .... Little Rock

US District Court
Eastern District of Arkansas

PACER sign-up number is 800-676-6856. Both civil and criminal case records are available online.

www.are.uscourts.gov

Jonesboro Division, PO Box 7080, Jonesboro, AR 72403, 870-972-4610, Fax: 870-972-4612

Helena Division, c/o Little Rock Division, PO Box 869, Little Rock, AR 72203, 501-324-5351

Little Rock Division, Room 402, 600 W Capitol, Little Rock, AR 72201, 501-324-5351

Batesville Division, c/o Little Rock Division, PO Box 869, Little Rock, AR 72201, 501-324-5351

Pine Bluff Division, PO Box 8307, Pine Bluff, AR 71611-8307, 870-536-1190, Fax: 870-536-6330

US Bankruptcy Court
Eastern District of Arkansas

PACER sign-up number is 800-676-6856.

Little Rock Division, PO Drawer 3777, Little Rock, AR 72203, 501-918-5500, Fax: 501-918-5520.

US District Court
Western District of Arkansas

PACER sign-up number is 501-783-6833. Both civil and criminal case records are available online.

http://156.119.80.100/index.html

El Dorado Division, PO Box 1566, El Dorado, AR 71731, 870-862-1202

Harrison Division, c/o Fayetteville Division, PO Box 6420, Fayetteville, AR 72702, 501-521-6980, Fax: 501-575-0774.

Fayetteville Division, PO Box 6420, Fayetteville, AR 72702, 501-521-6980, Fax: 501-575-0774.

Fort Smith Division, PO Box 1523, Fort Smith, AR 72902, 501-783-6833, Fax: 501-783-6308.

Hot Springs Division, PO Drawer I, Hot Springs, AR 71902, 501-623-6411.

Texarkana Division, PO Box 2746, Texarkana, AR 75504, 501-773-3381.

US Bankruptcy Court
Western District of Arkansas

PACER sign-up number is 800-676-6856.

Fayetteville Division, PO Box 3097, Fayetteville, AR 72702-3097, 501-582-9800, Fax: 501-582-9825.

California

Governor's Office
State Capitol, 1st Floor   916-445-2841
Sacramento, CA 95814   Fax 916-445-4633
www.ca.gov/s/governor

Attorney General's Office
Justice Department   916-445-9555
PO Box 944255   Fax 916-324-5205
Sacramento, CA 94244-2550   8AM-5PM
caag.state.ca.us

State Archives
Secretary of State   916-653-7715
State Archives   Fax 916-653-7134
1020 "O" St   9:30AM-4PM
Sacramento, CA 95814
ss.ca.gov/archives/archives.htm

Capital:	Sacramento
	Sacramento County
Time Zone:	PST
Number of Counties:	58
Population:	32,268,301
Web Site:	www.state.ca.us

State Court Administrator
Admin. Office of Courts   415-396-9100
303 2nd St, S Tower   Fax 415-396-9349
San Francisco, CA 94107   8AM-5PM
courtinfo.ca.gov

State Agencies Online

Corporation Records
Limited Liability Company Records
Limited Partnerships
Secretary of State, Information Retrieval Unit, 1500 11th Street, Sacramento, CA 95814; 916-657-5448, 916-653-3794 (LLCs), 916-653-3365 (LPs), 8AM-4:30PM.

General Information: New records are available for inquiry immediately.

Online search: The state offers a corporate online system. There is a $300 set-up fee and usage charges of $1.00 for the first screen and $.25 thereafter. The system is available 24 hours a day. For more information, call (916) 953-8905

Uniform Commercial Code
Federal Tax Liens
State Tax Liens
www.ca.gov

UCC Division, Secretary of State, PO Box 942835, Sacramento, CA 94235-0001; (1500 11th St, 2nd Fl, Sacramento, CA 95814); 916-653-3516, 8AM-5PM.

General Information: Records are available for current records and expired records up to 1 year after expiration. The search includes federal and some state tax liens on businesses. Federal tax liens on individuals are filed at the county level, state tax liens are filed at either location.

Online search: Direct Access provides dial-up searching via PC and modem. Fees range from $1-3 dollars, depending on type of search. Each page scroll is $.25. Requesters operate from a prepaid account

Driver Records
Department of Motor Vehicles, Information Services, PO Box 944247, Mail Station G199, Sacramento, CA 94244-2470; (Courier: Bldg East-First Floor, 2415 First Ave, Sacramento, CA 95818); 916-657-8098, 916-657-5564 (Alternate Telephone), 8AM-5PM.

General Information: Records are available for 3 years for accidents and minor moving violations, 4 years for fatal accidents and major violations, and 10 years for DWIs. It takes 10 days or more before new records are available for inquiries. Commercial requesters/users who meet certain criteria maintain a Commercial Requester

Account, which may require a $50,000 bond if confidential address information is released. For more information about a Requester Account call (916) 657-5564.

Online search: The department offers online access, but a $10,000 one-time setup fee is required. The system is open 24 hours, 7 days a week. Fee is $2 per record. For more information call the Analysis and Coordination Unit at (916) 657-5582.

Vehicle Ownership
Vehicle Identification
Boat & Vessel Ownership
Boat & Vessel Registration

Department of Motor Vehicle, Public Contact Unit, PO Box 944247, Sacramento, CA 94244-2470; (Courier: Bldg East-First Floor, 2415 First Ave, Sacramento, CA 95818); 916-657-8098 (Walk-in/Mail-in Phone), 916-657-7914 (Commercial Accounts), 916-657-6739 (Vessel Registration), 916-657-9041 (Fax), 8AM-5PM.

General Information: Records are available for three years. Beyond that, a subpoena is required. All watercraft must be registered if over 8 ft (except rowboats). There are two types of requesters: "casual requesters" and "requester account holders."

Online search: Online access is limited to certain Authorized Vendors. Fee is $2 per record, most records. Hours are 6 AM to midnight. Requesters are may not use the data for direct marketing, solicitation, nor resell for those purposes. For more information, call 916-657-5582. Release of information is denied for commercial marketing purposes.

Legislation-Current/Pending
Legislation-Passed

www.leginfo.ca.gov

California State Legislature, State Capitol, Room B-32 (Legislative Bill Room), Sacramento, CA 95814; 916-445-2323 (Current/Pending Bills), 916-653-7715 (State Archives), 8AM-5PM.

Online search: The Internet site has all legislative information back to 1993. The site also gives access to state laws.

Information About County Agencies

Court Structure

As of September 1995, all justice courts were eliminated and converted to municipal courts. Operations, judges, and records became part of the municipal court system.

California continues the process of combining and consolidating Superior and Municipal Courts.

Municipal Courts may try minor felonies not included under our felony definition.

About the County Courts

Online Access

There is no statewide online computer access available, internal or external, however, a number of counties have developed their own online systems, allowing access to their internal case management systems by county residents. The State Judicial Council is investigating the feasibility, cost, and coverage of such a system statewide. Two percent of all fines, penalties, and forfeitures in criminal cases is being set aside in an automation fund to be used exclusively to pay for the automation of court record keeping and case management systems for criminal cases. However, activity is at the planning and pilot level.

Searching Hints

If there is more than one court of a type within a county, where the case is tried and where the record is held depends on how a citation is written, where the infraction occurred, or where the filer chose to file the case.

Some courts—see Alameda County—now require signed releases from the subject in order to perform criminal searches, and will no longer allow the public to conduct such searches.

Personal checks are acceptable by state law.

Although fees are set by statute, courts interpret them differently. For example, the search fee is supposed to be $5.00 per name per year searched, but many courts charge only $5.00 per name. Certification fee is now $6.00 per document.

About the Recorder's Office

Organization

58 counties, 58 recording offices. The recording officer is County Recorder. Recordings are usually located in a Grantor/Grantee or General index. The entire state is in the Pacific Time Zone (PST).

Real Estate Records

Most counties do not perform real estate searches. Copy fees and certification fees vary.

UCC Records

Financing statements are filed at the state level, except for consumer goods, crops, and real estate related collateral, which are filed only with the County Recorder. All counties will perform UCC searches. Use search request form UCC-11. Search fees are usually $15.00 per debtor name. Copy costs vary.

Other Lien Records

Federal and state tax liens on personal property of businesses are filed with the Secretary of State. Other federal and state tax liens are filed with the County Recorder. Some counties will perform separate tax lien searches. Fees vary for this type of search.

Other liens are: judgment (Note: many judgments are also filed with the Secretary of State), child support, mechanics.

County Courts & Recording Offices Online

Contra Costa County

Civil Cases

www.co.contra-costa.ca.us

Superior Court, 725 Court St Rm 103, Martinez CA 94553, 925-646-2950. Civil Phone: 925-646-2951. Hours: 8AM-4PM

General Information: The web site includes all municipal courts within the county.

Online search: Access is available for free through a remote dial-up system. This includes all municipal courts within the county. Accessible information includes: parties names, court dates, court calendars and a list of all documents filed. Required to search: name, years to search. Cases indexed by defendant, plaintiff.

Civil Actions Under $25,000, Eviction, Small Claims

Mt Diablo Municipal Court-Civil Division, 2970 Willow Pass Rd, Concord CA 94519, 925-646-5410. Fax: 925-646-5205.

Hours: 8AM-4PM (PST). Includes Avon, Clayton, Clyde, Concord, Martinez, Pacheco, Pleasant Hill.

Misdemeanor, Civil Actions Under $25,000, Eviction, Small Claims

Delta Municipal Court, 45 Civic Ave, Pittsburg CA 94565-0431. Civil Phone: 510-427-8159. Hours: 8AM-4:30PM. Includes Antioch, Bethel Island, Bradford Island, Brentwood, Byron, Coney Island, Discovery Bay, Holland Tract, Jersey Island, Knightsen, Oakley, Pittsburg, Quimby Island, Shore Acres, Webb Tract, West Pittsburg, and parts of Clayton.

All the following Contra-Costa County courts have records that can be accessed from the web site listed here.

Misdemeanor, Civil Actions Under $25,000, Eviction, Small Claims

Bay Municipal Court, 100 37th St Rm 185, Richmond CA 94805. Civil Phone: 510-374-3138. Hours: 8AM-4PM (PST). Includes Crockett, El Cerrito, El Sobrante, Hercules, Kensington, North Richmond, Pinole, Point Richmond, Port Costa, Richmond, Rodeo, Rollingwood and San Pablo.

Misdemeanor, Civil Actions Under $25,000, Eviction, Small Claims

Walnut Creek-Danville Municipal Court, 640 Ygnacio Valley Rd, Walnut Creek CA 94596-1128, 925-646-6578. Civil Phone: 925-646-6579. Hours: 8:30AM-4:30PM (PST). Includes Alamo, Canyon, Danville, Lafayette, Moraga, Orinda, Rheem, San Ramon, St Mary's College, Walnut Creek and Ygnacio Valley.

Los Angeles County

Superior & Trial Court Cases

All consolidated courts throughout Los Angeles County

www.latrialcourts.org/civil.htm

WEBCOURT online access is available for these courts in the county from the Internet Site. (Traffic records are also available.)

Civil Cases, Traffic, Misdemeanors

Los Angeles Municipal Courts throughout Los Angeles County.

www.lamuni.org

In Los Angeles County, **Superior & Trial Court** cases can be found at: www.latrialcourts.org/civil.htm

Civil Cases, Traffic & Misdemeanors can be found at: www.lamuni.org;.

An exception is **Burbank Municipal Courts**, which offers only directory info at www.courts.org

Misdemeanor, Civil Actions Under $25,000, Eviction, Small Claims

Site used by Burbank Municipal Court:

www.courts.org

Burbank Municipal Court, 300 E Olive, PO Box 750, Burbank CA 91503, 818-557-3461. Civil Phone: 818-557-2461. Criminal Phone: 818-557-3466.

Online search:

www.court.org is a generic state Internet site used by the Burbank Court and no actual Civil and Criminal records are available online, but directory information is available.

Orange County

Civil Actions Over $25,000.

www.oc.ca.gov/superior/civil.htm

Superior Court-Civil, 700 Civic Center Dr W, Santa Ana CA 92702, 714-834-2208. Hours: 9AM-5PM (PST).

Civil Actions Under $25,000, Eviction, Small Claims.

www.oc.ca.gov/southcourt

South Orange County Municipal Court-Civil Division, 23141 Moulton Pkwy 2nd Fl, Laguna Hills CA 92653-1206, 949-472-6964. Hours: 8AM-5PM (PST).

Misdemeanor

www.oc.ca.gov/southcourt

South Orange County Municipal Court-Criminal Division, 30143 Crown Valley Parkway, Laguna Niguel CA 92677, 949-249-5113. Hours: 8AM-5PM (PST).

Riverside County

Felony, Misdemeanor

www.co.riverside.ca.us/depts/courts

Consolidated Courts - Criminal Division, 4100 Main St, Riverside CA 92501, 909-275-2300. Fax: 909-275-4007.

Online search: A county-wide computer network contains indexed cases for all courts in the county. Online access is available by modem at $225.00 plus $16.00 per hour. Civil, family law, probate and traffic cases are also included on the system. Call Melinda Pierpoint at 909-275-5940 for more information.

All the Courts listed for Riverside County have records that can be accessed from the web site listed here.

Civil, Probate

www.co.riverside.ca.us/depts/courts

Consolidated Courts-Civil Division, 4050 Main St, Riverside CA 92501, 909-275-1960. Fax: 909-275-1751. Hours: 8AM-5PM (PST).

Misdemeanor, Civil Actions Under $25,000, Eviction, Small Claims

Banning Department-Municipal Court, 155 E Hayes St, Banning CA 92220. Civil Phone: 909-922-7155. Criminal Phone: 909-922-7145. Fax: 909-922-7160. Includes Banning, Cabazon, Highland Springs, Poppet Flatt, Silent Valley, Beaumont, Calimesa, Cherry Valley and Whitewater.

Desert Division-Blythe Consolidated Courts, 260 N Spring St, Blythe CA 92225, 760-921-7828. Fax: 760-921-7941. Hours: 7:30AM-5PM (PST). Includes Blythe, Ripley.

Consolidated Courts-Corona Branch, 505 S Buena Vista Rm 201, Corona CA 91720, 909-270-5020 (Traffic & Minor Offenses). Civil Phone: 909-272-5620. Criminal Phone: 909-272-5630. Fax: 909-272-5651 (Civil) 272-5691 (Criminal). Hours: 7:30AM-5PM. Includes Corona, El Cerrito, Home Gardens, Norco, Santa Ana Canyon.

Hemet Department-Municipal Court, 880 N State St, Hemet CA 92543, 909-766-2321. Criminal Phone: 909-766-2310. Fax: 909-766-2317. Hours: 7:30AM-4:30PM; Criminal, Civil/SC. Includes Aguanga, Anza, Gilman Hot Springs, Hemet, Idylwild, Mountain Center, Pine Cove, Redec, Sage, San Jacinto, Sobba Hot Spring, Valle Vista and Winchester.

Desert Division-Indio Consolidated Courts, 46200 Oasis St, Indio CA 92201. Civil: 760-863-8208. Criminal: 760-863-8206. Fax: 760-863-8707. Includes Desert Center, Eagle Mountain, Indio, La Quinta, Coachella, Bermuda Dunes, Mecca, North Shore, Pinyon Pines, Palm Springs, Salton Sea, Oasis, Thermal. Most Palm Springs records are here.

Civil Actions Under $25,000, Eviction, Small Claims.

Three Lakes District-Lake Elsinore Branch-Municipal Court, 117 S Langstaff, Lake Elsinore CA 92530, 909-245-3370. Fax: 909-245-3366. Hours: 7:30AM-Noon, 1-5PM (PST).

Three Lakes District-Temecula Branch-Municipal Court, 41002 County Center Dr, Temecula CA 92591, 909-694-5160. Fax: 909-694-5084. Hours: 7:30AM-Noon,1-4PM.

Misdemeanor, Civil Actions Under $25,000, Eviction, Small Claims

Consolidated Courts-Moreno Valley Branch, 13800 Heacock Ave Ste D201, Moreno Valley CA 92553-3338, 909-697-4504 (small claims). Civil Phone: 909-341-8876 (traff). Fax: 909-697-4526. Hours: 7:30AM-5PM (PST).

Misdemeanor

Desert Division-Palm Springs Consolidated Courts, 3255 Tahkuits Canyon Way, Palm Springs CA 92262, 760-778-2315. Fax: 760-863-8114. Hours: 7:30AM-5PM. Includes Cathedral City, Palm Springs, Rancho Mirage, Thousand Palms, Indian Wells, Palm Desert, Desert Hot Springs. See also Indio Court.

Felony, Misdemeanor, Civil Actions Under $25,000, Eviction, Small Claims.

Three Lakes District-Perris Department-Municipal Court, 277 N "D" St., Perris CA 92370, 909-940-6820; 940-6830 (Traffic). Civil Phone: 909-940-6820. Criminal Phone: 909-940-6840. Fax: 909-940-6810. Hours: 7:30AM-5PM (PST). Holds all records for Three Lakes District. Records are for past 10 years.

Ventura County

Felony, Misdemeanor, Civil, Eviction, Small Claims, Probate

www.ventura.org/courts/vencrts.htm

East County Superior & Municipal Court, PO Box 1200, Simi Valley CA 93062-1200, 805-582-8080. Hours: 8AM-5PM.

Online search: Online access is open 24 hours daily and is the same system as below. Civil and criminal records on computer since 1991. No adoption, mental health, paternity actions, juvenile, medical, probation or sealed records released.

Felony, Misdemeanor, Civil, Eviction, Small Claims, Probate

www.ventura.org/courts/vencrts.htm

Ventura County Superior & Municipal Courts, 800 S Victoria Ave PO Box 6489, Ventura CA 93006-6489, 805-662-6620. Fax: 805-650-4032. Hours: 8AM-5PM (PST).

Online search: Contact Gloria Moreno at 805-654-3745 for information about remote access. Cost is $100 for civil and $100 for criminal access plus $60 per user key. The system is open 24 hours daily.

Federal Courts Online

County-to-Court Cross Reference (Bankruptcy Court locations in Parenthesis if different)

County	District	Court Location
Alameda	Northern	San Jose (Oakland)
Alpine	Eastern	Sacramento
Amador	Eastern	Sacramento
Butte	Eastern	Sacramento
Calaveras	Eastern	Sacramento (Modesto)
Colusa	Eastern	Sacramento
Contra Costa	Northern	San Jose (Oakland)
Del Norte	Northern	San Jose (Santa Rosa)
El Dorado	Eastern	Sacramento
Fresno	Eastern	Fresno
Glenn	Eastern	Sacramento
Humboldt	Northern	San Jose (Santa Rosa)
Imperial	Southern	San Diego
Inyo	Eastern	Fresno
Kern	Eastern	Fresno
Kings	Eastern	Fresno
Lake	Northern	San Jose (Santa Rosa)
Lassen	Eastern	Sacramento
Los Angeles	Central	Los Angeles (Western)
Madera	Eastern	Fresno
Marin	Northern	San Jose (Santa Rosa)
Mariposa	Eastern	Fresno
Mendocino	Northern	San Jose (Santa Rosa)
Merced	Eastern	Fresno
Modoc	Eastern	Sacramento
Mono	Eastern	Sacramento
Monterey	Northern	San Jose
Napa	Northern	San Jose (Santa Rosa)
Nevada	Eastern	Sacramento
Orange	Central	Santa Ana (Southern)
Placer	Eastern	Sacramento
Plumas	Eastern	Sacramento
Riverside	Central	Riverside (Eastern)
Sacramento	Eastern	Sacramento
San Benito	Northern	San Jose
San Bernardino	Central	Riverside (Eastern)
San Diego	Southern	San Diego
San Francisco	Northern	San Jose (San Francisco)
San Joaquin	Eastern	Sacramento (Modesto)
San Luis Obispo	Central	Los Angeles (Western)
San Mateo	Northern	San Jose (San Francisco)
Santa Barbara	Central	Los Angeles (Western)
Santa Clara	Northern	San Jose
Santa Cruz	Northern	San Jose
Shasta	Eastern	Sacramento
Sierra	Eastern	Sacramento
Siskiyou	Eastern	Sacramento
Solano	Eastern	Sacramento
Sonoma	Northern	San Jose (Santa Rosa)
Stanislaus	Eastern	Fresno (Modesto)
Sutter	Eastern	Sacramento
Tehama	Eastern	Sacramento
Trinity	Eastern	Sacramento
Tulare	Eastern	Fresno
Tuolumne	Eastern	Fresno (Modesto)
Ventura	Central	Los Angeles (Western)
Yolo	Eastern	Sacramento
Yuba	Eastern	Sacramento

US District Court
Central District of California

www.cacd.uscourts.gov

PACER sign-up number is 800-676-6856. Both civil and criminal case records are available online.

Los Angeles (Western) Division, US Courthouse, Attn: Correspondence, 312 N Spring St, Room G-8, Los Angeles, CA 90012, 213-894-5261

Riverside (Eastern) Division, US Courthouse, PO Box 13000, Riverside, CA 92502-3000, 909-276-6170

Santa Ana (Southern) Division, 751 W Santa Ana Blvd, Room 101, Santa Ana, CA 92701-4599, 714-836-2468

US Bankruptcy Court
Central District of California

www.cacb.uscourts.gov

PACER sign-up number is 800-676-6856.

Los Angeles Division, 255 E Temple St, , Los Angeles, CA 90012, 213-894-3118, Fax: 213-894-1261

Riverside Division, 3420 12th St, Riverside, CA 92501-3819, 909-774-1000

San Fernando Valley Division, 21041 Burbank Blvd, Woodland Hills, CA 91367, 818-587-2900

Santa Ana Division, PO Box 12600, Santa Ana, CA 92712, 714-836-2993

Santa Barbara (Northern) Division, 1415 State St, Santa Barbara, CA 93101, 805-884-4800

US District Court
Eastern District of California

www.caed.uscourts.gov

PACER sign-up number is 800-676-6856. Both civil and criminal case records are available online.

Fresno Division, US Courthouse, Room 5000, 1130 "O" St, Fresno, CA 93721-2201, 209-498-7483, Record Room: 209-498-7372, Civil Docket Section: 209-498-7235, Criminal Docket Section: 209-498-7235

Sacramento Division, 2546 United States Courthouse, 650 Capitol Mall, Sacramento, CA 95814-4797, 916-498-5470, Record Room: 916-498-5415, Fax: 916-498-5469

US Bankruptcy Court
Eastern District of California

www.caeb.uscourts.gov

PACER sign-up number is 800-676-6856.

Fresno Division, Room 2656, 1130 O Street, Fresno, CA 93721, 209-498-7217

Modesto Division, PO Box 5276, Modesto, CA 95352, 209-521-5160

Sacramento Division, 8308 US Courthouse, 650 Capitol Mall, Sacramento, CA 95814, 916-498-5525

US District Court
Northern District of California

PACER sign-up number is 800-676-6856. Both civil and criminal case records are available online.

San Jose Division, Room 2112, 280 S 1st St, San Jose, CA 95113, 408-535-5364.

US Bankruptcy Court
Northern District of California

www.canb.uscourts.gov

PACER sign-up number is 800-676-6856.

Oakland Division, PO Box 2070, Oakland, CA 94604, 510-879-3600

San Francisco Division, PO Box 7341, San Francisco, CA 94120-7341, 415-268-2300

San Jose Division, Room 3035, 280 S 1st St, San Jose, CA 95113-3099, 408-535-5118

Santa Rosa Division, 99 South E St, Santa Rosa, CA 95404, 707-525-8539, Fax: 707-579-0374

US District Court
Southern District of California

San Diego Division, Room 4290, 880 Front St, San Diego, CA 92101-8900, 619-557-5600, Record Room: 619-557-7362, Fax: 619-557-6684

www.casd.uscourts.gov/

Although charges of 7 cents per page are planned for this site, at last check you could use this site freely by entering your own PACER ID and password, *or* use p135 as an ID and "pass" as the password, then search for dockets by case number, name, SSN, or tax ID number.

The regular PACER sign-up number is 800-676-6856. Both civil and criminal case records are available online.

US Bankruptcy Court
Southern District of California

New "PACER-Net"

http://207.222.24.5/bc/chlogin.html

As a member of the PACER-Net project, PACER data may be obtained via the Internet. The PACER sign-up number is 800-676-6856. Only civil case records are available online.

San Diego Division, Office of the Clerk, US Courthouse, 325 West "F" St., San Diego, CA 92101, 619-557-5620.

Colorado

Governor's Office
136 State Capitol Bldg   303-866-2471
Denver, CO 80203-1792   Fax 303-866-2003
www.state.us/gov_dir/governor_office.html

Attorney General's Office
1525 Sherman St, 5th Floor   303-866-4500
Denver, CO 80203   Fax 303-866-5691
www.state.us/gov_dir/dol/index.htm

State Archives
Colorado Information   303-866-2055
Technology Services   Fax 303-866-2257
Archives & Public Records   9AM-4:30PM
1313 Sherman St, Room 1B20
Denver, CO 80203
www.state.us/gov_dir/gss/archives/index.html

Capital:	Denver
	Denver County
Time Zone:	MST
Number of Counties:	63
Population:	3,892,644
Web Site:	www.state.co.us

State Court Administrator
State Court Administrator   303-861-1111
1301 Pennsylvania St, Ste. 300 Fax 303-837-2340
Denver, CO 80203   8AM-5PM
www.courts.state.us

State Agencies Online

Criminal Records
Bureau of Investigation, State Repository, Identification Unit, 690 Kipling St, Suite 3000, Denver, CO 80215; 303-239-4230, 303-239-0865 (Fax), 8AM-5PM.

General Information: The following data is not available - sealed records or juvenile records.

Online search: There is a remote access system available called the Electronic Clearance System (ECS). This is an overnight batch system, open M-F from 7AM to 4PM. The fee is $7.00 per record. There is no set-up fee, but requesters must register. Billing in monthly. For more information, call (303) 239-4230

Corporation Records
Trademarks/Servicemarks
Fictitious Name
Limited Liability Company Records
Assumed Name
Secretary of State, Corporation Division, 1560 Broadway, Suite 200, Denver, CO 80202; 303-894-2251

(Corporations), 900-555-1717 (Status-Name), 303-894-2242 (Fax), 8:30AM-5PM.

General Information: Records are available for all active companies. Inactive company records are archived. New records are available for inquiry immediately.

Online search: Online access is gatewayed through another agency -The Colorado Central Indexing System, (303) 894-2175. The system can be accessed from their web site (www.cocis.com) or from a separate dial-up mode. There is an annual $29.50 registration fee. Accounts can be set up to pay on a per search basis or for unlimited access. There are two plans, one including corporate officers and directors, and one not (corporate name searching only). The system holds UCC records from both the Secretary of State and the counties as well vehicle lien records.

Uniform Commercial Code
Federal Tax Liens
State Tax Liens

UCC Division, Secretary of State, 1560 Broadway, Suite 200, Denver, CO 80202; 303-894-2200, 900-555-1717 Status-Name, 303-894-2242 (Fax), 8:30AM-5PM.

Online search: The online access is available through the Colorado Central Indexing System (CIS). It is available from the Internet at www.cocis.com or by direct dial-up. The fee is $15.00 to search by name or $2,500 per 6 months for unlimited access. There is no fee to search notice of farm product liens or for the sales tax by address locator. This system has filings from the state and the counties and lien records from the DMV. CIS can be reached at (303) 894-2175. They do not permit mail, phone, or in person searching.

Legislation-Current/Pending
Legislation-Passed

www.state.us/gov_dir/stateleg.html

Colorado General Assembly, State Capitol, 200 E Colfax Ave, Denver, CO 80203-1784; 303-866-3055 (Bill Data (during session), 303-866-2358 (Archives),.

Online search: The web site gives access to bills, status, journals, the two latest sessions, and much more.

Information About County Agencies

Court Structure

The District and County Courts have overlapping jurisdiction over civil cases involving less than $10,000. District and County Courts are combined in most counties. Combined courts usually search both civil or criminal indexes for a single fee, except as indicated in the profiles. Denver is the only county with a separate Probate Court. Municipal courts only have jurisdiction over traffic, parking, and ordinance violations.

About the
County Courts

Searching Hints

A statewide online computer system is under development in Colorado.

Co-located with seven district courts are divisions known as "Water Courts." The Water Courts are located in Weld, Pueblo, Alamosa, Montrose, Garfield, Routt, and La Platta counties; see the District Court discussion for those counties to determine the jurisdictional area for the Water Court. Water Court records are maintained by the Water Clerk and fees are similar to those for other court records. To retrieve a Water Court record, one must furnish the Case Number or the Legal Description (section, township, and range) or the Full Name of the respondent (note that the case number or legal description are preferred).

About the
Recorder's Office

Organization

63 counties, 63 recording offices. The recording officer is County Clerk and Recorder. The entire state is in the Mountain Time Zone (MST).

Real Estate Records

Counties do not perform real estate searches. Copy fees are usually $1.25 per page and certification fees are usually $1.00 per document. Tax records are located in the Assessor's Office.

UCC Records

Financing statements are filed at the state level, except for consumer goods, farm and real estate related collateral, which are filed with the

County Clerk and Recorder. All counties will perform UCC searches. Use search request form UCC-11. Search fees are usually $5.00 per debtor name for the first year and $2.00 for each additional year searched (or $13.00 for a five year search). Copies usually cost $1.25 per page.

Other Lien Records

Federal and some state tax liens on personal property are filed with the Secretary of State. Other federal and state tax liens are filed with the County Clerk and Recorder. Many counties will perform tax lien searches, usually at the same fees as UCC searches. Copies usually cost $1.25 per page. Other liens are: judgments, motor vehicle, mechanics.

County Courts & Recording Offices Online

Although a statewide online computer system is under development in Colorado, there are presently no courts or recording offices online.

Federal Courts Online

US District Court
District of Colorado

Denver Division, US Courthouse, Room C-145 (Civil) Room C-161 (Criminal), 1929 Stout St, Denver, CO 80294-3589, 303-844-3433, Civil Docket Section: 303-844-3434, Criminal Docket Section: 303-844-2115. This court services all Colorado counties.

PACER sign-up number is 800-676-6856. Both civil and criminal case records are available online.

US Bankruptcy Court
District of Colorado

Denver Division, US Custom House, Room 114, 721 19th St, Denver, CO 80202-2508, 303-844-4045, Record Room: 303-844-0235. This court services all Colorado counties.

www.ck10.uscourts.gov/cobk

PACER sign-up number is 800-676-6856.

Connecticut

Governor's Office
State Capitol,
210 Capitol Ave, Rm 202   860-566-4840
Hartford, CT 06106   Fax 860-566-4677
www.state.ct.us/governor

Attorney General's Office
55 Elm St   860-808-5318
Hartford, CT 06106   Fax 860-808-5387
www.cslnet.ctstateu.edu/attygenl

State Archives
Connecticut State Library   860-566-3692
History & Genealogy Unit   Fax 860-566-2133
231 Capitol Ave   9:30AM-5PM M-F
Hartford, CT 06106
www.cslet.ctstateu.edu/archives.htm

Capital:	Hartford
	Hartford County
Time Zone:	EST
Number of Counties:	8
Population:	3,269,858
Web Site:	www.state.ct.us

State Court Administrator
Chief Court Administrator   860-566-4461
231 Capitol Ave   Fax 860-566-3308
Hartford, CT 06106   9AM-5PM

State Agencies Online

Corporation Records
Limited Partnership Records
Trademarks/Servicemarks
Limited Liability Company Records
www.state.ct.us/sots

Secretary of State, Commercial Recording Division, 30 Trinity St, Hartford, CT 06106; 860-509-6003, 860-509-6068 (Fax), 8:45AM-3PM.

General Information: New records are available for inquiry immediately. Assumed names are found at the county level.

Online search: There is no set-up fee, but a "bank" of $500.00 must be established. The communications network is AAMVAnet and charges are incurred. The cost to view a screen of data figures to less than $.01. The system supports baud rates to 28.8. Call David Pritchard at (860) 509-6154 for more information.

Driver Records
Department of Motor Vehicles, Copy Records Section, 60 State St, Room 305, Wethersfield, CT 06109-1896; 860-566-3720, 8:30AM-4:30PM T,W,F; 8:30AM-7:30PM Th; 8:30AM-12:30 S.

General Information: Records are available for 5 years to present at the commissioner's discretion. Accidents and arrests under the "Per Se" suspension are not reported. A DWI first offense violation will not appear if the offender attends an "Accelerated Alcohol Class." It takes 5 days before new records are available for inquiries.

Online search: Online access is provided to approved businesses that enter into written contract. The system is open 24 hours a day, 7 days a week. The fee is $10 per record. The address is part of the record. For more information, call (860) 566-3596

Vehicle Ownership
Vehicle Identification
Department of Motor Vehicles, Copy Record Unit, 60 State St, Branch Operations, Wethersfield, CT 06109-1896; 860-566-3720, 8:30AM-4:30PM T,W,F; 8:30AM-7:30 PM Th; 8:30AM-12:30 S.

General Information: Records are available for 3 years to present. Any records prior to this period may be destroyed at the discretion of the commissioner. Businesses that enter into a contract with the DMV may obtain records.

Online search: The Department has started a pilot program for online access that is not yet open to the general business public. This program, when available to all, will have the same restrictions and criteria as described in the Driving Records Section.

Legislation-Current/Pending Legislation-Passed

www.cga.state.ct.us

Connecticut General Assembly, State Library, 231 Capitol Ave, Bill Room, Hartford, CT 06106; 860-566-5736, 860-566-2133 (Fax), 9:30AM-5PM.

Online search: From the web site you can track bills, find update or status, and print copies of bills.

Information About County Agencies

Court Structure

The Superior Court is the sole court of original jurisdiction for all causes of action, except for matters over which the probate courts have jurisdiction as provided by statute. The "Geographic Area Courts" are actually divisions of the Superior Court given jurisdiction over lesser offenses and actions. The Superior Court has five divisions: Criminal, Civil, Family, Juvenile, and Administrative Appeals.

About the County Courts

Online Access

An online system called Civil/Family System, which provides direct access to Superior Court records, is available through CATER, the Connecticut Administrative Center. CATER users can access data concerning all civil and family cases statewide. The system is available from 8AM to 5PM Eastern Time Monday through Friday except on holidays. The fee is $30 per month network charge, $10.00 per use per month user authorization fee, plus a per minute usage fee. For an information brochure or subscription information call the CT JIS Office at 860-566-8580. There is currently no online access to criminal records. However, there is a central records repository (see below).

Searching Hints

Personal checks must have name and address printed on the check; if requesting in person, check must have same address as drivers' license.

Many clerks state that they will send an extract of a record without copying originals or certification at no charge.

About the Recorder's Office

Organization

8 counties and 170 towns/cities. The recording officer is Town/City Clerk. Counties have no administrative offices. Be careful not to confuse searching in the following towns/cities as equivalent to a county-wide search : Fairfield, Hartford, Litchfield, New Haven, New London, Tolland, and Windham. The entire state is in the Eastern Time Zone (EST).

Real Estate Records

Towns do not perform real estate searches. Copy fees are usually $1.00 per page. Certification fees are usually $1.00 per document or per page.

UCC Records

Financing statements are filed at the state level, except for real estate related collateral, which are filed only with the Town/City Clerk. Towns will not perform UCC searches. Copies usually cost $1.00 per page.

Other Lien Records

All federal and state tax liens on personal property are filed with the Secretary of State. Federal and state tax liens on real property are filed with the Town/City Clerk. Towns will not perform tax lien searches. Other liens are: mechanics, judgments, lis pendens, municipal, welfare, carpenter, sewer & water, city/town.

County Courts & Recording Offices Online

An online system called Civil/Family System, which provides direct access to Superior Court records, is available through CATER, the Connecticut Administrative Center. CATER users can access data concerning all civil and family cases statewide. The system is available from 8AM to 5PM Eastern Time Monday through Friday except on holidays. The fee is $30 per month network charge, $10.00 per use per month user authorization fee, plus a per minute usage fee. For an information brochure or subscription information call the CT JIS Office at 860-566-8580. There is currently no online access to criminal records.

No remote online access is available from real estate recorder's office in Connecticut.

Federal Courts Online

County-to-Court Cross Reference (Bankruptcy Court locations in Parenthesis if different)

Fairfield	Bridgeport		New Haven	New Haven
Hartford	Hartford		New London	New Haven
Litchfield	New Haven (Hartford)		Tolland	Hartford
Middlesex	New Haven (Hartford)		Windham	Hartford

US District Court
District of Connecticut

PACER sign-up number is 800-676-6856. Both civil and criminal case records are available online.

Bridgeport Division, Office of the Clerk, Room 400, 915 Lafayette Blvd, Bridgeport, CT 06604, 203-579-5861.

Hartford Division, 450 Main St, Hartford, CT 06103, 860-240-3200.

New Haven Division, 141 Church St, New Haven, CT 06510, 203-773-2140.

Waterbury Division, c/o New Haven Division, 141 Church St, New Haven, CT 06510, 203-773-2140.

US Bankruptcy Court
District of Connecticut

PACER sign-up number is 800-676-6856.

Bridgeport Division, 915 Lafayette Blvd, Bridgeport, CT 06604, 203-579-5808, Record Room: 203-579-5808.

Hartford Division, 450 Main St, Hartford, CT 06103, 860-240-3675.

New Haven Division, The Connecticut Financial Center, 157 Church St, 18th Floor, New Haven, CT 06510, 203-773-2009.

Delaware

Governor's Office
820 N. French St,
Carvel State Bldg   302-577-3210
Wilmington, DE 19801   Fax 302-577-3118
www.state.de.us

Attorney General's Office
Carvel State Office Bldg   302-577-3047
820 N French St, 7th floor   Fax 302-577-3090
Wilmington, DE 19801   8:30AM-4:30PM
www.state.de.us

State Archives
Delaware Public Archives   302-739-5318
Hall of Records   Fax 302-739-2578
Public Archives   8:30AM-4:15PM
Dover, DE 19903
www.state.de.us

Capital:	Dover
	Kent County
Time Zone:	EST
Number of Counties:	3
Population:	731,581
Web Site:	www.state.de.us

State Court Administrator
Admin. Office of the Courts   302-577-2480
PO Box 8911   Fax 302-577-3139
Wilmington, DE 19899   8:30AM-5PM
www.state.de.us

State Agencies Online

Driver Records
Division of Motor Vehicles, Driver Services, PO Box 698, Dover, DE 19903; (Courier: 303 Transportation Circle, Dover, DE 19901); 302-739-4343, 302-739-2602 (Fax), 8AM-4:30PM M-T-Th-F; 12:00PM-8PM W.

General Information: Records are available for 3 years to present for public record purposes. It takes 2-3 weeks before new records are available for inquiries.

Online search: Online searching is single inquiry only, no batch request mode is offered. Searching is done by driver's license number or name and DOB. A signed contract application and valid "business license" is required. Hours of operation are 8AM to 4:30PM. Access is provided through AT&T's 900 number at a fee of $1.00 per minute, plus a cost of $4 per record. For more information, call (302) 739-4435.,

Vehicle Ownership
Vehicle Identification
Division of Motor Vehicles, Correspondence Section, PO Box 698, Dover, DE 19903; (Courier: 303 Transportation Circle, Dover, DE 19901); 302-739-3147, 302-739-2042 (Fax), 8:30AM-4:30PM M-T-Th-F; 12-8PM W.

General Information: Records are available for 3 years to present. It takes 2-3 weeks before new records are available for inquiries. Delaware allows individuals to request that the DMV exclude their name and address from lists compiled, sold, or supplied by the division for direct-mail advertising purposes. Casual requesters can obtain records, but with no personal information.

Access by: mail, visit, online

Online search: Cost is $4 per record plus there is an additional $1.00 per minute fee for using the online "900 number" system. The system is single inquiry mode and is open from 8 am to 4:30PM. For more information, call (302) 739-4435.

Information About County Agencies

Court Structure

Superior Courts have jurisdiction over felonies and all drug offenses, the Court of Common Pleas has jurisdiction over all misdemeanors except those involving drug offenses. The Common Pleas courts handle some minor "felonies" as defined in state statutes. Probate is handled by the Register of Wills within the Court of Chancery. The Municipal Court of Wilmington merged with the Court of Common Pleas in New Castle in 1998.

Online Access

About the County Courts

An online system called CLAD, developed by Mead Data Central and the New Castle Superior Court, (302) 577-6470) is currently available in Delaware. CLAD contains only toxic waste, asbestos, and class action cases; however, based on CLAD's success, Delaware may pursue development of online availability of other public records by working in conjunction with private information resource enterprises.

Searching Hints

Effective 1/15/95, the civil case limit of the Justice of the Peace Courts increased from $5,000 to $15,000; the Courts of Common Pleas' limit went from $15,000 to $50,000.

Criminal histories are available with a signed release from the offender at the State Bureau of Identification in Dover. For information on criminal history retrieval requirements, call 302-739-5880.

About the Recorder's Office

Organization

Delaware has 3 counties and 3 recording offices. The recording officer is County Recorder in both jurisdictions. Delaware is in the Eastern Time Zone.

Real Estate Records

Counties do not perform real estate searches.

UCC Records

Financing statements are filed at the state level, except for real estate related collateral, which are filed only with the County Recorder. All counties perform UCC searches.

Other Lien Records

Federal tax liens on personal property of businesses are filed with the Secretary of State. Other federal and all state tax liens on personal property are filed with the County Recorder.

County Courts & Recording Offices Online

For online access to court records, see "Online Access" on the previous page.

No remote online access is available from real estate recorder's offices in Delaware.

Federal Courts Online

US District Court
District of Delaware

Wilmington Division, US Courthouse, Lock Box 18, 844 N King St, Wilmington, DE 19801, 302-573-6170, Record Rm.: 302-573-6158. This court serves all Delaware Counties.

PACER sign-up number is 800-676-6856. Both civil and criminal case records are available online.

US Bankruptcy Court
District of Delaware

Wilmington Division, 824 Market St, 5th Floor, Marine Midland Plaza, Wilmington, DE 19801, 302-573-6174. This court serves all Delaware Counties.

PACER sign-up number is 800-676-6856.

District of Columbia

Mayor's Office
One Judiciary Square,   202-727-2980
441 4th St NW #1100   Fax 202-727-2975
Washington, DC 20001
www.ci.washington.dc.us

Time Zone: EST

Population: 528-964

Web Site: www.capcityon-line.com

District Archives
Secretary of the District   202-727-2052
Office of Archives/   Fax 202-727-6076
Public Records
1300 Naylor Ct NW
Washington, DC 20001-4225

District Court Administrator
Executive Office   202-879-1700
500 Indiana Ave NW,   Fax 202-879-4829
Room 1500
Washington, DC 20001   8:30AM-5PM

District Agencies Online

Driver Records
Department of Motor Vehicles, Driver Records Division, 301 "C" St, NW, Washington, DC 20001; 202-727-6761, 8:15AM-4PM M-T-Th-F; 8:15AM-7:00PM W.

General Information: Records are available for 3 years for moving violations, suspensions/revocations for 7 years, and DWIs for an indefinite period. Accidents are listed on the record if there is a conviction, but fault is not indicated.

Online search: Online requests are taken throughout the day and are available the next morning after 8:15AM. There is no minimum order requirement, the fee is $5.00 per record. Overnight tape-to-tape batches are not available. Billing is a "bank" system that draws from pre-paid account. Requesters are restricted to high volume, ongoing users. Each requester must be approved and sign a contract. For more information, call (202) 727-5692.

Information About County Agencies

Court Structure
The Superior Court in DC is divided into 17 divisions, including: Criminal, Civil, Family, and Tax-Probate. Probate is handled by the Tax-Probate Division of the Superior Court.

About the County Courts

Online Access
The Court of Appeals maintains a bulletin board system for various court notices, and can be dialed from computer at 202-626-8863.

About the Recorder's Office

Organization

District of Columbia is in the Eastern Time Zone (EST).

Real Estate Records

The District does not perform real estate searches.

UCC Records

Financing statements are filed at the state level, except for real estate related collateral, which are filed only with the Recorder. UCC searches performed.

Other Lien Records

Federal tax liens on personal property of businesses are filed with the Secretary of State. Other federal and all state tax liens on personal property are filed with the Recorder.

Courts & Recording Offices Online

There is no online access to court records. However, the Court of Appeals maintains a bulletin board system for various court notices, and can be dialed from computer at 202-626-8863.

Real estate and lien records are not offered online.

Federal Courts Online

US District Court
District of Columbia

US Courthouse, Clerk's Office, Room 1225, 3rd & Constitution Ave NW, Washington, DC 20001, 202-273-0555, Record Room: 202-273-0520, Civil Docket Section: 202-273-0564, Criminal Docket Section: 202-273-0503, Fax: 202-273-0412.

PACER sign-up number is 800-676-6856. Both civil and criminal case records are available online.

US Bankruptcy Court
District of Columbia

E Barrett Prettyman Courthouse, Room 4400, 333 Constitution Ave NW, Washington, DC 20001, 202-273-0042.

PACER sign-up number is 800-676-6856.

Governor's Office

The Capitol   850-488-4441
Tallahassee, FL 32399-0001 Fax 850-487-0801
www.fcn.state.fl.us/eog

Attorney General's Office

Legal Affairs Department   850-488-2526
The Capitol, PL-01   Fax 850-487-2564
Tallahassee, FL 32399-1050 8AM-5PM
legal.firn.edu

State Archives

Library & Information Services Division
Archives & Records   850-487-2073
R A Gray Bldg,   Fax 850-488-4894
500 S Bronough   8AM-5PM M-F
Tallahassee, FL 32399-0250 9AM-3PM SA
www.dos.state.fl.us/dlis/barm/
archives.html

Capital: Tallahassee
Leon County

Time Zone: EST*

* Florida's ten western-most counties are CST:
They are: Bay, Calhoun, Escambia, Gulf, Holmes,
Jackson, Okaloosa, Santa Rosa, Walton, Washington.

Number of Counties: 67

Population: 14,653,945

Web Site: www.state.fl.us

State Court Administrator

Office of State Courts Administrator
Supreme Court Bldg,   850-922-5082
500 S Duval   Fax 850-488-0156
Tallahassee, FL 32399-1900 8AM-5PM
www.flcourts.org

State Agencies Online

Corporation Records
Limited Partnership Records
Trademarks/Servicemarks
Assumed Name
Fictitious Names
www.dos.state.fl.us

Division of Corporations, Department of State, PO Box 6327, Tallahassee, FL 32314; (Courier: 409 E Gaines St, Tallahassee, FL 32399); 850-488-9000 (Telephone Inquires), 850-487-6053 (Copy Requests), 850-487-6056 (Annual Reports), 8:30AM-4:30PM.

General Information: New records are available for inquiry immediately. Addresses of judges and police are not released. This agency recommends use of a retriever service or to come in person for documents; for general information they recommend accessing the Internet site.

Online search: The state has an excellent Internet site which gives detailed information for no charge on all corporate, fictitious names, partnerships, and UCC records. They also offer electronic filing. The site is available from 7 AM to 7 PM, EST Monday-Friday. Recently, they have added a corporations document image delivery system which includes fictitious name filings and corporation annual reports since 01/96, all other corporation filings since 11/97, and all partnership filings.

Criminal Records

Florida Department of Law Enforcement, User Services Bureau, PO Box 1489, Tallahassee, FL 32302; (Courier: 2331 Phillip Rd, Tallahassee, FL 32308); 850-488-6236, 850-488-1413 (Fax), 8AM-5PM.

Online search: Access is available for pre-approved, pre-paid accounts. This is a batch inquiry system. All criminal history records are available; the fee is $15.00 per individual. There is no sign-up fee, but requesters must establish an escrow account. The turnaround time is 48 hours. For more information, call Julie Boland at (850) 488-6236.

Uniform Commercial Code
Federal Tax Liens
www.dos.state.fl.us

UCC Division, Secretary of State, PO Box 5588, Tallahassee, FL 32314; (Courier: 409 E Gaines St, Tallahassee, FL 32399); 850-487-6055, 850-487-6013 (Fax), 8AM-4:30PM.

General Information: Records filed by electronic process are available in image format. Federal tax liens on businesses are filed here, state tax liens are not. It is suggested to search tax liens at the county level.

Online search: The state has a great Internet site which allows access for no charge. The site is open 7AM to 7PM M-F (EST). The collateral for the UCC filing is not mentioned in this database. The state also has a document image delivery system on the web site. This includes all UCC filings since 01/97 and all documents that were filed electronically since 03/95.

Driver Records
www.hsmv.state.fl.us

Department of Highway Safety & Motor Vehicles, Division of Drivers Licenses, PO Box 5775, Tallahassee, FL 32314-5775; (Courier: 2900 Apalachee Pky, Rm B-239, Neil Kirkman Bldg, Tallahassee, FL 32399); 850-488-0250, 850-487-7080 (Fax), 8AM-4:30PM.

General Information: Accidents will appear only if a citation is issued, but the record will not show fault. It takes no more than 10 days after conviction before new records are available for inquiries. Driving records are deemed public information and no restrictions to requests or usage are maintained, as long as the usage is of a legal nature. Casual requesters cannot obtain personal information if the subject opted out

Online search: Online requests are $2.10 for a three year record and $3.10 for a seven year record. There is also a $.10 transaction fee per record. The system is open 24 hours a day, 7 days a week. The state differentiates between high and low volume users. Call Information Systems Administration at 850-488-6264 for details.

Vehicle Ownership
Vehicle Identification
www.hsmv.state.fl.us

Division of Motor Vehicles, Information Research Section, Neil Kirkman Bldg, A-126, Tallahassee, FL 32399; 850-488-5665, 850-488-8983 (Fax), 8AM-4:30PM.

General Information: Florida imposes no access restrictions as long as the request is of a legal nature. However, casual requesters cannot obtain personal information if the subject has opted out

Online search: Florida has contracted to release vehicle information through TML Information Services (800) 743-7891, accounts must be approved by the state first. For each record accessed, the charge is $.50 plus a transactional fee based on access and software. Users must work from an estimated 2 1/2 month pre-paid bank. New subscribers to TML must contact the company prior to completing an application with the Department (850) 488-6193.

Legislation-Current/Pending
Legislation-Passed
www.leg.state.fl.us

Joint Legislative Mgmt Committee, Legislative Information Division, 111 W Madison St, Pepper Bldg, Rm 704, Tallahassee, FL 32399-1400; 850-488-4371, 850-487-5285 (Senate Bills), 850-488-7475 (House Bills), 850-488-8427 (Session Laws), 850-921-5334 (Fax), 8AM-5PM.

Online search: Their Internet site contains full text of bills and a bill history session outlining actions taken on bills. The site is updated every day at 11 PM. Records go back to 1995. There is a more extensive online information service available from the Legislative Data Center at (850) 488-8326. This system also information on lobbyists. Fees are involved.

Information About County Agencies

Court Structure
All counties have combined Circuit and County Courts.

About the
County Courts

Online Access
There is a statewide, online computer system for internal use only; there is no external access available nor planned currently. A number of courts offer online access to the public.

Searching Hints

All courts have one address and switchboard; however, the divisions within the court(s) are completely separate. Requesters should specify which court and which division, e.g., Circuit Civil, County Civil, etc., the request is directed to, even though some counties will automatically check both with one request.

Fees are set by statute and are as follows:

Search Fee — $1.00 per name per year   Certification Fee — $1.00 per document plus copy fee

Copy Fee — $1.00 per certified page; $.15 per non-certified page.

Most courts have very lengthy phone recording systems.

About the Recorder's Office

Organization

67 counties, 67 recording offices. The recording officer is Clerk of the Circuit Court. All transactions are recorded in the "Official Record," a grantor/grantee index. A number of counties make their records available on-line. Some counties will search by type of transaction while others will return everything on the index. 57 counties are in the Eastern Time Zone (EST) and 10 are in the Central Time Zone (CST).

Real Estate Records

Any name searched in the "Official Records" will usually include all types of liens and property transfers for that name. Most counties will perform searches. In addition to the usual $1.00 per page copy fee, certification of documents usually cost $1.00 per document. Tax records are located at the Property Appraiser Office.

UCC Records

Financing statements are filed at the state level, except for farm and real estate related collateral. All but a few counties will perform UCC searches. Use search request form UCC-11. Search fees are usually $1.00 per debtor name per year searched and include all lien and real estate transactions on record. Copies usually cost $1.00 per page.

Other Lien Records

Federal tax liens on personal property of businesses are filed with the Secretary of State. All other federal and state tax liens on personal property are filed with the county Clerk of Circuit Court. Usually tax liens on personal property are filed in the same index with UCC financing statements and real estate transactions. Most counties will perform a tax lien as part of a UCC search. Copies usually cost $1.00 per page. Other liens are: judgments, hospital, mechanics, sewer, ambulance.

County Courts & Recording Offices Online

Alachua County

Criminal, Civil, Eviction, Small Claims, Probate

Circuit and County Courts, PO Box 600, Gainesville FL 32602, 352-374-3611. Fax: 352-338-3201. Hours: 8:30AM-5PM (EST).

Online search: For information about the remote access system and requesting searches by e-mail, fax a request to Jack Crosetti at 352-338-7365. The annual fee is $360 plus a one time setup fee of $50. The system is open 24 hours daily. Records can be searched by name or case number.

Brevard County

Civil, Eviction, Small Claims, Probate, Liens, Vital Records

www.clerk.co.brevard.fl.us

Circuit Court, PO Box H, 700 S Park Ave, Titusville FL 32780, 407-264-5245. Fax: 407-264-5246. Hours: 8AM-5PM

Online search: The annual fee for online access to the Indexing and ORM systems is $25.00, which includes unlimited use of the databases. The system is open 24 hours daily. Search by name or case number. Contact Lori Raulerson at 407-264-5241 for information about remote access.

Real Estate

www.appraiser.co.brevard.fl.us

County Appraisers, 400 South St 5th Fl, Titusville, FL 32780, 407-264-6700.

Online search: Access is free through the Internet. One may search by owner name or address.

Broward County

Criminal, Civil, Eviction, Small Claims, Probate

Circuit and County Court, 201 SE 6th St, Ft Lauderdale FL 33301, 954-831-5729. Criminal Phone: 954-765-4573. Fax: 954-831-7166. Hours: 9AM-4PM (EST).

Online search: The online system has a $40.00 setup fee plus security deposit. The monthly access fee is $49.00 which includes 2 free hours, afterward there is a $.34 per minute charge. Search by name or case number or case type. Call 954-357-7022 for more data.

Real Estate

www.bcpa.net/search_1.htm

Broward County Property Appraiser, 115 S Andrews #111, Ft Lauderdale, FL 33301-1899.

Online search: Access is free through the Internet.

Clay County

Criminal, Civil Actions Over $15,000, Probate, Liens, Real Estate

www.state.fl.us/clayclerk

Circuit Court, PO Box 698, Green Cove Springs FL 32043, 904-284-6302, Fax: 904-284-6390. Hours: 8:30AM-4:30PM.

Online search: The setup fee is $500 and there is a monthly usage fee of $50. Any VT 100 emulation software will work. The records date back to 1984. The system operates 24 hours daily and supports baud rates up to 33.6. One may search by name, case number, Grantee/Grantor and book and page. Lending agency information is available. Records include domestic and traffic. For further information, contact Carol Johnson at 904-284-6371.

Criminal, Civil Actions Over $15,000

www.state.fl.us/clayclerk

County Court, PO Box 698, Green Cove Springs FL 32043, 904-284-6316, Fax: 904-284-6390. Hours: 8:30AM-4:30PM.

Online search: This is the same system used by the Circuit Court in Clay County.

Collier County

Criminal, Civil Actions Over $15,000, Probate

Circuit and County Court, PO Box 413044, Naples FL 34101-3044, 941-732-2646. Hours: 8AM-5PM (EST).

Online search: The online access system has a $100.00 setup fee, a monthly $10.00 fee and a $.05 per minute access charge. The system is open 24 hours daily. Records include probate, traffic and domestic. Call 941-774-8339 for more information. No sealed by court or statute records released.

Liens, Real Estate, Birth Records, Death Records, Marriage Records, Divorce Records

County Clerk of the Circuit Court, 3001 Tamiami Trail, Administration Building, 4th Floor, Naples, FL 34122 , 941-774-8261. Fax: 941-774-8408.

Online search: The subscription fee is $100, plus a $50 deposit. The monthly fee is $10, plus $.05 per minute. The records date back to 1986. The system operates 24 hours daily and supports baud rates up to 9,600. One may search by name and Grantee/Grantor. Lending agency information is available. For additional information, contact Judy Stephenson at 941-774-8339.

Dade County

Civil, Eviction, Small Claims, Probate

Circuit and County Courts, 73 W Flagler St, Miami FL 33130, 305-275-1155. Fax: 305-375-5819. Hours: 9AM-4PM (EST).

Online search: Online access includes a $125.00 setup fee, $52.00 monthly and $.25 per minute after the first 208 minutes each month. Open 24 hours daily, docket information can be searched by case number or name. Call 305-596-8148 for more information.

Liens, Real Estate, Marriage Records, Tax Assessor Records

County Clerk, 44 W Flagler St, Miami FL 33130, 305-275-1155. Fax: 305-372-7775.

Online search: An initial setup fee of $125 is required, and there is a minimum monthly fee of $52, which includes 208 minutes of use. Additional minutes are $.25 each. The records date back to 1975. The system operates 24 hours daily, and supports a baud rate of 56k. 11 databases are available to search, including property appraisal, building permits, tax collection and permit public hearings, and others. One can search by name, Grantee/Grantor, folio number, address and by date. For info, contact Jerry Kiernan at 305-596-8148.

Duval County

Criminal, Civil, Eviction, Small Claims, Probate

www.ci.jax.fl.us/pub/clerk/default.htm

Circuit and County Courts, 330 E Bay St, Rm M106, Jacksonville FL 32202, 904-630-2039 (Civil), 904-630-2070 (Criminal) Fax: 904-630-7505. Hours: 8AM-5PM (EST).

Online search: Contact Mike O'Brien at 904-630-1140 for information about remote access. Costs include $100 setup, $30 per month and $0.25 per minute. System available 24 hours per day at minimum 9600 baud. Records back to 1992.

Escambia County

Liens, Real Estate, Divorce Records

County Clerk of the Circuit Courts, 223 Palafox Place, Old Courthouse, Pensacola FL 32501, 850-595-3930. Fax: 850-595-3925.

Online search: An initial subscription fee of $150 is required. The monthly fee of $42 is all inclusive. The records date back to 4/82. The system operates 24 hours daily. One may search by name, Grantee/Grantor or by document type. Lending agency information is available. No addresses can be viewed. For additional information, contact Joanne Duckworth at 850-595-3923.

Gadsden County

Liens, Real Estate, Death Records, Marriage Records, Divorce Records

Clerk of the Circuit Court, 10 E Jefferson St, Quincy FL 32351, 850-875-8603. Fax: 850-875-8612.

Online search: A written request needs to be sent to the Clerk of the Court to sign up for online access. The subscription fee varies, as does the monthly fee. The records date back to 1985. The system operates 24 hours daily. A baud rate of 19.2 is supported. The database can be searched by name, Grantee/Grantor, file number, date and document type. Lending agency information is available. For additional information, contact Jim Cleek at 904-875-8629.

Hernando County

Criminal, Civil, Liens, Real Estate, Marriage Records

Circuit and County Courts, 20 N Main St, Brooksville FL 34601, 352-754-4201. Fax: 352-754-4239. Hours: 8AM-5PM

Online search: A refundable deposit is required. The monthly minimum fee is $5.00, with a per minute charge of $.10. The records date back to 1983. The system operates 24 hours daily and supports baud rates up to 28.8. The database can be searched by name, Grantee/Grantor, book and page, instrument number, and parcel and case. Lending agency information is available. A fax back service for specific pages is available for $1-$1.25 per page. Plans are underway to move the public record access to the Internet. For more information, contact Bob Piercy at 352-754.

Hillsborough County

Criminal, Civil, Eviction, Small Claims, Probate, Liens, Real Estate

Circuit and County Courts, 419 Pierce St, Tampa FL 33602, 813-276-8100 X7252. Fax: 813-272-7707. Hours: 8AM-5PM (EST).

Online search: Online access has a $50.00 setup fee which includes software. Access is $.25 per minute or $5.00 per month, whichever is greater. Traffic and domestic records included. Contact the help desk at 813-276-8100, Ext. 7000 for more information.

Indian River County

Liens, Real Estate, Birth Records, Death Records, Marriage Records, Divorce Records

County Clerk of the Circuit Court, 2000 16th Ave, Vero Beach FL 32960, 561-770-5174. Fax: 561-770-7008. Hours: 8:30AM-5PM (EST).

Online search: There is a $200 all inclusive monthly fee. The records date back to the mid 1980s. The system operates 24 hours daily. The system supports baud rates up to 33.6. All records recorded in this office are available online. One may search by name, Grantee/Grantor and case number. For further information, contact Gary Tummond at 561-567-8000.

Jacksonville City

Real Estate

www.ci.jax.fl.us/pub/depot.htm#prop

Neighborhood Services Division, 904-630-7398.

Online search: The Jacksonville Public Data Depot is a free access to property records for the city of Jacksonville, Florida.

Jefferson County

Criminal, Civil, Eviction, Small Claims, Probate

Circuit and County Courts, Jefferson County Courthouse, Rm 10, PO Box 547, Monticello FL 32345, 850-342-0191. Fax: 850-997-4855. Hours: 8:30AM-5PM (EST).

Online search: Contact Dale Boatwright for information about remote access. Required to search: name, years to search, DOB; also helpful-address, SSN, race, sex. Criminal records on computer since 1989. General search fee: $1.00 per name per year.

Lake County

Liens, Real Estate, Marriage Records

County Clerk of the Circuit Court, 550 W Main St or PO Box 7800, Tavares FL 32778, 352-742-4114. Fax: 352-742-4166. Hours: 8:30AM-5PM (EST).

Online search: There is a set up fee of $75, plus an annual renewal fee of $50. The system operates from 8:30AM-5PM M-F and supports a baud rate of 19.2. The records date back to 1974. One may search by name and book and page. Lending agency information is available. For further information, contact Sandra Squires at 352-742-4156

Lee County

Criminal, Civil, Eviction, Small Claims, Probate

Circuit and County Courts, PO Box 2469, Ft Myers FL 33902, 941-335-2283. Hours: 7:45AM-5PM (EST).

Online search: Online access entails a $150.00 setup, $15.00 per month fee and a per minute charge based on usage. The system is open 24 hours daily and includes probate records. Call Natalie at 941-335-2975 for more information.

Leon County

Civil Cases, Criminal Cases

www.clerk.leon.fl.us

Circuit and County Courts, PO Box 726, Tallahassee FL 32302, 850-488-7534. Civil Phone: 850-488-7539. Criminal Phone: 850-488-2131. Probate Phone: 850-488-7667. Fax: 850-488-8863. Hours: 8:30AM-5PM (EST).

Online search: There is both a free and access to online records. Search the Internet for free by name or instrument code (not all records up). The pay system, which is much more thorough, is $100 setup and $100 per month. The system is open 8am to 7pm daily. Records date back to 1984.

Liens, Real Estate, Marriage Records

www.clerk.leon.fl.us

County Clerk of the Circuit Court, 301 S Monroe St, Rm 123, Tallahassee FL 32301, 850-488-7538. Fax: 850-921-1310. Hours: 8:30AM-5PM (EST).

Online search: Access is through their Internet site, there is no fee. One can search by name, Grantee/Grantor, type of document, recording date, document and instrument code. Information is available for no fee in their site. A search by lending agency gives a range of that agency's loans and dates. The earliest date documents are available is 01/01/84.

Manatee County

Civil, Criminal, Real Estate, Probate

Circuit and County Courts, PO Box 1000, Bradenton FL 34206, 941-749-1800. Fax: 941-741-4082. Hours: 8:30AM-5PM (EST).

Online search: Remote online access system, CHIPS, costs $50 for setup with an annual fee of $120. System includes civil and criminal indexes as well as property appraiser, tax assessor, probate and domestic data. Modem rates up to 9600. Call Terry Turner at 941-741-4003 for more information.

Real Estate, Death Records, Marriage Records, Divorce Records

County Clerk, 1115 Manatee Avenue W, Bradenton FL 34206, 941-741-4041. Fax: 941-749-7194. Hours: 8:30AM-5PM (EST),

Online search: There are no fees to view, but you are limited to 2 hours access per day. The records date back to 1978. The system operates 24 hours daily. One can search by name, Grantee/Grantor, book and page, case number and instrument type. Lending agency information is available. They also offer a fax back service for a fee, which requires a $400 deposit. For further information, contact Martha Pope at 941-741-4051.

Martin County

Criminal, Civil, Eviction, Small Claims, Probate

Circuit and County Courts, PO Box 9016, Stuart FL 34995, 561-288-5576. Fax: 561-288-5990; 288-5991 (civil). Hours: 8AM-5PM (EST).

Online search: Online access entails a $100.00 setup fee (half of which is refundable), a monthly fee of $40.00, and access fee of $.10 per minute. The system is open during working hours only. ProComm Plus is required. Records available include traffic and domestic. The system offers a fax back option for actual page copies for $1-1.25 per page. For more information, call 561-288-5985.

Okaloosa County

Criminal, Civil, Probate, Liens, Vital Records, Real Estate

Circuit and County Courts, 1250 Eglin Pkwy, Shalimar FL 32579, 850-651-7200. Fax: 850-651-7230. Hours: 8AM-5PM.

Online search: The system has a flat monthly usage fee of $100. The system operates 24 hours daily and supports baud rates up to 28.8. The records date back to 1982. One may search by name, Grantee/Grantor, book and page and by document type. Lending agency information is available. Records include traffic and domestic records. For further information contact, Don Howard at 850-689-5821.

Orange County

Civil, Criminal, Probate

Circuit and County Courts, 37 N Orange Ave #550, Orlando FL 32801, 407-836-2060. Hours: 8AM-5PM (EST).

Online search: The Teleclerk remote online system costs $100 one time fee and $30 per month, including 5 hours of online time. Additional time is charged at $0.25 per minute. The system is open 24 hours daily and includes traffic and domestic records. For more information call 407-836-2064. Required to search: name, years to search. Cases indexed by defendant, plaintiff.

Misdemeanor, Civil Actions Under $15,000, Eviction, Small Claims

County Court-Apopka Branch 1111 N Rock Springs Rd, Apopka FL 32712, 407-889-4176. Fax: 407-836-2225. Hours: 8AM-5PM (EST).

Online search: Same online system as described above.

Misdemeanor, Civil Actions Under $15,000, Eviction, Small Claims

County Court-NE Orange Division , 450 N Lakemont Ave, Winter Park FL 32792, 407-671-1116. Hours: 8AM-5PM.

Online search: Same county court remote online system.

Liens, Real Estate, Marriage Records

www.comptroller.co.orage.fl.us

County Comptroller (Recorder), 401 S Rosalind Av, Orlando FL 32801. 407-836-5115, 407-836-5101 (Fax).

Online search: Access to public records is through the Internet, there is no fee. Records date back to 1955. Marriage records are available beginning 3/98. One can search by name or book and page. Lending agency information is available.

Palm Beach County

Criminal. Civil, Probate

Circuit and County Courts, 205 North Dixie, Room 3.2400, West Palm Beach FL 33401, 561-355-2519 (Criminal), 561-355-2986 (Civil), Fax: 561-355-3802. Hours: 8AM-5PM.

Online search: Contact Betty Jones at 561-355-6783 for information about remote access. Fees include $145 setup and $65 per month. Civil records available back to 1988. Other records available include traffic and domestic. System is open 18 hours daily.

Pasco County

Criminal, Civil, Probate

Circuit and County Courts, 38053 Live Oak Ave, Dade City FL 33523, 352-521-4482 (Civil), 352-521-4482 (Criminal). Hours: 8:30AM-5PM (EST).

Online search: Online access requires a $100 deposit, $50 annual fee and minimum of $10.00 per month. There is a $.10 per screen charge. The system is open 24 hours daily. Search by name or case number. Call Barbara Alford at 352-521-4201 for more information.

Liens, Real Estate, Marriage Records

County Clerk of the Circuit Court, 38053 Live Oak Ave, Dade City FL 33523-3894, 352-521-4464.

Online search: To sign up, there is a $25 annual fee plus a $50 deposit. One is billed at the rate of $.05 per minute from 7AM-6PM, and $.03 per minute at all other times. There is a $3.00 monthly minimum. The records date back to 1975. Baud rates up to 56k are supported. There is a fax back service and the cost per page is $1.25. One may search by name, Grantee/Grantor and by date. No addresses are listed. Lending agency information is available. For further information, contact Mike Stubs at 352-521-4529.

Pinellas County

Civil, Eviction, Small Claims, Probate

Circuit and County Courts – Civil Division, 315 Court St, Clearwater FL 33756, 813-464-3267. Fax: 813-464-4070.

Criminal Cases

County Court – Criminal Division, 14250 49th St N, Clearwater FL 34622, 813-464-6800. Fax: 813-464-6072.

Online search: Contact Sue Maskeny at 813-464-3779 for information about remote access. Setup fee is $60 plus per minute charges. The civil index goes back to 1973, the

criminal index goes back to 1972. The system is open 24 hours daily and includes probate and traffic records.

Polk County

Civil Actions Over $15,000, Probate

Circuit and County Courts, PO Box 9000, Bartow FL 33831-9000, 941-534-4000. Fax: 941-534-4089. Hours: 8AM-5PM.

Online search: Online access requires a $150 setup fee and $.15 per minute with a $50 per quarter minimum. Call Ann Hoaks at 941-534-7575 for more information.

Putnam County

Civil, Criminal, Real Estate

Circuit and County Courts, PO Box 758, Palatka FL 32178, Civil 904-329-0361, Criminal 904-329-0249, Fax: 904-329-0888.

Online search: Write Lonnie Thompson to register; include a check for $400 as a setup fee. The monthly charge is $40 plus $0.05 per minute over 20 hours. Criminal records go back to 1972. Civil index goes back to 1984. The system operates 24 hours daily. No juvenile records released.

Liens, Real Estate, Marriage Records, Divorce Records, Tax Assessor Records

County Clerk, 518 St. Johns Ave, Bldg. 1-E, Palatka FL 32177, 904-329-0258. Fax: 904-329-0889.

Online search: The initial online access fee is $400. There is a $40 per month fee, which includes 20 hours of use. Additional minutes are billed at $.05 per minute. Records date back to 10/83. The system operates 24 hours daily and supports baud rates up to 33.6. One can search by name, Grantee/Grantor, instrument number and 911 street address. For additional information, contact Lonnie Thompson at 904-329-0353.

Sarasota County

Civil, Eviction, Small Claims, Probate

Circuit and County Courts – Civil Division, PO Box 3079, Sarasota FL 34230, 941-951-5206. Hours: 8:30AM-5PM (EST).

Online search: Contact Tom Kay for information about remote access. Cost is $15 per month minimum against $.15 per minute, with an initial deposit of $300. System operates 8-5 daily at 9600 baud. Index goes back to 1983. Domestic records included. Required to search: name, years to search. Cases indexed by defendant, plaintiff. No adoption or juvenile, sealed records released.

St. Johns County

Civil Cases, Criminal Cases

Circuit and County Courts, PO Drawer 300, St Augustine FL 32085-0300, 904-823-2333. Fax: 904-823-2294. Hours: 8AM-5PM (EST).

Online search: Online access requires dedicated phone line. Setup is $200 and there is a monthly fee of $50. The system is

Volusia County

Civil Cases, Criminal Cases

Circuit and County Courts, PO Box 43, De Land FL 32721, 904-736-5915. Fax: 904-822-5711. Hours: 8AM-4:30PM.

Online search: Online access is available from 8am to 4:30pm. Setup is $125 and the monthly fee is $25. Windows 95 or 98 is required. Search by name or case number back to 1988. Call Tom White for more information. No sealed records released.

Liens, Real Estate, Death Records, Marriage Records, Divorce Records

County Clerk, 235 New York Ave, De Land FL 32720, 904-736-5912. Fax: 904-740-5104.

Online Search: The initial set up fee is $125, with a flat monthly fee of $25. Once you sign up, you are given the commercial Internet site used for access. The records date back to 1988. You can search by name, Grantee/Grantor, case number, document type, and parcel number since 1995. Lending agency information is available. For further information, contact Virginia Threlkeld at 904-822-5710.

Walton County

Civil, Criminal, Probate, Liens, Real Estate, Death Records, Divorce Records

Circuit and County Courts, PO Box 1260, De Funiak Springs FL 32433, 850-892-8115. Fax: 850-892-7551. Hours: 8AM-4:30PM (CST).

Online search: The initial set up fee ranges between $300-$450, with a flat monthly access fee of $100. The records date back to 1800. The system operates 24 hours daily and baud rates up to 28.8 are supported. One can search by name, Grantee/Grantor and recording date. Lending agency information is available. For further information, contact either David Langford or Alex Alford at 850-892-8115. No sealed, expunged, or pre-sentence investigation records released.

Federal Courts Online

County-to-Court Cross Reference (Bankruptcy Court locations in Parenthesis if different)

Alachua	Northern	Gainesville (Tallahassee)
Baker	Middle	Jacksonville
Bay	Northern	Panama City (Tallahassee)
Bradford	Middle	Jacksonville
Brevard	Middle	Orlando
Broward	Southern	Fort Lauderdale (Miami)
Calhoun	Northern	Panama City (Tallahassee)
Charlotte	Middle	Fort Myers (Tampa)
Citrus	Middle	Ocala (Jacksonville)
Clay	Middle	Jacksonville
Collier	Middle	Fort Myers (Tampa)
Columbia	Middle	Jacksonville
Dade	Southern	Miami
De Soto	Middle	Fort Myers (Tampa)
Dixie	Northern	Gainesville (Tallahassee)
Duval	Middle	Jacksonville
Escambia	Northern	Pensacola
Flagler	Middle	Jacksonville
Franklin	Northern	Tallahassee
Gadsden	Northern	Tallahassee
Gilchrist	Northern	Gainesville (Tallahassee)
Glades	Middle	Fort Myers (Tampa)
Gulf	Northern	Panama City (Tallahassee)
Hamilton	Middle	Jacksonville
Hardee	Middle	Tampa
Hendry	Middle	Fort Myers (Tampa)
Hernando	Middle	Tampa
Highlands	Southern	Fort Pierce (Miami)
Hillsborough	Middle	Tampa
Holmes	Northern	Panama City (Tallahassee)
Indian River	Southern	Fort Pierce (Miami)
Jackson	Northern	Panama City (Tallahassee)
Jefferson	Northern	Tallahassee
Lafayette	Northern	Gainesville (Tallahassee)
Lake	Middle	Ocala (Orlando)
Lee	Middle	Fort Myers (Tampa)
Leon	Northern	Tallahassee
Levy	Northern	Gainesville (Tallahassee)
Liberty	Northern	Tallahassee
Madison	Northern	Tallahassee
Manatee	Middle	Tampa
Marion	Middle	Ocala (Jacksonville)
Martin	Southern	Fort Pierce (Miami)
Monroe	Southern	Key West (Miami)
Nassau	Middle	Jacksonville
Okaloosa	Northern	Pensacola
Okeechobee	Southern	Fort Pierce (Miami)
Orange	Middle	Orlando
Osceola	Middle	Orlando
Palm Beach	Southern	W. Palm Beach (Miami)
Pasco	Middle	Tampa
Pinellas	Middle	Tampa

Pasco	Middle	Tampa
Pinellas.................	Middle	Tampa
Polk	Middle	Tampa
Putnam	Middle	Jacksonville
Santa Rosa	Northern...........	Pensacola
Sarasota................	Middle	Tampa
Seminole	Middle	Orlando
St. Johns	Middle	Jacksonville
St. Lucie...............	Southern...........	Fort Pierce (Miami)

Sumter..................	Middle...............	Ocala (Jacksonville)
Suwannee	Middle...............	Jacksonville
Taylor...................	Northern...........	Tallahassee
Union	Middle...............	Jacksonville
Volusia.................	Middle...............	Orlando (Jacksonville)
Wakulla	Northern...........	Tallahassee
Walton	Northern...........	Pensacola
Washington	Northern............	Panama City (Tallahassee)

US District Court
Middle District of Florida

PACER sign-up number is 800-676-6856. Both civil and criminal case records are available online.

Fort Myers Division, 2110 First St, Room 2-194, Fort Myers, FL 33901, 941-461-2000.

Jacksonville Division, PO Box 53558, Jacksonville, FL 32201, 904-232-2854.

Ocala Division, c/o Jacksonville Division, PO Box 53558, Jacksonville, FL 32201, 904-232-2854.

Orlando Division, Room 218, 80 North Hughey Ave, Orlando, FL 32801, 407-648-6366.

Tampa Division, Office of the Clerk, US Courthouse, Room B-100, 611 N Florida Ave, Tampa, FL 33602, 813-228-2105, Record Room: 813-228-2105.

US Bankruptcy Court
Middle District of Florida

www.flmb.uscourts.gov

PACER sign-up number is 800-676-6856.

Jacksonville Division, PO Box 559, Jacksonville, FL 32201, 904-232-2852

Orlando Division, Suite 950, 135 W Central Blvd, Orlando, FL 32801, 407-648-6365

Tampa Division, 801 N Florida Ave #727, Tampa, FL 33602, 813-243-5162

US District Court
Northern District of Florida

PACER sign-up number is 800-676-6856. Both civil and criminal case records are available online.

Gainesville Division, 401 SE First Ave, Room 243, Gainesville, FL 32601, 352-380-2400, Fax: 352-380-2424.

Panama City Division, c/o Pensacola Division, 1 N Palafox St, #226, Pensacola, FL 32501, 850-435-8440, Fax: 850-433-5972.

Pensacola Division, US Courthouse, 1 N Palafox St, #226, Pensacola, FL 32501, 850-435-8440, Fax: 850-433-5972.

Tallahassee Division, Suite 122, 110 E Park Ave, Tallahassee, FL 32301, 850-942-8826, Fax: 850-942-8830.

US Bankruptcy Court
Northern District of Florida

PACER sign-up number is 904-435-8475.

Pensacola Division, Suite 700, 220 W Garden St, Pensacola, FL 32501, 904-435-8475.

Tallahassee Division, Room 3120, 227 N Bronough St, Tallahassee, FL 32301-1378, 850-942-8933.

US District Court
Southern District of Florida

PACER sign-up number is 800-676-6856. Both civil and criminal case records are available online.

Fort Lauderdale Division, 299 E Broward Blvd, Fort Lauderdale, FL 33301, 954-769-5400.

Miami Division, Room 150, 301 N Miami Ave, Miami, FL 33128-7788, 305-536-4131.

Key West Division, c/o Miami Division, Room 150, 301 N Miami Ave, Miami, FL 33128-7788, 305-536-4131.

Fort Pierce Division, c/o Miami Division, Room 150, 301 N Miami Ave, Miami, FL 33128, 305-536-4131.

West Palm Beach Division, Room 402, 701 Clematis St, West Palm Beach, FL 33401, 561-803-3400.

US Bankruptcy Court
Southern District of Florida

PACER sign-up number is 800-676-6856.

Fort Lauderdale Division, 299 E Broward Blvd, Room 310, Fort Lauderdale, FL 33301, 954-769-5700.

Miami Division, Room 1517, 51 SW 1st Ave, Miami, FL 33130, 305-536-5216.

West Palm Beach Division, Federal Bldg, Room 202, 701 Clematis St, West Palm Beach, FL 33401, 561-655-6774.

Georgia

Governor's Office
203 State Capitol   404-656-1776
Atlanta, GA 30334   Fax 404-657-7332
www.ganet.org/governor

Attorney General's Office
40 Capitol Square SW   404-656-3300
Atlanta, GA 30334-1300   Fax 404-651-9148
www.ganet.org/ago

State Archives
Secretary of State   404-656-2393
Archives & History Dept.   Fax 404-651-9270
330 Capitol Ave SE   8 AM-4:45 PM
Atlanta, GA 30334
www.sos.state.ga.us/archives/default.htm

Capital:	Atlanta
	Fulton County
Time Zone:	EST
Number of Counties:	159
Population:	7,486,242
Web Site:	www.state.ga.us

State Court Administrator
Admin. Office of the Courts   404-656-5171
244 Washington St SW,
Suite 550   Fax 404-651-6449
Atlanta, GA 30334   8:30AM-5PM
www.state.ga.us/courts/supreme/aochp.htm

State Agencies Online

Legislation-Current/Pending
Legislation-Passed
www.ganet.org/services/leg

General Assembly of Georgia, State Capitol, Atlanta, GA 30334; 404-656-5040 (Senate), 404-656-5015 (House), 404-656-2370 (Archives), 404-656-5043 (Fax).

Online search: The Internet site has bill information back to 1995. Statutes are not available online.

Corporation Records
Limited Partnership Records
Limited Liability Company Records
www.sos.state.ga.us/corporations

Secretary of State, Corporation Division, 2 M L King Dr, Suite 315, W Tower, Atlanta, GA 30334-1530; 404-656-2817, 404-656-2817 (Filing Questions), 404-651-9059 (Fax), 8AM-5PM.

General Information: Trade names, Fictitious Names and Assumed Names are found at the county level. DBAs are also found at the county level.

Online search: Records are available from the Internet site. The corporate database can be searched by entity name or registered agent for no fee. There is a $10.00 charge for a Certificate of Existence (Good Standing) or a Certified copy of Corporate Charter. Other services include name reservation, filing procedures, downloading of forms and applications.

Uniform Commercial Code
gsccca.org

Superior Court Clerks' Cooperative Authority, 1875 Century Blvd, #100, Atlanta, GA 30345; 404-327-9058, 404-327-7877 (Fax), 9AM-5PM.

General Information: As of January 1, 1995, new UCC filings are indexed statewide (older filings are only available at the county).

Online search: Online access is available for regular, ongoing requesters. There is a $50.00 set-up fee, a monthly charge of $25.00, and a $.32 per minute access fee. Billing is monthly. The system is open 24 hours a day, 7 days a week. Minimum baud rate is 9600; 28.8 is supported. Information from 01/01/95 forward is available. Call (800) 304-5175 or (404) 327-9058 for a subscription package.

Information About County Agencies

Court Structure

There is a Superior Court in each county, which assumes the role of State Court if the county does not have one.
The Magistrate Court has jurisdiction over one type of misdemeanor related to passing bad checks. This court also issues arrest warrants and sets bond on all felonies.

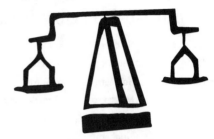

Online Access

There is no online access available locally or statewide.

About the County Courts

About the Recorder's Office

Organization

159 counties, 159 recording offices. The recording officer is Clerk of Superior Court. All transactions are recorded in a "General Execution Docket." The entire state is in the Eastern Time Zone (EST).

Real Estate Records

Most counties will not perform real estate searches. Copy fees are the same as for UCC. Certification fees are usually $2.00 per document—$1.00 for seal and $1.00 for stamp—plus $.50 per page.

UCC Records

Financing statements are filed only with the Clerk of Superior Court in each county. A new system is in effect as of January 1, 1995, which merges all new UCC filings into a central statewide database, and which allows statewide searching for new filings only from any county office. However, filings prior to that date will remain at the county offices. Only a few counties will perform local UCC searches. Use search request form UCC-11 for local searches. Search fees vary from $2.50 to $25.00 per debtor name. Copies usually cost $.25 per page if you make it and $1.00 per page if the county makes it.

Other Lien Records

All tax liens on personal property are filed with the county Clerk of Superior Court in a "General Execution Docket" (grantor/grantee) or "Lien Index." Most counties will not perform tax lien searches. Copy fees are the same as for UCC. Other liens are: judgments, hospital, materialman, county tax, lis pendens, child support, labor, mechanics.

County Courts & Recording Offices Online

There is no online access available for county courts.

No remote online access is available from real estate recorder's office in Georgia.

Federal Courts Online

County-to-Court Cross Reference (Bankruptcy Court locations in Parenthesis if different)

Appling	Southern	Brunswick (Savannah)
Atkinson	Southern	Waycross (Savannah)
Bacon	Southern	Waycross (Savannah)
Baker	Middle	Albany/Americus (Macon)
Baldwin	Middle	Macon
Banks	Northern	Gainesville
Barrow	Northern	Gainesville
Bartow	Northern	Rome
Ben Hill	Middle	Albany/Americus (Macon)
Berrien	Middle	Valdosta (Columbus)
Bibb	Middle	Macon
Bleckley	Middle	Macon
Brantley	Southern	Waycross (Savannah)
Brooks	Middle	Thomasville (Columbus)
Bryan	Southern	Savannah
Bulloch	Southern	Statesboro (Augusta)
Burke	Southern	Augusta
Butts	Middle	Macon
Calhoun	Middle	Albany/Americus (Macon)
Camden	Southern	Brunswick (Savannah)
Candler	Southern	Statesboro (Augusta)
Carroll	Northern	Newnan
Catoosa	Northern	Rome
Charlton	Southern	Waycross (Savannah)
Chatham	Southern	Savannah
Chattahoochee	Middle	Columbus
Chattooga	Northern	Rome
Cherokee	Northern	Atlanta
Clarke	Middle	Athens (Macon)
Clay	Middle	Columbus
Clayton	Northern	Atlanta
Clinch	Middle	Valdosta (Columbus)
Cobb	Northern	Atlanta
Coffee	Southern	Waycross (Savannah)
Colquitt	Middle	Thomasville (Columbus)
Columbia	Southern	Augusta
Cook	Middle	Valdosta (Columbus)
Coweta	Northern	Newnan
Crawford	Middle	Macon
Crisp	Middle	Albany/Americus (Macon)
Dade	Northern	Rome
Dawson	Northern	Gainesville
De Kalb	Northern	Atlanta
Decatur	Middle	Thomasville (Columbus)
Dodge	Southern	Dublin (Augusta)
Dooly	Middle	Macon
Dougherty	Middle	Albany/Americus (Macon)
Douglas	Northern	Atlanta
Early	Middle	Albany/Americus (Macon)
Echols	Middle	Valdosta (Columbus)
Effingham	Southern	Savannah
Elbert	Middle	Athens (Macon)
Emanuel	Southern	Statesboro (Augusta)
Evans	Southern	Statesboro (Augusta)
Fannin	Northern	Gainesville
Fayette	Northern	Newnan
Floyd	Northern	Rome
Forsyth	Northern	Gainesville
Franklin	Middle	Athens (Macon)
Fulton	Northern	Atlanta
Gilmer	Northern	Gainesville
Glascock	Southern	Augusta
Glynn	Southern	Brunswick (Savannah)
Gordon	Northern	Rome
Grady	Middle	Thomasville (Columbus)
Greene	Middle	Athens (Macon)
Gwinnett	Northern	Atlanta
Habersham	Northern	Gainesville
Hall	Northern	Gainesville
Hancock	Middle	Macon
Haralson	Northern	Newnan
Harris	Middle	Columbus
Hart	Middle	Athens (Macon)
Heard	Northern	Newnan
Henry	Northern	Atlanta
Houston	Middle	Macon

County	Region	Court (Location)
Irwin	Middle	Valdosta (Columbus)
Jackson	Northern	Gainesville
Jasper	Middle	Macon
Jeff Davis	Southern	Brunswick (Savannah)
Jefferson	Southern	Augusta
Jenkins	Southern	Statesboro (Augusta)
Johnson	Southern	Dublin (Augusta)
Jones	Middle	Macon
Lamar	Middle	Macon
Lanier	Middle	Valdosta (Columbus)
Laurens	Southern	Dublin (Augusta)
Lee	Middle	Albany/Americus (Macon)
Liberty	Southern	Savannah
Lincoln	Southern	Augusta
Long	Southern	Brunswick (Savannah)
Lowndes	Middle	Valdosta (Columbus)
Lumpkin	Northern	Gainesville
Macon	Middle	Macon
Madison	Middle	Athens (Macon)
Marion	Middle	Columbus
McDuffie	Southern	Augusta
McIntosh	Southern	Brunswick (Savannah)
Meriwether	Northern	Newnan
Miller	Middle	Albany/Americus (Macon)
Mitchell	Middle	Albany/Americus (Macon)
Monroe	Middle	Macon
Montgomery	Southern	Dublin (Augusta)
Morgan	Middle	Athens (Macon)
Murray	Northern	Rome
Muscogee	Middle	Columbus
Newton	Northern	Atlanta
Oconee	Middle	Athens (Macon)
Oglethorpe	Middle	Athens (Macon)
Paulding	Northern	Rome
Peach	Middle	Macon
Pickens	Northern	Gainesville
Pierce	Southern	Waycross (Savannah)
Pike	Northern	Newnan
Polk	Northern	Rome
Pulaski	Middle	Macon
Putnam	Middle	Macon
Quitman	Middle	Columbus
Rabun	Northern	Gainesville
Randolph	Middle	Columbus
Richmond	Southern	Augusta
Rockdale	Northern	Atlanta
Schley	Middle	Albany/Americus (Macon)
Screven	Southern	Statesboro (Augusta)
Seminole	Middle	Thomasville (Columbus)
Spalding	Northern	Newnan
Stephens	Northern	Gainesville
Stewart	Middle	Columbus
Sumter	Middle	Albany/Americus (Macon)
Talbot	Middle	Columbus
Taliaferro	Southern	Augusta
Tattnall	Southern	Statesboro (Augusta)
Taylor	Middle	Columbus
Telfair	Southern	Dublin (Augusta)
Terrell	Middle	Albany/Americus (Macon)
Thomas	Middle	Thomasville (Columbus)
Tift	Middle	Valdosta (Columbus)
Toombs	Southern	Statesboro (Augusta)
Towns	Northern	Gainesville
Treutlen	Southern	Dublin (Augusta)
Troup	Northern	Newnan
Turner	Middle	Albany/Americus (Macon)
Twiggs	Middle	Macon
Union	Northern	Gainesville
Upson	Middle	Macon
Walker	Northern	Rome
Walton	Middle	Athens (Macon)
Ware	Southern	Waycross (Savannah)
Warren	Southern	Augusta
Washington	Middle	Macon
Wayne	Southern	Brunswick (Savannah)
Webster	Middle	Albany/Americus (Macon)
Wheeler	Southern	Dublin (Augusta)
White	Northern	Gainesville
Whitfield	Northern	Rome
Wilcox	Middle	Macon
Wilkes	Southern	Augusta
Wilkinson	Middle	Macon
Worth	Middle	Albany/Americus (Macon)

US District Court
Middle District of Georgia

PACER sign-up number is 800-676-6856. Both civil and criminal case records are available online.

Albany/Americus Division, PO Box 1906, Albany, GA 31702, 912-430-8432, Fax: 912-430-8538.

Athens Division, PO Box 1106, Athens, GA 30603, 706-227-1094, Fax: 706-546-2190.

Columbus Division, PO Box 124, Columbus, GA 31902, 706-649-7816.

Macon Division, PO Box 128, Macon, GA 31202-0128, 912-752-3497, Fax: 912-752-3496.

Valdosta Division, PO Box 68, Valdosta, GA 31603, 912-242-3616, Fax: 912-244-9547.

Thomasville Division, c/o Valdosta Division, PO Box 68, Valdosta, GA 31601, 912-242-3616.

US Bankruptcy Court
Middle District of Georgia

www.gamb.uscourts.gov

PACER sign-up number is 800-676-6856.

Columbus Division, PO Box 2147, Columbus, GA 31902, 706-649-7837

Macon Division, PO Box 1957, Macon, GA 31202, 912-752-3506, Fax: 912-752-8157

US District Court
Northern District of Georgia

http://ecf.ganb.uscourts.gov/

The above web site permits free searching of some cases. The PACER sign-up number is 800-676-6856. Both civil and criminal case records are available online.

Atlanta Division, 2211 US Courthouse, 75 Spring St SW, Atlanta, GA 30303-3361, 404-331-6496, Civil Docket Section: 404-331-6613, Criminal Docket Section: 404-331-4227.

Gainesville Division, Federal Bldg, Room 201, 121 Spring St SE, Gainesville, GA 30501, 770-534-5954.

Newnan Division, PO Box 939, Newnan, GA 30264, 770-253-8847.

Rome Division, PO Box 1186, Rome, GA 30162-1186, 706-291-5629.

US Bankruptcy Court
Northern District of Georgia

http://ecf.ganb.uscourts.gov/

The above web site permits free searching of some cases. The PACER sign-up number is 800-676-6856.

Atlanta Division, 1340 US Courthouse, 75 Spring St SW, Atlanta, GA 30303-3361, 404-215-1000

Gainesville Division, 121 Spring St SE, Room 203-C, Gainesville, GA 30501, 770-536-0556

Newnan Division, Clerk, PO Box 2328, Newnan, GA 30264, 770-251-5583

Rome Division, Clerk, 600 E 1st St, Room 339, Rome, GA 30161-3187, 706-291-5639

US District Court
Southern District of Georgia

PACER sign-up number is 800-676-6856. Both civil and criminal case records are available online.

Augusta Division, PO Box 1130, Augusta, GA 30903, 706-722-2074.

Dublin Division, c/o Augusta Division, PO Box 1130, Augusta, GA 30903, 706-722-2074.

Brunswick Division, PO Box 1636, Brunswick, GA 31521, 912-265-1758.

Savannah Division, PO Box 8286, Savannah, GA 31412, 912-650-4020, Fax: 912-650-4030.

Statesboro Division, c/o Savannah Division, PO Box 8286, Savannah, GA 31412, 912-650-4020.

Waycross Division, c/o Savannah Division, PO Box 8286, Savannah, GA 31412, 912-650-4020.

US Bankruptcy Court
Southern District of Georgia

PACER sign-up number is 800-676-6856.

Augusta Division, PO Box 1487, Augusta, GA 30903, 706-724-2421.

Savannah Division, PO Box 8347, Savannah, GA 31412, 912-650-4100, Record Room: 912-650-4107.

99

Hawaii

Governor's Office

Leiopapa A Kamehameha Bldg   808-586-0034
235 S Beretania St   Fax 808-586-0006
Honolulu, HI 96813   7:30AM-5:30PM
hoohana.aloha.net/~gov

Attorney General's Office

425 Queen St   808-586-1500
Honolulu, HI 96813   Fax 808-586-1239
www.state.hi.us/ag

State Archives

State Archives   808-586-0329
Iolani Palace Grounds   Fax 808-586-0330
Honolulu, HI 96813   9AM-4PM

Capital: Honolulu
                                            Honolulu County

Time Zone: HT (Hawaii Standard Time)

Number of Counties: 4

Population: 1,186,602

Web Site: www.state.hi.us

State Court Administrator

Admin. Director of Courts   808-539-4900
PO Box 2560   Fax 808-539-4855
Honolulu, HI 96804   7:45AM-4:30PM
www.state.hi.us\jud

State Agencies Online

Corporation Records
Fictitious Name
Limited Partnership Records
Assumed Name
Trademarks/Servicemarks
www.state.hi.us/dbedt/start.html

Business Registration Division, PO Box 40, Honolulu, HI
96810; (1010 Richard St, 1st Floor, Honolulu, HI 96813);
808-586-2727, 808-586-2733 (Fax), 7:45AM-4:30PM.

General Information: There are no access restrictions.
Records are open to the public.

Online search: Online access is available through
Hawaii FYI (a state agency) at 808-587-4800. There are
no fees, the system is open 24 hours. For assistance
during business hours, call 808-586-1919.

Legislation-Current/Pending
Legislation-Passed
www.hawaii.gov

Hawaii Legislature, 415 S Beretania St, Honolulu, HI
96813; 808-587-0700 (Bill # and Location), 808-586-
6720 (Clerk's Office-Senate), 808-586-6400 (Clerk's
Office-House), 808-586-0690 (State Library), 808-587-
0720 (Fax), 7AM-6PM.

Access by: phone, visit, online.

Online search: To dial online for current year bill
information line, call 808-296-4636. Or, access the
information through the Internet site. There is no fee, the
system is up 24 hours.

Information About County Agencies

Court Structure

There are 4 circuits in Hawaii: #1, #2, #3, and #5. The 4th Circuit merged with the 3rd Circuit in 1943. There are no records available for minor traffic offenses after 7/1/94. The 7 District Courts handle some minor "felonies."

Online Access

There is no online access, but most courts offer a public access terminal to search records at the courts themselves.

About the County Courts

- - - - - - - - - - - - - - -

About the Recorder's Office

Organization

159 counties, 159 recording offices. The recording officer is Clerk of Superior Court. All transactions are recorded in a "General Execution Docket." The entire state is in the Hawaii Time Zone.

Real Estate Records

Most counties will not perform real estate searches. Copy fees are the same as for UCC. Certification fees are usually:

$2.00 per document—$1.00 for seal and $1.00 for stamp—plus $.50 per page.

UCC Records

Financing statements are filed only with the Clerk of Superior Court in each county. A new system is in effect as of January 1, 1995, which merges all new UCC filings into a central statewide database, and which allows statewide searching for new filings only from any county office. However, filings prior to that date will remain at the county offices. Only a few counties will perform local UCC searches. Use search request form UCC-11 for local searches. Search fees vary from $2.50 to $25.00 per debtor name. Copies usually cost $.25 per page if you make it and $1.00 per page if the county makes it.

Other Lien Records

All tax liens on personal property are filed with the county Clerk of Superior Court in a "General Execution Docket" (grantor/grantee) or "Lien Index." Most counties will not perform tax lien searches. Copy fees are the same as for UCC. Other liens are: judgments, hospital, materialman, county tax, lis pendens, child support, labor, mechanics.

County Courts & Recording Offices Online

There is no online access to court records in Hawaii.

No remote online access is available from real estate recorder's offices in Hawaii.

Federal Courts Online

US District Court
District of Hawaii

Honolulu Division, Box 50129, Honolulu, HI 96850, 808-541-1300, Civil Docket Section: 808-541-1287, Criminal Docket Section: 808-541-1301, Fax: 808-541-1303.

www.hid.uscourts.gov

PACER sign-up number is 800-676-6856. Both civil and criminal case records are available online.

US Bankruptcy Court
District of Hawaii

Honolulu Division, 1132 Bishop St, Suite 250-L, Honolulu, HI 96813, 808-522-8100.

PACER sign-up number is 800-676-6856.

Idaho

Governor's Office
PO Box 83720   208-334-2100
Boise, ID 83720-0034   Fax 208-334-2175
www.state.id.us/gov/govhmpg.htm

Attorney General's Office
PO Box 83720   208-334-2400
Boise, ID 83720-0010   Fax 208-334-2530
www.state.id.us/ag/homepage.htm

Capital: Boise
                                                 Ada County

Time Zone: MST*
* Idaho's ten northwestern-most counties are PST:
They are: Benewah, Bonner, Boundary, Clearwater,
Idaho, Kootenai, Latah, Lewis, Nez Perce, Shoshone.

Number of Counties: 44

Population: 1,210,232

Web Site: www.state.id.us

State Archives
Idaho State Historical Society   208-334-3356
Historical Library & Archives   Fax 208-334-3198
450 N 4th Street   9AM-5PM
Boise, ID 83702-6027
www.state.id.us/ishs/index.html

State Court Administrator
Admin. Director of the Courts   208-334-2246
451 W State St,   Fax 208-334-2146
Supreme Court Bldg   9AM-5PM
Boise, ID 83720
www.idwr.state.id.us/judicial/judicial
.html

State Agencies Online

Corporation Records
Limited Partnerships
Trademarks/Servicemarks
Limited Liability Company Records
Fictitious Names, Trade Names
idsos.state.id.us

Secretary of State, Corporation Division, PO Box 83720, Boise, ID 83720-0080; (Courier: 700 W Jefferson, Boise, ID 83720); 208-334-2301, 208-334-2847 (Fax), 8AM-5PM.

General Information: Effective 1/1/97, fictitious or assumed names are found at this office. (Previously they had recorded at the county level.)

Online search: The system is named PAIS. To subscribe, you must become a pre-paid customer. An initial deposit of $200 is requested. There is a monthly subscription of $10.00 and an online usage charge of $.10 per minute. Their current baud rate is 9600. The system is

available from 8 AM to 5 PM, M-F. If PAIS is only used for corporation recaps and UCC, then initial deposit is only $25.

Uniform Commercial Code
Federal Tax Liens
www.idsos.state.id.us

UCC Division, Secretary of State, PO Box 83720, Boise, ID 83720-0080; (Courier: 700 W Jefferson, Boise, ID 83720); 208-334-3191, 208-334-2847 (Fax), 8AM-5PM.

General Information: Federal tax liens on individuals and all state tax liens are filed at the county level. Include debtor name in your request.

Online search: The deposit is $25-200 is required with a monthly subscription fee of $10.00 and a usage fee of $.10 per minute. This is the same system described under Corporation Records.

Driver Records

www.state.id.us/itd/dmv.html

Idaho Transportation Department, Driver's Services, PO Box 34, Boise, ID 83731-0034, 208-334-8736, 208-334-8739 (Fax), 8:30AM-5PM.

General Information: Records are available for at least 3 years for moving violations, DWIs and suspensions. Accidents are not shown on the record. It takes 5 days from receipt before new records are available for inquiries. Casual requesters cannot obtain records with personal information if the subject has opted out.

Online search: Idaho offers online access (CICS) to the driver license files to approved vendors through the AAMVAnet/Advantis network. The system is interactive and open 24 hours per day. The fee if $4 per record. There is a minimum of 1,000 requests per month: however, this may change. The system not only permits access to driver records, but also to non-CDL title and registration records; it also offers a dealer inquiry screen. For more information, call (208) 334-8761.

Vehicle Ownership
Vehicle Identification

www.state.id.us/itd/dmv.htm

Idaho Transportation Department, Vehicle Services, PO Box 34, Boise, ID 83731-0034; 208-334-8773, 208-334-8542 (Fax), 8:30AM-5PM.

General Information: It takes 5 days before new records are available for inquiries. Personal information is released to casual requesters unless subject has opted out.

Online search: Idaho offers online access (CICS) to the registration and title files to approved vendors through the same system used for driving record requests. At present, only non-commercial information is available. The system is open 24 hours daily. The fee if $4 per record. A dealer inquiry screen is also offered. For more information, call 208-334-8659.

Legislation-Current/Pending
Legislation-Passed

www.state.is.us/legislat/legislat.html

Legislature Services Office, Research and Legislation, PO Box 83720, Boise, ID 83720-0054; (Courier: 700 W Jefferson, Lower Level, East, Boise, ID 83720); 208-334-2475, 208-334-2125 (Fax), 8AM-5PM.

General Information: The current and previous years are available on the Internet.

Online search: Statutes and bill information can be accessed from their web site.

Information About County Agencies

Court Structure

Small claims are handled by the Magistrate Division of the District Court. Probate is handled by the Magistrate Division of the District Court.

Online Access

There is no statewide computer system offering external access. ISTARS is a statewide intra-court/intra-agency system run and managed by the State Supreme Court. All counties are on ISTARS, and all courts provide public access terminals on-site.

**About the
County Courts**

Searching Hints

A statewide court administrative rule states that record custodians do not have a duty to "compile or summarize information contained in a record, nor...to create new records for the requesting party." Under this rule, some courts will not perform searches.

Many courts require a signed release for employment record searches. *(Continued)*

The following fees are mandated statewide: Search Fee—none; Certification Fee—$1.00 per document plus copy fee; Copy Fee—$1.00 per page. Not all jurisdictions currently follow these guidelines.

About the Recorder's Office

Organization

44 counties, 44 recording offices. The recording officer is County Recorder. Many counties utilize a grantor/grantee index containing all transactions recorded with them. 34 counties are in the Mountain Time Zone (MST), and 10 are in the Pacific Time Zone (PST).

Real Estate Records

Most counties will not perform real estate searches. Certification of copies usually costs $1.00 per document.

UCC Records

Financing statements are filed at the state level except for real estate related filings. All counties will perform UCC searches. Use search request form UCC-4. Search fees are usually $6.00 per debtor name for a listing of filings and $12.00 per debtor name for a listing plus copies at no additional charge. Separately ordered copies usually cost $1.00 per page.

Other Lien Records

Federal tax liens on personal property of businesses are filed with the Secretary of State. Other federal and all state tax liens on personal property are filed with the County Recorder. Some counties will perform a combined tax lien search for $5.00 while others will not perform tax lien searches. Other liens are: judgments, hospital, labor, mechanics.

County Courts & Recording Offices Online

No statewide computer system offers external access. ISTARS is a statewide intra-court/intra-agency system run and managed by the State Supreme Court. All counties are on ISTARS, and courts provide public access terminals on-site.

No remote online access is available from real estate recorder's offices in Idaho.

Federal Courts Online

County-to-Court Cross Reference (Bankruptcy Court locations in Parenthesis if different)

County	Court	County	Court
Ada	Boise	Gem	Boise
Adams	Boise	Gooding	Boise
Bannock	Pocatello	Idaho	Pocatello (Moscow)
Bear Lake	Pocatello	Jefferson	Pocatello
Benewah	Coeur d' Alene	Jerome	Boise
Bingham	Pocatello	Kootenai	Coeur d' Alene
Blaine	Boise	Latah	Moscow
Boise	Boise	Lemhi	Pocatello
Bonner	Coeur d' Alene	Lewis	Moscow
Bonneville	Pocatello	Lincoln	Boise
Boundary	Coeur d' Alene	Madison	Pocatello
Butte	Pocatello	Minidoka	Boise
Camas	Boise	Nez Perce	Moscow
Canyon	Boise	Oneida	Pocatello
Caribou	Pocatello	Owyhee	Boise
Cassia	Boise	Payette	Boise
Clark	Pocatello	Power	Pocatello
Clearwater	Moscow	Shoshone	Coeur d' Alene
Custer	Pocatello	Teton	Pocatello
Elmore	Boise	Twin Falls	Boise
Franklin	Pocatello	Valley	Boise
Fremont	Pocatello	Washington	Boise

US District Court
District of Idaho

www.id.uscourts.gov

The above URL offers limited free searching. PACER sign-up number is 208-334-9342. Both civil and criminal case records are available online.

Coeur d' Alene Division, c/o Boise Division, MSD 039, Federal Bldg, 550 W Fort St, Room 400, Boise, ID 83724, 208-334-1361.

Moscow Division, c/o Boise Division, Box 039, Federal Bldg, 550 W Fort St, Boise, ID 83724, 208-334-1361.

Boise Division, MSC 039, Federal Bldg, 550 W Fort St, Room 400, Boise, ID 83724, 208-334-1361, Fax: 208-334-9362.

Pocatello Division, c/o Boise Division, Box 039, Federal Bldg, 550 W Fort St, Boise, ID 83724, 208-334-1361.

On its RACER online system, Idaho offers US District and Bankruptcy records free on the Internet at:

www.id.uscourts.gov.

Records are searchable by name, SSN, and date range.

US Bankruptcy Court
District of Idaho

www.id.uscourts.gov

The above URL offers limited free searching. PACER sign-up number is 208-334-9342.

Boise Division, MSC 042, US Courthouse, 550 W Fort St, Room 400, Boise, ID 83724, 208-334-1074, Fax: 208-334-9362.

Coeur d' Alene Division, 205 N 4th St, 2nd Floor, Coeur d'Alene, ID 83814, 208-664-4925, Fax: 208-765-0270.

Moscow Division, 220 E 5th St, Moscow, ID 83843, 208-882-7612, Fax: 208-883-1576.

Pocatello Division, 250 S 4th Ave, Room 263, Pocatello, ID 83201, 208-236-6912, Fax: 208-232-9308.

Illinois

Governor's Office
207 Statehouse   217-782-0244
Springfield, IL 62706   Fax 217-524-4049
www.state.il.us/gov

Attorney General's Office
500 S 2nd St   217-785-2771
Springfield, IL 62706   Fax 217-785-2551
www.ag.state.il.us

State Archives
Secretary of State   217-782-4682
Archives Division   Fax 217-524-3930
Norton Bldg, Capitol Complex 8AM-4:30PM M-F
Springfield, IL 62756   11AM-3:30PM SA
www.sos.state.il.us/depts/archives/arc
_home.html

Capital:	Springfield
	Sangamon County
Time Zone:	CST
Number of Counties:	102
Population:	11,895,849
Web Site:	www.state.il.us

State Court Administrator
Administrative Ofc. of Courts 312-793-3250
222 N. Lasalle - 13th Floor   Fax 312-793-1335
Chicago, IL 60601   8AM-4PM

State Agencies Online

Criminal Records
www.state.il.us/isp/isphpage.htm

Illinois State Police, Bureau of Identification, 260 N Chicago St, Joliet, IL 60432-4075; 815-740-5164, 815-740-5193 (Fax), 8AM-4PM M-F.

General Information: No records are released without a disposition of conviction. Fingerprint cards are an option.

Online search: Online access costs $7.00 per page. Upon signing an interagency agreement with ISP and establishing an escrow account, users can submit inquiries over modem. Replies are still sent via U.S. mail. Turnaround time is approximately 4 business days for a "no record" response. Modem access is available from 7AM-4PM M-F, excluding holidays. Users must utilize LAPLINK for windows, version 6.0 or later. The system is called UCIA - Uniform Conviction Information Act

Corporation Records
Limited Partnership Records
Trade Names
Assumed Name
Limited Liability Company Records
www.sos.state.il.us/depts/bus_serv/fea
ture.htm

Department of Business Services, Corporate Department, Howlett Bldg, 3rd Floor, Copy Section, Springfield, IL 62756; (Courier: Corner of 2nd & Edwards Sts, Springfield, IL 62756); 217-782-7880, 212-782-4528 (Fax), 8AM-4:30PM.

Online search: Potential users must submit in writing what the purpose of the requests will be. Submit to: Sharon Thomas, Dept. of Business Srvs, 330 Howlett Bldg, Springfield, IL 62756. Also, call (217) 782-4104 for more information.

Legislation-Current/Pending
Legislation-Passed

Illinois General Assembly, State House, House (or Senate) Bills Division, Springfield, IL 62706; 217-782-3944 (Bill Status Only), 217-782-7017 (Index Div-Older Bills), 217-782-5799 (House Bills), 217-782-9778 (Senate Bills), 217-524-6059 (Fax), 8AM-4:30PM.

Online search: The Legislative Information System is available for subscription through a standard modem. The sign-up fee is $500.00, which includes 100 free minutes of access. Thereafter, access time is billed at $1.00 per minute. The hours of availability are 8 AM - 10 PM when in session and 8 AM - 5 PM when not in session, M-F. Contact Craig Garret at (217) 782-4083-set-up an account. There is no Internet site available.

Information About County Agencies

Court Structure

Illinois is divided into 22 judicial circuits; 3 are single county Cook, Du Page (18th Circuit) and Will (12th Circuit). The other 19 consist of 2 or more contiguous counties. The civil part of Circuit Court in Cook County is divided as follows: civil cases over $30,000 and civil cases under $30,000. The criminal part of Circuit Court in Cook County is divided into a criminal section and a misdemeanor section. The case indexes are maintained in one location. Felony and misdemeanor cases are heard at

About the County Courts

six locations within Cook County. All felony cases are maintained at one central location; misdemeanor case files are located at each of the hearing locations, as follows:

Felony Division, 2600 S. California, Chicago, IL 60608 (See court profile)
District 2, 5600 Old Orchard Rd, Skokie, IL 60077, 708-470-7200
District 3, 2121 Euclid Ave, Rolling Meadows, IL 60008, 708-818-3000
District 4, 1500 Maybrook Dr, Maywood, IL 60153, 708-865-5186
District 5, 10220 S. 76th Ave, Bridgeview, IL 60455, 708-974-6282
District 6, 16501 S. Kedzie, Markham, IL 60426, 708-210-4551

Probate is handled by the Circuit Court in all counties.

Online Access

While there is no statewide public online system available, a number of Circuit Courts offer online access.

Searching Hints

The search fee is set by statute and has three levels based on the county population. The higher the population, the larger the fee. In most courts, both civil and criminal data is on computer from the same starting date. In most Illinois courts the search fee is charged on a per name per year basis.

About the Recorder's Office

Organization

102 counties, 103 recording offices. Cook County has separate offices for UCC and real estate recording. The recording officer is Recorder of Deeds. Many counties utilize a grantor/grantee index containing all transactions. The entire state is in the Central Time Zone.

Real Estate Records

Most counties will not perform real estate searches. Cost of certified copies varies widely, but many counties charge the same as the cost of recording the document. Tax records are usually located at the Treasurer's Office.

UCC Records

Financing statements are filed at the state level except for real estate related filings. Most counties will perform UCC searches. Use search request form UCC-11. Search fees are usually $10.00 per debtor name/address combination. Copies usually cost $1.00 per page.

Other Lien Records

Federal tax liens on personal property of businesses are filed with the Secretary of State. Other federal and all state tax liens on personal property are filed with the County Recorder of Deeds. Some counties will perform tax lien searches for $5.00-$10.00 per name (state and federal are separate searches in many of these counties) and $1.00 per page of copy. Other liens are: judgments, mechanics, contractor, medical, lis pendens, oil & gas, mobile home.

County Courts & Recording Offices Online

Champaign County

Felony, Misdemeanor, Civil, Eviction, Small Claims

Circuit Court, 101 E Main, Urbana IL 61801. Civil Phone: 217-384-3725. Criminal Phone: 217-384-3727. Fax: 217-384-3879. Hours: 8:30AM-4:30PM (CST).

Online search: Online available for cases back to 1992. The system is called PASS. There is a setup fee and an annual user fee. Contact Jo Kelly at 217-384-3767 for information.

De Kalb County

Liens, Real Estate

County Recorder, 110 E Sycamore St, Sycamore IL 60178. 815-895-7156.

Online search: A $350 subscription fee is required to sign up and there is a per minute charge of $.25, $.50 if printing. The records date back to 1980. The system operates from 8:30AM-4:30PM and supports a baud rate of 28.8. One may search by name, Grantee/Grantor, lot block subdivision, section, township and range, file number and parcel number. Lending agency information is available. For further information, contact Sheila Larson at 815-895-7152.

Felony, Misdemeanor, Civil, Small Claims, Probate

Circuit Court, 133 W State St, Sycamore IL 60178. Civil Phone: 815-895-7131. Criminal Phone: 815-895-7138. Fax: 815-895-7140. Hours: 8:30AM-4:30PM (CST).

Online search: Court planning to offer online access. Call 1-800-307-1100 for more information.

Du Page County

Liens, Real Estate, Tax Assessor Records

www.co.dupage.il.us.org

County Recorder, 421 N County Farm Road, Wheaton IL 60187. 630-682-7200. Fax: 630-682-7214.

Online search: While the web site listed here does not offer access to records, it does provide helpful county directory information. For records access. one must lease a live interface telephone line from AT&T or a similar carrier to establish a connection. The only other fee is a $.05 per transaction charge. An IBM 3270 emulator is also required. The system operates from 12AM-6:30PM and supports a baud rate of 56K. Records date back to 1977. One may search by name, Grantee/Grantor or document number. For further information, contact Fred Kieltcka at 630-682-7030.

Kane County

Felony, Misdemeanor, Civil, Small Claims, Probate

Circuit Court, PO Box 112, Geneva IL 60134, 630-232-3400. Civil Phone: 630-208-3323. Criminal Phone: 630-208-3319. Fax: 630-208-2172. Hours: 8:30AM-4:30PM (CST).

Online search: Court is planning to offer online access. Call 1-800-307-1100 for more information.

Kendall County

Felony, Misdemeanor, Civil, Small Claims, Probate

Circuit Court, PO Drawer M, 807 W John St, Yorkville IL 60560, 630-553-4183. Hours: 8AM-4:30PM (CST).

Online search: Court is planning to offer online access. Call 1-800-1100 for more information

Macon County

Felony, Misdemeanor, Civil, Eviction, Small Claims

www.court.co.macon.il.us

Circuit Court, 253 E Wood St, Decatur IL 62523, 217-424-1454. Fax: 217-424-1350. Hours: 8AM-4:30PM (CST).

Online search: The online system is open 24 hours daily on the Internet. Docket information is viewable since 04/96. Search by name or case number. There is no fee.

McHenry County

Felony, Misdemeanor, Civil, Eviction, Small Claims

www.co.mchenry.il.us

Circuit Court, 2200 N Seminary Ave, Woodstock IL 60098, 815-338-2098. Fax: 815-338-8583. Hours: 8AM-4:30PM.

Online search: Online is available 24 hours daily, there are no fees. Records date back to 1990. Civil, criminal, probate, traffic, and domestic records are available. For more information, call Bill Case at 815-334-4302.

Liens, Real Estate

www.co.mchenry.il.us

County Recorder, 2200 N Seminary Ave, Room A280, Woodstock IL 60098, 815-344-4110. Fax: 815-338-9612.

Online search: A subscription fee of $350 applies. In addition, there is a monthly fee of $25.00 and a per minute charge of $.25. Name search results can be printed for $1.00. Records date back to 1987. The hours of operation are 7AM-12PM and baud rates of up to 28.8 are supported. Searches can be made by name, Grantee/Grantor, tax ID number, legal description and recorded document number. Lending agency information is available. For further information, contact Phyllis Walters at 815-344-4110.

Rock Island County

Felony, Misdemeanor, Civil, Small Claims, Probate

Circuit Court, 210 15th St, PO Box 5230, Rock Island IL 61204-5230, 309-786-4451. Fax: 309-786-3029. Hours: 8AM-4:30PM (CST).

Online search: Online access is open 24 hours daily. There is a $200 setup fee and additional deposit required. The access fee is $1.00 per minute. Civil, criminal, probate, traffic, and domestic records can be accessed by name or case number. No juvenile or adoption records released.

Federal Courts Online

County-to-Court Cross Reference (Bankruptcy Court locations in Parenthesis if different)

County	District	Location
Adams	Central	Springfield
Alexander	Southern	Benton
Bond	Southern	East St Louis
Boone	Northern	Rockford
Brown	Central	Springfield
Bureau	Central	Peoria
Calhoun	Southern	East St Louis
Carroll	Northern	Rockford
Cass	Central	Springfield
Champaign	Central	Danville/Urbana (Danville)
Christian	Central	Springfield
Clark	Southern	Benton (East St Louis)
Clay	Southern	Benton (East St Louis)
Clinton	Southern	East St Louis
Coles	Central	Danville/Urbana (Danville)
Cook	Northern	Chicago (Eastern)
Crawford	Southern	Benton (East St Louis)
Cumberland	Southern	Benton
De Kalb	Northern	Rockford
De Witt	Central	Springfield

County	Region	Court
Douglas	Central	Danville/Urbana (Danville)
Du Page	Northern	Chicago (Eastern)
Edgar	Central	Danville/Urbana (Danville)
Edwards	Southern	Benton
Effingham	Southern	Benton (East St Louis)
Fayette	Southern	East St Louis
Ford	Central	Danville/Urbana (Danville)
Franklin	Southern	Benton
Fulton	Central	Peoria
Gallatin	Southern	Benton
Greene	Central	Springfield
Grundy	Northern	Chicago (Eastern)
Hamilton	Southern	Benton
Hancock	Central	Peoria
Hardin	Southern	Benton
Henderson	Central	Rock Island (Peoria)
Henry	Central	Rock Island (Peoria)
Iroquois	Central	Danville/Urbana (Danville)
Jackson	Southern	Benton
Jasper	Southern	Benton (East St Louis)
Jefferson	Southern	Benton
Jersey	Southern	East St Louis
Jo Daviess	Northern	Rockford
Johnson	Southern	Benton
Kane	Northern	Chicago (Eastern)
Kankakee	Central	Danville/Urbana (Danville)
Kendall	Northern	Chicago (Eastern)
Knox	Central	Peoria
La Salle	Northern	Chicago (Eastern)
Lake	Northern	Chicago (Eastern)
Lawrence	Southern	Benton (East St Louis)
Lee	Northern	Rockford
Livingston	Central	Peoria (Danville)
Logan	Central	Springfield
Macon	Central	Danville/Urbana (Sprngfld)
Macoupin	Central	Springfield
Madison	Southern	East St Louis
Marion	Southern	East St Louis
Marshall	Central	Peoria
Mason	Central	Springfield
Massac	Southern	Benton
McDonough	Central	Peoria
McHenry	Northern	Rockford
McLean	Central	Peoria (Springfield)
Menard	Central	Springfield
Mercer	Central	Rock Island (Peoria)
Monroe	Southern	East St Louis
Montgomery	Central	Springfield
Morgan	Central	Springfield
Moultrie	Central	Danville/Urbana (Danville)
Ogle	Northern	Rockford
Peoria	Central	Peoria
Perry	Southern	Benton
Piatt	Central	Danville/Urbana (Danville)
Pike	Central	Springfield
Pope	Southern	Benton
Pulaski	Southern	Benton
Putnam	Central	Peoria
Randolph	Southern	East St Louis
Richland	Southern	Benton (East St Louis)
Rock Island	Central	Rock Island (Peoria)
Saline	Southern	Benton
Sangamon	Central	Springfield
Schuyler	Central	Springfield
Scott	Central	Springfield
Shelby	Central	Springfield
St. Clair	Southern	East St Louis
Stark	Central	Peoria
Stephenson	Northern	Rockford
Tazewell	Central	Peoria
Union	Southern	Benton
Vermilion	Central	Danville/Urbana (Danville)
Wabash	Southern	Benton
Warren	Central	Rock Island (Peoria)
Washington	Southern	East St Louis (Benton)
Wayne	Southern	Benton
White	Southern	Benton
Whiteside	Northern	Rockford
Will	Northern	Chicago (Eastern)
Williamson	Southern	Benton
Winnebago	Northern	Rockford
Woodford	Central	Peoria

US District Court
Central District of Illinois

PACER sign-up number is 800-676-6856. Both civil and criminal case records are available online.

Danville/Urbana Division, 201 S Vine, Room 218, Urbana, IL 61801, 217-373-5830.

Peoria Division, US District Clerk's Office, 305 Federal Bldg, 100 NE Monroe St, Peoria, IL 61602, 309-671-7117.

Rock Island Division, US District Clerk's Office, Room 40, Post Office Bldg, 211 19th St, Rock Island, IL 61201, 309-793-5778.

Springfield Division, Clerk, 151 US Courthouse, 600 E Monroe, Springfield, IL 62701, 217-492-4020.

US Bankruptcy Court
Central District of Illinois

PACER sign-up number is 800-676-6856.

Danville Division, 201 N Vermilion #130, Danville, IL 61832-4733, 217-431-4820.

Peoria Division, 131 Federal Bldg, 100 NE Monroe, Peoria, IL 61602, 309-671-7035.

Springfield Division, 226 US Courthouse, , Springfield, IL 62701-4551, 217-492-4551, Fax: 217-492-4560.

US District Court
Northern District of Illinois

www.ilnd.uscourts.gov

PACER sign-up number is 800-676-6856. Both civil and criminal case records are available online.

Chicago (Eastern) Division, 20th Floor, 219 S Dearborn St, Chicago, IL 60604, 312-435-5698, Record Room: 312-435-5863

Rockford Division, Room 211, 211 S Court St, Rockford, IL 61101, 815-987-4355

US Bankruptcy Court
Northern District of Illinois

www.ilnb.uscourts.gov

PACER sign-up number is 800-676-6856.

Chicago (Eastern) Division, 219 S Dearborn St, Chicago, IL 60604-1802, 312-435-5694, Record Room: 312-435-5862

Rockford Division, Room 110, 211 S Court St, Rockford, IL 61101, 815-987-4350, Fax: 815-987-4205

US District Court
Southern District of Illinois

PACER sign-up number is 800-676-6856.

Benton Division, 301 W Main St, Benton, IL 62812, 618-438-0671.

East St Louis Division, PO Box 249, East St Louis, IL 62202, 618-482-9371, Record Room: 618-482-9371.

US Bankruptcy Court
Southern District of Illinois

PACER sign-up number is 800-676-6856.

Benton Division, 301 W Main, Benton, IL 62812, 618-435-2200.

East St Louis Division, PO Box 309, East St Louis, IL 62202-0309, 618-482-9400.

Indiana

Governor's Office
206 State House   317-232-4567
Indianapolis, IN 46204   Fax 317-232-3443
www.state.in.us/gov

Attorney General's Office
State House, Rm 219   317-232-6201
Indianapolis, IN 46204   Fax 317-232-7979
www.ai.org/atty_gen/index.html

State Archives
Indiana State Archives   317-232-3660
Commission on Public Records
402 W Washington St   Fax 317-232-3154
IGCS, W472   8AM-4:30PM
Indianapolis, IN 46204
http://www.ai.org/icpr/index.html

Capital: Indianapolis
Marion County

Time Zone: EST*
* Indiana's 11 northwestern-most counties are CST:
They are: Gibson, Jasper, Laporte, Lake, Newton, Porter,
Posey, Spencer, Starke, Vanderburgh, Warrick.

Number of Counties: 92

Population: 5,864,108

Web Site: www.state.in.us

State Court Administrator
State Court Administrator   317-232-2542
115 W Washington St, #1080   Fax 317-233-6586
Indianapolis, IN 46204   8AM-4:30PM
www.ai.org

State Agencies Online

Corporation Records
Limited Partnerships
Fictitious Name
Assumed Name
Limited Liability Company Records
Limited Liability Partnerships
www.state.in.us/sos

Corporation Division, Secretary of State, 302 W Washington St, Room E018, Indianapolis, IN 46204; 317-232-6576, 317-233-3387 (Fax), 8AM-5:30PM M-F.

General Information: There are no restrictions, all information is public record. This agency also holds Agricultural Cooperative and Business Trust records.

Online search: This subscription service is available from the Access Indiana Information Network gateway over the Internet at www.ai.org. In general, search fees are $1.00 each. For more info, visit the web site.

Uniform Commercial Code
Access Indiana Information Network gateway:
www.ai.org/sos

Indiana secretary of State:
www.state.in.us/sos

UCC Division, Secretary of State, 302 West Washington St, Room E-018, Indianapolis, IN 46204; 317-233-3984, 317-233-3387 (Fax), 8AM-5:30PM.

Online search: This subscription service is available from the Access Indiana Information Network gateway over the Internet. The search fee is $3.00 with an additional $.50 to view an image of the lien. For more information, visit the web site.

Driver Records
www.ai.org

Bureau of Motor Vehicles, Driver Records, Indiana Government Center North, Room N405, Indianapolis, IN 46204; 317-232-2894, 8:15AM-4:30PM.

General Information: Records are available for 7 years (10 years for habitual violators) for moving violations; 10 years for DWIs and suspensions. Accidents reported to the state police appear on the record. It takes 1-3 weeks before new records are available for inquiries. Personal information is not disclosed to casual requesters. Further, a driver's Social Security Number, driver's license number or Federal ID number is not disclosed to all non-governmental requesters.

Online search: Online access costs $5.00 per record. Access Indiana Information Network (AIIN) is the state owned interactive information and communication system which provides batch and interactive access to driving records. There is an additional $.10 fee if accessing through AIIN's 800 number. However, there is no access fee if you come in through the Internet (www.ai.org). The system is open 24 hours per day, 7 days a week. Generally, batch transmissions are available 6 hours after request is made. For more information, call AIIN at 317-233-2010.

General Information: Records are available for 3 years on computer and up to ten years on microfilm. All boats valued over $3,000 when new and all motorized boats must be titled and registered. Casual requesters can obtain records, but no personal information is released on subjects who have opted out. Vehicle owner's SSN, driver's license number, and Federal ID number cannot be disclosed to all non governmental requesters. There are five types of records available for search; title inquiry, title history, registration inquiry, registration history, and registration copy. The title history will show liens. The title inquiry will show current listed lienholder.

Online search: The Access Indiana Information network at www.ai.org (AIIN) and (317) 233-2010 is the state appointed vendor. The fee is $5.00 per record plus an access fee of $.10 per minute if through an 800 number or no access fee if via the Internet (record fee still applies). The system is open 24 hours 7 days a week. Both interactive and batch (6 hour turnaround time) are available.

Vehicle Ownership & Identification
Boat & Vessel Ownership
Boat & Vessel Registration
www.ai.org

Bureau of Motor Vehicles, Records, 100 N Senate Ave, Room N404, Indianapolis, IN 46204; 317-233-6000, 8:15AM-4:45PM.

Legislation-Current/Pending
Legislation-Passed
www.state.in.us

Legislative Services Agency, State House, 200 W Washington, Room 302, Indianapolis, IN 46204-2789; 317-232-9856, 8:15AM-4:45PM.

Online search: All legislative information is available over the Internet. The Indiana Code is also available.

Information About County Agencies

Court Structure

Note that Small Claims in Marion County are heard at the township and records are maintained at that level. The phone number for the township offices are indicated in Marion County.

Online Access

No online access computer system, internal or external, is available, except for Marion and Adams Counties. CivicNet/Access Indiana Information Network, is available on the Internet (www.civicnet.net). An account and password is required. There is no charge for civil court name searches. Fees range from $2.00 to $5.00 for civil case summaries, civil justice name searches, criminal case summaries, and party booking details.

**About the
County Courts**

Searching Hints

The Circuit Court Clerk/County Clerk in every county is the same individual and is responsible for keeping all county judicial records. However, it is recommended that, when requesting a record, the request indicate which court heard the case (Circuit, Superior, or County). Many courts are no longer performing searches, especially criminal, based on a 7/96 statement by the State Board of Accounts.

Certification and copy fees are set by statute as $1.00 per document plus copy fee for certification and $1.00 per page for copies.

About the Recorder's Office

Organization

92 counties, 92 recording offices. The recording officer is County Recorder (Circuit Clerk for state tax liens on personal property). Many counties utilize a "Miscellaneous Index" for tax and other liens. 81 counties are in the Eastern Time Zone (EST), and 11 are in the Central Time Zone (CST).

Real Estate Records

Most counties will not perform real estate searches. Copies usually cost $1.00 per page, and certification usually $5.00 per document.

UCC Records

Financing statements are filed at the state level except for consumer goods, farm related and real estate related filings. All counties will perform UCC searches. Use search request form UCC-11. Search fees are usually $1.00 per debtor name. Copies usually cost $.50 per page. Most counties also charge $.50 for each financing statement reported on a search.

Other Lien Records

All federal tax liens on personal property are filed with the County Recorder. State tax liens on personal property are filed with the Circuit Clerk, who is in a different office from the Recorder. Most counties will **not** perform tax lien searches. Other liens are: judgments, mechanics, hospital, sewer, utility, innkeeper.

County Courts & Recording Offices Online

Adams County

Felony, Misdemeanor, Civil, Eviction, Small Claims

www.civicnet.net

Circuit & Superior Court, 2nd St Courthouse, Decatur IN 46733, 219-724-2600 X206. Fax: 219-724-3848. Hours: 8AM-4:30PM (EST).

Online search: Online access is available through www.civicnet.net. Fees vary by search, the system is open 24 hours. Civil records date back to 1991, criminal to 1988. No juvenile, adoption, mental health or sealed records released.

Elkhart County

Liens, Real Estate, Tax Assessor Records

County Recorder, 117 N 2nd St, Rm 205, Goshen IN 46526.

Online search: The annual fee is $50, plus a minimum of $20 per month if you use the system. The minimum fee gives 2 hours of access. Additional usage is billed at $10 per hour. The system operates 24 hours daily and supports baud rates up to 9,600. One can search by name, Grantee/Grantor and instrument type. Lending agency information is available. For further information, contact Nick Cenova at 219-535-6777.

Felony, Misdemeanor, Civil, Eviction, Small Claims

www.civicnet.net

Circuit and Superior Court, 200 E Washington St, Indianapolis IN 46204, 317-327-4600. Civil Phone: 317-327-4724. Criminal Phone: 317-327-4733. Hours: 8AM-4:30PM (EST).

The Municipal Court of Marion County is housed in the same building, phone is 317-327-4600. They handle civil actions under $25,000 and Class D felony records.

Online search: Remote access available through www.civicnet.net (Internet). The setup fee is $50, other fees vary by Criminal records go back to 1988.

Liens, Real Estate

www.indygov.net

County Recorder, 200 E Washington St, Suite 721, Indianapolis IN 46204, 317-327-4020. Fax: 317-327-4733.

Online search: The set up fee is $200, plus one is required to maintain an escrow balance of at least $100. Additional charges are $.50 per minute, $.25 display charge for the 1st page and $.10 for each additional page. The system operates 24 hours daily. Records date back to 1987 and images from 2/24/93. Search by name, Grantee/Grantor and document type. Federal tax liens and UCC information are available. The fax back service is $2 per page. For more information, contact Mike Kerner at 317-327-4587.

Federal Courts Online

County-to-Court Cross Reference (Bankruptcy Court locations in Parenthesis if different)

County	District	Court
Adams	Northern	Fort Wayne
Allen	Northern	Fort Wayne
Bartholomew	Southern	Indianapolis
Benton	Northern	Lafayette (Hammond at Lafayette)
Blackford	Northern	Fort Wayne
Boone	Southern	Indianapolis
Brown	Southern	Indianapolis
Carroll	Northern	Lafayette (Hammond at Lafayette)
Cass	Northern	South Bend
Clark	Southern	New Albany
Clay	Southern	Terre Haute
Clinton	Southern	Indianapolis
Crawford	Southern	New Albany
Daviess	Southern	Evansville
DeKalb	Northern	Fort Wayne
Dearborn	Southern	New Albany
Decatur	Southern	Indianapolis
Delaware	Southern	Indianapolis
Dubois	Southern	Evansville
Elkhart	Northern	South Bend
Fayette	Southern	Indianapolis
Floyd	Southern	New Albany
Fountain	Southern	Indianapolis
Franklin	Southern	Indianapolis
Fulton	Northern	South Bend
Gibson	Southern	Evansville
Grant	Northern	Fort Wayne
Greene	Southern	Terre Haute
Hamilton	Southern	Indianapolis
Hancock	Southern	Indianapolis
Harrison	Southern	New Albany
Hendricks	Southern	Indianapolis
Henry	Southern	Indianapolis
Howard	Southern	Indianapolis
Huntington	Northern	Fort Wayne
Jackson	Southern	New Albany
Jasper	Northern	Lafayette (Hammond at Lafayette)
Jay	Northern	Fort Wayne
Jefferson	Southern	New Albany
Jennings	Southern	New Albany
Johnson	Southern	Indianapolis
Knox	Southern	Terre Haute
Kosciusko	Northern	South Bend
La Porte	Northern	South Bend
LaGrange	Northern	Fort Wayne
Lake	Northern	Hammond (Hammond at Gary)
Lawrence	Southern	New Albany
Madison	Southern	Indianapolis
Marion	Southern	Indianapolis
Marshall	Northern	South Bend
Martin	Southern	Evansville
Miami	Northern	South Bend
Monroe	Southern	Indianapolis
Montgomery	Southern	Indianapolis
Morgan	Southern	Indianapolis
Newton	Northern	Lafayette (Hammond at Lafayette)
Noble	Northern	Fort Wayne
Ohio	Southern	New Albany
Orange	Southern	New Albany
Owen	Southern	Terre Haute
Parke	Southern	Terre Haute
Perry	Southern	Evansville
Pike	Southern	Evansville
Porter	Northern	Hammond (Hammond. at Gary)
Posey	Southern	Evansville
Pulaski	Northern	South Bend
Putnam	Southern	Terre Haute
Randolph	Southern	Indianapolis

Ripley	Southern	New Albany
Rush	Southern	Indianapolis
Scott	Southern	New Albany
Shelby	Southern	Indianapolis
Spencer	Southern	Evansville
St. Joseph	Northern	South Bend
Starke	Northern	South Bend
Steuben	Northern	Fort Wayne
Sullivan	Southern	Terre Haute
Switzerland	Southern	New Albany
Tippecanoe	Northern	Lafayette (Hammond at Lafayette)
Tipton	Southern	Indianapolis
Union	Southern	Indianapolis
Vanderburgh	Southern	Evansville
Vermillion	Southern	Terre Haute
Vigo	Southern	Terre Haute
Wabash	Northern	South Bend
Warren	Northern	Lafayette (Hammond at Lafayette)
Warrick	Southern	Evansville
Washington	Southern	New Albany
Wayne	Southern	Indianapolis
Wells	Northern	Fort Wayne
White	Northern	Lafayette (Hammond at Lafayette)
Whitley	Northern	Fort Wayne

US District Court
Northern District of Indiana

PACER sign-up number is 800-676-6856. Both civil and criminal case records are available online.

Fort Wayne Division, Room 1108, Federal Bldg, 1300 S Harrison St, Fort Wayne, IN 46802, 219-424-7360.

Hammond Division, Room 101, 507 State St, Hammond, IN 46320, 219-937-5235.

Lafayette Division, PO Box 1498, Lafayette, IN 47902, 765-420-6250.

South Bend Division, Room 102, 204 S Main, South Bend, IN 46601, 219-246-8000, Fax: 219-246-8002.

US Bankruptcy Court
Northern District of Indiana

www.innb.uscourts.gov

PACER sign-up number is 800-676-6856.

Fort Wayne Division, PO Box 2547, Fort Wayne, IN 46801-2547, 219-420-5100

Hammond at Lafayette Division, c/o Fort Wayne Division, PO Box 2547, Fort Wayne, IN 46801-2547, 219-420-5100

Hammond at Gary Division, 221 Federal Bldg, 610 Connecticut St, Gary, IN 46402-2595, 219-881-3335, Fax: 219-881-3307

South Bend Division, PO Box 7003, South Bend, IN 46634-7003, 219-236-8247, Fax: 219-236-8886

US District Court
Southern District of Indiana

The following courts recently began offering free Internet access to civil and criminal docket information as well as party names and counsel, at:

www.insd.uscourts.gov

Evansville Division 304 Federal Bldg, 101 NW Martin Luther King Blvd, Evansville, IN 47708, 812-465-6426, Record Rm: 812-465-6427, Fax: 812-465-6428.

Indianapolis Division Clerk, Room 105, 46 E Ohio St, Indianapolis, IN 46204, 317-229-3700, Fax: 317-229-3959.

New Albany Division Room 210, 121 W Spring St, New Albany, IN 47150, 812-948-5238.

Terre Haute Division 207 Federal Bldg, 30 N 7th St, Terre Haute, IN 47808, 812-234-9484.

US Bankruptcy Court
Southern District of Indiana

The following courts intent to offer free Internet access to docket information as well as party names and counsel in 1999, at:

www.insd.uscourts.gov

PACER sign-up number is 317-229-3845.

Evansville Division, 352 Federal Building, 101 NW Martin Luther King Blvd, Evansville, IN 47708, 812-465-6440.

Indianapolis Division, 116 US Courthouse, 46 E Ohio St, Indianapolis, IN 46204, 317-229-3800.

New Albany Division, 110 Federal Bldg, 121 W Spring St, New Albany, IN 47150, 812-948-5254.

Terre Haute Division, 207 Federal Bldg, 30 N 7th St, Terre Haute, IN 47808, 812-238-1550.

Governor's Office
State Capitol Bldg   515-281-5211
Des Moines, IA 50319   Fax 515-281-6611
www.state.ia.us/government/governor/index.html

Attorney General's Office
Hoover Bldg   515-281-5164
1305 E Walnut St, 2nd fl   Fax 515-281-4209
Des Moines, IA 50319   8AM-4:30PM
www.state.ia.us/government/ag/index.html

State Archives
State Historical Society of Iowa 515-281-5111
Library/Archives   Fax 515-282-0502
600 E. Locust,   9AM-4:30PM
Capitol Complex   T-SA
Des Moines, IA 50319-0290
www.uiowa.edu/~shsi/index.htm

Capital:	Des Moines
	Polk County
Time Zone:	CST
Number of Counties:	99
Population:	2,852,423
Web Site:	www.state.ia.us

State Court Administrator
State Court Administrator   515-281-5241
State Capitol   Fax 515-242-6164
Des Moines, IA 50319   8AM-4:30PM

State Agencies Online

Corporation Records
Limited Liability Company Records
Fictitious Name
Limited Partnership Records
Assumed Name
Trademarks/Servicemarks
sos.state.ia.us

Secretary of State, Corporation Division, 2nd Floor, Hoover Bldg, Des Moines, IA 50319; 515-281-5204, 515-242-6556 (other Fax line), 515-242-5953 (Fax), 8AM-4:30PM.

Online search: The state offers the DataShare Online System. Fees are $175.00 per year. plus $.30 per minute. The system is open 5 AM to 8 PM daily. All records are available, including UCCs. Call 515-281-5204 and ask for Cheryl Allen for more information.

Uniform Commercial Code
Federal Tax Liens
sos.state.ia.us

UCC Division, Secretary of State, Hoover Bldg, East 14th & Walnut, Des Moines, IA 50319; 515-281-5204, 515-242-5953 (Other Fax Line), 515-242-6556 (Fax), 8AM-4:30PM.

Online search: Online access is available at $.30 per minute with a $175.00 annual fee. The system is up daily from 5 AM to 8 PM and is the system used to obtain corporation records online

Legislation-Current/Pending
Legislation-Passed
www.legis.state.ia.us

Iowa General Assembly, Legislative Information Office, State Capitol, Des Moines, IA 50319; 515-281-5129, 8AM-4:30PM.

General Information: Records are available for the current year. For copies of older bills, it is suggested to go to a local law library.

Online search: Access is available through the Legislative Computer Support Bureau or through their web site. Note that the agency is going to discontinue the Bureau access and make all information available through the Internet site.

Information About County Agencies

Court Structure

Effective 7/1/95, the Small Claims limit was increased to $4000 from $3000.

Vital records are being moved from courts to the County Recorder's office in each county. There is no scheduled completion date for this conversion.

Online Access

There is a statewide online computer system called the Iowa Court Information System (ICIS), which is for internal use only. There is no public access system.

About the County Courts

Searching Hints

In most courts, the Certification Fee is $10.00 plus copy fee. Copy Fee is $.50 per page. Many courts do not do searches and recommend either in person searches or use of a record retriever.

Courts that accept written search requests do require an SASE. Credit cards are not accepted statewide. Most courts have a public access terminal for access to that court's records.

- - - - - - - - - - - - - - - -

About the Recorder's Office

Organization

99 counties, 100 recording offices. The recording officer is County Recorder. Many counties utilize a grantor/grantee index containing all transactions recorded with them. Lee County has two recording offices. See the notes under the county for how to determine which office is appropriate to search. The entire state is in the Central Time Zone (CST).

Real Estate Records

Most counties are hesitant to perform real estate searches, but some will provide a listing from the grantor/grantee index with the understanding that it is not certified in the sense that a title search is. Certification of copies usually costs $2.00 per document.

UCC Records

Financing statements are filed at the state level, except for consumer goods and real estate related filings. All counties will perform UCC searches. Use search request form UCC-11. Search fees are usually $5.00 per debtor name ($6.00 if the standard UCC-11 form is not used). Copies usually cost $1.00 per page.

Other Lien Records

Federal tax liens on personal property of businesses are filed with the Secretary of State. Other federal and all state tax liens on personal property are filed with the County Recorder. County search practices vary widely, but most provide some sort of tax lien search for $6.00 per name. Other liens are: home improvement, job service.

County Courts & Recording Offices Online

There is no online access available to the public for county court records.

No remote online access is available from real estate recorder's offices in Iowa.

Federal Courts Online

County-to-Court Cross Reference (Bankruptcy Court locations in Parenthesis if different)

County	District	Court
Adair	Southern	Council Bluffs (Des Moines)
Adams	Southern	Council Bluffs (Des Moines)
Allamakee	Northern	Dubuque (Cedar Rapids)
Appanoose	Southern	Des Moines (Central)
Audubon	Southern	Council Bluffs (Des Moines)
Benton	Northern	Cedar Rapids
Black Hawk	Northern	Dubuque (Cedar Rapids)
Boone	Southern	Des Moines (Central)
Bremer	Northern	Dubuque (Cedar Rapids)
Buchanan	Northern	Dubuque (Cedar Rapids)
Buena Vista	Northern	Sioux City (Cedar Rapids)
Butler	Northern	Sioux City (Cedar Rapids)
Calhoun	Northern	Sioux City (Cedar Rapids)
Carroll	Northern	Sioux City (Cedar Rapids)
Cass	Southern	Council Bluffs (Des Moines)
Cedar	Northern	Cedar Rapids
Cerro Gordo	Northern	Cedar Rapids
Cherokee	Northern	Sioux City (Cedar Rapids)
Chickasaw	Northern	Dubuque (Cedar Rapids)
Clarke	Southern	Council Bluffs (Des Moines)
Clay	Northern	Sioux City (Cedar Rapids)
Clayton	Northern	Dubuque (Cedar Rapids)
Clinton	Southern	Council Bluffs (Des Moines)
Crawford	Northern	Sioux City (Cedar Rapids)
Dallas	Southern	Des Moines (Central)
Davis	Southern	Des Moines (Central)
Decatur	Southern	Council Bluffs (Des Moines)
Delaware	Northern	Dubuque (Cedar Rapids)
Des Moines	Southern	Des Moines (Central)
Dickinson	Northern	Sioux City (Cedar Rapids)
Dubuque	Northern	Dubuque (Cedar Rapids)
Emmet	Northern	Sioux City (Cedar Rapids)
Fayette	Northern	Dubuque (Cedar Rapids)
Floyd	Northern	Dubuque (Cedar Rapids)
Franklin	Northern	Sioux City (Cedar Rapids)
Fremont	Southern	Council Bluffs (Des Moines
Greene	Southern	Des Moines (Central)
Grundy	Northern	Cedar Rapids
Guthrie	Southern	Des Moines (Central)
Hamilton	Northern	Sioux City (Cedar Rapids)
Hancock	Northern	Sioux City (Cedar Rapids)
Hardin	Northern	Cedar Rapids
Harrison	Southern	Council Bluffs (Des Moines)
Henry	Southern	Davenport (Des Moines)
Howard	Northern	Dubuque (Cedar Rapids)
Humboldt	Northern	Sioux City (Cedar Rapids)
Ida	Northern	Sioux City (Cedar Rapids)
Iowa	Northern	Cedar Rapids
Jackson	Northern	Dubuque (Cedar Rapids)
Jasper	Southern	Des Moines (Central)
Jefferson	Southern	Des Moines (Central)
Johnson	Southern	Davenport (Des Moines)
Jones	Northern	Cedar Rapids
Keokuk	Southern	Des Moines (Central)
Kossuth	Northern	Sioux City (Cedar Rapids)
Lee	Southern	Davenport (Des Moines)

Linn	Northern	Cedar Rapids
Louisa	Southern	Davenport (Des Moines)
Lucas	Southern	Council Bluffs (Des Moines)
Lyon	Northern	Sioux City (Cedar Rapids)
Madison	Southern	Des Moines (Central)
Mahaska	Southern	Des Moines (Central)
Marion	Southern	Des Moines (Central)
Marshall	Southern	Des Moines (Central)
Mills	Southern	Council Bluffs (Des Moines)
Mitchell	Northern	Dubuque (Cedar Rapids)
Monona	Northern	Sioux City (Cedar Rapids)
Monroe	Southern	Des Moines (Central)
Montgomery	Southern	Council Bluffs (Des Moines)
Muscatine	Southern	Davenport (Des Moines)
O'Brien	Northern	Sioux City (Cedar Rapids)
Osceola	Northern	Sioux City (Cedar Rapids)
Page	Southern	Council Bluffs (Des Moines)
Palo Alto	Northern	Sioux City (Cedar Rapids)
Plymouth	Northern	Sioux City (Cedar Rapids)
Pocahontas	Northern	Sioux City (Cedar Rapids)
Polk	Southern	Des Moines (Central)
Pottawattamie	Southern	Council Bluffs (Des Moines)
Poweshiek	Southern	Des Moines (Central)
Ringgold	Southern	Council Bluffs (Des Moines)
Sac	Northern	Sioux City (Cedar Rapids)
Scott	Southern	Davenport (Des Moines)
Shelby	Southern	Council Bluffs (Des Moines)
Sioux	Northern	Sioux City (Cedar Rapids)
Story	Southern	Des Moines (Central)
Tama	Northern	Cedar Rapids
Taylor	Southern	Council Bluffs (Des Moines)
Union	Southern	Council Bluffs (Des Moines)
Van Buren	Southern	Davenport (Des Moines)
Wapello	Southern	Des Moines (Central)
Warren	Southern	Des Moines (Central)
Washington	Southern	Davenport (Des Moines)
Wayne	Southern	Council Bluffs (Des Moines)
Webster	Northern	Sioux City (Cedar Rapids)
Winnebago	Northern	Sioux City (Cedar Rapids)
Winneshiek	Northern	Dubuque (Cedar Rapids)
Woodbury	Northern	Sioux City (Cedar Rapids)
Worth	Northern	Sioux City (Cedar Rapids)
Wright	Northern	Sioux City (Cedar Rapids)

US District Court
Northern District of Iowa

PACER sign-up number is 800-676-5856. Both civil and criminal case records are available online.

Cedar Rapids Division, Court Clerk, PO Box 74710, Cedar Rapids, IA 52407-4710, 319-286-2300.

Dubuque Division, c/o Cedar Rapids Division, PO Box 74710, Cedar Rapids, IA 52407-4710, 319-286-2300.

Sioux City Division, Room 301, Federal Bldg, 320 6th St, Sioux City, IA 51101, 712-233-3900.

US Bankruptcy Court
Northern District of Iowa

www.ianb.uscourts.gov

PACER sign-up number is 800-676-6856.

Cedar Rapids Division, PO Box 74890, Cedar Rapids, IA 52407-4890, 319-286-2200, Fax: 319-286-2280

US District Court
Southern District of Iowa

www.iasd.uscourts.gov/

PACER sign-up number is 800-676-6856. Both civil and criminal case records are available online.

Council Bluffs Division, PO Box 307, Council Bluffs, IA 51502, 712-328-0283, Fax: 712-328-1241

Davenport Division, PO Box 256, Davenport, IA 52805, , Civil Docket Section: 319-322-3223, Criminal Docket Section: 515-284-6248, Fax: 319-322-2962

Des Moines (Central) Division, PO Box 9344, Des Moines, IA 50306-9344, , Civil Docket Section: 515-284-6447, Criminal Docket Section: 515-284-6248, Fax: 515-284-6210

US Bankruptcy Court
Southern District of Iowa

PACER sign-up number is 800-676-6856.

Des Moines Division, PO Box 9264, Des Moines, IA 50306-9264, 515-284-6230, Fax: 515-284-6404.

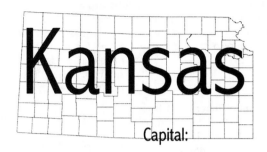

Governor's Office
State Capitol Bldg,
Room 212S   785-296-3232
Topeka, KS 66612-1590   Fax 785-296-7973
www.ink.org/public/governor

Attorney General's Office
Kansas Judicial Center   785-296-2215
301 SW 10th Ave, 2nd Floor   Fax 785-296-6296
Topeka, KS 66612-1597   8AM-5PM
lawlib.wuacc.edu/ag/homepage.html

State Archives
Kansas State Historical Society 785-272-8681
Library & Archives Division   Fax 785-272-8682
6425 SW 6th Ave   9AM-4:30PM M-S
Topeka, KS 66615-1099
http://history.cc.ukans.edu/heritage/k
shs/kshs1.html

Capital: Topeka
                                              Shawnee County

Time Zone: CST*
   * Kansas' five western-most counties are MST:
They are: Greeley, Hamilton, Kearny, Sherman, Wallace.

Number of Counties: 105

Population: 2,594,840

Web Site: www.state.ks.us

State Court Administrator
Judicial Administrator   785-296-4873
Kansas Judicial Center,   Fax 785-296-7076
301 W 10th St   8AM-5PM
Topeka, KS 66612-1507
www.law.ukans.edu/kscourts/kscourts.html

State Agencies Online

Legislation-Current/Pending
Legislation-Passed
www.ink.org

Kansas State Library, Capitol Bldg, 300 SW 10th Ave, Topeka, KS 66612; 785-296-2149, 785-296-6650 (Fax).

Online search: The web site has bill information for the current session. Site also contains access to state statutes.

Corporation Records
Limited Partnerships
Limited Liability Company Records
www.ink.org/public/sos

Secretary of State, Corporation Division, 300 SW 10th St, 2nd Floor, Topeka, KS 66612-1594; 785-296-4564, 785-296-4570 (Fax), 8AM - 5PM.

Online search: Corporate data can be ordered from The Information Network of Kansas (INK), a state sponsored interface. Both independent online and Internet (www.ink.org) access modes are offered. The system

is open 24 hours a day, 7 days a week. Corporation records are $.25 per search. There is a $.10 a minute access charge, unless you connect through the Internet where there is no connect charge. Minimum baud rate is 14.4. For more information, call INK at 800-452-6727.

Uniform Commercial Code
Federal Tax Liens
www.ink.org/public/sos

UCC Division, Secretary of State, State Capitol, 300 W Tenth, 2nd Floor, Topeka, KS 66612-1594; 785-296-3650, 785-296-3659 (Fax), 8AM-5PM.

General Information: The search includes federal tax liens on businesses. Federal tax liens on individuals can be filed here or at county, all state tax liens are filed at the county level.

Online search: Online service is provided the Information Network of Kansas (INK). The system is open 24 hours daily. There is an annual fee. Network charges are $.10 a minute unless access is through their

Internet site (www.ink.org) which has no network fee. UCC records are $8.00 per record. This is the same online system used for corporation records. For more information, call INK at 800-452-6727.

Driver Records

Department of Revenue, Driver Control Bureau, PO Box 12021, Topeka, KS 66612-2021; (Docking State Office Building, 915 Harrison, 1st Floor, Topeka, KS 66612); 785-296-3671, 785-296-6851 (Fax), 8AM-4:45PM.

General Information: Records are available for 3 years for minor violations and 5 years for DWIs. The state does not record speeding violations of 10 mph or less over in a 70 speed zone or 5 mph or less in all other speed zones. It takes 2-21 days before new records are available for inquiries. Casual requesters cannot obtain records. Statutes prohibit acquiring records for the purpose of obtaining addresses and lists for the sale of property or services.

Online search: Kansas has contracted with the Information Network of Kansas (INK) (800-452-6727) to service all electronic media requests of driver license histories. INK offers connection through an "800

number" or can be reached via the Internet (www.ink.org). Cost is $4.00 for batch records or $4.50 for interactive records with a $.10 charge per minute if using the 800 number, and a $50 annual subscription fee. There is a $15 minimum requirement per month, unless you pay by credit card. The system is open 24 hours a day, 7 days a week. Batch requests are available at 7:30 am (if ordered by 10PM previous day).

Vehicle Ownership
Vehicle Identification

Division of Vehicles, Title and Registration Bureau, 915 Harrison, Topeka, KS 66612; 285-296-3621, 285-296-3852 (Fax), 7:30AM-4:45PM.

General Information: Records are restricted from purchase for the purpose of obtaining address mail lists for selling property or services.

Online search: Online batch inquires are $3.00 per record; online interactive requests are $4.00 per record. See the Driving Records Section for a complete description of The Information Network of Kansas (800-452-6727), the state authorized vendor.

Information About County Agencies

Court Structure

If an individual in Municipal Court wants a jury trial, the request must be filed de novo in a District Court.

About the County Courts

Online Access

Online computer access is available for District Court Records in 4 counties—Johnson, Sedgwick, Shawnee, and Wyandotte—through the Information Network of Kansas (INK) Services. Franklin and Finney counties are to be available in 1999. There is also a wide range of other state information available through INK. A user can access INK through their Internet site at www.ink.org. The INK subscription fee is $75.00, and the annual renewal fee is $60.00. There is no per minute connect charge, but there is a transaction fee. Drivers License, Title, Registration, Lien, and UCC searches are also available by PC through the Internet or through a toll-free number. For additional information or a registration packet, call 800-452-6727.

Searching Hints

Cowley, Crawford, Labette, Montgomery and Neosho Counties have two hearing locations, but only one record center. Many Kansas courts not do searches and will refer any criminal request to the Kansas Bureau of Investigation.

━ ━ ━ ━ ━ ━ ━ ━ ━ ━ ━ ━

About the Recorder's Office

Organization

105 counties, 105 recording offices. The recording officer is Register of Deeds. Many counties utilize a "Miscellaneous Index" for tax and other liens, separate from real estate records. 100 counties are in CST and 5 are in the MST.

Real Estate Records

Most counties will not perform real estate searches, although some will do as an accommodation with the understanding that they are not "certified." Some counties will also do a search based upon legal description to determine owner. Copy fees vary, and certification fees are usually $1.00 per document. Tax records are located at the Appraiser's Office.

UCC Records

Financing statements are filed at the state level except for consumer goods and real estate related filings. All counties will perform UCC searches. Use search request form UCC-3. Search fees are usually $8.00 per debtor name. Copies usually cost $1.00 per page.

Other Lien Records

Federal tax liens on personal property of businesses are filed with the Secretary of State. Other federal tax liens and all state tax liens on personal property are filed with the county Register of Deeds. Most counties automatically include tax liens on personal property with a UCC search. Tax liens on personal property may usually be searched separately for $8.00 per name. Other liens are: mechanics, harvesters, lis pendens, threshers.

County Courts & Recording Offices Online

Finney County

Felony, Misdemeanor, Civil, Small Claims, Probate

District Court, PO Box 798, Garden City KS 67846. Civil Phone: 316-271-6120. Criminal Phone: 316-271-6123. Fax: 316-271-6140 (Civil) 271-6141 (Criminal). 8AM-4:30PM.

Online search: Online access via the Information Network of Kansas (INK) is intended in 1999.

Franklin County

Felony, Misdemeanor, Civil, Small Claims, Probate

District Court, PO Box 637, Ottawa KS 66067, 785-242-6000. Fax: 785-242-5970. Hours: 8AM-5PM (CST).

Online search: Online access via the Information Network of Kansas (INK) is intended in 1999.

Johnson County

Civil, Eviction, Small Claims, Probate.

District Court, 100 N Kansas, Olathe KS 66061, 913-764-8484 X5015. Fax: 913-791-5826. Hours: 8:30AM-5PM.

Online search: Index online through Information Network of Kansas. (INK). See www.ink.org for subscription info.

Sedgwick County

Felony, Misdemeanor, Civil, Small Claims, Probate, Liens, Real Estate, Tax Assessor Records

District Court, 525 N Main, Wichita KS 67203, 316-383-7302. Civil Phone: 316-383-7311. Criminal Phone: 316-383-7253. Fax: 316-383-8070 (Civil) 383-8071 (Criminal).

Online search: The setup fee is $225. There is a monthly fee of $49 and a per transaction charge of $.03-$.04. Records date back to 1980. The system operates 24 hours daily and supports

baud rates up to 28.8. System connections can be made using Windows 95/98. The database can be searched by name, Grantee/Grantor, address, key number and book and page. Lending agency information is available. For further information, contact John Zukovich at 316-383-7384.

Shawnee County

Felony, Misdemeanor, Civil, Small Claims, Probate.

District Court, 200 E 7th Rm 209, Topeka KS 66603, 785-233-8200 X4327. Fax: 785-291-4911. Hours: 8:30AM-5PM.

Online search: Access available through INK of Kansas. See www.ink.org for subscription information.

Wyandotte County

Felony, Misdemeanor, Civil, Small Claims, Probate

District Court, 710 N 7th St, Kansas City KS 66101. Civil Phone: 913-573-2901. Criminal Phone: 913-573-2905. Fax: 913-573-4134. Hours: 8AM-5PM (CST).

Online search: Online access requires specific software and a $20 setup fee. Transactions are $.05 each. The system is open 8am to 10pm M-F, and 8-4 on Sat. For more information call 913-573-2885.

Liens, Real Estate, Death Records, Marriage Records, Divorce Records

Register of Deeds, 710 N 7th St, Kansas City KS 66101. 913-573-2841. Fax: 913-573-3075.

Online search: A setup fee of $20 applies. The monthly fee is $5 and $.05 after the first 100 transactions. VT 100 emulation software is required. Records date back to 1/97. The system operates 8AM-10PM M-F and 8AM-4PM S and supports a baud rate of 9,600. Searches can be made by name, Grantee/Grantor, plat or subdivision name. Lending agency info available. Contact Louise Sachen at 913-573-2885.

Federal Courts Online

County-to-Court Cross Reference (Bankruptcy Court locations in Parenthesis if different)

County	Court	County	Court	County	Court
Allen	Topeka	Greeley	Wichita	Osborne	Wichita
Anderson	Topeka	Greenwood	Wichita	Ottawa	Topeka
Atchison	Kansas City	Hamilton	Wichita	Pawnee	Wichita
Barber	Wichita	Harper	Wichita	Phillips	Wichita
Barton	Wichita	Harvey	Wichita	Pottawatomie	Topeka
Bourbon	Kansas City	Haskell	Wichita	Pratt	Wichita
Brown	Kansas City	Hodgeman	Wichita	Rawlins	Wichita
Butler	Wichita	Jackson	Topeka	Reno	Wichita
Chase	Topeka	Jefferson	Wichita	Republic	Topeka
Chautauqua	Wichita	Jewell	Topeka	Rice	Wichita
Cherokee	Kansas City	Johnson	Kansas City	Riley	Topeka
Cheyenne	Wichita	Kearny	Wichita	Rooks	Wichita
Clark	Wichita	Kingman	Wichita	Rush	Wichita
Clay	Topeka	Kiowa	Wichita	Russell	Wichita
Cloud	Topeka	Labette	Kansas City	Saline	Topeka
Coffey	Topeka	Lane	Wichita	Scott	Wichita
Comanche	Kansas City (Wichita)	Leavenworth	Kansas City	Sedgwick	Wichita
Cowley	Wichita	Lincoln	Topeka	Seward	Wichita
Crawford	Kansas City	Linn	Kansas City	Shawnee	Topeka
Decatur	Wichita	Logan	Wichita	Sheridan	Wichita
Dickinson	Topeka	Lyon	Topeka	Sherman	Wichita
Doniphan	Kansas City	Marion	Topeka	Smith	Wichita
Douglas	Topeka	Marshall	Kansas City	Stafford	Wichita
Edwards	Wichita	McPherson	Wichita	Stanton	Wichita
Elk	Wichita	Meade	Wichita	Stevens	Wichita
Ellis	Wichita	Miami	Kansas City	Sumner	Wichita
Ellsworth	Wichita	Mitchell	Topeka	Thomas	Wichita
Finney	Wichita	Montgomery	Wichita	Trego	Wichita
Ford	Wichita	Morris	Topeka	Wabaunsee	Topeka
Franklin	Topeka	Morton	Wichita	Wallace	Wichita
Geary	Topeka	Nemaha	Kansas City	Washington	Topeka
Gove	Wichita	Neosho	Topeka	Wichita	Wichita
Graham	Wichita	Ness	Wichita	Wilson	Topeka
Grant	Wichita	Norton	Wichita	Woodson	Topeka
Gray	Wichita	Osage	Topeka	Wyandotte	Kansas City

US District Court
District of Kansas

www.ksd.uscourts.gov

PACER sign-up number is 800-676-6856. Both civil and criminal case records are available online.

Kansas City Division, Clerk, 500 State Ave, Kansas City, KS 66101, 913-551-6719

Topeka Division, Clerk, US District Court, Room 490, 444 SE Quincy, Topeka, KS 66683, 913-295-2610

Wichita Division, 204 US Courthouse, 401 N Market, Wichita, KS 67202-2096, 316-269-6491.

US Bankruptcy Court
District of Kansas

www.ksb.uscourts.gov

PACER sign-up number is 800-676-6856.

Kansas City Division, 500 State Ave, Room 161, Kansas City, KS 66101, 913-551-6732

Topeka Division, 240 Federal Bldg, 444 SE Quincy, Topeka, KS 66683, 785-295-2750

Wichita Division, 167 US Courthouse, 401 N Market, Wichita, KS 67202, 316-269-6486

Governor's Office

700 Capitol Ave, Room 100   502-564-2735
Frankfort, KY 40601   Fax 502-564-2517
www.state.ky.us/agencies/gov/govmenu6.htm

Attorney General's Office

Capitol Building   502-696-5300
Frankfort, KY 40601   Fax 502-696-8317
www.law.state.ky.us

State Court Administrator

Admin. Office of Courts   502-573-2350
100 Mill Creek Park   Fax 502-573-1448
Frankfort, KY 40601   8AM-4PM
www.state.ky.us/agencies/aoc/default

State Archives

Libraries & Archives Dept.   502-564-8300
300 Coffee Tree Rd   Fax 502-564-5773
Frankfort, KY 40601   8AM-4PM T-SA
www.kdla.state.ky.us

Capital: Frankfort
Franklin County

Time Zone: EST*

Kentucky's forty western-most counties are CST: They are: Adair, Allen, Ballard, Barren, Breckinridge, Butler, Caldwell, Calloway, Carlisle, Christian, Clinton, Crittenden, Cumberland, Daviess, Edmonson, Fulton, Graves, Grayson, Hancock, Hart, Henderson, Hickman, Hopkins, Livingstone, Logan, Marshall, McCracken, McLean, Metcalfe, Monroe, Muhlenberg, Ohio, Russell, Simpson, Todd, Trigg, Union, Warren, Wayne, Webster.

Number of Counties: 120

Population: 3,908.124

Web Site: www.state.ky.us

State Agencies Online

Corporation Records
Limited Partnerships
Assumed Name
Limited Liability Company Records

www.sos.state.ky.us/

Secretary of State, Corporate Records, PO Box 718, Frankfort, KY 40602-0718; (Courier: 700 Capitol Ave, Room 156, Frankfort, KY 40601); 502-564-7330, 502-564-4075 (Fax), 8AM-4PM,

General Information: Computer records are limited, they contain name, dates, current registered agent and initial incorporators and initial directors.

Online search: The Internet site, open 24 hours, has a searchable database with over 340,000 KY businesses. The site also offers downloading of filing forms.

Uniform Commercial Code

www.sos.state.ky.us

UCC Division, Secretary of State, PO Box 718, Frankfort, KY 40602-0718; (Courier: State Capitol Bldg, Rm 79, Frankfort, KY 40601); 502-564-2848 401, 502-564-4075 (Fax), 8AM-4:30PM.

General Information: Important--only out-of-state debtor filings are at this agency. All in-state filings are at the county level. All tax liens are filed at the county level.

Online search: Only information on out-of-state debtors can be obtained from their web site , there is no charge.

Marriage, Divorce & Death Records

http://ukcc.uky.edu:80/~vuitalrec

Department for Public Health, Vital Records, 275 E Main St-IE-A, Frankfort, KY 40621-0001; 502-564-4212, 502-227-0032 (Fax), 8AM-3PM.

Online search: In cooperation with the University of Kentucky, a searchable index is available on the Internet at http://ukcc.uky.edu:80/~vitalrec. The index runs from 1973 through 1993. The exception is the death index; it runs from 1911 to 1992. These online records are for non-commercial use only and are free.

Driver Records

Division of Driver Licensing, State Office Bldg, MVRS, 501 High Street, 2nd Floor, Frankfort, KY 40622; 502-564-6800 2250, 502-564-5787 (Fax), 8AM-4:30PM.

General Information: Records are available for 3 years for moving violations, DWIs and suspensions. Accidents are not reported. Any entry over 3 years old is "masked for insurance and employers." Records of surrendered licenses are available for 3 years.

Online search: This is a batch method for higher volume users. There is a minimum order of 150 requests per batch. The fee is $3 per record. Input received by 3 PM will be available the next morning. Either the Drivers License number or SSN is needed for ordering. The state will bill monthly. For more information, call (502) 564-6800, ext. 2111.

Vehicle Ownership
Vehicle Identification

Department of Motor Vehicles, Division of Motor Vehicle Licensing, State Office Bldg, 3rd Floor, Frankfort, KY 40622; 502-564-4076, 502-564-1686 (Fax), 8AM-4:30PM.

General Information: Vehicle and ownership records are made available to the public; however, those whom have opted out will not have their personal information released to the general public or for marketing purposes. This agency will not do a search by SSN.

Online search: Online access costs $2.00 per record. The online mode is interactive. Title, lien and registration searches are available. Records include those for mobile homes. For more information, contact Gale Warfield at the number listed above.

Legislation-Current/Pending
Legislation-Passed

www.lrc.state.ky.us

Kentucky General Assembly, Legislative Research Commission, 700 Capitol Ave, Room 300, Frankfort, KY 40601; 502-372-7181 (Bill Status Only), 502-564-8100 (Bill Room), 502-564-8100 (LRC Library), 502-223-5094 (Fax), 8AM-4:30PM,

Online search: The web site has an extensive searching mechanism for bills, actions, summaries, and statutes.

Information About County Agencies

Court Structure

56 Judicial Circuits and 59 Judicial Districts are organized into 140 courts. Circuit Courts handle felony actions.

Online Access

A statewide, online computer system called SUSTAIN is available for internal judicial/state agency use only.

Searching Hints

About the County Courts

Many courts refer requests for criminal searches to the Administrative Office of Courts (AOC) due to lack of personnel for searching at the court level. AOC maintains records on an internal system called COURTNET, which contains information on opening, closing, proceedings, disposition, and parties to including individual defendants. Felony convictions are accessible back to 1978, and Misdemeanors back five years. Until 1978, county judges handled all cases; therefore, in many cases, District and Circuit Court records go back only to 1978. Records prior to that time are archived.

The required Release Form is available from the AOC at the number shown above. A check or money order for the Search Fee of $10.00 per requested individual is payable to the State Treasurer of Kentucky, and an SASE must accompany the request.

- - - - - - - - - - - - - - - -

About the Recorder's Office

Organization

120 counties, 122 recording offices. The recording officer is County Clerk. Jefferson and Kenton Counties each have two recording offices. See the notes under each county for how to determine which office is appropriate to search. 80 counties are in the Eastern Time Zone (EST) and 40 are in the Central Time Zone.

Real Estate Records

Most counties will not perform real estate searches. Copy fees vary. Tax records are maintained by the Property Valuation Administrator, designated "Assessor" in this section.

UCC Records

Financing statements are filed with the County Clerk, except for non-resident debtors, which are filed at the state level. Many counties will not perform UCC searches. Use search request form UCC-11. Search fees and copy fees vary widely.

Other Lien Records

All federal and state tax liens on personal property are filed with the County Clerk, often in an "Encumbrance Book." Most counties will not perform tax lien searches. Other liens are: judgments, motor vehicle, mechanics, lis pendens, bail bond.

County Courts & Recording Offices Online

While there are no court records available online for the public, two Kentucky counties allow online access to County Clerk information.

Boyd County

Liens, Real Estate

County Clerk, 2800 Louisa ST, Courthouse, Catlettsburg KY 41129, 606-739-5116. Fax: 606-739-6357.

Online search: The usage fee is $10 monthly. The system operates 24 hours daily and supports baud rates up to 56K. Records date back to 1/79. One may search by name, Grantee/Grantor and book and page. Lending agency information is available. for further information, contact Maxine Selbee or Kathy Fisher at 606-739-5166.

Oldham County

Liens, Real Estate, Marriage Records, Tax Assessor Records

County Clerk, 100 W Jefferson, La Grange KY 40031, 502-222-9311. Fax: 502-222-3208.

Online search: The set up fee is $200, plus a monthly fee of $65. The system operates 24 hours daily. Records date back to 1980 and viewable images date back to 1/95. One may search by name, Grantee/Grantor, book and page, instrument number, subdivision and date. Lending agency information is available. For further information, contact Donna Schroeder at 502-222-9311.

Federal Courts Online

County-to-Court Cross Reference (Bankruptcy Court locations in Parenthesis if different)

County	District	Court
Adair	Western	Bowling Green (Louisville)
Allen	Western	Bowling Green (Louisville)
Anderson	Eastern	Frankfort (Lexington)
Ballard	Western	Paducah (Louisville)
Barren	Western	Bowling Green (Louisville)
Bath	Eastern	Lexington
Bell	Eastern	London (Lexington)
Boone	Eastern	Covington (Lexington)
Bourbon	Eastern	Lexington
Boyd	Eastern	Ashland (Lexington)
Boyle	Eastern	Lexington
Bracken	Eastern	Covington (Lexington)
Breathitt	Eastern	Pikeville (Lexington)
Breckinridge	Western	Louisville
Bullitt	Western	Louisville
Butler	Western	Bowling Green (Louisville)
Caldwell	Western	Paducah (Louisville)
Calloway	Western	Paducah (Louisville)
Campbell	Eastern	Covington (Lexington)
Carlisle	Western	Paducah (Louisville)
Carroll	Eastern	Frankfort (Lexington)
Carter	Eastern	Ashland (Lexington)
Casey	Western	Bowling Green (Louisville)
Christian	Western	Paducah (Louisville)
Clark	Eastern	Lexington
Clay	Eastern	London (Lexington)
Clinton	Western	Bowling Green (Louisville)
Crittenden	Western	Paducah (Louisville)
Cumberland	Western	Bowling Green (Louisville)
Daviess	Western	Owensboro (Louisville)
Edmonson	Western	Bowling Green (Louisville)
Elliott	Eastern	Ashland (Lexington)
Estill	Eastern	Lexington
Fayette	Eastern	Lexington
Fleming	Eastern	Lexington
Floyd	Eastern	Pikeville (Lexington)
Franklin	Eastern	Frankfort (Lexington)
Fulton	Western	Paducah (Louisville)
Gallatin	Eastern	Covington (Lexington)
Garrard	Eastern	Lexington
Grant	Eastern	Covington (Lexington)
Graves	Western	Paducah (Louisville)
Grayson	Western	Owensboro (Louisville)
Green	Western	Bowling Green (Louisville)
Greenup	Eastern	Ashland (Lexington)
Hancock	Western	Owensboro (Louisville)
Hardin	Western	Louisville
Harlan	Eastern	London (Lexington)
Harrison	Eastern	Lexington
Hart	Western	Bowling Green (Louisville)
Henderson	Western	Owensboro (Louisville)
Henry	Eastern	Frankfort (Lexington)
Hickman	Western	Paducah (Louisville)
Hopkins	Western	Owensboro (Louisville)
Jackson	Eastern	London (Lexington)
Jefferson	Western	Louisville
Jessamine	Eastern	Lexington
Johnson	Eastern	Pikeville (Lexington)
Kenton	Eastern	Covington (Lexington)
Knott	Eastern	Pikeville (Lexington)
Knox	Eastern	London (Lexington)
Larue	Western	Louisville
Laurel	Eastern	London (Lexington)
Lawrence	Eastern	Ashland (Lexington)
Lee	Eastern	Lexington
Leslie	Eastern	London (Lexington)
Letcher	Eastern	Pikeville (Lexington)
Lewis	Eastern	Ashland (Lexington)
Lincoln	Eastern	Lexington
Livingston	Western	Paducah (Louisville)
Logan	Western	Bowling Green (Louisville)
Lyon	Western	Paducah (Louisville)
Madison	Eastern	Lexington
Magoffin	Eastern	Pikeville (Lexington)
Marion	Western	Louisville
Marshall	Western	Paducah (Louisville)
Martin	Eastern	Pikeville (Lexington)
Mason	Eastern	Covington (Lexington)
McCracken	Western	Paducah (Louisville)
McCreary	Eastern	London (Lexington)
McLean	Western	Owensboro (Louisville)
Meade	Western	Louisville
Menifee	Eastern	Lexington
Mercer	Eastern	Lexington
Metcalfe	Western	Bowling Green (Louisville)
Monroe	Western	Bowling Green (Louisville)

Montgomery......... Eastern.......... Lexington
Morgan.................. Eastern.......... Ashland (Lexington)
Muhlenberg......... Western .... Owensboro (Louisville)
Nelson .... Western .... Louisville
Nicholas............... Eastern.......... Lexington
Ohio...................... Western .... Owensboro (Louisville)
Oldham .... Western .... Louisville
Owen..................... Eastern.......... Frankfort (Lexington)
Owsley .... Eastern.......... London (Lexington)
Pendleton .... Eastern.......... Covington (Lexington)
Perry .... Eastern.......... Pikeville (Lexington)
Pike...................... Eastern.......... Pikeville (Lexington)
Powell .... Eastern.......... Lexington
Pulaski.................. Eastern.......... London (Lexington)
Robertson.............. Eastern.......... Covington (Lexington)
Rockcastle .... Eastern.......... London (Lexington)
Rowan................... Eastern.......... Ashland (Lexington)
Russell.................. Western .... Bowling Green (Louisville)

Scott .... Eastern .... Lexington
Shelby .... Eastern .... Frankfort (Lexington)
Simpson................ Western .... Bowling Green (Louisville)
Spencer .... Western .... Louisville
Taylor.................... Western .... Bowling Green (Louisville)
Todd .... Western .... Bowling Green (Louisville)
Trigg..................... Western .... Paducah (Louisville)
Trimble .... Eastern .... Frankfort (Lexington)
Union .... Western .... Owensboro (Louisville)
Warren .... Western .... Bowling Green (Louisville)
Washington .... Western .... Louisville
Wayne................... Eastern .... London (Lexington)
Webster................. Western .... Owensboro (Louisville)
Whitley .... Eastern .... London (Lexington)
Wolfe .... Eastern .... Lexington
Woodford .... Eastern .... Lexington

US District Court
Eastern District of Kentucky

PACER sign-up number is 800-676-6856. Both civil and criminal case records are available online.

Ashland Division, Suite 336, 1405 Greenup Ave, Ashland, KY 41101, 606-329-2465.

Covington Division, Clerk, PO Box 1073, Covington, KY 41012, 606-655-3810.

Frankfort Division, Room 313, 330 W Broadway, Frankfort, KY 40601, 502-223-5225.

Lexington Division, PO Box 3074, Lexington, KY 40596-3074, 606-233-2503, Civil Docket Section: 606-233-2762, Criminal Docket Section: 606-233-2503.

London Division, PO Box 5121, London, KY 40745-5121, 606-864-5137.

Pikeville Division, Office of the Clerk, 203 Federal Bldg, 102 Main St, Pikeville, KY 41501-1144, 606-437-6160.

US Bankruptcy Court
Eastern District of Kentucky

Lexington Division, PO Box 1111, Lexington, KY 40589-1111, 606-233-2608.

PACER sign-up number is 800-676-6856.

US District Court
Western District of Kentucky

www.kywd.uscourts.gov

PACER sign-up number is 800-676-6856. Both civil and criminal case records are available online.

Bowling Green Division, US District Court, 241 E Main St, Room 120, Bowling Green, KY 42101-2175, 502-781-1110

Louisville Division, Clerk, US District Court, 450 US Courthouse, 601 W Broadway, Louisville, KY 40202, 502-582-5156, Fax: 502-582-6302

Owensboro Division, Federal Bldg, Room 126, 423 Frederica St, Owensboro, KY 42301, 502-683-0221, Fax: 502-685-4601

Paducah Division, 127 Federal Building, 501 Broadway, Paducah, KY 42001, 502-443-1337

US Bankruptcy Court
Western District of Kentucky

Louisville Division, 546 US Courthouse, 601 W Broadway, Louisville, KY 40202, 502-582-5145.

PACER sign-up number is 800-676-6856.

Louisiana

Governor's Office
PO Box 94004   225-342-7015
Baton Rouge, LA 70804-9004 Fax 225-342-7099
www.gov.state.la.us/

Attorney General's Office
LA Department of Justice   225-342-7013
PO Box 94005   Fax 225-342-7335
Baton Rouge, LA 70804-9005 8:30AM-5PM
www.laag.com

State Archives
Secretary of State   225-922-1184
Division of Archives, Records Fax 225-922-0433
Management, & History   8AM-4:30PM, 9-5
SA 1-5 SU
3851 Essen Lane
Baton Rouge, LA 70809-2137
www.sec.state.la.us/arch-1.htm

Capital: Baton Rouge
                          East Baton Rouge Parish

Time Zone: CST

Number of Parishes: 64

Population: 4,351,769

Web Site: www.state.la.us

State Court Administrator
Judicial Administrator   225-568-5747
Judicial Council of the Supreme Court
301 Loyola Ave, Room 109
New Orleans, LA 70112   9AM-5PM
www.lasc.org

State Agencies Online

Corporation Records
Limited Partnership Records
Limited Liability Company Records
Trademarks/Servicemarks
www.sec.state.la.us/crping.htm

Commercial Division, Corporation Department, PO Box 94125, Baton Rouge, LA 70804-9125; (Courier: 3851 Essen Lane, Baton Rouge, LA 70809); 225-925-4704, 225-925-4726 (Fax), 8AM-4:30PM.

General Information: Fictitious Names and Assumed Names are found at the parish level.

Online search: The dial-up system is $360 per year for unlimited access. Almost any communications software will work with up to a 14,400 baud rate. The system is open from 6:30 am to 11pm. For more information, call Brenda Wright at (225) 922-1475. There is also free searching available from the Internet site. This information is limited when compared to the pay system.

Uniform Commercial Code
Secretary of State, UCC Records, PO Box 94125, Baton Rouge, LA 70804-9125; 800-256-3758, 225-342-5542 (Fax), 8AM-4:30PM.

General Information: All tax liens and financial statements are filed at the parish level. IRS liens show up on UCC records.

Online search: An annual $400 fee gives unlimited access to UCC filing information. The dial-up service is open from 6:30AM-11PM daily. Minimum baud rate is 9600. Most any software communications program can be configured to work. For further information, call Brenda Wright at (225) 922-1475.

Driver Records
Dept of Public Safety and Corrections, Office of Motor Vehicles, PO Box 64886, Baton Rouge, LA 70896; (Courier: 109 S Foster, Baton Rouge, LA 70806); 225-925-6009, 225-922-2814 (Alternate Telephone), 225-925-6915 (Fax), 8AM-4:30PM M-F.

General Information: Records are available for 3 years for moving violations, 10 years from date of conviction for DWIs and 5 years for suspensions. Accidents are reported, but fault is not shown. It takes 2-3 weeks before new records are available for inquiries. Casual requesters can obtain driving records, but personal information is not released if subject opted out.

Online search: An online, interactive mode is available from 7 AM to 9:30 PM daily. Records are $6.00 each. There is a minimum order requirement of 2,000 requests per month. A bond or large deposit is required. For more information, call 225-925-6032.

Vehicle Ownership
Vehicle Identification
www.dps.state.la.us/laomv.html

Department of Public Safety & Corrections, Office of Motor Vehicles, PO Box 64884, Baton Rouge, LA 70896; (Courier: 109 S Foster Dr, Baton Rouge, LA 70806); 225-925-6146, 225-925-3979 (Fax), 8AM-4PM.

General Information: Casual requesters can obtain records, but personal information is not released if subject has opted out. The following data is not available-Social Security Numbers.

Online search: Online access costs $6.00 per record. Minimum usage is 2,000 requests per month. The online system operates similar to the system for driving records. For more information: Dept. of Public Safety and Corrections, PO Box 66614, Baton Rouge, LA 70896 (225) 925-6032, Attn: Jimmy Thibodeaux.

Legislation-Current/Pending
Legislation-Passed
www.legis.state.la.us/

Louisiana House (Senate) Representative, State Capitol, 2nd Floor, PO Box 44486, Baton Rouge, LA 70804; 225-342-2456 (Information Help Desk), 225-342-2365 (Senate Documents (Room 205)), 225-342-6458 (House Documents (Room 207)), 800-256-3793 (General Information, In-state), 8AM-5PM.

General Information: Sessions are from the last Monday in March for 60 days in even numbered years, for 85 days in odd numbered years. The PO Box above is for the House; the PO Box for Senate bills is 94183.

Online search: The Internet has a wealth of information about sessions and bills.

Information About County Agencies

Court Structure

A District Court Clerk in each Parish holds all the records for that Parish. Each Parish has its own clerk and courthouse.

Online Access

The online computer system—Case Management Information System (CMIS)—is operating and development is continuing. It is for internal use only; there is no plan to permit online access to the public. There are a number of Parishes that do offer a means of remote online access, see their individual entries for more information.

About the
County Courts

About the
Recorder's Office

Organization

64 parishes (not counties), 64 recording offices. The recording officer is the Clerk of Court. Many parishes include tax and other non-UCC liens in their mortgage records. The entire state is in the Central Time Zone (CST).

Real Estate Records

Most parishes will perform a mortgage search. Some will provide a record owner search. Copy and certification fees vary widely.

UCC Records

Financing statements are filed with the Clerk of Court in any parish in the state and are entered onto a statewide computerized database of UCC financing statements available for searching at any parish office. All parishes perform UCC searches for $15.0 per debtor name. Use search request form UCC-11. Cop fees are $.50-1.00 per page.

Other Lien Records

All federal and state tax liens are filed with the Clerk of Court. Parishes usually file tax liens on personal property in their UCC or mortgage records, and most will perform tax lien searches for varying fees. Some parishes will automatically include tax liens on personal property in a mortgage certificate search. Other liens are: judgments, labor, material, hospital.

County Courts & Recording Offices Online

Caddo Parish

Liens Real Estate, Marriage Records

Parish Clerk of the Court, 501 Texas St, Rm 103, Shreveport LA 71101-5408, 318-226-6780. Fax: 318-227-9080. Hours: 8:30AM-5PM.

Online search: The set up fee is $50, plus a monthly fee of $30.The system operates 24 hours daily and supports baud rates up to 19.2. Record dates vary. Mortgages and indirect conveyances date back to 1981, Direct conveyances date back to 1914. One may search by name, Grantee/Grantor and registry number. Lending agency information is available. UCC information is available through the Secretary of State. For further information, contact Susan Twohig at 318-226-6523.

East Baton Rouge Parish

Felony, Misdemeanor, Civil, Probate

19th District Court, PO Box 1991, Baton Rouge LA 70821, 225-389-3950. Fax: 225-389-3392. Hours: 7:30AM-5:30PM.

Online search: The online system is open 24 hours daily. The setup fee is $100, the monthly minimum is $15 at $.33 per minute. Civil, criminal, probate (1988 forward), traffic and domestic index information is available by name or case number. Call Wendy Gibbs at 504-389-5295 for more information.

Liens, Real Estate

Clerk of Court, 222 St. Louis St, Baton Rouge LA 70821, 225-389-3958. Fax: 225-389-3392.

Online search: The setup fee is $100. There is a monthly fee of $15 and a per minute fee of $.33. Four years worth of data is kept active on the system. The system operates 24 hours daily and supports a baud rate of 9,600. Searches are done by name. UCC information is located at the Secretary of State. Lending agency information is available. For further information, contact Wendy Gibbs at 504-398-5295.

Iberia Parish

Civil, Probate, Liens, Real Estate, Marriage Records, Divorce Records

16th District Court, PO Drawer 12010, New Iberia LA 70562-2010, 318-365-7282. Fax: 318-365-0737. Hours: 8:30AM-4:30PM.

Online search: A monthly usage fee of $50 applies. Records date back to 1959. The system operates 24 hours daily and supports baud rates up to 56k. Searches can be made by name, Grantee/Grantor and Book and Page. UCC lien information is available through the office of the Secretary of State. Lending agency information is available. For further information, contact Mike Thibodeaux at 318-365-7282.

Lafayette Parish

Felony, Misdemeanor, Civil, Probate

www.lafayettecourthouse.com

15th District Court, PO Box 2009, Lafayette LA 70502, 318-233-0150. Fax: 318-269-6392. Hours: 8:30AM-4:30PM.

Online search: Remote access available for $100 setup fee plus $15 per month and $0.50 per minute. Modem speeds up to 9600 supported 24 hours per day. For more information, call Mike Prejean at 318-291-6232.

Liens, Real Estate, Marriage Records

www.lafayettecourthouse.com

Parish Clerk of Court, 800 S Buchanan St, Lafayette LA 70501, 318-233-0150. Fax: 318-269-6392.

Online search: The set up fee is $100. A monthly fee of $15 applies, plus $.50 per minute. The system operates 24 hours daily and supports baud rates up to 9,600. Conveyances date back to 1936, mortgages back to 1948 and all other records back to 1986. One may search by name, file number and date range. Tax and UCC lien information is for this parish only. Lending agency information is available. For further information, contact Derek Comeaux at 318-291-6433.

Felony, Misdemeanor, Civil, Probate, Liens, Real Estate

4th District Court, Courthouse, 100 East Madison, Bastrop LA 71220-3893, 318-281-3343/3346/3349. Fax: 318-281-3775. Hours: 8:30AM-4:30PM.

Online search: Remote online access will be available sometime in 1999. It will be similar in service and fees to the Lafayette Parish (above).

Orleans Parish

Civil, Probate

Civil District Court, 421 Loyola Ave, Rm 402, New Orleans LA 70112, 504-592-9100 X122. Fax: 504-592-9128. Hours: 8AM-5PM.

Online search: CDC Remote provides access to civil cases from 1985 and First City Court cases from 1988, as well as mortgage and conveyance indexes for the county. The setup fee is $100, and usage is charged at $.25 per minute. Call 504-592-9264 for more information.

Liens, Real Estate

Recorder of Mortgages, 421 Loyola Ave, B-1, New Orleans LA 70112, 504-592-9176. Fax: 504-592-9192.

Online search: The setup fee is $100 and a $300 deposit for 1,200 minutes of usage is required. One is billed $.25 per minute. Records date back to 9/87. The system operates 24 hours daily and supports baud rates of 9,600-19.2. Searches can be made by name, lot number and district number. No lending agency information is available. For further information, contact John Rabb at 504-592-9264.

St. Tammany Parish

Liens, Real Estate

Stp.pa.st-tammany.la.us

Parish Clerk of Court, 510 Boston St, Covington LA 70434, 504-898-2430.

Online search: The set up fee is $100, plus a $.30 per minute fee. The system operates 24 hours daily and supports baud rates up to 33.6. Records date back to 1961. Viewable images are available for conveyances back to 1985 and Mortgages back to 8/93. One may search by name, Grantee/Grantor and instrument number. UCC lien information is with the Secretary of State. For further information, contact Mark Cohn at 504-898-2890 or Christy Howell at 504-898-2491.

Tangipahoa Parish

Civil, Probate

21st District Court, PO Box 667, Amite LA 70422, 504-748-4146. Fax: 504-748-6503. Hours: 8:30AM-4:30PM.

Online search: Online access is $125 per month and is available 24 hours daily. Civil and probate information can be searched by name. For more information, call 504-748-4146.

Liens, Real Estate, Marriage Records

Parish Clerk of Court, 110 N Bay St, Amite LA 70422, 504-549-1611. Fax: 504-748-6503.

Online search: A monthly fee of $125 applies. The system operates 24 hours daily and supports baud rates up to 28.8. Record dates vary. One may search by name, Grantee/Grantor, book and page, document type, instrument type and number and date. Lending agency information is available. For further information, contact Alison Carona at 504-549-1611.

Federal Courts Online

Parish-to-Court Cross Reference (Bankruptcy Court locations in Parenthesis if different)

Parish	District	Court
Acadia Parish	Western	Lafayette
(Lafayette-Opelousas)		
Allen Parish	Western	Lake Charles
Ascension Parish	Middle	Baton Rouge
Assumption Parish	Eastern	New Orleans
Avoyelles Parish	Western	Alexandria
Beauregard Parish	Western	Lake Charles
Bienville Parish	Western	Shreveport
Bossier Parish	Western	Shreveport
Caddo Parish	Western	Shreveport
Calcasieu Parish	Western	Lake Charles
Caldwell Parish	Western	Monroe
Cameron Parish	Western	Lake Charles
Catahoula Parish	Western	Alexandria
Claiborne Parish	Western	Shreveport
Concordia Parish	Western	Alexandria
De Soto Parish	Western	Shreveport
E. Baton Rouge Parish	Middle	Baton Rouge
East Carroll Parish	Western	Monroe
East Feliciana Parish	Middle	Baton Rouge
Evangeline Parish	Western	Lafayette
(Lafayette-Opelousas)		
Franklin Parish	Western	Monroe
Grant Parish	Western	Alexandria
Iberia Parish	Western	Lafayette
(Lafayette-Opelousas)		
Iberville Parish	Middle	Baton Rouge
Jackson Parish	Western	Monroe
Jefferson Davis Parish	Western	Lake Charles
Jefferson Parish	Eastern	New Orleans
La Salle Parish	Western	Alexandria
Lafayette Parish	Western	Lafayette
(Lafayette-Opelousas)		
Lafourche Parish	Eastern	New Orleans

Lincoln Parish .... Western .... Monroe
Livingston Parish .... Middle .... Baton Rouge
Madison Parish .... Western .... Monroe
Morehouse Parish .... Western .... Monroe
Natchitoches Parish .... Western .... Alexandria
Orleans Parish .... Eastern .... New Orleans
Ouachita Parish .... Western .... Monroe
Plaquemines Parish .... Eastern .... New Orleans
Pointe Coupee Parish .... Middle .... Baton Rouge
Rapides Parish .... Western .... Alexandria
Red River Parish .... Western .... Shreveport
Richland Parish .... Western .... Monroe
Sabine Parish .... Western .... Shreveport
St. Bernard Parish .... Eastern .... New Orleans
St. Charles Parish .... Eastern .... New Orleans
St. Helena Parish .... Middle .... Baton Rouge
St. James Parish .... Eastern .... New Orleans
St. John Baptist Parish .. Eastern .... New Orleans

St. Landry Parish .... Western .... Lafayette
(Lafayette-Opelousas)
St. Martin Parish .... Western .... Lafayette
(Lafayette-Opelousas)
St. Mary Parish .... Western .... Lafayette
(Lafayette-Opelousas)
St. Tammany Parish ...... Eastern .... New Orleans
Tangipahoa Parish .... Eastern .... New Orleans
Tensas Parish .... Western .... Monroe
Terrebonne Parish .... Eastern .... New Orleans
Union Parish .... Western .... Monroe
Vermilion Parish .... Western .... Lafayette
(Lafayette-Opelousas)
Vernon Parish .... Western .... Alexandria
Washington Parish .... Eastern .... New Orleans
Webster Parish .... Western .... Shreveport
W. Baton Rouge Parish Middle .... Baton Rouge
West Carroll Parish ...... Western .... Monroe
West Feliciana Parish .... Middle .... Baton Rouge
Winn Parish .... Western .... Alexandria

US District Court
Eastern District of Louisiana

New Orleans Division, Clerk, Room 151, 500 Camp St, New Orleans, LA 70130, 504-589-7650.

PACER sign-up number is 800-676-6856. Both civil and criminal case records are available online.

US Bankruptcy Court
Eastern District of Louisiana

New Orleans Division, Hale Boggs Federal Bldg, 501 Magazine St, #601, New Orleans, LA 70130, 504-589-7878

www.laeb.uscourts.gov/

PACER sign-up number is 800-676-6856.

US District Court
Middle District of Louisiana

Baton Rouge Division, PO Box 2630, Baton Rouge, LA 70821-2630, 504-389-3500, Fax: 504-389-3501

www.lamd.uscourts.gov/

PACER sign-up number is 800-676-6856. Both civil and criminal case records are available online.

US Bankruptcy Court
Middle District of Louisiana

Baton Rouge Division, Room 119, 707 Florida St, Baton Rouge, LA 70801, 504-389-0211.

PACER sign-up number is 800-676-6856

US District Court
Western District of Louisiana

PACER sign-up number is 800-676-6856. Both civil and criminal case records are available online.

Alexandria Division, PO Box 1269, Alexandria, LA 71309, 318-473-7415, Records: 318-676-4273, Civil Dockets: 318-676-4273, Crim. Dockets 318-676-4272, Fax 318-473-7345.

Lafayette Division, Room 113, Federal Bldg, 705 Jefferson St, Lafayette, LA 70501, 318-262-6613.

Lake Charles Division, 611 Broad St, Suite 188, Lake Charles, LA 70601, 318-437-3870.

Monroe Division, PO Drawer 3087, Monroe, LA 71210, 318-322-6740.

Shreveport Division, US Courthouse, Suite 1167, 300 Fannin St, Shreveport, LA 71101-3083, 318-676-4273.

US Bankruptcy Court
Western District of Louisiana

www.lawb.uscourts.gov

PACER sign-up number is 800-676-6856.

Alexandria Division, Hemenway Bldg, 300 Jackson St, Suite 116, Alexandria, LA 71301-8357, 318-445-1890.

Lafayette-Opelousas Division, PO Box J, Opelousas, LA 70571-1909, 318-948-3451, Fax: 318-948-4426.

Lake Charles Division, c/o Lafayette-Opelousas Division, PO Box J, Opelousas, LA 70571-1909, 318-948-3451

Shreveport Division, Suite 2201, 300 Fannin St, Shreveport, LA 71101-3089, 318-676-4267

Monroe Division, c/o Shreveport Division, Suite 2201, 300 Fannin St, Shreveport, LA 71101, 318-676-4267

Maine

Governor's Office
1 State House Station, Rm 236 207-287-3531
Augusta, ME 04333-0001 Fax 207-287-1034
www.state.me.us/governor/govhome.htm

Attorney General's Office
6 State House Station 207-626-8800
Augusta, ME 04333 Fax 207-626-8828

State Archives
State Archives 207-287-5790
State House Station Fax 207-287-5739
Augusta, ME 04333-0084 8:30AM-4PM

Capital: Augusta
Kennebec County

Time Zone: EST

Number of Counties: 16

Population: 1,242,051

Web Site: www.state.me.us

State Court Administrator
State Court Administrator 207-822-0792
PO Box 4820 Fax 207-822-0781
Portland, ME 04112 8AM-4PM
www.courts.state.me.us

State Agencies Online

Corporation Records
Limited Partnerships
Trademarks/Servicemarks
Assumed Name
Limited Liability Company Records
www.state.me.us/sos/corpinfo.htm

Secretary of State, Reports & Information Division, 101 State House Station, Augusta, ME 04333-0101; (Courier: Room 221, State Office Bldg, Corner Capitol & Seward Sts, Augusta, ME 04333); 207-287-4190, 207-287-4195 (Main Number), 207-287-5874 (Fax), 8AM - 5PM.

Online search: The Internet site gives basic information about the entity including address, corp ID, agent, and status.

Driver Records
www.state.me.us/sos/bmv/mbv.htm

Bureau of Motor Vehicles, Driver License & Control, 29 State House Station, Augusta, ME 04333-0029; 207-287-9005, 207-287-2592 (Fax), 8AM-5PM.

General Information: Records are available for 3 years for moving violations, DWIs and 3 years after the reinstatement of suspensions. Accidents are indicated on the record. It takes up to 30 days before new records are available for inquiries. Driving records and ticket information is released per DPPA guidelines. Personal information is not available to the general public when subject opts out.

Online search: The fee is $5.00 per request. The system is a PC modem access mode and is open 24 hours daily. There is a 10 minute or 10 transaction limit per session. Call (207) 287-8590 for further details.

Vehicle Ownership
Vehicle Identification
www.state.me.us/sos/bmv/bmv.htm

Department of Motor Vehicles, Registration Section, 29 State House Station, Augusta, ME 04333-0029; 207-287-9000, 207-287-5219 (Fax), 8AM-5PM M-T,Th-F; 8AM-4PM W.

General Information: Records are available from 1977. It takes up to 30 days before new records are available for inquiries. Casual requesters can obtain records, but not personal information if subject has opted out

Online search: Maine offers online access to title records via PC and modem. To use the dial-in system, you must set up an account at (207) 287-8590. The fee is $5 per record, and the system is available 24 hours a day.

Legislation-Current/Pending
Legislation-Passed
www.state.me.us/legis

Maine Legislature, 2 State House Station, Legislative Document Room, 3rd Floor, Augusta, ME 04333-0002; 207-287-1692 (Bill Status or LD #), 207-287-1408 (Document Room), 207-287-1456 (Fax), 8AM-5PM.

General Information: Records are available for the current session only. Older passed bills are found at the State Law Library, 207-287-1600.

Online search: There is a Link Service that requesters can subscribe to. Call Information Systems at 207 287-1692. Also, the web site offers bills, status, and access to text of state laws.

Information About County Agencies

Court Structure

Circuit Courts may accept civil cases involving claims less than $30,000. District courts handle some minor "felonies." The small claims limit was raised from $3000 to $4500 as of 7/1/97.

Probate Courts are part of the county court system, not the state system. Even though the Probate Court may be housed with other state courts, it is on a different phone system and calls may not be transferred.

**About the
County Courts**

Online Access

Online computer access is not currently available. Development of a statewide judicial computer system is in progress and will be available statewide sometime in the future. The system will be initially for judicial and law enforcement agencies and will not include public access in the near term.

Searching Hints

Most courts will refer written requests for criminal searches to the Maine State Police.

**About the
Recorder's Office**

Organization

16 counties, 18 recording offices. The recording officer is County Register of Deeds. Counties maintain a general index of all transactions recorded. Aroostock and Oxford Counties each have two recording offices. There are no county assessors; each town has its own. The entire state is in the Eastern Time Zone.

Real Estate Records

Counties do not usually perform real estate searches, but some will look up a name informally. Copy and certification fees vary widely. Assessor and tax records are located at the town/city level.

UCC Records

Financing statements are filed both at the state level, except for real estate related filings, which are filed only with the Register of Deeds. Counties do not perform UCC searches. Copy fees are usually $1.00 per page.

Other Lien Records

All tax liens on personal property are filed with the Secretary of State. All tax liens on real property are filed with the Register of Deeds. Other liens are: municipal, bail bond, mechanics.

County Courts & Recording Offices Online

There is no online access to county court records.

No remote online access is available from real estate recorder's offices in Maine.

Federal Courts Online

County-to-Court Cross Reference (Bankruptcy Court locations in Parenthesis if different)

Androscoggin...........................Portland
Aroostook................................Bangor
Cumberland.............................Portland
Franklin...................................Bangor
Hancock...................................Bangor
Kennebec.................................Bangor
Knox.......................................Portland (Bangor)
Lincoln...................................Portland (Bangor)

Oxford.....................................Portland
Penobscot ....Bangor
Piscataquis..............................Bangor
Sagadahoc ....Portland
Somerset.................................Bangor
Waldo......................................Bangor
Washington ....Bangor
York..Portland

US District Court
District of Maine

www.med.uscourts.gov

PACER sign-up number is 800-676-6856. Both civil and criminal case records are available online.

Bangor Division, Court Clerk, PO Box 1007, Bangor, ME 04402-1007, 207-945-0575.

Portland Division Court Clerk, 156 Federal St, Portland, ME 04101, 207-780-3356.

US Bankruptcy Court
District of Maine

www.meb.uscourts.gov/

PACER sign-up number is 800-676-6856.

Bangor Division, PO Box 1109, Bangor, ME 04402-1109, 207-945-0348, Fax: 207-945-0304

Portland Division, 537 Congress St, Portland, ME 04101, 207-780-3482, Fax: 207-780-3679

Maryland

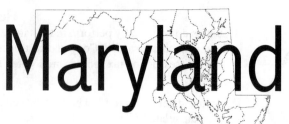

Governor's Office
State House   410-974-3901
Annapolis, MD 21401   Fax 410-974-3275
www.gov.state.md.us

Attorney General's Office
200 St Paul Place, 16th Floor   410-576-6300
Baltimore, MD 21202   Fax 410-576-7003
www.aog.state.md.us

State Archives
State Archives   410-974-3914
Hall of Records   Fax 410-974-3895
350 Rowe Blvd   8AM-4:30PM T-F;
Annapolis, MD 21401   8:30-4:30 SA
www.mdarchives.state.md.us

Capital: Annapolis
                                 Anne Arundel County

Time Zone: EST

Number of Counties: 23

Population: 5,094,289

Web Site: www.mec.state.md.us

State Court Administrator
Admin. Office of the Courts   410-260-1400
Court of Appeals Bldg,   Fax 410-974-2169
361 Rowe Blvd   8:30AM-4:30PM
Annapolis, MD 21401
www.courts.state.md.us

State Agencies Online

Criminal Records
Civil Case Records
Land Records
www.courts.state.md.us

Administrative Office of the Courts, Court of Appeals Bldg., 361 Rowe Blvd, Annapolis, MD 21404, 410-260-1400, 410-974-2169 (Fax),

Online search: The State Court Administrator's office has online access to criminal records from all state district courts, 2 circuit courts, and 1 city court. The system, called JIS, is available 24 hours daily. There is a one-time $50 fee to register and a $.50 per minute fee. Call 410-260-1031 for a registration package.

Trademarks & Service Marks
www.sos.state.md.us/sos

Secretary of State, State House, Ananapolis, MD 21401, 410-974-5531.

Online search: Trademarks and service marks may be searched free of charge at the web site above.

Corporation Records
Limited Partnerships
Trade Names
Limited Liability Company Records
Fictitious Name
www.dat.state.md.us/datanote.html

Department of Assessments and Taxation, Corporations Division, 301 W Preston St, Room 809, Baltimore, MD 21201; 410-767-1340, 410-767-1330 (Charter Information), 410-333-7097 (Fax). 8AM-4:30PM.

Online search: At press time, this site was under construction, but the indication is it will be up and running sometime in mid 1999. The site currently provides a statewide search of real estate records and UCC records; however, a name search cannot be performed. Note: there is a secondary web site in the state with corporate information at: www.dat.state.md.us/datanote.html.

Uniform Commercial Code
Real Property Records
www.dat.state.md.us/bsfd

UCC Division, Department of Assessments & Taxation, 301 West Preston St, Baltimore, MD 21201; 410-767-1340, 410-333-7097 (Fax), 8AM-4:30PM.

General Information: Records are available for all active files. All tax liens are filed at the county level and will not show on the UCC records

Online search: The Internet site offers free access to UCC index information. There is also a related site offering access to real property data for the whole state at www.dat.state.md.us/realprop.

Workers' Compensation Records

Workers Compensation Commission, Six N Liberty St, Baltimore, MD 21201; 410-767-0900, 410-333-8122 (Fax), 8AM-4:30PM.

General Information: Records are available for past 10 years are on computer. New records are available for inquiry immediately.. The following data is not available-medical records.

Online search: Request for online hook-up must be in writing on letterhead. There is no search fee, but there is a $7 set-up fee, $5 monthly fee and a $.01-03 per minute connect fee. The system is open 24 hours a day. Write to the Commission at address above, care of Information Support Division, or call Lili Joseph at (410) 767-0713.

Driver Records
mva.state.md.us

MVA, Driver Records Unit, 6601 Ritchie Hwy, NE, Glen Burnie, MD 21062; 410-787-7758, 8:15AM-4:30PM.

General Information: Accidents are indicated. It takes 5-10 days before new records are available for inquiries. An opt-out provision is place. Casual requesters may obtain records with personal information if subject did not opt-out. Records may not be resold or used for direct mail advertising or selling.

Online search: The network is available 6 days a week, twenty-four hours a day to qualified and bonded individuals and businesses. Access is through PC and modem at up to 9600 baud. The communication network is the Public Data Network (Bell Atlantic). The driver's license number, name, and DOB are needed when ordering. The fee is $5.00 per record. For signup, call 410-768-7234.

Vehicle Ownership
Vehicle Identification
mva.state.us

Department of Motor Vehicles, Vehicle Registration Division, Room 206, 6601 Ritchie Hwy, NE, Glen Burnie, MD 21062; 410-768-7520, 410-768-7653 (Fax), 8:15AM-4:30PM.

General Information:. All vehicle/ownership records are open to the public; however, personal information is not released on subjects who have opted out. The following data is not available-medical information.

Online search: The state offers vehicle and ownership data over the same online network utilized for driving record searches. The fee is $5 per record. Line charges will be incurred. For more info, call 410-768-7234.

Legislation-Current/Pending
Legislation-Passed
http://mlis.state.md.us

Maryland General Assembly, Dept of Legislative Services, 90 State Circle, Annapolis, MD 21401-1991; 410-841-3810 (Bill Status Only), 410-841-3000 (Alternate Telephone), 800-492-7122 (In-state), 410-841-3850 (Fax), 8AM-5PM.

Online search: The Internet site has complete information regarding bills and status.

Information About County Agencies

Court Structure

Certain categories of minor felonies are handled by the District Courts. However, all misdemeanors and felonies that require a jury trial are handled by a Circuit Courts.

The Circuit Court handles Probate in Montgomery and Harford counties. In other counties, Probate is handled by the Register of Wills and is a county, not a court, function.

Online Access

About the County Courts

An online computer system called the Judicial Information System (JIS) provides access to civil and criminal case information from the following:

All District Courts   Baltimore City Court   Anne Arundel & Carroll County Circuit Courts

Inquiries may be made to: the District Court traffic system for case information data, calendar information data, court schedule data, or officer schedule data; the District Court criminal system for case information data or calendar caseload data; the District Court civil system for case information data, attorney name and address data; the land records system for land and plat records. The one-time fee for JIS access is $50.00, which must be included with the application. There is a charge of $.50 per minute for access time. For additional information or to receive a registration packet, write or call Judicial Information Systems, Security Administrator, 2661 Riva Rd., Suite 900, Annapolis, MD 21401, 410-260-1031.

About the Recorder's Office

Organization

23 counties and one independent city, 24 recording offices. The recording officer is Clerk of the Circuit Court. Baltimore City has a recording office separate from the county of Baltimore. See the City/County Locator section at the end of this chapter for ZIP Codes that include both the city and the county. The entire state is in the Eastern Time Zone (EST).

Real Estate Records

Counties will not perform real estate searches. Copies usually cost $.50 per page, and certification fees $5.00 per document.

UCC Records

This is a dual filing state until July 1995. As of July 1995, all new UCC filings are submitted only to the central filing office. Financing statements are usually filed both at the state level and with the Clerk of Circuit Court, except for consumer goods, farm related and real estate related filings, which will still be filed with the Clerk after June 1995. Only one county performs UCC searches. Copy fees vary.

Other Lien Records

All tax liens are filed with the county Clerk of Circuit Court. Counties will not perform searches. Other liens are: judgment, mechanics, county, hospital, condominium.

County Courts & Recording Offices Online

A statewide system is available. See Online Access in the previous section for details.

No remote online access is available from real estate recorder's offices in Maryland.

Federal Courts Online

County-to-Court Cross Reference (Bankruptcy Court locations in Parenthesis if different)

Allegany.................................... Baltimore (Rockville)	Harford .... Baltimore
Anne Arundel.......................... Baltimore	Howard.................................. Baltimore
Baltimore .... Baltimore	Kent... Baltimore
Baltimore City City .... Baltimore	Montgomery .... Greenbelt (Rockville)
Calvert..................................... Greenbelt (Rockville)	Prince George's...................... Greenbelt (Rockville)
Caroline................................... Baltimore	Queen Anne's.......................... Baltimore
Carroll .... Baltimore	Somerset................................. Baltimore
Cecil .... Baltimore	St. Mary's................................ Greenbelt (Rockville)
Charles .... Greenbelt (Rockville)	Talbot...................................... Baltimore
Dorchester .... Baltimore	Washington .... Baltimore (Rockville)
Frederick................................. Baltimore (Rockville)	Wicomico................................ Baltimore
Garrett .... Baltimore (Rockville)	Worcester .... Baltimore

US District Court
District of Maryland

PACER sign-up number is 800-676-6856. Both civil and criminal case records are available online.

Baltimore Division, Clerk, 4th Floor, Room 4415, 101 W Lombard St, Baltimore, MD 21201, 410-962-2600.

Greenbelt Division, Clerk, Room 240, 6500 Cherrywood Lane, Greenbelt, MD 20770, 301-344-0660.

US Bankruptcy Court
District of Maryland

PACER sign-up number is 800-676-6856.

Baltimore Division, 8515 US Courthouse, 101 W Lombard St, Baltimore, MD 21201, 410-962-2688.

Rockville Division, 6500 Cherrywood Ln, #300, Greenbelt, MD 20770, 301-344-8018.

Massachusetts

Governor's Office
State House, Room 360   617-727-6250
Boston, MA 02133   Fax 617-727-9725
magnet.state.ma.us/gov/gov.htm

Attorney General's Office
One Ashburton Pl, Rm 2010   617-727-2200
Boston, MA 02108-1698   Fax 617-727-5768
www.magnet.state.ma.us/ag

State Archives
Massachusetts Archives
at Columbia Point   617-727-2816
Archives Division   Fax 619-288-8429
220 Morrissey Blvd   9AM-5PM M-F
Boston, MA 02125   9-3 SA
www.magnet.state.ma.us/sec/arc

Capital:	Boston
	Suffolk County
Time Zone:	EST
Number of Counties:	14
Population:	6,117,520
Web Site:	www.state.ma.us

State Court Administrator
Chief Justice for
Admin & Mgmt   617-742-8575
2 Center Plaza, Room 540   Fax 617-742-0968
Boston, MA 02108   8:30AM-5PM

State Agencies Online

Corporation Records
Trademarks/Servicemarks
Limited Liability Partnerships
Limited Partnership Records
state.ma.us/sec/cor/coridx.htm

Secretary of the Commonwealth, Corporation Division, One Ashburton Pl, 17th Floor, Boston, MA 02108; 617-727-9640 (Corporations), 617-727-2850 (Records), 617-727-8329 (Trademarks), 617-727-9440 (Forms request line), 617-742-4538 (Fax), 8:45AM-5PM.

General Information: Records are available for corporations and business entities organized since 1978 on computer.

Online search: The agency offers "Direct Access." The annual subscription fee is $149.00 and there is a $.40 a minute access fee. System is available from 8 AM to 9:50 PM. This systems also provides UCC record data. Call (617) 727-2853 for a sign-up packet

Uniform Commercial Code
Federal Tax Liens
State Tax Liens

UCC Division, Secretary of the Commonwealth, One Ashburton Pl, Room 1711, Boston, MA 02108; 617-727-2860, 8:45AM-5PM.

General Information: Records are available from 09/01/81 on computer and 01/01/84 on microfiche. Federal tax liens are filed at the US District Courts, PO & Courthouse Bldg, Boston, MA 02109 (617-233-9152). A list of state tax liens is available here, but must be searched in person separately from UCC filings.

Online search: "Direct Access" is available for $149 per year plus a $.40 per minute network fee. The system is open from 8 AM to 9:50 PM. Call (617) 727-2853-obtain information packet.

Vehicle Ownership
Vehicle Identification

Registry of Motor Vehicles, Customer Assistance-Mail List Dept., PO Box 199100, Boston, MA 02119-9100;

617-351-9384, 617-351-9524 (Fax), 8AM-4:30PM M-T-W-F; 8AM-7PM Th.

General Information: In general, license, ownership, and registration information is available to the public. If subject has opted out, personal information is not available to casual requesters. Lien information is provided as part of the record.

Online search: Permissible users are limited to Massachusetts based insurance companies and agents for the purpose of issuing or renewing insurance. This system is not open to the public. There is no fee, but line charges will be incurred.

Legislation-Current/Pending
Legislation-Passed
www.state.ma.us/legis.legis.htm

Massachusetts General Court, State House, Beacon St, Room 428 (Document Room), Boston, MA 02133; 617-722-2860 (Document Room), 9AM-5PM.

Online search: The web site has bill information for the current session and the previous session.

Information About County Agencies

Court Structure

The various court sections are called "Departments." The small claims limit changed in 1993 to $2000 from $1500.

About the
County Courts

While Superior and District Courts have concurrent jurisdiction in civil cases, the practice is to assign cases less than $25,000 to the District Court and those over $25,000 to Superior Court.

In addition to misdemeanors, the District Courts and Boston Municipal Courts have jurisdiction over certain minor felonies.

There are more than 20 Probate and Family Court locations in MA — one per county plus 2 each in Plymouth and Bristol, a Middlesex satellite in Cambridge, and a satellite in Lawrence.

Online Access

There is no online access computer system, internal or external.

About the
Recorder's Office

Organization

14 counties, 312 towns, and 39 cities; 21 recording offices and 365 UCC filing offices. Each town/city profile indicates the county in which the town/city is located. Filing locations vary depending upon the type of document, as noted below. Berkshire and Bristol Counties have three different recording offices; Essex, Middlesex and Worcester Counties each have two separate recording offices. Be careful to distinguish the following names that are identical for both a town/city and a county—Barnstable, Essex, Franklin, Hampden, Nantucket, Norfolk, Plymouth and Worcester. Recording officers are Town/City Clerk (UCC), County Register of Deeds (real estate), and Clerk of US District Court (federal tax liens). The entire state is in the Eastern Time Zone (EST).

Real Estate Records

Real estate records are located at the county level. Each town/city profile indicates the county in which the town/city is located. Counties will not perform searches. Copy fee with certification is usually $.75 per page. Each town also has Assessor/Tax Collector/Treasurer offices from which real estate ownership and tax information is available.

UCC Records

This is a dual filing state. Financing statements are usually filed both with the Town/City clerk and at the state level, except for real estate related collateral, which is recorded at the county Register of Deeds. All but twenty recording offices perform searches. Use search request form UCC-11. Search fees are usually $10.00 per debtor name. Copy fees vary widely.

Other Lien Records

Federal tax liens on personal property were filed with the Town/City Clerks prior to 1970. Since that time, federal tax liens on personal property are filed with the US District Court in Boston as well as with the towns/cities. Following is how to search the central index for federal tax liens—

Address: US District Court, Post Office/Courthouse Bldg, Boston, MA 02109 (617-223-9152)

The federal tax liens are indexed here on a computer system. Searches are available by mail or in person. Do not use the telephone. The court suggests including the Social Security number and/or address of individual names in your search request in order to narrow the results. A mail search costs $15.00 and will take about two weeks. Copies are included. Make your check payable to Clerk, US District Court. You can do the search yourself at no charge on their public computer terminal. State tax liens on personal property are filed with the Town/City Clerk or Tax Collector. All tax liens against real estate are filed with the county Register of Deeds. Some towns file state tax liens on personal property with the UCC index and include tax liens on personal property automatically with a UCC search. Others will perform a separate state tax lien search, usually for a fee of $10.00 plus $1.00 per page of copies. Other liens are: medical, town/city tax, child support.

County Courts & Recording Offices Online

Barnstable County

Liens, Real Estate

www.bcrd.co.barnstable.ma.us

County Register of Deeds, 3195 Route 6A, Barnstable, MA 02630, 508-362-7733, 508-362-5065 Fax.

Online search: A $50 annual fee applies along with a $.50 per minute charge. The system operates 24 hours daily and supports a baud rate of 56K. The records date back to 1976. One may search by name, Grantee/Grantor, street address and document number. Lending information is available. For information, contact Janet Hoben at 508-362-7733.

Berkshire County

Liens, Real Estate

County Register of Deeds (Southern District), 334 Main Street, Great Barrington, MA 01230, 413-528-0146, 413-528-6878 Fax.

County Register of Deeds (Middle District), 44 Bank Row, Pittsfield, MA 01201, 413-433-7438, 413-448-6025 Fax.

County Register of Deeds (Northern District), 65 Park St, Adams, MA 01220, 413-743-0035, 413-743-1003 Fax.

Online search: A one time signup fee of $100 is required and there is a $.50 per minute charge. This system provides access to all three District Recorders' records in the county. The records date back to 1985. The system operates 24 hours daily and supports baud rates up to 9,600. Searchable indexes are recorded land, plans and registered land. You can search by name and Grantee/Grantor. Lending agency information is available. For further information, contact Sharon Henault at 413-443-7438.

Bristol County

Liens, Real Estate

County Register of Deeds (Southern District), 25 N 6th Street, New Bedford, MA 02740, 508-993-2605, 508-997-4250 Fax.

County Register of Deeds (Northern District), 11 Court Street, Taunton, MA 02780, 508-822-0502, 508-880-4975 Fax.

County Register of Deeds (Fall River District), 441 N Main Street, Fall River, MA 02720, 508-673-1651, 508-673-7633 Fax.

Online search: There is a set up fee of $100, and at $.50 per minute access fee. All three districts are on this system. The record dates vary by district. The system operates 24 hours daily and supports baud rates up to

9,600. At this time one can only search by name and Grantee/Grantor. There are plans to expand search capabilities sometime in 1999. Lending agency information is available. For further information, contact Rosemary at 508-993-2605.

Essex County

Liens, Real Estate

http://207.244.88.10/RecLandLookup.asp

County Register of Deeds (Northern District), 381 Common Street, Lawrence, MA 01840, 978-683-2745, 978-688-4679 Fax.

Online search: Online access requires a $25 deposit, with a per minute charge of $.25 per minute. The records date back to 1981. The system operates 24 hours daily and supports baud rates up to 9,600. You can search by name and Grantee/Grantor. Lending agency information is available. For info, call David Burke at 978-683-2745.

Liens, Real Estate

County Register of Deeds (Southern District), 36 Federal St, Salem, MA 01970, 978-741-0201, 978-744-5865 Fax.

Online search: Public record information available on the Internet for no fee. Images are available from 01/92 to present. Index includes records from 01/84 to present. Search by name, Grantee/ Grantor, street address, book and page, town, date. Lending agency info is available.

Hampden County

Liens, Real Estate

County Register of Deeds, 50 State Street, Hall of Justice, Springfield, MA 01103, 413-748-8662, 413-731-8190 Fax.

Online search: A $50 annual fee applies along with a per minute charge of $.50. The records date back to 1965. The system operates 24 hours daily and supports a baud rate of 28.8. Searchable indexes are bankruptcy (downloaded from PACER), unregistered land site and registered land site. One may search by name, Grantee/Grantor and address. Lending agency information is available. For information, contact Donna Brown at 413-748-7945.

Hampshire County

Liens, Real Estate

County Register of Deeds, Hall of Records, 33 King Street, Northampton, MA 01060, 413-584-3637, 413-584-4136 Fax.

Online search: A $100 annual fee applies and per minute charges are $.50 for in-state and $.60 for out-of-state. The records date back to 9/2/86. The system operates 24 hours daily and supports baud rates up to 9,600. One may search by name, Grantee/Grantor, town location and book and page. Lending agency information is available. For further info, contact MaryAnn Foster at 413-584-3637.

Middlesex County

Liens, Real Estate

www.tiac.net/users/nmrd

County Register of Deeds (Northern District), 360 Gorham Street, Lowell, MA 01852, 978-458-8474, 978-458-7765 Fax.

Online search: The system is called "Telesearch." The set up fee is $100, plus a $50 deposit and access is billed at $.20 per minute. To connect, one must be able to emulate the Wang screen. Wang emulation software is $95. The system operates from 5AM-10:30PM. One can search the Grantee/Grantor index, recorded land plans, registered land documents and recording information. Records date back to 1976. A fax back service is available. For further information, contact customer service at 978-458-8474.

Liens, Real Estate

County Register of Deeds (Southern District), 208 Cambridge St, E. Cambridge, MA 02141, 617-494-4550.

Online search: The system is called "LandTrack." The Annual fee is $100, plus $.50 per minute. One also needs Wang 2110/2110A terminal emulation software. The system operates 24 hours daily. A minimum baud rate of 9,600 is recommended. One may search by name, Grantee/Grantor, address, document detail, book and page, date and instrument number, plans, and registered owner files. Lending agency information is available. They have a fax back service for documents since 1987. For further info, contact Grace Abruzzio: 617-494-4510.

Norfolk County

Liens, Real Estate

County Register of Deeds, 649 High Street, Dedham, MA 02026, 781-461-6122, 781-326-4742 Fax.

Online search: There is a set up fee of $25.00, $1.00 fee for the first minute and $.50 per minute thereafter per session. The system operates from 2AM-10:30PM M-F and 24 hours on weekends and holidays. The system is only accessible from within Massachusetts. The system supports a baud rate of 9,600. One may search by Grantee/Grantor, plan index by proprietor, town and street, tax index and by land court index. Lending agency information is available. For further information, contact Pam at 781-461-6116.

Plymouth County

Liens, Real Estate

County Register of Deeds, 7 Russell Street, Plymouth, MA 02360, 508-830-9200, 508-830-9280 Fax.

Online search: To access "Online Titleview" there is a usage charge of $.60 per minute. The records date back to 1971. The system operates 24 hours daily and supports baud rates up to 14.4. One may search by name,

Grantee/Grantor, tax lien and land courts. Lending agency information is available. They have a fax back service. There is a service charge of $3.00 plus $1.00 per page (in county). If out of county, the service charge is $4.00, plus $1.00 per page. For further information contact, Sandy, Cynthia or Graham at 508-830-9287.

Suffolk County

Liens, Real Estate

County Register of Deeds, 1 Pemberton Square, The Old Courthouse, Boston, MA 02108, 617-725-8575, 617-720-4163 Fax.

Online search: To gain access to the online access system, you must sent a written request to Paul R. Tierney, Register of Deeds. Online charges are $.50 per minute. The records date back to 1/1/79. The system operates 24 hours daily and supports a baud rate of 19.2. One may search by name, Grantee/Grantor, address, type of document, date, district and town. They have a fax back service. For area codes 617, 781 and 508, the fee is $3.00 for the first page and $1.00 for the remainder. For all other area codes, the first page is $5.00 and $1.00 for the remainder.

Worcester County

Liens, Real Estate, Death Records, Marriage Records

County Register of Deeds (Worcester North), Courthouse, 84 Elm Street, Fitchburg, MA 01420, 978-342-2634., 978-345-2865 Fax.

Online search: The annual fee for "Northfield" is $50, plus $.25 per minute. The records date back to 1983. The system operates 24 hours daily and supports baud rates from 1,200-9,600. Viewable images are available from 1995. One may search by name, Grantee/Grantor, book and page, document number and date. Lending agency information is available. A fax back service is available. For info, contact Ruth Piermarini at 978-342-2637.

Liens, Real Estate

County Register of Deeds (Worcester District), 2 Main Street, Courthouse, Worcester, MA 01608, 508-798-7713, 508-798-7746 Fax.

Online search: The "Landtrack System" annual fee is $50, plus $.25 per minute. The index records date back to 1966. The system operates 24 hours daily and supports baud rates up to 19.2. One may search by name and book and page. Lending agency information is available. Fax back service is available at $.50 per page. Images are viewable from 1974. For further information, contact Joe Ursoleo at 508-798-7713 X233.

Federal Courts Online

County-to-Court Cross Reference (Bankruptcy Court locations in Parenthesis if different)

Barnstable	Boston	Hampshire	Springfield (Worcester)
Berkshire	Springfield (Worcester)	Middlesex	Boston
Bristol	Boston	Nantucket	Boston
Dukes	Boston	Norfolk	Boston
Essex	Boston	Plymouth	Boston
Franklin	Springfield (Worcester)	Suffolk	Boston
Hampden	Springfield (Worcester)	Worcester	Worcester

US District Court
District of Massachusetts

PACER sign-up number is 800-676-6856. Both civil and criminal case records are available online.

Boston Division, Post Office & Courthouse Bldg, 90 Devonshire, Room 700, Boston, MA 02109, 617-223-9152, Record Room: 617-223-9086, Fax: 617-223-9096.

Springfield Division, 1550 Main St, Springfield, MA 01103, 413-785-0214, Civil Docket Section: 413-785-0215, Criminal Docket Section: 413-785-0216, Fax: 413-785-0204.

Worcester Division, 595 Main St., Room 502, Worcester, MA 01608, 508-793-0552.

US Bankruptcy Court
District of Massachusetts

www.mab.uscourts.gov

PACER sign-up number is 800-676-6856.

Boston Division, Room 1101, 10 Causeway, Boston, MA 02222-1074, 617-565-6051, Fax: 617-565-6087

Worcester Division, 595 Main St, Room 211, Worcester, MA 01608, 508-770-8900, Fax: 508-793-0541

Michigan

Governor's Office
PO Box 30013   517-373-7858
Lansing, MI 48909   Fax 517-335-6863
www.migov.state.mi.us

Attorney General's Office
PO Box 30212   517-373-1110
Lansing, MI 48909   Fax 517-373-4213

State Archives
State Archives of Michigan   517-373-1408
Michigan Historical Center   Fax 517-291-1658
Michigan Library
717 W Allegan   10AM-4PM
Lansing, MI 48918-1837
http://www.sos.state.mi.us/history/arc
hive/archive.html

Capital: Lansing
    Ingham County

Time Zone: EST*

* Four north-western Michigan counties are CST:
They are: Dickinson, Gogebic, Iron, Menominee.

Number of Counties: 83

Population: 9,773,892

Web Site: www.state.mi.us

State Court Administrator
State Court Administrator   517-373-2222
309 N Washington Sq   Fax 517-373-2112
Lansing, MI 48909   8AM-4:30PM

State Agencies Online

Legislation-Current/Pending
Legislation-Passed
www.michiganlegislature.org

Michigan Legislature Document Room, State Capitol, PO Box 30036, Lansing, MI 48909; (North Capitol Annex, Lansing, MI 48909); 517-373-0169, 8:30AM-5PM.

Online search: Access is available from their Internet site. Adobe Acrobat Reader is required. Information available includes status of bills, bill text, joint resolution text, journals, and calendars.

Driver Records
www.sos.state.mi.us/dv

Department of State Police, Record Look-up Unit, 7064 Crowner Dr, Lansing, MI 48918; 517-322-1624, 517-322-1181 (Fax), 8AM-4:45PM.

General Information: Records are available for 7 years from conviction date; unless there is an alcohol or controlled substance conviction, which will remain on record for 10 years. Accidents are reported on the record only if the driver is cited. It takes 14 days before new records are available for inquiries. Michigan has an opt-out policy. Casual requesters can only obtain records without personal information.

Online search: Online ordering is available on an interactive basis. The system is open 7 days a week. Ordering is by DL or name and DOB. An account must be established and billing is monthly. Access is also available from the Internet. Call Carol Lycos at 517-322-1591 for more information. The records are $6.55 each.

Vehicle Ownership
Vehicle Identification
Boat & Vessel Ownership
Boat & Vessel Registration
www.sos.state.mi.us/dv

Department of State Police, Record Look-up Unit, 7064 Crowner Dr, Lansing, MI 48918; 517-322-1624, 517-322-1181 (Fax), 8AM-4:45PM.

General Information: Records are available for 10 years to present for vehicle information and 3 years to present for registration information. Vessel titles are on computer since 1974. All motorized boats must be registered, if 20 ft or over they must also be titled. It takes 14 days before new records are available for inquiries.

Online search: Online searching is single inquiry and requires a VIN or plate number. A $25,000 surety bond is required. Direct dial-up or Internet access is offered. The records are $6.55 each. For information, call Carol Lycos at 517-322-1591.

Information About County Agencies

Court Structure

District Courts and Municipal Courts have jurisdiction over certain minor felonies.

About the County Courts

There is a Court of Claims in Lansing which is a function of the 30th Circuit Court with jurisdiction over claims against the state of Michigan. A Recorder's Court in Detroit was abolished as of October 1, 1997. As of January 1, 1998, the Family Division of the Circuit Court was created. Domestic relations actions and juvenile cases, including criminal and abuse/neglect, formerly adjudicated in the Probate Court, were transferred to the Family Division of the Circuit Court. Mental health and estate cases continue to be handled by the Probate Courts. As of January 1, 1998, the limit for civil actions brought in District Court was raised from $10,000 to $25,000. The minimum for civil actions brought in Circuit Court was raised to $25,000 at that time.

Online Access

Some Michigan courts provide public access terminals in clerk's offices, and some courts are developing off-site electronic filing and searching capabilities.

Court records are considered public except for specific categories: controlled substances, spousal abuse, Holmes youthful trainee, set aside convictions and probation, and sealed records. Courts will, however, affirm that cases exist and provide case numbers.

Some courts will not conduct criminal searches. Rather, they refer requests to the State Police. Note that costs, search requirements, and procedures vary widely because each jurisdiction may create its own administrative orders.

Searching Hints

Online computerization of the judicial system varies from "none" to "fairly complete," but there is no statewide network and no individual courts are online.

About the Recorder's Office

Organization

83 counties, 83 recording offices. The recording officer is County Register of Deeds. 79 counties are in the Eastern Time Zone (EST) and 4 are in the Central Time Zone (CST).

Real Estate Records

Some counties will perform real estate searches. Copies usually cost $1.00 per page. and certification fees vary. Ownership records are located at the Equalization Office, designated "Assessor" in this section. Tax records are located at the Treasurer's Office.

UCC Records

Financing statements are filed at the state level except for consumer goods, farm related and real estate related filings. All counties will perform UCC searches. Use search request form UCC-11. Search fees are usually $3.00 per debtor name if federal tax identification number or Social Security number are given, or $6.00 without the number. Copies usually cost $1.00 per page.

Other Lien Records

Federal and state tax liens on personal property of businesses are filed with the Secretary of State. Other federal and state tax liens are filed with the Register of Deeds. Most counties search each tax lien index separately. Some charge one fee to search both, while others charge a separate fee for each one. When combining a UCC and tax lien search, total fee is usually $9.00 for all three searches. Some counties require tax identification number as well as name to do a search. Copy fees are usually $1.00 per page. Other liens are: construction, lis pendens.

County Courts & Recording Offices Online

Jackson County

Liens, Real Estate

County Register of Deeds, 120 W Michigan Avenue, 11th Floor, Jackson, MI 49201, 517-788-4350, 517-788-4686 Fax.

Online search: The per minute fee is $1.00. The system is being upgraded in 1999 and fees may change. The system operates 24 hours daily and supports a baud rate of 28.8. The records date back to 1985. The indexes that are available are Grantee/Grantor, deeds and mortgages. One may search by name, Grantee/Grantor, book and page, legal description, document type, date and address. Lending agency information is available. Vital records will be added to the system when it is upgraded. For information, contact Mindy at 517-768-6682.

Livingston County

Liens, Real Estate, Tax Assessor Records

County Register of Deeds, Courthouse, Howell, MI 48843, 517-546-0270, 517-546-5966 Fax.

Online search: For the occasional user, the annual fee is $400, plus $.000043 per second. A dedicated line is available for $1,200. Records date back to 10/84. The system operates from 5:30AM-11PM daily. The system supports a baud rate of 28.8. One may search by name, Grantee/Grantor, legal description, instrument type, tax code and address. Lending agency information is available. For further information, contact Judy Eplee at 517-546-2530.

Montcalm County

Liens, Real Estate, Death Records

County Register of Deeds, 211 W Main Street, Courthouse, Stanton, MI 48888, 517-831-7337, 517-831-7320 Fax.

Online Search: They have two public record access systems available. To view only the index, the monthly fee is $250. To view both the index and the document image, the monthly fee is $650. These fees are all inclusive. The records date back to 1/1/88. The system operates 24 hours daily and supports baud rates up to 28.8. One may search by name, Grantee/Grantor, legal description and book and page. Lending agency information is available. For further information, contact Laurie Wilson at 517-831-7321.

Federal Courts Online

County-to-Court Cross Reference (Bankruptcy Court locations in Parenthesis if different)

County	District	Court
Alcona	Eastern	Bay City
Alger	Western	Marquette-Northern (Marquette)
Allegan	Western	Kalamazoo (Grand Rapids)
Alpena	Eastern	Bay City
Antrim	Western	Grand Rapids
Arenac	Eastern	Bay City
Baraga	Western	Marquette-Northern (Marquette)
Barry	Western	Grand Rapids
Bay	Eastern	Bay City
Benzie	Western	Grand Rapids
Berrien	Western	Kalamazoo (Grand Rapids)
Branch	Western	Lansing (Grand Rapids)
Calhoun	Western	Kalamazoo (Grand Rapids)
Cass	Western	Kalamazoo (Grand Rapids)
Charlevoix	Western	Grand Rapids
Cheboygan	Eastern	Bay City
Chippewa	Western	Marquette-Northern (Marquette)
Clare	Eastern	Bay City
Clinton	Western	Lansing (Grand Rapids)
Crawford	Eastern	Bay City
Delta	Western	Marquette-Northern (Marquette)
Dickinson	Western	Marquette-Northern (Marquette)
Eaton	Western	Lansing (Grand Rapids)
Emmet	Western	Grand Rapids
Genesee	Eastern	Flint
Gladwin	Eastern	Bay City
Gogebic	Western	Marquette-Northern (Marquette)
Grand Traverse	Western	Grand Rapids
Gratiot	Eastern	Bay City
Hillsdale	Western	Lansing (Grand Rapids)

Houghton .... Western .... Marquette-Northern (Marquette)
Huron .... Eastern .... Bay City
Ingham .... Western .... Lansing (Grand Rapids)
Ionia.................. Western .... Grand Rapids
Iosco .... Eastern .... Bay City
Iron .... Western .... Marquette-Northern (Marquette)
Isabella .... Eastern .... Bay City
Jackson.............. Eastern .... Ann Arbor (Detroit)
Kalamazoo .... Western .... Kalamazoo (Grand Rapids)
Kalkaska .... Western .... Grand Rapids
Kent.................. Western .... Grand Rapids
Keweenaw .... Western .... Marquette-Northern (Marquette)
Lake.................. Western .... Grand Rapids
Lapeer .... Eastern .... Flint
Leelanau............ Western .... Grand Rapids
Lenawee............ Eastern .... Ann Arbor (Detroit)
Livingston......... Eastern .... Flint
Luce.................. Western .... Marquette-Northern (Marquette)
Mackinac .... Western .... Marquette-Northern (Marquette)
Macomb............ Eastern .... Detroit
Manistee............ Western .... Grand Rapids
Marquette.......... Western .... Marquette-Northern (Marquette)
Mason .... Western .... Grand Rapids
Mecosta............ Western .... Grand Rapids
Menominee ...... Western .... Marquette-Northern (Marquette)
Midland............. Eastern .... Bay City
Missaukee......... Western .... Grand Rapids

Monroe .... Eastern .... Ann Arbor (Detroit)
Montcalm .... Western .... Grand Rapids
Montmorency .. Eastern .... Bay City
Muskegon......... Western .... Grand Rapids
Newaygo .... Western .... Grand Rapids
Oakland .... Eastern .... Ann Arbor (Detroit)
Oceana.............. Western .... Grand Rapids
Ogemaw .... Eastern .... Bay City
Ontonagon........ Western .... Marquette-Northern (Marquette)
Osceola .... Western .... Grand Rapids
Oscoda.............. Eastern .... Bay City
Otsego............... Eastern .... Bay City
Ottawa.............. Western .... Grand Rapids
Presque Isle ..... Eastern .... Bay City
Roscommon..... Eastern .... Bay City
Saginaw .... Eastern .... Bay City
Sanilac.............. Eastern .... Detroit
Schoolcraft ...... Western .... Marquette-Northern (Marquette)
Shiawassee ...... Eastern .... Flint
St. Clair............ Eastern .... Detroit
St. Joseph.......... Western .... Kalamazoo (Grand Rapids)
Tuscola .... Eastern .... Bay City
Van Buren .... Western .... Kalamazoo (Grand Rapids)
Washtenaw....... Eastern .... Ann Arbor (Detroit)
Wayne............... Eastern .... Detroit
Wexford............ Western .... Grand Rapids

US District Court
Eastern District of Michigan

PACER sign-up number is 800-676-6856. Both civil and criminal case records are available online.

Ann Arbor Division, PO Box 8199, Ann Arbor, MI 48107, 734-741-2380, Fax: 734-741-2065.

Bay City Division, PO Box 913, Bay City, MI 48707, 517-894-8800, Fax: 517-894-8804.

Detroit Division, 564 Theodore Levin US Courthouse, 231 W Lafayette Blvd, Detroit, MI 48226, 313-234-5050, Record Room: 313-234-5010, Fax: 313-234-5393.

Port Huron Division, c/o Detroit Division, 564 Theodore Levin US Courthouse, 231 W Lafayette Blvd, Detroit, MI 48226, 313-234-5050.

Flint Division, Clerk, Federal Bldg, Room 140, 600 Church St, Flint, MI 48502, 810-341-7840.

US Bankruptcy Court
Eastern District of Michigan

PACER sign-up number is 800-676-6856.

Bay City Division, PO Box 911, Bay City, MI 48707, 517-894-8840.

Detroit Division, Clerk, 21st Floor, 21 W Fort St, Detroit, MI 48226, 313-234-0065, Record Room: 313-234-0051.

Flint Division, 226 W 2nd St, Flint, MI 48502, 810-235-4126.

US District Court
Western District of Michigan

www.miw.uscourts.gov

PACER sign-up number is 800-676-6856. Both civil and criminal case records are available online.

Grand Rapids Division, 452 Federal Bldg, 110 Michigan St NW, Grand Rapids, MI 49503, 616-456-2381

Kalamazoo Division, B-35 Federal Bldg, 410 W Michigan Ave, Kalamazoo, MI 49007, 616-349-2922

Lansing Division, 113 Federal Bldg, 315 W Allegan, Lansing, MI 48933, 517-377-1559

Marquette-Northern Division, PO Box 698, Marquette, MI 49855, 906-226-2021, Fax: 906-226-6735

US Bankruptcy Court
Western District of Michigan

www.miw.uscourts.gov

PACER sign-up number is 800-676-6856.

Grand Rapids Division, PO Box 3310, Grand Rapids, MI 49501, 616-456-2693, Fax: 616-456-2919

Marquette Division, PO Box 909, Marquette, MI 49855, 906-226-2117, Fax: 906-226-7388

Minnesota

Governor's Office
130 Capitol Bldg,
75 Constitution Ave   651-296-3391
St Paul, MN 55155   Fax 651-296-2089
www.state.mn.us/ebranch/governor/index
.html

Attorney General's Office
102 State Capitol   651-296-6196
St Paul, MN 55155   Fax 651-297-4193
www.ag.state.mn.us

Capital:	St. Paul
	Ramsey County
Time Zone:	CST
Number of Counties:	87
Population:	4,685,549
Web Site:	www.state.mn.us

State Archives
Historical Society   651-296-6126
Divison of Library & Archives   Fax 651-297-7436
345 Kellogg Blvd, W   9AM-5PM M-W,
St Paul, MN 55102-1906   F-SA;
www.mnhs.org   9AM-9PM Th

State Court Administrator
State Court Administrator   651-296-2474
135 Minnesota Judicial Center,   Fax 651-297-5636
25 Constitution Ave   8AM-4:30PM
St Paul, MN 55155
www.courts.state.mn.us

State Agencies Online

Corporation Records
Limited Liability Company Records
Assumed Name
Trademarks/Servicemarks
Limited Partnerships
www.sos.state.mn.us

Business Records Services, Secretary of State, 180 State Office Bldg, 100 Constitution Ave, St Paul, MN 55155-1299; 651-296-2803 (Information), 651-297-9102 (Copies), 651-215-0683 (Fax), 8AM-4:30PM.

General Information Part II of foreign corporation annual reports are not released.

Online search: The program is called Direct Access and is available 24 hours. There is an annual subscription fee of $50.00. Records are $1-4, depending on item needed. Please call 651-297-9100 or 612-297-9097 for more information.

Legislation-Current/Pending
Legislation-Passed
www.leg.state.mn.us

Minnesota Legislature, State Capitol, House-Room 211, Senate-Room 231, St Paul, MN 55155; 651-296-2887 (Senate Bills), 651-296-6646 (House Bill Status), 651-296-2314 (House Bill Copies), 651-296-1563 (Fax).

Online search: Information available through the Internet site includes full text of bills, status, previous 4 years of bills, and bill tracking.

Driver Records
www.dps.state.mn.us/dvs

Driver & Vehicle Services, Records Section, 445 Minnesota St, #180, St Paul, MN 55101; 651-296-6911, 8AM-4:30PM.

General Information: Records are available for 5 years minimum for moving violations and suspensions; 10 years for open revocation; retained indefinitely for DWIs for 2 or more convictions. Accidents and up to 10 mph over in a 55 zone on interstate roads are not shown. It takes no more than 15 days before new records are available for inquiries.

Online search: Online access costs $2.50 per record. Online inquiries can be processed either as interactive or as batch files (overnight) 24 hours a day, seven days a week. Requesters operate off of a "bank." Records are accessed by either DL number or full name and DOB. For more information, call (651) 297-1714.

Uniform Commercial Code
Federal Tax Liens
State Tax Liens

www.sos.state.mn.us

UCC Division, Secretary of State, 180 State Office Bldg, St Paul, MN 55155-1299; 651-296-2803, 651-297-5844 (Fax), 8 AM-4:30 PM.

General Information: All tax liens on individuals are filed at the county level.

Online search: The program is called Direct Access and is available 24 hours. There is a subscription fee is

$50.00 per year, plus $4.00 per search. Call 651-297-9100 or 612-297-9097 for more information.

Vehicle Ownership
Vehicle Identification

Driver & Vehicle Services, Records Section, 445 Minnesota St, St Paul, MN 55101; 651-296-6911 (General Information), 8AM-4:30PM.

General Information: Records are available from 1990 to present. It takes 5 days before new records are available for inquiries. The state places no restrictions on obtaining vehicle or ownership information; however, the licensee has the option to restrict access to his/her record from sale to mail list vendors or to individual requesters not on DPPA approval list.

Online search: Online access costs $2.50 per record. There is an additional monthly charge for dial-in access. The system is the same as described for driving record requests. It is open 24 hours a day, 7 days a week. Lien information is included.

Information About County Agencies

Court Structure

There are 97 district courts in 87 counties.

Online Access

There is an online system in place that allows internal and external access. Some criminal information is available online from St Paul through the Bureau of Criminal Apprehension (BCA), 1246 University Ave, St. Paul, MN 55104. Additional information is available from BCA by calling 651-642-0670.

Searching Hints

Statewide certification and copy fees are as follows: Certification Fee: $10.00 per document, Copy Fee: $5.00 per document (not per page).

An exact name is required to search, e.g., a request for "Robert Smith" will not result in finding "Bob Smith." The requester must request both names and pay two search and copy fees. When a search is permitted by "plaintiff or defendant," most jurisdictions stated that a case is indexed by only the 1st plaintiff or defendant, and a 2nd or 3rd party would not be sufficient to search. The 3rd, 5th, 8th and 10th Judicial Districts no longer will perform criminal record searches for the public.

About the County Courts

About the Recorder's Office

Organization

87 counties, 87 recording offices. The recording officer is County Recorder. The entire state is in the Central Time Zone.

Real Estate Records

Some counties will perform real estate searches, especially short questions over the telephone. Copy fees vary, but do not apply to certified copies. Certification fees are usually $1.00 per page with a minimum of $5.00.

UCC Records

Financing statements are filed at the state level except for consumer goods, farm related and real estate related filings. Counties enter all non-real estate filings into a central statewide database which can be accessed from any county office. All counties will perform UCC searches. Use search request form UCC-11. Search fees are usually $15.00 per debtor name if the standard UCC-12 request form is used, or $20.00 if a nonstandard form is used. A UCC search can include tax liens. Search fee usually includes 10 listings or copies. Extra copies usually cost $1.00 per page.

Other Lien Records

Federal and state tax liens on personal property of businesses are filed with the Secretary of State. Other federal and state tax liens are filed with the County Recorder. A special search form UCC-12 is used for separate tax lien searches. Some counties search each tax lien index separately. Some charge one $15.00 fee to search both indexes, but others charge a separate fee for each index searched. Search and copy fees vary. Other liens are: mechanics, hospital, judgment, attorneys.

County Courts & Recording Offices Online

Anoka County

Real Estate, Tax Assessor Records

County Recorder, 2100 3rd Avenue, Anoka, MN 55303, 612-323-5400, 612-323-5421 Fax.

Online search: The set up fee is $250. The monthly fee is $20, plus $.25 per transaction. The system operates from 8AM-4:30PM M-F, and supports baud rates up to 33.6. The records date back to 1995. One may search by name, Grantee/Grantor and document number. Lending agency information is available. For further information, contact Pam LeBlanc at 612-323-5424.

Hennepin County

Liens, Real Estate

www.co.hennepin.mn.us/pins/main.htm

County Recorder, 300 S 6th Street, 8-A Government Center, Minneapolis, MN 55487, 612-348-3066.

Online search: The annual fee is $35. One is charged $5.00 per hour between 7AM-7PM and $4.15 the balance of the time. The system operates 24 hours daily and supports baud rates up to 28.8. Records date back to 1988. One may search by name, Grantee/Grantor, legal description, document number and address. Property tax information is at the treasurer's office. Only state UCC information is available. Lending agency information is available. For further information, contact Jerry Erickson at 612-348-3856.

Washington County

Liens, Real Estate, Tax Assessor Records

County Recorder, 14949 62nd Street N, Stillwater, MN 55082, 651-430-6755, 651-430-6753 Fax.

Online search: The set up fee is $250. No fees apply to recorders office information. Fees may apply to other indexes on the system. The system operates 24 hours daily and supports baud rates up to 28.8. Records date back 3 years. One may search by name, Grantee/Grantor, geo code and legal description. UCC information is on a separate system. Lending agency information is available. For further information: Larry Haseman 651-430-6423.

Federal Courts Online

County-to-Court Cross Reference (Bankruptcy Court locations in Parenthesis if different)

Aitkin	Duluth	Carlton	Duluth
Anoka	Minneapolis	Carver	Minneapolis
Becker	Minneapolis (Fergus Falls)	Cass	Duluth
Beltrami	Minneapolis (Fergus Falls)	Chippewa	Minneapolis
Benton	Duluth	Chisago	Minneapolis (St Paul)
Big Stone	Minneapolis (Fergus Falls)	Clay	Minneapolis (Fergus Falls)
Blue Earth	Minneapolis (St Paul)	Clearwater	Minneapolis (Fergus Falls)
Brown	Minneapolis (St Paul)	Cook	Duluth

Cottonwood	Minneapolis (St Paul)	Nobles	Minneapolis (St Paul)
Crow Wing	Duluth	Norman	Minneapolis (Fergus Falls)
Dakota	Minneapolis (St Paul)	Olmsted	Minneapolis (St Paul)
Dodge	Minneapolis (St Paul)	Otter Tail	Minneapolis (Fergus Falls)
Douglas	Minneapolis (Fergus Falls)	Pennington	Minneapolis (Fergus Falls)
Faribault	Minneapolis (St Paul)	Pine	Duluth
Fillmore	Minneapolis (St Paul)	Pipestone	Minneapolis (St Paul)
Freeborn	Minneapolis (St Paul)	Polk	Minneapolis (Fergus Falls)
Goodhue	Minneapolis (St Paul)	Pope	Minneapolis (Fergus Falls)
Grant	Minneapolis (Fergus Falls)	Ramsey	St Paul
Hennepin	Minneapolis	Red Lake	Minneapolis (Fergus Falls)
Houston	Minneapolis (St Paul)	Redwood	Minneapolis (St Paul)
Hubbard	Minneapolis (Fergus Falls)	Renville	Minneapolis
Isanti	Minneapolis	Rice	Minneapolis (St Paul)
Itasca	Duluth	Rock	Minneapolis (St Paul)
Jackson	Minneapolis (St Paul)	Roseau	Minneapolis (Fergus Falls)
Kanabec	Duluth	Scott	Minneapolis (St Paul)
Kandiyohi	Minneapolis	Sherburne	Minneapolis
Kittson	Minneapolis (Fergus Falls)	Sibley	Minneapolis (St Paul)
Koochiching	Duluth	St. Louis	Duluth
Lac qui Parle	Minneapolis (St Paul)	Stearns	Minneapolis (Fergus Falls)
Lake	Duluth	Steele	Minneapolis (St Paul)
Lake of the Woods	Minneapolis (Fergus Falls)	Stevens	Minneapolis (Fergus Falls)
Le Sueur	Minneapolis (St Paul)	Swift	Minneapolis
Lincoln	Minneapolis (St Paul)	Todd	Minneapolis (Fergus Falls)
Lyon	Minneapolis (St Paul)	Traverse	Minneapolis (Fergus Falls)
Mahnomen	Minneapolis (Fergus Falls)	Wabasha	Minneapolis (St Paul)
Marshall	Minneapolis (Fergus Falls)	Wadena	Minneapolis (Fergus Falls)
Martin	Minneapolis (St Paul)	Waseca	Minneapolis (St Paul)
McLeod	Minneapolis	Washington	Minneapolis (St Paul)
Meeker	Minneapolis	Watonwan	Minneapolis (St Paul)
Mille Lacs	Duluth	Wilkin	Minneapolis (Fergus Falls)
Morrison	Duluth	Winona	Minneapolis (St Paul)
Mower	Minneapolis (St Paul)	Wright	Minneapolis
Murray	Minneapolis (St Paul)	Yellow Medicine	Minneapolis (St Paul)
Nicollet	Minneapolis (St Paul)		

US District Court
District of Minnesota

PACER sign-up number is 800-676-6856. Both civil and criminal case records are available online.

Duluth Division, Clerk's Office, 417 Federal Bldg, Duluth, MN 55802, 218-529-3500, Fax: 218-720-5622.

Minneapolis Division, Court Clerk, Room 202, 300 S 4th St, Minneapolis, MN 55415, 612-664-5000.

St Paul Division, 708 Federal Bldg, 316 N Robert, St Paul, MN 55101, 612-290-3212, Fax: 651-290-3817.

US Bankruptcy Court
District of Minnesota

www.mnb.uscourts.gov

PACER sign-up number is 800-676-6856. Only civil case records are available online.

Duluth Division, 416 US Courthouse, 515 W 1st St, Duluth, MN 55802, 218-720-5253

Fergus Falls Division, 204 US Courthouse, 118 S Mill St, Fergus Falls, MN 56537, 218-739-4671

Minneapolis Division, 301 US Courthouse, 300 S 4th St, Minneapolis, MN 55415, 612-664-5200, Record Room: 612-664-5209

St Paul Division, 200 Federal Bldg, 316 N Robert St, St Paul, MN 55101, 651-290-3184

Mississippi

Governor's Office
PO Box 139
Jackson, MS 39205-0139
www.govoff.state.ms.us

601-359-3150
Fax 601-359-3741

Attorney General's Office
PO Box 220
Jackson, MS 39201-0220
www.ago.state.ms.us

601-359-3680
Fax 601-359-3796

State Archives
Archives & History Department
Archives & Library Division
PO Box 571
8AM-5PM T-F;
Jackson, MS 39205-0571
www.mdah.state.ms.us

601-359-6850
Fax 601-359-6905
9AM-5PM M;

8AM-1PM SA

Capital:	Jackson
	Hinds County
Time Zone:	CST
Number of Counties:	82
Population:	2,730,501
Web Site:	www.state.ms.us

State Court Administrator
Court Administrator
Supreme Court, Box 117
Jackson, MS 39205
www.mssc.state.ms.us

601-359-3697
Fax 601-359-2443
8AM-5PM

State Agencies Online

Corporation Records
Limited Partnership Records
Limited Liability Company Records
Trademarks/Servicemarks
www.sos.state.ms.us

Corporation Commission, Secretary of State, PO Box 136, Jackson, MS 39205-0136; (Courier: 202 N Congress, Suite 601, Jackson, MS 39201); 601-359-1633, 800-256-3494 (Alternate Telephone), 601-359-1607 (Fax), 8AM-5PM.

Online search: The system is called "Success" and is open 24 hours daily. There is a $250 set-up fee and usage fee of $.10 per screen. Users are billed quarterly. Once registered, users can access through the Internet and avoid toll charges. Call (601) 359-1548 for more information (ask for Tobie Curry).

Driver Records

Department of Public Safety, Driver Records, PO Box 958, Jackson, MS 39205; (Courier: 1900 E Woodrow Wilson, Jackson, MS 39216); 601-987-1274, 8AM-5PM.

General Information: Records are available for 3 years for moving violations, DUIs and suspensions. Accidents do appear on driving records. The driver's address is provided on the record. It takes 45 days or more before new records are available for inquiries. Casual requesters can obtain personal information, unless subject has opted out.

Online search: Both interactive and batch delivery is offered for high volume users only. Billing is monthly. Hook-up is through the Advantis System, fees apply. Lookup is by name only – not by driver license number. The fee is $7.00 per name searched. For more information, contact Donna Smith at 601-987-1337.

Uniform Commercial Code
Federal Tax Liens
www.sos.state.ms.us

UCC Division, Secretary of State, PO Box 136, Jackson, MS 39205-0136; (Courier: 202 N Congress St, Suite 601, Magnolia Federal Bank Bldg, Jackson, MS 39201); 601-

359-1350, 800-256-3494 (Alternate Telephone), 601-359-1607 (Fax), 8AM-5PM.

General Information: The search includes federal tax liens on businesses. Federal tax liens on individuals and all state tax liens are filed at the county level.

Online search: The PC system is called "Success" and is open 24 hours daily. There is a $250 set-up fee and usage fee of $.10 per screen. Users can access via the Internet to avoid any toll charges. Customers are billed quarterly. For more info, call Tobie Curry at (601) 359-1548.

Legislation-Current/Pending Legislation-Passed

www.als.state.ms.us

Mississippi Legislature, Documents, PO Box 1018, Jackson, MS 39215; (Courier: New Capitol, 3rd Floor, Jackson, MS 39215); 601-359-3229 (Senate), 601-359-3358 (House), 8AM – 5PM.

Online search: The Internet site has an excellent bill status and measure information program. Data included is for both the current and previous session.

Information About County Agencies

Court Structure

Justice Courts were first created in 1984, replacing the Justice of the Peace. Prior to 1984, records were kept separately by each Justice of the Peace, so the location of such records today is often unknown. Probate is handled by the Chancery Courts as are property matters.

Online Access

A pilot program for a statewide online computer system is in progress, and it is expected to be implemented within the next year. This system is intended for internal use only. A number of Mississippi counties have two Circuit Court Districts. A search of either court in such a county will include the index from the other court.

About the County Courts

Searching Hints

Full Name is a search requirement for all courts. DOB and SSN are very helpful for differentiating between like-named individuals.

About the Recorder's Office

Organization

82 counties, 92 recording offices. The recording officers are Chancery Clerk and Clerk of Circuit Court (state tax liens). Ten counties have two separate recording offices—Bolivar, Carroll, Chickasaw, Craighead, Harrison, Hinds, Jasper, Jones, Panola, Tallahatchie, and Yalobusha. See the notes under each county for how to determine which office is appropriate to search. The entire state is in the Central Time Zone (CST).

Real Estate Records

A few counties will perform real estate searches. Copies usually cost $.50 per page and certification fees $1.00 per document. The Assessor maintains tax records.

UCC Records

This is a dual filing state. Financing statements are filed both at the state level and with the Chancery Clerk, except for consumer goods, farm related and real estate related filings, which are filed only with the Chancery Clerk. All but one county will perform UCC searches. Use search request form UCC-11. Search fees are usually $5.00 per debtor name. Copy fees vary per page.

Other Lien Records

Federal tax liens on personal property of businesses are filed with the Secretary of State. Federal tax liens on personal property of individuals are filed with the county Chancery Clerk. State tax liens on personal property are filed with the county Clerk of Circuit Court. Refer to *The Sourcebook of County Court Records* for information about Mississippi Circuit Courts. State tax liens on real property are filed with the Chancery Clerk. Most Chancery Clerk offices will perform a federal tax lien search for a fee of $5.00 per name. Copy fees vary. Other liens are: mechanics, lis pendens, judgment (Circuit Court), construction.

County Courts & Recording Offices Online

There are no county courts that offer online access to records.

No remote online access is available from real estate recorder's offices in Mississippi.

Federal Courts Online

County-to-Court Cross Reference (Bankruptcy Court locations in Parenthesis if different)

County	District	Court
Adams	Southern	Vicksburg (Jackson)
Alcorn	Northern	Aberdeen-Eastern (Aberdeen)
Amite	Southern	Jackson
Attala	Northern	Aberdeen-Eastern (Aberdeen)
Benton	Northern	Oxford-Northern (Aberdeen)
Bolivar	Northern	Clarksdale/Delta (Aberdeen)
Calhoun	Northern	Oxford-Northern (Aberdeen)
Carroll	Northern	Greenville (Aberdeen)
Chickasaw	Northern	Aberdeen-Eastern (Aberdeen)
Choctaw	Northern	Aberdeen-Eastern (Aberdeen)
Claiborne	Southern	Vicksburg (Jackson)
Clarke	Southern	Meridian (Biloxi)
Clay	Northern	Aberdeen-Eastern (Aberdeen)
Coahoma	Northern	Clarksdale/Delta (Aberdeen)
Copiah	Southern	Jackson
Covington	Southern	Hattiesburg (Biloxi)
De Soto	Northern	Clarksdale/Delta (Aberdeen)
Forrest	Southern	Hattiesburg (Biloxi)
Franklin	Southern	Jackson
George	Southern	Biloxi-Southern (Biloxi)
Greene	Southern	Hattiesburg (Biloxi)
Grenada	Northern	Oxford-Northern (Aberdeen)
Hancock	Southern	Biloxi-Southern (Biloxi)
Harrison	Southern	Biloxi-Southern (Biloxi)
Hinds	Southern	Jackson
Holmes	Southern	Jackson
Humphreys	Northern	Greenville (Aberdeen)
Issaquena	Southern	Vicksburg (Jackson)
Itawamba	Northern	Aberdeen-Eastern (Aberdeen)
Jackson	Southern	Biloxi-Southern (Biloxi)
Jasper	Southern	Meridian (Biloxi)
Jefferson	Southern	Vicksburg (Jackson)
Jefferson Davis	Southern	Hattiesburg (Biloxi)
Jones	Southern	Hattiesburg (Biloxi)
Kemper	Southern	Meridian (Biloxi)
Lafayette	Northern	Oxford-Northern (Aberdeen)
Lamar	Southern	Hattiesburg (Biloxi)
Lauderdale	Southern	Meridian (Biloxi)
Lawrence	Southern	Hattiesburg (Biloxi)
Leake	Southern	Jackson
Lee	Northern	Aberdeen-Eastern (Aberdeen)
Leflore	Northern	Greenville (Aberdeen)
Lincoln	Southern	Jackson
Lowndes	Northern	Aberdeen-Eastern (Aberdeen)

Madison	Southern	Jackson
Marion	Southern	Hattiesburg (Jackson)
Marshall	Northern	Oxford-Northern (Aberdeen)
Monroe	Northern	Aberdeen-Eastern (Aberdeen)
Montgomery	Northern	Oxford-Northern (Aberdeen)
Neshoba	Southern	Meridian (Biloxi)
Newton	Southern	Meridian (Biloxi)
Noxubee	Southern	Meridian (Biloxi)
Oktibbeha	Northern	Aberdeen-Eastern (Aberdeen)
Panola	Northern	Clarksdale/Delta (Aberdeen)
Pearl River	Southern	Biloxi-Southern (Biloxi)
Perry	Southern	Hattiesburg (Biloxi)
Pike	Southern	Jackson
Pontotoc	Northern	Oxford-Northern (Aberdeen)
Prentiss	Northern	Aberdeen-Eastern (Aberdeen)
Quitman	Northern	Clarksdale/Delta (Aberdeen)
Rankin	Southern	Jackson
Scott	Southern	Jackson
Sharkey	Southern	Vicksburg (Jackson)
Simpson	Southern	Jackson
Smith	Southern	Jackson
Stone	Southern	Biloxi-Southern (Biloxi)
Sunflower	Northern	Greenville (Aberdeen)
Tallahatchie	Northern	Clarksdale/Delta (Aberdeen)
Tate	Northern	Clarksdale/Delta (Aberdeen)
Tippah	Northern	Oxford-Northern (Aberdeen)
Tishomingo	Northern	Aberdeen-Eastern (Aberdeen)
Tunica	Northern	Clarksdale/Delta (Aberdeen)
Union	Northern	Oxford-Northern (Aberdeen)
Walthall	Southern	Hattiesburg (Biloxi)
Warren	Southern	Vicksburg (Jackson)
Washington	Northern	Greenville (Aberdeen)
Wayne	Southern	Meridian (Biloxi)
Webster	Northern	Oxford-Northern (Aberdeen)
Wilkinson	Southern	Vicksburg (Jackson)
Winston	Northern	Aberdeen-Eastern (Aberdeen)
Yalobusha	Northern	Oxford-Northern (Aberdeen)
Yazoo	Southern	Vicksburg (Jackson)

US District Court
Northern District of Mississippi

www.msnd.uscourts.gov

PACER sign-up number is 800-676-6856. Both civil and criminal case records are available online.

Aberdeen-Eastern Division, PO Box 704, Aberdeen, MS 39730, 601-369-4952

Greenville Division, PO Box 190, Greenville, MS 38702-0190, 601-335-1651, Fax: 601-332-4292

Oxford-Northern Division, PO Box 727, Oxford, MS 38655, 601-234-1971, Record Room: 601-234-1351

Clarksdale/Delta Division, c/o Oxford-Northern Division, PO Box 727, Oxford, MS 38655, 601-234-1971, Record Room: 601-234-1351

US Bankruptcy Court
Northern District of Mississippi

PACER sign-up number is 800-676-6856.

Aberdeen Division, PO Drawer 867, Aberdeen, MS 39730-0867, 601-369-2596, Record Room: 601-369-2596.

US District Court
Southern District of Mississippi

www.mssd.uscourts.gov

PACER sign-up number is 800-676-6856.

Biloxi-Southern Division, Room 243, 725 Washington Loop, Biloxi, MS 39530, 601-432-8623, Fax: 601-436-9632

Jackson Division, Suite 316, 245 E Capitol St, Jackson, MS 39201, 601-965-4439

Meridian Division, c/o Jackson Division, Suite 316, 245 E Capiton St, Jackson, MS 39201, 601-695-4439

Vicksburg Division, c/o Jackson Division, Suite 316, 245 E Capitol St, Jackson, MS 39201, 601-965-4439

US Bankruptcy Court
Southern District of Mississippi

PACER sign-up number is 800-676-6856.

Biloxi Division, Room 117, 725 Washington Loop, Biloxi, MS 39530, 601-432-5542.

Jackson Division, PO Drawer 2448, Jackson, MS 39225-2448, 601-965-5301.

Missouri

Governor's Office
PO Box 720   573-751-3222
Jefferson City, MO 65102   Fax 573-751-1495
www.state.mo.us/gov/index.htm

Attorney General's Office
PO Box 899   573-751-3321
Jefferson City, MO 65102   Fax 573-751-0774
services.state.mo.us/ago/homepg.htm

State Archives
Secretary of State   573-751-3280
Archives Division   Fax 573-526-7333
PO Box 778   8-5 M-F
Jefferson City, MO 65102-0778   (till 9PM on Th);
         8:30-3:30 SA
mosl.sos.state.mo.us/rec-man/arch.html

Capital:	Jefferson City
	Cole County
Time Zone:	CST
Number of Counties:	114
Population:	5,402,058
Web Site:	www.state.mo.us

State Court Administrator
Court Administrator   573-751-4377
2112 Industrial Dr   Fax 573-751-5540
PO Box 104480
Jefferson City, MO 65109   8AM-5PM
www.state.mo.us/courts/Judicial2.nsf

State Agencies Online

Corporation Records
Fictitious Name
Limited Partnership Records
Assumed Name
Trademarks/Servicemarks
Limited Liability Company Records
http://mosl.sos.state.mo.us

Secretary of State, Corporation Services, PO Box 778, Jefferson City, MO 65102; (Courier: 600 W Main, Jefferson City, MO 65101); 573-751-4153, 573-751-5841 (Fax), 8AM-5PM.

Online search: Searching can be done from the Internet site. Either the corporate name, the agent name or the charter number is required to search. The site will indicate the currency of the data.

Driver Records
http://dor.state.mo.us

Department of Revenue, Driver License Bureau, PO Box 200, Jefferson City, MO 65105-0200; (Courier: Harry S Truman Bldg, 301 W High St, Room 470, Jefferson City, MO 65105); 573-751-4300, 573-526-4769 (Fax), 7:45AM-4:45PM.

General Information: Records are available for 5 years for moving violations and suspensions, permanent for DWIs. Zero point violations are not shown on the record. Accidents are stored in the state computer, but are not shown on the driving record, unless suspension or revocation action taken. The state complies with DPPA. Casual requesters can obtain records without personal information if subject opted out. If restricted, the photograph, SSN, telephone number, DL#, and medical information is not released. Online searchers can only submit name and DL#.

Online search: Online access costs $1.25 per page. Online inquiries can be put in Missouri's "mailbox" any time of the day. These inquiries are then picked up at 2 AM the following morning, and the resulting MVRs are sent back to each customer's "mailbox" approximately two hours later. The system is designed to be accessed by both PCs and main frames. All network access charges are billed directly by Advantis. For further information, call (573) 751-4391.

Legislation-Current/Pending
Legislation-Passed

www.moga.state.mo.us

Legislative Library, 117A State Capitol, Jefferson City, MO 65101; 573-751-4633 (Bill Status Only), 8:30AM-4:30PM.

Online search: The web site offers access to bills and statutes. One can search or track bills by key words, bill number, or sponsors.

Information About County Agencies

Court Structure

Missouri has 114 Circuit Courts, 114 Associated Courts and 406 Municipal Courts. Municipal Courts only have jurisdiction over traffic and ordinance violations.

Online Access

A limited, statewide, online internal computer access is available on a system called Banner Case Management System. There is legal permission to expand coverage and access using a $7.00 per case fee to be collected, but, there are no implementation plans for the near term.

About the County Courts

Searching Hints

All Circuit and Associate Circuit Courts will have public access terminals available onsite by the end of 1999.

About the Recorder's Office

Organization

114 counties and one independent city, 115 recording offices. The recording officer is Recorder of Deeds. The City of St. Louis has its own recording office. The entire state is in the Central Time Zone (CST).

Real Estate Records

A few counties will perform real estate searches. Copy and certification fees vary.

UCC Records

This is a dual filing state. Financing statements are filed both at the state level and with the Recorder of Deeds, except for consumer goods, farm related and real estate related filings, which are filed only with the Recorder. All but one county will perform UCC searches. Use search request form UCC-11. Search fees are usually $14.00 per debtor name without copies and $28.00 with copies. Copies usually cost $.50 per page.

Other Lien Records

All federal and state tax liens are filed with the county Recorder of Deeds. They are usually indexed together. Some counties will perform tax lien searches. Search and copy fees vary widely. Other liens are: mechanics, judgment, child support.

County Courts & Recording Offices Online

Cass County

Liens, Real Estate

County Recorder of Deeds, 102 E Wall Street, County Court House, Harrisonville, MO 64701, 816-380-1510, 816-380-5136 Fax.

Online search: The monthly fee is $250, plus $.10 per minute after 50 minutes usage. The system operates 24 hours daily. The records date back to 1990. One may search by name, Grantee/Grantor and book and page. Images are viewable and one may print the image for $1.00. A fax back service is also available at $1.00 per page. For further information, contact John Kohler at 816-380-1510.

Jackson County

Civil, Eviction, Small Claims, Probate

www.state.mo.us/sca/circuit16

Independence Circuit Court-Civil Annex 308 W Kansas, Independence MO 64050, 816-881-4497. Fax: 816-881-4410. Hours: 8AM-5PM (CST).

This court is on the same computer system as Kansas City for civil cases, but files maintained separately.

Online search: Contact Becki Fortune at 816-881-3411 for information about remote access. No fee for service, but request to sign up must be on company letterhead and include indication of the business you are in. Fax requests to 816-851-3148. The county has indicated it may place the records on the Internet sometime in 1999.

Civil, Small Claims, Probate

Circuit Court, 415 E 12th, Kansas City MO 64106, 816-881-3926; 881-3522. Hours: 8AM-5PM (CST).

There is a combined computer system with the Independence civil court.

Online search: Contact Becki Fortune at 816-881-3411 for information about remote access. No fee for service, but request to sign up must be on company letterhead and include indication of the business you are in. Fax requests to 816-851-3148. The county has indicated it may place the records on the Internet sometime in 1999.

St. Louis City

Civil, Eviction, Small Claims, Probate.

Circuit & Associate Circuit Courts, 10 N Tucker, Civil Courts Bldg, St Louis MO 63101, 314-622-4367/622-4405. Fax: 314-622-4537. Hours: 8:00AM-5:00PM.

Online search: Remote access is through MoBar Net and is open only to attorneys. Call 314-535-1950 for more information. Required to search: name, years to search. Cases indexed by defendant, plaintiff. No sealed or confidential records released.

Federal Courts Online

County-to-Court Cross Reference (Bankruptcy Court locations in Parenthesis if different)

County	District	Court
Adair	Eastern	Hannibal (St Louis)
Andrew	Western	St Joseph (Kansas City - Western)
Atchison	Western	St Joseph (Kansas City - Western)
Audrain	Eastern	Hannibal (St Louis)
Barry	Western	Joplin-Southwestern (Kansas City)
Barton	Western	Joplin-Southwestern (Kansas City)
Bates	Western	Kansas City - Western
Benton	Western	Jefferson City-Central (Kansas City)
Bollinger	Eastern	Cape Girardeau (St Louis)
Boone	Western	Jefferson City-Central (Kansas City)
Buchanan	Western	St Joseph (Kansas City - Western)
Butler	Eastern	Cape Girardeau (St Louis)
Caldwell	Western	St Joseph (Kansas City - Western)
Callaway	Western	Jefferson City-Central (Kansas City)
Camden	Western	Jefferson City-Central (Kansas City)
Cape Girardeau	Eastern	Cape Girardeau (St Louis)
Carroll	Western	Kansas City - Western
Carter	Eastern	Cape Girardeau (St Louis)
Cass	Western	Kansas City - Western
Cedar	Western	Springfield-Southern (Kansas City)

Chariton .... Eastern ..... Hannibal (St Louis)

Christian .... Western .... Springfield-Southern (Kansas City)

Clark .... Eastern ..... Hannibal (St Louis)

Clay .... Western .... Kansas City - Western

Clinton .... Western .... St Joseph (Kansas City - Western)

Cole .... Western .... Jefferson City-Central (Kansas City)

Cooper .... Western .... Jefferson City-Central (Kansas City)

Crawford .... Eastern ..... St Louis

Dade .... Western .... Springfield-Southern (Kansas City)

Dallas .... Western .... Springfield-Southern (Kansas City)

Daviess .... Western .... St Joseph (Kansas City - Western)

De Kalb .... Western .... St Joseph (Kansas City - Western)

Dent .... Eastern ..... St Louis

Douglas .... Western .... Springfield-Southern ((Kansas City)

Dunklin .... Eastern ..... Cape Girardeau (St Louis)

Franklin .... Eastern ..... St Louis

Gasconade .... Eastern ..... St Louis

Gentry .... Western .... St Joseph (Kansas City - Western)

Greene .... Western .... Springfield-Southern (Kansas City)

Grundy .... Western .... St Joseph (Kansas City - Western)

Harrison .... Western .... St Joseph (Kansas City - Western)

Henry .... Western .... Kansas City - Western

Hickory .... Western .... Jefferson City-Central (Kansas City)

Holt .... Western .... St Joseph (Kansas City - Western)

Howard .... Western .... Jefferson City-Central (Kansas City)

Howell .... Western .... Springfield-Southern (Kansas City)

Iron .... Eastern ..... St Louis

Jackson .... Western .... Kansas City – Western

Jasper .... Western .... Joplin-Southwestern (Kansas City)

Jefferson .... Eastern ..... St Louis

Johnson .... Western .... Kansas City - Western

Knox .... Eastern ..... Hannibal (St Louis)

Laclede .... Western .... Springfield-Southern (Kansas City

Lafayette .... Western .... Kansas City - Western

Lawrence .... Western .... Joplin-Southwestern (Kansas City)

Lewis .... Eastern ..... Hannibal (St Louis)

Lincoln .... Eastern ..... St Louis

Linn .... Eastern ..... Hannibal (St Louis)

Livingston .... Western .... St Joseph (Kansas City - Western)

Macon .... Eastern ..... Hannibal (St Louis)

Madison .... Eastern ..... Cape Girardeau (St Louis)

Maries .... Eastern ..... St Louis

Marion .... Eastern ..... Hannibal (St Louis)

McDonald .... Western .... Joplin-Southwestern (Kansas City)

Mercer .... Western .... St Joseph (Kansas City - Western)

Miller .... Western .... Jefferson City-Central (Kansas City)

Mississippi .... Eastern ..... Cape Girardeau (St Louis)

Moniteau .... Western .... Jefferson City-Central (Kansas City)

Monroe .... Eastern ..... Hannibal (St Louis)

Montgomery .... Eastern ..... Hannibal (St Louis)

Morgan .... Western ... Jefferson City-Central (Kansas City)

New Madrid ..... Eastern ..... Cape Girardeau (St Louis)

Newton .... Western ... Joplin-Southwestern (Kansas City)

Nodaway .... Western ... St Joseph (Kansas City - Western)

Oregon .... Western ... Springfield-Southern (Kansas City)

Osage .... Western ... Jefferson City-Central (Kansas City)

Ozark .... Western ... Springfield-Southern (Kansas City)

Pemiscot .... Eastern ..... Cape Girardeau (St Louis)

Perry .... Eastern ..... Cape Girardeau (St Louis)

Pettis .... Western ... Jefferson City-Central (Kansas City)

Phelps .... Eastern .... St Louis

Pike .... Eastern ..... Hannibal (St Louis)

Platte .... Western ... St Joseph (Kansas City - Western)

Polk .... Western ... Springfield-Southern (Kansas City)

Pulaski .... Western ... Springfield-Southern (Kansas City)

Putnam .... Western ... St Joseph (Kansas City - Western)

Ralls .... Eastern ..... Hannibal (St Louis)

Randolph .... Eastern ..... Hannibal (St Louis)

Ray .... Western ... Kansas City - Western)

Reynolds .... Eastern ..... Cape Girardeau (St Louis)

Ripley .... Eastern ..... Cape Girardeau (St Louis)

Saline .... Western ... Kansas City - Western

Schuyler .... Eastern ..... Hannibal (St Louis)

Scotland .... Eastern ..... Hannibal (St Louis)

Scott .... Eastern ..... Cape Girardeau (St Louis)

Shannon .... Eastern ..... Cape Girardeau (St Louis)

Shelby .... Eastern ..... Hannibal (St Louis)

St. Charles .... Eastern ..... St Louis

St. Clair .... Western ... Kansas City - Western

St. Francois .... Eastern ..... St Louis

St. Louis .... Eastern ..... St Louis

St. Louis City ... Eastern ..... St Louis

Ste. Genevieve . Eastern ..... St Louis

Stoddard .... Eastern ..... Cape Girardeau (St Louis)

Stone .... Western ... Joplin-Southwestern (Kansas City)

Sullivan .... Western ... St Joseph (Kansas City - Western)

Taney .... Western ... Springfield-Southern (Kansas City)

Texas .... Western ... Springfield-Southern (Kansas City)

Vernon .... Western ... Joplin-Southwestern (Kansas City)

Warren .... Eastern ..... St Louis

Washington ...... Eastern ..... St Louis

Wayne .... Eastern ..... Cape Girardeau (St Louis)

Webster .... Western ... Springfield-Southern (Kansas City)

Worth .... Western ... St Joseph (Kansas City - Western)

Wright .... Western ... Springfield-Southern (Kansas City)

US District Court
Eastern District of Missouri

www.moed.uscourts.gov

PACER sign-up number is 800-676-6856. Both civil and criminal case records are available online.

Cape Girardeau Division, 339 Broadway, Room 240, Cape Girardeau, MO 63701, 573-335-8538, Fax: 573-335-0379

St Louis Division, Room 260, 1114 Market St, St Louis, MO 63101, 314-539-2315, Record Room: 314-539-7336, Fax: 314-539-2929

Hannibal Division, c/o St Louis Division, Room 260, 1114 Market St, St Louis, MO 63101, 314-539-2315, Fax: 314-539-2929

US Bankruptcy Court
Eastern District of Missouri

St Louis Division, 7th Floor, 211 N Broadway, St Louis, MO 63102-2734, 314-425-4222, Fax: 314-425-4063

www.moeb.uscourts.gov

PACER sign-up number is 800-676-6856.

US District Court
Western District of Missouri

As a member of the PACER-Net project, the District Court of the Western District of Missouri may make some documents available to the public.

www.law.umkc.edu/fdcwm/ecf/ecfmenu.html

Jefferson City-Central Division, 131 W High St, Jefferson City, MO 65101, 573-636-4015, Fax: 573-636-3456.

PACER sign-up number is 800-676-6856. Both civil and criminal case records are available online.

Kansas City-Western Division, Clerk of Court, 201 US Courthouse, 811 Grand Ave, Kansas City, MO 64106, 816-426-2811, Fax: 816-426-2819.

Joplin-Southwestern Division, c/o Kansas City Division, 201 US Courthouse, 811 Grand Ave, Kansas City, MO 64106, 816-426-2811, Fax: 816-426-2819.

Springfield-Southern Division, 222 N John Q Hammons Pkwy, Suite 1400, Springfield, MO 65806, 417-865-3869, Fax: 417-865-7719.

St Joseph Division, PO Box 387, 201 S 8th St, St Joseph, MO 64501, Civil Docket Section: 816-279-2428, Criminal Docket Section: 816-426-2811, Fax: 816-279-0177.

US Bankruptcy Court
Western District of Missouri

Kansas City-Western Division, Room 913, 811 Grand Ave, Kansas City, MO 64106, 816-426-3321, Fax: 816-426-3364.

PACER sign-up number is 800-676-6856.

Montana

Governor's Office
State Capitol   406-444-3111
Helena, MT 59620-0801   Fax 406-444-5529
www.mt.gov/governor/governor.htm

Attorney General's Office
PO Box 201401   406-444-2026
Helena, MT 59620   Fax 406-444-3549

State Archives
Montana Historical Society   406-444-2694
Library/Archives Division   Fax 406-444-2696
225 N Roberts St   8AM-5PM M-F;
Helena, MT 59620-1201   9AM-4:30PM
www.his.state.mt.us   1st SA/month

Capital:	Helena
	Lewis and Clark County
Time Zone:	MST
Number of Counties:	56
Population:	878,810
Web Site:	www.mt.gov

State Court Administrator
Court Administrator, Rm 315   406-444-2621
215 N Sanders, Justice Bldg,   Fax 406-444-0834
Helena, MT 59620-3002   8AM-5PM

State Agencies Online

Uniform Commercial Code
Federal Tax Liens
www.mt.gov/sos

Business Services Bureau, Secretary of State, PO Box 202801, Helena, MT 59620-2801; (Courier: State Capitol, Rm 225, Helena, MT 59620); 406-444-3665, 406-444-3976 (Fax), 8AM-5PM.

General Information: Records are available from 1965, indexed on computer and on microfiche. Terminated or expired financing statements are not available with the exception of notices of federal tax liens. The search includes notice of federal tax liens on businesses and individuals. All state tax liens are filed at the county level. Include debtor name in your request.

Online search: The online system costs $25 per month plus $.50 per page if copies of filed documents are requested. A prepaid account is required. The system is open 24 hours daily.

Legislation-Current/Pending
Legislation-Passed
www.mt.gov/leg/branch/branch.htm

State Legislature of Montana, State Capitol, Room 138, Helena, MT 59620-1706; 406-444-3064, 406-444-3036 (Fax), 8AM-5PM.

Online search: Information is available on the Internet. There is also a BBS which contains additional information such as actions taken on a bill. Special software is needed. Call (406) 444-1626 for more information. Committee minutes and exhibits will be available on CD-ROM in the future; price has yet to be determined.

Information About County Agencies

Court Structure

Montana has 56 district courts, 66 justice of the peace courts and 83 city courts.

Searching Hints

There is no statewide internal or external online computer system available. Those courts with computer systems use them for internal purposes only.

**About the
County Courts**

About the
Recorder's Office

Organization

57 counties, 56 recording offices. The recording officer is County Clerk and Recorder (Clerk of District Court for state tax liens). Yellowstone National Park is considered a county, but is not included as a filing location. The entire state is in the Mountain Time Zone (MST).

Real Estate Records

Some counties will perform real estate searches. Search and copy fees vary. Certification usually costs $2.00 per document.

UCC Records

Financing statements are filed at the state level, except for consumer goods and real estate related collateral. All counties will perform UCC searches. Use search request form UCC-11. Search fees are usually $7.00 per debtor name. Copy fees vary.

Other Lien Records

Federal tax liens on personal property of businesses are filed with the Secretary of State. Other federal tax liens are filed with the county Clerk and Recorder. State tax liens are filed with the Clerk of District Court. Usually tax liens on personal property filed with the Clerk and Recorder are in the same index with UCC financing statements. Most counties will perform tax lien searches, some as part of a UCC search and others for a separate fee, usually $7.00 per name. Copy fees vary. Other liens are: mechanics, thresherman, judgment, lis pendens, construction, logger.

County Courts & Recording Offices Online

There is no online access to court records.

No remote online access is available from real estate recorder's offices in Montana.

Federal Courts Online

County-to-Court Cross Reference (Bankruptcy Court locations in Parenthesis if different)

Beaverhead	Butte
Big Horn	Billings (Butte)
Blaine	Great Falls (Butte)
Broadwater	Helena (Butte)
Carbon	Billings (Butte)
Carter	Billings (Butte)
Cascade	Great Falls (Butte)
Chouteau	Great Falls (Butte)
Custer	Billings (Butte)
Daniels	Billings (Butte)
Dawson	Billings (Butte)
Deer Lodge	Butte
Fallon	Billings (Butte)
Fergus	Great Falls (Butte)
Flathead	Missoula (Butte)
Gallatin	Butte
Garfield	Billings (Butte)
Glacier	Great Falls (Butte)
Golden Valley	Billings (Butte)
Granite	Missoula (Butte)
Hill	Great Falls (Butte)
Jefferson	Helena (Butte)
Judith Basin	Great Falls (Butte)
Lake	Missoula (Butte)
Lewis and Clark	Helena (Butte)
Liberty	Great Falls (Butte)
Lincoln	Missoula (Butte)
Madison	Butte
McCone	Billings (Butte)
Meagher	Helena (Butte)
Mineral	Missoula (Butte)
Missoula	Missoula (Butte)
Musselshell	Billings (Butte)
Park	Billings (Butte)
Petroleum	Billings (Butte)
Phillips	Billings (Butte)
Pondera	Great Falls (Butte)
Powder River	Billings (Butte)
Powell	Helena (Butte)
Prairie	Billings (Butte)
Ravalli	Missoula (Butte)
Richland	Billings (Butte)
Roosevelt	Billings (Butte)
Rosebud	Billings (Butte)
Sanders	Missoula (Butte)
Sheridan	Billings (Butte)
Silver Bow	Butte
Stillwater	Billings (Butte)
Sweet Grass	Billings (Butte)
Teton	Great Falls (Butte)
Toole	Great Falls (Butte)
Treasure	Billings (Butte)
Valley	Billings (Butte)
Wheatland	Billings (Butte)
Wibaux	Billings (Butte)
Yellowstone	Billings (Butte)
Yellowstone Nat. Park (part)	Billings (Butte)

US District Court
District of Montana

PACER sign-up number is 800-676-6856. Both civil and criminal case records are available online.

Billings Division, Clerk, Room 5405, Federal Bldg, 316 N 26th St, Billings, MT 59101, 406-247-7000, Fax: 406-247-7008.

Butte Division, Room 273, Federal Bldg, Butte, MT 59701, 406-782-0432, Fax: 406-782-0537.

Great Falls Division, Clerk, PO Box 2186, Great Falls, MT 59403, 406-727-1922, Fax: 406-727-7648.

Helena Division, Federal Bldg, Drawer 10015, Helena, MT 59626, 406-441-1355, Fax: 406-441-1357.

Missoula Division, Russell Smith Courthouse, PO Box 8537, Missoula, MT 59807, 406-542-7260, Fax: 406-542-7272.

US Bankruptcy Court
District of Montana

Butte Division, PO Box 689, Butte, MT 59703, 406-782-3354, Fax: 406-782-0537.

PACER sign-up number is 800-676-6856.

Nebraska

Governor's Office
PO Box 94848   402-471-2244
Lincoln, NE 68509-4848   Fax 402-471-6031
gov.nol.org

Attorney General's Office
2115 State Capitol   402-471-2682
Lincoln, NE 68509   Fax 402-471-3297

State Court Administrator
Court Administrator   402-471-2643
PO Box 98910   Fax 402-471-2197
Lincoln, NE 68509-8910   8AM-4:30PM

State Archives
Historical Society   402-471-4771
Archives   Fax 402-471-3100
PO Box 82554   9:30AM-4:30PM
Lincoln, NE 68501-2554   M-F; 8-5 SA;
www.nebraskahistory.org   1:30PM-5PM SU

Capital: Lincoln
                                         Lancaster County

Time Zone: CST*

* Nebraska's 19 western-most counties are MST:
Arthur, Banner, Box Butte, Chase, Cherry, Cheyenne,
Dawes, Deuel, Dundy, Garden, Grant, Hooker, Keith,
Kimball, Morrill, Perkins, Scotts Bluff, Sheridan, Sioux.

Number of Counties: 93

Population: 1,656,870

Web Site: www.state.ne.us

State Agencies Online

Corporation Records
Limited Liability Company Records
Limited Partnerships
Trade Names
Trademarks/Servicemarks
www.nol.org.home/SOS

Secretary of State, Corporation Commission, 1301 State
Capitol Bldg, Lincoln, NE 68509; 402-471-4079, 402-
471-3666 (Fax), 8AM - PM.

Online search: The state has designated Nebrask@
Online (800-747-8177) to facilitate online retrieval of
records. Access is through both a dial-up system and the
Internet; however an account and payment is required.
The state Internet site has general information only.

Uniform Commercial Code
Federal Tax Liens

UCC Division, Secretary of State, PO Box 95104,
Lincoln, NE 68509; (Courier: 1305 State Capitol Bldg,
Lincoln, NE 68509); 402-471-4080, 402-471-4429 (Fax),
7:30AM-5PM.

General Information: State tax liens are filed at the
county level. Some federal tax liens are filed here
(primarily on individuals) and some at the county level.

Online search: Access is outsourced to Nebrask@
Online. The system is available 24 hours daily. There is
an annual $50 fee and a $.12 per minute access charge.
The access charge can be avoided by using their Internet
site at www.nol.org. Call (800) 747-8177 for more
information.

Workers' Compensation Records

Workers' Compensation Court, PO Box 98908, Lincoln, NE 68509-8908; (Courier: State Capitol, 13th Floor, Lincoln, NE 68509); 402-471-6468, 800-599-5155 (Instate), 402-471-2700 (Fax), 8AM-5PM.

General Information: Must have a release form for medical or correspondence records. All other records are public record.

Online search: Access to data is available on Nebrask@ Online. There is a $50 set-up fee and $.12 per minute charge, unless you access through their Internet site at www.nol.org. This web site provides court information, name and address lists, and forms.

Driver Records

www.nol.org/home/dmv/driverec.htm

Department of Motor Vehicles, Driver Records Division, PO Box 94789, Lincoln, NE 68509-4789; (Courier: 301 Centennial Mall, S, Lincoln, NE 68509); 402-471-4343, 8AM - 5PM.

General Information: Records are available for 4 years for moving violations and suspensions; lifetime for DWIs. Accidents are reported on the record, but fault is not indicated. The general public and insurance companies are restricted to accessing only 4 year records. Social Security Numbers will not be released.

Online search: Nebraska outsources all online and tape record requests through Nebrask@ Online (800-747-8177). The online system is interactive and open 24 hours a day, 7 days a week. There is an annual fee of $50.00

and a $.40 per minute connect fee or $.12 if through the Internet, plus $3.00 per record.

Vehicle Ownership
Vehicle Identification
Boat & Vessel Ownership

Department of Motor Vehicles, Titles and Registration Section, PO Box 94789, Lincoln, NE 68509-4789; (Courier: 301 Centennial Mall, S, Lincoln, NE 68509); 402-471-3918, 8AM-5PM.

General Information An opt-out provision is in force. If a subject opts out, personal information is not released to casual requesters.

Online search: Electronic access is through Nebrask@ Online. There is a start-up fee and line charges are incurred in addition to the $1.00 per record fee. The system is open 24 hours a day, 7 days a week. Call (800) 747-8177 for more information.

Legislation-Current/Pending
Legislation-Passed

www.unicam.state.ne.us

Clerk of Legislature Office, PO Box 94604, Lincoln, NE 68509-4604; (Courier: State Capitol, 1445 K Street, Room 2018, Lincoln, NE 68509); 402-471-2271, 402-471-2126 (Fax), 8AM-5PM.

Online search: The web site features the state statutes, legislative bills for the present and past sessions, and a legislative journal.

Information About County Agencies

Court Structure

The number of judicial districts went from 21 to the current 12 in July 1992.

County Courts have juvenile jurisdiction in all but 3 counties. Douglas, Lancaster, and Sarpy counties have separate Juvenile Courts. Probate is handled by County Courts. Many have records on microfiche back to the mid/late 1800s.

About the County Courts

Online Access

Implementation of a statewide, internal online access system is underway. The goal is statewide access by 2000. Access by the public will be considered in the future. All internal online courts allow public access at their offices.

Searching Hints

All Nebraska courts require the public to do their own in-person searches and will not respond to written search requests. The State Attorney General has recommended that courts not perform searches because of the time involved and possible legal liability concerns.

About the Recorder's Office

Organization

93 counties, 109 recording offices. The recording officers are County Clerk (UCC and some state tax liens) and Register of Deeds (real estate and most tax liens). Most counties have a combined Clerk/Register office, which are designated "County Clerk" in this section. Sixteen counties have separate offices for County Clerk and for Register of Deeds—Adams, Cass, Dakota, Dawson, Dodge, Douglas, Gage, Hall, Lancaster, Lincoln, Madison, Otoe, Platte, Sarpy, Saunders, and Scotts Bluff. In combined offices, the Register of Deeds is frequently a different person from the County Clerk. 74 counties are in the Central Time Zone (CST) and 19 are in the Mountain Time Zone (MST).

Real Estate Records

Many counties will perform real estate searches, including owner of record from the legal description of the property. Address search requests and make checks payable to the Register of Deeds, not the County Clerk. Fees vary.

UCC Records

Financing statements are filed at the state level, except for consumer goods and farm related collateral, which are filed with the County Clerk, and real estate related collateral, which are filed with the County Clerk. All non-real estate UCC filings are entered into a statewide database that is accessible from any county office. All but five counties will perform UCC searches. Use search request form UCC-11. The UCC statute allows for telephone searching. Search fees are usually $3.50 per debtor name. Copy fees vary.

Other Lien Records

All federal and some state tax liens are filed with the County Register of Deeds. Some state tax liens on personal property are filed with the County Clerk. Most counties will perform tax lien searches, some as part of a UCC search, and others for a separate fee, usually $3.50 per name in each index. Copy fees vary. Other liens are: mechanics, artisans, judgment, motor vehicle, agricultural.

County Courts & Recording Offices Online

No remote online access is available from real estate recorder's offices in Nebraska.

Douglas County

Civil Records

Douglas County Court, 1819 Farnam, 2nd Fl, Omaha NE 68183, 402-444-5425. Hours: 8AM-4:30PM (CST).

Online search: Online access is $25 per month for the first 250 transactions and $.10 per transaction thereafter. The system is open 24 hours daily and can be searched by name or case number. Call Jo Williams at 402-444-7705 for more information.

Federal Courts Online

County-to-Court Cross Reference (Bankruptcy Court locations in Parenthesis if different)

County	Court	County	Court	County	Court
Adams	Lincoln	Frontier	North Platte	Nance	Lincoln
Antelope	Lincoln	Furnas	North Platte	Nemaha	Lincoln
Arthur	North Platte	Gage	Lincoln	Nuckolls	Lincoln
Banner	North Platte	Garden	North Platte	Otoe	Lincoln
Blaine	North Platte	Garfield	North Platte	Pawnee	Lincoln
Boone	Lincoln	Gosper	North Platte	Perkins	North Platte
Box Butte	North Platte	Grant	North Platte	Phelps	Lincoln
Boyd	Lincoln	Greeley	Lincoln	Pierce	Omaha
Brown	North Platte	Hall	Lincoln	Platte	Lincoln
Buffalo	Lincoln	Hamilton	Lincoln	Polk	Lincoln
Burt	Omaha	Harlan	Lincoln	Red Willow	North Platte
Butler	Lincoln	Hayes	North Platte	Richardson	Lincoln
Cass	Lincoln	Hitchcock	North Platte	Rock	North Platte
Cedar	Omaha	Holt	Lincoln	Saline	Lincoln
Chase	North Platte	Hooker	North Platte	Sarpy	Omaha
Cherry	North Platte	Howard	Lincoln	Saunders	Lincoln
Cheyenne	North Platte	Jefferson	Lincoln	Scotts Bluff	North Platte
Clay	Lincoln	Johnson	Lincoln	Seward	Lincoln
Colfax	Lincoln	Kearney	Lincoln	Sheridan	North Platte
Cuming	Omaha	Keith	North Platte	Sherman	Lincoln
Custer	North Platte	Keya Paha	North Platte	Sioux	North Platte
Dakota	Omaha	Kimball	North Platte	Stanton	Omaha
Dawes	North Platte	Knox	Omaha	Thayer	Lincoln
Dawson	North Platte	Lancaster	Lincoln	Thomas	North Platte
Deuel	North Platte	Lincoln	North Platte	Thurston	Omaha
Dixon	Omaha	Logan	North Platte	Valley	North Platte
Dodge	Omaha	Loup	North Platte	Washington	Omaha
Douglas	Omaha	Madison	Lincoln	Wayne	Omaha
Dundy	North Platte	McPherson	North Platte	Webster	Lincoln
Fillmore	Lincoln	Merrick	Lincoln	Wheeler	Lincoln
Franklin	Lincoln	Morrill	North Platte	York	Lincoln

US District Court
District of Nebraska

www.nfinity.com/~usdcne

PACER sign-up number is 800-676-6856. Both civil and criminal case records are available online.

Lincoln Division, PO Box 83468, Lincoln, NE 68501, 402-437-5225

North Platte Division, c/o Lincoln Division, PO Box 83468, Lincoln, NE 68501, 402-221-4761, Fax: 402-221-3160

Omaha Division, PO Box 129, DTS, Omaha, NE 68101, 402-221-4761, Fax: 402-221-3160

US Bankruptcy Court
District of Nebraska

PACER sign-up number is 800-676-6856.

Lincoln Division, 460 Federal Bldg, 100 Centennial Mall N, Lincoln, NE 68508, 402-437-5100, Fax: 402-437-5454.

Omaha Division, PO Box 428, DTS, Omaha, NE 68101-4281, 402-221-4687.

North Platte Division, c/o Omaha Division, PO Box 129, DTS, Omaha, NE 68101, 402-221-4687.

Nevada

Governor's Office
Executive Chambers,
Capitol Complex　　775-687-5670
Carson City, NV 89710　　Fax 775-687-4486
www.state.nv.us/gov/gov.htm

Attorney General's Office
Capitol Complex　　775-687-4170
Carson City, NV 89710　　Fax 775-687-5798
www.state.nv.us/executive/ag.htm

State Archives
State Library & Archives　　775-687-5160
100 N Stewart St　　Fax 775-687-8311
Carson City, NV 89701-4285　　8AM-5PM M-F
www.clan.lib.nv.us

Capital:	Carson City
	Carson City County
Time Zone:	PST
Number of Counties:	[#]
Number of Filing Locations:	[#]
Population:	1,676,809
Web Site:	www.state.nv.us

State Court Administrator
Supreme Court of Nevada　　775-687-5076
Admin. Office of the Courts　　Fax 775-687-5079
201 S Carson St, #250　　8AM-5PM
Carson City, NV 89701-4702

State Agencies Online

Corporation Records
Limited Partnerships
Limited Liability Company Records
Limited Partnership Records
http://sos.state.nv.us

Secretary of State, Status Division, 101 N Carson, #3, Carson City, NV 89701-4786; 775-687-5203, 900-535-3355 (Status Line), 775-687-3471 (Fax), 8AM-5PM.

Online search: Online access is offered on the Internet site for no charge. You can search by corporate name, resident agent, corporate officers, or by file number.

Uniform Commercial Code
Federal Tax Liens
State Tax Liens

UCC Department, Secretary of State, Capitol Complex, Carson City, NV 89710; 775-687-5203, 775-687-3471 (Fax), 8AM-5PM.

General Information: Since there is no state income tax, most state liens are on unemployment withholding.

Online search: This is a PC dial-up system. The fee is $24.50 per hour or $10.75 per hour on an 800 number for unlimited access. There is a $50.00 minimum deposit. The system is up from 7 AM to 5 PM. Call (702) 687-4357 for a packet.

Legislation-Current/Pending
Legislation-Passed
www.leg.state.nv.us

Nevada Legislature, 401 S Carson St, Carson City, NV 89710; 775-687-6825 (Bill Status Only), 775-687-6800 (Main Number), 775-687-6835 (Publications), 775-687-6827 (Research Library), 775-687-3048 (Fax), 8AM-5PM.

Online search: Bills and bill status information is available via this agency's web site.

Information About County Agencies

Court Structure

There are 9 judicial districts comprised of 17 district courts.

Online Access

Some Nevada Courts have internal online computer systems, but none have external access nor is such access planned in the near future. As of June, 1998, planning began for a statewide court automation system, with implementation planned within 2-3 years.

**About the
County Courts**

Searching Hints

Many Nevada Justice Courts are small and have very few records. Their hours of operation vary widely and contact is difficult. It is recommended that requesters call ahead for information prior to submitting a written request or attempting an in-person retrieval.

About the Recorder's Office

Organization

16 counties and one independent city, 17 recording offices. The recording officer is County Recorder. Carson City has a separate filing office. The entire state is in the Pacific Time Zone (PST).

Real Estate Records

Most counties will not provide real estate searches. Copies cost $1.00 per page and certification fees are usually $3.00 per document.

UCC Records

Financing statements are filed at the state level, except for consumer goods, crops and real estate related collateral, which are filed only with the County Recorder. All recording offices will perform UCC searches. Search fees are $15.00 per debtor name using the approved UCC-3 request form and $20.00 using a non-Nevada. Copies cost $1.00 per page.

Other Lien Records

Federal tax liens on personal property of businesses are filed with the Secretary of State. Federal tax liens on personal property of individuals are filed with the County Recorder. Although not called state tax liens, employment withholding judgments have the same effect and are filed with the County Recorder. Most counties will provide tax lien searches for a fee of $15.00 per name—$20.00 if the standard UCC request form is not used. Other liens are: mechanics.

County Courts & Recording Offices Online

There is no online access to court records.

Clark County

Liens, Tax Assessor Records, Real Estate, Birth Records, Death Records, Marriage Records, Divorce Records

County Recorder
www.co.clark.nv.us/RECORDER/or_srch.htm

Marriage Records
www.co.clark.nv.us/RECORDER/mar.srch.htm

County Recorder, 500 S Grand Central, 2nd Floor, Las Vegas, NV 89106, 702-455-4336

Access to public records is through the Internet. There is no fee. The records date back to 1988. You can search by name, Grantee/Grantor, book and instrument type, document type, UCC, and address. Lending agency information is available.

Federal Courts Online

County-to-Court Cross Reference (Bankruptcy Court locations in Parenthesis if different)

Carson City	Reno (Reno-Northern)
Churchill	Reno (Reno-Northern)
Clark	Las Vegas
Douglas	Reno (Reno-Northern)
Elko	Reno (Reno-Northern)
Esmeralda	Las Vegas
Eureka	Reno (Reno-Northern)
Humboldt	Reno (Reno-Northern)
Lander	Reno (Reno-Northern)
Lincoln	Las Vegas
Lyon	Reno (Reno-Northern)
Mineral	Reno (Reno-Northern)
Nye	Las Vegas
Pershing	Reno (Reno-Northern)
Storey	Reno (Reno-Northern)
Washoe	Reno (Reno-Northern)
White Pine	Reno (Reno-Northern)

US District Court
District of Nevada

There is no electronic access to the US District Court in Nevada (however, there is ready access to the Bankruptcy Court). This District Court is scheduled to go online sometime in 1999, at

www.nvb.uscourts.gov

Las Vegas Division Room 4425, 300 Las Vegas Blvd S, Las Vegas, NV 89101, 702-388-6351.

Reno Division Room 301, 400 S Virginia St, Reno, NV 89501, 702-686-5800, Record Room: 702-686-5909, Civil Docket Section: 702-686-5845, Criminal Docket Section: 702-686-5844, Fax: 702-686-5851.

US Bankruptcy Court
District of Nevada

Las Vegas Division, Room 2130, 300 Las Vegas Blvd S, Las Vegas, NV 89101, 702-388-6257

www.nvb.uscourts.gov

PACER sign-up number is 800-676-6856.

Reno-Northern Division, Room 4005, 300 Booth St, Reno, NV 89509, 775-784-5559

www.nvb.uscourts.gov

PACER sign-up number is 800-676-6856.

New Hampshire

Governor's Office

State House
107 N Main St, Rm 208
Concord, NH 03301
www.state.nh.us

603-271-2121
Fax 603-271-2130
8:30AM-5PM

Attorney General's Office

33 Capitol St
Concord, NH 03301-6397
www.state.nh.us/oag/ag.html

603-271-3658
Fax 603-271-2110

State Archives

Department of State
Div of Records Management
   & Archives
71 S Fruit St
Concord, NH 03301
www.state.nh.us/state/archives.htm

603-271-2236
Fax 603-271-2272

8AM-4:30PM

Capital:	Concord
	Merrimack County
Time Zone:	EST
Number of Counties:	10
Population:	1,172,709
Web Site:	www.state.nh.us

State Court Administrator

Admin. Office of Courts
Supreme Court Bldg, Noble Dr
Concord, NH 03301-6160
www.state.nh.us/courts/home.htm

603-271-2521
Fax 603-271-3977
8AM-5PM

State Agencies Online

Driver Records

Department of Motor Vehicles, Driving Records, 10 Hazen Dr, Concord, NH 03305; 603-271-2322, 8:15AM-4:15PM.

General Information: Records are available for 5 years for moving violations and 7 for DWIs. Surrendered license information remains on the system at least 5 years after the expiration date. An opt-out provision in place, so the state is very restrictive as to release of records.

Online search: Online access is offered for commercial accounts. The system is open 22 hours a day. Searches are by license number or by name and DOBand are $7.00 per record. For more information, call Chuck DeGrace at 603-271-2314.

Legislation-Current/Pending
Legislation-Passed

www.state.nh.us/gencourt/gencourt.htm

New Hampshire State Library, 20 Part St, Concord, NH 03301; 603-271-2239, 603-271-2205 (Fax), 8AM-4:30PM.

Online search: Information can be viewed from the web site. A dial-up system is also available. There is a $100 set-up fee, software is $75, and a $.75 charge per minute after the first month. This system offers more than web site. Call (603) 271-2180 and ask Stan Kelly for more information.

Information About County Agencies

Court Structure

Felony cases, which are found at superior courts, include Class A misdemeanors.

Filing a civil case in the monetary "overlap" area between the Superior Court minimum and the District Court maximum is at the discretion of the filer.

There are only 2 Municipal Courts left in New Hampshire: Rye and Greenville. They may remain in operation for as long as 7 years. These courts are closed as the judge retires. The case load and records are absorbed by the nearest District Court.

**About the
County Courts**

Online Access

There is no remote online computer access available

Searching Hints

A statutory search fee has been implemented in the District Courts, as follows:

Computer search—$10.00 for up to 10 names in one request; $25.00 for 10 or more names in one request; $25.00 per hour for search time beyond one hour.

Manual search—$25.00 per hour.

If the search requires both types, the fee is the total for each.

About the Recorder's Office

Organization

238 cities/towns and 10 counties, 10 recording offices and 242 UCC filing offices. The recording officers are Town/City Clerk (UCC) and Register of Deeds (real estate only). Each town/city profile indicates the county in which the town/city is located. Be careful to distinguish the following names that are identical for both a town/city and a county—Grafton, Hillsborough, Merrimack, Strafford, and Sullivan. Many towns are so small that their mailing addresses are within another town. The following unincorporated towns do not have a Town Clerk, so all liens are located at the corresponding county: Cambridge (Coos), Dicksville (Coos), Green's Grant (Coos), Hale's Location (Carroll), Millsfield (Coos), and Wentworth's Location (Coos). The entire state is in the Eastern Time Zone (EST).

Real Estate Records

Real estate transactions are recorded at the county level, and property taxes are handled at the town/city level. Local town real estate ownership and assessment records are usually located at the Selectman's Office. Each town/city profile indicates the county in which the town/city is located.

Most counties will not perform real estate searches. Copy fees vary. Certification fees generally are $2.00 per document.

UCC Records

This is a dual filing state. Financing statements are filed at the state level and with the Town/City Clerk, except for consumer goods and farm related collateral, which are filed only with the Town/City Clerk, and real estate related collateral, which are filed with the county Register of Deeds. Most recording offices will perform UCC searches. Use search request form UCC-11. Search fees are usually $5.00 per debtor name using the standard UCC-11 request form and $7.00 using a non-standard form. Copy fees are usually $.75 per page.

Other Lien Records

Federal and state tax liens on personal property of businesses are filed with the Secretary of State. Other federal and state tax liens on personal property are filed with the Town/City Clerk. Federal and state tax liens on real property are filed with the county Register of Deeds. There is wide variation in indexing and searching practices among the recording offices. Where a search fee of $7.00 is indicated, it refers to a non-standard request form such as a letter. Other liens are: condominium, town tax, mechanics, welfare.

County Courts & Recording Offices Online

Except for Grafton County Register of Deeds who makes liens and real estate records available online, there is no remote online computer access available.

Grafton County

Liens, Real Estate

County Register of Deeds, Route 10, North Haverhill, NH 03774, 603-787-6921, 603-787-2363 Fax.

Online search: The set up fee is $100, plus a monthly fee of $40. Two years of data are kept on the system. Prior years are stored on CD-ROM. The system operates 24 hours daily and supports a baud rate of 9,600. One can search by name and Grantee/Grantor. Lending agency information is available. There is a fax back service for in-state only. The first page is $4.00, the second $3.00 and $2.00 for any additional pages. For further information contact Carol Elliott at 603-787-6921.

Federal Courts Online

US District Court
District of New Hampshire

Concord Division, Warren B Rudman Courthouse, 55 Pleasant St, #110, Concord, NH 03301, 603-225-1423. This court handles all counties in New Hampshire.

PACER sign-up number is 800-676-6856. Both civil and criminal case records are available online.

US Bankruptcy Court
District of New Hampshire

Manchester Division, Room 404, 275 Chestnut St, Manchester, NH 03101, 603-666-7532, Record Room: 603-666-7626, Fax: 603-666-7408. This court handles all counties in New Hampshire.

PACER sign-up number is 800-676-6856.

New Jersey

Governor's Office
125 W State St, CN001 609-292-6000
Trenton, NJ 08625-0001 Fax 609-292-3454
www.state.nj.us/governor/office.htm

Attorney General's Office
Law & Public Safety Dept. 609-292-8740
25 Market St, CN-080 Fax 609-292-3508
Trenton, NJ 08625-0080 8:30AM-5PM
www.state.nj.us/lps

Capital: Trenton
Mercer County

Time Zone: EST

Number of Counties: 21

Population: 8,052,849

Web Site: www.state.nj.us

State Archives
New Jersey State Archives 609-633-8334
185 W. State Street, Fax 609-396-2454
PO Box 307 8:30AM-4:30PM
Trenton, NJ 08625-0307 T-F
www.state.nj.us/state/darm/darmidx.html

State Court Administrator
Admin. Office of Courts 609-984-0275
RJH Justice Complex Fax 609-984-6968
Courts Bldg, 7th Floor, CN037
Trenton, NJ 08625 8:30AM-4:30PM
www.state.nj.us/judiciary/ctmen.htm

State Agencies Online

Corporation Records
Limited Liability Company Records
Fictitious Name
Limited Partnerships
accessnet.state.nj.us/state/index.asp

Department of Treasury, Division of Commercial Recording, PO 450, Trenton, NJ 08625; (Courier: 820 Bear Tavern Rd, West Trenton, NJ 08628); 609-530-6400, 609-530-6432 (Copies), 609-530-8290 (Fax), 8:30AM-5:00PM.

Online search: The New Jersey Business Gateway Service (NJBGS) provides Internet online searching for business entities records. Fees are involved. The system is open 24 hours daily. NGBGS is planning to offer UCC records online in the future. For more information, call 609-530-6419.

Driver Records
www.state.nj.us/mvs

Motor Vehicle Services, Driver's Abstract Section, CN142, Trenton, NJ 08666; 609-292-6500, 888-486-3339 (In-state only), 609-292-6500 (Suspensions), 8AM-5PM.

General Information: Non-moving violations are not reported on the record. Accidents are reported, but fault is not shown.

Online search: Fee is $4.00 per record. Access is limited to insurance, bus and trucking companies, parking authorities, and approved vendors. There is a minimum of 400 requests per quarter.

Legislation-Current/Pending
Legislation-Passed
www.njleg.state.nj.us

New Jersey State Legislature, State House Annex, CN-068, Room B06, Trenton, NJ 08625-0068; 609-292-4840 (Bill Status), 609-292-6395 (Copy Room), 800-792-8630 (In State Only), 609-777-2440 (Fax), 8:30AM-5PM.

Online search: Limited online access is available for insurance companies, bus and trucking companies, highway/parking authorities, and approved vendors for these businesses. Participation requires a minimum of 100 requests per calendar quarter at $4.00 per request.

Vehicle Ownership/Identification
Boat & Vessel Ownership/Registration

www.state.nj.us/mvs

Motor Vehicle Services, Certified Information Unit, CN146, Trenton, NJ 08666; 609-292-6500, 888-486-3339 (In-state), 8AM-5PM.

General Information: Records are available from 1986 for most records. All boats 12 ft and over must be titled and registered. All motorized boats and sailboats under 12 ft must be registeredSSNs and medical information are not currently released and more restrictions are forthcoming. Casual requesters cannot obtain records.

Online search: Limited online access is available for insurance companies, bus and trucking companies, highway/parking authorities, and approved vendors for these businesses. Participation requires a minimum of 100 requests per calendar quarter at $4.00 per request.

Information About County Agencies

Court Structure

Each Superior Court has a Civil Division and a Criminal Division. Search requests should be addressed separately to each division.

About the County Courts

The Special Civil Part of the Superior Court acts like a division of the court, and handles only the smaller civil claims. The small claims limit is now $2,000, up from $1,500 in 1994. The Superior Court designation refers to the court where criminal cases and civil claims over $10,000 are heard. Probate is handled by Surrogates.

Online Access

Online computer access is available through the ACMS, AMIS, and FACTS systems. ACMS (Automated Case Management System) contains data on all active civil cases statewide from the Law Division-Civil Part, Chancery Division-Equity Part, the Special Civil Part for 21 counties, and the Appellate Division. AMIS (Archival Management Information System) contains closed case information. FACTS (Family Automated Case Tracking System) contains information on dissolutions from all counties. The fee is $1.00 per minute of use. For further information and/or an *Inquiry System Guidebook* containing hardware and software requirements and an enrollment form, write to: Superior Court Clerk's Office, Electronic Access, Program, 25 Market St, CN971, Trenton NJ 08625, FAX 609-292-6564, or call 609-292-4987.

Searching Hints

Effective 1/1/95, all court employees became state employees and each section is responsible for its own fees.

Note that Cape May County offices are located in the city of Cape May Court House, and not in the city of Cape May.

About the Recorder's Office

Organization

21 counties, 21 recording offices. The recording officer title varies depending upon the county. It is either Register of Deeds or County Clerk. The Clerk of Circuit Court records the equivalent of some state tax liens. The entire state is in the Eastern Time Zone (EST).

Real Estate Records

No counties will provide real estate searches. Copy and certification fees vary. Assessment and tax offices are at the municipal level.

UCC Records

Financing statements are filed at the state level, except for consumer goods, farm related and real estate related collateral, which are filed only with the County Clerk. Only 12 recording offices will perform UCC searches. Use search request form UCC-11. Search fees are usually $25.00 per debtor name and copy fees vary.

Other Lien Records

All federal tax liens are filed with the County Clerk/Register of Deeds and are indexed separately from all other liens. State tax liens comprise two categories—certificates of debt are filed with the Clerk of Superior Court (some, called docketed judgments are filed specifically with the Trenton court), and warrants of execution are filed with the County Clerk/Register of Deeds. Few counties will provide tax lien searches. Refer to *The Sourcebook of County Court Records* for information about New Jersey Superior Courts. Other liens are: judgment, mechanics, bail bond.

County Courts & Recording Offices Online

All County Superior Courts - Special Civil Part

Superior Court Clerk's Office, Electronic Access Program, 25 Market St, CN971, Trenton, NJ 08625, 609-292-4987, 609-292-6564 Fax.

Online access is available through 3 systems (ACMS, AMIS, and FACTS). ACMS contains data on all active civil cases from the 21 counties. AMIS contains closed case information. FACTS contains information on dissolutions from all counties. The fee is $1.00 per minute. For more information and an enrollment form, call 609-292-4987.

No remote online access is available from real estate recorder's offices in New Jersey.

Federal Courts Online

County-to-Court Cross Reference (Bankruptcy Court locations in Parenthesis if different)

County	Court	County	Court	County	Court
Atlantic	Camden	Hudson	Newark	Salem	Camden
Bergen	Newark	Hunterdon	Trenton	Somerset	Trenton
Burlington	Camden	Mercer	Trenton	Sussex	Newark
Camden	Camden	Middlesex	Newark (Trenton)	Union	Newark
Cape May	Camden	Monmouth	Newark (Trenton)	Warren	Trenton
Cumberland	Camden	Morris	Newark		
Essex	Newark	Ocean	Trenton		
Gloucester	Camden	Passaic	Newark		

US District Court
District of New Jersey

www.njuscourts.org

PACER sign-up number is 800-676-6856. Both civil and criminal case records are available online.

Camden Division, Clerk, PO Box 2797, Camden, NJ 08101, 609-757-5021, Fax: 609-757-5370

Newark Division, ML King, Jr Federal Bldg. & US Courthouse, 50 Walnut St, Room 4015, Newark, NJ 07101, 973-645-3730, Record Room: 973-645-6465

Trenton Division, Clerk, US District Court, Room 2020, 402 E State St, Trenton, NJ 08608, 609-989-2065

US Bankruptcy Court
District of New Jersey

www.njuscourts.org

PACER sign-up number is 800-676-6856. Only civil case records are available online.

Camden Division, 15 N 7th St, 3rd Fl, Camden, NJ 08102, 609-757-5485

Newark Division, ML King Jr Federal Bldg, 50 Walnut St, 3rd Fl, Newark, NJ 07102, 973-645-4764

Trenton Division, Clerk of Court, 402 E State St, 1st Fl, Trenton, NJ 08608, 609-989-2128

New Mexico

Governor's Office

State Capitol, Room 400   505-827-3000
Santa Fe, NM 87503   Fax 505-827-3026
www.governor.state.nm.us

Attorney General's Office

PO Drawer 1508   505-827-6000
Santa Fe, NM 87504-1508   Fax 505-827-5826
www.nol.org/home/ag

State Archives

State Records Ctr. & Archives   505-476-7908
1205 Camino Carols Rey   Fax 505-476-7909
Santa Fe, NM 87505   8AM-5PM
www.state.nm.us/cpr

Capital:	Santa Fe
	Santa Fe County
Time Zone:	MST
Number of Counties:	33
Population:	1,729,751
Web Site:	www.state.nm.us

State Court Administrator

Admin. Office of the Courts   505-827-4800
Supreme Court Bldg, Room 25   Fax 505-827-7549
Santa Fe, NM 87503   8AM-5PM

State Agencies Online

Corporation Records
Limited Liability Company Records

www.state.nm.us/scc/sccfind.htm

State Corporation Commission, Corporate Department, PO Box 1269, Santa Fe, NM 87504-1269; (Courier: 1120 Paseo de Peralta, Pera Bldg 4th Fl, Rm 418, Santa Fe, NM 87501); 505-827-4502 (Main Number), 800-947-4722 (In-state Only), 505-827-4510 (Good Standing), 505-827-4513 (Copy Request), 505-827-4387 (Fax), 8AM-12:00: 1PM-5PM.

Online search: There is no charge to view records at the Internet site.

Uniform Commercial Code

www.sos.state.nm.us/ucc/ucchome.htm

UCC Division, Secretary of State, State Capitol Bldg, Rm 420, Santa Fe, NM 87503; 505-827-3610, 505-827-3611 (Fax), 8AM – 5PM.

General Information: The system does not give information on collateral

Online search: The web site permits searches. A more extensive online access is available through a state appointed vendor New Mexico Technet. There is a $50 set-up fee and 3 levels of service with various access charges. Call 505-345-6555 for information.

Driver Records

Motor Vehicle Division, Driver Services Bureau, PO Box 1028, Santa Fe, NM 87504-1028; (Courier: Joseph M. Montoya Bldg, 1100 S St. Francis Dr, 2nd Floor, Santa Fe, NM 87504); 505-827-2234, 505-827-2267 (Fax), 8AM-5PM.

General Information: Records are available for 3 years for moving violations; 25 years DWIs. Accidents are not reported on the record. Neither are violations less than 10 mph over the limit in 55 or 65 zones.

Online search: New Mexico Technet is the state authorized vendor for access. The costs are $2.50 per record for interactive, $1.50 per record for batch, plus a $.25 per minute network fee. The system is open 24 hours a day, batch requesters must wait 24 hours. There is a $35.00 set-up fee, also. Technet bills users on a monthly basis. All users must first be approved and sign a contract with the Director of the Motor Vehicle Division. Technet can be reached at 505-345-6555.

Vehicle Ownership
Vehicle Identification
Boat & Vessel Ownership
Boat & Vessel Registration

Motor Vehicle Division, Vehicle Services Bureau, PO Box 1028, Santa Fe, NM 87504-1028; (Courier: Joseph M. Montoya Bldg, 1100 S St. Francis Dr, 2nd Floor, Santa Fe, NM 87504); 505-827-4636, 505-827-1004 (Alternate Telephone), 505-827-0395 (Fax), 8AM-5PM.

General Information: Records are available for a minimum of 3 years on boats and 6 years on vehicles. All motorized boats, sailboats, and jet skis must be both titled and registered if over 10 ft, and only registered if 10 ft or less. It takes 30 days before new records are available for inquiries.

Online search: Records are available, for authorized users, from the state's designated vendor New Mexico Technet. Cost is $2.50 per record plus a $.25 per minute network charge. Call (505) 345-6555 for more information.

Legislation-Current/Pending
Legislation-Passed
legis.state.nm.us

Legislative Council Service, State Capitol Bldg, Room 311, Santa Fe, NM 87501; 505-986-4600, 505-986-4350 (Bill Room (During Session Only)), 505-986-4610 (Fax).

Online search: The Internet site is a complete source of information about bills and legislators. There is also a link to some state statute sites.

Information About County Agencies

Court Structure

Magistrate Courts and the Bernalillo Metropolitan Court have jurisdiction in cases up to $5000. Probate Courts handle "informal" (uncontested) probate cases, and the District Courts handle "formal" (contested) probate cases.

About the County Courts

Online Access

Online computer access is available for 3 counties through New Mexico Technet. There is a $50.00 set up fee, a $.50 per minute connect time fee, and other fees based on type of search. The system is on 24 hours a day. Call 505-345-6555 for information.

Searching Hints

All magistrate courts and the Bernalillo Metropolitan Court have public access terminals to access civil records only. There are some "shared" courts, with one county handling cases arising in another.

About the Recorder's Office

Organization

33 counties, 33 recording offices. The recording officer is County Clerk. Most counties maintain a grantor/grantee index and a miscellaneous index. The entire state is in the MST.

Real Estate Records

Financing statements are filed at the state level, except for consumer goods, farm related and real estate related collateral, which are filed only with the County Clerk. Only a few recording offices will perform UCC searches. Use search request form UCC-11. Search and copy fees vary.

UCC Records

All federal and state tax liens are filed with the County Clerk. Most counties will not provide tax lien searches.

Other Lien Records

Most counties will not perform real estate searches. Copy and certification fees vary. Other liens are: judgment, mechanics, lis pendens, contractors, hospital.

County Courts & Recording Offices Online

Bernalillo County

Civil Cases, Criminal Cases

2nd Judicial District Court, PO Box 488, Albuquerque NM 87103, 505-841-7425 (Administration). Civil Phone: 505-841-7437. Criminal Phone: 505-841-7459. Probate Phone: 505-841-7404. Fax: 505-841-7446. Hours: 8AM-5PM (MST).

Online search: Online access available through New Mexico Technet. There is a setup fee and an access fee. Civil records go back 7 years. Search by name, case number, SSN or arrest number. Call 505-345-6555 for information.

Civil Cases, Criminal Cases

www.metrocourt.nmcjnet.org

Metropolitan Court, 401 Roma NW, Albuquerque NM 87102, 505-841-8110/841-8142. Fax: 505-841-8192. Hours: 8AM-5PM (MST).

Online search: Online access available through New Mexico Technet. Call 505-345-6555 for information. A setup fee and access fees apply.

Dona Ana County

Civil Cases, Criminal Cases

3rd Judicial District Court, 201 W Puecho, Suite A, Las Cruces NM 88005, 505-523-8200. Fax: 505-523-8290. Hours: 8AM-Noon, 1-5PM

Online search: Remote access available through New Mexico Technet. Call 505-345-6555 for information. A setup fee and access fees apply.

Liens, Real Estate

www.co.dona-ana.nm.us/newspages/assr/txparcel.html

Assessor's Office, 251 W Amador, Room 103, Las Cruces NM 87504, 505-646-7421. Fax: 647-523-7464.

Online search: Records date back to 1990. Records can be searched by name or street address or parcel number. For further information, contact Dan at 505-647-7449 or Cindy at 505-647-7426.

San Juan County

Civil Cases, Criminal Cases

11th Judicial District Court, 103 S. Oliver, Aztec NM 87410, 505-334-6151. Fax: 505-334-1940. Hours: 8AM-Noon, 1-5.

Online search: Remote access to Civil cases through New Mexico Technet. Call 505-345-6555 for information. There is a setup fee and access fees apply. Required to search: name, years to search; also helpful-address. Cases indexed by defendant, plaintiff.

Santa Fe County

Liens, Real Estate

County Clerk, 102 Grant Ave, Santa Fe NM 87504, 505-986-6280. Fax: 505-995-2767.

Online search: The monthly fee is $20, plus $5.00 per hour. The system operates 24 hours daily and supports baud rates up to 9,600. The records date back to 1990. One may search by name, Grantee/Grantor, book and page and document number. Lending agency information is available. For further information, contact, Mary Quintana at 505-995-2782.

Federal Courts Online

US District Court
District of New Mexico

www.nmcourt.fed.us

PACER sign-up number is 800-676-6856. Both civil and criminal case records are available online.

Albuquerque Division, PO Box 689, Albuquerque, NM 87103, 505-248-8052, Record Room: 505-248-8045, Civil Docket Section: 505-248-8128, Criminal Docket Section: 505-248-8128, Fax: 505-248-8124.

Las Cruces Division, 200 E Griggs, Room C-242, Las Cruces, NM 88001, 505-527-6800, Fax: 505-527-6817

Santa Fe Division, PO Box 2384, Santa Fe, NM 87504-2384, 505-988-6481, Fax: 505-988-6473

US Bankruptcy Court
District of New Mexico

This Bankruptcy Court services all counties in New Mexico.

Albuquerque Division, PO Box 546, Albuquerque, NM 87103, 505-248-6500, Fax: 505-248-6540

www.nmcourt.fed.us

PACER sign-up number is 800-676-6856.

New York

Governor's Office

Executive Chamber   518-474-8390
State Capitol   Fax 518-474-8390
Albany, NY 12224
www.state.ny.us/governor

Attorney General's Office

State Capitol   518-474-7330
Albany, NY 12224   Fax 518-474-0714
www.oag.state.ny.us

State Archives

State Archives &
Records Administration   518-474-8955
Empire State Plaza   Fax 518-473-9985
Cultural Education Center
Room 11D40   9AM-5PM
Albany, NY 12230
www.nysed.gov

Capital:	Albany
	Albany County
Time Zone:	EST
Number of Counties:	62
Population:	18,137,226
Web Site:	www.state.ny.us

State Court Administrator-NYC

NY State Office of
Court Administration   212-428-2100
New York City Office   Fax 212-428-2190
270 Broadway, Room 1400   9AM-5PM
New York, NY 10007
www.ucs.ljx.com

State Agencies Online

Corporation Records
Limited Partnership Records
Limited Liability Company Records
Limited Liability Partnerships

www.dos.state.ny.us

Division of Corporations, Department of State, 41 State St, Albany, NY 12231; 518-473-2492 (General Information), 900-835-2677 (Corporate Searches), 8AM-4:30PM.

Online search: While there is no direct online access, requests are accepted via e-mail at

info@dos.state.ny.us.

Driver Records

www.nydmv.state.ny.us

Department of Motor Vehicles, MV-15 Processing, 6 Empire State Plaza, Room 430, Albany, NY 12228; 518-474-0642, 518-473-5595 (Alternate Telephone), 8AM-5PM.

General Information: Records are available for 3 years in addition to the current year for moving violations, 10 years for DWIs, and indefinitely for open (4 years for closed) suspensions. Most non-moving violations are not shown on record. New York restricts personal information on the access of driving records for casual requesters.

Online search: Online access costs $4.00 per record. NY has implemented a "Dial-In Inquiry" system which enables customers to obtain data online 24 hours a day. The DL# or name, DOB and sex are required to retrieve. If the DOB and sex are not entered, the system defaults to a limited group of 5 records. These may be expanded for an additional fee. Billing is pre-paid. The agency also offers a batch inquiry method for higher volume requesters with about a 6 hour turnaround time. For more information, call (518) 474-4293.

Vehicle Ownership
Vehicle Identification
Boat & Vessel Ownership
Boat & Vessel Registration
www.nydmv.state.ny.us/index.htm

Department of Motor Vehicles, MV-15 Processing, 6 Empire State Plaza, Room 430, Albany, NY 12228, Albany, NY 12228-0430; 518-474-0710, 518-474-8510 (Alternate Telephone), 8AM-5PM.

General Information: Records are available for a minimum of 4 years on computer. All motorized vessels must be registered; titles are not issued. Generally, vehicle and ownership information is available. However, accessed is restricted in adherence to the Drivers' Privacy Protection Act and casual requesters cannot obtain records.

Online search: New York offers plate, VIN and ownership data through the same online network discussed in the Driving Record Section. The system is interactive and open 24 hours a day, with the exception of 10 hours on Sunday. The fee is $4.00 per record. Call 518-474-4293 for more information.

Legislation-Current/Pending
Legislation-Passed
www.senate.state.ny.us

NY Senate Document Room, State Capitol, Room 317, State and Washington Sts, Albany, NY 12247; 518-455-7545 (Bill Status Only), 518-455-2312 (Senate Document Room), 518-455-3216 (Calls Without Bill Numbers), 518-455-5164 (Assembly Document Room), 9AM - 5PM.

Online search: Both the New York Senate (senate.state.ny.us) and the Assembly (assembly.state.ny.us) have web sites to search for a bill or specific bill text. A much more complete system is the LRS online system. This offers complete state statutes, agency rules and regulations, bill text, bill status, summaries and more. For more information, call Barbara Lett at 800-356-6566.

Information About County Agencies

Court Structure

"Supreme" Courts are the highest trial courts in the state, equivalent to Circuit or District Courts in other states; they are not appeals courts. Many New York City courts are indexed by plaintiff only.

Records for Supreme and County Courts are maintained by County Clerks. In most counties, the address for the clerk is the same as for the court.

About the County Courts

Online Access

Civil case information from the 13 largest counties is available through DataCase, a database index of civil case information publicly available at terminals located at Supreme and County courts. In addition to the civil case index, DataCase also includes judgment docket and lien information, New York County Clerk system data, and the New York State attorney registration file. Remote access is also available at a fee of $1.00 per minute. Call 800-494-8981 for more remote access information.

Searching Hints

The New York State Office of Court Administration (address below) will perform an electronic search for criminal history information from a database of criminal case records from the boroughs and counties of Bronx, Dutchess, Erie, Kings, Nassau, New York, Orange, Putnam, Queens, Richmond, Rockland, Suffolk and Westchester. A separate form, illustrated with instructions on the next eight pages, is required for each county to be searched. The request must include complete name and date of birth, and, for mail requests, be accompanied by two (2) self addressed stamped return envelopes. The fee, payable by check, is $16.00 per name per county. Mail and in person requests go to

Office of Court Administration
Criminal History Search
25 Beaver St, 8th Floor
New York, NY 10004
212-428-2810

Supreme and County Court records are generally maintained in the County Clerk's Office, which outside of New York City may index civil cases by defendant, whereas the court itself maintains only a plaintiff index.

Fees for Supreme and County Courts are generally as follows: $5.00 per 2 year search per name for a manual search, and $16.00 per name for a computer or OCA search; $.50 per page (minimum $1.00) for copies; and $4.00 for certification. City Courts charge $5.00 for certification. Effective 4-1-95, no New York court will accept credit cards for any transaction.

About the Recorder's Office

Organization

62 counties, 62 recording offices. The recording officers are County Clerk (New York City Register in the counties of Bronx, Kings, New York, and Queens). The entire state is in the Eastern Time Zone (EST).

Real Estate Records

Some counties will perform real estate searches. Certified copy fees are usually $1.00 per page with a $4.00 minimum. Tax records are located at the Treasurer's Office.

UCC Records

This is a dual filing state. Financing statements are filed both at the state level and with the County Clerk, except for consumer goods, cooperatives (as in cooperative apartments), farm related and real estate related collateral, which are filed only with the County Clerk. All counties will perform UCC searches. Use search request form UCC-11. Search fees are usually $7.00 per debtor name using the approved UCC-11 request form and sometimes $12.00 using a non-New York form. Copies usually cost $1.50 per page.

Other Lien Records

Federal tax liens on personal property of businesses are filed with the Secretary of State. Other federal tax liens are filed with the County Clerk. State tax liens are filed with the County Clerk, with a master list—called state tax warrants—available at the Secretary of State's office. Federal tax liens are usually indexed with UCC Records. State tax liens are usually indexed with other miscellaneous liens and judgments. Some counties include federal tax liens as part of a UCC search, and others will search tax liens for a separate fee. Search fees and copy fees vary. Other liens are: judgment, mechanics, welfare, hospital, matrimonial, wage assignment, lis pendens.

County Courts & Recording Offices Online

Bronx County

Liens, Real Estate, Tax Assessor Records

City Register, 1932 Arthur Av, Bronx, NY 10457, 718-579-6828. Fax: 718-579-6832.

Online search: This service supports the Boroughs of Brooklyn, Queens, Staten Island, Bronx and Manhatten. There is a $250 monthly fee and a fee of $5.00 per transaction. Records are kept for 2-5 years. The system operates from 9AM-5PM M-F. One may search by name, Grantee/Grantor and address. For information, contact Richard Reskin at 718-935-6523.

Kings County

Liens, Real Estate, Tax Assessor Records

City Register, 210 Joralemon St, Municipal Bldg, Brooklyn, NY 11201, 718-802-3590. Fax: 718-802-3745.

Online search: This service supports the Boroughs of Brooklyn, Queens, Staten Island, Bronx and Manhatten. There is a $250 monthly fee and a fee of $5.00 per transaction. Records are kept for 2-5 years. The system operates from 9AM-5PM M-F. One may search by name, Grantee/Grantor and address. For information, contact Richard Reskin at 718-935-6523.

Monroe County

Civil, Criminal

Supreme and County Court, 39 W Main St, Rochester NY 14614, 716-428-5151. Fax: 716-428-5447. Hours: 9AM-5PM

Online search: The online system is open 7am to 7pm daily. No special software is need. Access is $50 per hour. Fax back is available for $.50 per page. Plans are underway to place viewable images on the Internet sometime in late 1999. Call Tom Fiorilli for information.

New York County

Liens, Real Estate, Tax Assessor Records

City Register, 31 Chambers St, Room 202, New York, NY 10007, 212-788-8529, 212-788-8521 Fax.

Online search: This service supports the Boroughs of Brooklyn, Queens, Staten Island, Bronx and Manhatten. There is a $250 monthly fee and a fee of $5.00 per transaction. Records are kept for 2-5 years. The system operates from 9AM-5PM M-F. One may search by name, Grantee/Grantor and address. For information, contact Richard Reskin at 718-935-6523.

Queens County

Liens, Real Estate, Tax Assessor Records

City Register, 90-27 Sutphin Boulevard, Jamaica, NY 11435, 718-298-7000.

Online search: This service supports the Boroughs of Brooklyn, Queens, Staten Island, Bronx and Manhatten. There is a $250 monthly fee and a fee of $5.00 per transaction. Records are kept for 2-5 years. The system operates from 9AM-5PM M-F. One may search by name, Grantee/Grantor and address. For information, contact Richard Reskin at 718-935-6523.

Rockland County

Felony, Civil, Liens, Real Estate

Supreme and County Court, 27 New Hempstead Rd, New City NY 10956, 914-638-5070. Fax: 914-638-5647. Hours: 7AM-6PM (EST).

Online search: Online system includes criminal index since 1982 plus civil judgments, real estate records and tax warrants. Online access is available 24 hours daily. Setup is $250, which includes software, and there is a minimum of $150 per month for access. Case file pages can be ordered and faxed back. The system includes criminal index since 1982 plus civil judgments, real estate records and tax warrants. One may search by name, Grantee/Grantor, book and page and transaction number. Images are viewable from 6/96 and more are being added. Call Paul Pipearto at 914-638-5221 for more information. No retention records released.

Ulster County

Civil, Criminal

Supreme and County Court, PO Box 1800, Kingston NY 12401, 914-340-3288. Fax: 914-340-3299. Hours: 9AM-5PM.

Online search: The online system is open 24 hours daily. There is a minimum fee of $25 per month, 12 months required to signup. Search by name or case number. Call Valerie Harris for more information.

Liens, Real Estate, Divorce Records

County Clerk, 240-244 Fair St, County Office Bldg, Kingston NY 12401, 914-340-3000. Fax: 914-340-0754.

Online search: The monthly fee is $25 and you must commit to 1 year of service to sign up. The per minute usage fee is $.05. All software is included. Records date back to 1984. The system operates 24 hours daily and supports baud rates of 9,600-28.8. One may search by name and Grantee/Grantor. Lending agency information is available. For information, contact Valerie Harris at 914-340-5300.

Federal Courts Online

County-to-Court Cross Reference (Bankruptcy Court locations in Parenthesis if different)

County	District	Court
Albany	Northern	Albany
Allegany	Western	Buffalo
Bronx	Southern	New York City (New York)
Broome	Northern	Binghamton (Utica)
Cattaraugus	Western	Buffalo
Cayuga	Northern	Syracuse (Utica)
Chautauqua	Western	Buffalo
Chemung	Western	Rochester
Chenango	Northern	Binghamton (Utica)
Clinton	Northern	Albany
Columbia	Northern (Southern)	Albany (Poughkeepsie)
Cortland	Northern	Syracuse (Utica)
Delaware	Northern	Binghamton (Utica)
Dutchess	Southern	White Plains (Poughkeepsie)
Erie	Western	Buffalo
Essex	Northern	Albany
Franklin	Northern	Binghamton (Albany)
Fulton	Northern	Syracuse (Albany)
Genesee	Western	Buffalo
Greene	Northern (Southern)	Albany (Poughkeepsie)
Hamilton	Northern	Syracuse (Utica)
Herkimer	Northern	Syracuse (Utica)
Jefferson	Northern	Binghamton (Albany)
Kings	Eastern	Brooklyn
Lewis	Northern	Binghamton (Utica)
Livingston	Western	Rochester
Madison	Northern	Syracuse (Utica)
Monroe	Western	Rochester
Montgomery	Northern	Syracuse (Albany)
Nassau	Eastern	Brooklyn (Westbury)
New York	Southern	New York City (New York)
Niagara	Western	Buffalo
Oneida	Northern	Utica
Onondaga	Northern	Syracuse (Utica)
Ontario	Western	Rochester
Orange	Southern	White Plains (Poughkeepsie)
Orleans	Western	Buffalo
Oswego	Northern	Syracuse (Utica)
Otsego	Northern	Binghamton (Utica)
Putnam	Southern	White Plains (Poughkeepsie)
Queens	Eastern	Brooklyn
Rensselaer	Northern	Albany
Richmond	Eastern	Brooklyn
Rockland	Southern	White Plains
Saratoga	Northern	Albany
Schenectady	Northern	Albany
Schoharie	Northern	Albany
Schuyler	Western	Rochester
Seneca	Western	Rochester
St. Lawrence	Northern	Binghamton (Albany)
Steuben	Western	Rochester
Suffolk	Eastern	Hauppauge
Sullivan	Southern	White Plains (Poughkeepsie)
Tioga	Northern	Binghamton (Utica)
Tompkins	Northern	Syracuse (Utica)
Ulster	Northern (Southern)	Albany (Poughkeepsie)
Warren	Northern	Albany
Washington	Northern	Albany
Wayne	Western	Rochester
Westchester	Southern	White Plains
Wyoming	Western	Buffalo
Yates	Western	Rochester

US District Court
Eastern District of New York

As a member of the PACER-Net project, the District Court of the Eastern District of New York may make some documents available to the public. PACER sign-up number is 800-676-6856. Both civil and criminal case records are available online.

www.nyed.uscourts.gov/ECF/ecfnav.html

Brooklyn Division, Brooklyn Courthouse, 225 Cadman Plaza E, Room 130, Brooklyn, NY 11201, 718-260-2600, Record Room: 718-260-2285, Civil Docket Section: 718-260-2610, Criminal Docket Section: 718-260-2610

Hauppauge Division, 300 Rabro Dr, Hauppauge, NY 11788, 516-582-1100, Fax: 516-582-1417

Uniondale Division, 2 Uniondale Ave, Room 303, Uniondale, NY 11553, 516-485-6500

US Bankruptcy Court
Eastern District of New York

PACER sign-up number is 800-676-6856. **Brooklyn Division,** 75 Clinton St, Brooklyn, NY 11201, 718-330-2188.

Hauppauge Division, 601 Veterans Memorial Hwy, Hauppauge, NY 11788, 516-361-8038.

Westbury Division, 1635 Privado Rd, Westbury, NY 11590, 516-832-8801.

US District Court
Northern District of New York

www.nynd.uscourts.gov

PACER sign-up number is 800-676-6856. Both civil and criminal case records are available online.

Albany Division, 445 Broadway, Room 222, James T Foley Courthouse, Albany, NY 12207-2924, 518-431-0279

Binghamton Division, 15 Henry St, Binghamton, NY 13901, 607-773-2893, Civil Docket Section: 607-773-2638

Syracuse Division, PO Box 7367, Syracuse, NY 13261-7367, 315-448-0507

Utica Division, Alexander Pirnie Bldg, 10 Broad St, Utica, NY 13501, 315-793-8151

US Bankruptcy Court
Northern District of New York

www.nynb.uscourts.gov

PACER sign-up number is 800-676-6856.

Albany Division, James T Foley Courthouse, 445 Broadway #327, Albany, NY 12207, 518-431-0188

Utica Division, Room 230, 10 Broad St, Utica, NY 13501, 315-793-8101, Fax: 315-793-8128

US District Court
Southern District of New York

www.nysd.uscourts.gov

The PACER sign-up number is 800-676-6856. Both civil and criminal case records are available online.

New York City Division, 500 Pearl St, New York, NY 10007, 212-805-0136

White Plains Division, 300 Quarropas St, White Plains, NY 10601, 914-390-4000

US Bankruptcy Court
Southern District of New York

www.nysb.uscourts.gov

The above web site permits free record searching. The PACER sign-up number is 800-676-6856.

New York Division, Room 511, 1 Bowling Green, New York, NY 10004-1408, 212-668-2870

Poughkeepsie Division, 176 Church St, Poughkeepsie, NY 12601, 914-551-4200, Fax: 914-452-8375

White Plains Division, 300 Quarropas St, White Plains, NY 10601, 914-390-4060

US District Court
Western District of New York

PACER sign-up number is 800-676-6856. Both civil and criminal case records are available online.

Buffalo Division, Room 304, 68 Court St, Buffalo, NY 14202, 716-551-4211, Fax: 716-551-4850.

Rochester Division, Room 2120, 100 State St, Rochester, NY 14614, 716-263-6263, Fax: 716-263-3178.

US Bankruptcy Court
Western District of New York

PACER sign-up number is 800-676-6856.

Buffalo Division, 310 US Courthouse, 68 Court St, Buffalo, NY 14202, 716-551-4130.

Rochester Division, Room 1220, 100 State St, Rochester, NY 14614, 716-263-3148.

North Carolina

Governor's Office
116 W Jones St 919-733-4240
Raleigh, NC 27603-8001 Fax 919-715-3175
www.state.nc.us

Attorney General's Office
Justice Department 919-716-6400
PO Box 629 Fax 919-716-6750
Raleigh, NC 27602-0629 8AM-5PM
www.jus.state.nc.us/Justice

State Archives
Cultural Resources Dept. 919-733-3952
Archives & History Division Fax 919-733-1354
109 E Jones St 8AM-5:30PM T-F,
Raleigh, NC 27601-2807 9-5 SA
www.ah.dcr.state.nc.us

Capital:	Raleigh
	Wake County
Time Zone:	EST
Number of Counties:	100
Population:	7,425,183
Web Site:	www.state.nc.us

State Court Administrator
Admin. Office of Courts 919-733-7107
2 E Morgan St, Fax 919-715-5779
Justice Bldg, 4th Floor 8AM-5PM
Raleigh, NC 27602
www.aoc.state.nc.us

State Agencies Online

Corporation Records
Limited Partnerships
Limited Liability Company Records
Trademarks/Servicemarks
www.state.nc.us/secstate

Secretary of State, Corporations Section, 300 N Salisbury St, Raleigh, NC 27603-5909; 919-733-4201 (Corporations), 919-733-4129 (Trademarks), 919-733-1837 (Fax), 8AM-5PM.

General Information: Fictitious Names and Assumed Name records are found at the county Register of Deeds offices.

Online search: Access is available through a dial-up system. There is an initial registration fee of $185 and a charge of $.02 each time the "enter key" is pushed. To register, call Bonnie Elek at (919) 733-0418. Also, the web site offers a free limited search of status and registered agent by corporation name.

Uniform Commercial Code
Federal Tax Liens
www.secstate.state.nc.us/secstate/ucc.htm

UCC Division, Secretary of State, 300 North Salisbury St, #302, Raleigh, NC 27603-5909; 919-733-4205, 919-733-9700 (Fax), 7:30AM-5PM.

General Information: Federal tax liens on individuals and all state tax liens are filed at Superior Courts.

Online search: Dial-up access is offered. There is a one-time registration fee of $185 and a $.02 charge each time the "enter key" is pushed. The minimum baud rate is 9600. Call Bonnie at (919) 733-0418 for information.

Driver Records
www.dmv.dot.state.nc.us

Division of Motor Vehicles, Driver's License Section, 1100 New Bern Ave, Raleigh, NC 27697; 919-715-7000, 8AM-5PM.

General Information: Records are available for 5 years or more for moving violations, 10 years or more for

DWIs and suspensions. Records of surrendered licenses are kept for one year after the expiration date. Online requesters must have the license number to search. The following data is not available-medical information.

Online search: To qualify for online availability, a client must be an insurance agent or insurance company support organization. The mode is interactive and is open from 7 AM to 10 PM. The DL# and name are needed when ordering. The fee is $5.00 per record. A minimum $500 security deposit is required.

Legislation-Current/Pending
Legislation-Passed
www.ncga.state.nc.us

North Carolina General Assembly, State Legislative Bldg, 16 W. Jones Street, 1st Fl, Raleigh, NC 27603; 919-733-7779 (Bill Numbers), 919-733-3270 (Archives), 919-733-5648 (Order Desk), 8:30AM-5:30PM.

Online search: The Internet site has copies of bills, status, and state statutes.

Information About County Agencies

Court Structure

There are 100 combined superior-district courts in the state, one location per county.

Online Access

An internal online computer system links all North Carolina civil and criminal courts. There is no external access.

Searching Hints

About the County Courts

Most courts recommend that civil searches be done in person or by a retriever and that only criminal searches be requested in writing (for a $5.00 search fee). Many courts have archived their records prior to 1968 in the Raleigh State Archives, 919-733-5722.

About the Recorder's Office

Organization

100 counties, 100 recording offices. The recording officers are Register of Deeds and Clerk of Superior Court (tax liens). The entire state is in the Eastern Time Zone (EST).

Real Estate Records

Counties will not perform real estate searches. Copy fees are usually $1.00 per page. Certification usually costs $3.00 for the first page and $1.00 for each additional page of a document.

UCC Records

This is a dual filing state. Financing statements are filed both at the state level and with the Register of Deeds, except for consumer goods, farm related and real estate related collateral. All counties will perform UCC searches. Use search request form UCC-11. Search fees are usually $15.00 per debtor name. Copies usually cost $1.00 per page.

Other Lien Records

Federal tax liens on personal property of businesses are filed with the Secretary of State. Other federal and all state tax liens are filed with the county Clerk of Superior Court, not with the Register of Deeds. (Oddly, even tax liens on real property are also filed with the Clerk of Superior Court, not with the Register of Deeds.) Refer to *The Sourcebook of County Court Records* for information about North Carolina Superior Courts. Other liens are: judgment, mechanics (all at Clerk of Superior Court).

County Courts & Recording Offices Online

There is no online access to court records.

No remote online access is available from real estate recorder's offices in North Carolina.

Federal Courts Online

County-to-Court Cross Reference (Bankruptcy Court locations in Parenthesis if different)

Alamance	Middle	Greensboro
Alexander	Western	Statesville (Charlotte)
Alleghany	Western	Statesville (Charlotte)
Anson	Western	Charlotte
Ashe	Western	Statesville (Charlotte)
Avery	Western	Asheville (Charlotte)
Beaufort	Eastern	Greenville-Eastern (Wilson)
Bertie	Eastern	Elizabeth City (Wilson)
Bladen	Eastern	Wilmington (Wilson)
Brunswick	Eastern	Wilmington (Wilson)
Buncombe	Western	Asheville (Charlotte)
Burke	Western	Shelby (Charlotte)
Cabarrus	Middle	Greensboro
Caldwell	Western	Statesville (Charlotte)
Camden	Eastern	Elizabeth City (Wilson)
Carteret	Eastern	Greenville-Eastern (Wilson)
Caswell	Middle	Greensboro
Catawba	Western	Statesville (Charlotte)
Chatham	Middle	Greensboro
Cherokee	Western	Bryson City (Charlotte)
Chowan	Eastern	Elizabeth City (Wilson)
Clay	Western	Bryson City (Charlotte)
Cleveland	Western	Shelby (Charlotte)
Columbus	Eastern	Wilmington (Wilson)
Craven	Eastern	Greenville-Eastern (Wilson)
Cumberland	Eastern	Greenville-Eastern (Wilson)
Currituck	Eastern	Elizabeth City (Wilson)
Dare	Eastern	Elizabeth City (Wilson)
Davidson	Middle	Greensboro (Winston-Salem)
Davie	Middle	Greensboro
Duplin	Eastern	Wilmington (Wilson)
Durham	Middle	Greensboro
Edgecombe	Eastern	Raleigh (Wilson)
Forsyth	Middle	Greensboro (Winston-Salem)
Franklin	Eastern	Raleigh
Gaston	Western	Charlotte
Gates	Eastern	Elizabeth City (Wilson)
Graham	Western	Bryson City (Charlotte)
Granville	Eastern	Raleigh
Greene	Eastern	Greenville-Eastern (Wilson)
Guilford	Middle	Greensboro
Halifax	Eastern	Greenville-Eastern (Wilson)
Harnett	Eastern	Raleigh
Haywood	Western	Asheville (Charlotte)
Henderson	Western	Asheville (Charlotte)
Hertford	Eastern	Elizabeth City (Wilson)
Hoke	Middle	Greensboro
Hyde	Eastern	Greenville-Eastern (Wilson)
Iredell	Western	Statesville (Charlotte)
Jackson	Western	Bryson City (Charlotte)
Johnston	Eastern	Raleigh
Jones	Eastern	Greenville-Eastern (Wilson)
Lee	Middle	Greensboro
Lenoir	Eastern	Greenville-Eastern (Wilson)
Lincoln	Western	Statesville (Charlotte)
Macon	Western	Bryson City (Charlotte)
Madison	Western	Asheville (Charlotte)
Martin	Eastern	Greenville-Eastern (Wilson)
McDowell	Western	Shelby (Charlotte)
Mecklenburg	Western	Charlotte
Mitchell	Western	Asheville (Charlotte)
Montgomery	Middle	Greensboro
Moore	Middle	Greensboro
Nash	Eastern	Raleigh (Wilson)
New Hanover	Eastern	Wilmington (Wilson)
Northampton	Eastern	Elizabeth City (Wilson)
Onslow	Eastern	Wilmington (Wilson)
Orange	Middle	Greensboro
Pamlico	Eastern	Greenville-Eastern (Wilson)
Pasquotank	Eastern	Elizabeth City (Wilson)

Pender .... Eastern .... Wilmington (Wilson)
Perquimans .... Eastern .... Elizabeth City (Wilson)
Person .... Middle .... Greensboro
Pitt .... Eastern .... Greenville-Eastern (Wilson)
Polk .... Western .... Shelby (Charlotte)
Randolph .... Middle .... Greensboro
Richmond .... Middle .... Greensboro
Robeson .... Eastern .... Wilmington (Wilson)
Rockingham ..... Middle .... Greensboro
Rowan .... Middle .... Greensboro
Rutherford .... Western .... Shelby (Charlotte)
Sampson .... Eastern .... Wilmington (Wilson)
Scotland .... Middle .... Greensboro
Stanly .... Middle .... Greensboro
Stokes .... Middle .... Greensboro (Winston-Salem)

Surry .... Middle .... Greensboro (Winston-Salem)
Swain .... Western .... Bryson City (Charlotte)
Transylvania ..... Western .... Asheville (Charlotte)
Tyrrell .... Eastern .... Elizabeth City (Wilson)
Union .... Western .... Charlotte
Vance .... Eastern .... Raleigh
Wake .... Eastern .... Raleigh
Warren .... Eastern .... Raleigh
Washington ..... Eastern .... Elizabeth City (Wilson)
Watauga .... Western .... Statesville (Charlotte)
Wayne .... Eastern .... Raleigh (Wilson)
Wilkes .... Western .... Statesville (Charlotte)
Wilson .... Eastern .... Raleigh (Wilson)
Yadkin .... Middle .... Greensboro (Winston-Salem)
Yancey .... Western .... Asheville (Charlotte)

US District Court
Eastern District of North Carolina

PACER sign-up number is 800-676-6856. Both civil and criminal case records are available online.

Greenville-Eastern Division, Room 209, 201 S Evans St, Greenville, NC 27858-1137, 919-830-6009, Criminal Docket Section: 919-856-4370, Fax: 919-830-2793.

Raleigh Division, Clerk's Office, PO Box 25670, Raleigh, NC 27611, 919-856-4370, Civil Docket Section: 919-856-4422, Fax: 919-856-4160.

Elizabeth City Division, c/o Raleigh Division, PO Box 25670, Raleigh, NC 27611, 919-856-4370.

Wilmington Division, PO Box 338, Wilmington, NC 28402, 910-815-4663, Fax: 910-815-4518.

US Bankruptcy Court
Eastern District of North Carolina

www.nceb.uscourts.gov

PACER sign-up number is 800-676-6856.

Raleigh Division, PO Box 1441, Raleigh, NC 27602, 919-856-4752

Wilson Division, PO Drawer 2807, Wilson, NC 27894-2807, 919-237-0248

US District Court
Middle District of North Carolina

www.ncmd.uscourts.gov

PACER sign-up number is 800-676-6856. Both civil and criminal case records are available online.

Greensboro Division, Clerk's Office, PO Box 2708, Greensboro, NC 27402, 336-332-6000, Civil Docket Section: 336-332-6030, Criminal Docket Section: 336-332-6020

US Bankruptcy Court
Middle District of North Carolina

www.ncmb.uscourts.gov

PACER sign-up number is 800-676-6856.

Greensboro Division, PO Box 26100, Greensboro, NC 27420-6100, 336-333-5647

Winston-Salem Division, 226 S Liberty St, Winston-Salem, NC 27101, 910-631-5340

US District Court
Western District of North Carolina

PACER sign-up number is 800-676-6856.

Asheville Division, Clerk of the Court, Room 309, US Courthouse Bldg, 100 Otis St, Asheville, NC 28801-2611, 704-271-4648, Fax: 704-271-4343.

Bryson City Division, c/o Asheville Division, Clerk of the Court, Room 309, US Courthouse, 100 Otis St, Asheville, NC 28801-2611, 704-271-4648.

Shelby Division, c/o Asheville Division, Clerk of the Court, Room 309, US Courthouse, 100 Otis St, Asheville, NC 28801-2611, 704-271-4648.

Charlotte Division, Clerk, Room 210, 401 W Trade St, Charlotte, NC 28202, 704-350-7400.

Statesville Division, PO Box 466, Statesville, NC 28687, 704-873-7112, Fax: 704-873-0903.

US Bankruptcy Court
Western District of North Carolina

Charlotte Division, 401 W Trade St, Charlotte, NC 28202, 704-350-7500

www.ncbankruptcy.org

PACER sign-up number is 800-676-6856.

North Dakota

Governor's Office
State Capitol
600 E Boulevard Ave, 1st Fl
Bismarck, ND 58505-0001
www.ehs.health.state.nd.us/gov

701-328-2200
Fax 701-328-2205
8AM-5PM

Attorney General's Office
State Capitol - 1st Floor
600 E Boulevard Ave
Bismarck, ND 58505-0040
www.state.nd.us/ndag

701-328-2210
Fax 701-328-2226
8AM-5PM

State Archives
Historical Society
State Archives
& Historical Research Library
612 E Boulevard Ave
Bismarck, ND 58505-0830
www.state.nd.us/hist

701-328-2666
Fax 701-328-3710
8AM-5PM

Capital:	Bismark
	Burleigh County
Time Zone:	CST
Number of Counties:	53
Population:	640,883
Web Site:	www.state.nd.us

State Court Administrator
Court Administrator
North Dakota Supreme Court
1st Floor Judicial Wing,
600 E Blvd
Bismarck, ND 58505-0530

701-328-4216
Fax 701-328-4480

8AM-5PM

State Agencies Online

Legislation-Current/Pending
Legislation-Passed
www.state.nd.us/lr

North Dakota Legislative Council, State Capitol, 600 E Boulevard Ave, Bismarck, ND 58505; 701-328-2916, 701-328-2900 (Secretary of State), 701-328-2992 (Sec of State fax), 8AM-5PM.

Online search: Their Internet site offers an extensive array of legislative information at no charge

Driver Records
Department of Transportation, Driver License & Traffic Safety Division, 608 E Boulevard Ave, Bismarck, ND 58505-0700; 701-328-2603, 701-328-2435 (Fax).

General Information: Records are available for 3 years for moving violations, DWI and suspensions. Records available to the public will show neither violations less than 2 points nor accidents. The record will not show the driver's address. The Division sends an additional copy of the abstract to the driver whose record was requested,

accompanied by a statement identifying the requester. There is an opt-out provision and casual requesters do not receive personal info on opt-outs.

Online search: The system is interactive and is open 24 hours daily. Records are $3.00 each. For more information, call 701-328-4790.

Uniform Commercial Code
Federal Tax Liens
State Tax Liens
www.state.nd.us/sec

UCC Division, Secretary of State, 600 E Boulevard Ave, 1st Fl, Bismarck, ND 58505-0500; 701-328-3662, 701-328-4214 (Fax), 8AM-5PM.

General Information: The state has a Central Indexing System which allows UCC and tax lien searches at this office or at any of the county Register of Deeds (53).

Online search: Sign-up for access to the Central Indexing System includes an annual $125 fee and a one-time $50.00 subscription fee. The $7. search fee applies.

Information About County Agencies

Court Structure

In 1995, the County Courts were merged with the District Courts across the entire state. County Court records are maintained by the District Courts and may be requested from them. We recommend stating "include County Court cases" in search requests.

Online Access

A statewide computer system for internal purposes is in operation in most counties, with the main exception of Cass (Fargo), which has its own system. The Cass system will be converted to the statewide system by the end of 1999. No decision has been made whether to allow remote public access.

**About the
County Courts**

Searching Hints

In Summer, 1997, the standard search fee in District Courts increased to $10.00 per name, and the certification fee increased to $10.00 per document. Copy fees remain at $.50 per page.

About the Recorder's Office

Organization

53 counties, 53 recording offices. The recording officer is Register of Deeds. The entire state is in the Central Time Zone

Real Estate Records

Some counties will perform real estate searches by name or by legal description. Copy fees are usually $1.00 per page. Certified copies usually cost $5.00 for the first page and $2.00 for each additional page. Copies may be faxed.

UCC Records

Financing statements may be filed either at the state level or with any Register of Deeds, except for real estate related collateral, which are filed only with the Register of Deeds. All counties access a statewide computer database of filings and will perform UCC searches. Use search request form UCC-11. Various search options are available, including by federal tax identification number or Social Security number The search with copies costs $7.00 per debtor name, including three pages of copies and $1.00 per additional page. Copies may be faxed for an additional fee of $3.00.

Other Lien Records

Federal tax liens on personal property of businesses are filed with the Secretary of State. Other federal and all state tax liens are filed with the county Register of Deeds. All counties will perform tax lien searches. Some counties automatically include business federal tax liens as part of a UCC search because they appear on the statewide database. (Be careful—federal tax liens on individuals may only be in the county lien books, not on the statewide system.) Separate searches are usually available at $5.00-7.00 per name. Copy fees vary. Copies may be faxed. Other liens are: mechanics, judgment, hospital, repair, egg cutter.

County Courts & Recording Offices Online

There is no online access to court records in North Dakota.

No remote online access is available from real estate recorder's offices in North Dakota.

Federal Courts Online

County-to-Court Cross Reference (Bankruptcy Court locations in Parenthesis if different)

Adams	Bismarck-Southwestern (Fargo)
Barnes	Fargo-Southeastern (Fargo)
Benson	Grand Forks-Northeastern (Fargo)
Billings	Bismarck-Southwestern (Fargo)
Bottineau	Minot-Northwestern (Fargo)
Bowman	Bismarck-Southwestern (Fargo)
Burke	Minot-Northwestern (Fargo)
Burleigh	Bismarck-Southwestern (Fargo)
Cass	Fargo-Southeastern (Fargo)
Cavalier	Grand Forks-Northeastern (Fargo)
Dickey	Fargo-Southeastern (Fargo)
Divide	Minot-Northwestern (Fargo)
Dunn	Bismarck-Southwestern (Fargo)
Eddy	Fargo-Southeastern (Fargo)
Emmons	Bismarck-Southwestern (Fargo)
Foster	Fargo-Southeastern (Fargo)
Golden Valley	Bismarck-Southwestern (Fargo)
Grand Forks	Grand Forks-Northeastern (Fargo)
Grant	Bismarck-Southwestern (Fargo)
Griggs	Fargo-Southeastern (Fargo)
Hettinger	Bismarck-Southwestern (Fargo)
Kidder	Bismarck-Southwestern (Fargo)
La Moure	Fargo-Southeastern (Fargo)
Logan	Bismarck-Southwestern (Fargo)
McHenry	Minot-Northwestern (Fargo)
McIntosh	Bismarck-Southwestern (Fargo)
McKenzie	Minot-Northwestern (Fargo)
McLean	Bismarck-Southwestern (Fargo)
Mercer	Bismarck-Southwestern (Fargo)
Morton	Bismarck-Southwestern (Fargo)
Mountrail	Minot-Northwestern (Fargo)
Nelson	Grand Forks-Northeastern (Fargo)
Oliver	Bismarck-Southwestern (Fargo)
Pembina	Grand Forks-Northeastern (Fargo)
Pierce	Minot-Northwestern (Fargo)
Ramsey	Grand Forks-Northeastern (Fargo)
Ransom	Fargo-Southeastern (Fargo)
Renville	Minot-Northwestern (Fargo)
Richland	Fargo-Southeastern (Fargo)
Rolette	Minot-Northwestern (Fargo)
Sargent	Fargo-Southeastern (Fargo)
Sheridan	Minot-Northwestern (Fargo)
Sioux	Bismarck-Southwestern (Fargo)
Slope	Bismarck-Southwestern (Fargo)
Stark	Bismarck-Southwestern (Fargo)
Steele	Fargo-Southeastern (Fargo)
Stutsman	Fargo-Southeastern (Fargo)
Towner	Grand Forks-Northeastern (Fargo)
Traill	Grand Forks-Northeastern (Fargo)
Walsh	Grand Forks-Northeastern (Fargo)
Ward	Minot-Northwestern (Fargo)
Wells	Minot-Northwestern (Fargo)
Williams	Minot-Northwestern (Fargo)

US District Court
District of North Dakota

PACER sign-up number is 800-676-6856. Both civil and criminal case records are available online.

Bismarck-Southwestern Division, PO Box 1193, Bismarck, ND 58502, 701-250-4295, Fax: 701-250-4259.

PACER sign-up number is 800-676-6856. Both civil and criminal case records are available online.

Minot-Northwestern Division, c/o Bismarck Division, PO Box 1193, Bismarck, ND 58502, 701-250-4295, Fax: 701-250-4259.

Fargo-Southeastern Division, PO Box 870, Fargo, ND 58107, 701-239-5377, Fax: 701-239-5270.

Grand Forks-Northeastern Division, c/o Fargo-Southeastern Division, PO Box 870, Fargo, ND 58107, 701-239-5377, Fax: 701-239-5270.

US Bankruptcy Court
District of North Dakota

Fargo Division, PO Box 1110, Fargo, ND 58107, 701-239-5129.

PACER sign-up number is 800-676-6856.

Governor's Office

77 S High St, 30th Floor,   614-466-3555
Vern Riffe Center   Fax 614-466-9354
Columbus, OH 43215
www.state.oh.us/gov

Attorney General's Office

State office Tower   614-466-4320
30 E Broad St, 17th Floor   Fax 614-644-6135
Columbus, OH 43215-3428   8AM-5PM
www.ag.ohio.gov

Capital:	Columbus
	Franklin County
Time Zone:	EST
Number of Counties:	88
Population:	11,186,331
Web Site:	www.state.oh.us

State Archives

Historical Society   614-297-2300
Archives/Library   Fax 614-297-2546
1982 Velma Ave   9AM-5PM Th-SA
Columbus, OH 43211-2497
winslo.ohio.gov/ohswww/ohshome.html

State Court Administrator

Administrative Director   614-466-2653
Supreme Court of Ohio   Fax 614-752-8736
30 E Broad St, 3rd Floor   8AM-4:30PM
Columbus, OH 43266-0419
www.sconet.state.oh.us

State Agencies Online

Legislation-Current/Pending
Legislation-Passed

www.legislature.state.oh.us

Ohio House of Representatives, 77 S High Street, Columbus, OH 43266; (Courier: Ohio Senate, State House, Columbus, OH 43215); 614-466-8842 (In-State Only), 614-466-9745 (Out-of-State), 8:30AM-5PM.

Online search: The Internet site offers access to bill text, status, and enactment.

Driver Records

www.ohio.gov/odps

Department of Public Safety, Bureau of Motor Vehicles, 1970 W Broad St, Columbus, OH 43223-1102; 614-752-7600, 8AM-5:30PM M-T-W; 8AM-4:30PM Th-F.

General Information: Records are available for 5 years for moving violations, DWIs and suspensions. SSNs are not released unless provided by requester (except government agency requesters). Driver's address is included as part of the search report for permissible requesters, except for requests received from California.

Online search: The system is called "Defender System" and is suggested for requesters who order 100 or more motor vehicle reports per day in batch mode. Turnaround is in 4-8 hours. The DL# or SSN and name are needed when ordering. The fee is $2.00 per record. For more information, call (614) 752-7692.

Vehicle Ownership
Vehicle Identification

www.state.oh.us/odps/division/bmv/bmv/html

Bureau of Motor Vehicles, Motor Vehicle Title Records, 1970 W Broad St, Columbus, OH 43223-1102; 614-752-7671, 614-752-8929 (Fax), 8AM-5:30PM M-T-W; 8AM-4:30PM Th-F.

General Information: Records are available for the current year plus four. Lien information is not recorded on vehicle registration records in Ohio.

Online search: Ohio offers online access through AAMVAnet. All requesters must comply with a contractual agreement prior to release of data. The fee is $2.00 per record. Call (614) 752-7692 for information.

Information About County Agencies

Court Structure

Effective July 1, 1997, the dollar limits for civil cases in County and Municipal Courts were raised as follows: County Court—from $3,000 to $15,000; Municipal Court—from $10,000 to $15,000. In addition the small claims limit was raised from $2,000 to $3,000.

About the County Courts

Online Access

There is no statewide computer system, but a number of counties offer online access.

About the Recorder's Office

Organization

88 counties, 88 recording offices. The recording officer is County Recorder and Clerk of Common Pleas Court (state tax liens). The entire state is in the Eastern Time Zone (EST).

Real Estate Records

Counties will not perform real estate searches. Copy fees are usually $1.00 per page. Certification usually costs $50 per document. Tax records are located at the Auditor's Office.

UCC Records

This is a dual filing state. Financing statements are filed both at the state level and with the County Recorder, except for consumer goods, farm related and real estate related collateral, which are filed only with the County Recorder. All counties will perform UCC searches. Use search request form UCC-11. Search fees are usually $9.00 per debtor name. Copies usually cost $1.00 per page.

Other Lien Records

All federal tax liens are filed with the County Recorder. All state tax liens are filed with the Clerk of Common Pleas Court. Refer to *The Sourcebook of County Court Records* by BRB Publications Inc (1-800-929-3811) for information about Ohio courts. Federal tax liens are filed in the "Official Records" of each county. Most counties will not perform a federal tax lien search. Other liens are: mechanics, workers' comp, judgment.

County Courts & Recording Offices Online

Butler County

Civil Cases, Criminal Cases

Common Pleas Court, 130 High St, Hamilton OH 45011, 513-887-3996. Probate Phone: 513-887-3296. Fax: 513-887-3089. Hours: 8:30AM-4:30PM (EST).

Online search: Contact Vicki Robertson at 513-887-3280 for information about remote access. Free access number is 513-887-5689 24 hours per day using up to 28.8 modem with VT100 emulation software.

Hamilton County

Civil Cases, Criminal Cases

www.courtclerk.org/case.htm

Common Pleas Court, 1000 Main St, Room 315, Cincinnati OH 45202, 513-632-8283. Civil Phone: 513-632-8247. Criminal Phone: 513-632-8245. Probate Phone: 513-632-8277. Fax: 513-763-4860.

Online search: Access is free from the Internet site. Civil index goes back to 1991. Criminal index goes back to 1986. Municipal civil case information is also included.

Liens, Real Estate

www.hcro.org

County Recorder, 138 E Court St, Room 205, Cincinnati OH 45202, 513-946-4600. Fax: 513-946-4577. Hours: 8AM-4PM (EST).

Online search: An escrow account of $100 is required. It costs $1.00 to connect to the system and $.30 per minute. The system operates 6:30AM-10:30PM daily and supports baud rates up to 9,600. Records date back to 6/88. One may search by name, document number and book and page. Lending agency information is available. The fax back service fee is $2.00 per page. For info, call Vicky Jones at 513-946-4571.

Lawrence County

Liens, Real Estate

County Recorder, S 4th St, Courthouse, Ironton, OH 45638, 740-533-4314,-Fax: 740-533-4411.

Online search: The set up fee is $600-700, plus a monthly fee of $150. The system operates 24 hours daily and supports baud rates up to 28.8. Mortgage records date back to 1988 and deeds back to 1986. One may search by name and Grantee/Grantor. Only Federal tax liens are online; state liens are kept with the Clerk of the Court. UCC liens date back to 1989. Lending agency information is available. For further info, contact Kim Estep or Sue Deeds at 740-533-4314.

Lorain County

Liens, Real Estate

County Recorder, 226 Middle Avenue, Elyria, OH 44035, 440-329-5148,-Fax: 440-329-5199.

Online search: There is no set up fee and you are given 2 free months. Monthly charges are $10 for 2 hours, then one is billed $.10 per minute. The system operates 24 hours daily and supports baud rates up to 14.4. Records date back to 5/92. One may search by name, Grantee/Grantor and document number. Lending agency information is available. For further information, contact Rich Barrett at 440-329-5413.

Medina County

Civil Cases, Criminal Cases

Medina Municipal Court, 135 N Elmwood, Medina OH 44256, 330-723-3287. Fax: 330-225-1108.

Online search: Online access requires Procomm Plus. The system is open 24 hours daily. There are no fees. Search by either name or case number. The computer access number is 330-723-4337. For more info, call Judy Schwartz at ext. 227.

Wood County

Civil Cases, Criminal Cases

Perrysburg Municipal Court, 300 Walnut, Perrysburg OH 43551, 419-872-7900. Fax: 419-872-7905. Hours: 8AM-4:30PM (EST).

Online search: Contact Judy Daquano at 419-872-7906 for information about remote access. Access is free using up to 14.4 modem speed. Civil and criminal indexes go back to 1988. The system is open 24 hours daily.

Federal Courts Online

US District Court
Northern District of Ohio

www.ohnd.uscourts.gov

The above mentioned is a free access web site.

PACER sign-up number for the following courts is 800-676-6856. Both civil and criminal case records are available online.

Akron Division, 568 Federal Bldg, 2 S Main St, Akron, OH 44308, 330-375-5407

Cleveland Division, 201 Superior Ave, NE, Cleveland, OH 44114, 216-522-4355, Fax: 216-522-2140

Toledo Division, 114 US Courthouse, 1716 Spielbusch, Toledo, OH 43624, 419-259-6412

Youngstown Division, 337 Federal Bldg, 125 Market St, Youngstown, OH 44503, 330-746-1726, Fax: 330-746-2027

US Bankruptcy Court
Northern District of Ohio

www.ohnb.uscourts.gov

PACER sign-up number for the following courts is 800-676-6856.

Akron Division, 455 Federal Bldg, 2 S Main, Akron, OH 44308, 330-375-5840

Canton Division, Frank T Bow Federal Bldg, 201 Cleveland Ave SW, Canton, OH 44702, 330-489-4426, Fax: 330-489-4434

Cleveland Division, Key Tower, 31st Floor, 127 Public Square, Cleveland, OH 44114, 216-522-4373

Toledo Division, Room 411, 1716 Spielbusch Ave, Toledo, OH 43624, 419-259-6440

Youngstown Division, PO Box 147, Youngstown, OH 44501, 330-746-7027

US District Court
Southern District of Ohio

PACER sign-up number for the following courts is 800-676-6856. Both civil and criminal case records are available online.

Cincinnati Division, Clerk, US District Court, 324 Courthouse Bldg, 100 E 5th St, Cincinnati, OH 45202, 513-564-7500, Fax: 513-564-7505.

Columbus Division, Office of the Clerk, Room 260, 85 Marconi Blvd, Columbus, OH 43215, 614-719-3000, Fax: 614-469-5953.

Dayton Division, Federal Bldg, 200 W 2nd, Room 712, Dayton, OH 45402, 513-512-1400.

US Bankruptcy Court
Southern District of Ohio

PACER sign-up number for the following courts is 800-676-6856.

Cincinnati Division, Atrium Two, Suite 800, 221 E Fourth St, Cincinnati, OH 45202, 513-684-2572.

Columbus Division, 170 N High St, Columbus, OH 43215, 614-469-6638.

Dayton Division, 120 W 3rd St, Dayton, OH 45402, 937-225-2516.

County-to-Court Cross Reference (Bankruptcy Court locations in Parenthesis if different)

County	District	Court
Adams	Southern	Cincinnati
Allen	Northern	Toledo
Ashland	Northern	Cleveland (Canton)
Ashtabula	Northern	Cleveland (Youngstown)
Athens	Southern	Columbus
Auglaize	Northern	Toledo
Belmont	Southern	Columbus
Brown	Southern	Cincinnati
Butler	Southern	Cincinnati (Dayton)
Carroll	Northern	Akron (Canton)
Champaign	Southern	Dayton
Clark	Southern	Dayton
Clermont	Southern	Cincinnati
Clinton	Southern	Cincinnati (Dayton)
Columbiana	Northern	Youngstown
Coshocton	Southern	Columbus
Crawford	Northern	Cleveland (Canton)
Cuyahoga	Northern	Cleveland
Darke	Southern	Dayton
Defiance	Northern	Toledo
Delaware	Southern	Columbus
Erie	Northern	Toledo
Fairfield	Southern	Columbus
Fayette	Southern	Columbus
Franklin	Southern	Columbus
Fulton	Northern	Toledo
Gallia	Southern	Columbus
Geauga	Northern	Cleveland
Greene	Southern	Dayton
Guernsey	Southern	Columbus
Hamilton	Southern	Cincinnati
Hancock	Northern	Toledo
Hardin	Northern	Toledo
Harrison	Southern	Columbus
Henry	Northern	Toledo
Highland	Southern	Cincinnati
Hocking	Southern	Columbus
Holmes	Northern	Akron (Canton)
Huron	Northern	Toledo
Jackson	Southern	Columbus
Jefferson	Southern	Columbus
Knox	Southern	Columbus
Lake	Northern	Cleveland
Lawrence	Southern	Cincinnati
Licking	Southern	Columbus
Logan	Southern	Columbus
Lorain	Northern	Cleveland
Lucas	Northern	Toledo
Madison	Southern	Columbus
Mahoning	Northern	Youngstown
Marion	Northern	Toledo
Medina	Northern	Cleveland (Akron)
Meigs	Southern	Columbus
Mercer	Northern	Toledo
Miami	Southern	Dayton
Monroe	Southern	Columbus
Montgomery	Southern	Dayton
Morgan	Southern	Columbus
Morrow	Southern	Columbus
Muskingum	Southern	Columbus
Noble	Southern	Columbus
Ottawa	Northern	Toledo
Paulding	Northern	Toledo
Perry	Southern	Columbus
Pickaway	Southern	Columbus
Pike	Southern	Columbus
Portage	Northern	Akron
Preble	Southern	Dayton
Putnam	Northern	Toledo
Richland	Northern	Cleveland (Canton)
Ross	Southern	Columbus
Sandusky	Northern	Toledo
Scioto	Southern	Cincinnati
Seneca	Northern	Toledo
Shelby	Southern	Dayton
Stark	Northern	Akron (Canton)
Summit	Northern	Akron
Trumbull	Northern	Youngstown
Tuscarawas	Northern	Akron (Canton)
Union	Southern	Columbus
Van Wert	Northern	Toledo
Vinton	Southern	Columbus
Warren	Southern	Cincinnati (Dayton)
Washington	Southern	Columbus
Wayne	Northern	Akron (Canton)
Williams	Northern	Toledo
Wood	Northern	Toledo
Wyandot	Northern	Toledo

Oklahoma

Governor's Office

State Capitol, Suite 212   405-521-2342
Oklahoma City, OK 73105   Fax 405-521-3317
www.state.ok.us/~governor

Attorney General's Office

112 State Capitol   405-521-3921
Oklahoma City, OK 73105   Fax 405-521-6246

State Archives

Libraries Department   405-521-2502
Archives & Records Office   Fax 405-525-7804
200 NE 18th St   8AM-5PM
Oklahoma City, OK 73105-3298
www.state.ok.us/~odl

Capital:	Oklahoma City
	Oklahoma County
Time Zone:	CST
Number of Counties:	77
Population:	3,317,091
Web Site:	www.state.ok.us

State Court Administrator

Admin. Director of Courts   405-521-2450
1915 N Stiles, #305   Fax 405-521-6815
Oklahoma City, OK 73105   8AM-4PM

State Agencies Online

Legislation-Current/Pending
Legislation-Passed

www.state.ok.us/osfdocs/leghp.html

Oklahoma Legislature, State Capitol, Status Info-Room 309, Copies-Room 310, Oklahoma City, OK 73105; 405-521-5642 (Bill Status Only), 405-521-5515 (Bill Distribution), 405-528-2546 (Bills in Progress), 405-521-5507 (Fax), 8:30AM-4:30PM.

Online search: There are plans for an online system – "OLIS" – to be available sometime in 1999.

County Agencies Online

Court Structure

There are 80 district courts in the state. Cities with populations in excess of 200,000 (Oklahoma City and Tulsa) have municipal criminal courts of record. Cities with less than 200,000 do not have such courts.

Small claims limit was raised from $3000 to $4500 in 1998.

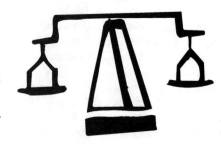

Online Access

Online computer access, for internal use only, is available through the Case Processing System (CPS) for 9 counties, with a goal of including all Oklahoma counties at some future time. Access is available only through a "state terminal."

About the County Courts

Case information is available in bulk form for downloading to computer. For information, call the Administrative Director of Courts, 405-521-2450.

About the Recorder's Office

Organization

77 counties, 77 recording offices. The recording officer is County Clerk. The entire state is in the Central Time Zone (CST).

Real Estate Records

Many counties will perform real estate searches by legal description. Copy fees are usually $1.00 per page. Certification usually costs $1.00 per document.

UCC Records

Financing statements are filed centrally with the County Clerk of Oklahoma County, except for consumer goods, which are dual filed, and farm related and real estate related collateral, which are filed with the County Clerk. All counties will perform UCC searches. Use search request form UCC-4. Search fees are usually $5.00 per debtor name for a written request and $3.00 per name by telephone. Copies usually cost $1.00 per page.

Other Lien Records

Federal tax liens on personal property of businesses are filed with the County Clerk of Oklahoma County, which is the central filing office for the state. Other federal and all state tax liens are filed with the County Clerk. Usually state and federal tax liens on personal property are filed in separate indexes. Some counties will perform tax lien searches. Search fees vary. Other lines are: judgment, mechanics, physicians, hospital.

County Courts & Recording Offices Online

There is no online access to court records in Oklahoma.

No remote online access is available from real estate recorder's offices in Oklahoma.

Federal Courts Online

County-to-Court Cross Reference (Bankruptcy Court Locations in Parenthesis)

County	District	Court (Bankruptcy)
Adair	Eastern	Muskogee (Okmulgee)
Alfalfa	Western	Oklahoma City
Atoka	Eastern	Muskogee (Okmulgee)
Beaver	Western	Oklahoma City
Beckham	Western	Oklahoma City
Blaine	Western	Oklahoma City
Bryan	Eastern	Muskogee (Okmulgee)
Caddo	Western	Oklahoma City
Canadian	Western	Oklahoma City
Carter	Eastern	Muskogee (Okmulgee)
Cherokee	Eastern	Muskogee (Okmulgee)
Choctaw	Eastern	Muskogee (Okmulgee)
Cimarron	Western	Oklahoma City
Cleveland	Western	Oklahoma City

Coal	Eastern	Muskogee (Okmulgee)
Comanche	Western	Oklahoma City
Cotton	Western	Oklahoma City
Craig	Northern	Tulsa
Creek	Northern	Tulsa
Custer	Western	Oklahoma City
Delaware	Northern	Tulsa
Dewey	Western	Oklahoma City
Ellis	Western	Oklahoma City
Garfield	Western	Oklahoma City
Garvin	Western	Oklahoma City
Grady	Western	Oklahoma City
Grant	Western	Oklahoma City
Greer	Western	Oklahoma City
Harmon	Western	Oklahoma City
Harper	Western	Oklahoma City
Haskell	Eastern	Muskogee (Okmulgee)
Hughes	Eastern	Muskogee (Okmulgee)
Jackson	Western	Oklahoma City
Jefferson	Western	Oklahoma City
Johnston	Eastern	Muskogee (Okmulgee)
Kay	Western	Oklahoma City
Kingfisher	Western	Oklahoma City
Kiowa	Western	Oklahoma City
Latimer	Eastern	Muskogee (Okmulgee)
Le Flore	Eastern	Muskogee (Okmulgee)
Lincoln	Western	Oklahoma City
Logan	Western	Oklahoma City
Love	Eastern	Muskogee (Okmulgee)
Major	Western	Oklahoma City
Marshall	Eastern	Muskogee (Okmulgee)
Mayes	Northern	Tulsa
McClain	Western	Oklahoma City
McCurtain	Eastern	Muskogee (Okmulgee)
McIntosh	Eastern	Muskogee (Okmulgee)
Murray	Eastern	Muskogee (Okmulgee)
Muskogee	Eastern	Muskogee (Okmulgee)
Noble	Western	Oklahoma City
Nowata	Northern	Tulsa
Okfuskee	Eastern	Muskogee (Okmulgee)
Oklahoma	Western	Oklahoma City
Okmulgee	Northern (Eastern)	Tulsa (Okmulgee)
Osage	Northern	Tulsa
Ottawa	Northern	Tulsa
Pawnee	Northern	Tulsa
Payne	Western	Oklahoma City
Pittsburg	Eastern	Muskogee (Okmulgee)
Pontotoc	Eastern	Muskogee (Okmulgee)
Pottawatomie	Western	Oklahoma City
Pushmataha	Eastern	Muskogee (Okmulgee)
Roger Mills	Western	Oklahoma City
Rogers	Northern	Tulsa
Seminole	Eastern	Muskogee (Okmulgee)
Sequoyah	Eastern	Muskogee (Okmulgee)
Stephens	Western	Oklahoma City
Texas	Western	Oklahoma City
Tillman	Western	Oklahoma City
Tulsa	Northern	Tulsa
Wagoner	Eastern	Muskogee (Okmulgee)
Washington	Northern	Tulsa
Washita	Western	Oklahoma City
Woods	Western	Oklahoma City
Woodward	Western	Oklahoma City

US District Court
Eastern District of Oklahoma

Muskogee Division, Clerk, PO Box 607, Muskogee, OK 74401, 918-687-2471, Fax: 918-687-2400.

PACER sign-up number is 800-676-6856. Both civil and criminal case records are available online.

US Bankruptcy Court
Eastern District of Oklahoma

Okmulgee Division, PO Box 1347, Okmulgee, OK 74447, 918-758-0126, Fax: 918-756-9248.

PACER sign-up number is 800-676-6856.

US District Court
Northern District of Oklahoma

Tulsa Division, 411 US Courthouse, 333 W 4th St, Tulsa, OK 74103, 918-699-4700, Fax: 918-699-4756.

PACER sign-up number is 800-676-6856. Both civil and criminal case records are available online.

US Bankruptcy Court
Northern District of Oklahoma

Tulsa Division, 224 S. Boulder, Tulsa, OK 74103, 918-581-7181, Fax: 918-581-7645.

PACER sign-up number is 800-676-6856.

US District Court
Western District of Oklahoma

Oklahoma City Division, Clerk, Room 1210, 200 NW 4th St, Oklahoma City, OK 73102, 405-231-4792, Criminal Docket Section: 405-231-4955.

PACER sign-up number is 800-676-6856. Both civil and criminal case records are available online.

US Bankruptcy Court
Western District of Oklahoma

Oklahoma City Division, 1st Floor, Old Post Office Bldg, 215 Dean A McGee Ave, Oklahoma City, OK 73102, 405-231-5141, Fax: 405-231-5866.

PACER sign-up number is 800-676-6856.

Governor's Office

160 State Capitol   503-378-3111
Salem, OR 97310-4001   Fax 503-378-8970
www.governor.state.or.us/governor.html

Attorney General's Office

Justice Department   503-378-4400
1162 Court St NE   Fax 503-378-4017
Salem, OR 97310   8AM-5PM
www.doj.state.or.us

State Archives

Secretary of State   503-373-0701
Archives Division   Fax 503-373-0953
800 Summer St NE   8AM-4:45PM
Salem, OR 97310
arcweb.sos.state.or.us

Capital:	Salem
	Marion County
Time Zone:	PST
Number of Counties:	36
Population:	3,243,487
Web Site:	www.state.or.us

State Court Administrator

Court Administrator   503-986-5500
Supreme Court Bldg,   Fax 503-986-5503
1163 State St   8AM-5PM
Salem, OR 97310

State Agencies Online

Legislation-Current/Pending
Legislation-Passed

www.leg.state.or.us

Oregon Legislative Assembly, State Capitol-Information Services, State Capitol, Rm 49, Salem, OR 97310; 503-986-1180 (Current Bill Information), 503-373-0701 (Archives), 503-373-1527 (Fax), 8AM-5PM.

Online search: Text and histories of measures can be found at the Internet site for no charge.

Criminal Records

Oregon State Police, Identification Services Section, PO Box 430034, Salem, OR 97208; (3772 Portland Rd NE, Salem, OR 97303); 503-378-3070, 503-378-2121 (Fax).

General Information: Information will include all convictions and all arrests within the past year without disposition. If record exists, person of record will be notified of the request and the record will not be released for 14 additional days.

Online search: This service is a bulletin board used for requesting and receiving criminal history reports. The hours are 10 AM to 1 PM and 5 PM to 7 AM. Results are posted as "No Record" or "In Process" which means a record will be mailed in 14 days. Users must complete an application and will be billed. The fee is $15.00 per record. Call (503) 373-1808, ext. 230 for application.

Corporation Records
Limited Partnership Records
Trademarks/Servicemarks
Fictitious Name / Assumed Name
Limited Liability Company Records

www.sos.state.or.us/corporation/corphp.htm

Corporation Division, Public Service Building, 255 Capital St NE, #151, Salem, OR 97310-1327; 503-986-2200, 503-378-4381 (Fax), 8AM-5PM.

General Information: Records are available on the computer screen for 10 years after inactive. Assumed names are only available for 5 years after inactive.

Online search: A dial-up system is available at $400 per year. Call 503-986-2343 for more information.

Uniform Commercial Code
Federal Tax Liens

www.sos.state.or.us/corporation/ucc/ucc.htm

UCC Division, Secretary of State, 255 Capitol St NE, Suite 151, Salem, OR 97310-1327; 503-986-2200, 503-373-1166 (Fax), 8AM - 5PM.

Online search: UCC index information can be obtained for free from the web site. You can search by debtor name or by lien number. You can also download forms from here.

County Agencies Online

Court Structure

Effective January 15, 1998, the District and Circuit Courts were combined into "Circuit Courts." At the same time, three new judicial districts were created by splitting existing ones. Probate is handled by the Circuit Court except in 6 counties (Gilliam, Grant, Harney, Malheur, Sherman, and Wheeler) where Probate in handled by County Courts.

Online Access

About the County Courts

Online computer access is available through the Oregon Judicial Information Network (OJIN). OJIN includes almost all cases filed in the Oregon state courts. Generally, the OJIN database contains criminal, civil, small claims, probate, and some, but not all, juvenile records. However, it does not contain any records from municipal nor county courts. There is a one time setup fee of $295.00, plus a monthly usage charge (minimum $10.00) based on transaction type, type of job, shift, and number of units/pages (which averages $10-13 per hour). For further information and/or a registration packet, write to: Oregon Judicial System, Information Systems Division, ATTN: Technical Support, 1163 State Street, Salem OR 97310, or call 800-858-9658.

Searching Hints

Many Oregon courts indicated that in person searches would markedly improve request turnaround time as court offices are understaffed or spread very thin. Most Circuit Courts that have records on computer do have a public access terminal which will speed up in-person or retriever searches.

About the Recorder's Office

Organization

36 counties, 36 recording offices. The recording officer is County Clerk. 35 counties are in the Pacific Time Zone (PST) and one is in the Mountain Time Zone (MST).

Real Estate Records

Some counties will not perform real estate searches. Search fees vary. Many counties search all liens together for $12.50 per name. Copy fees are usually $.25 per page. Certification usually costs $3.75 per document. The Assessor keeps tax and ownership records.

UCC Records

Financing statements are filed at the state level, except for real estate related collateral. All counties will perform UCC searches. Use search request form UCC-11. Search fees are usually $3.75 or $5.00.

Other Lien Records

All federal tax liens on personal property are filed with the Secretary of State. Other federal tax liens and all state tax liens are filed with the County Clerk. Most counties will perform tax lien searches and include both with a UCC search for an extra $7.50 per name. Search fees vary widely. Other liens are: county tax, public utility, construction, judgment, hospital.

County Courts & Recording Offices Online

Online computer access is available through the Oregon Judicial Information Network (OJIN) for almost all cases filed in the Oregon state courts. For online access to court records, see "Online Access" on the previous page.

Benton County

Liens, Real Estate, Tax Assessor Records

County Recorder, 120 NW 4th Street, Corvallis, OR 97330, 541-757-6831, 541-757-6757 Fax.

Online search: Access is through their Information Resources system. There are no fees. An Internet site will be available in March 1999, possibly sooner. The web site is www.co.benton.or.us. Records date back to 1988. The system operates 24 hours daily and supports baud rates up to 9,600. One can search by name, date of recording, map number, tax lot number, serial number and document type. For further information, contact Dan Miller at 541-757-6877.

Federal Courts Online

County-to-Court Cross Reference (Bankruptcy Court locations in Parenthesis if different)

Baker .... Portland	Harney .... Portland	Morrow .... Portland
Benton.................. Eugene	Hood River........... Portland	Multnomah .... Portland
Clackamas .... Portland	Jackson .... Medford (Eugene)	Polk .... Portland (Eugene)
Clatsop .... Portland	Jefferson .... Portland	Sherman .... Portland
Columbia .... Portland	Josephine.............. Medford (Eugene)	Tillamook .... Portland
Coos .... Eugene	Klamath................ Medford (Eugene)	Umatilla .... Portland
Crook................... Portland	Lake .... Medford (Eugene)	Union.................... Portland
Curry .... Medford (Eugene)	Lane .... Eugene	Wallowa............... Portland
Deschutes............. Eugene (Portland)	Lincoln .... Eugene	Wasco .... Portland
Douglas................ Eugene	Linn....................... Eugene	Washington .... Portland
Gilliam .... Portland	Malheur .... Portland	Wheeler................ Portland
Grant.................... Portland	Marion .... Eugene	Yamhill .... Portland

US District Court
District of Oregon

The District Court of Oregon makes documents available to the public, searchable by case number and type.

http://ecf.ord.uscourts.gov

Eugene Division, 100 Federal Bldg, 211 E 7th Ave, Eugene, OR 97401, 541-465-6423, Fax: 541-465-6344

PACER sign-up number is 800-676-6856. Both civil and criminal case records are available online.

Medford Division, 201 James A Redden US Courthouse, 310 W 6th St, Medford, OR 97501, 541-776-3926, Fax: 541-776-3925

Portland Division, Clerk, 740 US Courthouse, 1000 SW 3rd Ave, Portland, OR 97204-2902, 503-326-8000, Record Room: 503-326-8020, Civil Docket Section: 503-326-8008, Criminal Docket Section: 503-326-8003, Fax: 503-326-8010

US Bankruptcy Court
District of Oregon

PACER sign-up number is 800-676-6856.

Eugene Division, PO Box 1335, Eugene, OR 97440, 541-465-6448.

Portland Division, 1001 SW 5th Ave, #700, Portland, OR 97204, 503-326-2231.

Pennsylvania

Governor's Office
225 Main Capitol Bldg   717-787-2500
Harrisburg, PA 17120   Fax 717-772-8284
www.state.pa.us/PA_Exec/Governor/
overview.html

Attorney General's Office
Strawberry Square, 16th Floor   717-787-3391
Harrisburg, PA 17120   Fax 717-787-8242
www.attorneygeneral.gov

State Archives
PA Historical &
Museum Commission   717-783-3281
Bureau of Archives & History   Fax 717-787-4822
PO Box 1026   9AM-4PM T-SU
Harrisburg, PA 17108-1026
state.pa.us/PA_Exec/Historical_Museum/
DAM/psa.htm

Capital:	Harrisburg
	Dauphin County
Time Zone:	EST
Number of Counties:	67
Population:	12,019,661
Web Site:	www.state.pa.us

State Court Administrator
Admin. Office of Courts   717-795-2000
PO Box 719   Fax 717-795-2050
Mechanicsburg, PA 17055-0719   8AM-4:30PM
www.courts.state.pa.us

State Agencies Online

Driver Records

Department of Transportation, Driver Record Services, PO Box 68695, Harrisburg, PA 17106-8695; (Courier: 1101-1125 Front Street, Harrisburg, PA 17104); 717-391-6190, 800-932-4600 (In-state only), 7:30AM-4:30PM.

General Information: Records are available for minimum of 3 calendar years for moving violations and departmental actions, minimum of 7 years for DWIs, and indefinite for suspensions. Accidents are reported on record as involvement only. Casual requesters must have a signed, notarized release from the driver on Form DL-503. Large volume requesters must sign an agreement stating the individual authorizations are on file

Online search: The state is in the process of testing their online access system. This new interface will be available to high-volume requesters only. The fee is likely to be $5.00 per record.

Information About County Agencies

Court Structure

The civil records clerk of the Court of Common Pleas is called the Prothonotary. Small claims cases are, usually, handled by the District Justice Courts/Magistrates. However, all small claims actions are recorded through the Prothonotary Section (civil) of the Court of Common Pleas, which then holds the records. It is not necessary to check with each District Justice Court, but rather to check with the Prothonotary for the county. Probate is handled by the Register of Wills.

About the County Courts

Online Access

Pennsylvania has an online computer system for internal access only to criminal cases, though some courts provide remote online access systems.

Searching Hints

Fees vary widely among jurisdictions. Many courts will not conduct searches due to a lack of personnel or, if they do search, turnaround time may be excessively lengthy. Many courts have public access terminals for in-person searches.

About the Recorder's Office

Organization

67 counties, 67 recording offices and 134 UCC filing offices. Each county has two different recording offices: the Prothonotary —their term for "Clerk"—accepts UCC and tax lien filings, and the Recorder of Deeds maintains real estate records. The entire state is in the Eastern Time Zone (EST).

Real Estate Records

County Recorders of Deeds will not perform real estate searches. Copy fees and certification fees vary.

UCC Records

This is a dual filing state. Financing statements are filed both at the state level and with the Prothonotary, except for real estate related collateral, which are filed with the Recorder of Deeds. Some county offices will not perform UCC searches. Use search request form UCC-11. Search fees are usually $57.50 per debtor name. Copies usually cost $.50-$2.00 per page. Counties also charge $4.50 per financing statement found on a search.

Other Lien Records

All federal and state tax liens on personal property and on real property are filed with the Prothonotary. Usually, tax liens on personal property are filed in the judgment index of the Prothonotary. Some Prothonotaries will perform tax lien searches. Search fees are usually $5.00 per name. Other liens are: judgment, municipal, mechanics.

County Courts & Recording Offices Online

Berks County

Vital Records, Probate, Marriage Records, Birth Records

www.berksregofwills.com

Court of Common Pleas-Civil 2nd Floor, 633 Court St, Reading PA 19601, 610-478-6970. Fax: 610-478-6969.

Online search: The Register of Wills has a free searchable web site at www.berksregofwills.com which includes records both for the county and city of Reading. The birth and marriage records are extremely current.

Bucks County

Civil Cases, Criminal Cases, Liens, Real Estate, Marriage Records, Tax Assessor Records, Probate

Court of Common Pleas, 55 E Court St, Doylestown PA 18901, 215-348-6191 (Civil), 215-348-6389 (Criminal), 215-348-6209 (Recorder), 215-348-6379 (Fax).

Online search: To access their public records, one must have a Sprint ID number. The annual Sprint fee is $24. The user is charged .60 per minute (2 minute minimum). The records date back to 1980. The system operates from 8AM-9PM M-F and 8AM-5PM S-S and supports baud rates up to 9,600. One may search by name, Grantee/Grantor, address and book and page. Lending agency information is available, as well as the register of wills data. For further information contact Jack Morris at 215-348-6579. No mental, sealed records released.

Butler County

Criminal Cases

Court of Common Pleas-Criminal, Butler County Courthouse, PO Box 1208, Butler PA 16003-1208, 724-284-5233. Fax: 724-284-5244. Hours: 8:30AM-4:30PM (EST).

Online search: Call Infocon Corp. at 814-472-6066 for more information about the remote online system. No mental, sealed, juvenile (16 & under) victim records released.

Chester County

Liens, Real Estate, Marriage Records, Tax Assessor Records, Probate

County Recorder of Deeds, 235 W Market St, Ste. 100, West Chester PA 19382, 610-344-6330, 610-344-6408 Fax.

Online search: The sign up fee is $50, plus a $.30 per minute charge. The records date back to 1992. The system operates 24 hours daily and supports baud rates up to 9,600. One may

search by name, Grantee/Grantor and parcel number. Lending agency information is available, as is register of wills data. For further information, contact Lisa or Gail at 610-344-6884.

Civil Cases, Criminal Cases

Court of Common Pleas-Criminal, 2 North High St, Ste. 130, West Chester PA 19380, 610-344-6300. Hours: 8:30AM-4:30PM (EST).

Online search: Contact Gail Galliger at 610-344-6884 for information about remote access. Fee is $50 for subscription and $.30 per minute. Index goes back to 1990. Available 24 hours per day.

Delaware County

Real Estate, Tax Assessor Records

County Recorder of Deeds, 201 W Front St, Media PA 19063, 610-891-4148.

Online search: Access is free by dialing 610-566-1507. The system operates 24 hours daily. Records date back to 1990. For further info, contact Data Processing at 610-891-4675.

Civil Cases

Court of Common Pleas-Criminal/Civil, 201 W Front St, Media PA 19063, 610-891-5399. Hours: 8:30AM-4:30PM (EST).

Online search: There are no fees for online access. VT100 emulation is required. The system is open 24 hours daily. For more information, call 610-891-4675. The access number is 610-566-1507.

Indiana County

Felony, Misdemeanor, Civil, Eviction

Court of Common Pleas-Criminal/Civil, County Courthouse, 825 Philadelphia St, Indiana PA 15701, 724-465-3855/3858. Fax: 724-465-3968. Hours: 8AM-4:30PM (EST).

Online search: Records are expected to be online sometime in 1999.

Lancaster County

Liens, Real Estate, Marriage Records, Tax Assessor Records, Probate

County Recorder of Deeds, 50 N Duke St, Lancaster PA 17608, 717-299-8238.

Online search: A monthly fee of $25 applies, plus a per minute charge of $.18. Their system holds 5 years of data. Use of Windows is required. The system operates 8AM-6PM M-S and supports baud rates up to 56K. One may search by name, Grantee/Grantor and by index number. Lending agency information is available, as is the register of wills data. For further information, contact Nancy Malloy at 717-299-8252

Civil Cases

www.co.lancaster.pa.us

Court of Common Pleas-Civil, 50 N Duke St, PO Box 83480, Lancaster PA 17608-3480, 717-299-8282. Fax: 717-293-7210. Hours: 8:30AM-5PM (EST).

Online search: Online access is available 8am to 6pm M-Sat. There is a monthly fee of $25 and a per minute fee of $.18. by name or case number. Call Nancy Malloy at 717-299-8252 for more information

Lehigh County

Civil Cases, Criminal Cases

Court of Common Pleas, 455 W Hamilton St, Allentown PA 18101-1614, 610-782-3148 (Civil) 610-782-3077 (Criminal), Fax: 610-770-3840. Hours: 8:30AM-4:30PM (EST).

Online search: All types of county records, including criminal cases and real estate records are available online. The system is open 24 hours daily, fees are involved. Call Al Johnson at 610-782-3189 for more information. No sealed, impounded records released.

Liens, Real Estate, Marriage Records, Tax Assessor Records

County Recorder of Deeds, 455 W Hamilton St, Allentown PA 18101,. 610-782-3162, 610-820-2039 Fax.

Online search: The set up fee is $10 and the annual fee is $288. Online minutes are billed at $.05. The system operates 24 hours daily and supports baud rates up to 56K. Records date back to 1984. One may search by name, Grantee/Grantor and book and page. Lending agency information is available. For further information, contact Al Johnson at 610-782-3189.

Montgomery County

Liens, Real Estate, Tax Assessor Records

County Recorder of Deeds, One Montgomery Plaza, Ste. 303, Airy & Swede St, Norristown PA 19404, 610-278-3289, 610-278-3869 Fax.

Online search: The initial sign up fee is $10, plus a $.15 per minute usage charge. Their records date back to 1900. The system operates 24 hours daily and supports baud rates up to 14.4. Lending agency and prothonotary information are both available. One must contact the outside agency, Berkheimer Associates at 800-360-8989 to sign up for access to the system.

Civil Cases, Criminal Cases

www.montcopa.org.

Court of Common Pleas, PO Box 311, Airy & Swede St, Norristown PA 19404-0311, 610-278-3346. Fax: 610-278-5188.

Online search: For information about remote access, call 800-360-8989, extension 5. There is a $10 registration fee plus $0.15 per minute of usage. Index goes back 10 years.

Required to search: name, years to search, DOB. No impounded, sealed records released.

Washington County

Liens, Real Estate, Tax Assessor Records

County Recorder of Deeds, Washington County Courthouse, 1 S Main St, Washington PA 15301, 724-228-6806. Fax: 724-228-6737.

Online search: The system operates 24 hours daily and supports baud rates up to 56K. Records date back to 1952. One may search by name, Grantee/Grantor and book and page. Tax lien information in kept in the Prothonotarys office. The Register of Wills data is available, as is lending agency information. For further information, contact Jack Welty at 724-228-6766.

Civil Cases, Criminal Cases, Probate, Divorce

Court of Common Pleas, 1 S Main St Suite 1001, Washington PA 15301, 724-228-6770 (Civil), 724-228-6787 (Criminal), 724-Fax 228-6890.

Online search: Online access is open 24 hours daily, there are no fees. Criminal records date back to 1986. Call Sally Michalski at 724-228-6797 for more information

Westmoreland County

Liens, Real Estate

County Recorder of Deeds, Main St, Courthouse Sq, Rm 503, PO Box 1630, Greensburg PA 15601, 724-830-3526. Fax: 724-830-8757.

Online search: A setup fee of $100 applies, which includes software. In addition, there is a monthly fee of $20 and a per minute charge of $.50 after 40 minutes. Records date back to 1957. The system operates 24 hours daily and supports baud rates up to 19.2. Searches can be made by name, Grantee/Grantor, book and page and by street. No tax lien information is available, only UCC liens. For further information, contact Phil Svesnik at 724-830-3874.

Civil Cases, Criminal Cases

Court of Common Pleas, Courthouse Square, Greensburg PA 15601-1168, 724-830-3500, 724-830-3734 (Criminal), Fax: 724-830-3517.

Online search: Online access is open 24 hours daily. The $100 setup fee includes software, the minimum monthly fee is $20. Records are available from 1992 forward. For more information, call Phil Svesnik at 724-830-3874.

York County

Civil Cases, Criminal Cases

Court of Common Pleas-Civil, York County Courthouse, 28E Market St, York PA 17401, 717-771-9611. Hours: 8:30AM-4:30PM (EST).

Online search: The online system is available from 4AM-PM, M-F. The setup fee is $200.00 and the access fee is $.75 per minute. Criminal records from mid-1988 forward are available. For further information, call (717) 771-9321.

Federal Courts Online

County-to-Court Cross Reference (Bankruptcy Court locations in Parenthesis if different)

County	District	Court
Adams	Middle	Harrisburg
Allegheny	Western	Pittsburgh
Armstrong	Western	Pittsburgh
Beaver	Western	Pittsburgh
Bedford	Western	Johnstown (Pittsburgh)
Berks	Eastern	Allentown/Reading (Reading)
Blair	Western	Johnstown (Pittsburgh)
Bradford	Middle	Scranton (Wilkes-Barre)
Bucks	Eastern	Philadelphia
Butler	Western	Pittsburgh
Cambria	Western	Johnstown (Pittsburgh)
Cameron	Middle	Williamsport (Wilkes-Barre)
Carbon	Middle	Scranton (Wilkes-Barre)
Centre	Middle	Williamsport (Harrisburg)
Chester	Eastern	Philadelphia
Clarion	Western	Pittsburgh (Erie)
Clearfield	Western	Johnstown (Pittsburgh)
Clinton	Middle	Williamsport (Wilkes-Barre)
Columbia	Middle	Williamsport (Wilkes-Barre)
Crawford	Western	Erie
Cumberland	Middle	Harrisburg
Dauphin	Middle	Harrisburg
Delaware	Eastern	Philadelphia
Elk	Western	Erie
Erie	Western	Erie
Fayette	Western	Pittsburgh
Forest	Western	Erie
Franklin	Middle	Harrisburg
Fulton	Middle	Harrisburg
Greene	Western	Pittsburgh
Huntingdon	Middle	Harrisburg
Indiana	Western	Pittsburgh
Jefferson	Western	Pittsburgh (Erie)
Juniata	Middle	Harrisburg
Lackawanna	Middle	Scranton (Wilkes-Barre)
Lancaster	Eastern	Allentown/Reading (Reading)
Lawrence	Western	Pittsburgh
Lebanon	Middle	Harrisburg
Lehigh	Eastern	Allentown/Reading (Reading)
Luzerne	Middle	Scranton (Wilkes-Barre)
Lycoming	Middle	Williamsport (Wilkes-Barre)
McKean	Western	Erie
Mercer	Western	Pittsburgh (Erie)
Mifflin	Middle	Harrisburg
Monroe	Middle	Scranton (Wilkes-Barre)
Montgomery	Eastern	Philadelphia
Montour	Middle	Williamsport (Harrisburg)
Northampton	Eastern	Allentown/Reading (Reading)
Northumberland	Middle	Williamsport (Harrisburg)
Perry	Middle	Williamsport (Harrisburg)
Philadelphia	Eastern	Philadelphia
Pike	Middle	Scranton (Wilkes-Barre)
Potter	Middle	Williamsport (Wilkes-Barre)
Schuylkill	Eastern	Allentown/Reading (Reading)
Snyder	Middle	Williamsport (Harrisburg)
Somerset	Western	Johnstown (Pittsburgh)
Sullivan	Middle	Williamsport (Wilkes-Barre)
Susquehanna	Middle	Scranton (Wilkes-Barre)
Tioga	Middle	Williamsport (Wilkes-Barre)
Union	Middle	Williamsport (Harrisburg)
Venango	Western	Erie
Warren	Western	Erie
Washington	Western	Pittsburgh
Wayne	Middle	Scranton (Wilkes-Barre)
Westmoreland	Western	Pittsburgh
Wyoming	Middle	Scranton (Wilkes-Barre)
York	Middle	Harrisburg

US District Court
Eastern District of Pennsylvania

www.paed.uscourts.gov

PACER sign-up number is 215-597-5710. Both civil and criminal case records are available online.

Allentown/Reading Division, c/o Philadelphia Division, Room 2609, US Courthouse, 601 Market St, Philadelphia, PA 19106-1797, 215-597-7704, Record Room: 215-597-7721, Fax: 215-597-6390

Philadelphia Division, Room 2609, US Courthouse, 601 Market St, Philadelphia, PA 19106-1797, 215-597-7704, Record Room: 215-597-7721, Fax: 215-597-6390

US Bankruptcy Court
Eastern District of Pennsylvania

www.paeb.uscourts.gov

PACER sign-up number is 800-676-6856.

Philadelphia Division, 4th Floor, 900 Market St, Philadelphia, PA 19107, 215-408-2800

Reading Division, Suite 300, The Madison, 400 Washington St, Reading, PA 19601, 610-320-5255

US District Court
Middle District of Pennsylvania

PACER sign-up number is 800-676-6856. Both civil and criminal case records are available online.

Harrisburg Division, PO Box 983, Harrisburg, PA 17108-0983, 717-221-3920, Record Room: 717-221-3924, Fax: 717-221-3959.

Scranton Division, Clerk's Office, PO Box 1148, Scranton, PA 18501, 717-207-5600, Criminal Docket Section: 717-207-5606, Fax: 717-207-5650.

Williamsport Division, PO Box 608, Williamsport, PA 17703, 717-323-6380, Fax: 717-323-0636.

US Bankruptcy Court
Middle District of Pennsylvania

PACER sign-up number is 800-676-6856.

Harrisburg Division, PO Box 908, Harrisburg, PA 17101, 717-901-2800.

Wilkes-Barre Division, Room 217, 197 S Main St, Wilkes-Barre, PA 18701, 717-826-6450.

US District Court
Western District of Pennsylvania

PACER sign-up number is 800-676-6856. Both civil and criminal case records are available online.

Erie Division, PO Box 1820, Erie, PA 16507, 814-453-4829.

Johnstown Division, Penn Traffic Bldg, Room 208, 319 Washington St, Johnstown, PA 15901, 814-533-4504, Fax: 814-533-4519.

Pittsburgh Division, US Post Office & Courthouse, Room 829, 7th Ave & Grant St, Pittsburgh, PA 15219, 412-644-3527, Record Room: 412-644-3533.

US Bankruptcy Court
Western District of Pennsylvania

PACER sign-up number is 800-676-6856.

Erie Division, 717 State St, #501, Erie, PA 16501, 814-453-7580.

Pittsburgh Division, 600 Grant St #5414, Pittsburgh, PA 15219-2801, 412-644-2700.

Rhode Island

Governor's Office
State House, Room 143   401-222-2080
Providence, RI 02903   Fax 401-222-5894

Attorney General's Office
72 Pine St   401-274-4400
Providence, RI 02903   Fax 401-222-1302
www.sec.state.ri.us./genoff/pine.htm

State Archives
Office of Secretary of State   401-222-2353
State Archives   Fax 401-222-3199
& Public Records Admin.   8:30AM-4:30PM
337 Westminster St   M-SA
Providence, RI 02903

Capital:	Providence
	Providence County
Time Zone:	EST
Number of Counties:	5
Population:	987,429
Web Site:	www.state.ri.us

State Court Administrator
Court Administrator   401-222-3272
Supreme Court   Fax 401-222-3599
250 Benefit St   8:30AM-4:30PM
Providence, RI 02903

State Agencies Online

Corporation Records
Fictitious Name
Limited Partnerships
Limited Liability Company Records
Limited Liability Partnerships

Secretary of State, Corporations Division, 100 N Main St, Providence, RI 02903; 401-222-3040, 401-222-1309 (Fax), 8:30AM-4:30PM.

Online search: The direct access system is free; however, special Wang software is needed. The system is open 24 hours daily. Call 401-222-3040 for more information.

Legislation-Current/Pending
Legislation-Passed
www.state.ri.us

Rhode Island General Assembly, State House, Room 38, Public Information Center, Providence, RI 02903; 401-222-3983 (Bill Status Only), 401-222-2473 (State Library), 401-222-1308 (Fax Back Request Line), 401-222-1356 (Fax), 8:30AM-4:30PM.

Online search: The Internet system provides a means to search enactments and measures by key words.

Information About County Agencies

Court Structure

Rhode Island has five counties, but only four Superior/District Court Locations (2nd, 3rd, 4th, and 6th Districts). Bristol and Providence counties are completely merged at the Providence location. Civil claims between $5000 and $10,000 may be filed in either Superior or District Court at the discretion of the filer. Probate is handled by the Town Clerk at the 39 cities and towns across Rhode Island.

Online Access

An online computer system for internal use is under development which will eventually include all state courts.

About the Recorder's Office

About the County Courts

Organization

5 counties and 39 towns, 39 recording offices. The recording officer is Town/City Clerk (Recorder of Deeds). The Town/City Clerk usually also serves as Recorder of Deeds. There is no county administration in Rhode Island. The entire state is in the Eastern Time Zone (EST).

Real Estate Records

Towns will not perform real estate searches. Copy fees are usually $1.50 per page. Certification usually costs $3.00 per document.

UCC Records

Financing statements are filed at the state level, except for farm related and real estate related collateral, which are filed with the Town/City Clerk. Most recording offices will not perform UCC searches. Use search request form UCC-11. Copy fees are usually $1.50 per page.

Other Lien Records

All federal and state tax liens on personal property and on real property are filed with the Recorder of Deeds. Towns will not perform tax lien searches. Other liens are: Mechanics, municipal, lis pendens.

County Courts & Recording Offices Online

There is no online access to County Court records available in Rhode Island.

No remote online access is available from real estate recorder's offices in Rhode Island.

Federal Courts Online

US District Court
District of Rhode Island

Providence Division, Clerk's Office, One Exchange Terrace, Federal Bldg, Providence, RI 02903, 401-528-5100, Fax: 401-528-5112. This court handles all counties in Rhode Island.

PACER sign-up number is 800-676-6856. Both civil and criminal case records are available online.

US Bankruptcy Court
District of Rhode Island

Providence Division, 6th Floor, 380 Westminster Mall, Providence, RI 02903, 401-528-4477, Fax: 401-528-4470. This court handles all counties in Rhode Island.

PACER sign-up number is 800-676-6856.

South Carolina

Governor's Office

PO Box 11369   803-734-9818
Columbia, SC 29211   Fax 803-734-1598
www.state.sc.us/db

Attorney General's Office

PO Box 11549   803-734-3970
Columbia, SC 29211   Fax 803-734-4323
www.scattorneygeneral.org

State Archives

Archives & History Dept.   803-734-8577
1430 Senate St   Fax 803-734-8820
Columbia, SC 29211   9AM-9PM T-F, 9-
6 SA, 1-6 SU
www.scdah.sc.homepage.htm

Capital:	Columbia
	Richland County
Time Zone:	EST
Number of Counties:	46
Population:	3,760,181
Web Site:	www.state.sc.us

State Court Administrator

Court Administration   803-734-1800
1015 Sumter St, 2nd Floor   Fax 803-734-1821
Columbia, SC 29201   8:30AM-5PM M-F
www.judicialca.state.sc.us

State Agencies Online

Corporation Records
Trademarks/Servicemarks
Limited Partnerships
Limited Liability Company Records

Corporation Division, Capitol Complex, PO Box 11350, Columbia, SC 29211; (Courier: Edgar A. Brown Bldg, Room 525, Columbia, SC 29201); 803-734-2158, 803-734-2164 (Fax), 8:30PM-5PM.

General Information: Trademarks and service marks are not on the computer but are in this department.

Online search: Their program is called Direct Access. Information available includes corporate names, registered agents and addresses, date of original filings, and dates of amendments or merger filings. The system is open 24 hours daily and there are no fees. The system permits the retrieval of documents by fax return. For more information, call 803-734-2345.

Uniform Commercial Code

UCC Division, Secretary of State, PO Box 11350, Columbia, SC 29211; (Courier: Edgar Brown Bldg, 1205

Pendelton St #525, Columbia, SC 29201); 803-734-2175, 803-734-2164 (Fax), 8:30AM-5PM.

General Information:. All tax liens are filed at the county level.

Online search: "Direct Access" is open 24 hours daily, there are no fees. Inquiry is by debtor name. The system provides for copies to be faxed automatically (for a fee). Call 803-734-2345 for registration information

Driver License Information
Driver Records

Division of Motor Vehicles, Driver Records Section, PO Box 100178, Columbia, SC 29202-3178; (Courier: 955 Park St, Columbia, SC 29201); 803-737-2940, 803-737-1077 (Fax), 8:30AM-5PM.

General Information: Records provided to the public are limited to 3 or 10 years. The state will show moving violations regardless of whether the fine was not paid and license suspended. It takes 1-4 weeks before new records are available for inquiries. Identification card information is confidential by statute. The state has filed suit in the US District Court against DPPA. The court ruled that

DPPA was unconstitutional. Driving records are open; however, personal information is not released.

Online search: The online system offers basic driver data, as well as a 3 year and 10 year record. This is a single inquiry process. Network charges will be incurred as well as initial set-up and a security deposit. The fee is $2.00 per record. The system is up between 8 AM and 7 PM. Access is through the AAMVAnet (IBMIN), which requesters much "join."

Legislation-Current/Pending Legislation-Passed

www.leginfo.state.sc.us

South Carolina Legislature, 937 Assembly Street, Rm 220, Columbia, SC 29201; 803-734-2060, 803-734-2145 (Older Bills), 9AM - 5PM.

General Information: Records are available for current session only. The session is a 2 year session.

Online search: Bill text and status data can be found at the web site.

Information About County Agencies

Court Structure

There are 46 circuit courts. Magistrate and Municipal Courts only handle misdemeanor cases involving 30 days or less jail time. The maximum civil claim monetary amount for the Magistrate Courts increased from $2500 to $5000 as of January 1, 1996.

Online Access

There is no statewide online public access available.

Search Hints

About the County Courts

The Clerk of the Circuit Court maintains the records of both civil and criminal divisions of the Circuit Court, Court of General Sessions, and Court of Common Pleas as well as for the Family Court. General Sessions and Common Pleas are co-located in every county. If requesting a record in writing, it is recommended that the words "request that General Session, Common Pleas, and Family Court records be searched" be included in the request.

Most South Carolina courts will not conduct searches. However, if a name and case number are provided, many will pull and copy the record. Search fees vary widely as they are set by each county individually.

About the Recorder's Office

Organization

46 counties, 46 recording offices. The recording officer is Register of Mesne Conveyances or Clerk of Court (varies by county). The entire state is in the Eastern Time Zone (EST).

Real Estate Records

Most counties will not perform real estate searches. Copy and certification fees vary. The Assessor keeps tax records

UCC Records

Financing statements are filed at the state level, except for consumer goods, farm related and real estate related collateral, which are filed with the Register. All recording offices will perform UCC searches. Use search request form UCC-4. Searches fees are usually $5.00 per debtor name. Copy fees are usually $1.00 per page.

Other Lien Records

All federal and state tax liens on personal property and on real property are filed with the Register of Mesne Conveyances (Clerk of Court). Some counties will perform tax lien searches. Search fees and copy fees vary.

County Courts & Recording Offices Online

No remote online access is available from real estate recorder's offices in South Carolina.

Charleston County

Civil Cases, Criminal Cases

Circuit Court, PO Box 70219, Charleston SC 29415, 843-740-5700. Fax: 843-740-5887. Hours: 8:30AM-5PM (EST).

Online search: The Internet offers access to records from 4/92 forward. Search by name or case number. There is no fee.

Federal Courts Online

County-to-Court Cross Reference (Bankruptcy Court locations in Parenthesis if different)

County	Court
Abbeville	Greenwood (Columbia)
Aiken	Greenwood (Columbia)
Allendale	Greenwood (Columbia)
Anderson	Anderson (Columbia)
Bamberg	Greenwood (Columbia)
Barnwell	Greenwood (Columbia)
Beaufort	Beaufort (Columbia)
Berkeley	Charleston (Columbia)
Calhoun	Greenwood (Columbia)
Charleston	Charleston (Columbia)
Cherokee	Spartanburg (Columbia)
Chester	Spartanburg (Columbia)
Chesterfield	Florence (Columbia)
Clarendon	Charleston (Columbia)
Colleton	Charleston (Columbia)
Darlington	Florence (Columbia)
Dillon	Florence (Columbia)
Dorchester	Charleston (Columbia)
Edgefield	Greenwood (Columbia)
Fairfield	Greenwood (Columbia)
Florence	Florence (Columbia)
Georgetown	Charleston (Columbia)
Greenville	Greenville (Columbia)
Greenwood	Greenwood (Columbia)
Hampton	Beaufort (Columbia)
Horry	Florence (Columbia)
Jasper	Beaufort (Columbia)
Kershaw	Columbia
Lancaster	Greenwood (Columbia)
Laurens	Greenville (Columbia)
Lee	Columbia
Lexington	Columbia
Marion	Florence (Columbia)
Marlboro	Florence (Columbia)
McCormick	Greenwood (Columbia)
Newberry	Greenwood (Columbia)
Oconee	Anderson (Columbia)
Orangeburg	Greenwood (Columbia)
Pickens	Anderson (Columbia)
Richland	Columbia
Saluda	Greenwood (Columbia)
Spartanburg	Spartanburg (Columbia)
Sumter	Columbia
Union	Spartanburg (Columbia)
Williamsburg	Florence (Columbia)
York	Spartanburg (Columbia)

US District Court
District of South Carolina

PACER sign-up number is 800-676-6856. Both civil and criminal case records are available online.

Charleston Division, PO Box 835, Charleston, SC 29402, 803-579-1401, Fax: 803-579-1402.

Beaufort Division, c/o Charleston Division, PO Box 835, Charleston, SC 29402, 803-579-1401, Fax: 803-579-1402.

Columbia Division, 1845 Assembly St, Columbia, SC 29201, 803-765-5816.

Florence Division, PO Box 2317, Florence, SC 29503, 803-676-3820, Fax: 803-676-3831.

Greenville Division, PO Box 10768, Greenville, SC 29603, 864-241-2700.

Greenwood Division, c/o Greenville Division, PO Box 10768, Greenville, SC 29603, 864-241-2700.

Anderson Division, c/o Greenville Division, PO Box 10768, Greenville, SC 29603, 864-241-2700.

Spartanburg Division, c/o Greenville Division, PO Box 10768, Greenville, SC 29603, 864-241-2700.

US Bankruptcy Court
District of South Carolina

PACER sign-up number is 800-676-6856.

Columbia Division, PO Box 1448, Columbia, SC 29202, 803-765-5436. All counties are serviced by this court.

South Dakota

Governor's Office
State Capitol,
500 E Capitol Ave   605-773-3212
Pierre, SD 57501-5070   Fax 605-773-5844
www.state.sd.us/state/executive/
governor/governor.htm

Attorney General's Office
State Capitol,
500 E Capitol Ave   605-773-3215
Pierre, SD 57501-5070   Fax 605-773-4106
www.state.sd.us/state/executive/
attorney/attorney.html

State Archives
State Historical Society   605-773-3804
Cultural Heritage Center/   Fax 605-773-6041
State Archives   9AM-4:30PM
900 Governors Dr
Pierre, SD 57501-2217
www.state.sd.us/state/executive/
deca/cultural/archives.htm

Capital: Pierre
                            Hughes County

Time Zone: CST*

* South Dakota's 18 western-most counties are MST:
They are: Bennett, Butte, Corson, Custer, Dewey, Fall
River, Haakon, Harding, Jackson, Lawrence, Meade,
Mellette, Pennington, Perkins, Shannon, Stanley, Todd,
Ziebach,

Number of Counties: 66

Population: 737,973

Web Site: www.state.sd.us

State Court Administrator
State Court Administrator   605-773-3474
State Capitol Bldg   Fax 605-773-6128
500 E Capitol Ave   8AM-5PM
Pierre, SD 57501

State Agencies Online

Legislation-Current/Pending
Legislation-Passed
www.state.sd.us/state/legis/lrc.htm

South Dakota Legislature, Capitol Bldg-Legislative
Documents, 500 E Capitol Ave, Pierre, SD 57501; 605-
773-3835, 605-773-4576 (Fax), 8AM-5PM.

Online search: Information is available at their
web site at no charge. The site is very thorough and
has enrolled version of bills.

Uniform Commercial Code
Federal Tax Liens

UCC Division, Secretary of State, 500 East Capitol,
Pierre, SD 57501-5077; 605-773-4422, 605-773-4550
(Fax), 8AM-5PM.

General Information: The search includes federal tax
liens on businesses. Federal tax liens on businesses and

all state tax liens on individuals are filed at the county
level.

Online search: Online access costs $240.00 per year plus
a transaction charge over 200 keystrokes per month.
Prepayment is required. The system is open 24 hours per
day. Place request in writing to set up an account. The
state is considering an Internet site in the future.

Driver Records
www.state.sd.us/dcr/dl/sddriver.htm

Dept of Commerce & Regulation, Office of Driver
Licensing, 118 W Capitol, Pierre, SD 57501; 605-773-
6883, 605-773-3018 (Fax), 8AM-5PM.

General Information: Records are available for 3 years
for moving violations and DWIs. Speeding violations less
than 10 mph over and out-of-state speeding violations
(except for commercial drivers), suspensions and
revocations are not listed on the record. It takes 1-3

weeks before new records are available for inquiries. Casual requesters can only obtain records with the written permission of the subjects. All other requesters must certify for what reason they are obtaining the information.

Online search: The system is open for batch requests 24 hours a day. It generally takes 10 minutes to process a batch. The current fee is $4.00 per record and there is some start-up costs. For more information, call (605) 773-6883.

Information About County Agencies

Court Structure

There are 66 circuit courts.

About the County Courts

Online Access

There is no statewide online access computer system currently available. Larger courts are being placed on computer systems at a rate of 4 to 5 courts per year. Access is intended for internal use only. Smaller courts place their information on computer cards that are later sent to Pierre for input by the state office.

Searching Hints

Most South Dakota courts do not allow the public to perform searches, but rather require the court clerk to do them for a fee of $15.00 per name (increased from $5.00 as of July 1, 1997). A special Record Search Request Form must be used. Searches will be returned with a disclaimer stating that the clerk is not responsible for the completeness of the search. Clerks are not required to respond to telephone or Fax requests. Many courts are not open all day so they prefer written requests.

About the Recorder's Office

Organization

66 counties, 66 recording offices. The recording officer is Register of Deeds. 48 counties are in the Central Time Zone (CST) and 18 are in the Mountain Time Zone (MST).

Real Estate Records

Many counties will perform real estate searches. Search fees and copy fees vary. Certification usually costs $2.00 per document.

UCC Records

Financing statements are filed at the state level, except for real estate related collateral, which are filed with the Register of Deeds. All recording offices will perform UCC searches. All counties have access to a statewide database of UCC filings. Use search request form UCC-11. Searches fees are usually $10.00 per debtor name. Copy fees are usually $1.00 per page.

Other Lien Records

Federal and state tax liens on personal property of businesses are filed with the Secretary of State. Other federal and state tax liens are filed with the county Register of Deeds. Most counties will perform tax lien searches. Search fees vary. Other liens are: mechanics, motor vehicle, materials.

County Courts & Recording Offices Online

There is no online access to court records in South Dakota.

No remote online access is available from real estate recorder's offices in South Dakota

Federal Courts Online

County-to-Court Cross Reference (Bankruptcy Court locations in Parenthesis if different)

Aurora	Sioux Falls		Hyde	Pierre
Beadle	Sioux Falls		Jackson	Pierre
Bennett	Rapid City (Pierre)		Jerauld	Pierre
Bon Homme	Sioux Falls		Jones	Pierre
Brookings	Sioux Falls		Kingsbury	Sioux Falls
Brown	Aberdeen (Pierre)		Lake	Sioux Falls
Brule	Sioux Falls		Lawrence	Rapid City (Pierre)
Buffalo	Pierre		Lincoln	Sioux Falls
Butte	Aberdeen (Pierre)		Lyman	Pierre
Campbell	Aberdeen (Pierre)		Marshall	Aberdeen (Pierre)
Charles Mix	Sioux Falls		McCook	Sioux Falls
Clark	Aberdeen (Pierre)		McPherson	Aberdeen (Pierre)
Clay	Sioux Falls		Meade	Rapid City (Pierre)
Codington	Aberdeen (Pierre)		Mellette	Pierre
Corson	Aberdeen (Pierre)		Miner	Sioux Falls
Custer	Rapid City (Pierre)		Minnehaha	Sioux Falls
Davison	Sioux Falls		Moody	Sioux Falls
Day	Aberdeen (Pierre)		Pennington	Rapid City (Pierre)
Deuel	Aberdeen (Pierre)		Perkins	Rapid City (Pierre)
Dewey	Pierre		Potter	Pierre
Douglas	Sioux Falls		Roberts	Aberdeen (Pierre)
Edmunds	Aberdeen (Pierre)		Sanborn	Sioux Falls
Fall River	Rapid City (Pierre)		Shannon	Rapid City (Pierre)
Faulk	Pierre		Spink	Aberdeen (Pierre)
Grant	Aberdeen (Pierre)		Stanley	Pierre
Gregory	Pierre		Sully	Pierre
Haakon	Pierre		Todd	Pierre
Hamlin	Aberdeen (Pierre)		Tripp	Pierre
Hand	Pierre		Turner	Sioux Falls
Hanson	Sioux Falls		Union	Sioux Falls
Harding	Rapid City (Pierre)		Walworth	Aberdeen (Pierre)
Hughes	Pierre		Yankton	Sioux Falls
Hutchinson	Sioux Falls		Ziebach	Pierre

US District Court
District of South Dakota

New "PACER-Net"

www.sdd.uscourts.gov

As a member of the PACER-Net project, some District Court of South Dakota records may be via the Internet. The PACER sign-up number is 800-676-6856. Both civil and criminal case records are available online.

Aberdeen Division, c/o Pierre Division, Federal Bldg & Courthouse, 225 S Pierre St, Room 405, Pierre, SD 57501, 605-342-3066

Pierre Division, Federal Bldg & Courthouse, Room 405, 225 S Pierre St, Pierre, SD 57501, 605-224-5849, Fax: 605-224-0806

Rapid City Division, Clerk's Office, Room 302, 515 9th St, Rapid City, SD 57701, 605-342-3066

Sioux Falls Div., Rm 220, US Courthouse, 400 S Phillips Av, Sioux Falls, SD 57102, 605-330-4447, Fax: 605-330-4312

US Bankruptcy Court
District of South Dakota

www.sdb.uscourts.gov

PACER sign-up number is 800-676-6856.

Pierre Division, Clerk, Room 203, Federal Bldg, 225 S Pierre St, Pierre, SD 57501, 605-224-6013, Fax: 605-224-9808

Sioux Falls Division, PO Box 5060, Sioux Falls, SD 57117-5060, 605-330-4541, Fax: 605-330-4548

Tennessee

Governor's Office

State Capitol, 1st Floor   615-741-2001
Nashville, TN 37243-0001   Fax 615-532-9711
www.state.tn.us/governor

Attorney General's Office

425 5th Ave North   615-741-3491
Nashville, TN 37243-0497   Fax 615-741-2009

State Archives

Secretary of State   615-741-7996
State Library &   Fax 615-741-6471
Archives Division
403 7th Ave N   8AM-6PM M-SA
Nashville, TN 37243-0312
www.state.tn.us/sos/statelib/
tslahome.htm

Capital:	Nashville
	Davidson County
Time Zone:	CST*

* Tennessee's 29 eastern-most counties are EST:
They are: Anderson, Blount, Bradley, Campbell, Carter,
Claiborne, Cocke, Grainger, Greene, Hamilton, Hancock,
Hawkins, Jefferson, Johnson, Knox, Loudon, McMinn,
Meigs, Monroe, Morgan, Polk, Rhea, Roane, Scott,
Sevier, Sullivan, Unicoi, Union, Washington.

Number of Counties:	95
Population:	5,368,198
Web Site:	www.state.tn.us

State Court Administrator

Admin. Office of the Courts   615-741-2687
600 Nashville City Center   Fax 615-741-6285
511 Union St   8AM-4PM
Nashville, TN 37243-0607
www.tsc.state.tn.us

State Agencies Online

Legislation-Current/Pending
Legislation-Passed

www.legislature.state.tn.us

Tennessee General Assembly, Office of Legislative
Information Services, Rachel Jackson Bldg, 1st Floor,
Nashville, TN 37243; 615-741-3511 (Status), 615-741-
0927 (Bill Room), 8AM-4:30PM.

General Information: Records are available for the
current and past session only. Earlier records are
maintained in the State Library & Archives. Include the
following in your request-bill number, topic of bill.

Access by: mail, phone, visit, online.

Online search: Bill information can be viewed at the
Internet site. The Tennessee Code is also available.

Information About County Agencies

Court Structure

All General Sessions Courts have raised the maximum civil case limit to $15,000 from $10,000. The Chancery Courts, in addition to handling probate, also hear certain types of equitable civil cases.

Criminal cases are handled by the Circuit Courts and General Sessions Courts. Combined courts vary by county, and the counties of Davidson, Hamilton, Knox, and Shelby have separate Criminal Courts. Probate is handled in the Chancery or County Courts, except in Shelby and Davidson Counties where it is handled by the Probate Court.

About the County Courts

Online Access

There is currently no statewide, online computer system available, internal or external. The Tennessee Administrative Office of Courts (AOC) has provided computers and CD-ROM readers to state judges, and a computerization project (named TnCIS) to implement statewide court automation started in '97.

About the Recorder's Office

Organization

95 counties, 96 recording offices. The recording officer is Register of Deeds. Sullivan County has two offices. 66 counties are in the Central Time Zone (CST) and 29 are in the Eastern Time Zone (EST).

Real Estate Records

Counties will not perform real estate searches. Copy fees and certification fees vary. Tax records are kept at the Assessor's Office.

UCC Records

Financing statements are filed at the state level, except for consumer goods, farm and real estate related collateral, which are filed with the Register of Deeds. Most recording offices will not perform UCC searches. Use search request form UCC-11. Search fees and copy fees vary.

Other Lien Records

All federal tax liens are filed with the county Register of Deeds. State tax liens are filed with the Secretary of State or the Register of Deeds. Counties will not perform tax lien searches. Other liens are: judgment, materialman, mechanics, trustee.

County Courts & Recording Offices Online

There is no online access to court records in Tennessee.

No remote online access is available from real estate recorder's offices in Tennessee.

Federal Courts Online

County-to-Court Cross Reference (Bankruptcy Court locations in Parenthesis if different)

County	District	Court
Anderson	Eastern	Knoxville
Bedford	Eastern	Winchester (Chattanooga)
Benton	Western	Jackson
Bledsoe	Eastern	Chattanooga
Blount	Eastern	Knoxville
Bradley	Eastern	Chattanooga
Campbell	Eastern	Knoxville
Cannon	Middle	Nashville
Carroll	Western	Jackson
Carter	Eastern	Greeneville (Knoxville)
Cheatham	Middle	Nashville
Chester	Western	Jackson
Claiborne	Eastern	Knoxville
Clay	Middle	Cookeville (Nashville)
Cocke	Eastern	Greeneville (Knoxville)
Coffee	Eastern	Winchester (Chattanooga)
Crockett	Western	Jackson
Cumberland	Middle	Cookeville (Nashville)
Davidson	Middle	Nashville
De Kalb	Middle	Cookeville (Nashville)
Decatur	Western	Jackson
Dickson	Middle	Nashville
Dyer	Western	Memphis
Fayette	Western	Memphis
Fentress	Middle	Cookeville (Nashville)
Franklin	Eastern	Winchester (Chattanooga)
Gibson	Western	Jackson
Giles	Middle	Columbia (Nashville)
Grainger	Eastern	Knoxville
Greene	Eastern	Greeneville (Knoxville)
Grundy	Eastern	Winchester (Chattanooga)
Hamblen	Eastern	Greeneville (Knoxville)
Hamilton	Eastern	Chattanooga
Hancock	Eastern	Greeneville (Knoxville)
Hardeman	Western	Jackson
Hardin	Western	Jackson
Hawkins	Eastern	Greeneville (Knoxville)
Haywood	Western	Jackson
Henderson	Western	Jackson
Henry	Western	Jackson
Hickman	Middle	Columbia (Nashville)
Houston	Middle	Nashville
Humphreys	Middle	Nashville
Jackson	Middle	Cookeville (Nashville)
Jefferson	Eastern	Knoxville
Johnson	Eastern	Greeneville (Knoxville)
Knox	Eastern	Knoxville
Lake	Western	Jackson
Lauderdale	Western	Memphis
Lawrence	Middle	Columbia (Nashville)
Lewis	Middle	Columbia (Nashville)
Lincoln	Eastern	Winchester (Chattanooga)
Loudon	Eastern	Knoxville
Macon	Middle	Cookeville (Nashville)
Madison	Western	Jackson
Marion	Eastern	Chattanooga
Marshall	Middle	Columbia (Nashville)
Maury	Middle	Columbia (Nashville)
McMinn	Eastern	Chattanooga
McNairy	Western	Jackson
Meigs	Eastern	Chattanooga
Monroe	Eastern	Knoxville
Montgomery	Middle	Nashville
Moore	Eastern	Winchester (Chattanooga)
Morgan	Eastern	Knoxville
Obion	Western	Jackson
Overton	Middle	Cookeville (Nashville)
Perry	Western	Jackson
Pickett	Middle	Cookeville (Nashville)
Polk	Eastern	Chattanooga
Putnam	Middle	Cookeville (Nashville)
Rhea	Eastern	Chattanooga
Roane	Eastern	Knoxville
Robertson	Middle	Nashville
Rutherford	Middle	Nashville
Scott	Eastern	Knoxville
Sequatchie	Eastern	Chattanooga
Sevier	Eastern	Knoxville
Shelby	Western	Memphis
Smith	Middle	Cookeville (Nashville)
Stewart	Middle	Nashville
Sullivan	Eastern	Greeneville (Knoxville)
Sumner	Middle	Nashville
Tipton	Western	Memphis
Trousdale	Middle	Nashville
Unicoi	Eastern	Greeneville (Knoxville)
Union	Eastern	Knoxville
Van Buren	Eastern	Winchester (Chattanooga)
Warren	Eastern	Winchester (Chattanooga)
Washington	Eastern	Greeneville (Knoxville)
Wayne	Middle	Columbia (Nashville)
Weakley	Western	Jackson
White	Middle	Cookeville (Nashville)
Williamson	Middle	Nashville
Wilson	Middle	Nashville

US District Court
Eastern District of Tennessee

PACER System: Sign-up number is 800-676-6856. Both civil and criminal case records are available online.

Chattanooga Division Clerk's Office, PO Box 591, Chattanooga, TN 37401, (Courier address: Room 309, 900 Georgia Ave, Chattanooga, TN 37402), 423-752-5200.

Greeneville Division 101 Summer St W, Greenville, TN 37743, 423-639-3105.

Knoxville Division Clerk's Office, 800 Market St, Knoxville, TN 37902, 423-545-4228.

Winchester Division PO Box 459, Winchester, TN 37398, (Courier address: 200 S Jefferson St, Room 201, Winchester, TN 37397), 931-967-1444.

US Bankruptcy Court
Eastern District of Tennessee

PACER System: Sign-up number is 800-676-6856. Closed bankruptcy case records are available back to January 1986. Records are purged as deemed necessary. Special note: current information is available online after 1 day.

Chattanooga Division Historic US Courthouse, 31 E 11th St, Chattanooga, TN 37402, 423-752-5163.

Knoxville Division Suite 1501, 1st Tennessee Plaza, Knoxville, TN 37929, 423-545-4279.

US District Court
Middle District of Tennessee

edge.edge.net/~uscourts

PACER System: Sign-up number is 800-676-6856. Both civil and criminal case records are available online.

Nashville Division US Courthouse, Room 800, 801 Broadway, Nashville, TN 37203, 615-736-5498, Record Room: 615-736-5498, Civil Docket Section: 615-736-7178, Criminal Docket Section: 615-736-7396, Fax: 615-736-7488.

Cookeville Division c/o Nashville Division, US Courthouse Room 800, 801 Broadway, Nashville, TN 37203, 615-736-5498, Fax: 615-736-7488. Searches should be conducted at the Nashville Division.

Columbia Division c/o Nashville Division, US Courthouse Room 800, 801 Broadway, Nashville, TN 37203, 615-736-5498. Searches should be conducted at the Nashville Division.

US Bankruptcy Court
Middle District of Tennessee

Nashville Division Customs House, Room 200, 701 Broadway, Nashville, TN 37203, 615-736-5584.

edge.edge.net/~uscourts.

PACER System: Sign-up number is 615-736-5577. Special note: current information is available online after 1 day.

US District Court
Western District of Tennessee

PACER System: Sign-up number is 800-676-6856. Both civil and criminal case records are available online.

Jackson Division Federal Bldg, Room 101, 109 S Highland Ave, Jackson, TN 38301, 901-427-6586, Fax: 901-422-3367.

Memphis Division Federal Bldg, Room 242, 167 N Main, Memphis, TN 38103, 901-495-1200, Record Room: 901-495-1206, Fax: 901-495-1250.

US Bankruptcy Court
Western District of Tennessee

PACER System: Sign-up number is 800-676-6856. Closed bankruptcy case records are available back to 1989. Special note: current information is available online after 2 days.

Jackson Division Room 312, 109 S Highland Ave, Jackson, TN 38301, 901-424-9751.

Memphis Division Suite 413, 200 Jefferson Ave, Memphis, TN 38103, 901-544-3202, Record Room: 901-544-4429.

Governor's Office
PO Box 12428   512-463-2000
Austin, TX 78711   Fax 512-463-1849
www.governor.state.tx.us

Attorney General's Office
PO Box 12548   512-463-2100
Austin, TX 78711-2548 Fax 512-463-2063
www.oag.state.tx.us

State Archives
Library & Archives
Commission   512-463-5455
PO Box 12927   Fax 512-463-5436
Austin, TX 78711   8AM-5PM,
Genealogy 8-5 T-SA
www.tsl.state.tx.us

Capital:	Austin
	Travis County
Time Zone:	CST*

* Texas' two western-most counties are MST:
They are: El Paso and Hudspeth,

Number of Counties:	254
Population:	19,439,337
Web Site:	www.state.tx.us

State Court Administrator
Office of Court Admin.   512-463-1625
PO Box 12066   Fax 512-463-1648
Austin, TX 78711-2066   8AM-5PM
www.courts.state.tx.us

State Agencies Online

Criminal Records
txdps.state.tx.us

Crime Records Service, Correspondence Section, PO Box 15999, Austin, TX 78761-5999; (Courier: 5805 N Lamar, Austin, TX 78752); 512-424-2079, 8AM-5PM.

General Information: To obtain ALL arrest information (conviction and non-conviction), must have a signed release form from the person of record and full set of fingerprints of person of record.

Online search: Records can be pulled from the web site. Requesters must establish an account and have a pre-paid bank to work from. The fee established by the Department (Sec. 411.135(b)) is $3.09 per request plus an additional handling fee of $.57 to buy credits.

Legislation-Current/Pending
Legislation-Passed
www.capitol.state.tx.us

Legislative Reference Library, PO Box 12488, Austin, TX 78711-2488; (Courier: State Capitol Building, 2N.3,

1100 Congress, Austin, TX 78701); 512-463-1252 (Bill Status), 512-463-0252 (Senate Bill Copies), 512-463-1144 (House Bill Copies), 512-475-4626 (Fax).

Online search: The web is a thorough searching site of bills and status.

Corporation Records
www.window.texas.gov/taxinfo/coasintr.html

Fictitious Name
Limited Partnership Records
Limited Liability Company Records
Assumed Name
Trademarks/Servicemarks
www.sos.state.tx.us

Secretary of State, Corporation Section, PO Box 13697, Austin, TX 78711-3697; (Courier: J Earl Rudder Bldg, 1019 Brazos, B-13, Austin, TX 78701); 512-463-5555 (Information), 512-463-5578 (Copies), 512-463-5576 (Trademarks), 512-463-5709 (Fax), 8AM-5PM.

General Information: Records are available from the 1800s. New records are available immediately on the computer, but it takes 12 days before new records are available to be copied.

Online search: Dial-up access is available M-TH from 7 AM to 8 PM (6PM on Fridays). There is a $3.00 fee for each record searched (secured party searches are ($10.00) Filing procedures and forms are available from the web site or from 900-263-0060 ($1.00 per minute). To sign up for online access, call Tina Passell at 512-475-2755. A second way to access information, although somewhat limited, is through the Office of the Comptroller for certification of franchise tax account status. You can determine status of a corporation or an LLC and obtain list of officers or directors. Go to: www.window.texas.gov/taxinfo/coasintr.html.

Uniform Commercial Code
Federal Tax Liens
www.sos.state.tx.us

UCC Section, Secretary of State, PO Box 13193, Austin, TX 78711-3193; 512-475-2705, 512-475-2812 (Fax)

General Information: The search includes federal tax liens on businesses. Federal tax liens on individuals and all state tax liens are filed at the county level.

Online search: Direct dial-up is open from 7 AM to 6 PM. The fee is $3.00 per search, $10.00 for a secured party search. General information and forms can be found at the web site.

Vehicle Ownership
Vehicle Identification

Department of Transportation, Vehicle Titles and Registration, 40th St and Jackson, Austin, TX 78779; 512-465-7611, 512-465-7736 (Fax), 8AM-5PM.

General Information: Records are available for 5 years to present. The state does not permit searches based on name or vehicle owner. Personal information is not released on opt-outs to casual requesters

Online search: Online access is available for pre-approved accounts. A $200 deposit is required, there is a $23 charge per month and $.12 fee per inquiry. Searching by name is not permitted. For more information, call the number listed above.

Information About County Agencies

Court Structure

Generally, Texas District Courts have general civil jurisdiction and exclusive felony jurisdiction, along with typical variations such as contested probate and divorce.

About the County Courts

The County Court structure includes two forms of courts—"Constitutional" and "at Law"—which come in various configurations depending upon the county. County Courts' upper civil claims limit vary from $5,000 to $100,000. For civil matters up to $5000, we recommend searchers start at the Constitutional County Court as they, generally, offer a shorter waiting time for cases in urban areas. In addition, keep in mind that the Municipal Courts have, per the Texas manual, "limited civil penalties in cases involving dangerous dogs." In some counties the District Court or County Court handles evictions.

District Courts handle felonies. County Courts handle misdemeanors and general civil cases. Probate is handled in Probate Court in the 18 largest counties and in District Courts or County Courts at Law elsewhere. However, the County Clerk is responsible for the records in every county.

Online Access

There is no statewide, court-related online computer access available, internal or external. However, a number of counties offer online access.

About the Recorder's Office

Organization

254 counties, 254 recording offices. The recording officer is County Clerk. 252 counties are in the Central Time Zone (CST) and 2 are in the Mountain Time Zone (MST).

Real Estate Records

Some counties will perform real estate searches. Copy fees are usually $1.00 per page. Certification usually costs $5.00 per document. Each county has an "Appraisal District" which is responsible for collecting taxes.

UCC Records

Financing statements are filed at the state level, except for real estate related collateral, which are filed with the County Clerk. All recording offices will perform UCC searches. Searches fees are usually $10.00 per debtor name using the approved UCC-11 request form, plus $15.00 for using a non-Texas form. Copy fees are usually $1.00-1.50 per page with a minimum copy fee of $5.00.

Other Lien Records

Federal tax liens on personal property of businesses are filed with the Secretary of State. Other federal and all state tax liens are filed with the County Clerk. All counties will perform tax lien searches. Search fees and copy fees vary. Other liens are: mechanics, judgment, hospital, labor, lis pendens.

County Courts & Recording Offices Online

Bexar County

Civil Cases, Criminal Cases

County Court-Criminal, 300 Dolorosa, Suite 4101, San Antonio TX 78205, 210-220-2220. Hours: 8AM-5PM (CST).

Civil Cases, Criminal Cases

County Court-Criminal, 100 Dolorosa, County Courthouse, San Antonio TX 78205, 210-220-2083.

Online search: Online access is open 24 hours daily. The setup fee is $100, the monthly fee is $25 plus inquiry fees. Call Jennifer Mann at 210-335-0212 for more information.

Cameron County

Civil Cases

District Court, 974 Harrison St, Brownsville TX 78520, 956-544-0839.

Online search: Online access is available 24 hours daily. The $125 setup fee includes software, there is a $30 monthly access fee also. For more information, call Eric at 956-544-0838 X475.

Collin County

Civil Cases, Criminal Cases

District Clerk, PO Box 578, McKinney TX 75069, 972-548-4365. Hours: 8AM-5PM (CST).

Civil Cases, Criminal Cases

County Court, 210 S McDonald St Rm 542, McKinney TX 75069, 972-548-4529. Fax: 972-548-4698.

Online search: Online is available 7AM to 7PM M-Sat, 6 to 6 on Sun. The access fee is $.12 a minute, there is a monthly minimum of $31.13. Procomm Plus is suggested. Call Patty Ostrom for subscription information.

Dallas County

No civil claims limit as of 05/23/97 in Dallas County.

Civil Cases

County Court-Civil, 509 W Main 3rd Floor, Dallas TX 75202, 214-653-7131. Hours: 8AM-4:30PM (CST).

Online search: Public Access System allows remote access at $1.00 per minute invoiced to your telephone bill. Access number is 900-263-INFO. ProComm Plus is recommended. Call the Administrator at 214-653-7807 for more information. No juvenile, mental, sealed, or adoption records released.

Civil Cases

District Court-Civil, 600 Commerce, Dallas TX 75202-4606, 214-653-7421. Hours: 8AM-4:30PM (CST).

Online search: Public Access System allows remote access at $1.00 per minute to these and other court and public records. Access number is 900-263-INFO. ProComm Plus is recommended. The system is open 8AM to 4:30PM. Searching is by name or case number.

Criminal Cases

District Court-Criminal, 133 N Industrial Blvd, Dallas TX 75207-4313, 214-653-5950. Fax: 214-653-5986. Hours: 8AM-4:30PM (CST).

Online search: The Public Access System makes felony and other records available remotely at a cost of $1.00 per minute, billed on your telephone bill. Access number is 900-263-INFO. The system is open from 8AM to 4:30PM. Search by name or case number. For more info, call 214-653-6807.

Denton County

Civil Cases, Criminal Cases

http://justice.co.denton.tx.us

District Court PO Box 2146, Denton TX 76202, 940-565-8528. Fax: 940-565-8607. Hours: 8AM-4:30PM

Online search: Criminal searches are available on the web site at no charge. Records are available from 1998 forward. Access also includes sheriff bond and jail records. Search by name or cause number.

Fort Bend County

Liens, Real Estate, Birth & Death Records

County Clerk, 301 Jackson St, Richmond TX 77469, 281-341-8650. Fax: 281-341-4520. Hours: 8AM-4PM

Online search: A $100 escrow account is required. Monthly fee is $15, plus $.25 per minute. The system operates 24 hours daily and supports a baud rate of 14.4. Reach Out software is required to interface with their system. Records date back to the 1930's, viewable images back to 10/94. Images are printable for $.50, $.75 if long distance. One may search by name, Grantee/Grantor, book and page and instrument number. Lending agency information is available. For information, contact Linda Jordan at 281-341-8652.

Civil Cases, Criminal Cases

District and County Court, 301 Jackson St, Richmond TX 77469, 281-341-4562, 281-341-42 (Criminal), Fax: 281-341-4519.

Online search: Online searching available through a 900 number service. The access fee is $.55 per minute plus a deposit. Call 281-341-4522 for information

Galveston County

Liens, Real Estate, Marriage Records

County Clerk, 722 Moody Ave, Galveston TX 77550, 409-766-2292, Hours: 8AM-5PM (CST).

County Clerk (Leek City Annex), 174 Calder Dr, Suite 149, Leek City TX 77573, 281-316-8732, Fax: 281-316-8737

Online search: A $200 escrow account deposit is required. The monthly fee is $25, plus $.25 per minute. The system operates 8AM-12AM and supports baud rates up to 14.4. Index records date back to 1965. Viewable image documents date back to 1/95. One may search by name, Grantee/Grantor, date filed, instrument number and document type. A fax back service is available, $.75 per page for local, $1.00 long distance. Lending agency information is available. Reach out Software is required to interface with their system. For further information, contact Robert Dickinson at 409-770-5115.

Civil Cases, Criminal Cases

County Court, PO Box 2450, Galveston TX 77553-2450, 409-766-5112 (Misdemeanor). Civil Phone: 409-766-2203. Criminal Phone: 409-766-2206. Hours: 8AM-5PM

Online search: A $200 escrow account is required to open online access. The fee is $.25 per minute. The system is available 24 hours daily and gives fax back capability. For more information about GCNET call Mary Ann Daigle at 409-766-2200

Harris County

Civil Cases, Probate, Real Estate, Vital Records, Liens

County Court, PO Box 1525, Houston TX 77251-1525, 713-755-6421. Hours: 8AM-4:30PM (CST).

Online search: The online system is open 24 hours daily. There is a $300 deposit and access in $40.00 per hour. The online system also includes real property, assumed names, UCC, probate court dockets and marriages. For more information, call Ken Peabody at 713-755-7151.

Civil Cases, Criminal Cases

District Court, PO Box 4651, Houston TX 77210. Civil Phone: 713-755-5711. Criminal Phone: 713-755-5734. Fax: 713-755-5480 (civil). Hours: 8AM-5PM (CST).

Online search: Online access requires a separate deposit of $150 for both civil and criminal access plus access fees. Civil and criminal are in separate systems, however. The system is open 24 hours daily. Attendance at a training class is required. For more information, call Eric Engelking at 713-755-7815.

Tarrant County

Civil Cases, Probate

County Court, 100 W Weatherford Rm 250, Fort Worth TX 76196, 817-884-1076. Hours: 7:30AM-4:30PM (CST).

Online search: Online access is by subscription only. There is a setup fee, deposit and monthly minimum fees of $25 (based on $.05 per minute). The system is open 24 hours daily and also includes probate, misdemeanor and traffic. For further information, call Laura Yanes at 817-884-3202.

Civil Cases, Criminal Cases

District Court, 401 W Belknap, Fort Worth TX 76196-0402, 817-884-1574 (884-1265 Family Division). Civil Phone: 817-884-1240. Criminal Phone: 817-884-1342. Fax: 817-884-1484. Hours: 8AM-5PM (CST).

Online search: The online system is open 7:30 am to 7pm daily. The $50 setup includes software. The per minute fee is $.05 with a $25 minimum per month. Call Ms. Ziton at 817-884-1782 for more information.

Federal Courts Online

County-to-Court Cross Reference (Bankruptcy Court locations in Parenthesis if different)

Anderson ....Eastern ....Tyler
Andrews...........Western.............Midland (Midland/Odessa)
Angelina...........Eastern ....Texarkana (Beaumont)
Aransas ....Southern...........Corpus Christi
Archer ....Northern...........Wichita Falls
Armstrong........Northern...........Amarillo
Atascosa...........Western.............San Antonio
Austin...............Southern...........Houston
Bailey ....Northern...........Lubbock
Bandera...........Western.............San Antonio
Bastrop............Western.............Austin
Baylor...............Northern...........Wichita Falls
Bee...................Southern...........Corpus Christi
Bell ....Western.............Waco
Bexar................Western.............San Antonio
Blanco ....Western.............Austin
Borden..............Northern...........Lubbock
Bosque ....Western.............Waco
Bowie...............Eastern ....Texarkana
Brazoria...........Southern...........Galveston (Houston)
Brazos ....Southern...........Houston
Brewster...........Western.............Pecos (Midland/Odessa)
Briscoe ....Northern...........Amarillo
Brooks..............Southern...........Corpus Christi
Brown ....Northern...........San Angelo (Lubbock)
Burleson...........Western.............Austin
Burnet..............Western.............Austin
Caldwell...........Western.............Austin
Calhoun............Southern...........Victoria (Corpus Christi)
Callahan ....Northern...........Abilene (Lubbock)
Cameron ....Southern...........Brownsville (Corpus Christi)
Camp................Eastern ....Marshall
Carson ....Northern...........Amarillo
Cass ....Eastern ....Marshall
Castro ....Northern...........Amarillo
Chambers.........Southern...........Galveston (Houston)
Cherokee..........Eastern ....Tyler
Childress ....Northern...........Amarillo
Clay ....Northern...........Wichita Falls
Cochran............Northern...........Lubbock
Coke ....Northern...........San Angelo (Lubbock)
Coleman...........Northern...........San Angelo (Lubbock)
Collin................Eastern ....Sherman (Plano)
Collingsworth...Northern...........Amarillo
Colorado ....Southern...........Houston
Comal...............Western.............San Antonio
Comanche........Northern...........Fort Worth
Concho.............Northern...........San Angelo (Lubbock)
Cooke...............Eastern ....Sherman (Plano)
Coryell..............Western.............Waco
Cottle...............Northern...........Wichita Falls
Crane................Western.............Midland (Midland/Odessa)

Crockett ....Northern ....San Angelo (Lubbock)
Crosby..............Northern ....Lubbock
Culberson ....Western.............Pecos (Midland/Odessa)
Dallam ....Northern ....Amarillo
Dallas ....Northern ....Dallas
Dawson.............Northern ....Lubbock
De Witt ....Southern ....Victoria (Houston)
Deaf Smith ......Northern ....Amarillo
Delta................Eastern ....Sherman (Plano)
Denton ....Eastern ....Sherman (Plano)
Dickens............Northern ....Lubbock
Dimmit.............Western.............San Antonio
Donley ....Northern ....Amarillo
Duval................Southern ....Corpus Christi
Eastland ....Northern ....Abilene (Lubbock)
Ector................Western.............Midland (Midland/Odessa)
Edwards...........Western.............Del Rio (San Antonio)
El Paso ....Western.............El Paso
Ellis ....Northern ....Dallas
Erath.................Northern ....Fort Worth
Falls..................Western.............Waco
Fannin ....Eastern ....Sherman (Plano)
Fayette..............Southern ....Houston
Fisher ....Northern ....Abilene (Lubbock)
Floyd.................Northern ....Lubbock
Foard ....Northern ....Wichita Falls
Fort Bend.........Southern ....Houston
Franklin............Eastern ....Texarkana
Freestone ....Western.............Waco
Frio ....Western.............San Antonio
Gaines ....Northern ....Lubbock
Galveston..........Southern ....Galveston (Houston)
Garza................Northern ....Lubbock
Gillespie...........Western.............Austin
Glasscock ....Northern ....San Angelo (Lubbock)
Goliad ....Southern ....Victoria (Corpus Christi)
Gonzales...........Western.............San Antonio
Gray.................Northern ....Amarillo
Grayson ....Eastern ....Sherman (Plano)
Gregg ....Eastern ....Tyler
Grimes ....Southern ....Houston
Guadalupe ....Western.............San Antonio
Hale..................Northern ....Lubbock
Hall..................Northern ....Amarillo
Hamilton..........Western.............Waco
Hansford..........Northern ....Amarillo
Hardeman........Northern ....Wichita Falls
Hardin ....Eastern ....Beaumont
Harris ....Southern ....Houston
Harrison ....Eastern ....Marshall
Hartley ....Northern ....Amarillo
Haskell..............Northern ....Abilene (Lubbock)

County-to-Court Cross Reference (Bankruptcy Court locations in Parenthesis if different)

County	District	Court
Hays	Western	Austin
Hemphill	Northern	Amarillo
Henderson	Eastern	Tyler
Hidalgo	Southern	McAllen (Corpus Christi)
Hill	Western	Waco
Hockley	Northern	Lubbock
Hood	Northern	Fort Worth
Hopkins	Eastern	Sherman (Plano)
Houston	Eastern	Texarkana (Beaumont)
Howard	Northern	Abilene (Lubbock)
Hudspeth	Western	Pecos (Midland/Odessa)
Hunt	Northern	Dallas
Hutchinson	Northern	Amarillo
Irion	Northern	San Angelo (Lubbock)
Jack	Northern	Fort Worth
Jackson	Southern	Victoria (Corpus Christi)
Jasper	Eastern	Beaumont
Jeff Davis	Western	Pecos (Midland/Odessa)
Jefferson	Eastern	Beaumont
Jim Hogg	Southern	Laredo (Houston)
Jim Wells	Southern	Corpus Christi
Johnson	Northern	Dallas
Jones	Northern	Abilene (Lubbock)
Karnes	Western	San Antonio
Kaufman	Northern	Dallas
Kendall	Western	San Antonio
Kenedy	Southern	Corpus Christi
Kent	Northern	Lubbock
Kerr	Western	San Antonio
Kimble	Western	Austin
King	Northern	Wichita Falls
Kinney	Western	Del Rio (San Antonio)
Kleberg	Southern	Corpus Christi
Knox	Northern	Wichita Falls
La Salle	Southern	Laredo (Corpus Christi)
Lamar	Eastern	Sherman (Plano)
Lamb	Northern	Lubbock
Lampasas	Western	Austin
Lavaca	Southern	Victoria (Houston)
Lee	Western	Austin
Leon	Western	Waco
Liberty	Eastern	Beaumont
Limestone	Western	Waco
Lipscomb	Northern	Amarillo
Live Oak	Southern	Corpus Christi
Llano	Western	Austin
Loving	Western	Pecos (Midland/Odessa)
Lubbock	Northern	Lubbock
Lynn	Northern	Lubbock
Madison	Southern	Houston
Marion	Eastern	Marshall
Martin	Western	Midland (Midland/Odessa)
Mason	Western	Austin
Matagorda	Southern	Galveston (Houston)
Maverick	Western	Del Rio (San Antonio)
McCulloch	Western	Austin
McLennan	Western	Waco
McMullen	Southern	Laredo (Houston)
Medina	Western	San Antonio
Menard	Northern	San Angelo (Lubbock)
Midland	Western	Midland (Midland/Odessa)
Milam	Western	Waco
Mills	Northern	San Angelo (Lubbock)
Mitchell	Northern	Abilene (Lubbock)
Montague	Northern	Wichita Falls
Montgomery	Southern	Houston
Moore	Northern	Amarillo
Morris	Eastern	Marshall
Motley	Northern	Lubbock
Nacogdoches	Eastern	Texarkana (Beaumont)
Navarro	Northern	Dallas
Newton	Eastern	Beaumont
Nolan	Northern	Abilene (Lubbock)
Nueces	Southern	Corpus Christi
Ochiltree	Northern	Amarillo
Oldham	Northern	Amarillo
Orange	Eastern	Beaumont
Palo Pinto	Northern	Fort Worth
Panola	Eastern	Tyler
Parker	Northern	Fort Worth
Parmer	Northern	Amarillo
Pecos	Western	Pecos (Midland/Odessa)
Polk	Eastern	Texarkana (Beaumont)
Potter	Northern	Amarillo
Presidio	Western	Pecos (Midland/Odessa)
Rains	Eastern	Tyler
Randall	Northern	Amarillo
Reagan	Northern	San Angelo (Lubbock)
Real	Western	San Antonio
Red River	Eastern	Sherman (Plano)
Reeves	Western	Pecos (Midland/Odessa)
Refugio	Southern	Victoria (Corpus Christi)
Roberts	Northern	Amarillo
Robertson	Western	Waco
Rockwall	Northern	Dallas
Runnels	Northern	San Angelo (Lubbock)
Rusk	Eastern	Tyler
Sabine	Eastern	Texarkana (Beaumont)
San Augustine	Eastern	Texarkana (Beaumont)
San Jacinto	Southern	Houston
San Patricio	Southern	Corpus Christi
San Saba	Western	Austin
Schleicher	Northern	San Angelo (Lubbock)
Scurry	Northern	Lubbock
Shackelford	Northern	Abilene (Lubbock)
Shelby	Eastern	Texarkana (Beaumont)
Sherman	Northern	Amarillo
Smith	Eastern	Tyler
Somervell	Western	Waco
Starr	Southern	McAllen (Corpus Christi)
Stephens	Northern	Abilene (Lubbock)
Sterling	Northern	San Angelo (Lubbock)

County-to-Court Cross Reference (Bankruptcy Court locations in Parenthesis if different)

Stonewall ....Northern............Abilene (Lubbock)	Waller ....Southern ....Houston
Sutton ....Northern............San Angelo (Lubbock)	Ward ....Western............Pecos (Midland/Odessa)
Swisher ....Northern............Amarillo	Washington ......Western............Austin
Tarrant...............Northern............Fort Worth	Webb.................Southern ....Laredo (Houston)
Taylor ....Northern............Abilene (Lubbock)	Wharton............Southern ....Houston
Terrell...............Western............Del Rio (San Antonio)	Wheeler ....Northern ....Amarillo
Terry.................Northern............Lubbock	Wichita ....Northern ....Wichita Falls
Throckmorton ..Northern............Abilene (Lubbock)	Wilbarger.........Northern ....Wichita Falls
Titus..................Eastern ....Texarkana	Willacy.............Southern ....Brownsville (Corpus Christi)
Tom Green ......Northern............San Angelo (Lubbock)	Williamson......Western............Austin
Travis ....Western............Austin	Wilson..............Western............San Antonio
Trinity...............Eastern ....Texarkana (Beaumont)	Winkler............Western............Pecos (Midland/Odessa)
Tyler ....Eastern ....Texarkana (Beaumont)	Wise ....Northern ....Fort Worth
Upshur...............Eastern ....Marshall	Wood ....Eastern ....Tyler
Upton.................Western............Midland (Midland/Odessa)	Yoakum............Northern ....Lubbock
Uvalde...............Western............Del Rio (San Antonio)	Young ....Northern ....Wichita Falls
Val Verde ....Western............Del Rio (San Antonio)	Zapata ....Southern ....Laredo (Houston)
Van Zandt........Eastern ....Tyler	Zavala ....Western............Del Rio (San Antonio)
Victoria ....Southern............Victoria (Corpus Christi)	
Walker...............Southern............Houston	

US District Court
Eastern District of Texas

www.txed.uscourts.gov

PACER sign-up number for the following courts is 800-676-6856. Both civil and criminal case records are available online.

Beaumont Division, PO Box 3507, Beaumont, TX 77704, 409-654-7000

Marshall Division, PO Box 1499, Marshall, TX 75671-1499, 903-935-2912, Criminal Docket Section: 903-590-1000

Sherman Division, 101 E Pecan St, Sherman, TX 75090, 903-892-2921

Texarkana Division, Clerk's Office, 500 State Line Ave, Room 302, Texarkana, TX 75501, 903-794-8561, Fax: 903-794-0600

Tyler Division, Clerk, Room 106, 211 W Ferguson, Tyler, TX 75702, 903-590-1000

US Bankruptcy Court
Eastern District of Texas

PACER sign-up number for the following courts is 800-676-6856. Only civil case records are available online.

Beaumont Division, Suite 100, 300 Willow, Beaumont, TX 77701, 409-839-2617.

Texarkana Division, c/o Plano Division, Suite 300B, 660 N Central Expressway, Plano, TX 75074, 972-509-1240, Fax: 972-509-1245.

Plano Division, Suite 300B, 660 N Central Expressway, Plano, TX 75074, 972-509-1240, Fax: 972-509-1245.

Tyler Division, 200 E Ferguson, 2nd Floor, Tyler, TX 75702, 903-590-1212, Ext-210, Fax: 903-590-1226.

Marshall Division, c/o Tyler Division, 200 E Ferguson, Tyler, TX 75702, 903-590-1212, Ext-210, Fax: 903-590-1226.

US District Court
Northern District of Texas

New "PACER-Net"

http://207.203.50.52/dc/pacer100.html

As a member of the PACER-Net project, Northern District of Texas Court makes PACER available via the Internet.

PACER sign-up number is 800-676-6856. Both civil and criminal case records are available online.

Abilene Division, PO Box 1218, Abilene, TX 79604, 915-677-6311

Amarillo Division, 205 E 5th St, Amarillo, TX 79101, 806-324-2352

Dallas Division, Room 14A20, 1100 Commerce St, Dallas, TX 75242, 214-767-0787, Record Room: 214-767-0789

Fort Worth Division, Clerk's Office, 501 W Tenth St, Room 310, Fort Worth, TX 76102, 817-978-3132

Lubbock Division, Clerk, Room 105, 904 Broadway, Lubbock, TX 79401, 806-775-1300

San Angelo Division, Clerk's Office, Room 202, 33 E Twohig, San Angelo, TX 76903, 915-655-4506, Fax: 915-658-6826

Wichita Falls Division, PO Box 1234, Wichita Falls, TX 76307, 940-767-1902, Fax: 940-767-2526

US Bankruptcy Court
Northern District of Texas

New "PACER-Net"

www.txnb.uscourts.gov

As a member of the PACER-Net project, Northern District of Texas Court makes PACER available via the Internet.

PACER sign-up number is 800-676-6856

Amarillo Division, PO Box 15960, Amarillo, TX 79105, 806-324-2302

Dallas Division, 1100 Commerce St, Suite 12A24, Dallas, TX 75242-1496, 214-767-0814, Record Room: 214-767-3616

Wichita Falls Division, c/o Dallas Division, Suite 12A24, 1100 Commerce St, Dallas, TX 75242-1496, 214-767-0814, Record Room: 214-767-0814

Fort Worth Division, 501 W 10th, Suite 147, Fort Worth, TX 76102, 817-978-3802

Lubbock Division, 306 Federal Bldg, 1205 Texas Ave, Lubbock, TX 79401, 806-472-7336

US District Court
Southern District of Texas

www.txs.uscourts.gov

PACER sign-up number for the following courts is 800-676-6856. Both civil and criminal case records are available online.

Brownsville Division, PO Box 2299, Brownsville, TX 78522, 956-548-2500

Corpus Christi Division, Clerk's Office, 521 Starr St, Corpus Christi, TX 78401, 512-888-3142

Galveston Division, Clerk's Office, PO Drawer 2300, Galveston, TX 77553, 409-766-3530

Houston Division, PO Box 61010, Houston, TX 77208, 713-250-5500, Record Room: 713-250-5543, Civil Docket Section: 713-250-5786, Criminal Docket Section: 713-250-5598

Laredo Division, PO Box 597, Laredo, TX 78042-0597, 956-723-3542, Civil Docket Section: 956-726-2236, Criminal Docket Section: 956-726-2236, Fax: 956-726-2289

McAllen Division, Suite 1011, 10th Fl, 1701 W Business Hwy 83, McAllen, TX 78501, 956-618-8065

Victoria Division, Clerk US District Court, PO Box 1541, Victoria, TX 77902, 512-788-5000

US Bankruptcy Court
Southern District of Texas

PACER sign-up number is 800-676-6856.

Corpus Christi Division, Room 113, 615 Leopard St, Corpus Christi, TX 78476, 512-888-3484.

Houston Division, Room 1217, 515 Rusk Ave, Houston, TX 77002, 713-250-5500

US District Court
Western District of Texas

www.txwd.uscourts.gov

PACER sign-up number for the following courts is 800-676-6856. Both civil and criminal case records are available online.

Austin Division, Room 130, 200 W 8th St, Austin, TX 78701, 512-916-5896

Del Rio Division, Room L100, 111 E Broadway, Del Rio, TX 78840, 830-703-2054

El Paso Division, US District Clerk's Office, Room 350, 511 E San Antonio, El Paso, TX 79901, 915-534-6725

Midland Division, Clerk, US District Court, 200 E Wall St, Midland, TX 79701, 915-686-4001

Pecos Division, US Courthouse, 410 S Cedar St, Pecos, TX 79772, 915-445-4228

San Antonio Division, US Clerk's Office, 655 E Durango, Suite G-65, San Antonio, TX 78206, 210-472-6550

Waco Division, Clerk, PO Box 608, Waco, TX 76703, 254-750-1501

US Bankruptcy Court
Western District of Texas

PACER sign-up number for the following courts is 800-676-6856. Only civil case records are available online.

Austin Division, Homer Thornberry Judicial Bldg, 903 San Antonio, Room 322, Austin, TX 78701, 512-916-5237.

El Paso Division, PO Box 971040, El Paso, TX 79997-1040, 915-779-7362.

Midland/Odessa Division, US Post Office Annex, Room P-163, 100 E Wall St, Midland, TX 79701, 915-683-1650.

Pecos Division, 410 S. Cedar, Pecos, TX 79772, 915-445-4228.

San Antonio Division, PO Box 1439, San Antonio, TX 78295, 210-472-6720, Fax: 210-472-5916.

Waco Division, PO Box 687, Waco, TX 76703, 254-754-1481.

Governor's Office
210 State Capitol   801-538-1000
Salt Lake City, UT 84114   Fax 801-538-1528
www.governor.state.ut.us

Attorney General's Office
236 State Capitol   801-538-9600
Salt Lake City, UT 84114   Fax 801-366-0221
www.at.state.ut.us

Capital:	Salt Lake City
	Salt Lake County
Time Zone:	MST
Number of Counties:	29
Population:	2,059,148
Web Site:	www.state.ut.us

State Archives
Utah State Archives   801-538-3013
PO Box 141021   Fax 801-538-3354
Salt Lake City, UT 84114-1021
archives.state.ut.us   8AM-5PM M-F

State Court Administrator
Court Administrator   801-578-3800
230 S 500 E, #300   Fax 801-578-3843
Salt Lake City, UT 84102   8AM-5PM
courtlink.utcourts.gov

State Agencies Online

Legislation-Current/Pending
Legislation-Passed
www.le.state.ut.us

Utah Legislature, Research and General Counsel, 436 State Capitol, Salt Lake City, UT 84114; 801-538-1032, 801-538-1588 (Bill Room), 801-538-1032 (Older Passed Bills), 801-538-1712 (Fax), 8AM-5PM.

Online search: Web site contains bill information and also the Utah Codes.

Corporation Records
Limited Liability Company Records
Fictitious Name
Limited Partnership Records
Assumed Name
Trademarks/Servicemarks

Commerce Department, Corporate Division, PO Box 146705, Salt Lake City, UT 84114-6705; (Courier: 160 E 300 S, 2nd fl, Salt Lake City, UT 84111); 801-530-4849 (Administration), 801-530-6205 (Certified Records), 801-530-6034 (Non-Certified), 801-530-6363 (Good Standing), 801-530-6111 (Fax), 8AM-5PM.

General Information: Records are available for active companies only. This agency also has records of non-profit corporations.

Online search: The system is called "Datashare." User fee is $10.00 per month plus some records require search fees. The system is open 24 hours daily. A large variety of information is available including notary public commissions and state contractors licenses. Call (801) 530-6443 for more information.

Uniform Commercial Code
www.commerce.state.ut.us

Department of Commerce, UCC Division, Box 146705, Salt Lake City, UT 84114-6705; (Courier: 160 E 300 South, Heber M Wells Bldg, 2nd Floor, Salt Lake City, UT 84111); 801-530-6025, 801-530-6438 (Fax).

General Information: All tax liens are filed at the county level. The state hopes to have the UCC data available on the Internet by early 1999.

Online search: User fee is $10.00 per month. There is no additional fee at this time; however, the state is considering a certification fee. The system is open 24 hours daily and is the same system used for corporation records. Call (801) 530-6643 for details.

Information About County Agencies

Court Structure

Effective July 1, 1996, all Circuit Courts (the lower court) were combined with the District Courts (the higher court) in each county. It is reported that branch courts in larger counties such as Salt Lake which were formerly Circuit Courts have been elevated to District Courts, with full jurisdiction over felony as well as misdemeanor cases. Therefore, it may be necessary to search for felony records

at more courts than prior to July 1, 1996. In written requests to District Courts, we recommend including a statement asking to "include Circuit Court cases in the search" to assure that index records from the former court are checked.

About the County Courts

Online Access

Case index information from approximately 98% of all Utah Court records is available from XChange. Fees include a $55.00 registration fee and a $35.00 monthly usage fee. For more information, contact the Court Administrator's Office at 801-578-3843 or visit http://courtlink.utcourts.gov. Information about XChange and the subscription agreement can be found on the Utah Internet site.

Searching Hints

Personal checks are generally accepted across the state. SASE are, generally, required across the state. Fees are set by statute as follows:

Search Fee — $13.00 per hour;

Certification Fee — $2.00 per document plus $.50 per page;

Copy Fee — $.25 per page

About the Recorder's Office

Organization

29 counties 29 recording offices. The recording officers are County Recorder and Clerk of District Court (state tax liens).

The entire state is in the Mountain Time Zone (MST).

Real Estate Records

County Recorders will not perform real estate searches. Copy fees vary, and certification fees are usually $2.00 per document.

UCC Records

Financing statements are filed at the state level, except for real estate related collateral, which are filed with the Register of Deeds (and at the state level in certain cases). Filing offices will not perform UCC searches. Copy fees vary.

Other Lien Records

All federal tax liens are filed with the County Recorder. They do not per form searches. All state tax liens are filed with Clerk of District Court.

County Courts & Recording Offices Online

Case index information from approximately 98% of all Utah Court records is available from XChange. Fees include a $55.00 registration fee and a $35.00 monthly usage fee.

For more information, contact the Court Administrator's Office at 801-578-3843 or visit the web site at http://courtlink.utcourts.gov.

No remote online access is available from real estate recorder's offices in Utah.

Federal Courts Online

US District Court
District of Utah

Clerk's Office, Room 150, 350 S Main St, Salt Lake City, UT 84101, 801-524-6100, Fax: 801-526-1175. This court handles all counties in Utah.

www.utd.uscourts.gov

PACER sign-up number is 800-676-6856. Both civil and criminal case records are available online.

US Bankruptcy Court
District of Utah

Clerk of Court, Frank E Moss Courthouse, 350 S Main St, Room 301, Salt Lake City, UT 84101, 801-524-5157, Fax: 801-524-4409. This court handles all counties in Utah.

www.utb.uscourts.gov

PACER sign-up number is 800-676-6856. Only civil case records are available online.

Vermont

Governor's Office
Pavillion Office Bldg
5th Floor, 109 State St
Montpelier, VT 05609
www.state.vt.us/governor/index.htm

802-828-3333
Fax 802-828-3339
7:45AM-4:30PM

Attorney General's Office
109 State St
Montpelier, VT 05609-1001
www.state.vt.us/aty

802-828-3171
Fax 802-828-2154

State Archives
Secretary of State
State Papers Archives Div.
109 State St
Montpelier, VT 05609-1103
www.sec.state.vt.us/archives/archdex.htm

802-828-2308
Fax 802-828-2496
7:45AM-4:30PM

Capital:	Montpelier
	Washington County
Time Zone:	EST
Number of Counties:	14
Population:	588,978
Web Site:	www.state.vt.us

State Court Administrator
Court Administrator
Admin. Office of Courts
109 State St
Montpelier, VT 05609-0701
www.state.vt.us/courts

802-828-3278
Fax 802-828-3457
8AM-4:30PM

State Agencies Online

Corporation Records
Trademarks/Servicemarks
sec.state.vt.us/soshome.htm

Secretary of State, Corporation Division, 109 State St, Montpelier, VT 05609-1101; (Courier: 81 River St, Heritage Bldg, Montpelier, VT 05602); 802-828-2386, 802-828-2853 (Fax), 7:45AM-4:30PM.

Online search: Corporate and trademark records can be accessed from the Internet for no fee. All records are available except for LPs, LLCs, and Farm Product Liens (however, all of these records will eventually be up).

Uniform Commercial Code
sec.state.vt.us/seek/ucc_seek.htm

UCC Division, Secretary of State, 109 State St, Montpelier, VT 05609-1101; (Courier: 81 River St, Heritage One, Montpelier, VT 05602); 802-828-2386, 802-828-2853 (Fax), 7:45AM-4:30PM.

General Information: All tax liens are filed at the town/city level.

Online search: Searches are available from the Internet site. You can search by debtor name, there is no fee

Driver Records
Driver License Information

Department of Motor Vehicles, DI-Records Unit, 120 State St, Montpelier, VT 05603; 802-828-2050, 802-828-2098 (Fax), 7:45AM-4:30PM.

General Information: Online requesters need only the license number, but the last name and DOB are helpful. The following data is not available-addresses, Social Security Numbers, medical information or personal information (height, weight, sex, eye color, etc.). This office is closed on Wed. mornings.

Online search: Online access costs $4.00 per 3 year record. Two methods are offered-single inquiry and batch mode. The system is open 24 hours a day, 7 days a week (except for file maintenance periods). Only the license number is needed when ordering, but it is suggested to submit the name and DOB also. The system is oriented towards PC and modem users. For more information, call (802) 828-2053.

Legislation-Current/Pending
Legislation-Passed

www.leg.state.vt.us

Vermont General Assembly, State House-Legislative Council, 115 State Street, Drawer 33, Montpelier, VT 05633; 802-828-2231, 802-828-2424 (Fax), 8AM-4:30PM.

Online search: The web site offers access to bill information.

Information About County Agencies

Court Structure

As of September, 1996, all small claims came under the jurisdiction of Superior Court. Bennington District Court has a diversion program in which 1st offenders go through a process that includes a letter of apology, community service, etc. and, after 2 years, the record is expunged. These records are never released.

There is one Probate Court per county except in the four southern counties (Bennington, Rutland, Windsor, and Windham) which have two each.

About the
County Courts

Online Access

There is no online computer access, internal or external.

Searching Hints

There are statewide certification and copy fees, as follows:

Certification Fee — $5.00 per document plus copy fee;

Copy Fee — $.25 per page with a $1.00 minimum

About the
Recorder's Office

Organization

14 counties and 246 towns/cities, 246 recording offices. The recording officer is Town/City Clerk. There is no county administration in Vermont. Many towns are so small that their mailing addresses are in different towns. Four towns/cities have the same name as counties—Barre, Newport, Rutland, and St. Albans. The entire state is in the Eastern Time Zone (EST).

Real Estate Records

Most towns/cities will not perform real estate searches. Copy fees and certification fees vary. Certified copies are generally very expensive at $6.00 per page total. Deed copies usually cost $2.00.

UCC Records

This has been a dual filing state until December 31, 1994. As of January 1, 1995, only consumer goods and real estate related collateral are filed with Town/City Clerks. Most recording offices will perform UCC searches. Use search request form UCC-11. Search fees are usually $10.00 per name, and copy fees vary.

Other Lien Records

All federal and state tax liens on personal property and on real property are filed with the Town/City Clerk in the lien/attachment book and indexed in real estate records. Most towns/cities will not perform tax lien searches. Other liens are: mechanics, local tax, judgment, foreclosure.

County Courts & Recording Offices Online

There is no online access to court records in Vermont.

No remote online access is available from real estate recorder's offices in Vermont.

Federal Courts Online

County-to-Court Cross Reference (Bankruptcy Court locations in Parenthesis if different)

Addison..Rutland	Lamoille....................................... Burlington (Rutland)
Bennington ....Rutland	Orange .... Rutland
Caledonia....................................Burlington (Rutland)	Orleans.. Burlington (Rutland)
Chittenden ....Burlington (Rutland)	Rutland .... Rutland
Essex ....Burlington (Rutland)	Washington .... Burlington (Rutland)
Franklin......................................Burlington (Rutland)	Windham..................................... Rutland
Grand Isle ....Burlington (Rutland)	Windsor....................................... Rutland

US District Court
District of Vermont

PACER sign-up number is 800-676-6856. Both civil and criminal case records are available online.

Burlington Division, Clerk's Office, PO Box 945, Burlington, VT 05402-0945, 802-951-6301.

Rutland Division, PO Box 607, Rutland, VT 05702-0607, 802-773-0245.

US Bankruptcy Court
District of Vermont

www.usbcvt.court.fed.us

PACER sign-up number is 800-676-6856. Only civil case records are available online.

Rutland Division, PO Box 6648, Rutland, VT 05702, 802-747-7625, Record Room: 802-747-7625, Fax: 802-747-7629. This court handles all counties in Vermont.

Virginia

Governor's Office

Capitol Bldg, 3rd Floor   804-786-2211
Richmond, VA 23219   Fax 804-371-6351
www.state.va.us/governor

Attorney General's Office

900 E Main St   804-786-2071
Richmond, VA 23219   Fax 804-786-1991
www.state.va.us/noag/main.htm

State Archives

The Library of Virginia   804-692-3500
800 E. Broad St   Fax 804-692-3556
Richmond, VA 23219-1905   9AM-5PM M-SA
leo.vsla.edu

Capital:	Richmond
	Richmond City County
Time Zone:	EST
Number of Counties:	95
Population:	6,733,996
Web Site:	www.state.va.us

State Court Administrator

Executive Secretary   804-786-6455
Admin. Office of Courts   Fax 804-786-4542
100 N 9th St, 3rd Floor   9AM-5PM
Richmond, VA 23219
www.courts.state.va.us

State Agencies Online

Criminal Records

Virginia State Police, CCRE, PO Box C-85076, Richmond, VA 23261-5076; (Courier: 7700 Midlothian Turnpike, Richmond, VA 23235); 804-674-2084, 804-674-2277 (Fax), 8AM-5PM.

General Information: Arrest records one year old without a disposition are not released.

Online search: Certain entities, including screening companies, are entitled to online access. The system is ONLY available to IN-STATE accounts. Fees are same as manual submission with exception of required software package purchase. The system is windows oriented, but will not handle networks. The PC user must be a stand-alone system. There is a minimum usage requirement of 25 requests per month. The fee is $15.00 per record. Turnaround time is 24-72 hours.

Corporation Records
Limited Liability Company Records
Fictitious Name
Limited Partnership Records
Assumed Name

dit1.state.va.us/scc/division/clm/index.htm

State Corporation Commission, Clerks Office, PO Box 1197, Richmond, VA 23218-1197; (Courier: Tyler Bldg, 1st Floor, 1300 E Main St, Richmond, VA 23219); 804-371-9733, 804-371-9133 (Other fax), 804-371-9744 (Fax), 8:15AM - 5PM.

Online search: There is a dial-up system, called Direct Access, for registered accounts. There are no fees. A wealth of information is available on this system. For more data, call 804-371-9654.

Uniform Commercial Code
Federal Tax Liens

dit1.state.va.us/ecc/division/clk/
index.htm

UCC Division, State Corporation Commission, PO Box 1197, Richmond, VA 23218-1197; (Courier: 1300 E Main St, 1st Floor, Richmond, VA 23219); 804-371-9189, 804-371-9744 (Fax), 8:15AM-5PM.

General Information: Federal tax liens on individuals and all state tax liens are filed at the local level, which may be a county or independent city. The agency now accepts filing using EDI. For more information contact Wanda at 804 371-9380.

Online search: This is a free, non-Internet service. Accounts must be registered. This is the same system used for corporation records. Call (804) 371-9661 and ask Angela for a registration packet.

Driver Records

Department of Motor Vehicles, Motorist Records Services, PO Box 27412, Richmond, VA 23269; 804-367-0538, 8:30AM-5:30PM M-F; 8:30AM-12:30PM S.

General Information: Records are available for 3 years for moving violations and miscellaneous convictions, 5 years for speeding and unauthorized use of a motor vehicle, 11 years for 3 reckless driving offenses and DWI, and 24 months from the complied date for suspensions. There is no opt-out-casual requesters cannot obtain records without consent

Online search: Online service is provided by the Virginia Information Providers Network (VIPNet). Online reports are provided on an interactive basis 24 hours daily. There is a $50 annual administrative fee and records are $5.00 each. All accounts must be approved in

advance by the DMV and VIPNet. Call Rodney Willett at 804-786-4718 to request an information use agreement application.

Vehicle Ownership
Vehicle Identification

Motorist Records Services, Customer Records Request Section, PO Box 27412, Richmond, VA 23269; 804-367-0538, 8:30AM-5:30PM M-F; 8:30AM-12:30PM S.

General Information: Casual requesters cannot obtain records without consent. High volume requesters must sign an agreement or contract and will be assigned a user number. Records cannot be purchased and resold for marketing purposes. Lien information is only released to lending institutions and collection agencies.

Online search: Online access costs $4.00 per page. The online system, managed by the Virginia Information Providers Network (VIPNet), is an interactive system open 24 hours daily. There is an annual $50 administration fee and records are $5.00 each. All accounts must be approved by both the DMV and VIPNet. Contact Rodney Willett at 804-786-4718 to request an information use agreement application.

Legislation-Current/Pending
Legislation-Passed

http://legis.state.va.us/vaonline/v.htm

House of Delegates, Legislative Information, PO Box 406, Richmond, VA 23218; (Courier: 1st Floor, State Capitol Bldg, 9th and Grace Streets, Richmond, VA 23219); 804-698-1500, 804-786-3215 (Fax), 8AM-5PM.

Online search: Information can be found on the web site. There is no fee.

Information About County Agencies

Court Structure

Records of civil action from $1000 to $15,000 can be at either the Circuit or District Court as either can have jurisdiction. It is necessary to check both record locations as there is no concurrent database nor index.

The limit for civil actions in District Court was raised from $10,000 to $15,000 as of July 1, 1997.

Online Access

An online, statewide public access computer system is available, called Law Office Public Access System (LOPAS). The system allows remote access to the court case indexes and abstracts from most of the

About the
County Courts

state's courts. In order to determine which courts are on LOPAS, you must obtain an ID and password (instructions below), and search on the system.

The system contains opinions from the Supreme Court and the Court of Appeals, as well as criminal and civil case information from Circuit and District Courts. The number of years of information provided varies widely from court to court, depending on when the particular court joined the Courts Automated Information System (CAIS).

The preferred communication software for LOPAS access is PROCOMM+. There are no sign-up or other fees to use LOPAS. Access is granted on a request-by-request basis. Anyone wishing to establish an account or receive information on LOPAS must contact Ken Mittendorf, Director of MIS, Supreme Court of Virginia, 100 N 9th St, Richmond VA 23219 or by phone at 804-786-6455 or Fax at 804-786-4542.

Searching Hints

In most jurisdictions, the Certification Fee is $2.00 per document plus copy fee. The Copy Fee is $.50 per page.

About the Recorder's Office

Organization

95 counties and 41 independent cities, 123 recording offices. The recording officer is Clerk of Circuit Court. Fourteen independent cities share the Clerk of Circuit Court with the county—Bedford, Emporia (Greenville County), Fairfax, Falls Church (Arlington or Fairfax County), Franklin (Southhampton County), Galax (Carroll County), Harrisonburg (Rockingham County), Lexington (Rockbridge County), Manassas and Manassas Park (Prince William County), Norton (Wise County), Poquoson (York County), South Boston (Halifax County), and Williamsburg (James City County. Charles City and James City are counties, not cities. The City of Franklin is not in Franklin County, the City of Richmond is not in Richmond County, and the City of Roanoke is not in Roanoke County. The entire state is in the Eastern Time Zone.

Real Estate Records

Only a few Clerks of Circuit Court will perform real estate searches. Copy fees and certification fees vary. The independent cities may have separate Assessor Offices.

UCC Records

This is a dual filing state. Financing statements are filed at the state level and with the Clerk of Circuit Court, except for consumer goods, farm and real estate related collateral, which are filed only with the Clerk of Circuit Court. Some recording offices will perform UCC searches. Use search request form UCC-11. Searches fees and copy fees vary.

Other Lien Records

Federal tax liens on personal property of businesses are filed with the State Corporation Commission. Other federal and all state tax liens are filed with the county Clerk of Circuit Court. They are usually filed in a "Judgment Lien Book." Most counties will not perform tax lien searches. Other liens are: judgment, mechanics, hospital, lis pendens.

County Courts & Recording Offices Online

All Circuit and District Courts, Court of Appeals, Supreme Court

An online, statewide system called LOPAS allows remote access to the court case indexes and abstracts from most of state's courts. Although there are no fees involved, registration for an ID and password is required. Keep in mind that searching is by specific court; there is no combined index. Plus, a summary list of all included courts is not available. Anyone wishing to register should contact the Director of MIS, Supreme Court of VA, at 804-786-6455.

Danville City

Liens, Real Estate, Marriage Records

City Clerk of the Circuit Court, 212 Lynn Street, Danville, VA 24541, 804-799-5168, 804-799-6502 Fax.

Online search: There are no fees. The records date back to 1993. The system operates 24 hours daily. Search by name, Grantee/Grantor, instrument type, finance and statements (UCC) and wills. Lending agency information is a available. Contact Leigh Ann Thomas at 804-799-5168.

Wise County & City of Norton

Real Estate

www.courtbar.org

Clerk of the Circuit Court, 125 Main St, Courthouse, Wise, VA 24293, 540-328-6111, 540-328-0039 Fax.

Online search: There are no fees for access to this system. Record dates vary. The system operates 24 hours daily and supports baud rates up to 56K. One may search by name and Grantee/Grantor. Lending agency information is available. For further information, contact Vickie Ratliff at 540-328-6111. Note: this system also includes real estate information for the City of Norton.

Federal Courts Online

US District Court
Eastern District of Virginia

PACER sign-up number is 800-676-6856. Both civil and criminal case records are available online.

There is a free Internet site at:

http://ecf.vaeb.uscourts.gov/

Alexandria Division, 401 Courthouse Square, Alexandria, VA 22314, 703-299-2100, Record Room: 703-299-2128, Civil Docket Section: 703-299-2101, Criminal Docket Section: 703-299-2102.

Newport News Division, Clerk's Office, PO Box 494, Newport News, VA 23607, 757-244-0539.

Norfolk Division, US Courthouse, Room 193, 600 Granby St, Norfolk, VA 23510, Civil Docket Section: 757-441-3250, Criminal Docket Section: 757-441-3253.

Richmond Division, Lewis F Powell, Jr Courthouse Bldg, 1000 E Main St, Room 307, Richmond, VA 23219-3525, Civil Docket Section: 804-771-2611, Criminal Docket Section: 804-771-2612.

US Bankruptcy Court
Eastern District of Virginia

www.vaeb.uscourts.gov

PACER sign-up number is 800-676-6856.

Alexandria Division, PO Box 19247, Alexandria, VA 22320-0247, 703-557-1716

Newport News Division, 825 Diligence Dr, Suite 201, Newport News, VA 23606, 757-595-9805

Norfolk Division, PO Box 1938, Norfolk, VA 23501-1938, 757-441-6651

Richmond Division, Office of the Clerk, 1100 E Main St, Room 310, Richmond, VA 23219-3515, 804-771-2878

US District Court
Western District of Virginia

PACER sign-up number is 800-676-6856.

Abingdon Division, Clerk's Office, PO Box 398, Abingdon, VA 24212, 540-628-5116, Fax: 540-628-1028.

Big Stone Gap Division, PO Box 490, Big Stone Gap, VA 24219, 540-523-3557, Fax: 540-523-6214.

Charlottesville Division, Clerk, Room 304, 255 W Main St, Charlottesville, VA 22902, 804-296-9284.

Danville Division, PO Box 52, Danville, VA 24543-0053, 804-793-7147, Fax: 804-793-0284.

Harrisonburg Division, Clerk, PO Box 1207, Harrisonburg, VA 22801, 540-434-3181.

Lynchburg Division, Clerk, PO Box 744, Lynchburg, VA 24505, 804-847-5722.

Roanoke Division, Clerk, PO Box 1234, Roanoke, VA 24006, 540-857-2224, Civil Docket Section: 540-857-2224, Criminal Docket Section: 540-857-2661.

US Bankruptcy Court
Western District of Virginia

www.vawb.uscourts.gov

PACER sign-up number is 800-676-6856.

Harrisonburg Division, PO Box 1407, Harrisonburg, VA 22801, 540-434-8327, Fax: 540-434-9715

Lynchburg Division, PO Box 6400, Lynchburg, VA 24505, 804-845-0317

Roanoke Division, PO Box 2390, Roanoke, VA 24010, 540-857-2391

County-to-Court Cross Reference (Bankruptcy Court locations in Parenthesis if different)

County	District	Court
Accomack	Eastern	Norfolk
Albemarle	Western	Charlottesville (Lynchburg)
Alexandria City	Eastern	Alexandria
Alleghany	Western	Roanoke (Harrisonburg)
Amelia	Eastern	Richmond
Amherst	Western	Lynchburg
Appomattox	Western	Lynchburg
Arlington	Eastern	Alexandria
Augusta	Western	Harrisonburg
Bath	Western	Harrisonburg
Bedford	Western	Lynchburg
Bedford City	Western	Lynchburg
Bland	Western	Roanoke
Botetourt	Western	Roanoke
Bristol City	Western	Abingdon (Roanoke)
Brunswick	Eastern	Richmond
Buchanan	Western	Abingdon (Roanoke)
Buckingham	Western	Lynchburg
Buena Vista City	Western	Lynchburg (Harrisonburg)
Campbell	Western	Lynchburg
Caroline	Eastern	Richmond
Carroll	Western	Roanoke
Charles City	Eastern	Richmond
Charlotte	Western	Danville (Lynchburg)
Charlottesville City	Western	Charlottesville (Lynchburg)
Chesapeake City	Eastern	Norfolk
Chesterfield	Eastern	Richmond
Clarke	Western	Harrisonburg
Clifton Forge City	Western	Roanoke (Harrisonburg)
Colonial Heights City	Eastern	Richmond
Covington City	Western	Roanoke (Harrisonburg)
Craig	Western	Roanoke
Culpeper	Western	Charlottesville (Lynchburg)
Cumberland	Western	Lynchburg
Danville City	Western	Danville (Lynchburg)
Dickenson	Western	Big Stone Gap (Roanoke)
Dinwiddie	Eastern	Richmond
Emporia City	Eastern	Richmond
Essex	Eastern	Richmond
Fairfax	Eastern	Alexandria
Fairfax City	Eastern	Alexandria
Falls Church City	Eastern	Alexandria
Fauquier	Eastern	Alexandria
Floyd	Western	Roanoke
Fluvanna	Western	Charlottesville (Lynchburg)
Franklin	Western	Roanoke
Franklin City	Eastern	Norfolk
Frederick	Western	Harrisonburg
Fredericksburg City	Eastern	Richmond
Galax City	Western	Roanoke
Giles	Western	Roanoke
Gloucester	Eastern	Newport News
Goochland	Eastern	Richmond
Grayson	Western	Roanoke
Greene	Western	Charlottesville (Lynchburg)
Greensville	Eastern	Richmond
Halifax	Western	Danville (Lynchburg)
Hampton City	Eastern	Newport News
Hanover	Eastern	Richmond
Harrisonburg City	Western	Harrisonburg
Henrico	Eastern	Richmond
Henry	Western	Danville (Lynchburg)
Highland	Western	Harrisonburg
Hopewell City	Eastern	Richmond
Isle of Wight	Eastern	Norfolk
James City	Eastern	Newport News

County-to-Court Cross Reference (Bankruptcy Court locations in Parenthesis if different)

County	District	Court
King George	Eastern	Richmond
King William	Eastern	Richmond
King and Queen	Eastern	Richmond
Lancaster	Eastern	Richmond
Lee	Western	Big Stone Gap (Roanoke)
Lexington City	Western	Lynchburg (Harrisonburg)
Loudoun	Eastern	Alexandria
Louisa	Western	Charlottesville (Lynchburg)
Lunenburg	Eastern	Richmond
Lynchburg City	Western	Lynchburg
Madison	Western	Charlottesville (Lynchburg)
Manassas City	Eastern	Alexandria
Manassas Park City	Eastern	Alexandria
Martinsville City	Western	Lynchburg
Mathews	Eastern	Newport News
Mecklenburg	Eastern	Richmond
Middlesex	Eastern	Richmond
Montgomery	Western	Roanoke
Nelson	Western	Charlottesville (Lynchburg)
New Kent	Eastern	Richmond
Newport News City	Eastern	Newport News
Norfolk City	Eastern	Norfolk
Northampton	Eastern	Norfolk
Northumberland	Eastern	Richmond
Norton City	Western	Big Stone Gap (Roanoke)
Nottoway	Eastern	Richmond
Orange	Western	Charlottesville (Lynchburg)
Page	Western	Harrisonburg
Patrick	Western	Danville (Lynchburg)
Petersburg City	Eastern	Richmond
Pittsylvania	Western	Danville (Lynchburg)
Poquoson City	Eastern	Newport News
Portsmouth City	Eastern	Norfolk
Powhatan	Eastern	Richmond
Prince Edward	Eastern	Richmond
Prince George	Eastern	Richmond
Prince William	Eastern	Alexandria
Pulaski	Western	Roanoke
Radford City	Western	Roanoke
Rappahannock	Western	Charlottesville (Harrisonburg)
Richmond	Eastern	Richmond
Richmond City	Eastern	Richmond
Roanoke	Western	Roanoke
Roanoke City	Western	Roanoke
Rockbridge	Western	Lynchburg (Harrisonburg)
Rockingham	Western	Harrisonburg
Russell	Western	Abingdon (Roanoke)
Salem City	Western	Roanoke
Scott	Western	Big Stone Gap (Roanoke)
Shenandoah	Western	Harrisonburg
Smyth	Western	Abingdon (Roanoke)
South Boston City	Western	Danville (Lynchburg)
Southampton	Eastern	Norfolk
Spotsylvania	Eastern	Richmond
Stafford	Eastern	Alexandria
Staunton City	Western	Harrisonburg
Suffolk City	Eastern	Norfolk
Surry	Eastern	Richmond
Sussex	Eastern	Richmond
Tazewell	Western	Abingdon (Roanoke)
Virginia Beach City	Eastern	Norfolk
Warren	Western	Harrisonburg
Washington	Western	Abingdon (Roanoke)
Waynesboro City	Western	Harrisonburg
Westmoreland	Eastern	Richmond
Williamsburg City	Eastern	Newport News
Winchester City	Western	Harrisonburg
Wise	Western	Big Stone Gap (Roanoke)
Wythe	Western	Roanoke
York	Eastern	Newport News

Washington

Governor's Office
PO Box 40002
Olympia, WA 98504-0002
www.wa.gov/governor

360-902-4111
Fax 360-753-4110

Attorney General's Office
PO Box 40100
Olympia, WA 98504-0100
www.wa.gov.ago

360-753-6200
Fax 360-664-0228

Capital:	Olympia
	Thurston County
Time Zone:	PST
Number of Counties:	39
Population:	5,610,362
Web Site:	www.wa.gov

State Archives
Secretary of State
State Archives
PO Box 40238
Olympia, WA 98504-0238

360-753-5485
Fax 360-664-8814
8:30AM-4:30PM

State Court Administrator
Court Administrator
Temple of Justice
PO Box 41174
Olympia, WA 98504-1174.

360-357-2121
Fax 360-357-2127
8:30AM-4:30PM

State Agencies Online

Criminal Records
watch.wsp.wa.gov

Washington State Patrol, Identification Section, PO Box 42633, Olympia, WA 98504-2633; (Courier: 321 Cleveland Ave, #A, Tumwater, WA 98501); 360-705-5100, 360-664-9461 (Fax), 8AM-5PM.

General Information: They will release arrest records without disposition if less than 1 year old.

Online search: The State Court Administrator's office (see address and phone number on previous page) maintains a database of criminal records in their JIS-Link. Records do not include arrests unless case is filed. There is a $125.00 set-up fee and a $25.00 per hour access charge. Call 360-705-5277 for packet. This agency offers access through a system called WATCH, which can be accessed from their web site. The fee is $10.00. The correct DOB and exact spelling of the name is required. Credit cards are accepted for payment. To set up a WATCH account, call (360) 705-5100 or e-mail to criminhis@wsp.gov.

Corporation Records
Trademarks/Servicemarks
Limited Partnerships
Limited Liability Company Records
www.wa.gov/sec/corps.htm

Secretary of State, Corporations Division, PO Box 40234, Olympia, WA 98504-0234; (Courier: 505 E Union, 2nd Floor, Olympia, WA 98504); 360-753-7115, 900-463-6000 (Records), 360-664-8781 (Fax).

Online search: The Secretary of State has plans to make corporation information available via their Internet site sometime in 1999. However, information is available elsewhere.

From the Dept of Licensing. Subscription is $18 per month, access is $60 per hour plus line charges of $.09-37 per minute. A $200 deposit is required to start. Hours are from 5 AM to 9 PM. Call Darla at 360-753-2523 in Licensing for more information.

Also, there is a non-commercial use database available on the Internet from the Department of Revenue. This database contains state business records for tax license and registration. Go to:
www.wa.gov/dor/prd/cgi_bin/prd2gif1.cgi

Trade Names

www.gov.gov/dol/bpd/limsnet.htm

Department of Licensing, Business & Professional Div, PO Box 9034, Olympia, WA 98507-9034; (Courier: 1125 Washington Street, Olympia, WA 98507); 360-664-1400, 900-463-6000 (Tradename Search), 360-753-9668 (Fax), 8AM - 5PM.

Online search: This is the same system for corporation and UCC records. A deposit is required (depends on usage), access is $60 per hour plus a $.09-.37 phone charge. Hours are 5 AM to 9 PM daily. Call Fran at (360) 664-1400 to set up an account.

Uniform Commercial Code
Federal Tax Liens

www.wa.gov/dol/bpd/uccfront.htm

UCC Division, Department of Licensing, PO Box 9660, Olympia, WA 98507-9660; (Courier: 1125 Washington St SE, Olympia, WA 98501); 360-753-2523, 360-586-1404 (Fax), 8AM - 5PM.

General Information: Only currently active plus 1 full year are accessible. The search includes all notices of federal tax liens. State tax liens are filed at the county level.

Online search: Subscription fee is $18.00 per month. Online access costs $60.00 per hour. There is a deposit of $200 required which is replenished at end of the month. Line charges will vary from $.09-.37 per minute. Hours

are from 5 AM to 9 PM. Call Darla at (360) 753-2523 for more information.

Sales Tax Registrations

www.wa.gov/dor/wador.htm

Revenue Department, Taxpayer Account Administration, PO Box 47476, Olympia, WA 98504-7476; (Courier: 415 General Admin Bldg, Olympia, WA 98504); 360-902-7180, 800-647-7706 (Alternate Telephone), 360-586-5543 (Fax), 8AM-5PM.

Online search: The agency provides a state business records database with free access on the Internet at www.wa.gov/dor/prd. Lookups are by owner names, DBAs, and tax reporting numbers. Results show a myriad of data.

Legislation-Current/Pending
Legislation-Passed

http://leginfo.leg.wa.gov

Washington Legislature, State Capitol, Room 120, 1st Floor, Olympia, WA 98504-0600; 360-753-5000 (Information), 800-562-6000 (Local Only), 360-786-7573 (Bill Room), 360-786-1293 (Fax), 9AM-5PM.

General Information: Records are available for past 2 years.

Online search: The web site offers bill text and status look-up.

Information About County Agencies

Court Structure

District Courts retain civil records for 10 years from date of final disposition, then the records are destroyed. District Courts retain criminal records forever.

Washington has a mandatory arbitration requirement for civil disputes for $35,000 or less. However, either party may request a trial in Superior Court if dissatisfied with the arbitrator's decision.

The limit for civil actions in District Court was increased from $25,000 to $35,000.

**About the
County Courts**

Online Access

Appellate, Superior, and District Court records are available online. The Superior Court Management Information System (SCOMIS), the Appellate Records System (ACORDS) and the District/Municipal Court Information System (DISCIS) are on the Judicial Information System's JIS-Link. Case records available through JIS-Link from 1977 include criminal, civil, domestic, probate, and judgments. JIS-

Link is generally available Monday through Friday from 6:30AM to Midnight Washington time (PST or PDT). Equipment requirements are a PC running Windows or MS-DOS (3.3 or higher), and a Hayes-compatible modem (9600, 2400, or 1200 baud). There is a one-time installation fee of $125.00 per site, and a connect time charge of $25.00 per hour (approximately $.42 per minute). For additional information and/or a registration packet, contact: JISLink Coordinator, Office of the Administrator for the Courts, 1206 S Quince St., PO Box 41170, Olympia WA 98504-1170, 360-357-2407.

About the Recorder's Office

Organization

39 counties, 39 recording offices. The recording officer is County Auditor. County records are usually combined in a Grantor/Grantee index. The area code for some counties has been changed from 206 to 360, effective January 1, 1995. The entire state is in the Pacific Time Zone (PST).

Real Estate Records

Many County Auditors will perform real estate searches, including record owner. Search fees and copy fees vary. Copies usually cost $1.00 per page and $2.00 for certification per document. If the Auditor does not provide searches, contact the Assessor for record owner information. Contact the Treasurer (Finance Department in King County) for information about unpaid real estate taxes.

UCC Records

Financing statements are filed at the state level, except for real estate related collateral, which are filed with the County Auditor. Most recording offices will perform UCC searches. Use search request form UCC-11R. Searches fees and copy fees vary.

Other Lien Records

All federal tax liens on personal property are filed with the Department of Licensing. Other federal and all state tax liens are filed with the County Auditor. Most counties will perform tax lien searches. Search fees are usually $8.00 per hour.

County Courts & Recording Offices Online

All Superior and District Courts

Three separate statewide systems are available. See the "Online Access" in the previous agencies section for details.

King County

Liens, Real Estate, Marriage Records

County Records, 500 4th Ave, Administration Building, Room 311, Seattle, WA, 206-296-1570, 206-296-1535 Fax.

Online search: The set up fee is $200. Online charges are $.03 per minute for browsing and $.20 per minute for viewing images. Records date back to 1853. No new customers are being accepted at this time. The system operates from 6PM-4:30PM and supports baud rates up to 19.2. Lending agency information is available. For further information, contact Diane Mickunas at 206-296-1588.

Federal Courts Online

County-to-Court Cross Reference (Bankruptcy Court locations in Parenthesis if different)

County	District	Court
Adams	Eastern	Spokane
Asotin	Eastern	Spokane
Benton	Eastern	Spokane
Chelan	Eastern	Spokane
Clallam	Western	Tacoma (Seattle)
Clark	Western	Tacoma
Columbia	Eastern	Spokane
Cowlitz	Western	Tacoma
Douglas	Eastern	Spokane
Ferry	Eastern	Spokane
Franklin	Eastern	Spokane
Garfield	Eastern	Spokane
Grant	Eastern	Spokane
Grays Harbor	Western	Tacoma
Island	Western	Seattle
Jefferson	Western	Tacoma (Seattle)
King	Western	Seattle
Kitsap	Western	Tacoma (Seattle)
Kittitas	Eastern	Yakima (Spokane)
Klickitat	Eastern	Yakima (Spokane)
Lewis	Western	Tacoma
Lincoln	Eastern	Spokane
Mason	Western	Tacoma
Okanogan	Eastern	Spokane
Pacific	Western	Tacoma
Pend Oreille	Eastern	Spokane
Pierce	Western	Tacoma
San Juan	Western	Seattle
Skagit	Western	Seattle
Skamania	Western	Tacoma
Snohomish	Western	Seattle
Spokane	Eastern	Spokane
Stevens	Eastern	Spokane
Thurston	Western	Tacoma
Wahkiakum	Western	Tacoma
Walla Walla	Eastern	Spokane
Whatcom	Western	Seattle
Whitman	Eastern	Spokane
Yakima	Eastern	Yakima (Spokane)

US District Court
Eastern District of Washington

www.iea.com/~usdcwae

PACER sign-up number at the following courts is 800-676-6856. Both civil and criminal case records are available online.

Spokane Division, PO Box 1493, Spokane, WA 99210-1493, 509-353-2150

Yakima Division, PO Box 2706, Yakima, WA 98907, 509-575-5838

US Bankruptcy Court
Eastern District of Washington

www.waeb.uscourts.gov

PACER sign-up number is 800-676-6856.

Spokane Division, PO Box 2164, Spokane, WA 99210-2164, 509-353-2404

US District Court
Western District of Washington

www.wawd.uscourts.gov

PACER sign-up number at the following courts is 800-676-6856. Both civil and criminal case records are available online.

Seattle Division, Clerk of Court, 215 US Courthouse, 1010 5th Ave, Seattle, WA 98104, 206-553-5598, Record Room: 206-553-5598, Civil Docket Section: 206-553-4080, Criminal Docket Section: 206-553-4080

Tacoma Division, Clerk's Office, Room 3100, 1717 Pacific Ave, Tacoma, WA 98402-3200, 253-593-6313

US Bankruptcy Court
Western District of Washington

www.wawb.uscourts.gov

PACER sign-up number at the following courts is 800-676-6856. Only civil case records are available online.

Seattle Division, Clerk of Court, 315 Park Place Bldg, 1200 6th Ave, Seattle, WA 98101, 206-553-7545, Fax: 206-553-0131

Tacoma Division, Suite 2100, 1717 Pacific Ave, Tacoma, WA 98402-3233, 206-593-6310

West Virginia

Governor's Office
Office of the Governor   304-558-2000
State Capitol,   Fax 304-342-7025
1900 Kanawha Blvd E
Charleston, WV 25305   8AM-6PM M-TH;
8AM-5PM F
www.state.wv.us/governor

Attorney General's Office
State Capitol, Bldg 1,
Rm E-26   304-558-2021
Charleston, WV 25305-0220   Fax 304-558-0140
www.state.wv.us/wvag

State Archives
Division of Culture & History   304-558-0220
Archives & History Section   Fax 304-558-2779
1900 Kanawha Blvd E   9AM-5PM M-F,
Charleston, WV 25305-0300   1-5 SA
www.wvlc.wvnet.edu/history/historyw.html

Capital:	Charleston
	Kanawha County
Time Zone:	EST
Number of Counties:	55
Population:	1,815,787
Web Site:	www.state.wv.us

State Court Administrator
Administrative Office   304-558-0145
State Court of Appeals   Fax 304-558-1212
1900 Kanawha Blvd,
Bldg 1 E 100   9AM-4PM
Charleston, WV 25305-0830
www.state.wv.us/wvsca

State Agencies Online

Driver License Information
Driver Records
www.state.wv.us/dmv

Division of Motor Vehicles, Driver Improvement Unit, Building 3, State Capitol Complex, Charleston, WV 25317; 304-558-0238, 304-558-0037 (Fax), 8:30AM-4:30PM.

General Information: Records are available for 3 years for all violations including DWIs and suspensions. Convictions not shown on the record include speeding 10 mph or less over limit on interstate, driving on expired license, and overweight or overlength violations (truckers). Per the opt-out provision, casual requesters cannot obtain personal information on subjects who opted out. Accidents are not reported on records.

Online search: Online access is available in either interactive or batch mode. The system is open 24 hours a day. Batch requesters receive return transmission about 3 AM. Users must access through AAMVAnet. A contract is required and accounts must pre-pay. The fee is $5.00 per record. For more information, call Lacy Morgan at 304-558-3915.

Legislation-Current/Pending
Legislation-Passed
wvlc.wvnet.edu/legisinfo/legisht.html

West Virginia State Legislature, State Capitol, Documents, Charleston, WV 25305; 304-347-4830, 800-642-8650 (Local), 8:30AM - 4:30PM.

Online search: The Internet site allows one to search for status of bills. To receive full text, there is a fee of $80.00 per month. There is also a BBS system for non-web users. Call Carla Dyer at (304) 347-4820 for more information.

County Agencies Online

Court Structure

The upper limit for civil claims in the Magistrate Courts was changed to $5000 from $3000 effective July 1994. Probate is handled by the Circuit Court. Records are held at the County Commissioner's Office.

Online Access

There is no statewide online computer system, internal or external. Most courts with a computer system use FORTUNE software; however, no external access is permitted.

About the County Courts

Searching Hints

There is a statewide requirement that search turnaround times not exceed 10 days. However, most courts do far better than that limit. There is a discrepancy in what courts will and will not release with the decisions resting with the judges and clerks in the various jurisdictions

About the Recorder's Office

Organization

55 counties, 55 recording offices. The recording officer is County Clerk. The entire state is in the Eastern Time Zone (EST).

Real Estate Records

Most County Clerks will not perform real estate searches. Copy fees are usually $1.50 up to two pages and $1.00 for each additional page. Certification usually costs $1.00 per document.

UCC Records

Financing statements are filed at the state level, except for real estate related collateral, which are filed only with the Register of Deeds, and consumer goods, which are filed in both places. Many recording offices will perform UCC searches. Use search request form UCC-11. Searches fees and copy fees vary.

Other Lien Records

All federal and state tax liens are filed with the County Clerk. Most counties will not perform tax lien searches. Other liens are: judgment, mechanics, lis pendens.

County Courts & Recording Offices Online

There is no online access to court records in West Virginia.

No remote online access is available from real estate recorder's offices in West Virginia.

Federal Courts Online

County-to-Court Cross Reference (Bankruptcy Court locations in Parenthesis if different)

County	District	Court
Barbour	Northern	Elkins (Wheeling)
Berkeley	Northern	Martinsburg (Wheeling)
Boone	Southern	Charleston
Braxton	Northern	Clarksburg (Wheeling)
Brooke	Northern	Wheeling
Cabell	Southern	Huntington (Charleston)
Calhoun	Northern	Clarksburg (Wheeling)
Clay	Southern	Charleston
Doddridge	Northern	Clarksburg (Wheeling)
Fayette	Southern	Beckley (Charleston)
Gilmer	Northern	Clarksburg (Wheeling)
Grant	Northern	Elkins (Wheeling)
Greenbrier	Southern	Beckley (Charleston)
Hampshire	Northern	Martinsburg (Wheeling)
Hancock	Northern	Wheeling
Hardy	Northern	Elkins (Wheeling)
Harrison	Northern	Clarksburg (Wheeling)
Jackson	Southern	Parkersburg (Charleston)
Jefferson	Northern	Martinsburg (Wheeling)
Kanawha	Southern	Charleston
Lewis	Northern	Clarksburg (Wheeling)
Lincoln	Southern	Huntington (Charleston)
Logan	Southern	Charleston
Marion	Northern	Clarksburg (Wheeling)
Marshall	Northern	Wheeling
Mason	Southern	Huntington (Charleston)
McDowell	Southern	Bluefield (Charleston)
Mercer	Southern	Bluefield (Charleston)
Mineral	Northern	Elkins (Wheeling)
Mingo	Southern	Huntington (Charleston)
Monongalia	Northern	Clarksburg (Wheeling)
Monroe	Southern	Bluefield (Charleston)
Morgan	Northern	Martinsburg (Wheeling)
Nicholas	Southern	Beckley (Charleston)
Ohio	Northern	Wheeling
Pendleton	Northern	Elkins (Wheeling)
Pleasants	Northern	Clarksburg (Wheeling)
Pocahontas	Northern	Elkins (Wheeling)
Preston	Northern	Elkins (Wheeling)
Putnam	Southern	Charleston
Raleigh	Southern	Beckley (Charleston)
Randolph	Northern	Elkins (Wheeling)
Ritchie	Northern	Clarksburg (Wheeling)
Roane	Southern	Charleston
Summers	Southern	Bluefield (Charleston)
Taylor	Northern	Clarksburg (Wheeling)
Tucker	Northern	Elkins (Wheeling)
Tyler	Northern	Clarksburg (Wheeling)
Upshur	Northern	Elkins (Wheeling)
Wayne	Southern	Huntington (Charleston)
Webster	Northern	Elkins (Wheeling)
Wetzel	Northern	Wheeling
Wirt	Southern	Parkersburg (Charleston)
Wood	Southern	Parkersburg (Charleston)
Wyoming	Southern	Beckley (Charleston)

US District Court
Northern District of West Virginia

PACER sign-up number is 800-676-6856. Both civil and criminal case records are available online.

Clarksburg Division, PO Box 2857, Clarksburg, WV 26302-2857, 304-622-8513.

Elkins Division, PO Box 1518, Elkins, WV 26241, 304-636-1445, Fax: 304-636-5746.

Martinsburg Division, Room 207, 217 W King St, Martinsburg, WV 25401, 304-267-8225, Fax: 304-264-0434.

Wheeling Division, Clerk, PO Box 471, Wheeling, WV 26003, 304-232-0011, Fax: 304-233-2185.

US Bankruptcy Court
Northern District of West Virginia

PACER sign-up number is 800-676-6856.

Wheeling Division, PO Box 70, Wheeling, WV 26003, 304-233-1655.

US District Court
Southern District of West Virginia

PACER sign-up number is 800-676-6856. Both civil and criminal case records are available online.

Beckley Division, PO Drawer 5009, Beckley, WV 25801, 304-253-7481, Fax: 304-253-3252.

Bluefield Division, Clerk's Office, PO Box 4128, Bluefield, WV 24701, 304-327-9798.

Charleston Division, PO Box 2546, Charleston, WV 25329, 304-347-5114, Record Room: 304-347-5527.

Huntington Division, Clerk of Court, PO Box 1570, Huntington, WV 25716, 304-529-5588, Fax: 304-529-5131.

Parkersburg Division, Clerk of Court, PO Box 1526, Parkersburg, WV 26102, 304-420-6490, Fax: 304-420-6363.

US Bankruptcy Court
Southern District of West Virginia

Charleston Division, PO Box 3924, Charleston, WV 25339, 304-347-5114.

PACER sign-up number is 800-676-6856.

Wisconsin

Governor's Office
PO Box 7863
Madison, WI 53707-7863
www.wisgov.state.wi.us

608-266-1212
Fax 608-267-8983

Attorney General's Office
Justice Department
PO Box 7857
Madison, WI 53707-7857
www.doj.state.wi.us

608-266-1221
Fax 608-267-2779
8AM-5PM

Capital:	Madison
	Dane County
Time Zone:	CST
Number of Counties:	72
Population:	5,169,677
Web Site:	www.state.wi.us

State Archives
Historical Society
Archives Division
816 State St
Madison, WI 53706
www.wisc.edu/shs-archives

608-264-6450
Fax 608-264-6577
8AM-5PM M-F,
9-4 SA

State Court Administrator
Director of State Courts
Supreme Court
PO Box 1688
Madison, WI 53701-1688
www.courts.state.wi.us

608-266-6828
Fax 608-267-0980
8AM-4:30PM

State Agencies Online

Driver Records

Division of Motor Vehicles, Records and Licensing Section, PO Box 7995, Madison, WI 53707-7995, 608-266-2353, 608-267-3636 Fax.

General Information: Records are available for 5 years from date of conviction for moving violations and suspensions/revocations, 10 years from date of convictions for alcohol-related violations, and 20 years for revocation based on damage judgment. Persons can "opt-out" meaning they can have their personal identifiers withheld from casual record requester, per DPPA guidelines.

Online search: Online access is available for high volume users only. The fee is $3.00 per record. Call 608-266-2353 for more information.

Uniform Commercial Code
Federal Tax Liens
State Tax Liens

Department of Financial Institutions, CCS/UCC, PO Box 7847, Madison, WI 53707-7847; (Courier: 30 West Mifflin, 10th Fl, Madison, WI 53703); 608-261-9555, 608-264-7965 (Fax), 7:45AM-4:30PM.

General Information: The search includes federal tax liens on businesses. Federal tax liens on individuals and state tax liens are filed at the county level, but will show up if entered on the state-wide lien system

Online search: The system requires purchase of software to access a Wang system. There is an up front fee of $144 (prorated annually) and a $.50 charge per minute, billing monthly. All current, open records are available. The system is open from 12 PM to 5 PM. Call Linda Schmidt at 608-267-3741 for details.

Legislation-Current/Pending
Legislation-Passed
www.legis.state.wi.us

Wisconsin Legislative, Legislative Reference Bureau, PO Box 2037, Madison, WI 53701-2037; (100 N. Hamilton Street, Madison, WI 53703); 608-266-0341, 800-362-9472 (Bill Status), 608-266-5648 (Fax).

Online search: Information on current bills is available over the Internet. There is a Folio program to search text of previous session bills.

Information About County Agencies

Court Structure

There are 74 circuit courts.

Probate filing is a function of the Circuit Court; however, each county has a Register in Probate who maintains and manages the probate records. The Register in Probate, also, maintains guardianship and mental health records, most of which are sealed but may be opened for cause with a court order. In some counties, the Register also maintains termination and adoption records, but practices vary widely across the state.

**About the
County Courts**

Most Registers in Probate are putting pre-1950 records on microfilm and destroying the hard copies. This is done as "time and workloads permit," so microfilm archiving is not uniform across the state.

Online Access

The Circuit Court Automation Program (CCAP) is in place in all but two counties. Public access terminals are available at each court. Statewide remote online access may be provided in the future.

Searching Hints

The statutory fee schedule for the Circuit Courts is as follows: Search Fee—$5.00 per name; Copy Fee—$1.25 per page; Certification Fee—$5.00. In about half the Circuit Courts, no search fee is charged if the case number is provided. There is normally no search fee charged for in-person searches.

The fee schedule for probate is as follows:

Search Fee — $4.00 per name;

Certification Fee — $3.00 per document plus copy fee;

Copy Fee — $1.00 per page.

About the Recorder's Office

Organization

72 counties, 72 recording offices. The recording officers are Register of Deeds and Clerk of Court (state tax liens). The entire state is in the Central Time Zone (CST).

Real Estate Records

Registers will not perform real estate searches. Copy fees and certification fees vary. Assessor telephone numbers are for local municipalities or for property listing agencies. Counties do not have assessors. Copies usually cost $2.00 for the first page and $1.00 for each additional page. Certification usually costs $.25 per document. The Treasurer maintains property tax records.

UCC Records

Financing statements are filed at the state level, except for consumer goods, farm and real estate related collateral, which are filed only with the Register of Deeds. All recording offices will perform UCC searches, and many will accept a search by phone. Use search request form UCC-11 for mail-in searches. Searches fees are usually $10.00 per debtor name. Copy fees are usually $1.00 per page.

Other Lien Records

Federal tax liens on personal property of businesses are filed with the Secretary of State. Other federal tax liens are filed with the county Register of Deeds. State tax liens are filed with the Clerk of Court. Refer to *The Sourcebook of County Court Records* for information about Wisconsin courts. Many Registers will perform federal tax lien searches. Search fees and copy fees vary. Other liens are: judgment, mechanics, breeders.

County Courts & Recording Offices Online

Kenosha County

Liens, Real Estate, Birth Records, Death Records, Marriage Records

County Register of Deeds, 1010 56th St, Kenosha, WI 53140, 414-653-2414, 414-653-2564 Fax.

Online search: The set up fee is $500 and you are billed $6.00 per hour. The system operates 24 hours daily and supports baud rates from 14.4-56K. Records date back to 5/86. One can search by name, Grantee/Grantor, book and page, document number, legal description and track. Federal tax liens are listed. Lending agency information is available. For further information, contact Joellyn Storz at 414-653-2511.

Milwaukee (City)

Real Estate

www.ci.mil.wi.us/citygov/assessor/asse ssments.htm

Assessor's Office, 200 E Wells, Milwaukee WI 53202-3515, 414-286-3651, 414-286-8447 Fax.

Online search: The City of Milwaukee Assessor's Office provides an excellent Internet site for free property and assessment data.

Federal Courts Online

US District Court
Eastern District of Wisconsin

Milwaukee Division, Clerk's Office, Room 362, 517 E Wisconsin Ave, Milwaukee, WI 53202, 414-297-3372. PACER sign-up number is 800-676-6856.

US Bankruptcy Court
Eastern District of Wisconsin

Milwaukee Division, Room 126, 517 E Wisconsin Ave, Milwaukee, WI 53202, 414-297-3291, Record Room: 414-297-4111.

PACER sign-up number is 800-676-6856.

US District Court
Western District of Wisconsin

Madison Division, PO Box 432, Madison, WI 53701, 608-264-5156.

PACER sign-up number is 800-676-6856. Both civil and criminal case records are available online.

US Bankruptcy Court
Western District of Wisconsin

www.wiwb.uscourts.gov

PACER sign-up number is 800-676-6856.

Eau Claire Division, PO Box 5009, Eau Claire, WI 54702, 715-839-2980, Fax: 715-839-2996

Madison Division, PO Box 548, Madison, WI 53701, 608-264-5178

County-to-Court Cross Reference (Bankruptcy Court locations in Parenthesis if different)

County	District	Court
Adams	Western	Madison
Ashland	Western	Madison (Eau Claire)
Barron	Western	Madison (Eau Claire)
Bayfield	Western	Madison (Eau Claire)
Brown	Eastern	Milwaukee
Buffalo	Western	Madison (Eau Claire)
Burnett	Western	Madison (Eau Claire)
Calumet	Eastern	Milwaukee
Chippewa	Western	Madison (Eau Claire)
Clark	Western	Madison (Eau Claire)
Columbia	Western	Madison
Crawford	Western	Madison
Dane	Western	Madison
Dodge	Eastern	Milwaukee
Door	Eastern	Milwaukee
Douglas	Western	Madison (Eau Claire)
Dunn	Western	Madison (Eau Claire)
Eau Claire	Western	Madison (Eau Claire)
Florence	Eastern	Milwaukee
Fond du Lac	Eastern	Milwaukee
Forest	Eastern	Milwaukee
Grant	Western	Madison
Green	Western	Madison
Green Lake	Eastern	Milwaukee
Iowa	Western	Madison
Iron	Western	Madison (Eau Claire)
Jackson	Western	Madison (Eau Claire)
Jefferson	Western	Madison
Juneau	Western	Madison (Eau Claire)
Kenosha	Eastern	Milwaukee
Kewaunee	Eastern	Milwaukee
La Crosse	Western	Madison (Eau Claire)
Lafayette	Western	Madison
Langlade	Eastern	Milwaukee
Lincoln	Western	Madison (Eau Claire)
Manitowoc	Eastern	Milwaukee
Marathon	Western	Madison (Eau Claire)
Marinette	Eastern	Milwaukee
Marquette	Eastern	Milwaukee
Menominee	Eastern	Milwaukee
Milwaukee	Eastern	Milwaukee
Monroe	Western	Madison (Eau Claire)
Oconto	Eastern	Milwaukee
Oneida	Western	Madison (Eau Claire)
Outagamie	Eastern	Milwaukee
Ozaukee	Eastern	Milwaukee
Pepin	Western	Madison (Eau Claire)
Pierce	Western	Madison (Eau Claire)
Polk	Western	Madison (Eau Claire)
Portage	Western	Madison (Eau Claire)
Price	Western	Madison (Eau Claire)
Racine	Eastern	Milwaukee
Richland	Western	Madison
Rock	Western	Madison
Rusk	Western	Madison (Eau Claire)
Sauk	Western	Madison
Sawyer	Western	Madison (Eau Claire)
Shawano	Eastern	Milwaukee
Sheboygan	Eastern	Milwaukee
St. Croix	Western	Madison (Eau Claire)
Taylor	Western	Madison (Eau Claire)
Trempealeau	Western	Madison (Eau Claire)
Vernon	Western	Madison (Eau Claire)
Vilas	Western	Madison (Eau Claire)
Walworth	Eastern	Milwaukee
Washburn	Western	Madison (Eau Claire)
Washington	Eastern	Milwaukee
Waukesha	Eastern	Milwaukee
Waupaca	Eastern	Milwaukee
Waushara	Eastern	Milwaukee
Winnebago	Eastern	Milwaukee
Wood	Western	Madison (Eau Claire)

Wyoming

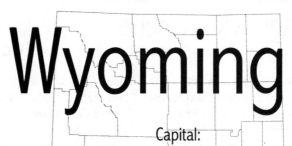

Governor's Office
State Capitol Bldg., Rm 124   307-777-7434
Cheyenne, WY 82002-0010   Fax 307-632-3909
www.state.wy.us/governor/
governor_home.html

Attorney General's Office
123 State Capitol   307-777-7841
Cheyenne, WY 82002   Fax 307-777-6869
www.state.wy.us/nag/index.html

Capital:	Cheyenne
	Laramie County
Time Zone:	MST
Number of Counties:	23
Population:	479,743
Web Site:	www.state.wy.us

State Archives
Department of Commerce   307-777-7826
Archives Division   Fax 307-777-7044
6101 Yellowstone Rd   8AM-5PM M-F;
Cheyenne, WY 82002   (Research Area:
   8AM-4:45PM)
http://commerce.state.wy.us/cr/archives

State Court Administrator
Court Administrator   307-777-7480
Supreme Court Bldg   Fax 307-777-3447
2301 Capitol Ave   8AM-5PM
Cheyenne, WY 82002
www.courts.state.wy.us

State Agencies Online

Corporation Records
http://soswy.state.wy.us/corporat/
webtips.htm

Limited Liability Company Records
Limited Partnership Records
Fictitious Name
Trademarks/Servicemarks
http://soswy.state.wy.us

Corporations Div., Sec. of State, State Capitol, Cheyenne, WY 82002; 307-777-7311, 307-777-5339 (Fax).
Online search: Information is available through the Internet site listed above. You can search by corporate name or even download the whole file. Also, they have an excellent 2 page tip document.

Uniform Commercial Code
Federal Tax Liens
UCC Division, Secretary of State, The Capitol, Cheyenne, WY 82002-0020; (Courier: Capitol Bldg, RM 110, Cheyenne, WY 82002); 307-777-5372, 307-777-5988 (Fax), 8AM-5PM.
General Information. The search includes federal tax liens on businesses. Federal tax liens on individuals and all state tax liens are filed at the county level.

Online search: Online search: All accounts must be approved by the Director and by Vendor Security. Fees include a $50 annual registration, $20 monthly, and long distant access fees of between $3 and $6 per hour. A word of caution, if user fails to log off the "clock" still keeps ticking and user is billed! The system is open 24 hours daily except 1:30AM to 5AM Monday through Sunday, and 4PM to 6PM on Sunday.

Legislation-Current/Pending
Legislation-Passed
legisweb.state.wy.us

Wyoming Legislature, State Capitol, Room 213, Cheyenne, WY 82002; 307-777-7881, 8AM-5PM.
Online search: The Internet site contains a wealth of information regarding the legislature and bills.

County Agencies Online

About the County Courts

Court Structure

Some counties have County Courts and others have Justice Courts, thus each county has a District Court and either a County or Justice Court. County Courts handle civil claims up to $7,000 while Justice Courts handle civil claims up to $3,000. The District Courts take cases over the applicable limit in each county, not just over $7,000. Three counties have two county courts each: Fremont, Park, and Sweetwater. Cases may be filed in either of the two courts in those counties, and records requests are referred between the two courts. The Park and Sublette County Justice Courts were eliminated in 1995 and were replaced by County Courts, where the prior records are now located. Probate is handled by the District Court.

Online Access

Wyoming's statewide case management system is for internal use only. Planning is underway for a new case management system that will ultimately allow public access.

About the Recorder's Office

Organization

23 counties, 23 recording offices. The recording officer is County Clerk. The entire state is in the Mountain Time Zone.

Real Estate Records

County Clerks will not perform real estate searches. Copy fees and certification fees vary. The Assessor maintains property tax records.

UCC Records

Financing statements are usually filed with the County Clerk. Accounts receivable and farm products require filing at the state level as well. All recording offices will perform UCC searches. Use search request form UCC-11. Searches fees are usually $10.00 per name. Copy fees vary.

Other Lien Records

Federal tax liens on personal property of businesses are filed with the Secretary of State. Other federal and all state tax liens are filed with the County Clerk. Most counties will perform tax lien searches. Search fees are usually $10.00 per name.

County Courts & Recording Offices Online

There is no online access to court records in Wyoming.

No remote online access is available from real estate recorder's offices in Wyoming.

Federal Courts Online

US District Court
District of Wyoming

www.ck10.uscourts.gov/wyoming/district

PACER sign-up number is 800-676-6856. Both civil and criminal case records are available online.

Casper Division, 111 South Wolcott, Room 121, Casper, WY 82601, 307-261-5440

Cheyenne Division, PO Box 727, Cheyenne, WY 82003, 307-772-2145

US Bankruptcy Court
District of Wyoming

www.wyb.uscourts.gov

PACER sign-up number is 800-676-6856. Only civil case records are available online.

Cheyenne Division, PO Box 1107, Cheyenne, WY 82003, 307-772-2191. This court services all counties.

This Bankruptcy Court division services the entire state of Wyoming.

Private Company Index

The company profiles are designed to give you a pertinent set of facts about each company that can be useful in choosing which company to call for a particular searching requirement. We anticipate that you will usually refer to the profiles after finding a potential company in the Company Information Index, which is designed to direct you to the public information category you need quickly and accurately.

Company Information Index

27 types of information found in online public record information are listed here in alphabetical order. A company listed under a specific category indicates that they offer access to information in that particular category.

We have indicated geographic coverage, including particular state, national, and international.

Also, we have indicated if the company maintains its own proprietary **database** or acts as an interactive **gateway** to another database.

27 Types of Public Record Information

Addresses & Telephone Numbers

Associations / Trade Groups

Aviation/Vessels

Bankruptcy

Corporate / Trade Name Data

Credit Information

Criminal Information

Driver and/or Vehicle

Education / Employment

Environmental

Foreign Country Information

Genealogical Information

Legislation/Regulation

Litigation/Judgment/Tax Liens

Military Service

News / Current Events

Professional Licenses/Registrations/Permits

Real Estate / Assessor

SEC / Other Financial

Social Security (Numbers)

Software / Training

Trademarks / Patents

Uniform Commercial Code

Vital Records

Voter Registration

Workers' Compensation

Wills / Probate

Addresses & Telephone Numbers

People Finders Company	Proprietary	Geographic Coverage
Access Louisiana	Gateway	LA
AcuSearch Investigations & Services LLC		US
Advanced Information Technologies		US
Amerestate Inc	Database	KY, MI, OH
American Business Information Inc	Database	US
American Information Network		US
American Research Bureau Inc		US
Ameridex Information Systems	Database	US
Anderson Research		US
ARISTOTLE	Database	US
Atlanta Attorney Services		US
Att Loss Prevention Inc		US
Avantext Inc	Database	US
BiblioData	Database	US
Bombet & Associates		US
Business Research Services		US
California Drivers Records		US
Cambridge Statistical Research Associates		US
Central Property Search Inc		US
ChoicePoint Inc		US
Cleo	Database	US
Commercial Information Systems Inc		OR
Compinstall Inc		US, International
CompuServe	Gateway	US
Computer Assisted Research Online		US
Condor Protective Services		US
CQ Staff Directories Ltd	Database	US
CrimeLine Information Systems		US
Daily Report, The	Database	CA
Database Technologies Inc	Database	US
Datalink		All
DataQuick		US
DCS Information Systems	Database	US
Delphic Information Systems		US
Don C. Haworth & Associates Inc		US
Dun & Bradstreet	Database	US
Empire Data Systems Inc		US
Equifax Credit Services Division	Database	US
Equity Title Search		US, CA
Everton Publishers	Database	US
Experian Consumer Credit	Database	US
Experian Target Marketing Services	Database	US
Find People Fast		US

People Finders Company	Proprietary	Geographic Coverage
Folks Finders Ltd		US
Gale Group Inc, The	Database	US, International
Global Intelligence Network Inc		US
Haines & Company Inc	Database	US
Hebert Land Services		US
Hoovers Inc	Database	US, International
Hylind Search Company Inc		
Idealogic		
IGB Associates Inc		US
Info-Pro Inc		US
Information America Inc	Database	US
Information Network Associates Inc		PA
Informus Corporation	Gateway	
Infotel Corp		TX
InfoTrack Information Services Inc		IL
INPRO		US
International Locate & Asset Services Inc		US
International Research Bureau		US
International Research Bureau Inc (IRB)		FL
Investigative Consultants Inc		US
Investigators Anywhere Resource Line	Database	US, International
IQ Data Systems		US
IRSC	Database	US
KeySearch Inc		US
KnowX	Database	US
Law Bulletin Information Network	Database	IL
LegalEase Inc		US
LegalTrieve Information Services Inc		US
Lloyds Maritime Information Services Inc		US, International
Locators International Inc		US
Logan Registration Service Inc		CA
Maine Public Record Services	Database	ME-6 counties
Martindale-Hubbell	Database	US, International
Merlin Information Services	Gateway	US
Merola Services		US
Metromail Corporation	Database	US
National Background Investigations Inc		US
National Credit Information Network NCI	Gateway	US
National Information Bureau Ltd		US
Nebrask@ Online	Gateway	NE
NEWSI		US
NightHawk International		US
Northwest Location Services		WA
Offshore Business News & Research		Bermuda, Caribbean
Online Search & Investigations		US
Online Systems Research		US, LA

People Finders Company	Proprietary	Geographic Coverage
OPEN (Online Professional Electronic Network)	Gateway	US
Owens Online Inc		US, International
Pallorium Inc		US
Paragon Document Research		MN, ND, SD, MT
Paul C Klumb, MLIS		US, WI
PeopleSearch		IL
PFC Information Services		US
Phoenix Research Corp		US
Pinnacle Research Inc		US
Plat System Services Inc	Database	MN-Minneapolis & St Paul
Professional Services Bureau	Database	LA, MS
Property Data Center Inc	Database	CO
PROTEC	Database	US
Public Record Research Library	Database	US
Public Records Research Service		US, International
Quest Information Service Inc		US-Detroit, MI
RC Information Brokers	Database	MA, US
Research Services & Recovery LLC		US
Research Specialists		US
Search Company of North Dakota LLC	Database	ND
Search Systems		US, CA
Search/America		US
Searching Registration Service		CA
Search-Net Management Corp		US
Security Research Consultants		US
SIC Inc		US
Sorensen Information Service		US
Staftrack Inc		US
State Information Bureau		US
Super Search Inc		TX
Tax Analysts	Database	US, International
T-R Information Services		US
Tracers Choice		US
Tracers Information Specialists Inc		US
Trans Union	Database	US
Unisyn Information Services		US
US Search & Background		US
Validata Inc		US
Vehicle Operator Searches		US
Western Regional Data Inc		NV
WinStar Telebase Inc	Gateway	US, International

Associations/Trade Groups

Associate/Groups Search Company Name	Proprietary	Geographic Coverage
Access Indiana Information Network		IN
Access/Information Inc		US, International
Avian Corporate Records Research Notary		TX
Cal Info		US, CA
Finder Group, The		US
Gale Group Inc, The	Database	US, International
Hebert Land Services		US
Independent Research, Inc		MI
Information Search Inc		FL, US
Progenitor		US
Public Data Corporation		NY-New York City
Tax Analysts		US
Virginia Information Providers Network		VA

Aviation/Vessels

Aviation/Vessels Search Company Name	Proprietary	Geographic Coverage
AccuSearch		AZ
Agentis Information Services Inc		Canada-BC
Avantext Inc	Database	US
Avian Corporate Records Research Notary		TX
Carolina Investigative Research		NC, SC
Commercial Information Systems Inc	Database	US
Datalink		All
Fairchild Record Search Ltd		US, AK, ID, OR, WA
Hylind Courthouse Retrieval Co		US
Hylind Search Company Inc		
Info-Pro Inc		US
Information America Inc		US
IRSC	Database	US
KnowX	Database	US
Lloyds Maritime Information Services Inc	Database	US, International
Motznik Computer Services Inc	Database	AK
Pallorium Inc	Database	AL, AZ, CA, CT, FL, GA, ID, IL, LA, MA, ME, MI, MS, NH, NJ, NM, NY, OH, OR, RI, TX, UT, VT, WA, US
Search Systems		US
SIC Inc		US
Vehicle Operator Searches		CA

Bankruptcy

Bankruptcy Records Company Name	Proprietary	Geographic Coverage
Access Louisiana		LA
Access Research		CA
Access/Information Inc		US
Accurate Background Checks Inc		US
Accurate Confidential Research Inc		FL-Southern Dist
AccuSearch		AZ
AccuSearch Inc	Database	CA, IL, TX
Action Court Service Inc		US
ADREM Profiles Inc		US
Advanced Background Check Inc		US
Advanced Information Technologies		US
AEGIS Consulting & Investigations		MT
Agentis Information Services Inc		Canada-BC
Alaska Public Records Search LLC		AK
Alert Credit Bureau		US, UT
All American Information Services		US
Alliant Inc		US
Alpha Records Search & Retrieval		CA-Southern
American Research Bureau Inc		US
American Research Unlimited		MO
AmeriSearch		US, CA
Anderson Research		US
Apex Information & Research Inc		TX
ASK Services Inc		US, MI, NC
Atlanta Attorney Services		US
Attorneys' Information Bureau		WA
Avian Corporate Records Research Notary		TX
Banko Document Retrieval (BDR)	Database	US
Barry Shuster & Associates		US, MA, RI
Blumberg Excelsior Corporate Services		US
Bombet & Associates		US
Bridge Services Corp		US, NY-New York City
Business Information Service	Database	TX-Austin, Colorado, Waller, Washington
Business Intelligence Inc		US
Business Research Services		US
Capitol District Information		DC, US
Capitol Lien Records & Research Inc		MN
Capitol Services Inc		US
CDB Infotek	Database	US
Centennial Coverages Inc		US
Central Indiana Paralegal Service Inc		IN-Southern District
Central Property Search Inc		PA, DE, NJ, MD, NY

Bankruptcy Records Company Name	Proprietary	Geographic Coverage
Charles Jones Inc		NJ
Chattel Mortgage Reporter Inc		US
ChoicePoint Inc	Database	US
Commercial Information Systems Inc		OR
Compinstall Inc		US
Computer Assisted Research Online		US
Condor Protective Services		US
Conrad Grundlehner Inc	Database	DC, MD, NC, VA, WV
CorpAmerica		DE
CorpAssist		US
Corporate Access Inc		US
Corpus Chirsti Court Services		TX-Southern District
Court Explorers Inc		US
Court House Legal Service		NJ-Southern, PA-Eastern
Court PC of Connecticut		US, CT
Court Record Research Inc		US, TX
Court Records Investigations		US
Court Records Research Group		OK, TX
Courthouse Connections		CA-Southern
CourtLink	Gateway	US
CQ Staff Directories Ltd		US
Credit-Facts of America		US
CSC, The United States Corporation Company		US
Daily Report, The		CA
Dane County Legal Notice		WI-Western Dist
Data Search Kentucky		KY
Disclosure Incorporated		US
Diversified Information Services Corp		AZ
Doc*U*Search Inc		US, MA, NH
Doc-U-Search Hawaii		US, HI
Don C. Haworth & Associates Inc		US
Dun & Bradstreet	Database	US
Electronic Property Information Corp (EPIC)	Database	NY-Northern & Western Districts
EL-RU Inc		GA
Empire Data Systems Inc		US
Experian Business Information Solutions	Database	US
Factel Inc		US-46 states
Fairchild Record Search Ltd		US, AK, ID, OR, WA
Ferrari		US
Fidelifacts		US
FIND/SVP Inc		US
FLA Search Company		FL
Global Intelligence Network Inc		US
Haines & Company Inc		US
Hebert Land Services		OK

Bankruptcy Records Company Name	Proprietary	Geographic Coverage
HIQ Companies		US
Hogan Information Services	Database	US
Hylind Courthouse Retrieval Co		US
Hylind Search Company Inc		US
ICDI		FL, Middle District/Orlando
Idealogic		Canada
IGB Associates Inc		US
Independent Research, Inc		US
Infinity Information Network Inc		US, OH
Info-Pro Inc		US
Information America Inc	Database	US
Information Management Systems Inc		US
Information Network Associates Inc		PA
Information Search Inc		FL
Infotel Corp		TX
InfoTrack Information Services Inc		Il
INPRO		US, MN
Intercounty Clearance Corporation		US
International Locate & Asset Services Inc		US
Intranet Inc	Database	TX
Investigative Consultants Inc		US
IQ Data Systems		US
IRSC	Gateway	US
Jess Barker Document Research/Retrieval		US, IL
Judicial Research & Retrieval Service Inc		US, FL
KeySearch Inc		US
KnowX	Database	US
Land Records of Texas		US-TX
Lawyers Aid Service Inc		TX
Legal Data Resources		US, IL
Legal Research		MI
LegalEase Inc		US, NY
LegalTrieve Information Services Inc		US
LEXIS Document Service		US
LIDA Credit Agency Inc		US
Maine Public Record Services		ME
McGinley Paralegal & Search Services Inc		IN
McGowan & Clark Services		WA
Merlin Information Services		US
Metro Clerking Inc		IL-Northern Dist
MLQ Attorney Services		US
Motznik Computer Services Inc	Database	AK
National Consumer Services Inc		KY-Jefferson
National Corporate Research Ltd		US
National Data Access Corp		US, SC
National Document Filing & Retrieval Inc		US

Bankruptcy Records Company Name	Proprietary	Geographic Coverage
National Information Bureau Ltd		US
National Service Information		US
Nationwide Court Services Inc		US
Nationwide Information Services		US
New Mexico Technet		NM
NM Factfinders Inc		US, NM
Northeast Court Services Inc		US
Offshore Business News & Research	Database	Bermuda, Cayman Islands
OPEN (Online Prof. Electronic Network)	Gateway	US
Origin Information & Services Inc		US
OTM Research Inc		US
Pacific Photocopy & Research		US, FL
Paper Chase Research		NY
Paragon Document Research		MN, ND, SD, MT
Paralegal Resource Center Inc		MA
PARASEC		US
PFC Information Services		US
Phoenix Research Corp		US
Prime Information Brokers Inc		US
Professional Services Bureau		LA, MS
Promesa Enterprises Inc		US
Prosearch of Texas		TX
Public Data Corporation		NY
Public Information Resource Inc		ME
Public Record Services		AL
Quest Research		AR
Quik Check Records		US
Rafael Jorge Investigations		CA
Record Access		CA
Record Finders		TX-Cameron
Record Information Services Inc	Database	IL
Record Search & Information Services		ID
Redi-Info Information Services	Database	US
Relyea Services Inc		NY, US
Research & Retrieval		US, CA
Research Data Service		US
Research Group, The		US-Dallas, Denton, Tarrant, Wichita
Research Services & Recovery LLC		US
Research Specialists		US
San Diego Daily Transcript/San Diego Source	Gateway	US
SEAFAX Inc		US, International
Search Associates Inc		WI
Search Company of North Dakota LLC	Database	ND
Search One Services		OH
Search Systems		US

Bankruptcy Records Company Name	Proprietary	Geographic Coverage
Search/America		US
SearchNY Inc		NY-New York City
SearchTec Inc		US, PA-Eastern Dist
Security Search & Abstract Co		US, PA, NJ
SIC Inc		US
SingleSource Services Corp		US
SKLD Information Services LLC		CO
Solons Legal Document Service Center		US
Sorensen Information Service		US
Southwest InfoNet		US-AZ
Specialty Services		AL, GA
Staftrack Inc		US
Suburban Record Research		MA
Super Search Inc		US, TX
Superior Information Services LLC	Database	DC, DE, MD, NC, NJ, NY, PA, VA
The Court System Inc		US, TX
The Pettit Company		US, VA
The Records Reviewer Inc		FL
The Search Company Inc		Canada
Thomas Paralegal Services		LA-Jefferson, New Orleans
Title Court Service		CA
Todd Wiegele Research Co Inc		US
T-R Information Services		US
Tracers Choice		US
UCC Retrievals Inc		VA
Unisearch Inc		US
Unisyn Information Services		US
US Corporate Services		US
US Search & Background		US
Washington Document Service, Inc		US

Corporate/Trade Name Data

Corporate/Trade Name Data Company	Proprietary	Geographic Coverage
Access Information Services Inc		US
Access Louisiana	Gateway	LA
Access/Information Inc		CO
AccuSearch		AZ
AccuSearch Inc	Database	CA, CT, IL, MA, MO, OH, OK, OR, PA, TX, WA
Accutrend Corporation	Database	US
Agentis Information Services Inc		Canada
Alaska Public Records Search LLC		AK
Alert Credit Bureau		UT

Corporate/Trade Name Data Company	Proprietary	Geographic Coverage
All American Information Services		US
Alliant Inc		
AmeriSearch		US, CA
Anderson Research		US
ASK Services Inc		US, MI, NC
Background Services		US, UT
Barry Shuster & Associates		US, MA, RI
Blumberg Excelsior Corporate Services		US
Business Intelligence Inc		US
Capital Connection Inc		FL
Capitol City Network		US
Capitol Document Services Inc		NM
Capitol Lien Records & Research Inc		MN
Capitol Services Inc		US
CDB Infotek	Database	US
Centennial Coverages Inc		US
Central Indiana Paralegal Service Inc		IN
Central Property Search Inc		US
Certified Document Retriever Bureau		NY
Chattel Mortgage Reporter Inc		US, IL
ChoicePoint Inc	Database	US
Colby Attorneys Service Co Inc		US, NY
Commercial Information Systems Inc	Database	CA, ID, OR, WA
Communications Systems Technology Inc		CO
Complete Corporate Services of Alaska		US, AK
Computer Assisted Research Online		US
Condor Protective Services		US
CorpAmerica		US, DE
CorpAssist		US
Corporate Access Inc		US
Corporate Creations International Inc		US
Court PC of Connecticut		CT
Court Records Research Group		OK, TX
CrimeLine Information Systems	Database	CA
CSC, The United States Corporation Company		US
Dane County Legal Notice		WI-Dane
Data Search Kentucky		KY
Database Technologies Inc	Database	US
DataQuick		US
Derwent Information	Database	US, International
Dialog Corporation, The	Gateway	US, International
Diversified Information Services Corp		AZ
Doc*U*Search Inc		US, MA, NH
Doc-U-Search Hawaii		US, HI
Don C. Haworth & Associates Inc		US
Dun & Bradstreet	Database	US

Corporate/Trade Name Data Company	Proprietary	Geographic Coverage
EL-RU Inc		GA
Empire Data Systems Inc		US
Experian Business Information Solutions	Database	US
Factel Inc		US-43 States
Fairchild Record Search Ltd		US, AK, ID, OR, WA
Ferrari		US
Gale Group Inc, The	Database	US, International
Government Liaison Services Inc		US
HIQ Companies		US
Hollingsworth Court Reporting Inc		LA, MS
Hoovers Inc	Database	US, International
Hylind Search Company Inc		US
Idealogic		Canada
IGB Associates Inc		US
Independent Research, Inc		MI
Info-Pro Inc		US
Information America Inc	Database	US
Information Network of Kansas	Gateway	KS
Information Search Associates		AZ
Information Search Inc		FL, US
Intercounty Clearance Corporation		US
International Research Bureau		US
International Research Bureau Inc (IRB)		FL
Investigative Consultants Inc		US
IQ Data Systems		US
IRSC	Database	US
KnowX	Database	US
Lawyers Aid Service Inc		TX-Travis
LegalTrieve Information Services Inc		US
Legislative Research Inc		TN
LEXIS Document Service		US
McGinley Paralegal & Search Services Inc		IN
Merlin Information Services	Database	CA
Merola Services		US
Motznik Computer Services Inc	Database	AK
National Corporate Research Ltd		US
National Data Access Corp		US, SC
National Document Filing & Retrieval Inc		US
National Fraud Center		US
National Information Bureau Ltd		US
National Service Information	Database	IN, OH, US
Nationwide Information Services		US
Nebrask@ Online	Gateway	NE
New Mexico Technet	Database	NM
NightHawk International		US
Offshore Business News & Research	Database	Bahamas, Bermuda, Cayman

Corporate/Trade Name Data Company	Proprietary	Geographic Coverage
		Islands
OPEN (Online Prof. Electronic Network)	Gateway	US
Pacific Photocopy & Research		FL
Paper Chase Research		NY
PARASEC		US
Penncorp Servicegroup Inc		US, PA
Pinnacle Research Inc		US
Prime Information Brokers Inc		US
Professional Services Bureau		LA, MS
Promesa Enterprises Inc		TX
Public Information Resource Inc		
Public Record Services		AL
Quest Information Service Inc		US-Detroit, MI
Quest Research		AR
Record Access		CA
Record Finders		TX-Cameron
Record Search & Information Services		ID
Records Research Inc		US
Relyea Services Inc		NY, US
Research & Retrieval		US
Research Data Service		US
Research Specialists		US
Sacramento Attorneys Service Inc		US, CA
SEAFAX Inc		US, International
Search Company of North Dakota LLC		ND
Search Network Ltd		US, IA, KS
Search Systems		US
Search/America		US
Search-Net Management Corp		US
SearchNY Inc		NY-New York City
SearchTec Inc		US
Security Research Consultants		US
Security Search & Abstract Co		US, PA, NJ
SIC Inc		US
Southwest InfoNet		US-AZ
Suburban Record Research		MA
Superior Information Services LLC	Database	NY, PA
Tax Analysts	Database	US
The Court System Inc		US
The Pettit Company		US, VA
The Search Company Inc		Canada
The Search Is On Inc		US, TN
Thomson & Thomson		US
Trans Union	Database	US
UCC Retrievals Inc		VA
UCC Search Inc		US, NM

Corporate/Trade Name Data Company	Proprietary	Geographic Coverage
Unisearch Inc		US
US Corporate Services		US
US Document Services Inc		US, SC, NC
West Group	Database	US
Western Regional Data Inc		NV
WinStar Telebase Inc	Gateway	US, International

Credit Information

Credit Information Company	Proprietary	Geographic Coverage
A Data Source		US
Accurate Background Checks Inc		US
AcuSearch Investigations & Services LLC		US
ADREM Profiles Inc		US
Advanced Information Technologies		US
Agency Records		US
Alert Credit Bureau		US, Canada
Alliant Inc		US
American Business Information Inc	Database	US
American Information Network		US
American Research Bureau Inc		US
Amherst Group Inc		US
Att Loss Prevention Inc		US
Background Research Services		US
Background Services		US, UT
Backtrack Inc		US
Business Research Services		US
Capitol Lien Records & Research Inc		MN
CDB Infotek		US
Central Property Search Inc		US
CMS Insight		US
Commercial Information Systems Inc		OR
Compinstall Inc		US
Confi-Chek		US
Corporate Access Inc		US
Corporate Information Services		US
Credit-Facts of America		US
DAC Services		US
Daily Report, The		CA-Kern
Dataprompt Corporation		US
DCS Information Systems	Database	TX, US
Delphic Information Systems		US
Don C. Haworth & Associates Inc		
Dun & Bradstreet	Database	US
E D Loven & Associates		US
Empire Data Systems Inc		US

Credit Information Company	Proprietary	Geographic Coverage
Equifax Credit Services Division	Database	US
Experian Consumer Credit	Database	US
FACS Information Service		US
Ferrari		US
Fidelifacts		US
Finder Group, The		US
Information Management Systems Inc		US
Informus Corporation		US
Infotel Corp		TX
International Locate & Asset Services Inc		US
International Research Bureau		US
International Research Bureau Inc (IRB)		FL
IQ Data Systems		US
IRSC	Database	US
KeySearch Inc		US
KnowX	Database	US
LIDA Credit Agency Inc		US, NY
Locators International Inc		US
Merlins Data Research		US, FL
MLQ Attorney Services		US
National Background Investigations Inc		US
National Consumer Services Inc		KY-Jefferson
National Credit Information Network NCI	Gateway	US
National Document Filing & Retrieval Inc		US
National Information Access Bureau		US
National Information Bureau Ltd	Database	US
Online Search & Investigations		US, Canada
OPEN (Online Prof. Electronic Network)	Gateway	US
Owens Online Inc		US, International
Pallorium Inc		US
Paragon Document Research		US
PFC Information Services		US
Phoenix Research Inc		US
Pinnacle Research Inc		US
Professional Services Bureau	Database	LA
Profiles International		US
Promesa Enterprises Inc		US
PROTEC		US
RC Information Brokers		US
Real Estate Guide Inc, The		
Redi-Info Information Services		US
Research Data Service		US
Research Services & Recovery LLC		US
SEAFAX Inc	Database	US
Search/America		US
Search-Net Management Corp		US

Credit Information Company	Proprietary	Geographic Coverage
SIC Inc		US
Sorensen Information Service		US
Staftrack Inc		US
Super Search Inc		US
Tenant Screening Services Inc		US
The Search Company Inc		Canada
Todd Wiegele Research Co Inc		US
T-R Information Services		US
Tracers Information Specialists Inc		US
Trans Union	Database	US
US Datalink Inc		US
Wholesale Information Network Inc		US
WinStar Telebase Inc	Gateway	US, International

Criminal Information

Criminal Record Search Company	Proprietary	Geographic Coverage
A Data Source		CA, US
Access Research		CA-Cook
Accurate Background Checks Inc		US
Accurate Confidential Research Inc		FL-Brow, Dade, Palm Beach
AccuSearch		AZ
Action Court Service Inc		US
AcuSearch Investigations & Services LLC	Gateway	US, CO
ADREM Profiles Inc		US
Advanced Background Check Inc		US
Agency Records	Database	CT, MN, US
Alaska Public Records Search LLC		AK
Alert Credit Bureau		UT
Alliant Inc		US
Allstate Legal Court Service		IA
Alpha Records Search & Retrieval		CA-Southern
American Information Network		US
Amherst Group Inc		US
ASK Services Inc		US, MI, NC
Atlanta Attorney Services		US
Att Loss Prevention Inc		US
Attorneys' Information Bureau		WA
Background Research Services		US
Background Services		US, UT
Bombet & Associates		LA
Business Information Service	Database	TX -Austin, Colorado, Waller, Washington Counties
Business Research Services		US, TN
Capitol District Information		DC, US
Capitol Lien Records & Research Inc		MN-Minneapolis/St Paul

Criminal Record Search Company	Proprietary	Geographic Coverage
Carolina Investigative Research		US
Chattel Mortgage Reporter Inc		US
ChoicePoint Inc		US
CMR Information Service		CA
CMS Insight		US
Commercial Information Systems Inc	Database	ID, OR, WA
Compinstall Inc		US
Computer Assisted Research Online		US, FL
Condor Protective Services		US
Confi-Chek	Database	US, CA
Corporate Information Services		US
Corpus Christi Court Services		TX-Nueces
Court House Legal Service		NJ, PA
Court PC of Connecticut	Database	CT
Court Records Research Group		OK, TX
Court Search Unlimited		US
Courthouse Connections		CA-San Diego
CourtLink		US, OR, WA
CrimeLine Information Systems	Gateway	AZ, CA, CO, US
CrimeSearch Inc		US
Criminal Information Services Inc	Database	AZ, OR, WA, ID, UT, TX
DAC Services	Database	US
Daily Report, The	Database	CA
Data Screen Inc		TX
Datalink		CA
Dataprompt Corporation		US, TX
DataQuick		US
DCS Information Systems	Database	TX
Delphic Information Systems		US
DJ Records		TN
Doc-U-Search Hawaii		US, HI
Don C. Haworth & Associates Inc		IL
Due Diligence Inc		US
E D Loven & Associates		US
EL-RU Inc		GA
Empire Data Systems Inc		US, CA, Puerto Rico
ExecuSearch		LA, TX
FACS Information Service		US
Factel Inc		US
Felonies R Us	Database	AR
Ferrari		US
Fidelifacts	Database	NY
FLA Search Company		FL
Folks Finders Ltd		US
GA Public Record Services Inc		US
Global Intelligence Network Inc		US

Criminal Record Search Company	Proprietary	Geographic Coverage
Hollingsworth Court Reporting Inc		US
Hylind Courthouse Retrieval Co		US
Idealogic		
IGB Associates Inc		US
Independent Research, Inc		US
Infinity Information Network Inc		US, OH
Infocon Corporation	Gateway	PA-12 Western Counties
Infonet Report Service		AZ
Info-Pro Inc		US
Information Inc	Database	TN-Nashville
Information Management Systems Inc		US
Information Network of Kansas	Gateway	KS- Sedgwick, Shawnee, Wyandotte
Information Search Associates		US, AZ-Pima
Information Search Inc		FL
Informus Corporation		US
InfoTrack Information Services Inc		IL
Innovative Enterprises Inc		US, VA
INPRO		US, MN
International Locate & Asset Services Inc		US
International Research Bureau		US
International Research Bureau Inc (IRB)		FL
IQ Data Systems		US
Judicial Research & Retrieval Service Inc		FL
KeySearch Inc		US
Knowledge Bank		US
Legal Data Resources		IL-Cook, Lake, DuPage
Legal Research		MI
LegalTrieve Information Services Inc		US
Locators International Inc		US
Logan Information Services		NC, VA
M & M Search Services		DC, MD
McGinley Paralegal & Search Services Inc		IN-Marion
McGowan & Clark Services		WA
Merlin Information Services	Database	CA
Merlins Data Research		US, FL
Merola Services		US
Michiana Searches, Inc		IN
MLQ Attorney Services		US
Motznik Computer Services Inc	Database	AK
National Background Investigations Inc		US
National Background Reports Inc		US, TN
National Consumer Services Inc		KY-Jefferson
National Document Filing & Retrieval Inc		US
National Fraud Center	Database	US, International
National Information Access Bureau		US

Criminal Record Search Company	Proprietary	Geographic Coverage
National Information Bureau Ltd		US
National Records Services		US, Canada, Puerto Rico, Guam
National Service Information		US
New Mexico Technet		NM
NightHawk International		US
NM Factfinders Inc		US, NM
Offshore Business News & Research		Bermuda, Caribbean
OPEN (Online Prof. Electronic Network)	Gateway	US, AL, IN, MI, MN, OH
Origin Information & Services Inc		US
OTM Research Inc		US
Pacific Photocopy & Research		FL
Pallorium Inc		US
Paper Chase Research		NY
Paragon Document Research		US
PARASEC		US
Paul C Klumb, MLIS		US
Peartree Information Services		AL, FL, UT, VA, WA
PFC Information Services		US
Phoenix Research Inc		US
Prime Information Brokers Inc		US
Professional Services Bureau	Database	LA, MS
Promesa Enterprises Inc		US, TX
Prosearch of Texas		TX
PROTEC		US
Public Records Research Service		US
Quest Information Service Inc		US-Detroit, MI
Quik Check Records		OR, WA
Rafael Jorge Investigations		US, CA
Record Finders		TX-Cameron, Willacy
Record Retrieval Services Inc		TX, US
Redi-Info Information Services	Database	US
Research & Retrieval		US
Research Data Service		US
Research Group, The		US-Dallas, Denton, Tarrant, Wichita
Research North Inc		MI
Research Specialists		US
Research World Unlimited		TX-Harris, Ft Bend, Montgomery
RIBackgrounds		RI
Search Associates Inc		WI
Search Company of North Dakota LLC	Database	ND
Search Systems		US
Search/America		US
SearchNY Inc		NY-New York City

Criminal Record Search Company	Proprietary	Geographic Coverage
Security Research Consultants		US
SIC Inc		US
SingleSource Services Corp		US, AL, DE, FL, MD, NC, SC, VA
Sleuth Research		GA
Solons Legal Document Service Center		US
Sorensen Information Service		US
Specialty Services	Gateway	US, AL, GA
Staftrack Inc		US
State Information Bureau		FL
Suburban Record Research		MA
Super Search Inc		TX
The Pettit Company		VA
The Records Reviewer Inc		FL
Thomas Paralegal Services		LA-Jefferson, New Orleans
Todd Wiegele Research Co Inc		US
T-R Information Services		US
Tracers Choice		US
Tracers Information Specialists Inc		US
Trax		RI
Unisyn Information Services		US
US Datalink Inc		US
US Search & Background		US
Vehicle Operator Searches		CA
Washington Document Service, Inc		US
Wholesale Information Network Inc		US

Driver and/or Vehicle

Driver/Vehicle Record Search Company	Proprietary	Geographic Coverage
Access Indiana Information Network	Gateway	IN
Access Information Services Inc		US
Access Research		CA
Accurate Background Checks Inc		US
Accurate Confidential Research Inc		FL-Brow, Dade, Palm Beach
AccuSearch		AZ
AcuSearch Investigations & Services LLC		US
ADREM Profiles Inc		US
Advanced Background Check Inc		US
Advanced Information Technologies		US, FL
Agency Records		US
Alaska Public Records Search LLC		AK
Alliant Inc		US
American Business Information Inc	Database	US
American Driving Records Inc	Gateway	US
American Information Network		US

Driver/Vehicle Record Search Company	Proprietary	Geographic Coverage
Amherst Group Inc		US
ARISTOTLE		US
ASK Services Inc		MI
Att Loss Prevention Inc		US
Avian Corporate Records Research Notary		TX
Background Research Services		US
Backgrounds Express LLC		US, TN
Barry Shuster & Associates		MA, RI
Blumberg Excelsior Corporate Services		US
Business Research Services		US, TN
California Drivers Records		US, CA
Capitol Lien Records & Research Inc		US, MN
Carfax	Database	US
Central Indiana Paralegal Service Inc		US
Certified Document Retriever Bureau		NY
Chattel Mortgage Reporter Inc		US
ChoicePoint Inc		US
CMS Insight		US
Colby Attorneys Service Co Inc		NY
Commercial Information Systems Inc	Database	ID, OR
Compinstall Inc		US, International
Complete Corporate Services of Alaska		AK
Computer Assisted Research Online		US
Condor Protective Services		US
Confi-Chek		28 states
CorpAmerica		US, DE
Corporate Access Inc		US
Corporate Creations International Inc		US
Court Records Research Group		OK, TX
CSC, The United States Corporation Company		US
DAC Services	Database	US
Dane County Legal Notice		WI
Data Screen Inc		TX
Database Technologies Inc	Database	US
Datalink	Gateway	US
Dataprompt Corporation		US, TX
DataSearch Inc		US
DCS Information Systems	Database	TX, US
Don C. Haworth & Associates Inc		IL
E D Loven & Associates		TX
Empire Data Systems Inc		US
Experian Target Marketing Services	Database	US
Experian Target Marketing Services		US
Explore Information Services	Gateway	CO, FL, IA, KY, ME, MN, MO, NE, NH, OH, TN, UT, WI
Factel Inc		US-28 states

Driver/Vehicle Record Search Company	Proprietary	Geographic Coverage
Fairchild Record Search Ltd		US, AK, ID, OR, WA
Fidelifacts		US
Find People Fast		US
Global Intelligence Network Inc		US
Hylind Courthouse Retrieval Co		US
Hylind Search Company Inc		US
Idealogic		Canada
IGB Associates Inc		US
Infinity Information Network Inc		US, OH
Infonet Report Service		AZ
Info-Pro Inc		US
Information America Inc	Gateway	AK, AL, CO, CT, DC, DE, FL, IA, ID, IL, KY, LA, MA, MD, ME, MI, MN, MO, MS, MT, ND, NE, NH, NM, NY, OH, SC, TN, UT, WI, WV, WY
Information Management Systems Inc		US
Information Network Associates Inc		PA
Information Network of Arkansas	Gateway	AR
Information Network of Kansas	Gateway	KS
Informus Corporation		US
Infotel Corp		TX
InfoTrack Information Services Inc		US, IL
INPRO		US, MN
Insurance Information Exchange (iiX)	Database, Gateway	US
Intercounty Clearance Corporation		US
International Locate & Asset Services Inc		US
International Research Bureau		US
International Research Bureau Inc (IRB)		FL
Investigative Consultants Inc		US
IQ Data Systems		US
IRSC	Gateway	US
IRSC		US
Judicial Research & Retrieval Service Inc		FL
KeySearch Inc		US
Legal Research		MI
LEXIS Document Service		US
LIDA Credit Agency Inc		NY
Locators International Inc		US
Logan Information Services	Gateway	CA, NC, VA
Logan Registration Service Inc		US
McGowan & Clark Services		WA
MDR/Minnesota Driving Records	Gateway	US
Merlins Data Research		US, FL
Merola Services		US, NY

Driver/Vehicle Record Search Company	Proprietary	Geographic Coverage
MLQ Attorney Services		US
Motznik Computer Services Inc	Database	AK
MVRs of Texas		US
National Background Investigations Inc		US
National Background Reports Inc		US, TN
National Corporate Research Ltd		US, NY
National Credit Information Network NCI	Gateway	US
National Data Access Corp		US, SC
National Document Filing & Retrieval Inc		AZ
National Information Access Bureau		US, Canada
National Information Bureau Ltd		US
National Records Services		US, Canada
Nationwide Court Services Inc		US
Nebrask@ Online	Gateway	NE
New Mexico Technet	Database	NM
NEWSI		US
NightHawk International		US
NM Factfinders Inc		US, NM
Online Search & Investigations		US
Online Systems Research		LA
OPEN (Online Professional Electronic Network)	Gateway	US
OTM Research Inc		US
Pacific Photocopy & Research		US, FL
Pallorium Inc	Database	AL, CA, CO, CT, FL, GA, ID, IL, LA, MA, ME, MI, MS, NH, NJ, NM, NY, OH, OR, RI, TX, UT, VT, WA
Paul C Klumb, MLIS		US, WI
Penncorp Servicegroup Inc		US, PA
Phoenix Research Corp		NY
Phoenix Research Inc		US
Prime Information Brokers Inc		US, FL, NY
Professional Services Bureau		LA, MS
Profiles International		US
Promesa Enterprises Inc		US, TX
PROTEC		US
Rafael Jorge Investigations		CA
RC Information brokers		US
Records Research Inc		US, CA
Redi-Info Information Services	Database	US
Research Data Service		US
Research Group, The		US
Research North Inc		MI
Research Services & Recovery LLC		US
Research Specialists		US

Driver/Vehicle Record Search Company	Proprietary	Geographic Coverage
Research World Unlimited		US
Search Company of North Dakota LLC	Database	ND
Searching Registration Service		CA
Security Research Consultants		US
SIC Inc		US
SingleSource Services Corp		US, FL
Sorensen Information Service		US
Staftrack Inc		US
State Information Bureau		FL
Texas Driving Record Express Service		TX
Texas Title Search		TX
The Search Company Inc		Canada-Ontario
The Search Is On Inc		US, TN
TML Information Services Inc	Gateway	AL, AZ, CA, CT, DC, FL, ID, IN, KS, KY, LA, MA, MD, MI, MN, MS, NC, ND, NE, NH, NJ, NY, OH, PA, SC, SD, VA, WI, WV
T-R Information Services		US
Tracers Information Specialists Inc		US
Trans Union	Gateway	US
Trax		FL, MA, ME, RI
UCC Retrievals Inc		VA
US Corporate Services		US
US Datalink Inc		US
Vehicle Operator Searches		US, CA
Virginia Information Providers Network	Gateway	VA
Wholesale Information Network Inc		US

Education/Employment

Education/Employment Records Company	Proprietary	Geographic Coverage
A Data Source		CA, US
Access Research		CA
ADREM Profiles Inc		US
Advanced Background Check Inc		US
Alliant Inc		US
American Research Bureau Inc		US
Amherst Group Inc		US
Avian Corporate Records Research Notary		TX-Bastrop, Hays, Travis, Williamson
Background Research Services		US
Background Services		US, UT
ChoicePoint Inc		US
CMS Insight		US
Compinstall Inc		US

Education/Employment Records Company	Proprietary	Geographic Coverage
Corporate Information Services		US
Court Records Research Group		OK, TX
DAC Services	Database	US
Dataprompt Corporation		US
Don C. Haworth & Associates Inc		US
E D Loven & Associates		US
Equifax Credit Services Division	Database	US
Fidelifacts		US
Global Intelligence Network Inc		US
Info-Pro Inc		US
Information Network Associates Inc		PA
InfoTrack Information Services Inc		IL
International Research Bureau		US
International Research Bureau Inc (IRB)		FL
IRSC	Database	US
KeySearch Inc		US
Knowledge Bank		US
LIDA Credit Agency Inc		US
Logan Information Services	Database	NC, VA
Martindale-Hubbell	Database	US, International
National Background Investigations Inc		US
National Background Reports Inc		US
NM Factfinders Inc		US, NM
OPEN (Online Professional Electronic Network)	Gateway	US
Paul C Klumb, MLIS		US, WI
Pinnacle Research Inc		US
Promesa Enterprises Inc		US, TX
PROTEC		US
Public Records Research Service		US
Quest Information Service Inc		US-Detroit, MI
Rafael Jorge Investigations		US
RC Information brokers		US
Record Retrieval Services Inc		US
Research Group, The		US
Research Services & Recovery LLC		US
Research Specialists		US
Research World Unlimited		US
Security Research Consultants		US
Specialty Services		AL, GA
Staftrack Inc		US
T-R Information Services		US
US Search & Background		US

Environmental

Environmental Search Company	Proprietary	Geographic Coverage
Access Indiana Information Network		IN
Agentis Information Services Inc		Canada-BC
American Research Unlimited		MO
Apex Information & Research Inc		TX
Avian Corporate Records Research Notary		TX
Cal Info		US, CA
Capitol City Network		US
Capitol District Information		DC
Centennial Coverages Inc		US
Charles Jones Inc		NJ
Commercial Information Systems Inc	Database	OR
DataQuick		US
Environmental Data Resources Inc	Database	US
Hebert Land Services		AR, OK
Information Management Systems Inc		US
IRSC	Database	US
Michiana Searches, Inc		IN
OSHA DATA		US
Pinnacle Research Inc		US
Prosearch of Texas		US
Public Data Corporation	Database	NY
Richland County Abstract Co		MN, ND
The Records Reviewer Inc		FL
VISTA Information Solutions	Database	US
Washington Document Service, Inc		US
West Group	Database	US

Foreign Country Information

Foreign Record Search Company	Proprietary	Geographic Coverage
American Business Information Inc	Database	
Corporate Information Services		
CQ Staff Directories Ltd		
DataTech Research		
Dialog Corporation, The	Gateway	International
FIND/SVP Inc		
Finder Group, The		Canada, Hong Kong, Sweden
Global Intelligence Network Inc		
Idealogic		
Information/Access Online		
Investigators Anywhere Resource Line		International
Offshore Business News & Research		Bermuda, Caribbean
Online Search & Investigations		International
Owens Online Inc		International

Foreign Record Search Company	Proprietary	Geographic Coverage
Pinnacle Research Inc		International
Progenitor		International
Search Resources Inc		Germany, Poland
SIC Inc		Europe
SingleSource Services Corp		UK, Europe
Thomson & Thomson	Database	International

Genealogical Information

Genealogical Search Company	Proprietary	Geographic Coverage
American Business Information Inc	Database	US
American Genealogical Research		US
American Research Unlimited		MO
Folks Finders Ltd	Gateway	CA, IL, US, International
MBK Consulting		US
Online Search & Investigations		US, Canada
PeopleSearch		US
Profiles International		MT
Progenitor	Database	US, Canada, International
Public Records Research Service		US, International
RC Information brokers		MA
Registry Research		MA-Berkshire
Search Resources Inc		US, CO, IL, MO
Search Systems		US
US Search & Background		US

Legislation/Regulation

Legislation/Regulation Records Company	Proprietary	Geographic Coverage
Access Indiana Information Network	Gateway	IN
Access/Information Inc		US, CO
Avantext Inc	Database	US
Avian Corporate Records Research Notary		TX
Blumberg Excelsior Corporate Services		US
Bombet & Associates		LA
Cal Info	Database	US, CA
Capitol City Network		US, CA
Capitol District Information		US, DC
CCH Washington Service Bureau		US
CMS Insight		US
Congressional Information Service Inc	Database	US
CQ Staff Directories Ltd		US
DataTech Research		US
Dialog Corporation, The	Gateway	US, International
Disclosure Incorporated		US
FIND/SVP Inc		US

Legislation/Regulation Records Company	Proprietary	Geographic Coverage
Inform Alaska Inc		AK
Information Network of Kansas	Gateway	KS
Lawyers Aid Service Inc		TX
Legal Data Resources		IL
Legalese		CA
Legi-Slate Inc	Gateway	US
Legislative Research Inc		TN
LEXIS-NEXIS	Database	US
Offshore Business News & Research	Database	Bermuda
OSHA DATA	Gateway	US
Paralegal Resource Center Inc		MA
Paul C Klumb, MLIS		US, WI
Pinnacle Research Inc		US
Public Record Research Library	Database	US
Public Record Services		AL
SEAFAX Inc		US, International
Search One Services		OH
Silver Plume	Database	US
Tax Analysts	Database	US, International
The Pettit Company		VA
Washington Document Service, Inc		US
West Group	Database	US
Western Regional Data Inc		NV

Litigation/Judgment/Tax Liens

Litigation/Judgment/Lien Search Company	Proprietary	Geographic Coverage
A Data Source		CA, US
Abstractor Associates Inc		MI-Wayne & Macomb
Access Indiana Information Network	Gateway	IN
Access Information Services Inc		US
Access Louisiana		LA
Access Research		CA
Access/Information Inc		CO
Accurate Background Checks Inc		US
Accurate Confidential Research Inc		FL-Dade, Miami
AccuSearch		AZ
AccuSearch Inc		CA, IL, TX
Action Court Service Inc		US
AcuSearch Investigations & Services LLC		US, CO-Denver
Advanced Background Check Inc		US
Agentis Information Services Inc		Canada
Alaska Public Records Search LLC		AK
Alert Credit Bureau		UT
All American Information Services		US
Alliant Inc		US
Allstate Legal Court Service		IA

Litigation/Judgment/Lien Search Company	Proprietary	Geographic Coverage
Alpha Records Search & Retrieval		CA-Southern
American Research Bureau Inc		US
American Research Unlimited		MO
AmeriSearch		US, CA
Amherst Group Inc		US
ASK Services Inc		MI, NC
Atlanta Attorney Services		US
Att Loss Prevention Inc		US
Attorneys' Information Bureau Inc		WA
Attorneys' Title Insurance Fund	Database	FL-31 counties
Background Research Services		US
Background Services		US, UT
Backgrounds Express LLC		TN-Shelby
Barry Shuster & Associates		US, MA, RI
Blumberg Excelsior Corporate Services		US
Bombet & Associates		LA
Bridge Services Corp		US, NY-New York City
Business Information Service	Database	TX -Austin, Colorado, Waller, Washington Counties
Business Intelligence Incorporated		US
Business Research Services		US, TN
Cal Info		US, CA
Capital Connection Inc		FL
Capitol City Network		US
Capitol District Information		DC, US
Capitol Lien Records & Research Inc		US, MN
Capitol Services Inc		US
Carolina Investigative Research		NC, SC
Case Record Info Services	Database	CA
CDB Infotek	Database	US
Centennial Coverages Inc		US
Central Indiana Paralegal Service Inc		IN-Southern District
Central Property Search Inc		US
Charles Jones Inc		NJ
Chattel Mortgage Reporter Inc		US, IL
ChoicePoint Inc	Database	US
ChoicePoint Inc		US
Colby Attorneys Service Co Inc		US, NY
Commercial Information Systems Inc		OR
Compinstall Inc		US
Condor Protective Services		US
Confi-Chek		US
Conrad Grundlehner Inc	Database	DC, MD, NC, VA, WV
CorpAmerica		US, DE
CorpAssist		US
Corporate Creations International Inc		US
Corpus Christi Court Services		TX-various counties

Litigation/Judgment/Lien Search Company	Proprietary	Geographic Coverage
Court Explorers Inc		US
Court House Legal Service		NJ, PA
Court PC of Connecticut	Database	CT
Court Record Consultants		US
Court Record Research Inc		TX
Court Records Investigations		US
Court Records Research Group		OK, TX
Court Search Unlimited		US
Courthouse Connections		CA-San Diego
CourtLink	Gateway	US, OR, WA
Credit-Facts of America		US
CrimeSearch Inc		US
CSC, The United States Corporation		US
Daily Report, The	Database	CA
Dane County Legal Notice		WI
Dane County Legal Notice		WI-Dane, Western Dist
Data Search Kentucky		KY
DataSearch Inc		US
Delphic Information Systems		US
Diversified Information Services Corp		AZ
Doc*U*Search Inc		US, MA, NH
Doc-U-Search Hawaii		US, HI
Don C. Haworth & Associates Inc		IL-Cook
Dun & Bradstreet	Database	US
E D Loven & Associates		TX-Tarrant
Electronic Property Information Corp (EPIC)	Database	NY-Erie, Monroe Counties
EL-RU Inc		GA
Empire Data Systems Inc		US
Experian Business Information Solutions	Database	US
Factel Inc		US
Fairchild Record Search Ltd		US, AK, ID, OR, WA
Fidelifacts		US
FIND/SVP Inc		US
FLA Search Company		FL
FOIA Group Inc		
Folks Finders Ltd		US
GA Public Record Services Inc		US
Global Intelligence Network Inc		US
Hebert Land Services		AR, OK
HIQ Companies		US
Hogan Information Services		US
Hollingsworth Court Reporting Inc	Database	AL, AR, FL, GA, IL, LA, MS, TN
Hylind Courthouse Retrieval Co		US
Hylind Search Company Inc		US
Idealogic		
IGB Associates Inc		US
Independent Research, Inc		MI

Litigation/Judgment/Lien Search Company	Proprietary	Geographic Coverage
Infinity Information Network Inc		US, OH
Infocon Corporation	Gateway	PA-12 Western Counties
Info-Pro Inc		US
Inform Alaska Inc		AK
Information America Inc	Database	US
Information Management Systems Inc		US
Information Network Associates Inc		PA
Information Network of Kansas	Gateway	KS-Johnson, Sedgwick
Information Search Associates		US, AZ-Pima
Information Search Inc		FL
Infotel Corp		TX
InfoTrack Information Services Inc		IL
INPRO		US, MN
Intercounty Clearance Corporation		US
International Research Bureau		US
International Research Bureau Inc (IRB)		FL
Intranet Inc		TX
Investigative Consultants Inc		US
IQ Data Systems		US
IRSC	Database	US
Jess Barker Document Research/Retrieval		US, IL
Judicial Research & Retrieval Service Inc		FL
Knowledge Bank		US
KnowX	Database	US
Kramer Research		DC
Land Records of Texas		US-TX
Law Bulletin Information Network	Database	IL-Central, North Counties
Lawyers Aid Service Inc		TX-Austin
Legal Data Resources		US, IL-Cook
Legal Research		MI
LegalEase Inc		US, NY
Legalese		CA
LegalTrieve Information Services Inc		US
Legislative Research Inc		TN
LEXIS Document Service		US
LEXIS-NEXIS	Database	US
LIDA Credit Agency Inc	Database	DE, NJ, NY, PA
Locators International Inc		US
Logan Information Services	Database	NC, VA
M & M Search Services		DC, MD
Maine Public Record Services	Database	ME-Cumberland, Knox, Lincoln, Waldo, York
MBK Consulting		OH
McGinley Paralegal & Search Services Inc		IL, IN, MI
McGowan & Clark Services		WA
Merlin Information Services	Database	CA
Metro Clerking Inc		IL-Cook
Michiana Searches, Inc		IN

Litigation/Judgment/Lien Search Company	Proprietary	Geographic Coverage
MLQ Attorney Services		US
Motznik Computer Services Inc	Database	AK
National Background Investigations Inc		US
National Background Reports Inc		US, TN
National Corporate Research Ltd		US
National Data Access Corp		US, SC
National Document Filing & Retrieval Inc		US
National Fraud Center		US
National Information Access Bureau		US
National Service Information		US
Nationwide Information Services		US
Nebrask@ Online	Gateway	NE
New Mexico Technet	Database	NM
NEWSI		US
NightHawk International		US
NM Factfinders Inc		US, NM
Northeast Court Services Inc		US
Offshore Business News & Research	Database	Bermuda, Cayman Islands
Origin Information & Services Inc		US
OTM Research Inc		US
Pacific Photocopy & Research		US, FL
Paper Chase Research		NY
Paragon Document Research		US
Paralegal Resource Center Inc		MA
PARASEC		US
Paul C Klumb, MLIS		US, WI
Peartree Information Services		AL, FL, UT, VA, WA
Penncorp Servicegroup Inc		US, PA
PeopleSearch		IL
PFC Information Services		US
Prime Information Brokers Inc		US
Pro Search Inc		CT
Professional Services Bureau		LA, MS
Promesa Enterprises Inc		US
Prosearch of Texas		US
PROTEC		US
Public Data Corporation	Database	NY
Public Information Resource Inc		ME
Public Record Services		AL
Quest Information Service Inc		US-Detroit, MI
Quest Research		AR
Quik Check Records		OR, WA
Raczak Inc		CO
Rafael Jorge Investigations		CA
RC Information brokers		MA
Record Finders		TX-Cameron, Willacy
Record Information Services Inc	Database	IL
Record Retrieval Services Inc		TX, US

Litigation/Judgment/Lien Search Company	Proprietary	Geographic Coverage
Record Search & Information Services		ID
Redi-Info Information Services	Database	US
Relyea Services Inc		NY, US
Research & Retrieval		US
Research Group, The		US
Research North Inc		MI
Research World Unlimited		TX-Harris, Ft Bend, Montgomery
RIBackgrounds		RI
Richland County Abstract Co	Database	MN, ND
Sacramento Attorneys Service Inc		US, CA
San Diego Daily Transcript/San Diego Source	Gateway	CA
Search Associates Inc		WI
Search Company of North Dakota LLC	Database	ND
Search Network Ltd		US, IA, KS
Search Systems		US
Search/America		US
Search-Net Management Corp		US
SearchNY Inc		NY-New York City
Security Search & Abstract Co		US, PA, NJ
SingleSource Services Corp		US, FL
SKLD Information Services LLC		CO-Metro Denver Counties
Solons Legal Document Service Center		US
Sorensen Information Service		US
Southwest InfoNet		US, AZ-Maricopa
Specialty Services	Gateway	US, AL, GA
State Information Bureau		FL
Suburban Record Research		MA
Super Search Inc		US, TX
Superior Information Services LLC	Database	DC, DE, MD, NC, NJ, NY, PA, VA
The Court System Inc		US, TX
The Pettit Company		VA, US
The Records Reviewer Inc		FL
The Search Is On Inc		US, TN
Thomas Paralegal Services		LA-Jefferson, New Orleans
Thomson & Thomson		US
Title Court Service		CA
Todd Wiegele Research Co Inc		US
T-R Information Services		US
Tracers Choice		US
Tracers Information Specialists Inc		US
Trans Union	Database	US
Trax		RI
UCC Retrievals Inc	Database	VA
UCC Search Inc		US, NM
Unisearch Inc		US

Litigation/Judgment/Lien Search Company	Proprietary	Geographic Coverage
Unisyn Information Services		US
US Corporate Services		US
US Datalink Inc		US
US Document Services Inc		US, SC, NC
US Search & Background		US
Wholesale Information Network Inc		US
WinStar Telebase Inc	Gateway	US

Military Service

Military Service Record Search Company	Proprietary	Geographic Coverage
Ameridex Information Systems	Database	US
Background Services		US, UT
CMS Insight		US
Corporate Information Services		US
DataTech Research		US
E D Loven & Associates		TX-Tarrant
Fidelifacts		US
Folks Finders Ltd		US
Military Information Enterprises Inc	Database	US
Online Search & Investigations		International
Progenitor		US
Public Records Research Service		US
Staftrack Inc		US

News/Current Events

News/Current Events Search Company	Proprietary	Geographic Coverage
A Data Source		CA, US
Access Indiana Information Network		IN
Access/Information Inc		US
Alpha Records Search & Retrieval		CA-Southern
American Business Information Inc	Database	US
Anderson Research		US, International
BiblioData	Database	US
Burrelle's Information Services	Database	US, International
Business Intelligence Incorporated		US
CCH Washington Service Bureau		US
CompuServe	Gateway	US
Computer Assisted Research Online		US
Dialog Corporation, The	Gateway	US
Federal Filings Inc	Gateway	US
FIND/SVP Inc		US
Hoovers Inc	Database	US, International
Inform Alaska Inc		AK
Information Search Associates		US

News/Current Events Search Company	Proprietary	Geographic Coverage
Information/Access Online		US
Legi-Slate Inc		US
MBK Consulting		US
Offshore Business News & Research		Bermuda, Caribbean
Paul C Klumb, MLIS		US, WI
Phoenix Research Corp		US
Prime Information Brokers Inc		US
SEAFAX Inc		US, International
UMI Company		US
WinStar Telebase Inc	Gateway	US, International

Professional Licenses/Registrations/Permits

Licensing/Registrations/Permits Records	Proprietary	Geographic Coverage
Access Indiana Information Network	Gateway	IN
Accutrend Corporation	Database	US
Advanced Information Technologies		US
AEGIS Consulting & Investigations		MT
Alert Credit Bureau		UT
All American Information Services		US
Alliant Inc		
Alpha Records Search & Retrieval		CA-Southern
Anderson Research		US
ASK Services Inc		US, MI, NC
Avian Corporate Records Research Notary		TX
Background Research Services		US
Bombet & Associates		LA
Centennial Coverages Inc		US
ChoicePoint Inc	Database	US
Commercial Information Systems Inc	Database	ID, OR, WA
Complete Corporate Services of Alaska		AK
Confi-Chek		40 states
Corporate Access Inc		US
Corporate Creations International Inc		US
Corporate Information Services		
CrimeLine Information Systems	Database	CA
Daily Report, The	Database	CA
DataTech Research		US
Environmental Data Resources Inc	Database	US
Ferrari		US
Fidelifacts		US
Idealogic		Canada
Inform Alaska Inc		AK
Information America Inc	Database	US, AZ, CA, CO, CT, FL, GA, IL, IN, LA, MA, MD, MI, NJ, OH, PA, SC, TN, TX, VA, WI

Licensing/Registrations/Permits Records	Proprietary	Geographic Coverage
Information Network Associates Inc		PA
Investigators Anywhere Resource Line		US
KnowX	Database	US
LegalEase Inc		US
Legalese		CA
Loren Data Corp		US
Merlin Information Services	Database	CA
Merlins Data Research		US, FL
Motznik Computer Services Inc	Database	AK
Nationwide Court Services Inc		US
NM Factfinders Inc		US, NM
Northwest Location Services	Gateway	WA
Penncorp Servicegroup Inc		US, PA
Phoenix Research Corp		NY, NJ, PA
Public Records Research Service		US
Quest Information Service Inc		US-Detroit, MI
Record Access		CA
Record Information Services Inc	Database	IL
Research Group, The		US
Research World Unlimited		US
Search Company of North Dakota LLC	Database	ND
Searching Registration Service		CA
Search-Net Management Corp		US
SingleSource Services Corp		US, FL
State Information Bureau		FL
Texas Driving Record Express Service		TX
The Pettit Company		US, VA
Thomson & Thomson	Database	US
Unisyn Information Services		US
Washington Document Service, Inc		US
Wholesale Information Network Inc		US

Real Estate/Assessor

Real Esate/Assessor Record Company	Proprietary	Geographic Coverage
A Data Source		CA, US
Abstractor Associates Inc		MI-Wayne & Macomb
Access Information Services Inc		US
Accurate Confidential Research Inc		FL-Dade, Miami
AccuSearch		AZ
AccuSearch Inc		CA-Los Angeles, TX-Harris & Dallas
Advanced Background Check Inc		OH
Agentis Information Services Inc		Canada
Alaska Public Records Search LLC		AK
All American Information Services		US

Real Esate/Assessor Record Company	Proprietary	Geographic Coverage
Allstate Legal Court Service		IA
Alpha Records Search & Retrieval		CA-Southern
Amerestate Inc	Database	KY, MI, OH
American Business Information Inc	Database	US
American Information Network		US
American Research Bureau Inc		US
American Research Unlimited		MO
AmeriSearch		US
Apex Information & Research Inc		TX
Atlanta Attorney Services		GA
Attorneys' Information Bureau Inc		WA
Attorneys' Title Insurance Fund	Database	FL-31 counties
Barry Shuster & Associates		MA, RI
Blumberg Excelsior Corporate Services		US
Bombet & Associates		LA
BRC Inc	Gateway	ME-17 county registries
Bridge Services Corp		US, NY-New York City
Business Information Service	Database	TX -Austin, Colorado, Waller, Washington Counties
California Drivers Records		CA
Capitol Lien Records & Research Inc		MN
Carolina Investigative Research		NC, SC
CDB Infotek	Database	US
Central Property Search Inc		PA, DE, NJ, MD, NY
Charles Jones Inc		NJ
Chattel Mortgage Reporter Inc		US
ChoicePoint Inc	Database	US
Commercial Information Systems Inc	Database	ID, NV, OR, WA
Confi-Chek		US
CorpAssist		US
Corpus Chirsti Court Services		TX
Court Record Consultants		US
Court Record Research Inc		TX
Court Records Research Group		OK, TX
Credit-Facts of America		US
Database Technologies Inc	Database	US
DataQuick	Database	US
DataQuick		US
DCS Information Systems	Database	US, TX
Diversified Information Services Corp	Database	AZ-Maricopa
Doc*U*Search Inc		NH
Electronic Property Information Corp (EPIC)	Database	NY-Erie, Monroe Counties
EL-RU Inc		GA
Environmental Data Resources Inc	Database	US
Equity Title Search		CA
FAR Retriever Bureau		MI

Real Esate/Assessor Record Company	Proprietary	Geographic Coverage
Ferrari		US
First American Real Estate Solutions	Database	AL, AZ, CA, CO, DC, DE, FL, GA, HI, IL, IN, LA, MA, MD, MI, MN, MS, NC, NJ, NM, NY, NV, OH, OK, OR, PA, SC, TN, TX, UT, VA, VI, WA, WI
FLA Search Company		FL
Haines & Company Inc	Database	US
Hebert Land Services		OK
Hogan Information Services		US
Hylind Courthouse Retrieval Co		US
Hylind Search Company Inc		US
ICDI		FL-Brevard, Duval, Orange, Seminole
IDM Corporation	Database	US
Infinity Information Network Inc		US, OH
Infocon Corporation	Gateway	PA-12 Western Counties
Infonet Report Service		AZ-Maricopa
Information America Inc	Database	US
Information Management Systems Inc		US
Information Network of Kansas	Gateway	KS
Information Search Associates		US, AZ-Pima
Information Search Inc		FL
InfoTrack Information Services Inc		IL
IQ Data Systems	Database	CA
IRSC	Database	US, AK, AL, AR, AZ, CA, CO, CT, DC, DE, FL, GA, HI, IL, KY, LA, MA, MD, MI, MN, MO, MS, NC, NJ, NV, NY, OH, OK, PA, SC, TN, TX, UT, VA, WI
Jess Barker Document Research/Retrieval		US
Land Records of Texas		US-TX
Law Bulletin Information Network	Database	IL-Cook
Legal Data Resources		IL-Cook
Legal Research		MI
LegalEase Inc		US, NY-New York City
LegalTrieve Information Services Inc		US
Locators International Inc		US
Logan Information Services		NC, VA
Logan Registration Service Inc		CA
M & M Search Services		DC, MD
Maine Public Record Services	Database	ME-Cumberland, Knox, Lincoln, Waldo, York
MBK Consulting		OH
McGinley Paralegal & Search Services Inc		IL, IN, MI
Merlin Information Services	Database	CA

Real Esate/Assessor Record Company	Proprietary	Geographic Coverage
Merola Services		US
Metro Clerking Inc		IL-Cook
Michiana Searches, Inc		IN
MLQ Attorney Services		US
Motznik Computer Services Inc	Database	AK
National Background Reports Inc		US, TN
National Corporate Research Ltd		US
National Data Access Corp		US, SC
National Document Filing & Retrieval Inc		US
National Fraud Center		US
Nationwide Court Services Inc		US
Offshore Business News & Research	Database	Bermuda
Online Search & Investigations		US
OPEN (Online Prof. Electronic Network)	Gateway	US
Origin Information & Services Inc		US
Paper Chase Research		NY
Paragon Document Research		MN, ND, SD, MT
Paralegal Resource Center Inc		MA
PARASEC		US
PFC Information Services		US
Plat System Services Inc	Database	MN-Minneapolis, St. Paul
Prime Information Brokers Inc		US
Pro Search Inc		CT
Professional Services Bureau		LA, MS
Promesa Enterprises Inc		US, TX
Property Data Center Inc	Database	CO
Prosearch of Texas		US
Public Data Corporation	Database	NY
Quest Research		AR
Real Estate Guide Inc, The	Database	US
Real Estate InfoService		VA
real-info Inc		NY-57 counties; not NYC
Record Finders		TX-Cameron, Willacy
Record Information Services Inc	Database	IL
Record Retrieval Services Inc		TX, US
Records Research Inc		CA
Registry Research		MA-Berkshire
Research & Retrieval		US
Research Data Service		US
Research North Inc		MI
Research Services & Recovery LLC		US
Richland County Abstract Co		MN, ND
Search Associates Inc		WI
Search/America		US
Search-Net Management Corp		US
SearchNY Inc		NY-New York City

Real Esate/Assessor Record Company	Proprietary	Geographic Coverage
SearchTec Inc		DE, NJ, PA
Security Search & Abstract Co	Database	US, NJ, PA
SKLD Information Services LLC		CO
Sorensen Information Service		US
Suburban Record Research		MA
Super Search Inc		US, TX
Superior Information Services LLC	Database	
The Pettit Company		VA
The Records Reviewer Inc		FL
The Search Company Inc	Database	Canada
Todd Wiegele Research Co Inc	Database	US, WI
T-R Information Services		US
Tracers Choice		US
Tracers Information Specialists Inc		US
Trans Union	Database	US
Vehicle Operator Searches		US
Western Regional Data Inc	Database	NV

SEC/Other Financial

SEC/Financial Records Company	Proprietary	Geographic Coverage
A.M. Best Company	Database	US
Access Louisiana	Gateway	LA
All American Information Services		US
Alpha Records Search & Retrieval		US
American Business Information Inc	Database	US
Anderson Research		US
Business Intelligence Incorporated		US
Cambridge Statistical Research Associates	Database	US
Capitol District Information		DC, US
Carolina Investigative Research		NC, SC
CCH Washington Service Bureau	Database	US
ChoicePoint Inc		US
Colby Attorneys Service Co Inc		US
Dialog Corporation, The	Gateway	US, International
Disclosure Incorporated	Database	US, Canada, International
Equifax Credit Services Division	Database	US
Everton Publishers	Database	US
FACS Information Service		US
Federal Filings Inc	Gateway	US
FIND/SVP Inc		US
Finder Group, The		US
Global Intelligence Network Inc		US
Government Liaison Services Inc		US
HIQ Companies		US
Hoovers Inc	Database	US

SEC/Financial Records Company	Proprietary	Geographic Coverage
Information Search Associates		US
Informus Corporation	Gateway	
IRSC	Database	US
Kramer Research		US
Legal Data Resources		US
National Credit Information Network NCI	Gateway	US
OPEN (Online Prof. Electronic Network)	Gateway	US
Pallorium Inc		US
Pinnacle Research Inc		US
Professional Services Bureau	Database	LA
PROTEC	Database	US
SEAFAX Inc		US, International
Search Company of North Dakota LLC	Database	ND
Silver Plume		US
Washington Document Service, Inc		US
WinStar Telebase Inc	Gateway	US, International

Social Security (Numbers)

Social Security Records Search Company	Proprietary	Geographic Coverage
A Data Source		US
Access Louisiana	Gateway	LA
Accurate Background Checks Inc		US
Accurate Confidential Research Inc		US, FL
AcuSearch Investigations & Services LLC		US
ADREM Profiles Inc		US
Advanced Information Technologies		US
Agency Records		US
American Research Bureau Inc		US
Amherst Group Inc		US
Anderson Research		US
Atlanta Attorney Services		US
Att Loss Prevention Inc		US
Background Research Services		US
California Drivers Records		US
Cambridge Statistical Research Associates	Database	US
Cleo		US
CMS Insight		US
Compinstall Inc		US
Condor Protective Services		US
Confi-Chek		US
Corporate Information Services		US
Court Explorers Inc		US
CrimeLine Information Systems		US
Dataprompt Corporation		US
DataSearch Inc		US

Social Security Records Search Company	Proprietary	Geographic Coverage
E D Loven & Associates		US
Equifax Credit Services Division	Database	US
Everton Publishers	Database	US
Ferrari		US
Find People Fast		US
Folks Finders Ltd		US
Informus Corporation	Gateway	
INPRO		US
International Research Bureau		US
International Research Bureau Inc (IRB)		FL
IRSC	Database	US
KeySearch Inc		US
Locators International Inc		US
Logan Registration Service Inc		US
MBK Consulting		OH
Merlin Information Services		US
Merola Services		US
National Background Investigations Inc		US
National Credit Information Network NCI	Gateway	US
National Information Access Bureau		US
National Information Bureau Ltd		US
Nationwide Court Services Inc		US
NEWSI		US
Online Search & Investigations		US
OPEN (Online Professional Electronic Network)	Gateway	US
Phoenix Research Corp		US
Phoenix Research Inc		US
Prime Information Brokers Inc		US
Professional Services Bureau	Database	LA
PROTEC	Database	US
Public Records Research Service		US
Quest Information Service Inc		US-Detroit, MI
RC Information brokers		US
Redi-Info Information Services		US
Research Data Service		US
Research Group, The		US
Research Services & Recovery LLC		US
Research Specialists		US
Search Company of North Dakota LLC	Database	ND
Search Resources Inc		US
Search-Net Management Corp		US
Security Research Consultants		US
Sorensen Information Service		US
State Information Bureau		US
Tracers Information Specialists Inc		US

Social Security Records Search Company	Proprietary	Geographic Coverage
Unisyn Information Services		US
US Search & Background		US

Software/Training

Software/Training Company Name	Proprietary	Geographic Coverage
FOIA Group Inc	Database	US
Carfax	Database	US
National Fraud Center	Database	US, International

Trademarks/Patents

Trademark/Patents Search Company	Proprietary	Geographic Coverage
Access Louisiana	Gateway	LA
Accurate Confidential Research Inc		FL-Dade, Miami
Alert Credit Bureau		UT
Amherst Group Inc		US
AmRent		US
Aurigin Systems Inc	Database	US, International
Backgrounds Express LLC		TN-Shelby
CompuServe	Gateway	US
Daily Report, The		CA-Kern
Dataprompt Corporation		US, TX
Derwent Information	Database	US, International
Dialog Corporation, The	Gateway	US, International
Equity Title Search		CA
Hogan Information Services		US
Hollingsworth Court Reporting Inc		AL, AR, FL, GA, IL, LA, MS, TN
LIDA Credit Agency Inc		US
MicroPatent USA	Database	US, International
OTM Research Inc		US
Phoenix Research Inc		US
Thomson & Thomson	Database, Gateway	US, International
WinStar Telebase Inc	Gateway	US, International

Uniform Commercial Code

UCC Records Company	Proprietary	Geographic Coverage
A Data Source		US, CA
Access Indiana Information Network	Gateway	IN
Access Information Services Inc		US
Access Louisiana	Gateway	LA
AccuSearch		AZ

UCC Records Company	Proprietary	Geographic Coverage
AccuSearch Inc	Database	CA, IL, OH, OR, MO, PA, TX, WA
Action Court Service Inc		US
Advanced Background Check Inc		IN, OH
Advanced Information Technologies		US
AEGIS Consulting & Investigations		MT
Alaska Public Records Search LLC		AK
Allstate Legal Court Service		IA
American Research Bureau Inc		US
American Research Unlimited		MO
AmeriSearch		US, CA
Anderson Research		US
ASK Services Inc		MI, NC
Atlanta Attorney Services		US
Attorneys' Information Bureau Inc		WA
Barry Shuster & Associates		US, MA, RI
Blumberg Excelsior Corporate Services		US
Bridge Services Corp		US, NY-New York City
Business Information Service	Database	TX -Austin, Colorado, Waller, Washington Counties
Business Intelligence Incorporated		US
Capitol City Network		US
Capitol Document Services Inc		NM
Capitol Lien Records & Research Inc	Database	MN
Capitol Services Inc		US
Carolina Investigative Research		NC, SC
CDB Infotek	Database	US
Centennial Coverages Inc		US
Central Indiana Paralegal Service Inc		IN
Central Property Search Inc		US
Chattel Mortgage Reporter Inc	Database	IL-Cook
ChoicePoint Inc		US
Colby Attorneys Service Co Inc		US, NY
Commercial Information Systems Inc	Database	CA, ID, OR, WA
Computer Assisted Research Online		US
Confi-Chek		US
CorpAmerica		US DE
CorpAssist		US
Corporate Creations International Inc		US
Corpus Christi Court Services		TX-Various counties
Court Explorers Inc		US
Court House Legal Service		NJ, PA
Court Record Research Inc		TX
Court Records Investigations		US
Court Records Research Group		OK, TX
Credit-Facts of America		US

UCC Records Company	Proprietary	Geographic Coverage
CSC, The United States Corporation Company		US
Daily Report, The		CA-Kern
Dane County Legal Notice		WI
Data Search Kentucky		KY
DataSearch Inc		US
Doc*U*Search Inc		US, MA, NH
Doc-U-Search Hawaii		US, HI
Dun & Bradstreet	Database	US
Electronic Property Information Corp (EPIC)	Database	NY-Erie, Monroe Counties
EL-RU Inc		GA
Experian Business Information Solutions	Database	US
Fairchild Record Search Ltd		US, AK, ID, OR, WA
FLA Search Company		FL
Hebert Land Services		AR, OK
HIQ Companies		US
Hogan Information Services		US
Hylind Courthouse Retrieval Co		US
Hylind Search Company Inc		US
ICDI		FL-Brevard, Duval, Orange, Seminole
IGB Associates Inc		US
Independent Research Inc		MI
Infinity Information Network Inc		US, OH
Inform Alaska Inc		AK
Information America Inc	Database	US
Information Management Systems Inc		US
Information Network Associates Inc		PA
Information Network of Kansas	Gateway	KS
Information Search Associates		US, AZ-Pima
Information Search Inc		US, FL
Infotel Corp		TX
INPRO		US, MN
Intercounty Clearance Corporation		US
International Locate & Asset Services Inc		US
Intranet Inc		TX
Investigative Consultants Inc		US
IQ Data Systems	Database	US
IRSC	Database	US
Jess Barker Document Research/Retrieval		US, IL
KnowX	Database	US
Lawyers Aid Service Inc		TX-Travis
Legal Data Resources		IL-Cook
Legal Research		MI
Legalese		CA
LegalTrieve Information Services Inc		US

UCC Records Company	Proprietary	Geographic Coverage
Legislative Research Inc		TN
LIDA Credit Agency Inc		New York City
Logan Information Services	Database	NC, VA
Logan Registration Service Inc		CA
M & M Search Services		DC, MD
MBK Consulting		OH
McGinley Paralegal & Search Services Inc		IL, IN, MI
McGowan & Clark Services		WA
Merlin Information Services	Gateway	CA
Merlins Data Research		US, FL
Metro Clerking Inc		IL-Cook
Michiana Searches Inc		IN
MLQ Attorney Services		US
Motznik Computer Services Inc	Database	AK
National Background Investigations Inc		US
National Background Reports Inc		US, TN
National Corporate Research Ltd		US
National Data Access Corp		US, SC
National Document Filing & Retrieval Inc		US
National Information Bureau Ltd		US
National Service Information	Database	IN, OH
National Service Information		US
Nationwide Information Services		US
Nebrask@ Online	Gateway	NE
Northeast Court Services Inc		US
OPEN (Online Prof. Electronic Network)	Gateway	US
Pacific Photocopy & Research		FL
Paper Chase Research		NY
Paragon Document Research	Database	US
Paralegal Resource Center Inc		MA
PARASEC		US
Penncorp Servicegroup Inc		US, PA
PFC Information Services		US
Phoenix Research Corp		US
Professional Services Bureau		LA, MS
Prosearch of Texas		TX
Public Data Corporation	Database	NY
Public Information Resource Inc		ME
Public Record Services		AL
Quest Research		AR
Quik Check Records		OR-Marion
Raczak Inc		CO
Rafael Jorge Investigations		CA
Record Access		CA
Record Finders		TX-Cameron
Record Search & Information Services		ID

UCC Records Company	Proprietary	Geographic Coverage
Relyea Services Inc		US, NY
Research & Retrieval		US
Research Group, The		US
Research North Inc		MI
Sacramento Attorneys Service Inc		US, CA
San Diego Daily Transcript/San Diego Source	Gateway	CA
Search Associates Inc		WI
Search Company of North Dakota LLC	Database	ND
Search Network Ltd	Database	US, IA, KS, MO
Search One Services		OH
Search Systems		US
Search/America		US
Searching Registration Service		CA
Search-Net Management Corp		US
SearchNY Inc		NY-New York City
SearchTec Inc		US
Security Search & Abstract Co		US, NJ, PA
SingleSource Services Corp		US, FL
Southwest InfoNet	Database	US, AZ-Maricopa, CA, IL, WA
Speciality Services		GA
State Information Bureau		FL
Suburban Record Research		MA
Super Search Inc		US, TX
Superior Information Services LLC	Database	PA
The Court System Inc		US, TX
The Pettit Company		US, VA
The Records Reviewer Inc		FL
The Search Is On Inc		US, TN
Todd Wiegele Research Co Inc		US
Tracers Choice		US
Tracers Information Specialists Inc		US
UCC Guide Inc, The	Database	US
UCC Retrievals Inc	Database	VA
UCC Search Inc		US, NM
Unisearch Inc	Database	AK, CA, ID, IL, MN, OR, UT, WA, WI
Unisyn Information Services		US
US Corporate Services	Database	WI
US Document Services Inc		US, NC, SC
Vehicle Operator Searches		CA
Washington Document Service Inc		US
West Group	Database	US
Western Regional Data Inc		NV
Wholesale Information Network Inc		US

Vital Records

Vital Records Company Name	Proprietary	Geographic Coverage
Access Research		CA
Action Court Service Inc		US
AcuSearch Investigations & Services LLC		US
ADREM Profiles Inc		US
Agentis Information Services Inc		Canada
All American Information Services		US
Alpha Records Search & Retrieval		CA-Southern
American Research Unlimited		MO
Attorneys' Information Bureau Inc		WA
Cambridge Statistical Research Associates		US
Carolina Investigative Research		NC, SC
Complete Corporate Services of Alaska		AK
Corporate Information Services		US
Court Record Consultants		US
Court Records Investigations		US
Credit-Facts of America		US
Daily Report, The		CA-Kern
Dane County Legal Notice		WI
Datalink		CA
DataSearch Inc		US
Doc*U*Search Inc		MA, NH
Doc-U-Search Hawaii		US, HI
Equity Title Search		CA
Fairchild Record Search Ltd		US, AK, ID, OR, WA
Find People Fast		US
Folks Finders Ltd	Database, Gateway	US, CA, NY-New York City, International
HIQ Companies		US
Hylind Courthouse Retrieval Co		US
IGB Associates Inc		US
Infocon Corporation	Gateway	PA-12 Western Counties
Inform Alaska Inc		
Information Search Associates		US, AZ-Pima
Information Search Inc		FL
INPRO		US, MN
International Locate & Asset Services Inc		US
Investigative Consultants Inc		US
Lawyers Aid Service Inc		TX
Legal Research		MI
LegalEase Inc		US, NY-New York City
LegalTrieve Information Services Inc		US
LIDA Credit Agency Inc		NY
Logan Registration Service Inc		CA
MBK Consulting		OH

Vital Records Company Name	Proprietary	Geographic Coverage
McGowan & Clark Services		WA
Merlin Information Services	Gateway	US
Metro Clerking Inc		IL
National Information Access Bureau		US
National Records Services		US
National Service Information		US
NM Factfinders Inc		US, NM
Pacific Photocopy & Research		FL
Pallorium Inc	Database	US, AL, AZ, CO, CT, FL, GA, ID, IL, LA, MA, ME, MI, MS, NH, NJ, NM, NY, OH, OR, RI, TX, UT, VT, WA
Paralegal Resource Center Inc		MA
PARASEC		US
Penncorp Servicegroup Inc		US, PA
Progenitor		US
Public Records Research Service		US
Quest Information Service Inc		US-Detroit, MI
RC Information brokers	Database	MA
Record Access		CA
Record Finders		TX-Cameron
Record Information Services Inc	Database	IL
Research & Retrieval		US
Research North Inc		MI
Research Specialists		US
Richland County Abstract Co		MN, ND
Search Company of North Dakota LLC		ND
Search Resources Inc		US
SearchNY Inc		NY-New York City
Security Search & Abstract Co		US
SingleSource Services Corp		US, FL
Suburban Record Research		MA
The Search Is On Inc		US, TN
Thomson & Thomson	Database	US
Tracers Choice		US
US Document Services Inc		
VitalChek Network	Gateway	US
Western Regional Data Inc	Database	NV
Wholesale Information Network Inc		US

Voter Registration

Voter Registration Records Company	Proprietary	Geographic Coverage
Access Louisiana	Gateway	LA
Amerestate Inc	Database	KY, MI, OH
American Business Information Inc	Database	US
Ameridex Information Systems	Database	US
ARISTOTLE	Database	US

Voter Registration Records Company	Proprietary	Geographic Coverage
Avantext Inc	Database	US
BiblioData	Database	US
Bombet & Associates		LA
Carolina Investigative Research		NC, SC
Cleo	Database	US
Court Records Investigations		US
CQ Staff Directories Ltd	Database	US
Daily Report, The	Database	CA
Database Technologies Inc	Database	US
DCS Information Systems	Database	US
Dun & Bradstreet	Database	US
E D Loven & Associates		TX-Dallas, Tarrant
EL-RU Inc		GA
Equity Title Search		CA
Everton Publishers	Database	US
Experian Consumer Credit	Database	US
Experian Target Marketing Services	Database	US
FLA Search Company		FL
Folks Finders Ltd	Gateway	US, CA, IL
Gale Group Inc, The	Database	US, International
Haines & Company Inc	Database	US, OH
Hoovers Inc	Database	US, International
Infonet Report Service		AZ-Maricopa
Inform Alaska Inc		
Investigators Anywhere Resource Line	Database	US, International
IRSC	Database	US
KnowX	Database	US
Logan Information Services	Database	NC, VA
Martindale-Hubbell	Database	US, International
Metro Clerking Inc		IL
Metromail Corporation	Database	US
National Credit Information Network NCI	Gateway	US
National Data Access Corp		US, SC
National Information Access Bureau		US
OPEN (Online Prof. Electronic Network)	Gateway	US
Pallorium Inc	Database	US, AL, AZ, CA, CO, CT, FL, GA, ID, IL, LA, MA, ME, MI, MS, NH, NJ, NM, NY, OR, RI, TX, UT, VT, WA
PFC Information Services		US
Professional Services Bureau	Database	LA
PROTEC	Database	US
Public Record Research Library	Database	US
RC Information brokers	Database	MA
Research Data Service		US
Research North Inc		MI
Search Company of North Dakota LLC	Database	ND

Voter Registration Records Company	Proprietary	Geographic Coverage
Staftrack Inc		AR
Trans Union	Database	US
Western Regional Data Inc		NV

Workers' Compensation

Workers' Compensation Records Company	Proprietary	Geographic Coverage
Agency Records	Database	FL
DAC Services	Database	AR, FL, IA, IL, KS, MA, MD, ME, MI, MS, ND, NE, OH, OK, OR, TX
Folks Finders Ltd	Database, Gateway	US, IL, CA, NY-New York City
Informus Corporation	Database	US, MS
IRSC	Gateway	AK, AL, AR, AZ, CA, CO, DC, DE, FL, IA, ID, IL, IN, KS, KY, MA, MD, ME, MI, MO, MT, NE, NH, NM, NV, OH, OK, OR, RI, SC, SD, TX, UT, VA, VT, WY
National Records Services		US-46 States
OPEN (Online Professional Electronic Network)	Gateway	US
Redi-Info Information Services	Database	US

Wills/Probate

Wills/Probate Records Company Name	Proprietary	Geographic Coverage
Bridge Services Corp		US, NY-New York City
Court Record Research Inc		TX
Court Records Investigations		TX
Electronic Property Information Corp (EPIC)	Database	NY-Erie, Monroe Counties
Equity Title Search		CA
Folks Finders Ltd		US
Hebert Land Services		AR, OK
ICDI		FL-Brevard, Duval, Orange, Seminole
MBK Consulting		OH
Northeast Court Services Inc		US
Paper Chase Research		NY
Prosearch of Texas		TX
Richland County Abstract Co		MN, ND
Search Resources Inc		US
Security Search & Abstract Co		US
Title Court Service		CA

Private Company Profiles

How to Read the Profiles

You can get a good sense a company's orientation by reviewing its profile. Here are some tips:

◆ **What Information Types does the company typically deal with?** Companies were given the opportunity to list up to 7 different public record categories of the 27 categories identified in the index.

◆ **Who are the Clientele of the company?** Distributors and search firms were given the opportunity to list up to seven markets in which they do significant business. Companies may specialize in a particular market or may have a broad base of customers.

◆ **What are typical Applications of the company's product or service?** We identified 17 application categories that are generally accepted in the public record industry as representative of the types of projects that require public record searches.

◆ **What organizations does the company belong to?** The kinds of organizations that the company belongs to, listed under Memberships, may also indicate the nature and focus of their services and products.

◆ **What are the Proprietary Products provided by the company?** Each entry for a company lists the name of the product, if it has one, and a brief clarifying description of the product content; the information type according to the categories defined in the Information Index; and the media in which the product is available.

You should note that some products cover very specific geography (e.g., Motznick in Alaska) or specific information types (e.g., ARISTOTLE) while others are sometimes vast conglomerations of various information types (e.g., IRSC). You may want to use the same information in one or the other of these products depending upon the breadth or depth of your search requirements.

♦ **Are there any other special characteristics of the company?** Each company was invited to submit a short description of special capabilities. This Statement of Capabilities may mention a service or other detail that you are looking for, including for example the availability of an online ordering system. Some of the other information you should notice as you review a profile include:

- When was the firm was founded? This industry is fast growing with a lot of new entrants with special experience and skills.

- A World Wide Web address for service or product information.

Visit www.publicrecordsources.com **for updated information about these and other companies.**

Editor's Note

These profiles were developed from a questionnaire sent to each company. When necessary, we completed the information about companies from our own knowledge where they failed to provide adequate details. We have tried to be as accurate as possible, we do not of course guarantee the complete accuracy of every profile. Companies can, and do, change products, and changes coverage areas.

To help you determine which vendor is best suited to your needs, we recommend reviewing 11 Questions to Ask an Online Vendor on pages 45-48.

A

A Data Source

7909 Walergard #112-205
Antelope, CA 95843
Telephone: **Fax:**
800-265-5657   916-726-4902
916-726-4636
www.adatasource.com
adatas@aol.com
Year Founded: 1996

Clientele: Attorney Firms, Business - General, Consumers (Individuals), Information - Brokers/Retrievers, Lending Institutions, Private Investigators, Public Record Research Firms

Applications: Background Info - Individuals, Employment Screening, Filing/Recording Documents, Litigation, Locating People/Businesses

Information Types:
Credit Information (US)
Criminal Information (CA,US)
Education/Employment (CA,US)
Litigation/Judgments/Tax Liens (CA,US)
News/Current Events (CA,US)
Real Estate/Assessor (CA,US)
Social Security (Numbers) (US)
Uniform Commercial Code (US, CA)

Membership: AIIP, PRRN

Statement of Capabilities: A Data Source specializes in courthouse searches and document retrieval. They cover 10 counties in Northern CA: Sacramento, Placer, Nevada, Solano, Yolo, Yuba, Sutter, San Joaquin, Stanislaus and El Dorado. Normal turnaround time is 24-48 hours. Additional services include: attorney support for the purpose of subject research, business and individual background checks, asset searches, Internet research, pre-employment screening and people locates. They structure searches around the client's specific needs by blending the unique characteristics of various online and off-line sources.

A.M. Best Company

Ambest Rd
Oldwick, NJ 08858-9988
Telephone: **Fax:**
908-439-2200   908-439-3296
www.ambest.com
Year Founded: 1899

Clientele: Insurance - Agents/Brokers, Insurance - General, Accountants, Attorney Firms, Lending Institutions, Libraries, Insurance - Underwriting

Applications: Insurance Underwriting, Insurance Ratings

Proprietary Products:
Name/Desc: Best Database Services
Info Provided: SEC/Other Financial
Media: Online Database, CD-ROM, Disk, Magnetic Tape, Call-back
Coverage: US

Statement of Capabilities: A.M. Best Company, known worldwide as The Insurance Information Source, was the first company to report on the financial condition of of insurance companies. A.M. Best strives to perform a constructive and objective role in the insurance industry toward the prevention and detection of insurer solvency. The company's exclusive Best's Ratings are the original and most recognized insurer financial strength ratings. A.M. Best provides quantitative and qualitative evaluations, and offers information through more than 50 reference publications and services. Since its inception a century ago, A.M. Best has provided financial services to professionals with timely, accurate and comprehensive insurance information. A.M. Best's London office can be reached at 011-44-171-264-2260. A.M. Best International, also based in London, can be reached at 011-44-181-579-1091.

Free Web Information:
Insurance company rating categories, links to insurance companies/associations, a glossary of insurance terms and descriptions of insurance policies.

Abstractor Associates Inc

18044 13 Mile Rd #400
Roseville, MI 48066
Telephone: **Fax:**
810-778-7554   810-778-9730

Year Founded: 1990

Clientele: Financial Institutions, Information - Brokers/Retrievers, Legal Profession, Legal Service Companies, Lending Institutions, Public Record Research Firms, Real Estate Owners/Managers

Applications: Asset/Lien Searching/Verification, Background Info - Business, Background Info - Individuals, Filing/Recording Documents, Real Estate Transactions

Information Types:
Litigation/Judgments/Tax Liens (MI-Wayne & Macomb)
Real Estate/Assessor (MI-Wayne & Macomb)

Membership: PRRN

Statement of Capabilities: Abstractor Associates specializes in title research and examining. Turnaround time is 24-48 hours. 40-100 year searches are possible with a 72 hour turnaround time.

Access Indiana Information Network
150 W Market #530
Indianapolis, IN 46204-2806
Telephone: **Fax:**
317-233-2106 317-233-2011
www.ai.org

Year Founded: 1995

Clientele: Business - General, Consumers (Individuals), Corporate Security, Insurance - Underwriting, Private Investigators, Attorney Firms, Employers (HR/Personnel Depts)

Applications: Employment Screening, Filing/Recording Documents, Government Document Retrieval, Insurance Underwriting, Legal Compliance

Information Types:
Environmental (IN)
News/Current Events (IN)
Associations/Trade Groups (IN)

Proprietary Products:

Name/Desc: Premium Services
Info Provided: Driver and/or Vehicle, Licenses/Registrations/Permits, Uniform Commercial Code, Litigation/Judgments/Tax Liens
Media: Internet, E-mail
Coverage: IN

Name/Desc: Free Services
Info Provided: Legislation/Regulation
Media: Internet, E-mail

Coverage: IN

Membership: NASIRE

Statement of Capabilities: AIIN is a comprehensive, one-stop source for electronic access to State of Indiana government information. This network is owned by the state of Indiana. Access to the public records listed here requires a subscription fee and per-use fee. Specialties include drivers records, vehicle title and lien information, vehicle registration records, physician and nurse license verification, Secretary of State records (including UCC and Corporation information) and information on the Indiana General Assembly. See the Internet site for more information.

Free Web Information:
The web site offers an myriad of information about Indiana and links state and local government sites. The web site also has a news and current events section and free Job Bank program.

Access Information Services Inc
1773 Western Ave
Albany, NY 12203
Telephone: **Fax:**
800-388-1598 800-388-1599
518-452-1873 518-452-0822
accessin@sprynet.com
Year Founded: 1994

Clientele: Legal Profession, Financial Institutions, Public Record Research Firms, Business - General

Applications: Filing/Recording Documents, Legal Compliance, Background Info - Business, Litigation

Information Types:
Uniform Commercial Code (US)
Corporate/Trade Name Data (US)
Litigation/Judgments/Tax Liens (US)
Driver and/or Vehicle (US)
Real Estate/Assessor (US)
Trademarks/Patents (US)

Membership: NPRRA, PRRN

Statement of Capabilities: Access Information specializes in UCC preparation, filing, and searching nationwide. President Jacqueline Lee is an editor of The UCC Filing Guide and has been in the industry since 1981. Access also provides a full range of public record searching and filing services for corporate, real property, and court documents.

Access Louisiana

400 Travis St #1308
Shreveport, LA 71101
Telephone: **Fax:**
800-489-5620   800-705-8953
318-227-9730

Clientele: Legal Profession, Secured Lenders, Professionals-Other

Applications: Asset/Lien Searching/Verification, Legal Compliance, Litigation

Information Types:
Bankruptcy (LA)
Litigation/Judgments/Tax Liens (LA)

Proprietary Products:

Name/Desc: LA UCC
Info Provided: Uniform Commercial Code, Addresses/Telephone Numbers and Social Security (Numbers)
Media: Printed Report
Coverage: LA

Name/Desc: LA Corporate Data
Info Provided: Corporate/Trade Name Data, Trademarks/Patents and Addresses/Telephone Numbers
Media: Printed Report
Coverage: LA

Membership: NPRRA, NFPA

Statement of Capabilities: Access Louisiana is a statewide legal research company with a physical presence in every Louisiana parish. Services include: public records (UCC, accounts, receivable, state/federal tax liens, suits, chattel mortgages, bankruptcy records), corporate filing/retrieval, court records and registered agent services. They have extensive knowledge of where information is recorded and how to effectively retrieve Louisiana public records.

Access Research

751 7th Ave #A
San Diego, CA 92103
Telephone: **Fax:**
800-456-9613   619-231-9338
619-231-8947
Year Founded: 1994

Clientele: Legal Profession, Business - General, Corporate Security, Employers (HR/Personnel

Depts), Information - Brokers/Retrievers, Private Investigators, Public Record Research Firms

Applications: Asset/Lien Searching/Verification, Filing/Recording Documents, General Business Information, Legal Compliance, Locating People/Businesses

Information Types:
Bankruptcy (CA)
Criminal Information (CA-Cook)
Driver and/or Vehicle (CA)
Education/Employment (CA)
Litigation/Judgments/Tax Liens (CA)
Vital Records (CA)
Workers' Compensation (CA-San Diego)

Statement of Capabilities: A "one-stop" source for public records throughout California. They have a large network of experienced researchers in the state and provide a normal turnaround time of 24-72 hours. They have correspondent relationships nationwide. They also offer employment/tenant screening. Credit accounts are accepted.

Access/Information Inc

900 E Louisiana Ave #209
Denver, CO 80210
Telephone: **Fax:**
800-827-7607   303-778-7691
303-778-7677
www.access-information.com
liz@csn.net
Year Founded: 1981

Clientele: Business - General, Government Agencies, Legal Profession, Libraries, Educational Institutions, Professionals-Other

Applications: Litigation, General Business Information, Background Info - Business, Competitive Intelligence

Information Types:
Litigation/Judgments/Tax Liens (CO)
Corporate/Trade Name Data (CO)
Legislation/Regulation (US, CO)
Associations/Trade Groups (US, International)
Bankruptcy (US)
News/Current Events (US)

Membership: AIIP, SLA

Statement of Capabilities: Several principals of Access/Information have extensive experience as law librarians and paralegals in a corporate setting. They provide comprehensive background information about a company or an entire industry in addition to providing public record information.

Accurate Background Checks Inc

31441 Santa Margarita Pkwy, #A-350
Rancho Santa Margarita, CA 92688
Telephone: **Fax:**
800-784-3911 800-784-3593
949-766-1660
www.accuratebackground.com

Year Founded: 1997

Clientele: Corporate Security, Employers (HR/Personnel Depts), Loss Prevention Specialists, Public Record Research Firms

Applications: Background Info - Business, Background Info - Individuals, Employment Screening, Tenant Screening

Information Types:
Bankruptcy (US)
Credit Information (US)
Litigation/Judgments/Tax Liens (US)
Criminal Information (US)
Driver and/or Vehicle (US)
Social Security (Numbers) (US)
Workers' Compensation (US)

Membership: PRRN

Statement of Capabilities: Accurate Background Checks is a nationwide information wholesaler of public records for the purpose of pre-employment screening. Primary clientele is composed of high volume pre-employment agencies, human resource and loss prevention divisions of large corporations. Facts are gathered by established national network of researchers. Normal turnaround time is 24-48 hours. They specialize in county level criminal and civil searches. Access by fax, electronically or with their software that is provided to clients.

Accurate Confidential Research Inc

677 SW 9 Ave #211
Miami, FL 33130
Telephone: **Fax:**
305-386-6677 305-383-2514
Year Founded: 1984

Clientele: Apartment Owners/Managers, Attorney Firms, Lending Institutions, Information - Brokers/Retrievers, Insurance - Claims, Private Investigators, Public Record Research Firms

Applications: Background Info - Business, Background Info - Individuals, Filing/Recording Documents, Government Document Retrieval, Locating People/Businesses

Information Types:
Bankruptcy (FL-Southern Dist)
Criminal Information (FL-Brow, Dade, Palm Beach)
Driver and/or Vehicle (FL-Brow, Dade, Palm Beach)
Litigation/Judgments/Tax Liens (FL-Dade, Miami)
Real Estate/Assessor (FL-Dade, Miami)
Social Security (Numbers) (US, FL)
Tenant History (FL-Dade, Miami)
Workers' Compensation (US, FL)

Statement of Capabilities: Accurate Confidential Research places emphasis on specialized complete and confidential on-site research of public records. They investigate in-person. Services include individual and group public record document retrieval. They offer daily turnaround time. Their professional experience spans over 21 years includes special assignments as Miami Dade Clerk in the Court Records Department.

AccuSearch

202 East McDowell Rd #151
Phoenix, AZ 85004-4532
Telephone: **Fax:**
800-462-7019 602-252-8109
602-252-8370
www.ACCUSEARCH-AZ.com

Year Founded: 1989

Clientele: Financial Institutions, Legal Profession, Public Record Research Firms, Legal Service Companies, Attorney Firms, Equipment Leasing Companies, Information - Brokers/Retrievers

Applications: Asset/Lien Searching/Verification, Background Info - Individuals, Employment Screening, Filing/Recording Documents, Lending/Leasing

Information Types:
Bankruptcy (AZ)
Litigation/Judgments/Tax Liens (AZ)
Corporate/Trade Name Data (AZ)
Uniform Commercial Code (AZ)
Criminal Information (AZ)
Real Estate/Assessor (AZ)

Aviation/Vessels (AZ)
Driver and/or Vehicle (AZ)

Membership: PRRN, NPRRA

Statement of Capabilities: Providing statewide services for Arizona, Accu Search will search and perform filing services in all jurisdictions of public record: federal, state, county, and local. Other services include criminal background searches, real property, motor vehicles, and daily abstracting. On a first order, they waive the service fee and up to $20 in costs. Turnaround time is 24-48 hours.

AccuSearch Inc

PO Box 3248
Houston, TX 77253-3248
Telephone: **Fax:**
800-833-5778   713-831-9891
713-864-7639
www.accusearchinc.com
accualr@accusearchinc.com
Year Founded: 1985

Clientele: Asset-Based Lenders, Attorney Firms, Lending Institutions, Credit Grantors, Equipment Leasing Companies, Financial Institutions, Legal Profession

Applications: Asset/Lien Searching/Verification, Filing/Recording Documents, Legal Compliance, Government Document Retrieval, Lending/Leasing

Information Types:
Litigation/Judgments/Tax Liens (CA, IL, TX)
Corporate/Trade Name Data (CT,IL,NV,MA, OK,PA,TX,WA)
Bankruptcy (CA,IL,TX)
UCC (CA,CO,IL,MA,MO,NV,NC,OH,OK, OR,PA,TX,WA,WI)
Real Estate/Assessor (CA-Los Angeles, TX-Harris & Dallas)

Proprietary Products:

Name/Desc: AccuSearch
Info Provided: Corporate/Trade Name, Uniform Commercial Code
Media: Direct Online
Coverage: TX,CA,PA,IL,WA,OH,OR,MO

Name/Desc: AccuSearch
Info Provided: Bankruptcy
Media: Online Database
Coverage: CA,IL,TX

Membership: NPRRA

Statement of Capabilities: AccuSearch provides immediate access to UCC, corporate, charter, real property and bankruptcy search services via IBM-compatible PCs or over the telephone. Instantaneous access is available for each online database listed. Each online or over-the-phone search is followed by same-day mailing or faxing of the search report and any copies requested. AccuSearch also performs any of the above searches for any county or state nationwide. AccuSearch's Direct Access system allows multi-page, formatted reports which eliminates print screens, and selective ordering of UCC copies.

Accutrend Corporation

6021 S Syracuse Wy #111
Denver, CO 80111
Telephone: **Fax:**
800-488-0011   303-488-0133
303-488-0011
www.accutrend.com
Year Founded: 1987

Applications: Direct Marketing, General Business Information

Proprietary Products:

Name/Desc: New Business Database
Info Provided:
Licenses/Registrations/Permits and Corporate/Trade Name Data
Media: CD-ROM, Internet, Magnetic Tape and Lists or labels
Coverage: US

Membership: DMA

Statement of Capabilities: Accutrend Corporation compiles a new business database monthly that contains 175 to 200 million new business registrations, licenses and incorporations. Data is collected from all levels of government and is enhanced with demographic overlays.

Action Court Service Inc

PO Box 309
Lake Elsinore, CA 92531
Telephone: **Fax:**
800-227-1174   800-227-1109
909-245-5872   909-245-0642
acs@actioncourt.com
Year Founded: 1992

Clientele: Legal Profession, Financial Institutions, Investigators - Fraud, Legal Service Companies, Mortgage Bankers, Private Investigators, Attorney Firms

Applications: Filing/Recording Documents, Genealogical Research, General Business Information, Government Document Retrieval, Litigation

Information Types:
Bankruptcy (US)
Criminal Information (US)
Litigation/Judgments/Tax Liens (US)
Uniform Commercial Code (US)
Vital Records (US)

Membership: ION

Statement of Capabilities: Action Court Services (ACS) has been in business for 6 years and are experienced in the courts, bankruptcy field and mortgage banking area. They have an average 7 day turnaround time. Rush orders (within 24-48 hours) are available. They return calls promptly.

AcuSearch Investigations & Services LLC

PO Box 100613
Denver, CO 80250
Telephone: **Fax:**
303-756-9687 303-756-9687
AcuSearch9@aol.com
Year Founded: 1997

Clientele: Attorney Firms, Business - General, Employers (HR/Personnel Depts), Legal Profession, Lending Institutions

Applications: Background Info - Business, Background Info - Individuals, Employment Screening, Filing/Recording Documents, Locating People/Businesses

Information Types:
Addresses/Telephone Numbers (US)
Credit Information (US)
Criminal Information (US)
Driver and/or Vehicle (US)
Litigation/Judgments/Tax Liens (US, CO-Denver)
Social Security (Numbers) (US)
Trademarks/Patents (US)
Vital Records (US)

Proprietary Products:
Name/Desc: CO Criminal Information
Info Provided: Criminal Information

Media: Call-back Only
Coverage: CO

Membership: NAIS, NAPPS

Statement of Capabilities: AcuSearch specializes in locating and obtaining pertinent information for financial institutions, businesses and individuals. Instant access to nationwide people, credit, and vehicle info. 24 hour turnaround time on all Colorado and Washington criminal/civil, driving/plate records, and process service. They provide in depth investigation in trademark matters. Owner Layla Flora is a Univ. of Colorado graduate and has extensive case investigation experience in civil and criminal matters. Guarantees quality and professional service.

ADREM Profiles Inc

5461 W Waters Ave #900
Tampa, FL 33634
Telephone: **Fax:**
800-281-1250 888-522-3736
813-890-0334
www.adpro.com
adrem-sales@adpro.com
Year Founded: 1992

Clientele: Business - General, Employers (HR/Personnel Depts), Information - Brokers/Retrievers, Investigators - Fraud, Legal Profession, Public Record Research Firms

Applications: Background Info - Business, Background Info - Individuals, Employment Screening, Litigation, Risk Management

Information Types:
Bankruptcy (US)
Credit Information (US)
Criminal Information (US)
Driver and/or Vehicle (US)
Education/Employment (US)
Social Security (Numbers) (US)
Vital Records (US)
Workers' Compensation (US)

Membership: SHRM

Statement of Capabilities: ADREM Profiles is an international, full service public records research and retrieval company. Their comprehensive retrieval network allows access to information repositories within the 3,347 counties and independent cities throughout the United States. They offer cost-plus pricing, a private label delivery system, compliance and technical support plus ADREM Advantage, their 24 hour Internet ordering and retrieval system. Their products and services are all designed to help achieve business objectives.

Advanced Background Check Inc.

259 Medford St
Dayton, OH 45410

Telephone: **Fax:**
888-264-4018   800-414-6212
937-254-9234   937-254-1171

Year Founded: 1993

Clientele: Attorney Firms, Banks, Business - General, Employers (HR/Personnel Depts), Insurance - General, Legal Profession, Financial Institutions

Applications: Asset/Lien Searching/Verification, Background Info - Business, Background Info - Individuals, Litigation, Locating People/Businesses

Information Types:
Bankruptcy (US)
Driver and/or Vehicle (US)
Education/Employment (US)
Uniform Commercial Code (IN, OH)
Workers' Compensation (KY, OH)
Criminal Information (US)
Litigation/Judgments/Tax Liens (US)
Real Estate/Assessor (OH)

Statement of Capabilities: Advanced Background Check has hand-picked civil and criminal information specialists throughout all fifty states. Their organization has an experienced core of real estate abstractors in all 88 Ohio counties.

Advanced Information Technologies

7028 Waters Ave #225
Tampa, FL 33634

Telephone: **Fax:**
813-269-7180   813-269-7180
www.aitresearch.com
datadiger@aol.com

Year Founded: 1995

Clientele: Attorney Firms, Educational Institutions, Information - Brokers/Retrievers, Private Investigators, Public Record Research Firms

Applications: Asset/Lien Searching/Verification, Background Info - Business, Background Info - Individuals, Employment Screening, Locating People/Businesses

Information Types:
Addresses/Telephone Numbers (US)
Bankruptcy (US)
Credit Information (US)
Driver and/or Vehicle (US, FL)
Social Security (Numbers) (US)
Licenses/Registrations/Permits (US)
Uniform Commercial Code (US)

Membership: AIIP

Statement of Capabilities: AIT Research provides accurate information to clients in a timely and discreet manner. A large percentage of searches can be returned the same or next business day. Most employees/providers have law enforcement backgrounds (FBI, police), helping insure proper business etiquette. Maintains a high level of customer service and satisfaction using the most up to date information available. Web site is available always.

AEGIS Consulting & Investigations

PO Box 9068
Helena, MT 59604

Telephone: **Fax:**
888-742-3447   888-742-3447
406-458-5369   406-458-5369
lswaegis@aol.com

Year Founded: 1995

Clientele: Business - General, Credit Reporting Agencies, Consulting Firms, Information - Brokers/Retrievers, Legal Profession, Private Investigators, Public Record Research Firms

Applications: Asset/Lien Searching/Verification, Background Info - Individuals, Employment Screening, Fraud Prevention/Detection, General Business Information

Information Types:
Bankruptcy (MT)
Licenses/Registrations/Permits (MT)
Uniform Commercial Code (MT)
Trademarks/Patents (MT)

Membership: ACFE

Statement of Capabilities: AEGIS provides a full array of public record and investigative services. Our staff supplies hands-on document retrieval requests for civil and criminal records in Lewis & Clark, Jefferson, and Broadwater counties with a 24 hour turnaround time. We welcome consumer requests and inquires regarding specific requests.

Agency Records

PO Box 310175
Newington, CT 06131
Telephone: **Fax:**
800-777-6655   860-666-4247
860-667-1490
www.agencyrecords.com

Year Founded: 1972

Clientele: Attorney Firms, Consulting Firms,
Corporate Security, Employers (HR/Personnel
Depts), Information - Brokers/Retrievers,
Insurance - General, Private Investigators

Applications: Background Info - Individuals,
Litigation, General Business Information,
Insurance Underwriting, Legal Compliance

Information Types:
Credit Information (US)
Criminal Information (US)
Workers' Compensation (FL)
Social Security (Numbers) (US)
Driver and/or Vehicle (US)

Proprietary Products:

Name/Desc: ARI
Info Provided: Criminal Information
Media: Direct Online, Gateway via Another
Online Svc, Automated Telephone Look-Up,
and Auto-Activated Fax-on-Demand
Coverage: CT

Name/Desc: MN Court Convictions (15 years)
Info Provided: Criminal Information
Media: Direct Online, Gateway via Another
Online Svc, Automated Telephone Look-Up,
and Auto-Activated Fax-on-Demand
Coverage: MN

Name/Desc: FL Workers' Compensation
Claims (20 years)
Info Provided: Workers' Compensation
Media: Direct Online, Gateway via Another
Online Svc, Automated Telephone Look-Up,
and Auto-Activated Fax-on-Demand
Coverage: FL

Statement of Capabilities: Agency Records
provides instant access to MVRs for FL, AL,
SC, NC, WV, NJ, NY, CT, VT, NH, and ME.
They also provide instant access to court
convictions for Connecticut and Minnesota.
They offer computer, fax and phone ordering
as well as volume discounts. Public companies
may be invoiced.

Agentis Information Services Inc

103-625 Agnes St
New Westminster, BC V3M 5Y4
Telephone: **Fax:**
604-257-1800   604-257-1888
www.agentis.com

info@agentis.com
Parent Company: Alouette Search Services Ltd
Year Founded: 1969

Clientele: Collection Agencies, Credit Reporting
Agencies, Equipment Leasing Companies,
Financial Institutions, Leasing Agents -
Personal Property, Legal Profession,
Government Agencies

Applications: Asset/Lien Searching/Verification,
Collections, Filing/Recording Documents,
Genealogical Research, Government
Document Retrieval

Information Types:
Aviation/Vessels (CD-BC)
Bankruptcy (CD-BC)
Corporate/Trade Name Data (CD)
Environmental (CD-BC)
Litigation/Judgments/Tax Liens (CD)
Real Estate/Assessor (CD)
Trademarks/Patents (CD)
Vital Records (CD)

Membership: NAPPS

Statement of Capabilities: Agentis
Information Services consists of professional
registry agents who service legal and financial
communities across Canada. They are brokers
of public information with access to private
property (real estate), personal property,
corporate, assessment, manufactured homes
and bankruptcy databases in Canada. They are
also an Internet service provider for the legal
community through BC Online. They have a
staff of 135 in offices in Vancouver, New
Westminster and Victoria, BC.

Alaska Public Records Search LLC

6648 E 16th St #B
Anchorage, AK 99504
Telephone: **Fax:**
800-808-5105   800-808-5155
907-333-5105   907-333-5155
http://members.aol.com/akrec
ords

akrecords@aol.com
Year Founded: 1993

Clientele: Public Record Research Firms, Mortgage Bankers, Attorney Firms, Bankers, Lending Institutions, Business - General, Asset-Based Lenders

Applications: Asset/Lien Searching/Verification, Real Estate Transactions, Litigation, Filing/Recording Documents, Legal Compliance

Information Types:
Uniform Commercial Code (AK)
Litigation/Judgments/Tax Liens (AK)
Bankruptcy (AK)
Corporate/Trade Name Data (AK)
Real Estate/Assessor (AK)
Driver and/or Vehicle (AK)
Criminal Information (AK)

Membership: PRRN, NPRRA

Statement of Capabilities: Alaska Public Records' founder has over 15 years experience in the public records industry. They conduct litigation searches, tax lien, judgment and current owner searches in all 34 county level recording districts of Alaska, including assessor/tax information. They conduct UCC searches and retrieve filings from Alaska state and all county level agencies. File UCC at the state and county level and record real property documents. Correspondents in key areas of the state. Their 800 number is accessible from Canada

Alert Credit Bureau

28 E 2100 South, #104
Salt Lake City, UT 84115
Telephone: **Fax:**
888-265-0400   888-265-0404
801-486-4945   801-486-5261

acbutah1@aol.com
Year Founded: 1997

Clientele: Apartment Owners/Managers, Business - General, Employers (HR/Personnel Depts), Lending Institutions, Private Investigators, Property Owners/Managers, Credit Grantors

Applications: Background Info - Individuals, Employment Screening, Lending/Leasing, Real Estate Transactions, Tenant Screening

Information Types:
Bankruptcy (US,UT)
Corporate/Trade Name Data (UT)
Credit Information (US, CD)
Criminal Information (UT)
Licenses/Registrations/Permits (UT)
Litigation/Judgments/Tax Liens (UT)
Tenant History (UT)

Statement of Capabilities: Alert Credit Bureau is able to provide: national and Canadian credit reports on individuals and businesses for personal use, mortgage qualification, credit extension, tenant and employment screening; credit reports are accessible by fax request or direct dialup; customized to fit client's needs; database of available Utah rental property; civil judgment and criminal background searches throughout most of Utah are completed within 4 hours; bankruptcy and federal case research; Utah state tax lien research; contractor license research (Utah); occupational licensing research (Utah).

All American Information Services

6015 Rustic Hills Dr #100
Rocklin, CA 95677
Telephone: **Fax:**
916-632-2149   916-632-1845

aais@mindsync.com
Year Founded: 1993

Clientele: Insurance - Agents/Brokers, Public Record Research Firms, Legal Profession, Business - General, Employers (HR/Personnel Depts), Consumers (Individuals)

Applications: Asset/Lien Searching/Verification, Locating People/Businesses, Fraud Prevention/Detection, Background Info - Business, General Business Information

Information Types:
Corporate/Trade Name Data (US)
Real Estate/Assessor (US)
SEC/Other Financial (US)
Bankruptcy (US)
Licenses/Registrations/Permits (US)
Litigation/Judgments/Tax Liens (US)
Vital Records (US)

Membership: AICPA, PRRN, AAIS

Statement of Capabilities: All American Information Services (AAIS) provides custom client research in the following areas: background research, asset location, business credit and litigation research. They also perform public record research and pre-employment screening. The principals have more than 20 years experience in research and investigation. They specialize in Placer

County, CA, on-site clerk, recorder, superior and municipal records.

Alliant Inc

5300 W Sahara #151
Las Vegas, NV 89102
Telephone: **Fax:**
800-731-1321 800-731-1321
verifyusa@aol.com
Year Founded: 1996

Clientele: Business - General, Corporate Security, Employers (HR/Personnel Depts), Loss Prevention Specialists

Applications: Background Info - Business, Background Info - Individuals, Competitive Intelligence, Employment Screening

Information Types:
Litigation/Judgments/Tax Liens (US)
Bankruptcy (US)
Corporate/Trade Name Data
Credit Information (US)
Criminal Information (US)
Driver and/or Vehicle (US)
Education/Employment (US)
Licenses/Registrations/Permits

Membership: SHRM, SCIP, AIIP, ASIS, NAIS

Statement of Capabilities: Alliant provides a wide range of nationwide services, including employment screening, background investigation, forensic toxicology, and business information reports to high technology and business companies including the Fortune 500, government agencies, and supporting organizations. They utilize a network of over 3000 court record researchers. Investigations are based on real time searches, eliminating errors due to outdated or incomplete information. They provide no-charge customized Windows-based software to order products and track in-process work status.

Allstate Legal Court Service

PO Box 485
Granger, IA 50109
Telephone: **Fax:**
888-260-2816 515-999-9267
515-999-2757
Parent Company: Allstate Legal Court Research
Year Founded: 1994

Clientele: Credit Grantors, Financial Institutions, Information - Brokers/Retrievers, Investment Bankers, Lending Institutions, Mortgage Bankers, Public Record Research Firms

Applications: Employment Screening, Filing/Recording Documents, Lending/Leasing, Real Estate Transactions, Tenant Screening

Information Types:
Criminal Information (IA)
Litigation/Judgments/Tax Liens (IA)
Real Estate/Assessor (IA)
Uniform Commercial Code (IA)

Membership: ABW, PRRN

Statement of Capabilities: Allstate Legal Court Services provides general and specialized research and document retrieval in Iowa, also tenant and pre-employment screening services.

Alpha Records Search & Retrieval

PO Box 2116
Toluca Lake, CA 91610-0116
Telephone: **Fax:**
323-851-5701 323-851-6611
Clientele: Attorney Firms, Lending Institutions, Legal Profession, Business - General, Corporate Counsel, Corporate Security, Private Investigators

Applications: Background Info - Business, Background Info - Individuals, Employment Screening, Litigation, Locating People/Businesses

Information Types:
Bankruptcy (CA-Southern)
Criminal Information (CA-Southern)
Litigation/Judgments/Tax Liens (CA-Southern)
Real Estate/Assessor (CA-Southern)
SEC/Other Financial (US)
Vital Records (CA-Southern)
Licenses/Registrations/Permits (CA-Southern)
News/Current Events (CA-Southern)

Membership: PRRN, SFSA

Statement of Capabilities: Alpha Record Search & Retrieval specializes in complicated, extraordinary, sensitive tasked, multiple search procedures, i.e., data base and/or on-site location searches, retrievals, report analyses. Company operations cover courts and recorder offices in Los Angeles, Kern, Orange, Venture, San Bernardino, Riverside counties. John F. Morrison, Alpha principal, directs the Alpha

Operation using his 25 years of investigative experience in all phases of investigation, record searches and retrievals.

Amerestate Inc

8160 Corporate Park Dr #200
Cincinnati, OH 45242
Telephone: **Fax:**
800-582-7300   513-489-4409
513-489-7300
www.amerestate.com

sales@amerestate.com
Year Founded: 1980

Clientele: Financial Institutions, Information - Brokers/Retrievers, Lending Institutions, Real Estate Owners/Managers, Direct Marketers, Appraisal Industry

Applications: Asset/Lien Searching/Verification, Direct Marketing, Filing/Recording Documents, Lending/Leasing, Real Estate Transactions

Proprietary Products:

Name/Desc: PaceNet for Windows
Info Provided: Real Estate/Assessor, Mortgage Data and Addresses/Telephone Numbers
Media: CD-ROM and Direct Online
Coverage: KY, MI, OH

Name/Desc: PaceNet Online
Info Provided: Real Estate Assessor, Real Estate Assessor (Mortgage Data)
Media: Direct Online
Coverage: KY, MI, OH

Name/Desc: Pace Books
Info Provided: Real Estate Assessor (Mortgage Data) and Addresses/Telephone Numbers
Media: Printed Report
Coverage: KY, MI, OH

Name/Desc: PaceNet Mortgage Heads
Info Provided: Real Estate Assessor (Mortgage Data) and Addresses/Telephone Numbers
Media: Direct Online
Coverage: KY, MI, OH

Name/Desc: Prospect Services
Info Provided: Real Estate Assessor (Mortgage Data) and Addresses/Telephone Numbers
Media: Disk, Lists or labels, Magnetic Tape and Printed Report

Coverage: KY, MI, OH
Membership: MBAA, NAR, REIPA

Statement of Capabilities: Amerestate maintains databases of existing real estate ownership and gathers and verifies data from courthouse public records and other sources on all real estate sales. They collect most information manually, assuring accuracy, completeness and timely information. Property addresses are standardized and updated quarterly to current CASS standards required by the USPS. Amerestate has recently introduced PaceNet Mortgage Leads, a product specifically designed for those in the lending industry who want to target prospects for refinance, lines of credit or seconds.

Free Web Information:
Offers real estate sales statistics for Kentucky, Michigan and Ohio and public school information.

American Business Information Inc

PO Box 27347
Omaha, NE 68127
Telephone: **Fax:**
800-808-4636   402-331-5990
402-593-4500
www.infousa.com

Parent Company: infoUSA
Clientele: Accountants, Business - General, Direct Marketers, Financial Institutions, Insurance - General, Libraries, Mortgage Bankers

Applications: Background Info - Business, Competitive Intelligence, Direct Marketing, General Business Information, Locating People/Businesses

Information Types:
Trademarks/Patents (US)

Proprietary Products:

Name/Desc: Business Sales Leads
Info Provided: Addresses/Telephone Numbers, Credit Information, Foreign Country Information, News/Current Events and SEC/Other Financial
Media: CD-ROM, Direct Online, Disk, Gateway Via Another Online Service, Internet, Lists or labels, Magnetic Tape, Printed Report, Publication/Directory and Software
Coverage: US

Name/Desc: Consumer Sales Leads

Info Provided: Addresses/Telephone Numbers, Credit Information, Driver and/or Vehicle, Genealogical Information and Real Estate Assessor
Media: CD-ROM, Direct Online, Disk, Gateway Via Another Online Service, Internet, Lists or labels, Magnetic Tape, Printed Report, Publication/Directory and Software
Coverage: US

Membership: ALA, DMA, SIIA, NACM, SLA

Statement of Capabilities: American Business Information compiles business information from telephone directories and other public sources. Over the past 20+ years, they have provided services to over 2 million customers. They telephone verify every name in their database before they offer it for sale. They phone-verify address changes from the USPS NCOA program. Their info is available in a variety of ways including online (SalesLeadsUSA.com), CD-ROM, and by telephone (Directory Assistance Plus). A division produces the Pro-CD Disk and another operates Digital Directory Assistance. For business leads call 800-555-5335. For SalesLeads USA call 402-593-4593.

Free Web Information:
Free lookup service (basic information) on business and consumers.

American Driving Records Inc

PO Box 160147
Sacramento, CA 95816-9998
Telephone: **Fax:**
800-766-6877 800-800-0817
916-456-3200 916-456-3332
www.mvrs.com
sales@mvrs.com
Year Founded: 1986

Clientele: Insurance - Underwriting, Insurance - Agents/Brokers, Attorney Firms, Employers (HR/Personnel Depts), Corporate Security

Proprietary Products:

Info Provided: Driver and/or Vehicle
Media: Online, Fax, Printed Report
Coverage: US

Statement of Capabilities: Amercian Driving Record (ADR) services include driving records, registration information, and special processing for the insurance industry such as automatic checking (ACH), calculating underwriting points, and ZapApp (TM) - an automated insurance application from the agency to the carrier. Driving records can be instant, same day or overnight, depending on the state.

American Genealogical Research

8 Whittier Pl #23G
Boston, MA 02114
Telephone: **Fax:**
617-742-6063 617-742-0746
Year Founded: 1988

Clientele: Legal Profession, Financial Institutions

Applications: Background Info - Individuals, Genealogical Research, Locating People/Businesses, Real Estate Transactions

Information Types:
Genealogical Information (US)

Membership: APG, NGS

Statement of Capabilities: American Genealogical Research finds missing persons. They are able to identify who the rightful heirs would be, locate them and provide court-quality documentation. Licensed, bonded, insured, certified and genealogical record specialists on staff.

American Information Network

205 W Saginaw
Lansing, MI 48933
Telephone: **Fax:**
800-871-5730 800-569-3950
www.ameri.com
Year Founded: 1995

Clientele: Consumers (Individuals), Employers (HR/Personnel Depts), Public Record Research Firms, Real Estate Owners/Managers, Private Investigators, Attorney Firms, Legal Profession

Applications: Locating People/Businesses, Background Info - Individuals, Employment Screening, General Business Information

Information Types:
Addresses/Telephone Numbers (US)
Driver and/or Vehicle (US)
Criminal Information (US)
Credit Information (US)
Real Estate/Assessor (US)

Statement of Capabilities: American Information Network provides information about companies and individuals from a variety of local, regional and national public record sources. They offer missing person locator ordering (known as Sherlock) via their Internet site.

American Research Bureau Inc

PO Box 36237
Denver, CO 80236
Telephone: **Fax:**
800-777-7860 303-980-5263
303-980-0955
www.arbi.com
arbi@arbi.com
Year Founded: 1979

Applications: Asset/Lien Searching/Verification, Background Info - Business, General Business Information, Collections, Employment Screening

Information Types:
Addresses/Telephone Numbers (US)
Bankruptcy (US)
Credit Information (US)
Education/Employment (US)
Litigation/Judgments/Tax Liens (US)
Real Estate/Assessor (US)
Social Security (Numbers) (US)
Uniform Commercial Code (US)

Statement of Capabilities: American Research Bureau has been in business for 20 years. ARB is insured for professional liability and is in strict compliance with the FCRA. Their company incorporates industry-leading techniques to produce industry leading success rates. Their average turnaround time is 10 days.

American Research Unlimited

5676 County Rd 120
Carthage, MO 64836
Telephone: **Fax:**
417-358-6494 417-359-5734
Year Founded: 1988

Clientele: Lending Institutions, Credit Grantors, Information - Brokers/Retrievers, Business - General, Public Record Research Firms

Applications: Asset/Lien Searching/Verification, Background Info - Business, Employment Screening, Filing/Recording Documents, Real Estate Transactions

Information Types:
Bankruptcy (MO)
Environmental (MO)
Litigation/Judgments/Tax Liens (MO)

Real Estate/Assessor (MO)
Uniform Commercial Code (MO)
Vital Records (MO)
Genealogical Information (MO)

Membership: PRRN

Statement of Capabilities: American Research Unlimited tries to give at maximum 48 hour turnaround time, faster for exceptional requests. The company runs on honesty, accuracy and speed.

Ameridex Information Systems

PO Box 51314
Irvine, CA 92619-1314
Fax:
714-731-2116
http://kadima.com
Year Founded: 1988

Clientele: Collection Agencies, Business - General, Credit Grantors, Employers (HR/Personnel Depts), Government Agencies, Professionals-Other, Investigators - Fraud

Applications: Background Info - Individuals, Locating People/Businesses, Genealogical Research

Proprietary Products:
Name/Desc: SSDI
Info Provided: Addresses/Telephone Numbers
Media: CD-ROM, Online, Lists
Coverage: US

Name/Desc: Military
Info Provided: Military Service
Media: CD-ROM, Online, List
Coverage: US

Name/Desc: Live Index
Info Provided: Addresses/Telephone Numbers
Media: CD-ROM, Online, Lists
Coverage: US

Statement of Capabilities: Ameridex presents several unique databases for people tracing on the Internet. Over 220 million names and 180 million with a date of birth are compiled from multiple public record sources. Specialty databases include a nationwide death index with supplements and an active military personnel database.

AmeriSearch

PO Box 2667

Sacramento, CA 95812

Telephone: **Fax:**
800-877-2877   800-877-3877
916-443-0795   916-443-1559

Year Founded: 1992

Clientele: Financial Institutions, Legal Profession, Public Record Research Firms, Equipment Leasing Companies, Legal Service Companies, Lending Institutions, Asset-Based Lenders

Applications: Asset/Lien Searching/Verification, Lending/Leasing, Legal Compliance, Litigation, Filing/Recording Documents

Information Types:
Bankruptcy (US, CA)
Litigation/Judgments/Tax Liens (US, CA)
Corporate/Trade Name Data (US, CA)
Uniform Commercial Code (US, CA)
Real Estate/Assessor (US)

Membership: NPRRA

Statement of Capabilities: AmeriSearch has a staff with over 35 years of combined experience in nationwide public record search and filing services. They specialize in the California area and can provide a California UCC search in five hours. They are online with various databases of UCC and corporate information, and maintain a nationwide network of correspondents to perform search and filing projects.

Amherst Group Inc

4804 Arlington Ave
Riverside, CA 92504

Telephone: **Fax:**
800-521-0237   909-785-5888
909-785-5777

www.amherst-group.com

a,herst@pe.net

Year Founded: 1982

Clientele: Accountants, Apartment Owners/Managers, Employers (HR/Personnel Depts), Business - General, Property Owners/Managers, Loss Prevention Specialists, Legal Profession

Applications: Background Info - Business, Background Info - Individuals, Litigation, Tenant Screening, Employment Screening

Information Types:
Credit Information (US)
Criminal Information (US)
Driver and/or Vehicle (US)

Education/Employment (US)
Litigation/Judgments/Tax Liens (US)
Social Security (Numbers) (US)
Tenant History (US)
Workers' Compensation (US)

Membership: APA, ASIS, NALI, NAPI

Statement of Capabilities: Founded in 1982, The Amerst Group, a national company with clients throughout the US, specializes in information services. They assist hundreds of organizations with their information needs. Their national network provides fast, accurate and reliable information. Placing orders for service may be accomplished by telephone, facsimile or the Internet. Tracking each order, their turnaround time is 24-72 hours with the majority being completed within 48 hours.

Anderson Research

4000 Summer Hollow Ct
Chantilly, VA 20151

Telephone: **Fax:**
703-449-1552   703-817-1744

iresearcher@compuserve.com

Year Founded: 1988

Clientele: Accountants, Attorney Firms, Consulting Firms, Investigators - Fraud, Private Investigators

Applications: Asset/Lien Searching/Verification, Background Info - Business, Litigation

Information Types:
Addresses/Telephone Numbers (US)
Corporate/Trade Name Data (US)
Bankruptcy (US)
Licenses/Registrations/Permits (US)
News/Current Events (US, International)
SEC/Other Financial (US)
Social Security (Numbers) (US)
Uniform Commercial Code (US)

Statement of Capabilities: In addition to regular hours, Anderson Research is available to work evenings and weekends, upon request.

Apex Information & Research Inc

16300 Katy Freeway #219
Houston, TX 77094

Telephone: **Fax:**
800-330-4525   281-398-6006
281-398-6000

airinc@flash.net

Clientele: Attorney Firms, Lending Institutions, Public Record Research Firms, Mortgage Bankers

Applications: Asset/Lien Searching/Verification, Employment Screening, Lending/Leasing, Real Estate Transactions, Background Info - Individuals

Information Types:
Bankruptcy (TX)
Real Estate/Assessor (TX)
Environmental (TX)

Membership: PRRN

Statement of Capabilities: Apex provides abstract information as it relates to real estate in Texas, with a turnaround time of 24-48 hours in Harris, Fort Bend, Brazoria, Galveston, and Montgomery counties (additional counties range from 4-5 working days). Their comprehensive search includes ownership, voluntary & involuntary liens, state and federal tax liens, and complete tax information. Their key personnel have 20 years and 16 years, respectively in the Title Insurance Industry in Texas and 10 years lending experience with a major lending institution. Their consulting department provides guidance to clients for resolving title problems.

ARISTOTLE

205 Pennsylvania Ave SW
Washington, DC 20003
Telephone: **Fax:**
800-296-2747   202-543-6407
202-543-8345
www.products.aristotle.org

Year Founded: 1981

Clientele: Government Agencies, Libraries, Legal Profession, Public Record Research Firms, Collection Agencies, Direct Marketers, Private Investigators

Applications: Background Info - Business, Legal Compliance, Direct Marketing, Government Document Retrieval, Locating People/Businesses

Information Types:
Driver and/or Vehicle (US)

Proprietary Products:

Name/Desc: ARISTOTLE
Info Provided: Voter Registration and Addresses/Telephone Numbers

Media: CD-ROM, Magnetic Tape and Online Database
Coverage: US

Statement of Capabilities: ARISTOTLE maintains a nationwide file of registered voters. Information obtained from 3,400 counties and municipalities is standardized and enhanced with listed phone number, postal correction and national change of address, census geography, and age and vote history. Twenty-six states have no significant restrictions on the commercial use of their voter registration information.

ASK Services Inc

PO Box 87127
Canton, MI 48187
Telephone: **Fax:**
734-416-1313   734-416-9433
www.ask-services.com
ASK@ask-services.com
Year Founded: 1990

Clientele: Attorney Firms, Lending Institutions, Consulting Firms, Employers (HR/Personnel Depts), Information Brokers/Retrievers, Public Record Research Firms

Applications: Asset/Lien Searching/Verification, Background Info - Individuals, Employment Screening, Lending/Leasing, Locating People/Businesses

Information Types:
Uniform Commercial Code (MI, NC)
Bankruptcy (US, MI, NC)
Corporate/Trade Name Data (US, MI, NC)
Criminal Information (US, MI, NC)
Driver and/or Vehicle (MI)
Licenses/Registrations/Permits (US, MI, NC)
Litigation/Judgments/Tax Liens (MI, NC)
Workers' Compensation (MI)

Membership: NPRRA, PRRN

Statement of Capabilities: ASK Services provides comprehensive public record searches and background profiles on companies and individuals. They provide 24-hour service in Michigan and North Carolina and offer an average 48-hour turnaround time nationwide. Initial profiles on any subject can usually be obtained same day, often within minutes. Searches and information available include, but are not limited to the following: current and former addresses, relatives, neighbors, phone numbers, SSN searches, DOB verifications, civil and criminal case histories, bankruptcies, real property ownership, vehicle ownership, driving records, professional licenses, educational verifications, corporate information, DBA, patents. Record requests can be ordered from their web site.

Atlanta Attorney Services

2625 Piedmont Rd #239
Atlanta, GA 30324
Telephone: **Fax:**
800-804-4078   404-237-6409
404-237-6407
www.attorneyservices.org
aas@attorneyservices.org
Parent Company: Attorney Services International Inc
Year Founded: 1996

Clientele: Legal Profession, Financial Institutions, Information - Brokers/Retrievers, Legal Service Companies, Public Record Research Firms, Attorney Firms

Applications: Asset/Lien Searching/Verification, Filing/Recording Documents, Litigation, Locating People/Businesses, Real Estate Transactions

Information Types:
Addresses/Telephone Numbers (US)
Bankruptcy (US)
Criminal Information (US)
Litigation/Judgments/Tax Liens (US)
Real Estate/Assessor (GA)
Social Security (Numbers) (US)
Uniform Commercial Code (US)

Membership: NAPPS, NFPA, NPRRA, PRRN

Statement of Capabilities: Atlanta Attorney Services provides a variety of attorney services to the legal professional. Services include document retrieval and filings in any jurisdiction in Georgia and the United States for use in civil, corporate, real estate, financial and criminal proceedings. Atlanta Attorney Services also conducts courthouse based searches such as UCC, lien and judgment searches, asset and criminal searches. Their staff are paralegal certified, with many years of relevant legal experience.

Att Loss Prevention Inc

PO Box 1681
Torrington, CT 06790
Telephone: **Fax:**
800-733-4405   860-482-0377
860-496-1472
www.attloss.com
attloss@javanet.com
Clientele: Attorney Firms, Lending Institutions, Collection Agencies, Corporate Security, Employers (HR/Personnel Depts), Government Agencies, Private Investigators

Applications: Background Info - Business, Background Info - Individuals, Fraud Prevention/Detection, Lending/Leasing, Employment Screening

Information Types:
Addresses/Telephone Numbers (US)
Credit Information (US)
Criminal Information (US)
Driver and/or Vehicle (US)
Litigation/Judgments/Tax Liens (US)
Social Security (Numbers) (US)
Workers' Compensation (US)

Membership: WAD

Statement of Capabilities: Att Loss Prevention is an information company that provides its services to businesses only. Att is known for hard to get information. Att also offers capabilities to retrieve reports for pre-employment background screening, workers compensation, SSNs, education, criminal histories in the US and out of country. A main specialty is CNSs on old numbers and locates. They offer services with no monthly fee or minimums.

Attorneys' Information Bureau Inc

516 Third Ave
C603 King Co Courthouse
Seattle, WA 98104
Telephone: **Fax:**
206-622-1909   206-622-2911
attsinfo@aol.com
Year Founded: 1929

Clientele: Insurance - Claims, Legal Profession, Legal Service Companies

Applications: Litigation, Real Estate Transactions

Information Types:
Bankruptcy (WA)

Criminal Information (WA)
Litigation/Judgments/Tax Liens (WA)
Real Estate/Assessor (WA)
Uniform Commercial Code (WA)
Vital Records (WA)

Attorneys' Title Insurance Fund

PO Box 628600
Orlando, FL 32862
Telephone:　　　　**Fax:**
800-336-3863　　　　407-240-1106
407-240-3863
www.thefund.com
Year Founded: 1948

Clientele: Attorney Firms, Asset-Based Lenders, Financial Institutions, Credit Grantors, Legal Service Companies, Lending Institutions

Applications: Real Estate Transactions, Asset/Lien Searching/Verification

Proprietary Products:

Name/Desc: The Fund
Info Provided: Real Estate Assessor, Litigation/Judgments/Tax Liens
Media: Online, Disk, Printed Report, Magnetic Tape
Coverage: FL-31 counties

Membership: ATLA

Statement of Capabilities: Although the primary business of The Fund (as they are called) is to issue title insurance, they offer access to over 100 million real estate records from 31 major counties in FL. The Fund has 14 branch offices and is expanding to SC and IL. Online users can access public records including mortgages, deeds, liens, assessments, right-of-way data, and even judgment and divorce proceedings.

Aurigin Systems Inc

1975 Landings Drive
Mountain View, CA 94043
Telephone:　　　　**Fax:**
650-237-0900　　　　650-237-0910
http://aurigin.com
info@aurigin.com
Year Founded: 1992

Clientele: Business - General, Corporate Counsel, Educational Institutions

Applications: Legal Compliance, Competitive Intelligence

Proprietary Products:

Name/Desc: SmartPatent
Info Provided: Trademarks/Patents
Media: Online, Software
Coverage: US, International

Membership: AIPLA, ABA, LES

Statement of Capabilities: Aurigin, formally known as SmartPatents Inc, offers the Aurigin IPAM System to manage a company's intellectual asset management needs. Other important products are SmartPatent Electronic Patents, indexed patents from the US Patent and Trademark Office, and the SmartPatent Workbench, a desktop software application.

Avantext Inc

Green Hills Corporate Center
2675 Morgantown Rd #3300
Reading, PA 19607
Telephone:　　　　**Fax:**
800-998-8857　　　　800-544-9252
610-796-2385　　　　610-796-2392
www.avantext.com
sales@avantex.com
Year Founded: 1992

Clientele: Direct Marketers, Information - Brokers/Retrievers, Business - General

Applications: Background Info - Business, Direct Marketing, Employment Screening, Legal Compliance

Proprietary Products:

Name/Desc: FAA Data
Info Provided: Aviation/Vessels, Addresses/Telephone Numbers, Legislation/Regulations
Media: CD-ROM
Coverage: US

Statement of Capabilities: Avantext product line includes 6 powerful CDs for the aviation industry. The FAA Data CD includes a full listing of pilots and aircraft owners, schools, technicians, dealers and much more.

Avian Corporate Records Research Notary

PO Box 161232
Austin, TX 78716
Telephone:　　　　**Fax:**
512-326-2638　　　　512-326-3354
avian@cclns.com

Year Founded: 1997

Clientele: Attorney Firms, Employers (HR/Personnel Depts), Information - Brokers/Retrievers, Legal Profession, Legal Profession, Mortgage Bankers, Public Record Research Firms

Applications: Asset/Lien Searching/Verification, Employment Screening, Filing/Recording Documents, Real Estate Transactions, Tenant Screening

Information Types:
Associations/Trade Groups (TX)
Aviation/Vessels (TX)
Bankruptcy (TX)
Driver and/or Vehicle (TX)
Education/Employment (TX-Bastrop, Hays, Travis, Williamson)
Environmental (TX)
Legislation/Regulation (TX)
Licenses/Registrations/Permits (TX)

Statement of Capabilities: Avian specializes in on-site court records searching and document retrieval. Their services include filing and processes services, tenant screening, employment screening/verification, real estate owner searches, driver records, judgment/lien searches, and evictions.

B

Background Research Services
PO Box 3
Willow Creek, CA 95573
Telephone: **Fax:**
800-707-1671   800-707-8849
530-629-2929   530-629-1199

brs@snowcrest.net
Year Founded: 1997

Clientele: Employers (HR/Personnel Depts), Private Investigators, Public Record Research Firms

Applications: Background Info - Business, Background Info - Individuals, Employment Screening, Lending/Leasing, Real Estate Transactions

Information Types:
Credit Information (US)
Criminal Information (US)
Driver and/or Vehicle (US)
Education/Employment (US)
Licenses/Registrations/Permits (US)
Litigation/Judgments/Tax Liens (US)
Social Security (Numbers) (US)
Workers' Compensation (CA)

Statement of Capabilities: BRS will provide some information within the first 24 hours, and fax a written report within 1-2 working days after all information is gathered. Hard copies mailed within the week. They access many sources of information to be sure clients have everything needed for informed decisions. BRS is affiliated with a PI to help BRS access and retrieve a wide range of information. A BRS partner is a past credit collector with a wide range of knowledge in information gathering. We try to provide our clients with personalized service and courtesy service.

Background Services
24981 Mockingbird Cir
West Valley City, UT 84119
Telephone: **Fax:**
801-967-6410   801-967-5797
Year Founded: 1993

Clientele: Apartment Owners/Managers, Business - General, Consulting Firms, Employers (HR/Personnel Depts), Insurance - Claims, Investigators - Fraud, Loss Prevention Specialists

Applications: Background Info - Business, Employment Screening, Fraud Prevention/Detection, Genealogical Research, Tenant Screening

Information Types:
Corporate/Trade Name Data (US, UT)
Credit Information (US, UT)
Criminal Information (US, UT)
Education/Employment (US, UT)
Litigation/Judgments/Tax Liens (US, UT)
Military Svc (US, UT)

Statement of Capabilities: Background Services offers a quick turnaround time, personal service and can customize their services to meet clients' needs.

Backgrounds Express LLC
100 N Main #402

Memphis, TN 38103
Telephone: **Fax:**
888-811-4667 888-811-4668
901-578-3287 901-578-7889
www.process-service.com
bchastain@process-
service.com
Parent Company: Alias Subpoena LLC
Year Founded: 1991

Clientele: Apartment Owners/Managers, Legal
Profession, Employers (HR/Personnel Depts),
Landlords, Legal Profession, Property
Owners/Managers, Attorney Firms

Applications: Background Info - Business,
Employment Screening, Filing/Recording
Documents, Locating People/Businesses,
Tenant Screening

Information Types:
UCC (TN-Shelby)
Workers' Compensation (TN)
Driver and/or Vehicle (US, TN)
Litigation/Judgments/Tax Liens (TN-Shelby)
Tenant History (TN-Shelby)

Proprietary Products:
Name/Desc: Forcible Detainer Filings (Real
Estate Suites)
Info Provided: Tenant History
Media: Fax-on-Demand
Coverage: TN-Shelby County

Membership: NAPPS

Statement of Capabilities: Backgrounds
Express offers same day service on requests
received by 2PM M-F. They also own and
update daily a database of all forcible detainers
filed in Shelby County, TN since January 1,
1996 (over 40,000 suits). They also have 14
private process servers and offer same day
delivery of court documents.

Free Web Information:
Nationwide referral of private process service.

Banko Document Retrieval (BDR)
PO Box 81146
San Diego, CA 92138-1146
Telephone: **Fax:**
800-969-2377 800-486-2377
619-232-9999 619-232-9998
www.bkauthority.com
Year Founded: 1989

Clientele: Financial Institutions, Government
Agencies, Legal Profession, Public Record
Research Firms, Collection Agencies

Applications: Lending/Leasing, Litigation, Real
Estate Transactions, Fraud
Prevention/Detection, Risk Management

Information Types:
Bankruptcy (US)

Proprietary Products:
Name/Desc: Bankruptcy
Info Provided: Bankruptcy
Coverage: US

Membership: MBA, USFN, ABI

Statement of Capabilities: Banko Document
Retrieval provides a single resource in
obtaining copies of documents from
bankruptcy files nationwide. They cover both
federal courts and federal record centers. BDR
has an online ordering system and a
customized case monitoring system.

Free Web Information:
Links to various bankruptcy sites, attorneys,
bankruptcy court sites, listings of all
bankruptcy courts, local rules for various
courts, and other new features. Like Internet
ordering and document delivery.

Banko Inc
607 Marquette Ave #500
Minneapolis, MN 55402
Telephone: **Fax:**
800-533-8897 612-321-0325
612-332-2427
www.BANKO.com
SALES@BANKO.com
Parent Company: Dolan Media Inc
Year Founded: 1987

Applications: Asset/Lien Searching/Verification,
Collections, Direct Marketing,
Filing/Recording Documents, General
Business Information
Membership: ACA, ICA, NACM, NPRRA

Statement of Capabilities: Banko Inc.
provides up to the minute information about
bankruptcy suppression and notification in a
variety of electronic formats.

Barry Shuster & Associates
PO Box 79578
North Dartmouth, MA 02747

Telephone: **Fax:**
800-367-8227   508-990-2665
508-999-5436
www.ucclien.com
barry@ucclien.com
Year Founded: 1981

Clientele: Financial Institutions, Government Agencies, Legal Profession, Public Record Research Firms

Applications: Asset/Lien Searching/Verification, Lending/Leasing, Employment Screening, Legal Compliance, Filing/Recording Documents

Information Types:
Bankruptcy (US, MA, RI)
Litigation/Judgments/Tax Liens (US, MA, RI)
Corporate/Trade Name Data (US, MA, RI)
Uniform Commercial Code (US, MA, RI)
Real Estate/Assessor (MA, RI)
Driver and/or Vehicle (MA, RI)

Membership: NPRRA

Statement of Capabilities: With more than 17 years of experience in the public document retrieval business, Barry Shuster & Associates perform UCC, tax lien, judgment, and litigation searches and obtain documents from all federal and state courts. They also serve as registered agent for corporations. Their services are useful to law firms, banks, leasing companies and government agencies. They provide fast turnaround time without adding expediting charges.

BiblioData

PO Box 61
Needham Heights, MA 02494
Telephone: **Fax:**
781-444-1154   781-449-4584
www.bibliodata.com
ina@bibliodata.com

Clientele: Business - General, Consumers (Individuals), Libraries

Applications: Current Events, Competitive Intelligence, Background Info - Individuals, Risk Management

Proprietary Products:
Name/Desc: BiblioData
Info Provided: News/Current Events, Addresses/Telephone Numbers
Media: Internet
Coverage: US

Statement of Capabilities: BiblioData publishes informative newsletters directly related to the online industry. Their products are targeted for researchers and librarians.

Free Web Information:
The Internet site offers subscription access to their database.

Blumberg Excelsior Corporate Services

62 White St
New York, NY 10013
Telephone: **Fax:**
800-221-2972   888-692-9256
212-431-5000
www.blumb.com

Parent Company: Blumberg Excelsior
Clientele: Accountants, Attorney Firms, Corporate Counsel, Legal Profession, Legal Service Companies

Applications: Asset/Lien Searching/Verification, Background Info - Business, Background Info - Individuals, Collections, General Business Information

Information Types:
Bankruptcy (US)
Corporate/Trade Name Data (US)
Driver and/or Vehicle (US)
Legislation/Regulation (US)
Litigation/Judgments/Tax Liens (US)
Real Estate/Assessor (US)
Trademarks/Patents (US)
Uniform Commercial Code (US)

Membership: NPRRA

Statement of Capabilities: Blumberg Excelsior Corporate Services is a nationwide provider of public record information services to the legal, corporate, financial and investigative markets. With both attorneys and paralegals on staff, they offer trademark search and application as well as copyright services.

Free Web Information:
Software demonstration and online ordering.

Bombet & Associates

12077 Old Hammond Hwy
Baton Rouge, LA 70816
Telephone: **Fax:**
800-256-5333   504-272-3631
504-275-0796

www.bombet.com
buddy@bombet.com
Year Founded: 1967

Clientele: Asset-Based Lenders, Attorney Firms, Business - General, Information - Brokers/Retrievers, Insurance - Claims, Investigators - Fraud, Public Record Research Firms

Applications: Asset/Lien Searching/Verification, Background Info - Business, Background Info - Individuals, Competitive Intelligence

Information Types:
Addresses/Telephone Numbers (US)
Bankruptcy (US)
Criminal Information (LA)
Legislation/Regulation (LA)
Licenses/Registrations/Permits (LA)
Litigation/Judgments/Tax Liens (LA)
Real Estate/Assessor (LA)
Voter Registration (LA)

Membership: COIN, CII, NALI, NAPPS, NASIR, NCISS

BRC Inc

PO Box 4889
Syracuse, NY 13221
Telephone:
315-437-1283

Clientele: Attorney Firms, Business - General, Credit Grantors, Financial Institutions, Information - Brokers/Retrievers, Mortgage Bankers

Applications: General Business Information, Real Estate Transactions

Proprietary Products:
Name/Desc: BRC
Info Provided: Real Estate/Assessor
Media: Direct Online
Coverage: ME-17 Counties

Statement of Capabilities: BRC specializes in online access to Maine Registries. Fees are involved. They are expanding into Illinois, also.

Bridge Services Corp

5 Beekman St #925
New York, NY 10038
Telephone: **Fax:**
800-225-2736   888-267-8680
212-267-8600   212-267-8687

Clientele: Legal Profession, Financial Institutions, Public Record Research Firms

Applications: Asset/Lien Searching/Verification, Filing/Recording Documents, Legal Compliance, Litigation, Lending/Leasing

Information Types:
Uniform Commercial Code (US, NY-New York City)
Real Estate/Assessor (US, NY-New York City)
Litigation/Judgments/Tax Liens (US, NY-New York City)
Bankruptcy (US, NY-New York City)
Wills/Probate (US, NY-New York City)

Membership: NPRRA, PRRN

Statement of Capabilities: Bridge Service Corp provides comprehensive research and recording services in the New York City area. They cover all federal, state and local agencies. They also provide national service through a network of agents.

Burrelle's Information Services

75 East Northfield Rd
Livingston, NJ 07039
Telephone:
800-631-1160
973-992-6600
http://burrelles.com
info@burrelles.com

Clientele: Business - General, Consulting Firms, Educational Institutions, Financial Institutions, Professionals-Other

Applications: Current Events, Background Info - Business, Competitive Intelligence

Proprietary Products:
Name/Desc: BIO
Info Provided: News/Current Events
Media: Online, CD-ROM, Publication
Coverage: US, International

Statement of Capabilities: For over 100 years Burrelle's has been monitoring, organizing, and delivering media data to clients. Products include Press Clipping, NewsExpress, NewsAlert, Media Direcories, Broadcast Transcripts, and Web Clips. The BIO - Burrelle's Information Office, is software to receive and use information from Burrelle's.

Business Information Service

531 S Holland
Bellville, TX 77418

Telephone: **Fax:**
409-865-2547 409-865-8918
Year Founded: 1995

Clientele: Financial Institutions, Employers (HR/Personnel Depts), Private Investigators, Public Record Research Firms

Applications: General Business Information, Lending/Leasing, Real Estate Transactions, Litigation, Employment Screening

Proprietary Products:

Name/Desc: Local Public Record
Info Provided: Real Estate/Assessor, Litigation/Judgments/Tax Liens, Uniform Commercial Code and Criminal Information
Media: Publication
Coverage: TX -Austin, Colorado, Waller, Washington Counties

Name/Desc: Bankruptcies
Info Provided: Bankruptcy
Media: Publication
Coverage: TX-Austin, Colorado, Waller, Washington

Statement of Capabilities: Business Information Service (BIS) provides its information in the form of monthly subscription publications

Business Intelligence Incorporated

55 Hilton Ave
Garden City, NY 11530
Telephone: **Fax:**
516-747-2660 516-747-0009
bii747@aol.com
Year Founded: 1998

Clientele: Accountants, Corporate Security, Insurance - General, Landlords, Mortgage Bankers, Employers (HR/Personnel Depts), Insurance - Agents/Brokers

Applications: Asset/Lien Searching/Verification, Background Info - Business, Background Info - Individuals, Employment Screening, Litigation

Information Types:
Bankruptcy (US)
Corporate/Trade Name Data (US)
Litigation/Judgments/Tax Liens (US)
News/Current Events (US)
SEC/Other Financial (US)
Trademarks/Patents (US)
Uniform Commercial Code (US)

Business Research Services

PO Box 31516
Knoxville, TN 37930
Telephone: **Fax:**
800-608-4636 423-690-8771
423-691-8778
www.bisresearch.com
bisinfo@bisresearch.com
Parent Company: Business Information Srvs Inc
Year Founded: 1989

Clientele: Legal Profession, Employers (HR/Personnel Depts), Insurance - General, Public Record Research Firms, Business - General

Applications: Background Info - Business, Employment Screening, Litigation, General Business Information, Background Info - Individuals

Information Types:
Addresses/Telephone Numbers (US)
Driver and/or Vehicle (US, TN)
Criminal Information (US, TN)
Litigation/Judgments/Tax Liens (US, TN)
Bankruptcy (US)
Credit Information (US)

Membership: ASIS, ION, PRRN, X-FBI, RFFI, NAIS

Statement of Capabilities: Business Research Services (BRS) provides online nationwide searching of public records as well as local document retrieval. Services include business and individual credit reports, driver history and MVR records, property, UCC and tax lien records, and voter registration records. The availability of credit reports is subject to a client agreement stipulating compliance with the Fair Credit Reporting Act.

C

Cal Info

316 W 2nd St #102
Los Angeles, CA 90012
Telephone: **Fax:**
213-687-8710 213-687-8778

`http://members.aol.com/calin`
`fola/`
`calinfola@aol.com`
Year Founded: 1986

Clientele: Business - General, Legal Profession, Consulting Firms, Mortgage Bankers, Private Investigators

Applications: Background Info - Business, Background Info - Individuals, Asset/Lien Searching/Verification

Information Types:
Litigation/Judgments/Tax Liens (US, CA)
Environmental (US, CA)
Legislation/Regulation (US, CA)
Associations/Trade Groups (US, CA)
Trademarks/Patents (US)

Proprietary Products:

Name/Desc: Guide to State Statutes
Info Provided: Legislation/Regulation (State Statutes)
Media: Directory
Coverage: US

Name/Desc: Administrative Guide to State Regulations
Info Provided: Legislation/Regulation
Media: Publication

Membership: AIIP, AALL

Statement of Capabilities: Cal Info offers an information research and retrieval service that finds answers to questions that affect law firms and businesses every day. Their personnel are trained to search computerized databases as well as the more traditional information sources, including libraries, publishers, government agencies, courts, trade unions and associations.. They provide company reports, financial data, product information, people information, journals and news stories, real estate information, legal research, public records research, government information and document retrieval.

California Drivers Records

PO Box 15314
Sacramento, CA 95851-1314
Telephone: **Fax:**
800-852-6219   800-488-0231
916-456-4757   916-451-2322
Year Founded: 1950

Clientele: Financial Institutions, Insurance - Agents/Brokers, Insurance - Agents/Brokers,

Legal Profession, Public Record Research Firms

Applications: Insurance Underwriting, Legal Compliance, Litigation, Asset/Lien Searching/Verification

Information Types:
Driver and/or Vehicle (US, CA)
Real Estate/Assessor (CA)
Addresses/Telephone Numbers (US)
Social Security (Numbers) (US)

Statement of Capabilities: California Drivers Records (CDR) provides a wide range of California and out of state DMV searches. Driving records may be obtained with DOB or a license number in California. Vehicle plate, VIN reports or name search are available for California and most other states. Other investigative searches include a national locator search, Social Security search and real estate searches. All clients ordering California DMV records must have the User Requester Code required by the state. CDR offers a computerized order entry system.

Cambridge Statistical Research Associates

53 Wellesley
Irvine, CA 92612
Telephone: **Fax:**
800-327-2772   800-327-2720
714-509-9900   714-509-9119
Year Founded: 1988

Clientele: Government Agencies, Insurance - General, Legal Profession, Professionals-Other, Public Record Research Firms

Applications: Locating People/Businesses, Fraud Prevention/Detection

Information Types:
Addresses/Telephone Numbers (US)
Vital Records (US)

Proprietary Products:

Name/Desc: Death Master File
Info Provided: Social Security (Numbers)
Media: CD-ROM, Online Database and Printed Report
Coverage: US

Statement of Capabilities: CSRA traces its origin to an actuarial and programming service established in 1979. In recent years, its efforts moved toward bringing large mainframe databases to the desktop computing platform, including CD-ROM. CSRA specializes in nationwide death index by name and Social Security Number, death auditing service, database consulting, genealogical and probate research, and address trace service.

Capital Connection Inc

417 E Virginia St #1
Talahassee, FL 32301
Telephone: **Fax:**
800-342-8062   850-222-1222
850-224-8870
Year Founded: 1983

Clientele: Accountants, Attorney Firms, Banks, Corporate Counsel, Legal Profession, Public Record Research Firms, Savings and Loans

Applications: Filing/Recording Documents, Government Document Retrieval

Information Types:
Corporate/Trade Name Data (FL)
Litigation/Judgments/Tax Liens (FL)

Membership: NAWBO, NPRRA

Statement of Capabilities: Capital Connection specializes in providing fast and accurate filings and retrievals for the legal profession. They also produce corporate kits and corporate supplies.

Capitol City Network

1191 Spruce Tree Cir
Sacramento, CA 95831
Telephone: **Fax:**
916-395-2917   916-429-2823

kmash9277@aol.com
Year Founded: 1985

Clientele: Financial Institutions, Legal Profession, Public Record Research Firms

Applications: Asset/Lien Searching/Verification, Legal Compliance, Litigation

Information Types:
Litigation/Judgments/Tax Liens (US)
Corporate/Trade Name Data (US)
Trademarks/Patents (US)
Environmental (US)
Legislation/Regulation (US)
Uniform Commercial Code (US)
Legislation/Regulation (CA)

Statement of Capabilities: Capitol City Network is managed by specialists who have daily access to county court houses, recording offices and Secretary of State offices. They

maintain correspondents in all 50 states. They also specialize in legislative research and bill tracking in California.

Capitol District Information

PO Box 67
Washington, DC 20044
Telephone: **Fax:**
800-494-5225   800-494-7512
202-265-1516   202-265-5006
www.capitoldistrict.com
capdisinf@radix.net
Year Founded: 1988

Clientele: Attorney Firms, Financial Institutions, Information - Brokers/Retrievers, Investment Bankers, Libraries, Public Record Research Firms, Legal Service Companies

Applications: Government Document Retrieval, General Business Information, Competitive Intelligence, Background Info - Business, Background Info - Individuals

Information Types:
Criminal Information (DC,US)
Bankruptcy (DC,US)
Environmental (DC)
Legislation/Regulation (DC,US)
Litigation/Judgments/Tax Liens (DC,US)
SEC/Other Financial (DC,US)
Trademarks/Patents (VA,DC)

Membership: PRRN

Capitol Document Services Inc

PO Box 1812
Albuquerque, NM 87103
Telephone: **Fax:**
800-255-4381   800-848-8511
505-248-1612   505-248-1646
www.capitolservices.com
Year Founded: 1985

Clientele: Asset-Based Lenders, Attorney Firms, Financial Institutions, Legal Profession, Public Record Research Firms

Applications: Asset/Lien Searching/Verification, Filing/Recording Documents, Real Estate Transactions, Lending/Leasing

Information Types:
Corporate/Trade Name Data (NM)
Uniform Commercial Code (NM)

Membership: PRRN, NPRRA

Capitol Lien Records & Research Inc

PO Box 65727
St Paul, MN 55165
Telephone: **Fax:**
800-845-4077   800-845-4080
612-222-2500   612-222-2110
Year Founded: 1990

Clientele: Financial Institutions, Legal Profession, Other Professionals

Applications: Competitive Intelligence, Background Info - Business, Employment Screening, Real Estate Transactions, Filing/Recording Documents

Information Types:
Litigation/Judgments/Tax Liens (US, MN)
Criminal Information (MN-Minneapolis/St Paul)
Driver and/or Vehicle (US, MN)
Real Estate/Assessor (MN)
Credit Information (MN)
Corporate/Trade Name Data (MN)
Bankruptcy (MN)

Proprietary Products:

Name/Desc: UCC
Info Provided: Uniform Commercial Code
Media: Disk
Coverage: MN

Statement of Capabilities: Capitol Lien Records & Research provides UCC, federal and state tax lien searches, environmental lien searches, Minnesota Watercraft, motor vehicle searches, bankruptcy, suit and judgment searches, corporate documents and a weekly tax lien report. They provide an online ordering system to clients.

Capitol Services Inc

PO Box 1831
Austin, TX 78767
Telephone: **Fax:**
800-345-4647   800-432-3622
512-474-8377   512-476-3678
www.capitolservices.com
Year Founded: 1978

Clientele: Asset-Based Lenders, Financial Institutions, Corporate Counsel, Equipment Leasing Companies, Legal Profession

Applications: Lending/Leasing, Real Estate Transactions, Asset/Lien

Searching/Verification, Filing/Recording Documents
Information Types:
Bankruptcy (US)
Litigation/Judgments/Tax Liens (US)
Corporate/Trade Name Data (US)
Uniform Commercial Code (US)

Membership: NPRRA, PRRN

Statement of Capabilities: Capitol Services probably has more offices than any other UCC and corporate service company in the Southwest, with nationwide capability for filing and retrieving documents. They provide fast service by direct online access to the UCC and corporate records of more than 20 states.

Carfax

3975 Fair Ridge Dr #200N
Fairfax, VA 22033
Telephone: **Fax:**
703-934-2664   703-218-2465
www.carfax.com

Parent Company: Blackburn Marketing Services Company
Year Founded: 1986

Clientele: Business - General, Financial Institutions, Insurance - General, Banks

Applications: Fraud Prevention/Detection, Risk Management

Proprietary Products:

Name/Desc: Vehicle History Service
Info Provided: Driver and/or Vehicle
Media: Internet and Direct Online
Coverage: US

Name/Desc: Motor Vehicle Title Information
Info Provided: Driver and/or Vehicle
Media: Online Database, Available on CompuServe and Call-in
Coverage: US

Name/Desc: VINde (VIN Validity Check Program)
Info Provided: Software/Training
Media: Disk
Coverage: US

Membership: AAMVA, DMA

Statement of Capabilities: With the largest online vehicle history database (728 million vehicle records), Carfax can generate a Vehicle History Report based on a VIN in less than one second. They collect data from a variety of sources including state DMVs and salvage pools. Reports include details from previous titles, city and state, odometer rollbacks, junk and flood damage, etc, reducing the risk of handling used vehicles with hidden problems that affect their value.

Free Web Information:
Tips on how to buy a used vehicle.

Carolina Investigative Research
106A Fountain Brook Cir
Cary, NC 27511
Telephone: **Fax:**
800-328-8981   919-460-5338
919-460-7799
car@bellsouth.net
Year Founded: 1998

Clientele: Attorney Firms, Educational Institutions, Insurance - Claims, Investigators - Fraud, Public Record Research Firms

Applications: Asset/Lien Searching/Verification, Background Info - Individuals, Locating People/Businesses, Employment Screening, Tenant Screening

Information Types:
Aviation/Vessels (NC, SC)
Litigation/Judgments/Tax Liens (NC, SC)
Real Estate/Assessor (NC,SC)
SEC/Other Financial (NC,SC)
Uniform Commercial Code (NC, SC)
Vital Records (NC, SC)
Voter Registration (NC, SC)
Criminal Information (US)

Membership: PRRN

Statement of Capabilities: Carolina Investigative Research offers "locates" and personnel research employment screening and public record searches utilizing online databases and physical onsite searches.

Case Record Info Services
2648 E Workman Ave #512
West Covina, CA 91791
Telephone: **Fax:**
626-967-6682   626-967-3782
caserecord@yahooo.com
Year Founded: 1994

Clientele: Collection Agencies, Credit Reporting Agencies, Direct Marketers, Public Record Research Firms

Applications: Collections, Direct Marketing
Proprietary Products:
Name/Desc: Judgment Lists
Info Provided: Litigation/Judgments/Tax Liens
Media: Disk, Lists or labels and Printed Report
Coverage: CA

Membership: PRRN

Statement of Capabilities: Case Record Info Services provides judgment lists in California. Their data is used by bulk data providers, collection and mediation companies. They are also members of the American Arbitration Association.

CCH Washington Service Bureau
655 15th Street NW
Washington, DC 20005
Telephone: **Fax:**
800-955-5219   202-508-0694
202-508-0600
www.wsb.com
custserve@wsb.com
Parent Company: Wolters Klower US
Year Founded: 1967

Clientele: Attorney Firms, Lending Institutions, Corporate Counsel, Government Agencies, Investment Bankers, Securities Industry

Applications: Background Info - Business, Background Info - Individuals, Competitive Intelligence, Filing/Recording Documents, Government Document Retrieval

Information Types:
Legislation/Regulation (US)
News/Current Events (US)

Proprietary Products:
Name/Desc: SECnet
Info Provided: SEC/Other Financial
Media: Direct Online and Internet
Coverage: US

Statement of Capabilities: With an average of over seven years of SEC document experience, their research specialists can tackle tough assignments and meet the most pressing deadlines. Whether clients require examples of precedent language or detailed intelligence on a specific firm or industry, CCH Washington Service Bureau will quickly provide the precise information. Using state-of-the-art proprietary databases, their research specialists quickly deliver a wide range of corporate and transactional information.

CDB Infotek

6 Hutton Centre Dr #600
Santa Ana, CA 92707

Telephone: **Fax:**
800-427-3747　　714-708-1000
714-708-2000
www.cdb.com

Clientele: Legal Profession, Government Agencies, Insurance - Agents/Brokers, Lending Institutions, Investigators - Fraud, Consumers (Individuals), Government Agencies

Applications: Locating People/Businesses, Asset/Lien Searching/Verification, Background Info - Business, Fraud Prevention/Detection, Lending/Leasing

Information Types:
Credit Information (US)

Proprietary Products:

Name/Desc: Real Property Ownership & Transfers
Info Provided: Real Estate/Assessor
Media: Online Database
Coverage: US

Name/Desc: Corporate & Limited Partnerships
Info Provided: Corporate/Trade Name Data
Media: Online Database
Coverage: US

Name/Desc: Uniform Commercial Code
Info Provided: Uniform Commercial Code
Media: Online Database
Coverage: US

Name/Desc: Bankruptcies, Tax Liens, Judgments, Notices of Default
Info Provided: Bankruptcy and Litigation/Judgments/Tax Liens
Media: Online Databases
Coverage: US

Membership: SIIA, NALV, NPRRA, ASIS, ACA

Statement of Capabilities: CDB Infotek offers nationwide public records information, including instant access to more than 3.5 billion records and 1,600 targeted databases to efficiently locate people or businesses, conduct background research, identify assets, control fraud, conduct due diligence, etc. Subscribers learn search strategies at free, year-round seminars and have toll-free access to customer service representatives for help. CDB Infotek also offers direct marketing lists, monitoring services, hard copy document retrieval and high-volume processing services.

Centennial Coverages Inc

6005 E Evans Ave #202
Denver, CO 80222

Telephone: **Fax:**
800-338-8221　　303-639-9651
303-639-9345

centennial@rmi.net
Year Founded: 1986

Clientele: Financial Institutions, Government Agencies, Employers (HR/Personnel Depts), Legal Profession, Public Record Research Firms

Applications: Filing/Recording Documents, Background Info - Business, Litigation, Asset/Lien Searching/Verification, Locating People/Businesses

Information Types:
Uniform Commercial Code (US)
Litigation/Judgments/Tax Liens (US)
Corporate/Trade Name Data (US)
Bankruptcy (US)
Licenses/Registrations/Permits (US)
Environmental (US)
Trademarks/Patents (US)

Membership: NPRRA, PRRN

Statement of Capabilities: Centennial provides complete/nationwide purchase money security and commercial filing and perfection procedures to national manufacturing and distribution concerns. In addition, Centennial provides nationwide public record research, asset research, credit file due diligence and whereabouts tracing services to public and private sector clients.

Central Indiana Paralegal Service Inc

55 Monument Cir #1424
Indianapolis, IN 46204

Telephone: **Fax:**
317-636-1311　　317-636-1426
www.cips1.com

Year Founded: 1992

Clientele: Financial Institutions, Legal Profession, Public Record Research Firms

Applications: Legal Compliance, Background Info - Business, Asset/Lien Searching/Verification, Filing/Recording Documents, Background Info - Individuals

Information Types:
Bankruptcy (IN-Southern District)
Corporate/Trade Name Data (IN)
Litigation/Judgments/Tax Liens (IN-Southern District)
Uniform Commercial Code (IN)
Driver and/or Vehicle (US)

Membership: NPRRA, NFPA, PRRN

Statement of Capabilities: Central Indiana Paralegal Service specializes in Marion County and State of Indiana document filings being completed on the day of ordering. Services are provided in most Indiana counties through correspondents.

Central Property Search Inc

9 Lawn Ave #200
Norristown, PA 19401
Telephone: **Fax:**
800-829-1779 610-630-8460
610-630-9340
www.cps.cncoffice.com
contact@cps.cnoffice.com
Year Founded: 1989

Clientele: Financial Institutions, Legal Service Companies, Public Record Research Firms, Government Agencies, Mortgage Bankers, Secured Lenders

Applications: Government Document Retrieval, Filing/Recording Documents, Real Estate Transactions, Lending/Leasing, Litigation

Information Types:
Litigation/Judgments/Tax Liens (US)
Bankruptcy (PA,DE,NJ,MD,NY)
Uniform Commercial Code (US)
Credit Information (US)
Real Estate/Assessor (PA,DE,NJ,MD,NY)
Corporate/Trade Name Data (US)
Addresses/Telephone Numbers (US)

Statement of Capabilities: Central Property Search offers a full range of "customizable" property and judgment reports. CPS also offers nationwide document retrieval and recording. CPS offers 24 hour turnaround in PA (48 hours outside PA). CPS offers flood zone determinations, flood insurance quotes and information.

Free Web Information:

CPS offer free flood insurance quotes and links to The National Flood Insurance Program.

Certified Document Retriever Bureau

PO Box 3150
Albany, NY 12203-0150
Telephone: **Fax:**
518-438-7956 518-438-0502
Year Founded: 1960

Clientele: Credit Reporting Agencies, Financial Institutions, Insurance - Agents/Brokers, Legal Profession, Public Record Research Firms, Professionals-Other

Applications: Insurance Underwriting, Locating People/Businesses

Information Types:
Corporate/Trade Name Data (NY)
Driver and/or Vehicle (NY)

Statement of Capabilities: Certified Document Retriever Bureau (CDRB) specializes in certified public record information from New York state. Their corporate searches include filings, name searches, reservations, certified documents on file, etc. Their extensive list of DMV searches include driving records, accident information by location, registration check, license plate check, insurance check, title searches, license copies and suspension and revocation orders. CDRB provides process service on all New York agencies including MVD, Department of State, Court of Claims and AG. Ordering is by telephone or fax. There is no enrollment or subscription fee.

Charles Jones Inc

PO Box 8488
Trenton, NJ 08650-8488
Telephone: **Fax:**
800-792-8888 800-883-0677
609-538-1000 609-883-0677
www.cji.com

Year Founded: 1911

Clientele: Financial Institutions, Legal Profession, Public Record Research Firms

Applications: Real Estate Transactions, Lending/Leasing, Litigation

Information Types:
Bankruptcy (NJ)
Litigation/Judgments/Tax Liens (NJ)

Environmental (NJ)
Real Estate/Assessor (NJ)

Membership: NPRRA, ICA, ALTA

Statement of Capabilities: Charles Jones Inc provides certified searches of judgments, liens and bankruptcies filed in New Jersey State Court and Federal Courts. From the early stages of manual indexing to the development of the first computerized system in 1969, Charles Jones has advanced the art and science of searching names and earned a solid reputation. Their numerous high-speed computers permit immediate access to millions of records. A staff of over 100 experts delivers millions of searches to thousands of satisfied customers. Special services include flood hazard searches, tidelands searches and 1099 reporting.

Chattel Mortgage Reporter Inc

300 W Washington #808
Chicago, IL 60606
Telephone: **Fax:**
312-214-1048   312-214-1054
www.chattelmtg.com

searches@chattelmtg.com
Year Founded: 1991

Clientele: Business - General, Credit Reporting Agencies, Financial Institutions, Legal Profession, Public Record Research Firms

Applications: Lending/Leasing, Filing/Recording Documents, Real Estate Transactions, Litigation

Information Types:
Real Estate/Assessor (US)
Corporate/Trade Name Data (US, IL)
Litigation/Judgments/Tax Liens (US, IL)
Bankruptcy (US)
Driver and/or Vehicle (US)
Criminal Information (US)

Proprietary Products:
Name/Desc: Chattel Mortgage Reporter
Info Provided: Uniform Commercial Code
Media: Call-in, Fax, Online and E-mail
Coverage: IL-Cook County

Membership: NPRRA, PRRN

Statement of Capabilities: CMR is a national public record service organization specializing in Illinois. They have more than 95 years of experience, with emphasis on public record research in Cook County, IL and the counties

surrounding the Chicago area. For fast copy retrieval, their UCC database for Cook County is backed up by microfilm dating back to 1973.

ChoicePoint Inc

1000 Alderman Dr
Alphretta, GA 30005
Telephone: **Fax:**
770-752-6000   770-752-6005
www.choicepointinc.com
Year Founded: 1997

Clientele: Business - General, Asset-Based Lenders, Employers (HR/Personnel Depts), Government Agencies, Secured Lenders, Legal Profession, Insurance - Claims

Applications: Background Info - Business, Employment Screening, Asset/Lien Searching/Verification, Background Info - Individuals, Litigation

Information Types:
Addresses/Telephone Numbers (US)
Bankruptcy (US)
SEC/Other Financial (US)
Education/Employment (US)
Criminal Information (US)
Driver and/or Vehicle (US)
Litigation/Judgments/Tax Liens (US)
Uniform Commercial Code (US)

Proprietary Products:
Name/Desc: Corp Data
Info Provided: Corporation/Trade Name Data
Media: Online Database
Coverage: US

Name/Desc: Bankruptcy
Info Provided: Bankruptcy
Media: Online
Coverage: US

Name/Desc: UCC
Info Provided: UCC Fillings and Tax Liens
Media: Online Database
Coverage: US

Name/Desc: Real Property
Info Provided: Real Estate/Assessor
Media: Online
Coverage: US

Name/Desc: Litigation
Info Provided: Litigation/Judgments/Tax Liens
Media: Online
Coverage: US

Name/Desc: Licenses

Info Provided:
Licenses/Registrations/Permits (Physicians)
Media: Online
Coverage: US

Name/Desc: Fict. Bus Names
Info Provided: Corporate/Trade Name Data
(Fictious Business Names)
Media: Online
Coverage: US

Membership: AALL, ABI, ASIS

Statement of Capabilities: ChoicePoint is a
leading provider of intelligence information to
help businesses, governments, and individuals
to better understand with whom they do
business. ChoicePoint services the risk
management information needs of the property
and casualty insurance market, the life and
health insurance market, and business and
government, including asset-based lenders and
professional service providers. The company,
with many branch offices nationwide, was spun
off/out from Equifax in 1997. They offer a
variety of useful online products.

Free Web Information:
Helpful information, directory and ordering
info.

Cleo
106 West 6th Ave
Rome, GA 30161
Telephone: **Fax:**
706-295-5777 706-295-9081
Parent Company: Fugitrac Systems, Inc
Year Founded: 1996

Clientele: Apartment Owners/Managers,
Attorney Firms, Collection Agencies,
Corporate Security, Credit Grantors,
Government Agencies, Insurance -
Agents/Brokers

Applications: Background Info - Individuals,
Employment Screening, Fraud
Prevention/Detection, Lending/Leasing,
Locating People/Businesses

Information Types:
Social Security (Numbers) (US)

Proprietary Products:

Name/Desc: Cleo
Info Provided: Addresses/Telephone
Numbers
Media: Direct Online and Fax
Coverage: US

Statement of Capabilities: Cleo has no long
distance charges for online access, and offers
30 seconds or less turnaround time. No
monthly minimum is required, but the client
agreement must identify the legal "need to
know." They offer a fraud detection program.

CMR Information Service
6560 La Praix
Highland, CA 92346
Telephone: **Fax:**
909-862-8908 909-864-8475
cmrinfo@aol.com
Year Founded: 1994

Clientele: Educational Institutions, Information -
Brokers/Retrievers, Insurance -
Agents/Brokers, Landlords, Private
Investigators, Public Record Research Firms

Applications: Background Info - Business,
Background Info - Individuals, Employment
Screening, Insurance Underwriting, Tenant
Screening

Information Types:
Criminal Information (CA)

Membership: PRRN

Statement of Capabilities: CMR Information
Service is a public record search service.
Primary services are criminal background
checks, felony and misdemeanor. They also
perform civil searches in most of the counties
in California. They have developed a network
of correspondents in all counties of California
who personally examine the indexes and
retrieve the necessary records to complete the
search. Same day service is available when
necessary.

CMS Insight
PO Box 100029
Roswell, GA 30077
Telephone: **Fax:**
800-714-5534 770-992-7162
770-992-9077
www.CMSINSIGHT.com
bbristol@cmsinsight.com
Year Founded: 1985

Information Types:
Credit Information (US)
Criminal Information (US)
Driver and/or Vehicle (US)
Education/Employment (US)

Legislation/Regulation (US)
Military Svc (US)
Social Security (Numbers) (US)
Workers' Compensation (US)

Membership: SHRM

Statement of Capabilities: CMS Insight compiles independent analytical assessments of employees and prospective employees from public record background search information. The detail depends on customer needs. They also provide credit risk analysis of businesses for credit departments.

Colby Attorneys Service Co Inc

41 State St #106
Albany, NY 12207
Telephone: **Fax:**
800-832-1220   518-434-2574
518-463-4426
Year Founded: 1939

Clientele: Legal Profession, Professionals-Other

Applications: Legal Compliance, Filing/Recording Documents, Background Info - Business, Litigation, Background Info - Individuals

Information Types:
Corporate/Trade Name Data (US, NY)
Driver and/or Vehicle (NY)
Uniform Commercial Code (US, NY)
Litigation/Judgments/Tax Liens (US, NY)
SEC/Other Financial (US)

Membership: NAPPS, NPRRA

Statement of Capabilities: Colby Attorneys Service is a New York-based company that provides service to the legal community for the filing and processing of legal documents, information and documents retrieval across the US, They have developed a working relationship with research specialists located strategically throughout the US, which allows them to provide service in any of the 50 states.

Commercial Information Systems Inc

4747 SW Kelly #110
Portland, OR 97201-4221
Telephone: **Fax:**
800-454-6575   503-222-7405
503-222-7422
www.cis-usa.com
cis@world1.worldstar.com

Year Founded: 1991

Clientele: Legal Profession, Collection Agencies, Employers (HR/Personnel Depts), Financial Institutions, Government Agencies, Insurance - Claims, Private Investigators

Applications: Asset/Lien Searching/Verification, Collections, Employment Screening, Fraud Prevention/Detection, Locating People/Businesses

Information Types:
Addresses/Telephone Numbers (OR)
Bankruptcy (OR)
Litigation/Judgments/Tax Liens (OR)
Credit Information (OR)

Proprietary Products:

Name/Desc: Aircraft Registrations
Info Provided: Aviation/Vessels
Media: Direct Online
Coverage: US

Name/Desc: UCCs
Info Provided: Uniform Commercial Code
Media: Direct Online
Coverage: CA, ID, OR, WA

Name/Desc: Corporations & Limited Partnerships
Info Provided: Corporate/Trade Name Data
Media: Direct Online
Coverage: CA, ID, OR, WA

Name/Desc: Professional Licenses
Info Provided:
Licenses/Registrations/Permits
Media: Direct Online
Coverage: ID, OR, WA

Name/Desc: Real Estate Records
Info Provided: Real Estate/Assessor
Media: Direct Online
Coverage: ID, NV, OR, WA

Name/Desc: Criminal Records
Info Provided: Criminal Information
Media: Direct Online
Coverage: ID, OR, WA

Name/Desc: Fish & Wildlife Records
Info Provided:
Licenses/Registrations/Permits
Media: Direct Online
Coverage: ID, OR

Name/Desc: Driver's License & Registration
Info Provided: Driver and/or Vehicle
Media: Direct Online
Coverage: ID, OR

Name/Desc: Hazardous Materials
Info Provided: Environmental
Media: Direct Online
Coverage: OR

Membership: SIIA, NACM, NALI

Statement of Capabilities: Commercial Information Systems (CIS) is an online/on-site database of public records serving business and government entities. They also provide direct access to selected public and private database records on a national level through special gateway relationships. The CIS integrated regional database aggregates, commingles and cross-matches records at the state level by name, address, city, state, ZIP Code, birth date, driver's license, vehicle plates and other identifiers with a search engine that allows a subscriber to return all related records on a common identifier. The CIS system is always available through a PC and modem. CIS provides the communication software. Internet access is expected. CIS also provides information on a manual retrieval basis, including credit bureau products and services as well as special data mining capabilities tailored to a clients' specific research or volume searching needs.

Communications Systems Technology Inc
5564 S Lee St
Littleton, CO 80127-1845
Telephone: **Fax:**
303-973-8111 303-973-1110
www.sni.net/~arte
Year Founded: 1988

Clientele: Financial Institutions, Legal Profession, Collection Agencies, Business - General

Applications: Lending/Leasing, Legal Compliance

Information Types:
Corporate/Trade Name Data (CO)

Statement of Capabilities: Communications Systems Technology (CST) provides access to Colorado public records through a BBS system. Available records include: corporate, trade names and trademarks.

Compinstall Inc
4710 Surf Ave

Brooklyn, NY 11224-1046
Telephone: **Fax:**
800-590-0900 800-590-5580
718-266-4116 718-266-7887
compinstall@compuserve.com
Year Founded: 1986

Clientele: Business - General, Collection Agencies, Employers (HR/Personnel Depts), Information - Brokers/Retrievers, Legal Profession, Private Investigators, Real Estate Owners/Managers

Applications: Asset/Lien Searching/Verification, Background Info - Business, Background Info - Individuals, Employment Screening, Locating People/Businesses

Information Types:
Addresses/Telephone Numbers (US, International)
Bankruptcy (US)
Credit Information (US)
Criminal Information (US)
Education/Employment (US)
Driver and/or Vehicle (US, International)
Litigation/Judgments/Tax Liens (US)
Social Security (Numbers) (US)

Membership: FOP

Statement of Capabilities: Compinstall has access to an established national network of research specialists and information brokers with extensive resources. To do business with Compinstall, "The Information Broker," No account is required. No sign up fees. No minimums. No monthly charges - and a computer or fax machine is not required as verbal and hard-copy reports are available. Personal service is provided at No additional cost.

Complete Corporate Services of Alaska
PO Box 33735
Juneau, AK 99801
Telephone: **Fax:**
877-790-4956 877-790-4956
907-790-4956 907-790-4954
chamiel@gci.net
Year Founded: 1991

Clientele: Accountants, Attorney Firms, Lending Institutions, Business - General, Consumers (Individuals), Public Record Research Firms, Legal Service Companies

Applications: Legal Compliance, Filing/Recording Documents, Registered Agent

Information Types:
Corporate/Trade Name Data (US, AK)
Driver and/or Vehicle (AK)
Licenses/Registrations/Permits (AK)
Vital Records (AK)

Membership: NPRRA

Statement of Capabilities: Complete Corporate Services of Alaska specializes in corporate document retrieval and filings within 24 to 48 hours. They are members of the National Registered Agents.

CompuServe
PO Box 20212
Columbus, OH 43220
Telephone: **Fax:**
800-848-8199   614-457-0348
614-457-8600
www.compuserve.com

Parent Company: America Online Inc
Clientele: Business - General, Consumers (Individuals)

Applications: General Business Information, Background Info - Business, Background Info - Individuals, Competitive Intelligence

Proprietary Products:

Name/Desc: Quest Research Center
Info Provided: Trademarks/Patents, News/Current Events,
Media: Internet
Coverage: US

Name/Desc: Phonefile
Info Provided: Addresses/Telephone Numbers
Coverage: US

Statement of Capabilities: Now a subsidiary of AOL, CompuServe is available in 185 countries and provides comprehensive services for serious Internet online users at home, in the workplace, and globally. Business and professional resources, latest news and information, are but a few of CompuServe's powerful communications capabilities.

Free Web Information:
Wide variety of valuable links, index, features, prices and discounts.

Computer Assisted Research Online
1166 NE 182nd St
Miami, FL 33162
Telephone:
800-329-6397
305-944-2111
Year Founded: 1983

Clientele: Legal Profession, Public Record Research Firms, Government Agencies, Business - General, Private Investigators

Applications: Background Info - Business, Background Info - Individuals, Competitive Intelligence, General Business Information, Locating People/Businesses

Information Types:
Bankruptcy (US)
Driver and/or Vehicle (US)
Workers' Compensation (US)
Criminal Information (US, FL)
Uniform Commercial Code (US)
Corporate/Trade Name Data (US)
Addresses/Telephone Numbers (US)
News/Current Events (US)

Membership: AIIP

Statement of Capabilities: Computer Assisted Research Online specializes in providing search services utilizing automated sources. Computer Assisted Research Online (C.A.R.O.L.) will do the search manually if an automated source is not available. Offices are staffed 24 hours per day.

Condor Protective Services
4101 N Andrews Ave #302
Ft Lauderdale, FL 33309
Telephone: **Fax:**
954-630-9888   954-630-0076
condorpro@aol.com
Year Founded: 1996

Clientele: Business - General, Credit Grantors, Government Agencies, Landlords, Legal Profession, Mortgage Bankers, Attorney Firms

Applications: Asset/Lien Searching/Verification, Background Info - Business, Collections, Competitive Intelligence, Litigation

Information Types:
Addresses/Telephone Numbers (US)
Bankruptcy (US)
Corporate/Trade Name Data (US)
Criminal Information (US)
Driver and/or Vehicle (US)

Litigation/Judgments/Tax Liens (US)
Social Security (Numbers) (US)

Statement of Capabilities: Condor Protective Services specializes in in-depth business and consumer intelligence reporting, exposing possible fraudulent business and consumer practices. With access to national and international database records, their Profile Analysis reports allow legal, financial, government and business communities to proactively manage their exposure to high risk. They also provide business and consumer intelligence reports. Condor Protective provides nationwide criminal, driving and social security reports. Their staff consists of former governmental intelligence officers, certified fraud examiners, security and information specialists, paralegals, process servers and document retrievers. Additionally, they have a special location division to help the public and private sections locate birth parents and the adopted.

Confi-Chek

1816 19th ST
Sacramento, CA 95814
Telephone: **Fax:**
800-821-7404 800-758-5859
916-443-4822 916-443-7420
www.Confi-chek.com

Year Founded: 1988

Clientele: Credit Reporting Agencies, Direct Marketers, Employers (HR/Personnel Depts), Financial Institutions, Insurance - General, Legal Profession, Private Investigators

Applications: Asset/Lien Searching/Verification, Background Info - Individuals, Competitive Intelligence, Litigation, Locating People/Businesses

Information Types:
Litigation/Judgments/Tax Liens (US)
Credit Information (US)
Real Estate/Assessor (US)
Uniform Commercial Code (US)
Criminal Information (US)
Driver and/or Vehicle (28 states/FIX)
Licenses/Registrations/Permits (40 states/FIX)
Social Security (Numbers) (US)

Proprietary Products:
Name/Desc: Confi-Chek Online
Info Provided: Criminal History
Media: Online Database

Coverage: CA

Membership: ION

Statement of Capabilities: Confi-Check provides instant access to national and local records throughout the US. They also offer asset services. Their web site has almost all state records. Dial-up and fax call-in services are also available.

Congressional Information Service Inc

4520 East-West Highway
Bethesda, MD 20814-3389
Telephone: **Fax:**
800-638-8380 301-654-4033
301-654-1550
www.cispubs.com

Year Founded: 1969

Clientele: Attorney Firms, Financial Institutions, Lending Institutions, Corporate Counsel, Legal Profession, Legal Service Companies

Applications: Legal Compliance, Government Document Retrieval, Current Events

Proprietary Products:
Name/Desc: Current Issues Sourcefile
Info Provided: Legislation/Regulations
Media: CD-ROM, Disk, Publication
Coverage: US

Statement of Capabilities: Congressional Information Service is an international publisher of reference, research, and current awareness information products and services. Many of their products deal with economic and demographic issues. Their multiple databases are offered in electronic format and through partners such as LEXIS-NEXIS.

Conrad Grundlehner Inc

8605 Brook Rd
McLean, VA 22102-1504
Telephone: **Fax:**
703-506-9648 703-506-9580
Year Founded: 1984

Clientele: Credit Reporting Agencies

Applications: Legal Compliance, Government Document Retrieval, Litigation

Proprietary Products:
Name/Desc: Conrad Grundlehner
Info Provided: Bankruptcy, Litigation/Judgments/Tax Liens

Media: Disk, Magnetic Tape
Coverage: DC, MD, NC, VA, WV

Membership: SIIA, NPRRA

Statement of Capabilities: Conrad Grundlehner Inc (CGI) was among the first companies to use portable computers to collect legal data at courts and recording offices. The use of notebook computers combined with electronic transmission of data to the customer reduces the time between data collection and its availability to the customer. CGI's information processing expertise also allows it to provide a high degree of customized service to its customers. Data can be delivered in a wide variety of ways on a broad spectrum of media.

CorpAmerica

PO Box 811
Dover, DE 19903-0811
Telephone: **Fax:**
888-736-4300   392-736-4301
302-736-4300
www.LawService.com

Year Founded: 1989

Clientele: Business - General, Legal Profession, Public Record Research Firms

Applications: Legal Compliance, General Business Information, Litigation, Real Estate Transactions

Information Types:
Litigation/Judgments/Tax Liens (US, DE)
Corporate/Trade Name Data (US, DE)
Driver and/or Vehicle (US, DE)
Uniform Commercial Code (US DE)
Bankruptcy (DE)

Membership: NALV, NPRRA, PRRN, NFPA

Statement of Capabilities: CorpAmerica offers a full range of corporate services including incorporation, qualification, registered agent, UCC filings and searches, and document retrieval in all 50 states, specializing in Delaware. Owner Carolyn McKown has more than 19 years of industry experience and previously served 5 years as a legal assistant with the Delaware AG. CorpAmerica is online with Delaware's Secretary of State and DMV databases. Instant Delaware incorporation is provided through the Internet site.
Free Web Information:
Cyber walk through incorporation process.

CorpAssist

1090 Vermont Ave NW #910
Washington, DC 20005
Telephone: **Fax:**
800-438-2996   202-371-1945
202-371-8090

corpDC@aol.com
Year Founded: 1992

Clientele: Financial Institutions, Government Agencies, Legal Profession, Libraries, Educational Institutions, Consumers (Individuals), Private Investigators

Applications: Filing/Recording Documents, General Business Information, Real Estate Transactions, Asset/Lien Searching/Verification

Information Types:
Real Estate/Assessor (US)
Litigation/Judgments/Tax Liens (US)
Uniform Commercial Code (US)
Corporate/Trade Name Data (US)
Trademarks/Patents (US)
Bankruptcy (US)

Membership: NPRRA, PRRN, NICA, NFPA

Statement of Capabilities: CorpAssist is staffed by paralegals and information retrieval specialists experienced in the following areas: all corporate preparation, filing and searching; registered agent services; all types of public record research services, including title examinations; federal and local government agency research and monitoring; document filing; and service of process.

Corporate Access Inc

1116-D Thomasville Rd
Tallahassee, FL 32303
Telephone: **Fax:**
800-969-1666   850-222-1666
850-222-2666
http://user.talstar.com/cai

Year Founded: 1994

Clientele: Lending Institutions, Attorney Firms, Information - Brokers/Retrievers, Public Record Research Firms, Legal Service Companies, Legal Profession

Applications: Asset/Lien Searching/Verification, Background Info - Business, Background Info - Individuals, Filing/Recording Documents, General Business Information

Information Types:
Bankruptcy (US)
Corporate/Trade Name Data (US)
Credit Information (US)
Driver and/or Vehicle (US)
Licenses/Registrations/Permits (US)
Trademarks/Patents (US)
UCC (US)

Statement of Capabilities: Most searches by Corporate Access are completed within 24 hours. They have over 30 years experience in the service of filing and retrieval services.

Corporate Creations International Inc

941 4th St #200
Miami Beach, FL 33139
Telephone: **Fax:**
800-672-9110   305-672-9110
305-672-0686
www.corpcreations.com

Year Founded: 1993

Clientele: Business - General, Legal Profession, Public Record Research Firms, Financial Institutions, Corporate Counsel, Accountants

Applications: Legal Compliance, Filing/Recording Documents, General Business Information, Background Info - Individuals, Locating People/Businesses

Information Types:
Corporate/Trade Name Data (US)
Trademarks/Patents (US)
Licenses/Registrations/Permits (US)
Uniform Commercial Code (US)
Litigation/Judgments/Tax Liens (US)
Driver and/or Vehicle (US)

Statement of Capabilities: Corporate Creations is an incorporation, trademark and general corporate service firm with search and filing capabilities throughout the US. They are owned by attorneys and staffed by attorney and non-attorney specialists. They provide online incorporation and trademark ordering through the Internet. Corporate filings can be completed in 24 hours or less in some states.

Corporate Information Services

PO Box 1717
Lilburn, GA 30048
Telephone: **Fax:**
770-931-3101   770-381-5977
www.opsecintl.com

Parent Company: Operation Security International
Clientele: Corporate Security, Employers (HR/Personnel Depts), Equipment Leasing Companies

Applications: Background Info - Business, Background Info - Individuals, Employment Screening

Information Types:
Credit Information (US)
Criminal Information (US)
Education/Employment (US)
Foreign Country Information
Licenses/Registrations/Permits
Vital Records (US)
Military Svc (US)
Social Security (Numbers) (US)

Membership: ASIS

Corpus Christi Court Services

PO Box 147
Corpus Christi, TX 78403-0147
Telephone: **Fax:**
512-887-8122   512-887-0335
Year Founded: 1985

Clientele: Legal Profession, Public Record Research Firms, Financial Institutions

Applications: Background Info - Individuals, Asset/Lien Searching/Verification, Litigation, Employment Screening, Filing/Recording Documents

Information Types:
Bankruptcy (TX-Southern District)
Litigation/Judgments/Tax Liens (TX-various counties)
Criminal Information (TX-Nueces)
Real Estate/Assessor (TX)
Uniform Commercial Code (TX-various counties)

Membership: PRRN

Statement of Capabilities: Corpus Christi Court Services is an independently owned and operated document retrieval and research company specializing in Texas public record retrieval.

Court Explorers Inc

300 Rector Pl
New York, NY 10280
Telephone: **Fax:**
212-945-6324   212-945-6325

cexplorers@aol.com
Year Founded: 1995

Clientele: Legal Profession, Financial Institutions, Insurance - Agents/Brokers

Applications: Filing/Recording Documents, Legal Compliance, Background Info - Business, Background Info - Individuals, General Business Information

Information Types:
Uniform Commercial Code (US)
Litigation/Judgments/Tax Liens (US)
Bankruptcy (US)
Social Security (Numbers) (US)

Membership: PRRN

Court House Legal Service
122 Haddontowne Ct #304
Cherry Hill, NJ 08034-3664
Telephone: **Fax:**
800-242-9779 609-428-5424
609-428-4700
Parent Company: Courthouse Couriers Inc
Year Founded: 1985

Clientele: Legal Profession, Public Record Research Firms

Applications: Lending/Leasing, Employment Screening, Litigation, Asset/Lien Searching/Verification, Real Estate Transactions

Information Types:
Bankruptcy (NJ-Southern, PA-Eastern)
Litigation/Judgments/Tax Liens (NJ, PA)
Criminal Information (NJ, PA)
Uniform Commercial Code (NJ, PA)

Membership: NAPPS

Statement of Capabilities: CHLS is a regional service company with 24 full-time employees. They cover eight counties in New Jersey and Pennsylvania with their own employees.

Court PC of Connecticut
PO Box 11081
Greenwich, CT 06831-1081
Telephone: **Fax:**
203-531-7866 203-531-6899
Year Founded: 1992

Clientele: Legal Profession, Public Record Research Firms, Insurance - General

Applications: Litigation, Background Info - Business, Asset/Lien Searching/Verification,

Locating People/Businesses, Background Info - Individuals

Information Types:
Bankruptcy (US, CT)
UCC (CT)
Corporate/Trade Name Data (CT)
Litigation/Judgments/Tax Liens (US)

Proprietary Products:
Name/Desc: Superior Index
Info Provided: Litigation/Judgments/Tax Liens, Criminal Information
Media: Fax-on-Demand and Printed Report
Coverage: CT

Membership: NPRRA

Statement of Capabilities: Court PC is Connecticut's comprehensive source of docket search information from Superior Court and US District Court cases. Their database contains records of civil filings from 1984, family/divorce from 1988, and criminal conviction data from 1991. Indexes are used to supplement PACER data from 1970 to present. They also provide current corporation, UCC and tax lien data from the Connecticut Secretary of State database, and statewide real estate information from computerized assessor lists.

Court Record Consultants
17029 Devonshire St #166
Northridge, CA 91325
Telephone: **Fax:**
818-366-1906 818-366-1985
Year Founded: 1985

Clientele: Financial Institutions, Government Agencies, Insurance - Agents/Brokers, Legal Profession, Public Record Research Firms

Applications: Asset/Lien Searching/Verification, Background Info - Business, Locating People/Businesses, Litigation

Information Types:
Litigation/Judgments/Tax Liens (US)
Real Estate/Assessor (US)
Vital Records (US)

Membership: NPRRA, NAFI, NNA, NAFE, NAIS

Statement of Capabilities: Court Record Consultants are specialists in court and property research and document retrieval at the state, county, and federal level.

Court Record Research Inc

PO Box 3796
Houston, TX 77253-3796
Telephone: **Fax:**
800-552-3353 888-395-8055
713-227-3353 713-236-1970
www.courtrecords.com

Year Founded: 1972

Clientele: Insurance - General, Public Record Research Firms, Legal Profession, Private Investigators, Attorney Firms, Title Companies

Applications: Real Estate Transactions, Litigation, Legal Compliance, General Business Information, Competitive Intelligence

Information Types:
Bankruptcy (US, TX)
Litigation/Judgments/Tax Liens (TX)
Real Estate/Assessor (TX)
Wills/Probate (TX)
Uniform Commercial Code (TX)

Membership: PRRN, NPRRA, NFPA

Statement of Capabilities: Court Record Research brings more than 45 years of experience to obtaining public records on behalf of clients. They specialize in the Houston/Gulf Coast area of Texas, with same day service in Harris County. They are licensed by the Texas Board of Private Investigators and Private Security Agencies Act.

Court Records Investigations

Route 5 Box 297 B-24
Lubbock, TX 79407
Telephone: **Fax:**
806-885-2602 806-885-1049
Year Founded: 1995

Clientele: Financial Institutions, Legal Profession, Government Agencies, Public Record Research Firms, Employers (HR/Personnel Depts)

Applications: Litigation, Asset/Lien Searching/Verification, Background Info - Individuals, Employment Screening, Insurance Underwriting

Information Types:
Bankruptcy (US)
Litigation/Judgments/Tax Liens (US)
Criminal Information (US)
Uniform Commercial Code (US)
Vital Records (US)

Voter Registration (US)
Wills/Probate (TX)

Statement of Capabilities: Court Records Investigations specializes in criminal history and civil litigation searches. They have correspondents nationwide.

Court Records Research Group

206 Westview Ter
Arlington, TX 76013
Telephone: **Fax:**
800-689-9030 800-687-7658
817-429-1972 817-459-1388
crrg3@airmail.net

Year Founded: 1993

Clientele: Apartment Owners/Managers, Legal Profession, Credit Reporting Agencies, Employers (HR/Personnel Depts), Financial Institutions, Landlords, Private Investigators

Applications: Asset/Lien Searching/Verification, Background Info - Business, Background Info - Individuals, Insurance Underwriting, Employment Screening

Information Types:
Bankruptcy (OK, TX)
Corporate/Trade Name Data (OK, TX)
Criminal Information (OK, TX)
Driver and/or Vehicle (OK, TX)
Education/Employment (OK, TX)
Litigation/Judgments/Tax Liens (OK, TX)
Real Estate/Assessor (OK, TX)
Uniform Commercial Code (OK, TX)

Membership: NPRRA, NAPSI

Statement of Capabilities: Court Records Research Group is a licensed investigation firm specializing in legal research. In every county in Texas and Oklahoma, they provide public record research. They offer 24 hour turnaround time in both states. They provide live in-person searches in every county. All work is quality controlled to insure complete accuracy.

Court Search Unlimited

55 Laurel Creel Ln
Laguna Hills, CA 92653
Telephone: **Fax:**
949-768-9061 949-362-0951
www.csuweb.com

Year Founded: 1997

Clientele: Attorney Firms, Consumers (Individuals), Insurance - Claims

Applications: Legal Compliance, Litigation

Information Types:
Criminal Information (US)
Litigation/Judgments/Tax Liens (US)

Statement of Capabilities: Court Search Unlimited specializes in determining if statutes of limitations for damages were properly protected by filing a lawsuit in the appropriate court. If a lawsuit is found, they furnish a copy of the compliant. Otherwise, they will advise the client in writing that no records are on file.

Courthouse Connections
3055 State Street
San Diego, CA 92103
Telephone: **Fax:**
619-692-3538   619-692-0931
isearch@abac.com
Year Founded: 1993

Clientele: Attorney Firms, Employers (HR/Personnel Depts), Private Investigators, Public Record Research Firms

Applications: Background Info - Business, Background Info - Individuals, Employment Screening

Information Types:
Bankruptcy (CA-Southern)
Criminal Information (CA-San Diego)
Litigation/Judgments/Tax Liens (CA-San Diego)

Statement of Capabilities: Courthouse Connections specializes in criminal background searches in San Diego County, CA. These searches are completed within 24 hours. Accounts are maintained regularly to assure the best quality of service.

CourtLink
400 112th Ave NE #250
Bellevue, WA 98004
Telephone: **Fax:**
800-774-7317   425-450-0394
425-450-0390
www.courtlink.com
panderson@courtlink.com
Parent Company: DataWest
Year Founded: 1986

Clientele: Legal Profession, Public Record Research Firms, Financial Institutions, News Media, Employers (HR/Personnel Depts), Insurance - Claims, Private Investigators

Applications: Background Info - Business, Background Info - Individuals, Litigation, Risk Management, Employment Screening

Information Types:
Litigation/Judgments/Tax Liens (US, OR, WA)
Criminal Information (US, OR, WA)
Bankruptcy (US)

Proprietary Products:
Name/Desc: CourtLink
Info Provided: Bankruptcy, Litigation/Judgments/Tax Liens
Media: Online Database, Printed Reports and Lists or Labels
Coverage: US

Membership: NACM

Statement of Capabilities: CourtLink has created an online gateway through which the user gains interactive access to all federal district and bankruptcy courts on PACER, also to OJIN (Oregon) and to SCOMIS (Washington State) using one Windows-based interface program. The user can search one court at a time or any combination of courts simultaneously. Federal and state court searches can be combined into one step.

CQ Staff Directories Ltd
815 Slaters Ln
Alexandria, VA 22314
Telephone: **Fax:**
800-252-1722   703-739-0234
703-739-0900
www.staffdirectories.com
Year Founded: 1959

Clientele: Libraries, Educational Institutions, Government Agencies, Business - General, Leasing Agents - Personal Property, Professionals-Other

Applications: Locating People/Businesses, Background Info - Individuals, Direct Marketing, Genealogical Research, Government Document Retrieval

Information Types:
Legislation/Regulation (US)
Bankruptcy (US)
Foreign Country Information

Proprietary Products:
Name/Desc: Congressional Staff Directory
Info Provided: Addresses/Telephone Numbers

Media: Publication, CD-ROM, Disk, and available on Lexis, LegiSlate and America Online
Coverage: US

Name/Desc: Federal Staff Directory
Info Provided: Addresses/Telephone Numbers
Media: Publication, CD-ROM and available on Lexis.
Coverage: US

Name/Desc: Judicial Staff Directory (Federal)
Info Provided: Addresses/Telephone Numbers
Media: Publication, CD-ROM and available on Lexis
Coverage: US

Name/Desc: Military Personnel (Active-US)
Info Provided: Addresses/Telephone Numbers
Media: CD-ROM
Coverage: US

Membership: AALL, ALA, SLA, PLA

Statement of Capabilities: Staff Directories is a leading publisher of directory information about federal employees, including Congress, the federal judiciary, and the US military.

Credit-Facts of America
650 Smithfield Street, #1850
Pittsburgh, PA 15222
Telephone: **Fax:**
800-233-4747   800-332-2317
412-232-3232   412-232-0903
www.cfacts.com

Clientele: Financial Institutions, Public Record Research Firms, Legal Profession

Applications: Asset/Lien Searching/Verification, Real Estate Transactions, Background Info - Individuals, Filing/Recording Documents

Information Types:
Real Estate/Assessor (US)
Litigation/Judgments/Tax Liens (US)
Uniform Commercial Code (US)
Bankruptcy (US)
Vital Records (US)
Credit Information (US)

Membership: NHEMA, NAC, MBAA

Statement of Capabilities: Credit-Facts of America is a national real estate information agency. For more than a decade they have offered abstract/property/title searches, other real estate related services, and a variety of document services to the financial services industry. They provide an online system for placing orders.

CrimeLine Information Systems
113 Latigo Lane
Canon City, CO 81212
Telephone: **Fax:**
800-332-7999   800-462-5823
www.cdrominvestigations.com
caligast@rmi.net
Parent Company: Interstate Data Corp
Year Founded: 1987

Clientele: Attorney Firms, Business - General, Credit Grantors, Collection Agencies, Government Agencies, Information - Brokers/Retrievers, Private Investigators

Applications: Background Info - Individuals, General Business Information, Legal Compliance, Litigation, Locating People/Businesses

Information Types:
Social Security (Numbers) (US)
Addresses/Telephone Numbers (US)
Criminal Information (US)

Proprietary Products:
Name/Desc: CA Criminal
Info Provided: Criminal Information
Media: CD-ROM, Direct Online and Call back
Coverage: AZ, CA, CO

Name/Desc: CA Professional Licenses
Info Provided: Licenses/Registration/Permits
Media: CD-ROM, Direct Online and Call back
Coverage: CA

Name/Desc: CA Corporate Records
Info Provided: Corporate/Trade Name Data
Media: CD-ROM, Direct Online and Call back
Coverage: CA

Statement of Capabilities: Crimeline provides a criminal background checking database as well as research on corporate requirements, professional licenses, Board of Equalization, fictitious business names, and others. Features online and CD-ROM technology at competitive prices.

Free Web Information:
Lists of investigators.

CrimeSearch Inc
4433 W Touhy Ave #402
Lincolnwood, IL 60646

Telephone: **Fax:**
888-679-9595   888-679-9616
847-679-9595   847-679-9616
www.crimesearch.com

custserv@crimesearch.com

Clientele: Government Agencies, Information - Brokers/Retrievers, Legal Profession, Private Investigators, Public Record Research Firms, Legal Service Companies

Applications: Background Info - Individuals, Employment Screening, Litigation, Government Document Retrieval, Tenant Screening

Information Types:
Criminal Information (US)
Litigation/Judgments/Tax Liens (US)
Workers' Compensation (il)

Membership: SHRM, ASIS

Statement of Capabilities: CrimeSearch provides access to criminal records through its network of more than 750 researchers. CrimeSearch obtains information that is valuable for future hiring decisions and is active with the courts, law enforcement, corrections, and prosecution fields. CrimeSearch processes thousands of requests monthly in a system designed with the customer in mind, taking the worry out of whether you are going to get results or not.

Criminal Information Services Inc
PO Box 7235
Aloha, OR 97007-7235

Telephone: **Fax:**
800-973-5500   503-642-7730
503-591-1355
www.criminalinfo.com/cris/in
    dex/htm

crim@earthlink.net

Year Founded: 1993

Clientele: Apartment Owners/Managers, Business - General, Information - Brokers/Retrievers, Credit Reporting Agencies, Tenant Screening Companies, Landlords, Employers (HR/Personnel Depts)

Applications: Background Info - Business, Background Info - Individuals, Employment Screening, Tenant Screening, Volunteer Screening

Proprietary Products:
Name/Desc: CRIS
Info Provided: Criminal Information
Media: Direct Online, Internet
Coverage: AZ, OR, WA, ID, UT, TX

Statement of Capabilities: Criminal Information Services Inc (CRIS) offers Internet access to state-wide Department of Corrections conviction history databases from six states including OR, WA, ID, UT, AZ and TX. More states will be added in the near future. Owned and operated by former criminal-justice professionals, CRIS provides real-time access to these databases, by alpha search and birthdate comparison, with "hits" providing conviction date, county of offense, offense description and sentencing information. Reports, including "No Record Found" reports are easy to print. Prices, based on a name check basis and monthly volume, are very inexpensive and affordable.

CSC, The United States Corporation Company
1013 Centre Rd
Wilmington, DE 19805

Telephone: **Fax:**
800-927-9800   302-998-7078
302-998-0595
www.cscinfo.com

Parent Company: Corporation Service Company
Year Founded: 1899

Clientele: Financial Institutions, Legal Profession, Public Record Research Firms

Applications: Legal Compliance, Asset/Lien Searching/Verification, Lending/Leasing, Litigation

Information Types:
Bankruptcy (US)
Litigation/Judgments/Tax Liens (US)
Corporate/Trade Name Data (US)
Driver and/or Vehicle (US)
Trademarks/Patents (US)
Uniform Commercial Code (US)

Membership: NPRRA

Statement of Capabilities: CSC provides national and international incorporating and registered agent services. In addition, they conduct UCC searches and retrieve file copies at state and county levels in all states. Their network of branches and correspondents in the

US and in foreign countries retrieves public information at all levels and on an expedited basis. CSC also offers Windows-based software to improve legal workload management, including CSCDIRECT for corporate filing and research, UCCXPRESS for UCC filings, and Secretariat for corporate secretary management.

Free Web Information:
Outlines for subscribers; subscription is free.

D

DAC Services
4110 S 100th East Ave
Tulsa, OK 74146-3639
Telephone: **Fax:**
800-331-9175   918-664-4366
918-664-9991
www.dacservices.com

Year Founded: 1981

Clientele: Employers (HR/Personnel Depts), Insurance - Agents/Brokers, Insurance - General

Applications: Insurance Underwriting, Employment Screening, Risk Management, Fraud Prevention/Detection

Information Types:
Credit Information (US)
Criminal Information (US)
Workers' Compensation (US)

Proprietary Products:

Name/Desc: Transportation Employment History; Drug/Alcohol Test Results, Security Guard Employment History
Info Provided: Education/Employment
Media: Online Database
Coverage: US

Name/Desc: Driving Records
Info Provided: Driver and/or Vehicle
Media: Online Database
Coverage: US

Name/Desc: 20/20 Insight
Info Provided: Criminal Information
Media: Online Database

Name/Desc: Claims and Injury Reports

Info Provided: Workers' Compensation
Media: Online Database
Coverage: AR, FL, IA, IL, KS, MA, MD, ME, MI, MS, ND, NE, OH, OK, OR, TX

Membership: SIIA, SHRM, AAMVA, ATA

Statement of Capabilities: DAC has serviced employers and insurance businesses for more than 15 years, providing employment screening and underwriting/risk assessment tools. CDLIST contains summary information on more than 6,000,000 drivers. Customers request information by PC and modem via toll-free lines. Computer access is available through networks and mainframe-to-mainframe connections. Customers may opt to call or fax requests to their service representative toll-free.

Daily Report, The
310 H Street
Bakersfield, CA 93304-2914
Telephone: **Fax:**
800-803-6127   805-322-9084
805-322-3226
www.thedailyreport.com
inquires@thedailyreport.com

Clientele: Accountants, Attorney Firms, Business - General, Financial Institutions, Consumers (Individuals), Legal Profession

Applications: Background Info - Business, Background Info - Individuals, Direct Marketing, Filing/Recording Documents, Competitive Intelligence

Information Types:
Addresses/Telephone Numbers (CA-Kern)
Bankruptcy (CA)
Credit Information (CA-Kern)
Litigation/Judgments/Tax Liens (CA-Kern)
Tenant History (CA-Kern)
Uniform Commercial Code (CA-Kern)
Vital Records (CA-Kern)

Proprietary Products:

Name/Desc: The Daily Report
Info Provided: Addresses/Telephone Numbers, Licenses/Registrations/Permits, Criminal Information, Litigation/Judgments/Tax Liens
Media: Internet
Coverage: CA

Free Web Information:
The Daily Report web site features a searchable database of information complied from courts and offices of Kern County. Most

of the information is placed on the site within 72 hours of filling or recording. Included are most documents recorded in Kern County, civil suits and judgments from Superior and Municipal Courts, plus bankruptcies, building permits and business licenses.

Dane County Legal Notice

139 W Wilson St #106
Madison, WI 53703

Telephone: **Fax:**
800-720-6871   608-251-8999
608-251-1181

Year Founded: 1977

Clientele: Legal Profession, Public Record Research Firms, Real Estate Owners/Managers

Applications: Locating People/Businesses, Background Info - Individuals, Filing/Recording Documents, Legal Compliance, Background Info - Business

Information Types:
Bankruptcy (WI-Western Dist)
Litigation/Judgments/Tax Liens (WI-Dane, Western Dist)
Corporate/Trade Name Data (WI-Dane)
Uniform Commercial Code (WI)
Litigation/Judgments/Tax Liens (WI)
Driver and/or Vehicle (WI)
Vital Records (WI)

Membership: NAPPS, NPRRA

Statement of Capabilities: Dane County Legal Notice primarily searches for information in local records such as UCC and criminal/civil records on both federal and circuit courts. They find and copy records at state level i.e. Commissioner of Insurance, Securities, Department of National Resources, Supreme Court, etc. They also do searches for driver and vehicle records and vital statistics for birth, death and marriage records. Most work is completed within 2 working days.

Data Screen Inc

6239 Oakmont Blvd #398
Ft Worth, TX 76132

Telephone: **Fax:**
817-294-7671   817-294-0773

Year Founded: 1991

Applications: Employment Screening, Tenant Screening

Information Types:
Criminal Information (TX)
Driver and/or Vehicle (TX)

Statement of Capabilities: Data Screen is a licensed investigations company specializing in criminal background checks in Texas. Reports from major counties are available in 24 hours or less. Most other counties are available in 24-48 hours. MVR reports are also available.

Data Search Kentucky

1374 Ouerbacker Ct
Louisville, KY 40208

Telephone: **Fax:**
502-637-4658   502-637-4495

Year Founded: 1989

Clientele: Financial Institutions, Legal Profession, Public Record Research Firms

Applications: Asset/Lien Searching/Verification, Legal Compliance, Background Info - Business, Litigation, Filing/Recording Documents

Information Types:
Uniform Commercial Code (KY)
Litigation/Judgments/Tax Liens (KY)
Bankruptcy (KY)
Corporate/Trade Name Data (KY)
Deed & Mortgage Research & Retrieval (KY)

Statement of Capabilities: Data Search Kentucky specializes in UCC, tax lien, and judgment searches as well as document filing at the Kentucky Secretary of State, and at counties in the state through correspondents. They also provide certificates of good standing for Kentucky corporations.

Database Technologies Inc

4530 Blue Lake Dr
Boca Raton, FL 33431

Telephone: **Fax:**
800-279-7710   561-982-5872
561-982-5000

Parent Company: DBT Online Inc

Clientele: Attorney Firms, Government Agencies, Corporate Security

Applications: Employment Screening, Fraud Prevention/Detection, General Business Information, Government Document Retrieval, Litigation

Proprietary Products:
Name/Desc: AutoTrack PLUS

Info Provided: Driver and/or Vehicle, Addresses/Telephone Numbers, Real Estate Assessor, Corporate/Trade Name Data
Media: Direct Online
Coverage: US

Name/Desc: AutoTrack XP
Info Provided: Driver and/or Vehicle
Media: Direct Online
Coverage: US

Statement of Capabilities: From a personal computer, Database Technologies' subscribers gain instant access to billions of publicly available records on individuals and companies. Information from both national and state sources includes: current/past addresses, telephone numbers, relatives, neighbors, assets, corporations and much more. Database Technologies offers these records in a uniquely integrated and cross-referenced system that is instantly accessible seven days a week, 24 hours a day. The system is available to qualified professionals in law enforcement, private investigation, insurance fraud investigation, legal professionals, news media and security investigations. Database Technologies offers two products. AutoTrack PLUS is a DOS-based system with a low per-minute rate. AutoTrack XP is a Windows-based system with a flat-rate for searches and reports.

Datalink

PO Box 188416
Sacramento, CA 95818
Telephone: **Fax:**
800-742-2375 916-452-5096
916-456-7454
www.datalinkservices.com
sales@datalinkservices.com
Year Founded: 1993

Clientele: Legal Profession, Financial Institutions, Collection Agencies, Information - Brokers/Retrievers, Private Investigators, Public Record Research Firms, Loss Prevention Specialists

Applications: Asset/Lien Searching/Verification, Background Info - Business, Employment Screening, Fraud Prevention/Detection, Insurance Underwriting

Information Types:
Addresses/Telephone Numbers (All)
Aviation/Vessels (All)

Criminal Information (CA)
Driver and/or Vehicle (US)
Vital Records (CA)

Proprietary Products:
Name/Desc: Driving, Vehicle & Dealer Records
Info Provided: Driver and/or Vehicle and Dealer Records
Media: Direct Online, Fax-on-Demand, Printed Report and Software
Coverage: US

Statement of Capabilities: Datalink is a public record research firm that accesses records nationwide. Located just 2 blocks from the California DMV, they provide fast, accurate information to clients. They provide electronic record retrieval for California driving and vehicle records and dealer searches through a proprietary software program. They use a nationwide database to access most state DMV records. A commitment to customer service is their top priority. Their staff has over 15 years in the record research industry, providing reliable technical support on searches.

Dataprompt Corporation

7850 Main St
Frisco, TX 75034
Telephone: **Fax:**
800-577-8157 800-340-3854
972-712-1748 972-712-1327
Year Founded: 1993

Clientele: Public Record Research Firms, Employers (HR/Personnel Depts)

Applications: Tenant Screening, Background Info - Business, Employment Screening, Direct Marketing

Information Types:
Credit Information (US)
Criminal Information (US, TX)
Driver and/or Vehicle (US, TX)
Education/Employment (US)
Social Security (Numbers) (US)
Tenant History (US, TX)

Statement of Capabilities: Dataprompt specializes in procuring public records, with the emphasis on criminal records. Using their own system they generate employment and residential background reports as well as develop raw databases for marketing purposes.

DataQuick

9171 Towne Centre Dr #600
San Diego, CA 92122
Telephone:
619-455-6900
www.dataquick.com

Parent Company: Axciom Corporation
Year Founded: 1978

Clientele: Business - General, Financial
Institutions, Real Estate Owners/Managers,
Government Agencies, Lending Institutions,
Mortgage Bankers

Applications: Real Estate Transactions,
Lending/Leasing, Asset/Lien
Searching/Verification, Direct Marketing,
Locating People/Businesses

Information Types:
Real Estate/Assessor (US)
Addresses/Telephone Numbers (US)
Criminal Information (US)
Corporate/Trade Name Data (US)
Environmental (US)

Proprietary Products:

Name/Desc: DataQuick
Info Provided: Real Estate/Assessor
Media: Online, Tape, Disk, Print
Coverage: US

Membership: REIPA

Statement of Capabilities: A leading name in
real property information products,
Axiom/DataCheck services the title, mortgage,
real estate and insurance industries. They
provide property details such as ownership and
address information; sale and loan details,
characteristics such as sq footage, etc; and
historical sales and data such as previous
transactions for marketing and research
purposes. They cover household development
demographics and market trend data.

Free Web Information:
Offers median home sale values by zip code,
allowing users to "trend" home prices.

DataSearch Inc

PO Box 15406
Sacramento, CA 95851
Telephone: **Fax:**
800-452-3282   916-922-5199
916-925-3282
Year Founded: 1930

Clientele: Financial Institutions, Insurance -
Claims, Legal Profession, Public Record
Research Firms, Insurance - Underwriting,
Investigators - Fraud, Private Investigators

Applications: Locating People/Businesses, Legal
Compliance, Litigation, Asset/Lien
Searching/Verification, Background Info -
Business

Information Types:
Bankruptcy (US)
Litigation/Judgments/Tax Liens (US)
Corporate/Trade Name Data (US)
Driver and/or Vehicle (US)
Uniform Commercial Code (US)
Vital Records (US)
Trademarks/Patents (US)
Social Security (Numbers) (US)

Membership: SIIA, NALI, NPRRA

Statement of Capabilities: With
representatives at virtually all levels of federal,
state, and local government, DataSearch is a
nationwide public information and document
retrieval/filing service to the legal, financial,
credit, insurance, investigative, and business
communities. With 14 branches, they provide
expedient delivery of time-sensitive documents
and information in any jurisdiction. They
provide direct online computer access to in-
house data and a growing library of
government records. Their Data Imaging
Center provides copies of official documents.

DataTech Research

726 Wilson Ave.
Green Bay, WI 54303
Telephone: **Fax:**
920-592-9617   920-592-9645
REILAND@NETNET.NET
Year Founded: 1998

Clientele: Business - General, Consulting Firms,
Government Agencies, Product Development
Managers

Applications: Competitive Intelligence, General
Business Information, Government Document
Retrieval

Information Types:
Foreign Country Information
Legislation/Regulation (US)
Licenses/Registrations/Permits (US)
Military Svc (US)

Membership: AIIP, NCMA

Statement of Capabilities: DataTech Research specializes in Federal and State procurement consulting and research, and provides daily observance of State and Federal acquisitions requests, and timely research of government agency forecasts and acquisitions in any market. Navy veteran Mark Reiland has worked with large and small companies in purchasing and defense contract administration. DataTech helps companies do business with the government, providing timely, accurate information on various government agencies.

DCS Information Systems

500 N Central Expressway #280
Plano, TX 75074
Telephone: **Fax:**
800-394-3274   800-299-3647
972-422-3600   972-422-3621
www.dnis.com
Year Founded: 1967

Clientele: Private Investigators, Public Record Research Firms, Insurance - General, Government Agencies, Collection Agencies, Financial Institutions

Applications: Locating People/Businesses, Background Info - Business, Fraud Prevention/Detection, Employment Screening, Asset/Lien Searching/Verification

Proprietary Products:

Name/Desc: DNIS
Info Provided: Addresses/Telephone Numbers, Credit Information (Header), Real Estate Assessor and Driver and/or Vehicle
Media: Online Database
Coverage: US

Name/Desc: Texas Systems
Info Provided: Driver and/or Vehicle, Criminal Convictions, Credit Information (Header) and Real Estate Assessor
Media: Online Database
Coverage: TX

Statement of Capabilities: DCS's premiere product, DNIS (DCS National Inquiry System) is a comprehensive skip tracing and locating tool. Both of their online systems utilize search technology that allows users access to information in ways not available from other providers. DCS offers customized information solutions for large volume users.

Delphic Information Systems

1855 S Pearl #20
Denver, CO 80201
Telephone: **Fax:**
303-777-1411   888-533-5744
                   303-777-2567
www.DELPHICINFO.com
CBRAY@DELPHICINFO.COM
Year Founded: 1997

Clientele: Business - General

Applications: Asset/Lien Searching/Verification, Background Info - Individuals, Background Info - Business, Current Events

Information Types:
Criminal Information (US)
Credit Information (US)
Addresses/Telephone Numbers (US)
Litigation/Judgments/Tax Liens (US)

Statement of Capabilities: Delphic Information Systems is a national provider of public records throughout the US, including civil, criminal, driving, vehicle, corporate, asset, real property, telephone and media (i.e. news and current events).

Derwent Information

1725 Duke Street #250
Alexandria, VA 22314
Telephone: **Fax:**
800-337-9368   703-838-0450
703-706-4220
www.derwent.com
info@derwent.com
Year Founded: 1952

Clientele: Business - General, Consulting Firms, Educational Institutions, Government Agencies, Information - Brokers/Retrievers, Product Development Managers, Corporate Counsel

Applications: Background Info - Business, Competitive Intelligence, Legal Compliance, Lending/Leasing, Current Events

Proprietary Products:

Name/Desc: Derwent World Patents Index Derwent World Patent Index
Info Provided: Trademarks/Patents, Corporate/Trade Name Data
Media: Direct Online, Internet, Publication/Directory, Printed Report,
Coverage: US, International

Name/Desc: Patent Explorer
Info Provided: Trademarks/Patents, Corporate/Trade Name Data
Media: US, International
Coverage: US, International

Statement of Capabilities: With offices in London, Tokyo, and Alexandria, Derwent provides international patent information and recruitment data oriented to chemicals, engineering, and pharmacies. They are the parent company to The Thomson Corporation. Online hosts include Dialog Corp, Questel.Orbit, DIMDI, and STN as well as their own various media and networks, some customized to client's needs.

Free Web Information:
Derwent's Patent Explorer is downloadable via web browser, offering access to patents easily.

Dialog Corporation, The

2440 W El Camino Real
Mountain View, CA 94040
Telephone: **Fax:**
800-334-2564   650-254-7070
650-254-7000
www.dialog.com

Year Founded: 1972

Clientele: Legal Profession, Financial Planners, Consulting Firms, Investment Bankers, Educational Institutions, Libraries, Information - Brokers/Retrievers

Applications: General Business Information, Competitive Intelligence, Direct Marketing, Government Document Retrieval, Background Info - Business

Proprietary Products:

Name/Desc: Profound; DIALOG Web
Info Provided: Foreign Country Information, Corporate/Trade Name Data, Trademarks/Patents, Legislation/Regulation, SEC/Other Financial
Media: Direct Online, Internet, CD-ROM, Software
Coverage: US, International

Name/Desc: Profound LiveWire
Info Provided: News/Current Events
Media: Online
Coverage: US

Statement of Capabilities: The Dialog Corporation provides comprehensive, authoritative sources of information to professionals worldwide. The company was created by the merger of MAID plc and Knight-Rider Information Inc. The Dialog Corporation's complete line of Internet, intranet, CD-ROM and Windows-based products and services have been designed to specifically address individual as well as enterprise-wide information solutions. They include DIALOGWeb, DataStar Web, DIALOG Select, Profound, DIALOG@Site, and Profound LiveWire.

Free Web Information:
Information and products lists.

Disclosure Incorporated

5161 River Rd
Bethesda, MD 20816
Telephone: **Fax:**
800-945-3647   301-657-1962
301-951-1300
www.disclosure.com

Year Founded: 1968

Clientele: Financial Institutions, Libraries, Educational Institutions, Accountants, Legal Profession, Consulting Firms, Attorney Firms

Applications: Background Info - Business, Competitive Intelligence, General Business Information, Legal Compliance, Litigation

Information Types:
Trademarks/Patents (US)
Bankruptcy (US)
Legislation/Regulation (US)

Proprietary Products:

Name/Desc: Compact D/SEC
Info Provided: SEC/Other Financial
Media: CD-ROM, Magnetic Tape, Online Database, Microfiche and Publication
Coverage: US

Name/Desc: Compact D/Canada
Info Provided: SEC/Other Financial
Media: CD-ROM and Publication
Coverage: CD

Name/Desc: Compact D/'33
Info Provided: SEC/Other Financial
Media: CD-ROM
Coverage: US

Name/Desc: Laser D SEC
Info Provided: SEC/Other Financial
Media: CD-ROM
Coverage: US

Name/Desc: Laser D International
Info Provided: SEC/Other Financial
Media: CD-ROM
Coverage: US, International

Name/Desc: Worldscope Global
Info Provided: SEC/Other Financial
Media: CD-ROM, Magnetic Tape, Online Database and Publication
Coverage: US, International

Membership: SIIA

Statement of Capabilities: Disclosure has specialized in public company information over the past 20 years. Their newest product, Global Access, provides online access to all EDGAR files. Disclosure's information products have grown from SEC documents filed by US public companies to include virtually every document available to the public. A subsidiary, FDR Information Centers, provides search and retrieval services. Disclosure was the first company to offer SEC documents via CD-ROM. Disclosure later teamed with Wright Investors' Service to provide Worldscope, an extensive database of international companies.

Diversified Information Services Corp
111 W Monroe St #720
Phoenix, AZ 85003-1720
Telephone: **Fax:**
602-256-0961   602-256-2074
www.discplats.qpg.com
discplats@aol.com
Year Founded: 1970

Clientele: Consulting Firms, Financial Institutions, Information - Brokers/Retrievers, Legal Service Companies, Lending Institutions, Mortgage Bankers, Public Record Research Firms

Applications: Asset/Lien Searching/Verification, Filing/Recording Documents, Insurance Underwriting, Real Estate Transactions

Information Types:
Bankruptcy (AZ)
Corporate/Trade Name Data (AZ)
Litigation/Judgments/Tax Liens (AZ)

Proprietary Products:
Name/Desc: Real Property Records
Info Provided: Real Estate/Assessor

Media: Online, Disk, CD-ROM, Printed Report, Fax
Coverage: AZ-Maricopa

Membership: ALTA

Statement of Capabilities: Diversified Information Services is owned by North American Title Agency, Old Republic Title Insurance Agency, Transnation Title, Lawyers Title of Arizona, Fidelity National Title Agency, Stewart Title & Trust of Phoenix, and Nations Title Agency.

DJ Records
PO Box 753597
Memphis, TN 38175-3597
Telephone: **Fax:**
901-795-6450   901-362-8320
Year Founded: 1996

Clientele: Employers (HR/Personnel Depts), Public Record Research Firms

Applications: Background Info - Individuals, Employment Screening, Tenant Screening

Information Types:
Criminal Information (TN)

Statement of Capabilities: DJ Records is a Tennessee search firm that specializes in researching for criminal information for use by employers and tenant screeners

Doc*U*Search Inc
PO Box 777
Concord, NH 03302-0777
Telephone: **Fax:**
800-332-3034   603-224-2794
603-224-2871
Year Founded: 1976

Clientele: Business - General, Financial Institutions, Legal Profession

Applications: Legal Compliance, Lending/Leasing, Real Estate Transactions, General Business Information

Information Types:
Bankruptcy (US, MA, NH)
Litigation/Judgments/Tax Liens (US, MA, NH)
Corporate/Trade Name Data (US, MA, NH)
Uniform Commercial Code (US, MA, NH)
Real Estate/Assessor (NH)
Vital Records (MA, NH)

Statement of Capabilities: Doc*U*Search provides information and document retrieval services at all federal, state, county and local offices, specializing in Massachusetts and New Hampshire public records.

Doc-U-Search Hawaii

1188 Bishop St #2212
Honolulu, HI 96813-3309
Telephone: **Fax:**
808-523-1200   808-533-3686

Applications: Asset/Lien Searching/Verification, Filing/Recording Documents, Background Info - Business, Legal Compliance, Litigation

Information Types:
Uniform Commercial Code (US, HI)
Litigation/Judgments/Tax Liens (US, HI)
Bankruptcy (US, HI)
Vital Records (US, HI)
Criminal Information (US, HI)
Corporate/Trade Name Data (US, HI)

Statement of Capabilities: Doc-U-Search Hawaii is located close to all city, state and federal agencies in Honolulu, providing clients with quick turnaround times.

Don C. Haworth & Associates Inc

53 W Jackson #715
Chicago, IL 60604
Telephone: **Fax:**
817-426-4278   312-362-0533
312-362-0530
www.falconpi.com
FALCONPI@aol.com
Year Founded: 1993

Clientele: Collection Agencies, Corporate Security, Employers (HR/Personnel Depts), Insurance - Claims, Legal Profession, Legal Service Companies, Private Investigators

Applications: Asset/Lien Searching/Verification, Background Info - Individuals, Employment Screening, Fraud Prevention/Detection, General Business Information

Information Types:
Addresses/Telephone Numbers (US)
Bankruptcy (US)
Corporate/Trade Name Data (US)
Credit Information
Criminal Information (IL)
Driver and/or Vehicle (IL)
Education/Employment (US)
Litigation/Judgments/Tax Liens (IL-Cook)

Membership: ACFE, ASIS, CII, NICA, NABEA

Statement of Capabilities: Don C. Haworth & Assoc provides a wide variety of database searches from the usual to the most unusual. They offer a wide array of investigative services throughout the Midwest.

Due Diligence Inc

PO Box 8366
Missoula, MT 59807
Telephone: **Fax:**
800-644-0107   406-728-0006
406-728-0001
www.diligence.com
rleblanc@diligence.com

Clientele: Consumers (Individuals), Employers (HR/Personnel Depts), Legal Service Companies, Information - Brokers/Retrievers, Public Record Research Firms, Educational Institutions

Applications: Background Info - Individuals, Employment Screening, General Business Information, Insurance Underwriting, Tenant Screening

Information Types:
Criminal Information (US)

Statement of Capabilities: Due Diligence Inc specializes in the acquisition of criminal records throughout the United States, directly utilizing a network of over 2000 local researchers. Orders may be placed by phone, fax, mail, e-mail, secure webform, FTP, Electronic Data Interchange, or through their proprietary CrimeCheck software. Their average turnaround time is 1.5 days.

Dun & Bradstreet

1 Diamond Hill Rd
Murray Hill, NJ 07974
Telephone:
800-234-3867
908-665-5000
www.dnb.com

Clientele: Business - General, Financial Institutions, Legal Profession

Applications: Risk Management, General Business Information, Asset/Lien Searching/Verification, Background Info - Business

Proprietary Products:

Name/Desc: D & B Public Record Search
Info Provided: Addresses/Telephone Numbers, Bankruptcy, Corporate/Trade Name Data, Credit Information, Litigation/Judgments/Tax Liens and Uniform Commercial Code
Media: Call-in Only, Direct Online, Internet, Printed Report, Software and Disk
Coverage: US

Name/Desc: Business Credit Information
Info Provided: Credit Information
Media: Online Database and Call-Back
Coverage: US

Membership: NPRRA

Statement of Capabilities: Dun & Bradstreet's Public Records Search database is one of the most extensive commercial public record information sites available. It is probably the only online database of corporate, UCC, litigation and tax lien information about businesses that covers all 50 states, the Virgin Islands, Puerto Rico and the District of Columbia. The 800 number listed above is for business credit information.

E

E D Loven & Associates

3033 Roberts Cutoff
Ft Worth, TX 76135
Telephone: **Fax:**
888-320-7684   817-847-9582
817-847-9581

mlpserv@flash.net
Year Founded: 1996

Clientele: Apartment Owners/Managers, Business - General, Consumers (Individuals), Legal Profession, Private Investigators, Public Record Research Firms, Employers (HR/Personnel Depts)

Applications: Background Info - Business, Background Info - Individuals, Employment Screening, Litigation, Tenant Screening

Information Types:
Credit Information (US)

Criminal Information (US)
Driver and/or Vehicle (TX)
Education/Employment (US)
Litigation/Judgments/Tax Liens (TX-Tarrant)
Military Svc (TX-Tarrant)
Social Security (Numbers) (US)
Voter Registration (TX-Dallas, Tarrant)

Statement of Capabilities: E D Loven & Assoc. DIS/FTWD, concentrates on employment screening, criminal/civil background checks, verifying employment and education, Texas MVR and Drivers' Licenses, SSNs, voter registration and credit reports for employment. Licensed, bonded, with 17 years experience in legal field, also 10 in USAF as Info Specialist. Can provide results within hours; very prompt and available.

EL-RU Inc

2141 Brooks Rd
Dacula, GA 30211
Telephone: **Fax:**
770-963-8023   770-682-1885
Year Founded: 1986

Clientele: Legal Profession, Financial Institutions, Public Record Research Firms, Credit Reporting Agencies

Applications: Background Info - Individuals, Employment Screening, Filing/Recording Documents, Litigation, Real Estate Transactions

Information Types:
Bankruptcy (GA)
Litigation/Judgments/Tax Liens (GA)
Corporate/Trade Name Data (GA)
Criminal Information (GA)
Real Estate/Assessor (GA)
Uniform Commercial Code (GA)
Voter Registration (GA)

Membership: NPRRA

Statement of Capabilities: EL-RU specializes in retrieving and filing documents in Georgia.

Electronic Property Information Corp (EPIC)

227 Alexander St #206
Rochester, NY 14607
Telephone: **Fax:**
716-454-7390   716-454-7409
Year Founded: 1987

Clientele: Financial Institutions, Insurance - Agents/Brokers, Insurance - General, Legal Profession, Public Record Research Firms

Applications: Real Estate Transactions, Insurance Underwriting, Asset/Lien Searching/Verification, Background Info - Business, Background Info - Individuals

Proprietary Products:

Name/Desc: OPRA
Info Provided: Real Estate Assessor, Uniform Commerical Code, Litigation/Judgments/Tax Liens and Wills/Probate
Media: Online Database
Coverage: NY-Erie, Monroe Counties

Name/Desc: OPRA
Info Provided: Bankruptcy
Media: Online Database
Coverage: NY-Northern & Western Districts

Statement of Capabilities: EPIC provides online access to their proprietary database of all public records affecting real property in Erie and Monroe Counties, NY and bankruptcy records for New York's Western and Northern Districts. In addition to helping create abstracts and write title insurance, the database has been used for collections, asset search, and individual and business screening applications.

Empire Data Systems Inc

2079-A Wantagh Ave #1
Wantagh, NY 11793
Telephone: **Fax:**
800-955-7448 800-955-7450
516-221-1900 516-221-1985
Year Founded: 1977

Clientele: Public Record Research Firms, Employers (HR/Personnel Depts), Legal Profession, Professionals-Other

Applications: Asset/Lien Searching/Verification, Employment Screening, Background Info - Business, Background Info - Individuals, Locating People/Businesses

Information Types:
Addresses/Telephone Numbers (US)
Bankruptcy (US)
Corporate/Trade Name Data (US)
Criminal Information (US, CA, PR)
Driver and/or Vehicle (US)
Credit Information (US)
Litigation/Judgments/Tax Liens (US)

Membership: NPRRA

Statement of Capabilities: Empire Data Systems accesses federal, national, state and municipal databases. Available information includes standard and demographic records. Credit information enables them to provide an instant locator service, SSN identification, address and resident data. Business searches include credit and business locator information. Also, they provide driving records and MV data for all states. No special software or equipment is necessary to use their service.

Environmental Data Resources Inc

3530 Post Rd
Southport, CT 06490
Telephone: **Fax:**
800-352-0050 800-231-6802
203-255-6606 203-255-1976
www.edrnet.com
Year Founded: 1991

Clientele: Financial Institutions, Legal Profession, Government Agencies, Real Estate Owners/Managers, Professionals-Other, Engineers

Applications: Real Estate Transactions, Risk Management

Proprietary Products:

Name/Desc: NEDIS, WasteMonitor, Sanborn Maps
Info Provided: Environmental, Licenses/Registratoins/Permits, and Real Estate Assessor
Media: Online Database, Call-in
Coverage: US

Statement of Capabilities: Environmental Data Resources (EDR) is an information company specializing in providing data on environmental liabilities associated with companies and properties. EDR provides this data to environmental consulting firms, banks, insurance companies, law firms, corporations and accounting firms. EDR has compiled and organized more than 600 separate government databases, obtained at the federal, state and local levels, into an environmental database referred to as NEDIS, the National Environmental Data Information System. The WasteMonitor database contains detailed information about more than 5000 non-hazardous waste disposal facilities and more than 500 hazardous treatment, storage and disposal facilities. EDR Sanborn owns the largest and most complete collection of fire insurance maps, with more than 12,000 communities surveyed, dating back to the 1800s.

Equifax Credit Services Division

1600 Peachtree St NW
Atlanta, GA 30309
Telephone:
888-202-4025
404-885-8000
www.equifax.com

Parent Company: Equifax Inc
Year Founded: 1899

Clientele: Business - General, Financial Institutions, Employers (HR/Personnel Depts), Insurance - General

Applications: Background Info - Individuals, Employment Screening, Lending/Leasing, Collections

Proprietary Products:

Name/Desc: Acrofile
Info Provided: Credit Information
Media: Direct Online, Internet
Coverage: US

Name/Desc: Persona
Persona
Info Provided: Addresses/Telephone Numbers, Education/Employment, Social Security (Numbers), Credit Information
Media: Direct Online, Internet
Coverage: US

Membership: AAMVA

Statement of Capabilities: Equifax, like its 2 major competitors Experian and Trans Union, provides a full range of consumer credit and related information. Equifax credit services include consumer credit, locate services, fraud detection, and accounts receivable management. They operate globally - in 18 countries with sales in 40. North American Information Services is an Equifax company. Media Relations telephone is 404-888-5452. Consumers may order a credit report at 800-685-1111 or discuss its content at 888-909-7304. Government entities can fax Equifax at 404-885-8215, or e-mail at govetrelequifax.com.

Free Web Information:
Descriptions of services, definitions, clients aides and protocols, request forms.

Equity Title Search

137 N Larchmont Blvd #545
Los Angeles, CA 90004
Telephone: **Fax:**
323-965-0759 323-965-1247
equitytitle@compuserve.com
Year Founded: 1986

Clientele: Collection Agencies, Financial Institutions, Legal Profession, Public Record Research Firms, Real Estate Owners/Managers

Applications: Asset/Lien Searching/Verification, Background Info - Individuals, General Business Information, Locating People/Businesses

Information Types:
Addresses/Telephone Numbers (US, CA)
Wills/Probate (CA)
Real Estate/Assessor (CA)
Tenant History (CA)
Vital Records (CA)
Voter Registration (CA)

Membership: NPRRA, WAD, APG, WIN, NAPPS

Statement of Capabilities: The firm is conveniently located near the main Los Angeles Court and the criminal and federal court buildings. They have immediate access to all California county courts and vital records in Southern California, including Orange, Riverside and San Diego counties. They can access most courts in the Bay area as well. They have a large microfiche library and access to most major databanks.

Everton Publishers

PO Box 368
Logan, UT 84323
Telephone: **Fax:**
800-443-6325
801-752-6022
www.everton.com

Applications: Genealogical Research

Proprietary Products:

Name/Desc: Everton's Online Search
Info Provided: Addresses/Telephone Numbers, Social Security (Numbers)
Media: Online Database
Coverage: US

Statement of Capabilities: Everton Publishers publish "The Genealogical Helper."

ExecuSearch

8910 Sidney Gautreaux
Abbeville, LA 70510
Telephone: **Fax:**
381-893-8712 318-893-1069

execusearch@hotmail.com

Clientele: Educational Institutions, Information - Brokers/Retrievers, Public Record Research Firms

Applications: Background Info - Individuals, Filing/Recording Documents

Information Types:
Criminal Information (LA, TX)

Statement of Capabilities: ExecuSearch offers 24 hour turnaround time in certain Texas counties Dallas, Burleson, Madison, Roberson, Grimes, and Brazos; and Louisiana counties Vermillion and Lafayette.

Experian Business Information Solutions

600 City Parkway West
8th FlOrange, CA 92868
Telephone:
800-831-5614
www.experian.com

Parent Company: Experian
Clientele: Business - General

Applications: Lending/Leasing, Asset/Lien Searching/Verification, Background Info - Business

Proprietary Products:
Name/Desc: Business Credit Information
Info Provided: Uniform Commercial Code, Bankruptcy, Litigation/Judgments/Tax Liens, Corporate/Trade Name Data
Media: Direct Online, Printed Report
Coverage: US

Statement of Capabilities: Experian Business Information Solutions is the business credit arm of Experian. Although this division is located in Orange, CA, they prefer inquiries to go through the main Experian switchboard (800-831-5614 in Allen, TX) first, then allow access to the California site at 714-385-7000.

Experian Consumer Credit

425 Martingale Rd #600
Schaumburg, IL 60173
Telephone:
800-831-5614
www.experian.com

Parent Company: Experian
Clientele: Business - General

Applications: Lending/Leasing, Employment Screening, Tenant Screening

Proprietary Products:
Name/Desc: Consumer File
Consumer File
Info Provided: Credit Information, Addresses/Telephone Numbers
Media: Direct Online, Printed Report
Coverage: US

Statement of Capabilities: As the consumer credit arm of Experian, formerly TRW, data from here may be used for a variety of purposes related to individuals, subject to permissible purposes. Individuals who need assistance with reports should call 888-397-3742.

Experian Target Marketing Services

701 Experian Parkway
Allen, TX 70013
Telephone: **Fax:**
800-527-3933 972-390-5001
972-390-5000
www.experian.com

Parent Company: Experian

Clientele: Business - General

Applications: Direct Marketing

Information Types:
Addresses/Telephone Numbers (US)
Driver and/or Vehicle (US)

Proprietary Products:
Name/Desc: Various Experian Databases
Various Experian Databases
Info Provided: Addresses/Telephone Numbers, Driver and/or Vehicle
Media: Disk, Magnetic Tape, Printed Report
Coverage: US

Statement of Capabilities: Experian Target Marketing Services is a list compiler that utilizes Experian's overall information - collected from such sources as the NCOA file - to provide support to direct marketers to businesses and individuals. Their MV database includes 42+ million vehicle owners and vehicle characteristics in 32 states and is available when and where legally permissible. Combining vehicle selections with their demographic, lifestyle, and other selections allows for higher focused targeting. Other Experian divisions are profiled separately.

Explore Information Services

4920 Moundview Dr
Red Wing, MN 55066

Telephone: **Fax:**
800-531-9125   612-385-2281
612-385-2284
www.exploredata.com

Clientele: Insurance - Agents/Brokers

Applications: Insurance Underwriting

Proprietary Products:

Name/Desc: EARS
Info Provided: Driver and/or Vehicle
Media: Online, Magnetic Tape and Disk
Coverage: CO, FL, IA, KY, ME, MN, MO, NE, NH, OH, TN, UT, WI

Statement of Capabilities: Their Electronically Accessed Reunderwriting Service (EARS), is a database of driver information, including violation history, that can be customized for use by insurance industry clients. RiskAlert is a service that identifies all licensed drivers in a household.

F

FACS Information Service

PO Box 33
Eastchester, NY 10709

Telephone: **Fax:**
800-424-9428   888-779-7038
914-779-5314   914-779-7038
ppi2@juno.com
Year Founded: 1971

Clientele: Financial Institutions, Legal Profession

Applications: General Business Information, Employment Screening

Information Types:
Credit Information (US)
Criminal Information (US)
SEC/Other Financial (US)
Trademarks/Patents (US)

Statement of Capabilities: Unlike other search firms, FACS Information Service can obtain specific parts of a filing such as an amendment or an exhibit of a 10K without requiring the client to take the entire report.

Factel Inc

3845 N Andrews Ave
Oakland Park, FL 33309

Telephone: **Fax:**
800-780-9888   888-432-2835
954-564-3282   954-564-9095
www.factel.com

Year Founded: 1991

Clientele: Attorney Firms, Insurance - Claims

Applications: Asset/Lien Searching/Verification, Background Info - Business, Background Info - Individuals, Fraud Prevention/Detection, Insurance Claims Investigation

Information Types:
Bankruptcy (US-46 states)
Corporate/Trade Name Data (US-43 States)
Criminal Information (US)
Driver and/or Vehicle (US-28 states)
Litigation/Judgments/Tax Liens (US)

Statement of Capabilities: Factel specializes in speedy reporting. Clients can select from any of 55 different 1-hour or same day services that include a captioned report and hard copy documentation of records found. Examples include: the Basic Asset and Liability Report that accesses 10 completely independent sources; the Basic Locate Report, providing results of searches from 7 different sources; and the Basic Background Report, comprising 16 individual searches, including county civil and criminal record checks. Clientele is limited to insurance companies, insurance attorneys, other insurance professionals and businesses.

Fairchild Record Search Ltd

PO Box 1368
Olympia, WA 98507

Telephone: **Fax:**
800-547-7007   800-433-3404
360-786-8775   360-943-6656
www.recordsearch.com

Year Founded: 1980

Applications: General Business Information, Filing/Recording Documents, Lending/Leasing, Locating People/Businesses, Real Estate Transactions

Information Types:
Uniform Commercial Code (US, AK, ID, OR, WA)
Corporate/Trade Name Data (US, AK, ID, OR, WA)
Litigation/Judgments/Tax Liens (US, AK, ID, OR, WA)
Bankruptcy (US, AK, ID, OR, WA)
Driver and/or Vehicle (US, AK, ID, OR, WA)
Aviation/Vessels (US, AK, ID, OR, WA)
Vital Records (US, AK, ID, OR, WA)

Membership: NPRRA, NFIB

Statement of Capabilities: Fairchild has specialized in public record retrieval in the US Northwest and in Alaska for more than 15 years. Primary capabilities include UCC/corporate document filing, retrieval and searching. Due to their long presence in the area they have established experience in filing and retrieval of virtually any public record documents in those states.

FAR Retriever Bureau

PO Box 377
Paw Paw, MI 49079
Telephone: **Fax:**
616-657-2166 616-657-6566
Year Founded: 1991

Clientele: Financial Institutions, Real Estate Owners/Managers, Investment Bankers, Mortgage Bankers

Applications: Filing/Recording Documents, Real Estate Transactions

Information Types:
Real Estate/Assessor (MI)

Statement of Capabilities: The owner of FAR has been in the public record retrieval business since 1968, specializing in SW lower Michigan.

Federal Filings Inc

601 Pennsylvania Ave NW
South Bldg #700Washington, DC 20004-2601
Telephone: **Fax:**
800-487-6162 202-393-0974

202-393-7400
www.fedfil.com
Parent Company: Dow Jones & Co
Year Founded: 1987

Clientele: Financial Institutions, Legal Profession, Business - General, Professionals-Other

Applications: General Business Information, Litigation, Legal Compliance

Proprietary Products:
Name/Desc: EDGAR
Info Provided: SEC/Other Financial
Media: Online Database
Coverage: US

Name/Desc: Federal Filings Business News
Info Provided: News/Current Events
Media: Online Database, Newsletters
Coverage: US

Statement of Capabilities: Federal Filings provides a number of different services based on access to federal records, including SEC filings, bankruptcy and civil court cases, and research at other federal agencies in Washington, DC such as the FCC. SEC services include monitoring specific public company filings. Court services include monitoring companies for new cases and new pleadings in existing cases. Copies of 10Ks and 10Qs may be ordered through their online system. Federal Filings also has a library of bankruptcy documents dating back to 1988.

Free Web Information:
Financial investment-oriented news and information.

Felonies R Us

1423 W 3rd #21
Little Rock, AR 72201
Telephone: **Fax:**
501-376-4719 510-376-4619
Year Founded: 1998

Applications: Employment Screening, Fraud Prevention/Detection, General Business Information, Litigation, Tenant Screening

Proprietary Products:
Name/Desc: AR Felonies
Info Provided: Criminal Information
Media: Fax-on-Demand and Printed Report
Coverage: AR

Statement of Capabilities: Felonies 'R' Us maintains an updated criminal database obtained from the Arkansas Administrative Office of the Courts. Able to run statewide searches, they retrieve documents desired by the client.

Ferrari

8 Tudor Ct
Buffalo, NY 14068
Telephone: **Fax:**
716-689-6577 716-689-6661
Year Founded: 1978

Clientele: Financial Institutions, Insurance - Agents/Brokers, Legal Profession, Public Record Research Firms, Insurance - Claims, Investigators - Fraud, Secured Lenders

Applications: Lending/Leasing, Employment Screening, Locating People/Businesses, Background Info - Business, Collections

Information Types:
Licenses/Registrations/Permits (US)
Corporate/Trade Name Data (US)
Credit Information (US)
Criminal Information (US)
Workers' Compensation (US)
Social Security (Numbers) (US)
Bankruptcy (US)
Real Estate/Assessor (US)

Membership: NCISS, WAD, ION, PRRN

Statement of Capabilities: Ferrari specializes in the location and identification of hidden, attachable and liquid assets held by individuals and businesses that are subject to seizure for collection, subrogation, bond salvage and other asset recovery matters. They often re-investigate matters already investigated by others.

Fidelifacts

50 Broadway
New York, NY 10004
Telephone: **Fax:**
800-678-0007 212-248-5619
212-425-1520

norton@fidelifacts.com
Year Founded: 1956

Clientele: Business - General, Financial Institutions, Employers (HR/Personnel Depts), Legal Profession, Real Estate Owners/Managers

Applications: Background Info - Business, Background Info - Individuals, Employment Screening, Litigation

Information Types:
Bankruptcy (US)
Litigation/Judgments/Tax Liens (US)
Credit Information (US)
Criminal Information (US)
Driver and/or Vehicle (US)
Education/Employment (US)
Licenses/Registrations/Permits (US)
Military Svc (US)

Proprietary Products:
Name/Desc: Fidelifacts Data Bank
Info Provided: Criminal Information
Media: Call-in
Coverage: NY

Membership: EMA, SHRM, NCISS, ASIS

Statement of Capabilities: Among the oldest companies engaged in the business of providing background reports on individuals for employment purposes and on companies, Fidelifacts has a network of offices around the country, and local personnel who examine public records in less populated areas. Fidelifacts specialty is conducting background investigations, reference checks, screening checks of job applicants and due diligence investigations. They also provide asset location services, skip tracing and other services on legal matters. Their in-house database lists 1,500,000 names of persons arrested, indicted, convicted, and otherwise had problems with the law. Data is primarily for metro New York area, but also includes SEC/NASD filings where unlawful activity may be a question. Note: their office is located 1/2 block from the NY State Office of Court Administration and they have personnel there on a daily basis.

Find People Fast

PO Box 20190
St Louis, MO 63123
Telephone: **Fax:**
800-829-1807 314-631-5785
314-544-5600
www.fpf.com

Parent Company: Infomax, Inc

Year Founded: 1991

Clientele: Attorney Firms, Private Investigators, Business - General, Collection Agencies,

Genealogists, Consumers (Individuals), Legal Profession

Applications: Background Info - Individuals, Litigation, Real Estate Transactions

Information Types:
  Addresses/Telephone Numbers (US)
  Driver and/or Vehicle (US)
  Social Security (Numbers) (US)
  Vital Records (US)

Statement of Capabilities: Find People Fast offers a computerized information service that provides assistance in locating adult individuals in the US. Their extensive database listing on 170 million adults plus multiple additional sources lets them provide very extensive database searches. In addition to maintaining current records, they retain archive records (5-7 years old), which often prove valuable in locating. They provide same day turnaround time for most requests and are reasonably priced. Special searches include death index, neighbor listings, and former participants in clinical studies.

FIND/SVP Inc

625 Avenue of the Americas
New York, NY 10011-2002
Telephone: **Fax:**
212-645-4500   212-645-7681
www.findsvp.com

Year Founded: 1969

Clientele: Business - General, Legal Profession

Applications: General Business Information, Background Info - Business, Competitive Intelligence, Locating People/Businesses, Asset/Lien Searching/Verification

Information Types:
  News/Current Events (US)
  Legislation/Regulation (US)
  Trademarks/Patents (US)
  Bankruptcy (US)
  Foreign Country Information
  Litigation/Judgments/Tax Liens (US)
  SEC/Other Financial (US)

Membership: AIIP, SCIP, SLA, ABA, AICPA, NALFM

Statement of Capabilities: FIND/SVP consultants help executives from all areas of business through their Quick Consulting & Research Service. FIND/SVP has more than 2,000 companies on retainer for whom they handle more than 7,000 questions posed by 13,000 executives every month. The service provides answers within 24-48 hours. One of ten consulting groups, the Legal Research Group, provides public record retrieval, jury verdict searches, legislative history research, legal document retrieval and current awareness services to determine how legislation may effect a particular industry.

Finder Group, The

PO Box 11740
Kansas City, KS 64138
Telephone: **Fax:**
800-501-8455   816-737-5225
816-737-5005

finder@solve.net

Parent Company: Insurance Information Services Inc

Year Founded: 1995

Clientele: Business - General, Collection Agencies, Consulting Firms, Insurance - General, Legal Profession, Consumers (Individuals), Corporate Counsel

Applications: Asset/Lien Searching/Verification, Background Info - Business, Background Info - Individuals, General Business Information, Locating People/Businesses

Information Types:
  Associations/Trade Groups (US)
  Credit Information (US)
  Foreign Country Information (FIX/Sweden, CD, Hong Kong)
  SEC/Other Financial (US)
  Trademarks/Patents (US)

Membership: NAIS, NALI, WAD, GIN

Statement of Capabilities: The Finder Group is a professional search firm designed to bridge the gap between end users and repositories. Economical access to public records includes criminal, civil, MVR, asset, background and address information. A web site is planned with links to sites for public record searching.

First American Real Estate Solutions

5601 E. La Palma Ave
Anaheim, CA 92807
Telephone: **Fax:**
800-345-7334   800-406-2907

714-701-2150   714-701-9231
www.firstAm.com

Parent Company: Formerly w/ Experian; now w/ First American Financial

Clientele: Financial Institutions, Public Record Research Firms, Real Estate Owners/Managers, Government Agencies

Applications: Real Estate Transactions, Lending/Leasing, Asset/Lien Searching/Verification, Background Info - Business, Background Info - Individuals

Proprietary Products:

Name/Desc: Real Property Database
Info Provided: Real Estate/Assessor
Media: Online Database, CD-ROM and Microfiche
Coverage: AL, AZ, CA, CO, DC, DE, FL, GA, HI, IL, IN, LA, MA, MD, MI, MN, MS, NC, NJ, NM, NY, NV, OH, OK, OR, PA, SC, TN, TX, UT, VA, VI, WA, WI

Statement of Capabilities: Now independent of Experian, First American Real Estate Solutions is now part of the First American Financial Corporation. They are a leading provider of real estate information from major counties in most US states. Call for specific coverage and access via online database, CD-ROM and microfiche information.

Free Web Information:
Directory, order forms, service descriptions

FLA Search Company

PO Box 5346
Lake Worth, FL 33466
Telephone: **Fax:**
561-969-6594   561-641-7516
Year Founded: 1985

Applications: Asset/Lien Searching/Verification, Litigation, Filing/Recording Documents, Real Estate Transactions, Background Info - Individuals

Information Types:
Uniform Commercial Code (FL)
Litigation/Judgments/Tax Liens (FL)
Bankruptcy (FL)
Criminal Information (FL)
Voter Registration (FL)
Real Estate/Assessor (FL)

Membership: NPRRA

Statement of Capabilities: FLA Search specializes in searching every court in Florida.

Collectively, employees have more than 50 years of experience in public record research. They are trained to answer any questions about the Florida courts.

FOIA Group Inc

1090 Vermont Ave NW # 800
Washington, DC 20005
Telephone: **Fax:**
202-408-7028   202-347-8419
www.FOIA.com
FOIA@FOIA.com
Year Founded: 1988

Clientele: Attorney Firms, Business - General, Consulting Firms, Corporate Counsel, Financial Institutions, Legal Profession, Libraries

Applications: Competitive Intelligence, Government Document Retrieval, Litigation

Information Types:
Litigation/Judgments/Tax Liens

Proprietary Products:

Name/Desc: FOIA-Ware
Info Provided: Software/Training
Media: Internet, Software and Disk
Coverage: US

Membership: ABA, SCIP

Statement of Capabilities: FOIA specializes in the Freedom of Information Act and State Open Records Act protocols. They help prepare and file FOIA requests, monitor and review documents, and service the legal profession and others seeking information through the Act. They also offer agency and customer competitive research and surveys. FOIA Group attorneys provide whistleblower assistance.

Free Web Information:
FOIA-ware info, forms, products lists

Folks Finders Ltd

PO Box 880, RR1
Neoga, IL 62447
Telephone: **Fax:**
800-277-3318   800-476-0782
217-895-2524   217-895-2418
www.pimall.com/folkfinders/f
olkfind.htm

Parent Company: Lenco Corp of Kentucky @ Paducah

Year Founded: 1974

Clientele: Insurance - General, Legal Profession, Employers (HR/Personnel Depts), Public Record Research Firms

Applications: Locating People/Businesses

Information Types:
Vital Records (US, International)
Social Security (Numbers) (US)
Addresses/Telephone Numbers (US)
Litigation/Judgments/Tax Liens (US)
Military Svc (US)
Criminal Information (US)
Wills/Probate (US)
Genealogical Information (US, International)

Proprietary Products:

Name/Desc: NYC Birth Index
Info Provided: Vital Records, Voter Registration, Workers' Compensation, Tenant History and Genealogical Information
Media: Printed Report
Coverage: NY-New York City

Name/Desc: IL Birth Index
Info Provided: Vital Records, Voter Registration, Workers' Compensation, Tenant History and Genealogical Information
Media: Printed Report
Coverage: IL

Name/Desc: CA Birth Index
Info Provided: Vital Records, Voter Registration, Workers' Compensation, Tenant History and Genealogical Information
Media: Printed Report
Coverage: CA

Name/Desc: Cemetery Internment
Info Provided: Vital Records, Voter Registration, Workers' Compensation, Tenant History and Genealogical Information
Media: Printed Report
Coverage: US

Membership: NAIS, ICFA, NFDA, PRRN

Statement of Capabilities: Folks Finders specializes in finding folks, missing persons, that may not object to being located. Most service charges are based on a "no find, no fee" philosophy. Categories of searches include no-name pension beneficiaries, health-related searches, and adoption searches. As part of their expertise, they obtain and provide vital records worldwide. They have begun "alternate identity" locating.

G

GA Public Record Services Inc
8035 ERL Thornton Fwy #415
Dallas, TX 75228
Telephone: **Fax:**
214-320-9836 214-320-2992
www.gaprs.com

Year Founded: 1989

Clientele: Insurance - Agents/Brokers, Insurance - General, Public Record Research Firms, Corporate Security, Information - Brokers/Retrievers, Private Investigators, Employers (HR/Personnel Depts)

Applications: Employment Screening, Background Info - Individuals, Fraud Prevention/Detection, Tenant Screening, Litigation

Information Types:
Criminal Information (US)
Litigation/Judgments/Tax Liens (US)

Membership: ASIS, SHRM, NPRRA

Statement of Capabilities: GA Public Record Services, a licensed investigation company, specializes in on-site criminal and civil background searches. They have a national network of experienced research professionals, whom they screen and audit on a regular basis to ensure that quality standards are met. They provide free software to allow for efficient and secure exchange of information.

Gale Group Inc, The
27500 Drake Rd
Framington Hills, MI 48331-3535
Telephone:
800-877-4253
248-699-4253
www.gale.com

Parent Company: Thomson Corporation
Year Founded: 1998

Clientele: Business - General, Educational Institutions

Applications: Background Info - Business, Current Events, Genealogical Research

Proprietary Products:

Name/Desc: GaleNet
Info Provided: Associations/Trade Groups, Addresses/Telephone Numbers and Corporate/Trade Name Data
Media: Online Database
Coverage: US, International

Statement of Capabilities: As a major publisher of academic, educational, and business research companies serving libraries, educational institutions, and businesses in all major international markets, The Gale Group provides much of its material online through products such as Associations Unlimited, Biography and Genealogy Master Index, Brands and Their Companies, Gale Business Resources, and Peterson's Publications. It was formed Sept. '98 with the merger of Gale Research, Information Access Co., and Primary Source Material.

Global Intelligence Network Inc

2293 Smoky Park Hwy
Candler, NC 28715
Telephone: **Fax:**
828-665-7115   828-665-7180
www.gini.net
gini@gini.net
Year Founded: 1995

Clientele: Leasing Agents - Personal Property, Employers (HR/Personnel Depts), Private Investigators, Investigators - Fraud, Attorney Firms, Landlords

Applications: Asset/Lien Searching/Verification, Background Info - Individuals, Employment Screening, Locating People/Businesses, Tenant Screening

Information Types:
Addresses/Telephone Numbers (US)
Bankruptcy (US)
Criminal Information (US)
Driver and/or Vehicle (US)
Education/Employment (US)
Foreign Country Information (US)
Litigation/Judgments/Tax Liens (US)
SEC/Other Financial (US)

Membership: ABW

Statement of Capabilities: Global Intelligence Network (GIN) provides reliable, up-to-date information. They specialize in asset location

and in assisting individuals and businesses with access to the information they need now. They have over 20 years of experience in investigations and public record research.

Government Liaison Services Inc

3030 Clarendon Blvd #209
Arlington, VA 22210
Telephone: **Fax:**
800-642-6564   703-525-8451
703-524-8200
www.trademarkinfo.com
GLS@trademarkinfo.com
Year Founded: 1957

Clientele: Business - General, Legal Profession

Applications: General Business Information, Legal Compliance

Information Types:
Corporate/Trade Name Data (US)
SEC/Other Financial (US)
Trademarks/Patents (US)

Membership: INTA

Statement of Capabilities: Government Liaison Services is one of the few firms that routinely searches trademarks in both computerized records and the paper records of the official Trademark Search Library. Today, paper records include about 40,000 recently-filed applications that are missing from the computer data distributed by the US Patent and Trademark Office which most other computerized search systems use. This amounts to more than 8 weeks of trademark application filings. Providing the most current information available, their searches can be performed in as little as four hours.

Free Web Information:
Free screening of registered trademarks.

Haines & Company Inc

8050 Freedom Ave
North canton, OH 44720
Telephone: **Fax:**
800-843-8452   330-494-0226

330-494-9111
www.haines.com
criscros@haines.com
Year Founded: 1932

Clientele: Legal Profession, Collection Agencies, Lending Institutions, Corporate Security, Government Agencies, Insurance - General, Real Estate Owners/Managers

Applications: Collections, Direct Marketing, Insurance Underwriting, Lending/Leasing, Locating People/Businesses

Information Types:
Voter Registration (OH)
Bankruptcy (US)
Addresses/Telephone Numbers (US)
Real Estate/Assessor (US)

Proprietary Products:

Name/Desc: Criss+Cross Directory
Info Provided: Addresses/Telephone Numbers
Media: Publication/Directory
Coverage: US

Name/Desc: Criss+Cross Plus CD-ROM
Info Provided: Address/Telephone Numbers
Media: CD-ROM
Coverage: US

Name/Desc: Criss+Cross Plus Real Estate
Info Provided: Real Estate/Assessor
Media: CD-ROM
Coverage: US

Name/Desc: Criss+Cross Plus Online
Info Provided: Address/Telephone Numbers, Real Estate/Assessor
Media: Direct Online
Coverage: US

Name/Desc: Criss+Cross Natl Look-Up Library
Info Provided: Addresses/Telephone Numbers
Media: Call-in Only
Coverage: US

Name/Desc: Americalist
Media: Disk, Lists or labels and Magnetic Tape
Coverage: US

Membership: NAR, REIPA, DMA

Statement of Capabilities: Varied products and full-service capabilities allow Haines & Company to satisfy the marketing and research needs of most industries. County Real Estate on CD-ROM has been noted for its ease of use, speed and marketing power. They also offer cross-reference directories in book form or on CD-ROM in 71 major markets, also business and residential lists on labels, manuscripts, CD-ROM, off the Internet or bulletin boards (24-hour turnaround time available). Using their target list or a customer-provided list, they can provide complete direct marketing services, graphic design, printing and database maintenance -- all in-house.

Hebert Land Services

109 N Witte
Poteau, OK 74953
Telephone: **Fax:**
918-647-9524   918-647-9524
Year Founded: 1981

Clientele: Legal Profession, Financial Institutions, Public Record Research Firms

Applications: Asset/Lien Searching/Verification, Real Estate Transactions, Locating People/Businesses, Filing/Recording Documents

Information Types:
Wills/Probate (AR, OK)
Uniform Commercial Code (AR, OK)
Associations/Trade Groups (US)
Real Estate/Assessor (OK)
Addresses/Telephone Numbers (US)
Bankruptcy (OK)
Litigation/Judgments/Tax Liens (AR, OK)
Environmental (AR, OK)

Membership: AAPL

HIQ Companies

516 N Charles St 5th Fl
Baltimore, MD 21201
Telephone: **Fax:**
800-564-5300   410-752-2808
410-752-8030

HQ@HIQ-AGENTS.COM
Parent Company: HIQ Corporate Services Inc
Year Founded: 1990

Clientele: Attorney Firms, Corporate Counsel, Equipment Leasing Companies, Financial Institutions, Legal Profession, Lending Institutions, Public Record Research Firms

Applications: Asset/Lien Searching/Verification, Filing/Recording Documents, Government Document Retrieval, Government Document Retrieval, Lending/Leasing

Information Types:
Bankruptcy (US)
Corporate/Trade Name Data (US)
Litigation/Judgments/Tax Liens (US)
SEC/Other Financial (US)
Uniform Commercial Code (US)
Vital Records (US)

Membership: NPRRA

Hogan Information Services

14000 Quail Springs Parkway #4000
Oklahoma, OK 73134
Telephone:
405-278-6954
www.hoganinfo.com
hogan.data@firstdatacorp.com
Parent Company: First Data Corp
Year Founded: 1990

Clientele: Business - General, Corporate
Security, Employers (HR/Personnel Depts),
Legal Profession, Public Record Research
Firms, Property Owners/Managers

Applications: Lending/Leasing, Risk
Management, Employment Screening, Tenant
Screening, Background Info - Individuals

Information Types:
Litigation/Judgments/Tax Liens (US)
Uniform Commercial Code (US)
Real Estate/Assessor (US)
Tenant History (US)

Proprietary Products:

Name/Desc: Hogan Online
Info Provided: Bankruptcy
Media: Online, Disk, Lists, Labels, Magnetic
Tape
Coverage: US

Statement of Capabilities: Hogan Information
Services provides high-quality national public
record information to credit bureaus, bankcard
issuers, collection agencies, retail institutions,
and other businesses through various First Data
business units. Founded in 1990, in 1996
Hogan Information Services became a business
unit of First Data Corp. Hogan gathers public
record information on laptop computers in over
8,000 courthouses nationwide for business to
business applications. They specialize in
helping businesses make smarter decisions and
manage risk by using public record
information.

Hollingsworth Court Reporting Inc

10761 Perkins Rd #A
Baton Rouge, LA 70810
Telephone: **Fax:**
504-769-3386   504-769-1814
www.hcrinc.com
Year Founded: 1983

Clientele: Credit Reporting Agencies, Employers
(HR/Personnel Depts), Insurance - General,
Public Record Research Firms, Apartment
Owners/Managers, Information -
Brokers/Retrievers, Product Development
Managers

Applications: General Business Information,
Background Info - Business, Employment
Screening, Government Document Retrieval,
Filing/Recording Documents

Information Types:
Tenant History (AL, AR, FL, GA, IL, LA, MS,
TN)
Corporate/Trade Name Data (LA, MS)
Criminal Information (US)

Proprietary Products:

Name/Desc: Public Record Report
Info Provided: Litigation/Judgments/Tax
Liens
Media: Online Database, Disk, and Magnetic
Tape
Coverage: AL, AR, FL, GA, IL, LA, MS, TN

Membership: NPRRA, PRRN

Statement of Capabilities: HCR collects and
compiles public record information in eight
states and makes it available in a variety of
formats, including call-in service. HCR
processes criminal record searches nationwide
with a 48-hour turnaround time. Orders may be
placed through an online system. Their
proprietary database is an excellent source of
eviction information for apartment owners and
managers. The principals of HCR have a
combined 40 years experience in the public
record field.

Hoovers Inc

1033 La Posada Drive #250
Austin, TX 78752
Telephone: **Fax:**
800-486-8666   512-374-4505
512-374-4500
www.hoovers.com
info@hoovers.com

Clientele: Business - General, Consumers (Individuals), Consulting Firms, Direct Marketers, Insurance - General

Applications: General Business Information, Background Info - Business, Competitive Intelligence, Locating People/Businesses

Proprietary Products:

Name/Desc: Hoover's Company Profiles
Info Provided: Addresses/Telephone Numbers, Corporate/Trade Name Data, News/Current Events
Media: Direct Online, Printed Report, Internet
Coverage: US, International

Name/Desc: Real-Time SEC Documents
Info Provided: SEC/Other Financial
Media: Direct Online, Printed Report, Internet
Coverage: US

Statement of Capabilities: Hoovers offers a wide range of company information, much for investing purposes. Their published materials are distributed electronically and in print, and they claim their databases are among the least expensive sources of information on operations, strategies, etc. of major US and global and private companies.

Free Web Information:
Ordering and general information is available on their site.

Hylind Courthouse Retrieval Co

151 Cold Stream Tr
Felton, PA 17322
Telephone: **Fax:**
888-790-2229   717-246-6739
717-246-6540
www.hylind.com
info@hylind.com
Year Founded: 1998

Clientele: Legal Profession, Business - General, Financial Institutions, Government Agencies, Information - Brokers/Retrievers, Legal Service Companies, Private Investigators

Applications: Asset/Lien Searching/Verification, Filing/Recording Documents, Government Document Retrieval, Litigation, Real Estate Transactions

Information Types:
Aviation/Vessels (US)
Bankruptcy (US)
Criminal Information (US)
Driver and/or Vehicle (US)
Litigation/Judgments/Tax Liens (US)

Real Estate/Assessor (US)
Uniform Commercial Code (US)
Vital Records (US)

Membership: NPRRA, PRRN

Statement of Capabilities: Hylind Courthouse Retrieval Company provides a comprehensive range of searches, filings and document preparation services within the major, corporate, real estate, legal and financial industries, not just in Pennsylvania but on a nationwide basis at all levels of government. Their network covers the spectrum of public records research and corporate document services: UCC, tax liens, litigation (civil and criminal), judgments, real estate title services, resident agent representation and beyond. They pride themselves on working expeditiously, accurately and cost efficiency. Orders can be placed on their web site.

Hylind Search Company Inc

307 Dolphin St #1A
Baltimore, MD 21217
Telephone: **Fax:**
888-449-5463   410-225-0016
410-225-0014
www.hylindsearch.com
Year Founded: 1996

Clientele: Legal Profession, Financial Institutions, Corporate Counsel, Information - Brokers/Retrievers, Equipment Leasing Companies, Public Record Research Firms, Attorney Firms

Applications: Asset/Lien Searching/Verification, Filing/Recording Documents, Lending/Leasing, Locating People/Businesses, Real Estate Transactions

Information Types:
Uniform Commercial Code (US)
Litigation/Judgments/Tax Liens (US)
Real Estate/Assessor (US)
Bankruptcy (US)
Corporate/Trade Name Data (US)
Driver and/or Vehicle (US)
Addresses/Telephone Numbers
Aviation/Vessels

Membership: NPRRA, PRRN

Statement of Capabilities: Hylind Search Company tailors asset/lien searches to each client's specific needs. They may now have an Internet site operating by which orders can be placed and results returned electronically.

I

ICDI

3822 Edgewater Dr
Orlando, FL 32804
Telephone: **Fax:**
407-299-6300 407-290-2032
Year Founded: 1992

Clientele: Financial Institutions, Legal Profession, Search Firsms - Title Companies

Applications: Real Estate Transactions, Asset/Lien Searching/Verification

Information Types:
Bankruptcy (FL, Middle District/Orlando)
Wills/Probate (FL, Brevard, Duval, Orange, Seminole)
Real Estate/Assessor (FL-Brevard, Duval, Orange, Seminole)
Uniform Commercial Code (FL-Brevard, Duval, Orange, Seminole)

Statement of Capabilities: Specializing in the state of Florida, the staff of ICDI has combined experience of 30 years in the search field.

Idealogic

505 University Ave #1603
Toronto, Ontario, CD M5G 1X3
Telephone: **Fax:**
800-265-0361 800-890-6971
416-506-9900 416-506-0700
www.idealogic.com

ideal@idealogic.com
Year Founded: 1980

Clientele: Legal Profession, Public Record Research Firms, Private Investigators, Attorney Firms, Consumers (Individuals), Equipment Leasing Companies, Legal Profession

Applications: Background Info - Business, General Business Information, Filing/Recording Documents, Litigation, Asset/Lien Searching/Verification

Information Types:
Bankruptcy (CD)
Licenses/Registrations/Permits (CD)
Corporate/Trade Name Data (CD)
Driver and/or Vehicle (CD)
Litigation/Judgments/Tax Liens
Addresses/Telephone Numbers
Criminal Information
Foreign Country Information

Membership: NPRRA, OAPSOR

Statement of Capabilities: Idealogic is a full service provider of public information from all jurisdictions in Canada. Corporate, personal property and other registry information is available. Idealogic has knowledge about how to translate public information available in the US to its Canadian counterpart.

IDM Corporation

3550 W Temple St
Los Angeles, CA 90004
Telephone: **Fax:**
877-436-3282 213-389-9569
213-389-2793
Year Founded: 1989

Clientele: Financial Institutions, Information - Brokers/Retrievers, Legal Profession, Lending Institutions, Direct Marketers

Applications: Asset/Lien Searching/Verification, Direct Marketing, Fraud Prevention/Detection, Lending/Leasing, Real Estate Transactions

Proprietary Products:
Name/Desc: Tax, Assessor and Recorders
Info Provided: Real Estate/Assessor
Media: Disk and Direct Online
Coverage: US

Membership: REIPA

Statement of Capabilities: IDM Corporation is one of the largest source providers of real estate public records. They convert 900 tax/assessor counties and 500 recorder's counties to a uniform format. Their assessment files are updated once per year, and recorder's are updated weekly.

IGB Associates Inc

1181 Shipwatch Cir
Tampa, FL 33602
Telephone: **Fax:**
813-226-8810 813-226-8710
Year Founded: 1993

Clientele: Attorney Firms, Collection Agencies, Credit Grantors, Information - Brokers/Retrievers, Legal Profession,

Mortgage Bankers, Public Record Research Firms

Applications: Government Document Retrieval, Asset/Lien Searching/Verification, Background Info - Business, Background Info - Individuals, Litigation

Information Types:
Bankruptcy (US)
Litigation/Judgments/Tax Liens (US)
Uniform Commercial Code (US)
Vital Records (US)
Corporate/Trade Name Data (US)
Addresses/Telephone Numbers (US)
Criminal Information (US)
Driver and/or Vehicle (US)

Membership: PRRN, NPRRA

Statement of Capabilities: IGB Associates provides nationwide legal research and document retrieval services. They specialize in a wide range of public record searches and can obtain pleadings for all court cases anywhere in the US.

Independent Research, Inc

2963 Wyndwicke Dr
St Joseph, MI 49085
Telephone: Fax:
616-429-9873 616-429-5693
Year Founded: 1989

Clientele: Credit Reporting Agencies, Employers (HR/Personnel Depts), Financial Institutions, Information - Brokers/Retrievers, Private Investigators, Public Record Research Firms

Applications: Asset/Lien Searching/Verification, Background Info - Individuals, Filing/Recording Documents, Government Document Retrieval, Real Estate Transactions

Information Types:
Associations/Trade Groups (MI)
Bankruptcy (US)
Corporate/Trade Name Data (MI)
Litigation/Judgments/Tax Liens (MI)
Uniform Commercial Code (MI)
Criminal Information (US)

Membership: PRRN

Statement of Capabilities: Independent Research provides public record research and retrieval in Michigan and nationally. They have correspondents in all states specializing in criminal background checks. They also provide real estate research locally.

Infinity Information Network Inc

4516 Kenny Rd #203
Columbus, OH 43220-3711
Telephone: Fax:
614-261-1213 614-268-3485
www.iinetwork.com

Year Founded: 1993

Clientele: Credit Reporting Agencies, Public Record Research Firms, Legal Profession, Information - Brokers/Retrievers, Private Investigators, Mortgage Bankers, Attorney Firms

Applications: Employment Screening, Background Info - Individuals, Fraud Prevention/Detection, Litigation, Tenant Screening

Information Types:
Bankruptcy (US, OH)
Litigation/Judgments/Tax Liens (US, OH)
Criminal Information (US, OH)
Real Estate/Assessor (US, OH)
Uniform Commercial Code (US, OH)
Workers' Compensation (US, OH)
Driver and/or Vehicle (US, OH)

Membership: AIIP, NPRRA, ION, PRRN

Statement of Capabilities: Infinity Information Network (IIN) is a full service research company designed to meet the many needs of their clients. IIN can conduct records research in almost every courthouse in the US. Most prices are on a flat-fee basis and average between $7-15 per name. In addition to records research, IIN offers a variety of other services to assist corporations, attorneys, investigators and other professionals. All of their services are available through the Internet.

Free Web Information:
Products, Services, and online ordering

Info-Pro Inc

PO Box 424
St Louis, MO 63088
Telephone: Fax:
314-225-3866 314-225-3866
infopromo@aol.com
Year Founded: 1996

Clientele: Attorney Firms, Lending Institutions, Employers (HR/Personnel Depts), Insurance - Claims, Legal Profession, Lending Institutions, Secured Lenders

Applications: Asset/Lien Searching/Verification, Background Info - Business, Locating People/Businesses, Collections, Background Info - Individuals

Information Types:
Addresses/Telephone Numbers (US)
Aviation/Vessels (US)
Bankruptcy (US)
Corporate/Trade Name Data (US)
Criminal Information (US)
Driver and/or Vehicle (US)
Education/Employment (US)
Litigation/Judgments/Tax Liens (US)

Membership: NCJHS, IASIU

Statement of Capabilities: Info-Pro Inc specializes in subject locating, background investigation, small business and the child-care industry. Info-Pro provides confidential sub-rosa inquires using multiple databases and external sources. All employees are former police investigators with degrees and have years of specialized training.

Infocon Corporation
PO Box 568
Ebensburg, PA 15931-0568
Telephone: **Fax:**
814-472-6066   814-472-5019
Clientele: Legal Profession, Business - General, Credit Grantors, Financial Institutions, Investigators - Fraud, Public Record Research Firms

Applications: Background Info - Individuals, Real Estate Transactions, Litigation, Risk Management, Genealogical Research

Proprietary Products:
Name/Desc: INFOCON County Access System
Info Provided: Criminal Information, Vital Records, Voter Registration, Litigation/Judgments/Tax Liens, Real Estate Assessor
Media: Direct Online
Coverage: PA-12 Western Counties

Statement of Capabilities: The Infocon County Access System offers online access to civil, criminal, real estate, and vital record information in Pennsylvania counties of Armstrong, Bedford, Blair, Butler, Clarion, Clinton, Erie, Huntingdon, Lawrence, Mifflin, Potter, and Pike. Fees are involved, access is through a remote 800 number.

Infonet Report Service
5532 E Grandview Rd
Scottsdale, AZ 85254
Telephone: **Fax:**
602-971-7481   602-971-8377
www.infonetreports.com
pi@infonetreports.com
Year Founded: 1991

Clientele: Attorney Firms, Lending Institutions, Employers (HR/Personnel Depts), Insurance - Claims, Insurance - General, Insurance Agents/Brokers, Legal Profession

Applications: Asset/Lien Searching/Verification, Background Info - Business, Employment Screening, Filing/Recording Documents, Insurance Underwriting

Information Types:
Criminal Information (AZ)
Driver and/or Vehicle (AZ)
Real Estate/Assessor (AZ-Maricopa)
Voter Registration (AZ-Maricopa)

Statement of Capabilities: Infonet Report Service has a 48 hour turnaround for all motor vehicle records, by VIN, plate or name, citation disposition, lien checks, civil and criminal searches, real property, searched by name, property address or legal descriptions. They have broad access to databases. Accident/criminal police reports depend upon the city's release date. They are fluent in European languages and services are available to other countries.

Inform Alaska Inc
PO Box 190908
Anchorage, AK 99519-0908
Telephone: **Fax:**
907-258-4636   907-277-8294
InformAlaska@att.net
Year Founded: 1985

Clientele: Business - General, Legal Profession, Professionals-Other, Private Investigators, Information - Brokers/Retrievers, Consumers (Individuals)

Applications: Background Info - Business, Background Info - Individuals, General Business Information, Litigation, Government Document Retrieval

Information Types:
Litigation/Judgments/Tax Liens (AK)

Legislation/Regulation (AK)
Licenses/Registrations/Permits (AK)
Uniform Commercial Code (AK)
News/Current Events (AK)
Vital Records
Voter Registration
Workers' Compensation

Membership: AIIP, ABI

Statement of Capabilities: Inform Alaska is probably the only company in Alaska that performs "retrospective" searches in prior-dated issues of Alaskan newspapers and Journals. Inform Alaska is the publisher of Alaska Court Review, a monthly summary and index of all the Alaska Supreme Court and Court of Appeals opinions. Sample copies are sent upon request. Owner is attorney with 20 years experience in state government, legal affairs, legislation, and agency administration.

Information America Inc

Marquis One Tower #1400
245 Peachtree Center Ave
Atlanta, GA 30303
Telephone: **Fax:**
800-235-4008 800-845-6319
404-479-6500
www.infoam.com

Year Founded: 1982

Clientele: Government Agencies, Legal Profession, Financial Institutions, Asset-Based Lenders, Corporate Security, Professionals-Other

Applications: Lending/Leasing, Background Info - Business, Asset/Lien Searching/Verification, Litigation, Locating People/Businesses

Information Types:
Driver and/or Vehicle (US)
Licenses/Registrations/Permits (US)

Proprietary Products:

Name/Desc: Bankruptcy Records
Info Provided: Bankruptcy
Media: Online Database and Call back
Coverage: US

Name/Desc: Corporations and Partnerships
Info Provided: Corporate/Trade Name Data
Media: Online Database and Call back
Coverage: US

Name/Desc: Lawsuits, Judgments, Liens

Info Provided: Litigation/Judgments/Tax Liens
Media: Online Database and Call back
Coverage: US

Name/Desc: Professional Licenses
Info Provided: Licenses/Registrations/Permits
Media: Online Database and Call back
Coverage: AZ, CA, CO, CT, FL, GA, IL, IN, LA, MA, MD, MI, NJ, OH, PA, SC, TN, TX, VA, WI

Name/Desc: Real Estate, Liens and Judgments
Info Provided: Real Estate Assessor, Litigation/Judgments/Tax Liens
Media: Online Database and Call back
Coverage: US

Name/Desc: UCCs
Info Provided: Uniform Commerical Code
Media: Online Database and Call back
Coverage: US

Name/Desc: Watercraft Locator/Aircraft Locator
Info Provided: Aviation/Vessels
Media: Online Database and Call back
Coverage: US

Name/Desc: Business Finder/People Finder
Info Provided: Addresses/Telephone Numbers
Media: Online Database, Internet and Call back
Coverage: US

Name/Desc: Motor Vehicle Records
Info Provided: Driver and/or Vehicle
Media: Direct Online
Coverage: AK, AL, CO, CT, DC, DE, FL, IA, ID, IL, KY, LA, MA, MD, ME, MI, MN, MO, MS, MT, ND, NE, NH, NM, NY, OH, SC, TN, UT, WI, WV, WY

Membership: NPRRA

Statement of Capabilities: Information America combines and links public records and courthouse documents with information from private sources to address the relationships between corporations, people and their assets. Banks, financial service companies, corporations, law firms and government agencies across the nation use their online and document retrieval services to obtain background data on businesses, locate assets and people, retrieve official public records and solve business problems. Information America was founded by a practicing attorney and a computer systems expert acquainted with the needs of government, legal and corporate customers. A related company, Document Resources, is a national search firm.

Free Web Information:
Free summary searches of their databases on www.free.knowx.com

Information Inc

PO Box 382
Hermitage, TN 37076
Telephone: **Fax:**
615-884-8000 615-889-6492
www.members.aol.com/infomant
n/info.html

infomantn@aol.com
Year Founded: 1992

Clientele: Business - General, Educational Institutions, Collection Agencies, Corporate Security, Private Investigators, Loss Prevention Specialists, Public Record Research Firms

Applications: Background Info - Individuals, Collections, Employment Screening, Litigation, Tenant Screening

Information Types:
Criminal Information (TN)

Proprietary Products:

Name/Desc: Arrest Database
Info Provided: Criminal Information
Media: Direct Online
Coverage: TN-Nashville

Membership: PRRN

Statement of Capabilities: Information Inc provides a real time criminal arrest database for Davidson County, TN. This includes all agencies in the 20th Judicial District of Tennessee.

Information Management Systems Inc

PO Box 2924
New Britain, CT 06050-2924
Telephone: **Fax:**
860-229-1119 860-225-5524
www.imswebb.com

Year Founded: 1989

Clientele: Business - General, Employers (HR/Personnel Depts), Attorney Firms, Information - Brokers/Retrievers, Private

Investigators, Property Owners/Managers, Public Record Research Firms

Applications: Asset/Lien Searching/Verification, Background Info - Business, Background Info - Individual, Employment Screening, Real Estate Transactions

Information Types:
Credit Information (US)
Criminal Information (US)
Driver and/or Vehicle (US)
Environmental (US)
Real Estate/Assessor (US)
Bankruptcy (US)
Litigation/Judgments/Tax Liens (US)
Uniform Commercial Code (US)

Membership: PRRN

Information Network Associates Inc

300 Hummel Ave
Lemoyne, PA 17043
Telephone: **Fax:**
800-443-0824 717-612-9700
717-612-9600
http://home.att.net/~infonetwo
rk

Clientele: Legal Profession, Business - General, Investigators - Fraud, Private Investigators, Public Record Research Firms, Attorney Firms

Applications: Asset/Lien Searching/Verification, Background Info - Business, Fraud Prevention/Detection, General Business Information, Litigation

Information Types:
Addresses/Telephone Numbers (PA)
Bankruptcy (PA)
Driver and/or Vehicle (PA)
Education/Employment (PA)
Licenses/Registrations/Permits (PA)
Litigation/Judgments/Tax Liens (PA)
Uniform Commercial Code (PA)

Membership: PRRN, IFTI, ACFE, ASIS, NAPPS, NALI

Statement of Capabilities: Information Network Associates (INA) is a problem solving and record retrieval service business. INA maintains a license to do private investigative work. Their clients identify the need and/or problem, and INA obtains the information required or identifies an alternate source for the information needed. INA is based in Pennsylvania and will provide services through its own employees, correspondents and/or other private investigators.

Information Network of Arkansas

425 West Capitol Ave #3565
Little Rock, AR 72201
Telephone:
800-392-6069
501-324-8900
www.state.ark.us/ina/about_ina.html

info@ark.org
Year Founded: 1998

Clientele: Business - General, Corporate Security, Employers (HR/Personnel Depts), Insurance - General, Investigators - Fraud, Legal Profession, Private Investigators

Applications: Background Info - Business, General Business Information, Employment Screening, Insurance Underwriting

Proprietary Products:

Name/Desc: INA
Info Provided: Driver and/or Vehicle
Media: Internet
Coverage: AR

Statement of Capabilities: Information Network of Arkansas was created by the Arkansas Legislature with the responsibility of assisting the state in permitting citizens to access public records. More categories of records will soon be available. There is a fee for driving record access; there may not be fees for other record categories.
Free Web Information:
The web site offers access various records and links to Arkansas government agencies.

Information Network of Kansas

534 S Kansas Ave #1210
Topeka, KS 66603
Telephone: **Fax:**
800-452-6727   785-296-5563
785-296-5059
www.ink.org

Clientele: Asset-Based Lenders, Business - General, Employers (HR/Personnel Depts), Insurance - General, Investigators - Fraud, Public Record Research Firms

Applications: General Business Information, Employment Screening, Insurance

Underwriting, Lending/Leasing, Legal Compliance
Proprietary Products:

Name/Desc: Premium Services
Info Provided: Driver and/or Vehicle, Uniform Commercial Code, Corporate/Trade Name Data, Legislation/Regulations, Real Estate Assessor
Media: Internet, Online
Coverage: KS

Name/Desc: Premium Services
Info Provided: Litigation/Judgements/Tax Liens
Media: Internet, Online
Coverage: KS-Johnson, Sedgwick, Shawnee, Wyandotte

Name/Desc: Premium Services
Info Provided: Criminal Information
Media: Online, Internet
Coverage: KS- Sedgwick, Shawnee, Wyandotte

Statement of Capabilities: INK is the official source for electronic access to the State of Kansas government information. Access to public record information listed here requires a subscription.
Free Web Information:
There is a plethora of data available about Kansas at the web site.

Information Search Associates

PO Box 32698
Tucson, AZ 85751-2698
Telephone: **Fax:**
888-448-4477   520-749-2074
520-749-4342
Year Founded: 1993

Clientele: Business - General, Legal Profession, Public Record Research Firms, Consumers (Individuals)

Applications: Background Info - Business, General Business Information, Asset/Lien Searching/Verification, Competitive Intelligence, Current Events

Information Types:
News/Current Events (US)
Real Estate/Assessor (US, AZ-Pima)
Litigation/Judgments/Tax Liens (US, AZ-Pima)
Criminal Information (US, AZ-Pima)
SEC/Other Financial (US)
Uniform Commercial Code (US, AZ-Pima)

Vital Records (US, AZ-Pima)
Corporate/Trade Name Data (AZ)

Membership: PRRN, AIIP

Statement of Capabilities: Information Search Associates, founded in 1993, specializes in efficient, cost-effective searches of the leading online information systems. Services include public records research and retrieval, current awareness, business intelligence, computer consulting and general research in a wide variety of subjects. Public record retrieval is available for Pima County (Tucson) AZ.

Information Search Inc

2929 Biarritz Dr
Palm Beach Gardens, FL 33410
Telephone: **Fax:**
561-624-5115   561-694-8281
http://infohotline.com
newman@flite.net
Year Founded: 1995

Clientele: Consulting Firms, Business - General, Direct Marketers, Information - Brokers/Retrievers, Lending Institutions, Private Investigators, Public Record Research Firms

Applications: Background Info - Business, Asset/Lien Searching/Verification, Direct Marketing, Government Document Retrieval, Real Estate Transactions

Information Types:
Bankruptcy (FL)
Associations/Trade Groups (FL,US)
Corporate/Trade Name Data (FL,US)
Criminal Information (FL)
Litigation/Judgments/Tax Liens (FL)
Real Estate/Assessor (FL)
Uniform Commercial Code (FL,US)
Vital Records (FL)

Membership: AIIP, PRRN

Statement of Capabilities: Information Search Inc's goal is to source or discover and retrieve or verify information concerning individuals, groups, organizations, companies, industries, business entities and informational topics for their clients. They have many distinct services. "Competitive Business Intelligence" concerns information solutions to critical problems and hard-to-find data. "Customized (non-standard) Business Lists" are targeted to specific needs or niches.

"Finding More Look-Alike Best Business Prospects-Clients" is based on analyzing existing clients, determining common characteristics and identifying similar prospects.

Information/Access Online

1909 E Barden Rd
Charlotte, NC 28226
Telephone:
704-364-7987
Year Founded: 1982

Clientele: Information - Brokers/Retrievers, Research & Development Directors

Applications: Background Info - Business, Competitive Intelligence, General Business Information

Information Types:
Foreign Country Information
News/Current Events (US)
Technical Information

Membership: AIIP, SLA

Statement of Capabilities: Information/Access Online is a chemical/technical information organization whose principal has 26 years of experience. They track people, corporations or technology through patent literature, technical literature, conferences, news and journal sources. Both online and manual sources are used. The principal has extensive knowledge in chemistry, textile and polymer fields. Personnel employment firms utilize Information/Access Online to locate people in specific positions within corporations.

Informus Corporation

2001 Airport Rd #201
Jackson, MS 39208
Telephone:
800-364-8380
601-664-1900
www.informus.com
Year Founded: 1990

Clientele: Employers (HR/Personnel Depts), Public Record Research Firms, Business - General, Corporate Counsel, Information - Brokers/Retrievers

Applications: Employment Screening, Locating People/Businesses, Background Info - Individuals, Collections

Information Types:
Criminal Information (US)
Driver and/or Vehicle (US)
Credit Information (US)

Proprietary Products:

Name/Desc: Informus
Info Provided: Workers' Compensation
Media: Online, Printed Report
Coverage: MS, US

Name/Desc: IntroScan
Info Provided: Addresses/Telephone
Numbers, Social Security (Numbers)
Media: US

Statement of Capabilities: Informus provides an online pre-employment screening and public record retrieval service. Online access is available through the Internet. Some searches provide instant information, depending on state and category.

Infotel Corp
5090 Richmond #94
Houston, TX 77056
Telephone: **Fax:**
888-244-7761   281-565-9831
281-565-9830
www.intotel.net
e-mail@infotel.net

Clientele: Legal Profession, Business - General, Consumers (Individuals), Equipment Leasing Companies, Property Owners/Managers, Investigators - Fraud, Attorney Firms

Applications: Asset/Lien Searching/Verification, Background Info - Business, Collections, Employment Screening, Fraud Prevention/Detection

Information Types:
Addresses/Telephone Numbers (TX)
Bankruptcy (TX)
Credit Information (YX)
Driver and/or Vehicle (TX)
Litigation/Judgments/Tax Liens (TX)
Uniform Commercial Code (TX)

Membership: ABW, AIIP, SIIA, NPRRA

Statement of Capabilities: Infotel was one of the first companies to provide the composite background check to the public.

InfoTrack Information Services Inc
1635 Barclay Blvd
Buffalo Grove, IL 60089

Telephone: **Fax:**
800-275-5594   800-275-5595
847-808-9990   847-808-7773
www.INFOTRACKING.com

Year Founded: 1990

Clientele: Attorney Firms, Employers (HR/Personnel Depts), Information - Brokers/Retrievers, Insurance - General, Mortgage Bankers, Private Investigators, Public Record Research Firms

Applications: Background Info - Business, Background Info - Individuals, Employment Screening, Locating People/Businesses, Real Estate Transactions

Information Types:
Litigation/Judgments/Tax Liens (IL)
Criminal Information (IL)
Driver and/or Vehicle (US, IL)
Real Estate/Assessor (IL)
Addresses/Telephone Numbers (IL)
Bankruptcy (Il)
Education/Employment (IL)
Workers' Compensation (IL)

Statement of Capabilities: InfoTrack Information Services provides personalized information retrieval services. Reports include immediate Illinois vehicle information and 24-48 hour civil and criminal information from Cook, Lake, DuPage, Will, Kane, Sangamon, Peoria, Tazewell, Christian, Menard, McLean, Woodford, McDonough, Knox, Warren, Fulton, and most other Illinois counties.

Innovative Enterprises Inc
PO Box 22506
Newport News, VA 23609-2506
Telephone: **Fax:**
888-777-9435   888-777-9436
www.knowthefacts.com
innovate@knowthefacts.com
Year Founded: 1996

Clientele: Apartment Owners/Managers, Attorney Firms, Educational Institutions, Information - Brokers/Retrievers, Public Record Research Firms

Applications: Background Info - Individuals, Employment Screening, Legal Compliance, Locating People/Businesses

Information Types:
Criminal Information (US, VA)

Statement of Capabilities: Innovative Enterprises' staff brings forward more than 55 years of combined Virginia judicial, law enforcement, and military experience, making them qualified to service client's background research needs. The first search performed for new clients is always free.

INPRO

14870 Granada Ave #323
Apple Valley, MN 55124-5514
Telephone: **Fax:**
800-476-4677 612-891-3618
612-891-3617
www.inpro.com
inproinc@aol.com
Year Founded: 1994

Clientele: Legal Profession, Business - General, Employers (HR/Personnel Depts), Insurance - Claims, Legal Profession, Private Investigators, Public Record Research Firms

Applications: Asset/Lien Searching/Verification, Background Info - Individuals, Employment Screening, Fraud Prevention/Detection, Locating People/Businesses

Information Types:
Addresses/Telephone Numbers (US)
Bankruptcy (US, MN)
Criminal Information (US, MN)
Driver and/or Vehicle (US, MN)
Litigation/Judgments/Tax Liens (US, MN)
Social Security (Numbers) (US)
Uniform Commercial Code (US, MN)
Vital Records (US, MN)

Membership: ASIS, ACFE, NALI, ION

Statement of Capabilities: INPRO provides a wide range of database information services to law firms, insurance companies, investigative professionals and businesses throughout the US. They can also provide immediate access to business filings, civil/criminal/judgment filings, DMV information, property records, etc. in Minnesota. Most requests are honored within 24-48 hours. They accept most major credit cards. No prepayment is required on cash accounts. INPRO is committed to providing their clientele with prompt service, personal attention and satisfactory results.

Free Web Information:
The INPRO web site offers free access to a wide range of information and database resources and links.

Insurance Information Exchange (iiX)

PO Box 30001
College Station, TX 77842-3001
Telephone: **Fax:**
800-683-8553 409-696-5584
www.iixx.com
Year Founded: 1966

Clientele: Insurance - General, Insurance - Agents/Brokers, Employers (HR/Personnel Depts), Public Record Research Firms

Applications: Insurance Underwriting

Proprietary Products:

Name/Desc: Motor Vehicle Reports
Info Provided: Driver and/or Vehicle
Media: Direct Online, Fax-on-Demand, Internet and Printed Report
Coverage: US

Name/Desc: UDI
Info Provided: Driver and/or Vehicle
Media: Direct Online, Fax-on-Demand, Internet and Printed Report
Coverage: US

Name/Desc: CLUE
Info Provided: Driver and/or Vehicle
Media: Direct Online
Coverage: US

Name/Desc: UNCLE
Info Provided: Driver and/or Vehicle
Media: Direct Online
Coverage: US

Name/Desc: A+
Info Provided: Driver and/or Vehicle
Media: Direct Online
Coverage: US

Name/Desc: MVP
Info Provided: Driver and/or Vehicle
Media: Direct Online
Coverage: US

Statement of Capabilities: iiX is an established provider of information systems to the insurance industry. Their services and products include MVR, claims, undisclosed driver, and other underwriting services. Users still call this system AMS or AMSI. They are one of the leading providers of driving records to search firms and investigators.

Intercounty Clearance Corporation

440 9th Ave 5th Fl
New York, NY 10001

Telephone: **Fax:**
800-229-4422   212-349-0145
212-594-0020
www.intercountyclearance.com

Year Founded: 1935

Clientele: Financial Institutions, Legal Profession, Public Record Research Firms, Professionals-Other

Applications: Lending/Leasing, Asset/Lien Searching/Verification, Filing/Recording Documents, Legal Compliance, Background Info - Business

Information Types:
Uniform Commercial Code (US)
Corporate/Trade Name Data (US)
Litigation/Judgments/Tax Liens (US)
Bankruptcy (US)
Driver and/or Vehicle (US)

Membership: NPRRA, PRRN

Statement of Capabilities: Intercounty Clearance Corporation provides nationwide lien searching and filing services to clients around the country. A specific representative is assigned to each client, and reports, invoices and statements can be customized. Intercounty has its own employees in the major metropolitan counties of New York and many of them have more experience than the staff of public records agencies. They accept American Express, Visa and MasterCard as well as open accounts.

Free Web Information:
They provide information by state regarding UCC filings and searches on their web site.

International Locate & Asset Services Inc

8795 W McNab Rd #307
Tamarac, FL 33321

Telephone: **Fax:**
888-484-4527   954-720-3374
954-722-4782
www.RSI-ILAS.COM

STAYLOR@RSI-ILAS.COM

Parent Company: Receivables Specialist Inc
Year Founded: 1988

Clientele: Accountants, Accountants, Lending Institutions, Collection Agencies, Landlords, Private Investigators, Savings and Loans

Applications: Asset/Lien Searching/Verification, Background Info - Business, Collections, Employment Screening, Tenant Screening

Information Types:
Addresses/Telephone Numbers (US)
Bankruptcy (US)
Credit Information (US)
Criminal Information (US)
Driver and/or Vehicle (US)
Uniform Commercial Code (US)
Vital Records (US)
Workers' Compensation (US)

Membership: ACA

Statement of Capabilities: International Locate and Asset Services provides a quick turnaround on missing person cases, such as old friends, adoption, longer on volume skip cases. However, most are cleared within a 30 day time frame. They have a combined 75 years of experience. Their sister company, Receivable Specialist Inc, is a leading company in the collection of bad debt along with skip tracing, collections and legal actions.

International Research Bureau

1331 E Lafayette St #A & B
Tallahassee, FL 32301

Telephone: **Fax:**
800-447-2112   800-814-7714
850-942-2500
www.irb-online.com

Year Founded: 1986

Clientele: Insurance - Agents/Brokers, Business - General, Legal Profession, Public Record Research Firms, Employers (HR/Personnel Depts), Financial Institutions, Private Investigators

Applications: Asset/Lien Searching/Verification, Locating People/Businesses, Background Info - Business, Background Info - Individuals, Employment Screening

Information Types:
Criminal Information (US)
Social Security (Numbers) (US)
Driver and/or Vehicle (US)
Addresses/Telephone Numbers (US)
Education/Employment (US)
Corporate/Trade Name Data (US)

Credit Information (US)
Litigation/Judgments/Tax Liens (US)

Statement of Capabilities: International Research Bureau (IRB) has been successfully providing fast and accurate nationwide employment and tenant backgrounds, asset searches, locates and other specialized public record services for over 12 years. Being conveniently headquartered in Florida's capital also enables them to obtain original documentation daily on an expedited basis from this state.

International Research Bureau Inc (IRB)

1331 E Lafayette St #A-B
Tallahassee, FL 32301
Telephone: **Fax:**
800-447-2112 800-814-7714
850-942-2500
www.IRB-ONLINE.com

Year Founded: 1986

Clientele: Insurance - General, Business - General, Legal Profession, Public Record Research Firms, Employers (HR/Personnel Depts), Financial Institutions, Private Investigators

Applications: Asset/Lien Searching/Verification, Locating People/Businesses, Background Info - Business, Employment Screening, General Business Information

Information Types:
Addresses/Telephone Numbers (FL)
Corporate/Trade Name Data (FL)
Credit Information (FL)
Criminal Information (FL)
Driver and/or Vehicle (FL)
Social Security (Numbers) (FL)
Litigation/Judgments/Tax Liens (FL)
Education/Employment (FL)

Statement of Capabilities: IRB has provided fast and accurate nationwide employment and tenant backgrounds, asset searches, locates and other specialized public record services for over 12 years. Being conveniently headquartered in Florida's capital enables IRB to obtain original documentation daily on an expedited basis.

Intranet Inc

107 E Erwin
Tyler, TX 75702

Telephone: **Fax:**
903-593-9817 903-593-8183

Clientele: Financial Institutions, Legal Profession, Public Record Research Firms, Investigators - Fraud

Applications: Asset/Lien Searching/Verification, Litigation, General Business Information, Direct Marketing

Information Types:
Litigation/Judgments/Tax Liens (TX)
Uniform Commercial Code (TX)

Proprietary Products:
Name/Desc: Bankscan
Info Provided: Bankruptcy
Media: Disk
Coverage: TX

Statement of Capabilities: Intranet specializes in bankruptcy research and retrieval services for the state of Texas.

Investigative Consultants Inc

2020 Pennsylvania Ave NW #813
Washington, DC 20006-1846
Telephone: **Fax:**
202-237-1500 020-237-8642
dberlin50@aol.com
Year Founded: 1977

Clientele: Business - General, Legal Profession, Public Record Research Firms, Employers (HR/Personnel Depts), Financial Institutions, Corporate Counsel, Attorney Firms

Applications: Background Info - Business, Asset/Lien Searching/Verification, Background Info - Individuals, Litigation, Locating People/Businesses

Information Types:
Addresses/Telephone Numbers (US)
Litigation/Judgments/Tax Liens (US)
Driver and/or Vehicle (US)
Uniform Commercial Code (US)
Vital Records (US)
Workers' Compensation (US)
Bankruptcy (US)
Corporate/Trade Name Data (US)

Membership: AIIP, ASIS, SIIA, PRRN

Statement of Capabilities: Drawing upon an extensive assortment of databases available in the US and abroad, LITDIS Group is an organization of professional researchers and investigators trained to collect and analyze information on individuals and corporations for law firms. It conducts database searches, develops an investigative strategy and provides litigation management services. In addition to standard data searches for relevant facts, LITDIS staff members with investigative and psychological training conduct penetrating and discreet background searches and evaluate the likely behavior of witnesses. The LITDIS name derives from their specialization in LITigation and DIScovery services.

Investigators Anywhere Resource Line

PO Box 40970
Mesa, AZ 85274-0970
Telephone: **Fax:**
800-338-3463   602-730-8103
602-730-8088
www.IONINC.com
ION@IONINC.com
Parent Company: ION Incorporated
Year Founded: 1987

Clientele: Business - General, Public Record Research Firms, Corporate Counsel, Corporate Security, Secured Lenders, Financial Institutions, Private Investigators

Applications: Risk Management, Litigation, Legal Compliance, Litigation, Fraud Prevention/Detection

Information Types:
Addresses/Telephone Numbers (US)
Foreign Country Information (International)
Licenses/Registrations/Permits (US)

Proprietary Products:
Name/Desc: Resource Line
Info Provided: Addresses/Telephone Numbers
Media: Call-in
Coverage: US, International

Membership: ASIS, CII, ION, NALI, NAPPS, NCISS

Statement of Capabilities: Investigators Anywhere Resources' Resource Line service provides access to over 30,000 investigators, prescreened for excellence of service levels. Callers are matched to appropriate investigators. No fee to the callers except for international and non-commercial projects.

IQ Data Systems

1401 El Camino Ave #220

Sacramento, CA 95815
Telephone: **Fax:**
800-264-6517   800-528-2813
916-576-1000   916-576-1005
www.IQDATA.com
Year Founded: 1996

Clientele: Attorney Firms, Corporate Security, Employers (HR/Personnel Depts), Government Agencies, Insurance - Underwriting, Legal Service Companies, Private Investigators

Applications: Asset/Lien Searching/Verification, Background Info - Business, Background Info - Individuals, Filing/Recording Documents, Locating People/Businesses

Information Types:
Addresses/Telephone Numbers (US)
Bankruptcy (US)
Corporate/Trade Name Data (US)
Credit Information (US)
Criminal Information (US)
Driver and/or Vehicle (US)
Litigation/Judgments/Tax Liens (US)

Proprietary Products:
Name/Desc: UCC Data
Info Provided: Uniform Commercial Code
Media: Online
Coverage: US**Info Provided:** Real Estate/Assessor
Media: Online
Coverage: CA

Membership: NPRRA

Statement of Capabilities: As a gateway and a compiler of some of their own data, IQ Data Systems offers over three billion public records, retrievable instantaneously via the Internet in an easy to use, point-&-click, full-color graphic interface. They offer UCC, tax lien, judgment searches in all states and can also hand search criminal and civil county records from every US county. Driver records are available from all 50 states.

Free Web Information:
Log-in, account application, service agreement.

IRSC

3777 N Harbor Blvd
Fullerton, CA 92835
Telephone: **Fax:**
800-640-4772   714-526-5836
714-526-8485
www.irsc.com

Year Founded: 1983

Clientele: Legal Profession, Financial Institutions, Employers (HR/Personnel Depts), Private Investigators, Corporate Security, Landlords, Insurance - Claims

Applications: Asset/Lien Searching/Verification, Background Info - Business, Competitive Intelligence, Fraud Prevention/Detection, Locating People/Businesses

Information Types:
Driver and/or Vehicle (US)
Litigation/Judgments/Tax Liens (US)
Workers' Compensation (US)
Real Estate/Assessor (US)

Proprietary Products:

Name/Desc: IRSC
Info Provided: Social Security (Numbers), Education/Employment, Aviation/Vessels, Credit Information, Addresses/Telephone Numbers, Environmental, Uniform Commercial Code and Litigation/Judgments/Tax Liens
Media: Online Database
Coverage: US

Name/Desc: IRSC
Info Provided: Corporate/Trade Name Data
Media: Online Database
Coverage: US

Name/Desc: IRSC
Info Provided: Bankruptcy
Media: Online Database
Coverage: US

Name/Desc: IRSC (Criminal Court Index)
Info Provided: Criminal Information
Media: Online Database
Coverage: US

Name/Desc: IRSC
Info Provided: Workers' Compensation
Media: Online Database
Coverage: Ak, AL, AR, AZ, CA, CO, DC, DE, FL, IA, ID, IL, IN, KS, KY, MA, MD, ME, MI, MO, MT, NE, NH, NM, NV, OH, OK, OR, RI, SC, SD, TX, UT, VA, VT, WY

Name/Desc: IRSC
Info Provided: Real Estate/Assessor
Media: Online Database
Coverage: AK, AL, AR, AZ, CA, CO, CT, DC, DE, FL, GA, HI, IL, KY, LA, MA, MD, MI, MN, MO, MS, NC, NJ, NV, NY, OH, OK, PA, SC, TN, TX, UT, VA, WI

Name/Desc: IRSC

Info Provided: Driver and/or Vehicle
Coverage: US

Membership: SIIA, NALI, NPRRA, ASIS, NCISS, SHRM

Statement of Capabilities: Information Resource Service Company (IRSC) has an investigative database that accesses more than one billion records about individuals and businesses. Their database is available online 24 hours a day. They do not charge for connect time. A Windows-based front end program is available.

J

Jess Barker Document Research/Retrieval

400 Shelby
Gillespie, IL 62033
Telephone: **Fax:**
217-839-3219 217-839-2901
Year Founded: 1993

Clientele: Financial Institutions, Insurance - Agents/Brokers, Legal Profession, Public Record Research Firms

Applications: Asset/Lien Searching/Verification, Litigation, Lending/Leasing, General Business Information, Legal Compliance

Information Types:
Real Estate/Assessor (US)
Bankruptcy (US, IL)
Litigation/Judgments/Tax Liens (US, IL)
Uniform Commercial Code (US, IL)

Membership: NFPA, NPRRA

Statement of Capabilities: Jess Barker Document Research/Retrieval specializes in retrieving real estate information for mortgage transactions (current owner property reports, deed & mortgage retrieval) from a variety of local, regional and national public record resources (national agent contacts, direct searching, online searching). Expedited service can be arranged.

Judicial Research & Retrieval Service Inc

17 NW Miami Ct
Miami, FL 33128

Telephone: **Fax:**
800-529-6226   888-529-3291
305-379-3900   305-379-4460

Judiciallaw@aol.com

Year Founded: 1996

Clientele: Accountants, Financial Institutions, Legal Profession, Libraries, Loss Prevention Specialists, Private Investigators, Public Record Research Firms

Applications: Asset/Lien Searching/Verification, Filing/Recording Documents, General Business Information, Litigation

Information Types:
Bankruptcy (US, FL)
Criminal Information (FL)
Driver and/or Vehicle (FL)
Litigation/Judgments/Tax Liens (FL)

Membership: ABA

Statement of Capabilities: Judicial Search & Retrieval Services Inc is permitted to use court computers when visiting the courts in-person.

K

KeySearch Inc

PO Box 380123
Birmingham, AL 35238-0123

Telephone: **Fax:**
205-408-0065   888-408-0071
205-408-0071

www.keysearchinc.com

ksearchinc@aol.com

Year Founded: 1997

Clientele: Financial Institutions, Business - General, Corporate Counsel, Employers (HR/Personnel Depts), Financial Institutions, Mortgage Bankers

Applications: Employment Screening

Information Types:
Addresses/Telephone Numbers (US)
Bankruptcy (US)

Credit Information (US)
Criminal Information (US)
Driver and/or Vehicle (US)
Education/Employment (US)
Social Security (Numbers) (US)
Workers' Compensation (US)

Statement of Capabilities: KeySearch Inc assists companies nationwide with their employment screening needs, enabling clients to utilize previous employment data and education confirmations. Their services included many types of searches, including: criminal records, federal, outstanding warrants, motor vehicle, credit reports, workers' compensation, civil, professional licenses and bankruptcy. They provide reference checks and assistance with drug policies.

Knowledge Bank

23679 Calabasas Rd #274
Calabasas, CA 91302-3306

Telephone: **Fax:**
818-224-5235 818-224-4827

Year Founded: 1993

Clientele: Legal Profession, Real Estate Owners/Managers, Public Record Research Firms, Employers (HR/Personnel Depts), Property Owners/Managers, Attorney Firms

Applications: Litigation, Employment Screening, Support for Attorneys, Legal Research for Attorneys, Employment Screening

Information Types:
Education/Employment (US)
Litigation/Judgments/Tax Liens (US)
Criminal Information (US)

Membership: NALA, ATLA, AIIP, SLA, LAPA

Statement of Capabilities: The Knowledge Bank is an independent paralegal managed information and legal research firm providing litigation support and public record searching both manually and through online database searches. The principal is a nationally certified legal assistant.

KnowX

245 Peachtree Center Ave #1400
Atlanta, GA 30303

www.knowx.com

support@knowx.com

Parent Company: Information America Inc; West Group; Thomson Corp

Clientele: Business - General, Legal Profession, Banks, Government Agencies, Real Estate Owners/Managers, Securities Industry

Applications: Asset/Lien Searching/Verification, Background Info - Business, Competitive Intelligence, Locating People/Businesses, Government Document Retrieval

Proprietary Products:

Name/Desc: KnowX

Info Provided: Addresses/Telephone Numbers, Credit Information, Bankruptcy, Licenses/Registrations/Permits, Corporate/Trade Name Data, Aviation/Vessels, Litigation/Judgments/Tax Liens, Uniform Commercial Code

Media: Direct Online, Internet

Coverage: US

Statement of Capabilities: KnowX, a division of Information America (owned by West Group and Thomson Corp.) is one of the most comprehensive sources of public records available on the Internet. Included is aircraft ownership, bankruptcies, business directories, partnerships, DBAs, DEAs, death records, Duns, judgments, liens, lawsuits, licensing, residencies, real property foreclosures & refinancings, tax records, property transfers, sales permits, stock ownership, UCC and watercraft records.

Free Web Information:
Links, information, and ordering

Kramer Research

1757 Lamont St NW
Washington, DC 20010
Telephone: **Fax:**
202-234-5410   202-234-6362
ALEXINDC@WORLDNET.ATT.NET
Year Founded: 1991

Clientele: Attorney Firms, Business - General, Information - Brokers/Retrievers, Investigators - Fraud, Legal Profession, Libraries, Private Investigators

Applications: Asset/Lien Searching/Verification, Background Info - Business, Competitive Intelligence, Government Document Retrieval, Locating People/Businesses

Information Types:
Litigation/Judgments/Tax Liens (DC)
SEC/Other Financial (US)

Membership: AIIP, SCIP

Statement of Capabilities: Kramer Research has easy access to many Federal agencies, National Archives and the Library of Congress. They have the knowledge and experience to get clients the public records they need for smart business.

Land Records of Texas

1945 Walnut Hill Ln
Irving, TX 75038
Telephone: **Fax:**
800-678-8016   800-678-8017
972-580-8575   972-518-2412
Parent Company: Fidelity National Title
Year Founded: 1985

Clientele: Legal Profession, Financial Institutions, Lending Institutions, Mortgage Bankers, Real Estate Owners/Managers, Savings and Loans, Secured Lenders

Applications: Asset/Lien Searching/Verification, Filing/Recording Documents, Real Estate Transactions

Information Types:
Bankruptcy (US-TX)
Litigation/Judgments/Tax Liens (US-TX)
Real Estate/Assessor (US-TX)

Membership: ALTA, NAR, NPRRA

Statement of Capabilities: Land Records of Texas specializes in property records research in Texas, but they can handle nationwide requests. They offer trustee and foreclosure services statewide, and their turnaround time is generally 3-5 days.

Law Bulletin Information Network

415 N State
Chicago, IL 60610-4674
Telephone: **Fax:**
312-644-7800   312-527-2890
www.lawbulletin.com

Clientele: Legal Profession, Credit Reporting Agencies, Financial Institutions, Insurance - General, Real Estate Owners/Managers

Applications: Asset/Lien Searching/Verification, Locating People/Businesses, Employment Screening

Information Types:
UCC (IL)

Proprietary Products:

Name/Desc: Access Plus
Info Provided: Real Estate/Assessor
Media: Online Database
Coverage: IL-Cook County

Name/Desc: Access Plus
Info Provided: Litigation/Judgments/Tax Liens
Media: Online Database
Coverage: IL-Central, North Counties

Name/Desc: Access Plus
Info Provided: Addresses/Telephone Numbers
Media: Online Database
Coverage: IL

Membership: NPRRA, NFPA, NALFM

Statement of Capabilities: The Law Bulletin Publishing Company's Information Network, called access Plus, provides both online and access to Illinois Courts, vital public record information, corporate documents, realty sales, etc. They offer other useful DocuCheck services online, and also licensed investigative services.

Lawyers Aid Service Inc
PO Box 848
Austin, TX 78767-0848
Telephone: **Fax:**
512-474-2002 512-474-4329
Clientele: Accountants, Attorney Firms, Information - Brokers/Retrievers

Applications: Asset/Lien Searching/Verification, Filing/Recording Documents, Government Document Retrieval, Litigation, Real Estate Transactions

Information Types:
Bankruptcy (TX)
Corporate/Trade Name Data (TX-Travis)
Legislation/Regulation (TX)
Litigation/Judgments/Tax Liens (TX-Austin)
Uniform Commercial Code (TX-Travis)

Vital Records (TX)
Workers' Compensation (TX)

Membership: NPRRA

Statement of Capabilities: Handling 14,000 filings, retrievals and outfits a year, Lawyer's Aid Service performs virtually any type of filing, retrieval, legal research or errand in Austin TX at a reasonable cost. Lawyer's Aid can draft filings for clients. Typical turnaround time: same or next day for retrievals and filings, 2-5 business days for legal research (rush available). For Instant Incorporations, call by 2PM, be chartered by 5PM. Customized corporate outfits are available.

Legal Data Resources
2816 W Summerdale Ave #200
Chicago, IL 60625
Telephone: **Fax:**
800-735-9207 773-561-2488
773-561-2468

legaldat@theramp.net
Year Founded: 1990

Clientele: Attorney Firms, Collection Agencies, Credit Grantors, Financial Institutions, Insurance - General, Legal Profession, Public Record Research Firms

Applications: Litigation, General Business Information, Asset/Lien Searching/Verification, Legal Compliance, Real Estate Transactions

Information Types:
Bankruptcy (US, IL)
Criminal Information (IL-Cook, Lake, DuPage)
Legislation/Regulation (IL)
Litigation/Judgments/Tax Liens (US, IL-Cook)
Real Estate/Assessor (IL-Cook)
SEC/Other Financial (US)
Trademarks/Patents
Uniform Commercial Code (IL-Cook County)

Membership: AIIP, NPRRA

Statement of Capabilities: Legal Data Resources provides all kinds of public records information, specializing in Illinois information. Their experienced searchers are trained to scrutinize the data and advise clients about items that are especially significant or exceptional. They access the Federal Records Center in Chicago regularly.

Legal Research

PO Box 250267
Franklin, MI 48025-0267
Telephone: **Fax:**
248-353-0990   248-356-4655
Year Founded: 1983

Clientele: Accountants, Legal Profession,
Corporate Security, Employers (HR/Personnel
Depts), Investigators - Fraud, Financial
Institutions, Corporate Counsel

Applications: Asset/Lien Searching/Verification,
Background Info - Business, Collections,
Employment Screening, Filing/Recording
Documents

Information Types:
Bankruptcy (MI)
Criminal Information (MI)
Driver and/or Vehicle (MI)
Litigation/Judgments/Tax Liens (MI)
Real Estate/Assessor (MI)
Uniform Commercial Code (MI)
Vital Records (MI)
Workers' Compensation (MI)

Statement of Capabilities: Legal Research
specializes in document retrieval from all
courts and worldwide process serving.

LegalEase Inc

139 Fulton St #1013
New York, NY 10038
Telephone: **Fax:**
800-293-1277   212-393-9796
212-393-9070
Year Founded: 1985

Clientele: Legal Profession, Public Record
Research Firms, Financial Institutions,
Libraries, Educational Institutions, Insurance -
Claims, Investigators - Fraud

Applications: Litigation, Filing/Recording
Documents, General Business Information,
Locating People/Businesses

Information Types:
Licenses/Registrations/Permits (US)
Bankruptcy (US, NY)
Addresses/Telephone Numbers (US)
Vital Records (US, NY-New York City)
Real Estate/Assessor (US, NY-New York City)
Litigation/Judgments/Tax Liens (US, NY)

Membership: NAPPS, AIIP, PRRN

Statement of Capabilities: LegalEase was
formed by a former US District Court Clerk
and an attorney to provide professional legal
services to the New York legal community.
Since 1985 they have expanded their services
to include nationwide document search and
retrieval services at all levels-federal, state and
local. They have a nationwide network of
agents to assist at all levels. Their own staff
covers much of the New York metropolitan
area. They can access several online databases
to provide quick and economical information
and go directly to the source when requested to
obtain copies of necessary documents. Their
staff has more than 35 years of experience in
serving process. Most services are completed
with 48 hours at no extra charge.

Legalese

1912 F Street #100
Sacramento, CA 95816
Telephone: **Fax:**
916-498-1999   916-498-1980
Year Founded: 1983

Clientele: Collection Agencies, Asset-Based
Lenders, Business - General, Consumers
(Individuals), Information - Brokers/Retrievers,
Legal Service Companies, Lending Institutions

Applications: Litigation, Asset/Lien
Searching/Verification, Collections,
Lending/Leasing, Locating People/Businesses

Information Types:
Bankruptcy (CA)
Bankruptcy (CA)
Litigation/Judgments/Tax Liens (CA)
Criminal Information (CA)
Uniform Commercial Code (CA)
Legislation/Regulation (CA)
Licenses/Registrations/Permits (CA)
Workers' Compensation (CA)

Membership: NAPPS, NALV, NPRRA, APS

Statement of Capabilities: Although the
information provided by Legalese is available
through several vendors, Legalese
distinguishes their services by assigning each
account to one person who is responsible to
become familiar with the nature and purpose of
the client's requests. The legal background of
the staff makes Legalese well-suited to
litigation support and financial and collection
matters.

LegalTrieve Information Services Inc

80 Randall St
N Easton, MA 02356
Telephone: **Fax:**
508-238-4227   508-238-4678
Year Founded: 1995

Clientele: Legal Profession, Government Agencies, Public Record Research Firms, Real Estate Owners/Managers

Applications: Asset/Lien Searching/Verification, Filing/Recording Documents, Real Estate Transactions, Litigation, Legal Compliance

Information Types:
Addresses/Telephone Numbers (US)
Corporate/Trade Name Data (US)
Criminal Information (US)
Litigation/Judgments/Tax Liens (US)
Real Estate/Assessor (US)
Uniform Commercial Code (US)
Vital Records (US)
Bankruptcy (US)

Membership: PRRN, NPRRA

Statement of Capabilities: LegalTrieve Information Services is a nationwide public information and document filing/retrieval company servicing the legal, financial, credit, investigative, and business communities. They utilize both a network of nationwide correspondents, their staff of six, and in-house access to online databases, allowing them to expedite completion of projects at all levels of government, including courts and agencies. The principal has more than ten years experience with two major public record companies.

Legi-Slate Inc

10 G Street NE #500
Washington, DC 20002
Telephone: **Fax:**
800-733-1131   202-898-3030
202-898-2300
www.legislate.com
legislate@legislate.com
Parent Company: Washington Post Company
Year Founded: 1978

Clientele: Attorney Firms, Consulting Firms, Government Agencies, Legal Profession, Public Record Research Firms

Applications: Current Events, Legal Compliance

Information Types:
News/Current Events (US)
Legislation/Regulation (US)

Proprietary Products:
Name/Desc: Legi-Slate
Info Provided: Legislation/Regulations
Media: Online Database
Coverage: US

Statement of Capabilities: Legi-Slate provides expert guidance on federal and state government issues. Includes federal regulations, analysis, news, and current events, with timely delivery and responsive customized support.

Legislative Research Inc

121 21st Ave N #207
Nashville, TN 37203
Telephone: **Fax:**
615-329-2362   615-329-2362
www.tnresearch.com
trnres@usit.net
Year Founded: 1985

Clientele: Attorney Firms, Government Agencies, Legal Profession, Legal Service Companies, Public Record Research Firms

Applications: Background Info - Business, Filing/Recording Documents, Government Document Retrieval, Litigation, Real Estate Transactions

Information Types:
Corporate/Trade Name Data (TN)
Legislation/Regulation (TN)
Litigation/Judgments/Tax Liens (TN)
Uniform Commercial Code (TN)
Workers' Compensation (TN)

Statement of Capabilities: Legislative Research Inc specializes in Tennessee legislative histories which include transcripts of House and Senate floor sessions and committees (when available), original bills and amendments, fiscal notes, special committee reports, etc. They also provide descriptions of each legislative document and its use.

Free Web Information:
Links to nationwide general assemblies, secretaries of state, codes and business forms. The site includes description of the Tennessee legislative process, definitions of legislative

terms and links to legal sites for Tennessee legislative documents.

LEXIS Document Service

801 Adlai Stevenson Dr
Springfield, IL 62703-4261

Telephone: **Fax:**
800-634-9738 800-842-4235
217-529-5599 217-492-0636
www.netlds.com

Year Founded: 1962

Clientele: Financial Institutions, Legal Profession, Asset-Based Lenders, Equipment Leasing Companies, Corporate Counsel

Applications: Asset/Lien Searching/Verification, Lending/Leasing, Legal Compliance, Real Estate Transactions, Filing/Recording Documents

Information Types:
Driver and/or Vehicle (US)
Bankruptcy (US)
Litigation/Judgments/Tax Liens (US)
Corporate/Trade Name Data (US)
UCC (US)

Membership: NPRRA, ELA

Statement of Capabilities: LEXIS Document Services is a national public record search firm with 9 US offices. In addition to handling all aspects of public record searching and corporate compliance, their focus is UCC searching and filing. A national network of correspondents can complete any public record project, including coverage in Canada and the Virgin Islands. They are responsible for obtaining documents ordered online through the LEXDOC feature of LEXIS/NEXIS.

LEXIS-NEXIS

PO Box 933
Dayton, OH 45401-0933

Telephone:
800-227-9597
937-865-6800
www.lexis-nexis.com

Parent Company: Reed Elsevier Inc
Year Founded: 1973

Clientele: Legal Profession, Accountants, Business - General, Consulting Firms, Attorney Firms, Educational Institutions, Government Agencies

Applications: Legal Compliance, Current Events, General Business Information, Competitive Intelligence, Government Document Retrieval

Proprietary Products:

Name/Desc: LEXIS Law Publishing
Info Provided: Litigation/Judgments/Tax Liens
Media: Direct Online, Internet
Coverage: US

Name/Desc: Shepard's
Info Provided: Litigation/Judgments/Tax Liens
Media: Direct Online, Internet
Coverage: US

Name/Desc: Congressional Information Service
Info Provided: Legislation/Regulation
Media: Direct Online, CD-ROM
Coverage: US

Statement of Capabilities: For more than 10 years, LEXIS-NEXIS has been building one of the largest collections of public records in the US, and today is an industry leader in providing information to a variety of professionals in law, law enforcement, business, research, and academia. Four main business units are LEXIS, NEXIS, Reed Technologies & Information Systems, and Martindale-Hubbell. Their Quick-Check provides clients with company news and credit rating changes, brokerage reports, SEC filings, trends and views/analysis of companies, their debts, equities, and earnings estimates, etc.

LIDA Credit Agency Inc

450 Sunrise Hwy
Rockville Centre, NY 11570

Telephone: **Fax:**
516-678-4600 516-678-4611
Year Founded: 1920

Clientele: Financial Institutions, Business - General, Consumers (Individuals), Legal Profession, Government Agencies, Credit Grantors, Securities Industry

Applications: Litigation, Real Estate Transactions, Background Info - Business, Asset/Lien Searching/Verification, Employment Screening

Information Types:
Credit Information (US, NY)
Vital Records (NY)

Uniform Commercial Code (New York City)
Bankruptcy (US)
Driver and/or Vehicle (NY)
Education/Employment (US)
Tenant History (US)

Proprietary Products:

Name/Desc: LIDA
Info Provided: Litigation/Judgments/Tax
Liens
Media: Printed Report and Call-back
Coverage: DE, NJ, NY, PA

Statement of Capabilities: LIDA's management averages more than 35 years in public record research, investigations and credit/financial reporting. Among their 17 member staff are five licensed and bonded private investigators. They specialize in Metro New York City, including the five boroughs and surrounding counties.

Lloyds Maritime Information Services Inc

1200 Summer St
Stamford, CT 06905
Telephone: **Fax:**
800-423-8672   203-358-0437
203-359-8383
www.lmis.com

Year Founded: 1986

Clientele: Business - General, Government Agencies, Legal Profession, Professionals-Other

Applications: General Business Information, Direct Marketing, Background Info - Business, Asset/Lien Searching/Verification

Information Types:
Addresses/Telephone Numbers (US, International)

Proprietary Products:

Name/Desc: SEADATA/MARDATA
Info Provided: Aviation/Vessels
Media: Online Database (available on Genie)
Coverage: US, International

Name/Desc: APEX (Analysis of Petroleum Exports)
Info Provided: Economic/Demographic
Media: Disk
Coverage: US, International

Name/Desc: LSA (Linear Shipping Analysis)
Info Provided: Economic/Demographic
Media: Disk
Coverage: US, International

Name/Desc: AS+ (Analysis Software +)
Info Provided: Economic/Demographic
Media: Disk
Coverage: US, International

Statement of Capabilities: Lloyd's Maritime Information Services is a joint venture company owned by Lloyd's Register, the world's premier Classification Society and LLP Ltd. Information is maintained on six computer databases, providing coverage of over 85,000 self-propelled seagoing merchant ships of 100 gross tonnage and above, comprising the world merchant fleet plus those on order, together with movements, casualties, charter fixtures, ownership details, all referenced by the unique Lloyd's Register Identity Number. Lloyd's Maritime provides the world's maritime and business community with some of the most comprehensive, up-to-date and validated maritime information available.

Locators International Inc

Bala Cynwyd, PA 19004
Telephone:
800-280-6664

Clientele: Accountants, Business - General, Employers (HR/Personnel Depts), Information - Brokers/Retrievers, Legal Profession, Private Investigators, Landlords

Applications: Asset/Lien Searching/Verification, Background Info - Business, Background Info - Individuals, Litigation, Locating People/Businesses

Information Types:
Addresses/Telephone Numbers (US)
Credit Information (US)
Criminal Information (US)
Driver and/or Vehicle (US)
Litigation/Judgments/Tax Liens (US)
Real Estate/Assessor (US)
Social Security (Numbers) (US)
Workers' Compensation (US)

Membership: ICA, NACM, NAIS

Statement of Capabilities: Locators International provides over 125 types of searches, both domestic and international. Most domestic searches are completed within 48 hours or less.

Logan Information Services

636-B Piney Forest Rd #172

Danville, VA 24540
Telephone: **Fax:**
888-640-8613 804-836-6709
804-791-0808

LISINC@gamewood.net
Parent Company: Lotel Inc
Year Founded: 1991

Clientele: Apartment Owners/Managers,
Lending Institutions, Mortgage Bankers, Public
Record Research Firms, Real Estate
Owners/Managers, Property
Owners/Managers, Employers (HR/Personnel
Depts)

Applications: Direct Marketing, Employment
Screening, Real Estate Transactions, Tenant
Screening, Asset/Lien Searching/Verification

Information Types:
Criminal Information (NC, VA)
Driver and/or Vehicle (NC, VA)
Real Estate/Assessor (NC, VA)

Proprietary Products:

Name/Desc: Driving Records
Info Provided: Driver and/or Vehicle
Media: Direct Online and Printed Report
Coverage: CA

Name/Desc: LIS 5
Info Provided: Litigation/Judgments/Tax
Liens, Tenant History, Uniform Commercial
Code, Voter Registration and
Education/Employment
Media: Printed Report and Internet
Coverage: NC, VA

Membership: NAIS, NASA, NPRRA

Statement of Capabilities: Logan Information
Services is an information retrieval and
verification company providing public records
research services to some of the country's
largest and best known corporations. Their
services include criminal, civil and real estate
record searches. One of the principals of the
organization was a key employee for a major
consumer information provider; he has trained
his staff to ensure that each report will be
accurately prepared and timely received.
Turnaround time on searches is 24-48 hours,
depending on the type of search requested.
"Rush" service is available on all searches.

Logan Registration Service Inc
PO Box 161644
Sacramento, CA 95816

Telephone: **Fax:**
800-524-4111 916-457-5789
916-457-5787
Year Founded: 1976

Clientele: Legal Profession, Financial
Institutions, Public Record Research Firms,
Insurance - Agents/Brokers, Private
Investigators, Collection Agencies, Lending
Institutions

Applications: Asset/Lien Searching/Verification,
Background Info - Business, Background Info -
Individuals

Information Types:
Driver and/or Vehicle (US)
Addresses/Telephone Numbers (CA)
Uniform Commercial Code (CA)
Social Security (Numbers) (US)
Real Estate/Assessor (CA)
Vital Records (CA)

Membership: NFIB

Statement of Capabilities: Logan has more
than 20 year experience working with
California driver and vehicle records. They are
an online vendor that allows their DMV
authorized clients to retrieve driver and vehicle
registration records in seconds with a computer
software program that is available free of
charge. Clients are also able to access needed
records via phone or fax.

Loren Data Corp
4640 Admiralty Way #430
Marina Del Rey, CA 90292
Telephone: **Fax:**
800-745-6736 310-574-6840
310-827-7400
www.LD.com

Clientele: Business - General, Consulting Firms,
Consumers (Individuals), Government
Agencies, Information - Brokers/Retrievers,
Libraries

Applications: Government Document Retrieval

Information Types:
Licenses/Registrations/Permits (US)

Statement of Capabilities: Loren Data Corp
provides customers with advice and access to
government business, helping make bids and
gain government contracts. They offer free
access and e-mail based subscription services
for their publication Commerce Business
Daily, CDB.

Free Web Information:
Access to back issues to January '95 with over 300,000 notices regarding contracting opportunities with the US federal government.

M

M & M Search Services
624 9th St NW #222
Washington, DC 20032
Telephone: **Fax:**
202-393-3144   202-393-3242
Clientele: Attorney Firms, Lending Institutions, Consumers (Individuals), Insurance - Underwriting, Investment Bankers, Public Record Research Firms, Real Estate Owners/Managers

Applications: Asset/Lien Searching/Verification, Background Info - Individuals, Filing/Recording Documents, Insurance Underwriting, Real Estate Transactions

Information Types:
Criminal Information (DC, MD)
Litigation/Judgments/Tax Liens (DC, MD)
Real Estate/Assessor (DC, MD)
Uniform Commercial Code (DC, MD)

Maine Public Record Services
PO Box 514
Moody, ME 04054
Telephone: **Fax:**
207-646-9065   207-646-9065
Year Founded: 1993

Clientele: Credit Reporting Agencies, Public Record Research Firms, Information - Brokers/Retrievers, Insurance - Agents/Brokers, Legal Profession, Lending Institutions, Mortgage Bankers

Applications: Real Estate Transactions, Asset/Lien Searching/Verification, Filing/Recording Documents, Competitive Intelligence, Background Info - Individuals

Information Types:
Addresses/Telephone Numbers (ME)

Bankruptcy (ME)
UCC (ME)

Proprietary Products:

Name/Desc: Maine Public Records
Info Provided: Real Estate Assessor, Litigation/Judgments/Tax Liens
Media: Disk, Printed Report, Lists or Labells and Call-in
Coverage: ME-Cumberland, Knox, Lincoln, Waldo, York

Name/Desc: Mortgage Filings
Info Provided: Addresses/Telephone Numbers
Media: Disk, Magnetic Tape and Lists or labels
Coverage: ME-6 counties

Membership: PRRN

Statement of Capabilities: Maine Public Records (MPRS) specializes in corporate services and public research at the federal, state and county level. They maintain a database of County Registrar information for nine Maine counties, primarily York and Cumberland. The database contains mortgage and other legal actions such as tax liens and foreclosure, affecting properties in those counties. The MPRS principals have banking, real estate, and investigative backgrounds.

Martindale-Hubbell
121 Chanlon Road
New Providence, NJ 07974
Telephone: **Fax:**
800-526-4902   908-464-3553
908-464-6800
www.martindale.com

info@martindale.com
Parent Company: Reed Elsevier PLC Group
Year Founded: 1868

Clientele: Business - General, Legal Profession, Libraries, Public Record Research Firms, Consumers (Individuals)

Applications: Background Info - Business

Proprietary Products:

Name/Desc: Martindale-Hubbell Law Directory (Attorneys and Law Firms)
Info Provided: Addresses/Telephone Numbers, Education/Employment
Media: Available on LEXIS, Publication, Printed Reports, CD-ROM and Lists or Labels
Coverage: US, International

Statement of Capabilities: Martindale-Hubbell's database is now regarded as the primary source for attorney and law firm information around the world. Their flagship product, Martindale-Hubbell Law Directory consists of more the 900,000 listings, organized by city, state, county, and province with extensive cross-references and indexes. Products are available in four media: hardbound print, CR-ROM, via LEXIS/NEXIS (a sister company) and Internet via the Martindale-Hubbell Lawyer Locator. Their data includes corporate law departments, legal-related services such as PIs, title search companies, law digests.

Free Web Information:
Contacts, feedback, site maps, lawyer locator, vendors.

MBK Consulting
60 N Harding Rd
Columbus, OH 43209-1524
Telephone: **Fax:**
614-239-8977 614-239-0599
mbkcons@netexp.net
Year Founded: 1991

Clientele: Public Record Research Firms, Legal Profession, Libraries, Educational Institutions, Professionals-Other, Legal Service Companies

Applications: General Business Information, Government Document Retrieval, Current Events, Locating People/Businesses, Filing/Recording Documents

Information Types:
Vital Records (OH)
Wills/Probate (OH)
Social Security (Numbers) (OH)
News/Current Events (US)
Genealogical Information (US)
Uniform Commercial Code (OH)
Real Estate/Assessor (OH)
Litigation/Judgments/Tax Liens (OH)

Membership: ALA, SLA, NGS, SAA, AASLH, PRRN

Statement of Capabilities: MBK Consulting provides access to major research libraries and public records in Ohio. Their professional librarian has more than 15 years research and reference experience. Historical research and public record retrieval and abstracting are specialties.

McGinley Paralegal & Search Services Inc
155 E Market St #750
Indianapolis, IN 46204
Telephone: **Fax:**
317-630-9721 317-630-9723
Year Founded: 1992

Applications: Asset/Lien Searching/Verification, Background Info - Business, Filing/Recording Documents, Real Estate Transactions, Current Events

Information Types:
Uniform Commercial Code (IL, IN, MI)
Corporate/Trade Name Data (IN)
Litigation/Judgments/Tax Liens (IL, IN, MI)
Bankruptcy (IN)
Real Estate/Assessor (IL, IN, MI)
Criminal Information (IN-Marion)

Membership: PRRN, NPRRA, Indiana Paralegal Association

Statement of Capabilities: McGinley Paralegal & Search Services specializes in assisting attorneys, financial institutions and other information service companies in research, filing and retrieval of documents. They offer nationwide service at a reasonable price.

McGowan & Clark Services
3295 115th Ave NE #163
Bellevue, WA 98004
Telephone: **Fax:**
888-727-6352 425-828-3616
425-827-6352
Year Founded: 1993

Applications: Asset/Lien Searching/Verification, Background Info - Business, Background Info - Individuals, Employment Screening

Information Types:
Bankruptcy (WA)
Criminal Information (WA)
Driver and/or Vehicle (WA)
Litigation/Judgments/Tax Liens (WA)
Uniform Commercial Code (WA)
Vital Records (WA)

Membership: ALA

Statement of Capabilities: McGowan & Clark Services searches every county in the state of Washington. Between alpha-numeric pagers, cell phones and a 24-hour answering service, they are able to offer their clients continual contact throughout business hours. Their turnaround time is within 24 hours.

MDR/Minnesota Driving Records

1710 Douglas Dr. N #103
Golden Valley, MN 55422-4313
Telephone: **Fax:**
800-644-6877 612-595-8079
612-755-1164
Clientele: Business - General, Insurance - Agents/Brokers, Insurance - General

Applications: Insurance Underwriting, Risk Management, Background Info - Individuals, Direct Marketing

Proprietary Products:

Name/Desc: MDR
Info Provided: Driver and/or Vehicle
Media: Automated Telephone Lookup, Printed Report and Lists or Labels
Coverage: US

Statement of Capabilities: MDR provides an automated touch-tone call-in service for driver information in Minnesota, letting clients retrieve a record with a verbal response in less than one minute, followed by a fax hard copy within minutes. Service available 24 hours a day every day. The service is endorsed by the Minnesota Insurance Agents Assoc.

Merlin Information Services

215 S Complex Dr
Kalispell, MT 59901
Telephone: **Fax:**
800-367-6646 406-755-8568
406-755-8550
www.merlindata.com/redirect.
asp

Year Founded: 1991

Clientele: Attorney Firms, Collection Agencies, Government Agencies, Insurance - Claims, Corporate Security, Private Investigators, Financial Institutions

Applications: Locating People/Businesses, Asset/Lien Searching/Verification, Background Info - Business, Collections, Fraud Prevention/Detection

Information Types:
Addresses/Telephone Numbers (US)
Corporate/Trade Name Data (CA)
Criminal Information (CA)
Bankruptcy (US)
Uniform Commercial Code (CA)
Licenses/Registrations/Permits (CA)
Real Estate/Assessor (CA)
Social Security (Numbers) (US)

Proprietary Products:

Name/Desc: California Criminal
Info Provided: Criminal Information
Media: CD-ROM and Internet
Coverage: CA

Name/Desc: CA Brides and Grooms
Info Provided: Vital Records
Media: CD-ROM and Internet
Coverage: CA

Name/Desc: CA Statewide Property
Info Provided: Real Estate/Assessor
Media: CD-ROM and Internet
Coverage: CA

Name/Desc: CA Civil Superior Indexes
Info Provided: Litigation/Judgments/Tax Liens
Media: CD-ROM and Internet
Coverage: CA

Name/Desc: CA Prof. License
Info Provided: Licenses/Registrations/Permits (Professional Licenses)
Media: CD-ROM and Internet
Coverage: CA

Name/Desc: UCC Index
Info Provided: Uniform Commercial Code (Filing Index)
Media: CD-ROM and Internet
Coverage: CA

Name/Desc: CA Corp
Info Provided: Corporation/Trade Name Data (LTD Partnerships)
Media: CD-ROM and Internet
Coverage: CA

Name/Desc: National People Finder
Info Provided: Addresses/Telephone Numbers, Vital Records
Media: CD-ROM and Internet
Coverage: US

Statement of Capabilities: Merlin Information Services produces unique search and retrieval systems to search public record and proprietary information databases. Merlin specializes in new technology for combined media search and retrieval using both CD-ROM and the Internet. Merlin's proprietary databases and several national databases are available on the Internet at their web site. They also sell public record related CD-ROM products produced by a number of other publishers, including voter registration records, DMV records, and Social Security death records.

Free Web Information:
Merlin' offers a free web search called "the ultimate weapon." This product gives the searcher a free index of information from a combined search into most of Merlin's proprietary databases.

Merlins Data Research
1031 #25 Loch Vail Dr
Apopka, FL 32712-2089
Telephone: **Fax:**
888-434-6337 407-886-5394
407-886-5354
www.MERLINSREPORTS.com
Year Founded: 1992

Clientele: Business - General, Consumers (Individuals), Financial Institutions, Professionals-Other, Public Record Research Firms, Real Estate Owners/Managers

Applications: Background Info - Business, Employment Screening, General Business Information, Civil, Federal, & Bankruptcy Courts

Information Types:
Credit Information (US, FL)
Driver and/or Vehicle (US, FL)
Uniform Commercial Code (US, FL)
Workers' Compensation (US, FL)
Criminal Information (US, FL)
Licenses/Registrations/Permits (US, FL)

Membership: NPRRA, NAIS, FALI, PIAF

Statement of Capabilities: With 40 years experience in Florida business, including real estate location, demographics, government and banking, Merlin's Data Research has affiliates in Florida, nationwide, and overseas. Reports available include criminal arrests/convictions, workers' compensation history, driving record, education, credit report, mortgage updates and assignments, Social Security, employment and earnings, and business credit. Other reports include name/address/phone number verification, FAA, FCC, and medical and teacher licenses.

Merola Services
PO Box 12216
Albany, NY 12212
Telephone: **Fax:**
518-869-8002 518-869-7755
AM MEROLA@aol.com
Year Founded: 1988

Clientele: Collection Agencies, Insurance - General, Legal Profession, Public Record Research Firms, Employers (HR/Personnel Depts)

Applications: Locating People/Businesses, Asset/Lien Searching/Verification, Background Info - Business, Employment Screening, Real Estate Transactions

Information Types:
Addresses/Telephone Numbers (US)
Driver and/or Vehicle (US, NY)
Social Security (Numbers) (US)
Corporate/Trade Name Data (US)
Criminal Information (US)
Real Estate/Assessor (US)

Statement of Capabilities: Merola Services is certified to provide New York State DMV records, police reports, MV 104s, abstracts, and vehicle information, with instant access to New York DMV and New Jersey driver/vehicle information, and Florida DMV. On a nationwide basis, Merola Services secure police reports, driver/vehicle and insurance information where available. Services include: locate missing witnesses to accidents, skip tracing, phone number ownership, surname scan by city, state and nationwide. Also, criminal records and real property records by county, asset searches, and pre-employment screening.

Metro Clerking Inc
134 N LaSalle #1826
Chicago, IL 60602
Telephone: **Fax:**
312-263-2977 312-263-2985
Year Founded: 1985

Clientele: Legal Profession, Public Record Research Firms

Applications: Filing/Recording Documents, Litigation, Real Estate Transactions, Employment Screening, Tenant Screening

Information Types:
Bankruptcy (IL-Northern Dist)
Litigation/Judgments/Tax Liens (IL-Cook)

Real Estate/Assessor (IL-Cook)
Uniform Commercial Code (IL-Cook)
Vital Records (IL)
Voter Registration (IL)
Workers' Compensation (IL)

Statement of Capabilities: Metro Clerking provides a full range of public records services, specializing in the Chicago area. They regularly access the Federal Records Center in Chicago, which houses all the Northern District closed civil and bankruptcy files.

Metromail Corporation
360 East 22nd St
Lombard, IL 60148
Telephone: **Fax:**
800-927-2238 708-916-1336
www.metromail.com

Parent Company: Experian sister company
Year Founded: 1941

Clientele: Financial Institutions, Collection Agencies, Insurance - General, Legal Profession

Applications: Locating People/Businesses, Fraud Prevention/Detection, Direct Marketing

Proprietary Products:

Name/Desc: MetroSearch
Info Provided: Addresses/Telephone Numbers
Media: CD-ROM
Coverage: US

Name/Desc: Cole Directory
Info Provided: Addresses/Telephone Numbers
Media: CD-ROM, Publication
Coverage: US

Membership: DMA, ACA, ALA

Statement of Capabilities: Their MetroNet product includes direct access to the electronic directory assistance databases of the Regional Bells (RBOCs). Regional editions of the MetroSearch CD-ROM products and call-in services are featured.

Michiana Searches, Inc
28916 Kehres
Elkhart, IN 46514
Telephone: **Fax:**
800-403-5207 219-266-8399
219-266-4652
jamibaker@prodigy.net

Year Founded: 1993

Clientele: Educational Institutions, Legal Profession, Legal Service Companies, Title Companies

Applications: Employment Screening, Filing/Recording Documents, Real Estate Transactions

Information Types:
Criminal Information (IN)
Environmental (IN)
Litigation/Judgments/Tax Liens (IN)
Real Estate/Assessor (IN)
Uniform Commercial Code (IN)

Statement of Capabilities: Michiana specializes in 5 Indiana counties (Elkhart, Kosciusko, Marshall, St Joseph, Starke), and has 24-48 hour turnaround time on property reports. Full title searches may take longer.

MicroPatent USA
250 Dodge Ave
East Haven, CT 06512
Telephone: **Fax:**
800-648-6787 203-466-5054
203-466-5055
http://micropat.com
info@micropat.com
Parent Company: Information Holdings Inc
Year Founded: 1989

Clientele: Consumers (Individuals), Educational Institutions, Information - Brokers/Retrievers, Legal Profession, Legal Service Companies, Libraries, Product Development Managers

Applications: Legal Compliance, Competitive Intelligence, General Business Information, Litigation, Research & Development

Proprietary Products:

Name/Desc: WPS
Info Provided: Trademarks/Patents
Media: Online, CD-ROM, E-mail
Coverage: US, International

Name/Desc: TradeMark Checker
Info Provided: Trademarks/Patents
Media: CD-ROM
Coverage: US, International

Name/Desc: Mark Search Plus
Info Provided: Trademark
Media: Online, CD-ROM
Coverage: US, International

Membership: AALL, ATLA, AIPLA, INTA, NALA, NLG

Statement of Capabilities: Micropatent is a global leader in the production and distribution of patent and trademark information. MicroPatent is committed to developing intellectual property systems with its sophisticated and talented programming staff. MicroPatent Europe is located in London, England.

Military Information Enterprises Inc
PO Box 17118
Spartanburg, SC 29301
Telephone: **Fax:**
800-937-2133   864-595-0813
864-595-0981
www.militaryusa.com
miepub@aol.com
Year Founded: 1988

Clientele: Legal Profession, Collection Agencies, Genealogists, Attorney Firms

Applications: Background Info - Individuals, Genealogical Research, Locating People/Businesses

Information Types:
Military Svc (US)

Proprietary Products:

Name/Desc: Nationwide Locator Online
Info Provided: Military Svc (Files and Military Service)
Media: Internet
Coverage: US

Statement of Capabilities: Military Information Enterprises specializes in current and former military locates and background checks. They also publish books on locating people. The principal served 28 years in the US Army and is a licensed private investigator in South Carolina and Texas.

Free Web Information:
From their web site, you can search their "Vietnam Veterans Database" for free. They also have a searchable list of over 7,200 military reunions.

MLQ Attorney Services
3200 Cobb Galleria Pkwy #225
Atlanta, GA 30339
Telephone: **Fax:**
800-466-8794   770-984-7049

770-984-7007
Parent Company: Lindsay Services, Inc.
Year Founded: 1983

Clientele: Legal Profession, Financial Institutions

Applications: Litigation, Asset/Lien Searching/Verification, Lending/Leasing, Locating People/Businesses, Employment Screening

Information Types:
Bankruptcy (US)
Litigation/Judgments/Tax Liens (US)
Real Estate/Assessor (US)
Uniform Commercial Code (US)
Driver and/or Vehicle (US)
Credit Information (US)
Criminal Information (US)

Membership: NAPPS, NPRRA

Statement of Capabilities: Since 1983, MLQ Attorney Services has provided a nationwide comprehensive packages of services. Staffed with fully-insured, experienced paralegals, MLQ performs nationwide service of process, subpoena preparation, legal research, document retrieval, environmental assessments, deposition summaries, bankruptcy services, online research and investigative services. MLQ performs title abstracting, also. Turnaround can be 24 hours or less, with immediate confirmations and telecommunication of results.

Motznik Computer Services Inc
8301 Briarwood St #100
Anchorage, AK 99518-3332
Telephone:
907-344-6254
Year Founded: 1976

Clientele: Collection Agencies, Financial Institutions, Government Agencies, Legal Profession, Business - General, Attorney Firms, Lending Institutions

Applications: Asset/Lien Searching/Verification, Locating People/Businesses, Real Estate Transactions, Litigation, Background Info - Business

Proprietary Products:

Name/Desc: Alaska Public Information Access System
Info Provided: Aviation/Vessels, Bankruptcy, Licenses/Registrations/Permits, Litigation/Judgments/Tax Liens, Criminal

Information, Corporate/Trade Name Data, Uniform Commercial Code, Real Estate Assessor, Voter Registration and Driver and/or Vehicle

Media: Online Database, Call back

Coverage: AK

Membership: NFIB

Statement of Capabilities: Motznik Computer Services' product is a comprehensive information research system that provides access to a wide selection of Alaska public files online. Information that can be researched includes: tax liens, UCC, address, real property, Anchorage civil suits, commercial fishing vessels, judgments, motor vehicles, partnerships, bankruptcies, aircraft, permanent fund filing, businesses, Anchorage criminal cases and commercial fishing permits. MV data does not include driver information.

MVRs of Texas

11555 Mulholland Dr
Stafford, TX 77477

Telephone: **Fax:**
281-568-1900   281-568-1185

Year Founded: 1987

Clientele: Employers (HR/Personnel Depts), Insurance - Underwriting, Insurance - General, Insurance - Agents/Brokers

Applications: Employment Screening, Fraud Prevention/Detection, Insurance Underwriting

Information Types:
Driver and/or Vehicle (US)

Statement of Capabilities: MVRs of Texas has been providing driving records nationwide since 1987. They offer computer access and fax-in/fax-back capability. Turnaround time is 1 day for Texas driving records and 1-2 days for most other states. Quick access is available for many states. Texas driving records include a three-year history of moving violations, accidents, suspensions and restrictions. Records also include the original date of application and current status of the license. Information varies on records from other states. Restrictions apply in some states.

N

National Background Investigations Inc

PO Box 156
Mayo, MD 21106

Telephone: **Fax:**
410-798-0072   410-798-7868

`nbi.2@aol.com`

Year Founded: 1994

Clientele: Apartment Owners/Managers, Business - General, Financial Institutions, Information - Brokers/Retrievers, Legal Service Companies, News Media, Private Investigators

Applications: Asset/Lien Searching/Verification, Background Info - Business, Background Info - Individuals, Collections, Employment Screening

Information Types:
Addresses/Telephone Numbers (US)
Credit Information (US)
Criminal Information (US)
Driver and/or Vehicle (US)
Education/Employment (US)
Litigation/Judgments/Tax Liens (US)
Social Security (Numbers) (US)
Uniform Commercial Code (US)

Membership: ABW, NAWBO, PRRN

Statement of Capabilities: National Background Investigations, Inc (NBI) is a pre- and post-employment screening company with direct access to county criminal and civil history records from nearly 4,000 courts nationwide. Our vast network of paralegals and legal researchers enter the myriad of county courts on a daily basis to retrieve the most current public record information. Other search services include motor vehicle records, financial reports, SSN and address verifications and comprehensive profiles. NBI is committed to a response time of 24-48 hours to aid in expediting processing of applications. NBI is comprised of a team of seasoned professionals with over 50 years of collective experience in tenant screening/property management, background screening, consumer fraud, business law and risk management. All in all,

NBI Inc provides quality reporting efficiently and accurately.

National Background Reports Inc
243 Adams Ave
Memphis, TN 38103
Telephone: **Fax:**
800-526-4654   901-526-4753
901-526-4654
www.nbri.com

Information Types:
Criminal Information (US, TN)
Litigation/Judgments/Tax Liens (US, TN)
Real Estate/Assessor (US, TN)
Uniform Commercial Code (US, TN)
Driver and/or Vehicle (US, TN)
Education/Employment (US)

Membership: PRRN, NPRRA, AIIP

Statement of Capabilities: NBRI is a licensed professional, full service public record research company, specializing in searches requiring adherence to the Fair Credit Reporting Act, such as criminal background reports on prospective employees and tenants.

National Consumer Services Inc
1018 S 4th St #125
Louisville, KY 40203
Telephone: **Fax:**
888-965-3892   502-585-5701
502-585-5499
Clientele: Asset-Based Lenders, Legal Profession, Financial Institutions, Attorney Firms

Applications: Collections, Employment Screening, Insurance Underwriting, Legal Compliance, Lending/Leasing

Information Types:
Bankruptcy (KY-Jefferson)
Credit Information (KY-Jefferson)
Criminal Information (KY-Jefferson)
Workers' Compensation (KY)

Membership: NFPA, PRRN

Statement of Capabilities: National Consumer Services specializes in retrieval of information from US Bankruptcy Courts and US District Courts. They also offer above standard turnaround times.

National Corporate Research Ltd
225 W 34th St #910

New York, NY 10122
Telephone: **Fax:**
800-221-0102   212-564-6083
212-947-7200
www.nationalcorp.com
info@nationalcorp.com
Year Founded: 1980

Clientele: Accountants, Legal Profession, Financial Institutions, Public Record Research Firms, Secured Lenders, Attorney Firms

Applications: Asset/Lien Searching/Verification, Filing/Recording Documents, Legal Compliance, Lending/Leasing, Real Estate Transactions

Information Types:
Bankruptcy (US)
Corporate/Trade Name Data (US)
Driver and/or Vehicle (US, NY)
Litigation/Judgments/Tax Liens (US)
Real Estate/Assessor (US)
Trademarks/Patents (US)
Uniform Commercial Code (US)

Membership: NPRRA

Statement of Capabilities: Since 1980, National Corporate Research Ltd, with full service offices in NYC, Albany, Delaware and California, has provided nationwide public record search and filing services. National takes a unique approach by providing personalized service to clients. Each client works with an assigned service specialist familiar with the specific requirements of each order. Orders can be placed by phone, fax or e-mail. Reports, invoices and statements can be customized to include client-specific reference information. Clients also receive regular status updates on their orders, keeping them on top of their projects.

National Credit Information Network NCI
PO Box 31221
Cincinnati, OH 45231-0221
Telephone: **Fax:**
800-374-1400   513-522-1702
513-522-3832
www.wdia.com

Parent Company: WDIA Corporation
Year Founded: 1983

Clientele: Business - General, Corporate Security, Employers (HR/Personnel Depts)

Applications: Background Info - Individuals, Locating People/Businesses, Employment Screening, Tenant Screening

Proprietary Products:

Name/Desc: Evictalert
Info Provided: Tenant History
Media: Printed Report, Fax and Call back
Coverage: IN, KY, OH

Name/Desc: NCI Network
Info Provided: Credit Information, Addresses/Telephone Numbers, Social Security (Numbers), Voter Registration, Driver and/or Vehicle
Media: Direct Online and Internet
Coverage: US

Statement of Capabilities: National Credit Information Network (NCI) specializes in interfacing with credit and public record databases for online searches with immediate response time. Online ordering is available for setup and for searches using a credit card. Access is available through their Internet site. A variety of packages include applicant identity, SSNs, DMVs, education, reference and credential verification, criminal history, bankruptcy and civil history, workers comp claims, and more.

Free Web Information:
Online ordering and information.

National Data Access Corp

PO Box 23123
Columbia, SC 29224
Telephone: **Fax:**
800-528-8790   800-542-7499
803-699-6130   803-699-6178
www.N-DAC.com

Year Founded: 1990

Clientele: Business - General, Legal Profession, Financial Institutions, Insurance - General, Private Investigators, Mortgage Bankers, Public Record Research Firms

Applications: Asset/Lien Searching/Verification, Filing/Recording Documents, Lending/Leasing, Litigation, Real Estate Transactions

Information Types:
Bankruptcy (US, SC)
Litigation/Judgments/Tax Liens (US, SC)
Corporate/Trade Name Data (US, SC)
Driver and/or Vehicle (US, SC)
Workers' Compensation (US, SC)

Uniform Commercial Code (US, SC)
Real Estate/Assessor (US, SC)
Voter Registration (US, SC)

Membership: NPRRA, NAPPS, PRRN

Statement of Capabilities: National Data Access is a public records retrieval and filing firm that covers all South Carolina offices of federal, state, county and municipal agencies. They offer online state UCC searches and have an on-site microfilm library for South Carolina UCC filings. Through correspondents, they are able to retrieve and file documents anywhere in the US and in some other countries.

National Document Filing & Retrieval Inc

3111 N Central #200
Phoenix, AZ 85012
Telephone: **Fax:**
800-933-8223   602-274-5573
602-274-5578
www.ndrinc.com

Year Founded: 1981

Clientele: Asset-Based Lenders, Attorney Firms, Banks, Corporate Counsel, Credit Grantors, Legal Profession, Public Record Research Firms

Applications: Filing/Recording Documents, Lending/Leasing, Real Estate Transactions, Corporate/Incorporations

Information Types:
Litigation/Judgments/Tax Liens (US)
Driver and/or Vehicle (AZ)
Uniform Commercial Code (US)
Bankruptcy (US)
Corporate/Trade Name Data (US)
Credit Information (US)
Criminal Information (US)
Real Estate/Assessor (US)

Membership: NPRRA

Statement of Capabilities: National Document Retrieval (NDR) provides due diligence research and investigative services, document retrieval (USS specialists) and computer research to financial, corporate and legal clients throughout the US. They provide documentation from Arizona and California Secretaries of State and Maricopa and Pima Counties (AZ), and in-house ownership of UCC indexes. NDR treats a husband and wife as one search in most cases, effectively providing half-price searches. Other services include Arizona driver histories and vehicle ownership, investigations for assets and liabilities, background inquiries, business activities, litigation histories, and witness location.

National Fraud Center

Four Horsham Business Center
300 Welsh Rd #200Horsham, PA 19044

Telephone: **Fax:**
800-999-5658   215-657-7071
215-657-0800
www.nationalfraud.com

Year Founded: 1981

Clientele: Financial Institutions, Government Agencies, Insurance - Agents/Brokers, Legal Profession, Insurance - General, Insurance - Claims

Applications: Fraud Prevention/Detection, Risk Management

Information Types:
Litigation/Judgments/Tax Liens (US)
Real Estate/Assessor (US)
Corporate/Trade Name Data (US)

Proprietary Products:

Name/Desc: NFC Online
Info Provided: Software/Training
Media: CD-ROM, Disk and Call-in
Coverage: US, International

Name/Desc: Bank Fraud Database
Info Provided: Criminal Information
Media: Online Database and Call-in
Coverage: US, International

Name/Desc: Insurance Fraud Database
Info Provided: Criminal Information
Media: Online Database and Call-in
Coverage: US, International

Name/Desc: Organized Crime Database
Info Provided: Criminal Information
Media: Online Database and Call-in
Coverage: US, International

Name/Desc: Government Fraud Database
Info Provided: Criminal Information
Media: Online Database and Call-in
Coverage: US, International

Name/Desc: The Fraud Bulletin
Info Provided: Criminal History
Media: Publication
Coverage: US

Name/Desc: Fraud Alert

Info Provided: Criminal Information
Media: Publication
Coverage: US

Name/Desc: Cellular Fraud Database
Info Provided: Criminal Information
Media: Online Database
Coverage: US

Name/Desc: Check Fraud Database
Info Provided: Criminal Information
Media: Online Database
Coverage: US

Membership: ASIS, IAAI, CII, IFS

Statement of Capabilities: National Fraud Center combines its diverse databases into a system: NFConline. They utilize a fraud prevention, an interdiction program, and risk management tools to discover and prevent fraud and risk. They also specialize in pro-active measures such as security policies, training, and installation of security devices to protect corporations from future losses.

National Records Services

17201 E 40 Hwy #211
Independence, MO 64055

Telephone: **Fax:**
888-840-7257   888-840-6164
816-373-1661   816-373-8071
chadweber@nationalrecords.net

Year Founded: 1997

Clientele: Apartment Owners/Managers, Lending Institutions, Educational Institutions, Information - Brokers/Retrievers, Private Investigators

Applications: Background Info - Individuals, Employment Screening, Tenant Screening

Information Types:
Criminal Information (US, Canada, Puerto Rico, Guam)
Driver and/or Vehicle (US, Canada)
Vital Records (US)
Workers' Compensation (US-46 States)

Statement of Capabilities: National Records Services specializes in reasonably priced background checks for pre-employment and tenant screening needs, and they can provide fast turnaround times of 24-48 hours.

National Information Access Bureau

1142 Auahi St #1524
Honolulu, HI 96814

Telephone: Fax:
800-787-6422   808-394-0849
808-394-0904
Year Founded: 1995

Clientele: Legal Profession, Consumers (Individuals), Employers (HR/Personnel Depts), Information - Brokers/Retrievers, Property Owners/Managers, Attorney Firms, Landlords

Applications: Asset/Lien Searching/Verification, Background Info - Individuals, Employment Screening, Locating People/Businesses, Tenant Screening

Information Types:
Credit Information (US)
Criminal Information (US)
Driver and/or Vehicle (US, CD)
Litigation/Judgments/Tax Liens (US)
Social Security (Numbers) (US)
Vital Records (US)
Voter Registration (US)
Workers' Compensation (US)

Statement of Capabilities: National Information Access Bureau specializes in nationwide public record searches, pre-employment background screening and asset/lien searches. Nationwide criminal and civil background searches for individuals are also available.

National Information Bureau Ltd
14 Washington Rd Bldg 2
Princeton Junction, NJ 08550
Telephone: **Fax:**
609-936-2900   609-936-2859
http://nib.com
Year Founded: 1993

Clientele: Financial Institutions

Applications: Background Info - Individuals, General Business Information, Lending/Leasing

Information Types:
Addresses/Telephone Numbers (US)
Bankruptcy (US)
Corporate/Trade Name Data (US)
Criminal Information (US)
Driver and/or Vehicle (US)
Social Security (Numbers) (US)
Uniform Commercial Code (US)

Proprietary Products:
Name/Desc: BACAS

Info Provided: Credit Information
Media: Online, Software
Coverage: US

Membership: SIIA

Statement of Capabilities: National Information Bureau (NIB) offers Courier, a combination of accessible to multiple databases for public record retrieval. Other state-of-the-art products include Ca$he, RTK, and BACAS.

National Service Information
145 Baker St
Marion, OH 43301
Telephone: **Fax:**
740-387-6806   740-382-1256
www.nsii.net
Year Founded: 1989

Clientele: Asset-Based Lenders, Financial Institutions, Public Record Research Firms, Secured Lenders, Equipment Leasing Companies, Legal Profession, Mortgage Bankers

Applications: Asset/Lien Searching/Verification, Filing/Recording Documents, Background Info - Business, Lending/Leasing, Legal Compliance

Information Types:
Uniform Commercial Code (US)
Corporate/Trade Name Data (US)
Bankruptcy (US)
Litigation/Judgments/Tax Liens (US)
Criminal Information (US)
Vital Records (US)

Proprietary Products:
Name/Desc: NSI - Online
Info Provided: Corporate/Trade Name Data, Uniform Commercial Code
Media: Internet
Coverage: IN, OH

Membership: NPRRA

Statement of Capabilities: Founded in 1989, National Service Information is engaged in the search, filing and document retrieval of public record information. Having offices in Marion, OH and Indianapolis, IN, they consider Ohio, Indiana and Kentucky their local market in addition to 4300 different jurisdictions they search nationwide. They recently unveiled a comprehensive database to allow clients to perform public record searches via the Web. Their web site allows you to perform state level UCC lien and corporate detail searches for Ohio, and state level UCCs for Indiana. NSI also provides the option of requesting copies of microfilmed UCC lien images.

Nationwide Court Services Inc

3340 Veterans Hwy
Bohemia, NY 11716

Telephone:	Fax:
888-941-1234	888-981-8522
516-981-4400	516-981-5514

anelsonlg@aol.com

Year Founded: 1994

Clientele: Attorney Firms, Lending Institutions, Financial Institutions, Legal Service Companies, Mortgage Bankers, Legal Profession

Applications: Asset/Lien Searching/Verification, Filing/Recording Documents, Real Estate Transactions

Information Types:
Bankruptcy (US)
Driver and/or Vehicle (US)
Licenses/Registrations/Permits (US)
Real Estate/Assessor (US)
Social Security (Numbers) (US)

Membership: ALTA, NAFE, NAPPS, NPRRA, PRRN

Statement of Capabilities: NCS employs 32 paralegals who have extensive experience in real estate law. NCS also maintains a network of 800 abstractors nationwide helping to guarantee a 48 hour turnaround time on property reports.

Nationwide Information Services

52 James St
Albany, NY 12207

Telephone:	Fax:
800-873-3482	800-234-8522
518-499-8429	518-449-8507

nis@nispsp.com

Year Founded: 1979

Clientele: Financial Institutions, Legal Profession, Public Record Research Firms, Attorney Firms

Applications: Lending/Leasing, Legal Compliance, Real Estate Transactions, Filing/Recording Documents

Information Types:
Bankruptcy (US)
Litigation/Judgments/Tax Liens (US)
Corporate/Trade Name Data (US)
Uniform Commercial Code (US)

Membership: NPRRA

Statement of Capabilities: Since 1979, NIS has provided public information document filing and retrieval. They handle projects on a national scope. Each client is assigned a client service rep with the ability to handle the entire service process.

Nebrask@ Online

301 South 13th #301
Lincoln, NE 68508

Telephone:	Fax:
800-747-8177	402-471-7817
402-471-7810	

www.nol.org
INFO@NOL.org

Year Founded: 1992

Clientele: Financial Institutions, Insurance - General, Legal Profession, Public Record Research Firms, Business - General

Applications: Asset/Lien Searching/Verification, Legal Compliance, Insurance Underwriting, Lending/Leasing, Direct Marketing

Proprietary Products:
Name/Desc: Nebrask@ Online
Info Provided: Driver and/or Vehicle, Corporate/Trade Name Data and Uniform Commercial Code
Media: Magnetic Tape and Online Database
Coverage: NE

Name/Desc: Nebrask@ Online
Info Provided: Litigation/Judgments/Tax Liens and Addresses/Telephone Numbers
Media: Online Database

Coverage: NE
Statement of Capabilities: Nebrask@ Online is a State of Nebraska information system that provides electronic access to state, county, local, association and other public information. Some agency and association data is updated daily, weekly or monthly, Subscribers connect via 800 #, local #s, or the Internet 24-hours per day. There are sign-up and connect fees if not accessing via the Internet.

New Mexico Technet

5921 Jefferson NE
Albuquerque, NM 87109

Telephone: **Fax:**
505-345-6555   505-345-6559
www.technet.nm.org

Year Founded: 1984

Clientele: Business - General, Insurance -
Agents/Brokers, Legal Profession, Libraries,
Financial Institutions

Information Types:
Bankruptcy (NM)
Criminal Information (NM)

Proprietary Products:

Name/Desc: New Mexico Technet
Info Provided: Driver and/or Vehicle,
Litigation/Judgments/Tax Liens and
Corporate/Trade Name Data
Media: Online
Coverage: NM

Statement of Capabilities: New Mexico
Technet is a self-supporting, non-profit
corporation operating to provide management
of a statewide fiber optic computer network
serving the needs of New Mexico, its state
universities and statewide research, educational
and economic-development interests. Technet
serves as the primary connection point to the
Internet for other Internet Service Providers,
business, government and private users in New
Mexico. Technet offers a full range of Internet
services from dial-up to direct connections and
web page services, to co-located services and
New Mexico MVR requests.

NEWSI

PO Box 3008
Newtown, CT 06470-3008
Telephone: **Fax:**
800-517-4636   203-270-9338
203-426-5784
Parent Company: New World Services
International Ltd
Year Founded: 1993

Clientele: Legal Profession, Business - General,
Consumers (Individuals), Public Record
Research Firms

Applications: Locating People/Businesses,
Asset/Lien Searching/Verification, Litigation,
Background Info - Individuals, General
Business Information

Information Types:
Addresses/Telephone Numbers (US)
Social Security (Numbers) (US)

Driver and/or Vehicle (US)
Litigation/Judgments/Tax Liens (US)

Membership: NAPPS, ATLA, CALPI

Statement of Capabilities: NEWSI staff
consists of either licensed private investigators
or experienced paralegals. They have extensive
experience using online resources to provide
information to clients.

NightHawk International

PO Box 360
Chiloquin, OR 97624-0360
Telephone: **Fax:**
541-783-3523   541-783-3517
www.nighthawk.com

Year Founded: 1989

Clientele: Employers (HR/Personnel Depts),
Legal Profession, Public Record Research
Firms

Applications: Locating People/Businesses,
Background Info - Business, Asset/Lien
Searching/Verification

Information Types:
Addresses/Telephone Numbers (US)
Criminal Information (US)
Driver and/or Vehicle (US)
Litigation/Judgments/Tax Liens (US)
Corporate/Trade Name Data (US)

Membership: NAIS, ISDA

Statement of Capabilities: NightHawk
International is a nationwide information
service. Requests may be made by fax, phone,
e-mail or mail. No special equipment or
training of staff is required and a computer is
not necessary. They provide a PC-based
interactive system where users can log on and
perform their own searches, traces and research
24 hours a day.

Free Web Information:
Free links to national and international
databases that provide addresses, licensing,
telephone numbers, business directories and
more.

NM Factfinders Inc

PO Box 1218
Peralta, NM 87042
Telephone: **Fax:**
505-869-4829   505-869-7721
Year Founded: 1990

Clientele: Legal Profession, Public Record Research Firms, Employers (HR/Personnel Depts), Business - General, Insurance - Agents/Brokers

Applications: Litigation, Background Info - Business, Employment Screening, Locating People/Businesses, Fraud Prevention/Detection

Information Types:
Criminal Information (US, NM)
Driver and/or Vehicle (US, NM)
Litigation/Judgments/Tax Liens (US, NM)
Education/Employment (US, NM)
Licenses/Registrations/Permits (US, NM)
Vital Records (US, NM)
Bankruptcy (US, NM)

Membership: ASIS, PRRN

Statement of Capabilities: NM Factfinders specializes in New Mexico public records. They also utilize correspondents nationally in other states for searches, investigations and service of process. They accept credit cards.

Northeast Court Services Inc

375 Park Ave
Scotch Plains, NJ 07076
Telephone: **Fax:**
800-235-0794   908-322-9098
908-322-5565
Year Founded: 1986

Clientele: Financial Institutions, Legal Profession, Public Record Research Firms

Applications: Background Info - Business, Litigation, Filing/Recording Documents, Legal Compliance

Information Types:
Bankruptcy (US)
Wills/Probate (US)
Uniform Commercial Code (US)
Litigation/Judgments/Tax Liens (US)

Membership: NAPPS, NPRRA, PRRN

Statement of Capabilities: Northeast Court Services has over a decade of experience operating daily, weekly, and on-demand schedules for state and federal courts and archives. Their staff consists of public records and document handling professionals joined together under the leadership of a former assistant managing attorney for a major New York law firm. Northeast Court Services provides nationwide and international services in document research, retrieval, filing, investigation, and process service.

Northwest Location Services

1416 E Main Ave #E
Puyallup, WA 98372
Telephone: **Fax:**
253-848-7767   253-848-4414
http://search.nwlocation.com/nwmain.htm
Year Founded: 1990

Clientele: Private Investigators, Attorney Firms, Legal Profession, Collection Agencies

Applications: Locating People/Businesses, Asset/Lien Searching/Verification, Collections, Litigation

Information Types:
Addresses/Telephone Numbers (WA)

Proprietary Products:

Name/Desc: Northwest Online
Northwest Online
Info Provided: Corporation/Trade Name Data
Media: Direct Online, Call back, Internet, Fax, E-mail
Coverage: WA, ID

Name/Desc: Gateway
Info Provided: Licenses/Registration/Permits
Media: Internet, Call Back, Fax, E-mail
Coverage: WA

Statement of Capabilities: Serving investigative, legal and business professionals, Northwest Location Services specializes in witness location, skip tracing, asset research and other information services, with an eye on protecting privacy and the public safety. Licensed and bonded in Washington. They are allied with Northwest Online and Digital Research Company who produces CD-ROM database products for investigators, attorneys and collection agencies.

Free Web Information:
Some corporate and contractor/license searches for Washington and Idaho,

O

Offshore Business News & Research

123 SE 3rd Ave #173
Miami, FL 33131
Telephone: **Fax:**
305-372-6267   305-372-8724
www.offshorebusiness.com
INFOOFFSHOREBUSINESS.com
Parent Company: Offshore Business News & Research Inc
Year Founded: 1996

Clientele: Accountants, banks, Financial Institutions, Insurance - Underwriting, Legal Profession, Private Investigators

Applications: Background Info - Business, Background Info - Individuals, Fraud Prevention/Detection, General Business Information, Litigation

Information Types:
Addresses/Telephone Numbers (Bermuda, Caribbean)
Criminal Information (Bermuda, Caribbean)
Foreign Country Information (Bermuda, Caribbean)
News/Current Events (Bermuda, Caribbean)

Proprietary Products:

Name/Desc: BE Supreme Court
Info Provided: Litigation/Judgments/Tax Liens and Bankruptcy
Media: Internet
Coverage: BE/Fix

Name/Desc: Grand Court of the CI
Info Provided: Litigation/Judgments/Tax Liens and Bankruptcy
Media: Internet
Coverage: CI/Fix

Name/Desc: BE Business
Info Provided: Corporate/Trade Name Data, Legislation/Regulation and Real Estate Assessor
Media: Internet
Coverage: BE/Fix

Name/Desc: Cayman Business
Info Provided: Corporate/Trade Name Data and Bankruptcy
Media: Internet

Coverage: CI/Fix

Name/Desc: BA Business
Info Provided: Corporate/Trade Name Data
Media: Internet
Coverage: Bahamas

Statement of Capabilities: Offshore owns litigation databases covering Bermuda and the Cayman Islands. They offer 24 hour/7 days a week access, year around via the Internet. They publish investigative newsletters covering Bermuda and the Caribbean.

Free Web Information:
One free copy of each of our two newsletters, Offshore Alert and Inside Bermuda, also some free searches of their databases.

Online Search & Investigations

3029 127th Pl SE
Bellevue, WA 98005
Telephone: **Fax:**
888-791-4636   425-865-8197
425-747-5387
osi@infoconex.com
Year Founded: 1997

Clientele: Attorney Firms, Insurance - Claims, Legal Profession

Applications: Asset/Lien Searching/Verification, Background Info - Individuals, Fraud Prevention/Detection, Litigation, Locating People/Businesses

Information Types:
Addresses/Telephone Numbers (US)
Credit Information (US, CD)
Genealogical Information (US, CD)
Foreign Country Information (Worldwide)
Military Svc (Worldwide)
Social Security (Numbers) (US)
Driver and/or Vehicle (US)
Real Estate/Assessor (US)

Statement of Capabilities: Online Search & Investigations offers same day turnaround on most information. They also offer an exclusive "No find, no fee" on locates, and may offer the same on some skip traces. They have been conducting criminal investigations since 1980, and maintain a network of investigators worldwide. Their specialty is criminal investigations and locating difficult to find individuals quickly and affordably.

Online Systems Research

PO Box 23302
Harahan, LA 70183
Telephone: **Fax:**
800-588-0444   504-738-3102
504-738-9709
Year Founded: 1976

Clientele: Insurance - General, Legal Profession, Insurance - Claims

Applications: Insurance Underwriting, Locating People/Businesses

Information Types:
Driver and/or Vehicle (LA)
Addresses/Telephone Numbers (US, LA)

Statement of Capabilities: Online Systems Research provides the insurance, legal and business communities with access to records and data from public and private sources. There are no sign-up costs or monthly fees for their services; a contract and agreement for services is required.. They provide reports for personal/business information, vehicle registration, criminal records and driving records. They offer insurance information by vehicle in Louisiana instantly. They comply with the FCRA and DPPA. Access is available by phone, fax, mail. Most reports are returned instantly, with Louisiana and Texas vehicle and/or driver information returned online.

OPEN (Online Professional Electronic Network)

PO Box 549
Columbus, OH 43216-0549
Telephone: **Fax:**
888-381-5656   614-481-6980
614-481-6999
www.openonline.com

Year Founded: 1992

Clientele: Apartment Owners/Managers, Corporate Security, Employers (HR/Personnel Depts), Insurance - Claims, Legal Profession, Private Investigators, Securities Industry

Applications: Background Info - Business, Locating People/Businesses, Employment Screening, Background Info - Individuals, Litigation

Proprietary Products:

Name/Desc: OPEN
OPEN

Info Provided: Real Estate Assessor, Bankruptcy, Uniform Commercial Code, Corporate/Trade Name Data, Addresses/Telephone Numbers, Social Security (Numbers), Workers' Compensation, Education/Employment, Credit Information, Criminal Information, Driver and/or Vehicle
Media: Direct Online
Coverage: US

Name/Desc: Arrest Records
Info Provided: Criminal Information
Media: Direct Online
Coverage: OH,IN,MN,AL,MI

Membership: ASIS, NCISS, NSA, SHRM

Statement of Capabilities: OPEN provides a wide range of access to nationwide public records and proprietary information such as driver records, commercial and consumer credit reports, and bankruptcies, liens and judgments. The service is subscription-based and is available to professionals for a variety of applications including background checks, skip-traces, verification of information such as addresses, phone numbers, SSNs, employment-educational background. OPEN provides free software and account start-up, and toll-free technical support with no monthly minimum.

Origin Information & Services Inc

233 Mitchell St SW #400
Atlanta, GA 30303
Telephone: **Fax:**
800-315-3492   800-315-3493
404-524-8400   404-524-8807
Year Founded: 1996

Clientele: Attorney Firms, Lending Institutions, Public Record Research Firms

Applications: Background Info - Business, Background Info - Individuals, Filing/Recording Documents, Lending/Leasing, Litigation

Information Types:
Bankruptcy (US)
Criminal Information (US)
Litigation/Judgments/Tax Liens (US)
Real Estate/Assessor (US)
UCC (US)

Membership: PRRN, NPRRA

Statement of Capabilities: Origin Information & Services is a full service public records research firm. They offer retrieval and filing services in the entire US. Two offices offer 24-48 hour turnaround time for most orders.

OSHA DATA

12 Hoffman St
Maplewood, NJ 07040-1114
Telephone:
973-378-8011
www.oshadata.com
mcarmel@oshadata.com
Year Founded: 1991

Clientele: Business - General, Direct Marketers, Employers (HR/Personnel Depts), Insurance - Underwriting, Legal Profession, Loss Prevention Specialists, News Media

Applications: Litigation, Legal Compliance, Direct Marketing, Background Info - Business, Government Document Retrieval

Information Types:
Environmental (US)
Legislation/Regulation (US)

Proprietary Products:

Name/Desc: OSHA Data Gateway
Info Provided: Legislation/Regulation
Media: Printed Report, Fax
Coverage: US

Membership: ASSE, AIHA

Statement of Capabilities: OSHA DATA's database contains corporate regulator violation records for every business inspected since July 1972. Information includes not only OSHA data, but also wage and hour, EEOC, insurance, NLRB asbestos and other regulatory types. The database is updated quarterly. Consultation and software for the utilization of the data are available.

Free Web Information:
Reference materials related to constructor pre-qualification screening and quarterly reports on OSHA enforcement activity.

OTM Research Inc

PO Box 685055
Austin, TX 78768
Telephone: **Fax:**
800-222-8199   512-320-5486
512-320-5485
otmteam@flash.net
Clientele: Employers (HR/Personnel Depts), Public Record Research Firms, Business - General, Apartment Owners/Managers, Leasing Agents - Personal Property, Financial Institutions

Applications: Employment Screening, Background Info - Individuals, Tenant Screening, Insurance Underwriting, Lending/Leasing

Information Types:
Bankruptcy (US)
Criminal Information (US)
Driver and/or Vehicle (US)
Litigation/Judgments/Tax Liens (US)
Tenant History (US)

Statement of Capabilities: OTM Research utilizes in-house court researchers across the country, with 24-72 hour turnaround for most counties. Orders and results can be sent via the Internet.

Owens Online Inc

251 Lyndhurst St
Dunedin, FL 34698-7577
Telephone: **Fax:**
800-745-4656   813-738-8275
813-738-1245
www.owens.com
email@owens.com
Year Founded: 1987

Clientele: Legal Profession, Financial Institutions, Collection Agencies, Government Agencies, Information - Brokers/Retrievers, Credit Grantors, Credit Reporting Agencies

Applications: Background Info - Business, Background Info - Individuals, General Business Information, Locating People/Businesses

Information Types:
Addresses/Telephone Numbers (US, International)
Credit Information (US, International)
Foreign Country Information (US, International)

Statement of Capabilities: Owens Online specializes in international credit reports on businesses and individuals. They provide worldwide coverage, with 9 million foreign credit reports online. Single orders are welcomed and there are no complex unit contracts.

Free Web Information:
Available are 200+ free directories and links to 90+ counties.

Pacific Photocopy & Research

1 NE 1st St #404
Miami, FL 33132
Telephone: **Fax:**
305-371-7694   305-371-9657
www.OBAR.ORG/ADHP/PACIFIC_PH
   OTOCOPY

Year Founded: 1972

Clientele: Legal Profession, Public Record Research Firms, Financial Institutions, Government Agencies, Legal Service Companies, Mortgage Bankers, Private Investigators

Applications: Filing/Recording Documents, Current Events, Asset/Lien Searching/Verification, Background Info - Individuals, Litigation

Information Types:
Bankruptcy (US, FL)
Litigation/Judgments/Tax Liens (US, FL)
Driver and/or Vehicle (US, FL)
Corporate/Trade Name Data (FL)
Criminal Information (FL)
Uniform Commercial Code (FL)
Vital Records (FL)
Workers' Compensation (FL)

Statement of Capabilities: Providing retrieval and photocopying service for more than 20 years, Pacific Photocopy covers all of Florida from eight locations. They specialize in federal and state court case retrieval for Florida, the US generally, also Puerto Rico and Canada. Florida branches include: Miami, Fort Lauderdale, West Palm Beach, Tampa, Orlando, Jacksonville, Tallahassee.

Pallorium Inc

PO Box 155-Midwood Station
Brooklyn, NY 11230
Telephone: **Fax:**
212-969-0286   800-275-4329

www.pallorium.com
Year Founded: 1979

Clientele: Government Agencies, Public Record Research Firms, Private Investigators

Applications: Asset/Lien Searching/Verification, Locating People/Businesses, Employment Screening, Risk Management, Litigation

Information Types:
SEC/Other Financial (US)
Credit Information (US)
Criminal Information (US)
Addresses/Telephone Numbers (US)

Proprietary Products:

Name/Desc: Skiptrace America
Info Provided: Aviation/Vessels, Driver and/or Vehicle, Vital Records and Voter Registration
Media: Direct Online
Coverage: US

Name/Desc: People Finder California
Info Provided: Aviation/Vessels, Driver and/or Vehicle, Vital Records and Voter Registration
Media: Direct Online
Coverage: CA

Name/Desc: People Finder Texas
Info Provided: Aviation/Vessels, Driver and/or Vehicle, Vital Records and Voter Registration
Media: Direct Online
Coverage: TX

Name/Desc: People Finder Tri-State
Info Provided: Aviation/Vessels, Driver and/or Vehicle, Vital Records and Voter Registration
Media: Direct Online
Coverage: CT, NJ, NY

Name/Desc: People Finder Florida
Info Provided: Aviation/Vessels, Driver and/or Vehicle, Vital Records and Voter Registration
Media: Direct Online
Coverage: FL

Name/Desc: People Finder Gulf Coast
Info Provided: Aviation/Vessels, Driver and/or Vehicle, Vital Records and Voter Registration
Media: Direct Online
Coverage: AL, GA, LA, MS

Name/Desc: People Finder West I & II

Info Provided: Aviation/Vessels, Driver and/or Vehicle, Vital Records and Voter Registration
Media: Direct Online
Coverage: AZ, CO, NM, OR, UT, WA

Name/Desc: People Finder Great Lakes
Info Provided: Aviation/Vessels, Driver and/or Vehicle, Vital Records and Voter Registration
Media: Direct Online
Coverage: ID, IL, MI, OH

Name/Desc: People Finder New England
Info Provided: Aviation/Vessels, Driver and/or Vehicle, Vital Records and Voter Registration
Media: Direct Online
Coverage: MA, ME, NH, RI, VT

Membership: ION, WAD, NAIS, BOMP, ASIS, NCISS

Statement of Capabilities: Pallorium (PallTech Online) services are divided into three areas: the electronic mail system, which links all users (800 investigative/security professionals); the bulletin board system, which provides a forum for the free exchange of information among all approved subscribers (public or private law enforcement only); and the investigative support system, which provides investigative support to approved users. PallTech's searches include aircraft record locator, national financial asset tracker, bankruptcy filings locator, business credit reports, consumer credit reports, NCOA trace, criminal records, national vehicle records, current employment locator, NYC registered voters by address, court and governmental jurisdiction identifier, ZIP Code locator and more searches in the US, Canada, Israel and Hong Kong. New products are CD-ROMs of addresses and personal information for a number of states, totaling more than one billion records.

Paper Chase Research

139 Fulton St #1004
New York, NY 10038
Telephone: **Fax:**
212-587-7071   212-587-7072

paperCh@aol.com
Year Founded: 1994

Clientele: Legal Profession, Legal Service Companies, Public Record Research Firms,
Employers (HR/Personnel Depts), Attorney Firms, Banks, Securities Industry

Applications: Litigation, Filing/Recording Documents, Employment Screening, Asset/Lien Searching/Verification, Real Estate Transactions

Information Types:
  Bankruptcy (NY)
  Real Estate/Assessor (NY)
  Corporate/Trade Name Data (NY)
  Criminal Information (NY)
  Litigation/Judgments/Tax Liens (NY)
  Uniform Commercial Code (NY)
  Wills/Probate (NY)

Statement of Capabilities: Paper Chase Research is an attorney/paralegal service company specializing in filing and document retrieval, civil case status analysis, and general court research throughout the US. They also provide real estate transaction information.

Paragon Document Research

PO Box 65216
St Paul, MN 55165
Telephone: **Fax:**
800-892-4235   800-847-7369
651-222-6844   651-222-2281
www.banc.com

Parent Company: PDR Inc
Year Founded: 1991

Clientele: Legal Profession, Lending Institutions, Private Investigators, Libraries, Direct Marketers, Credit Reporting Agencies, Equipment Leasing Companies

Applications: Asset/Lien Searching/Verification, Background Info - Business, Competitive Intelligence, Employment Screening, Litigation

Information Types:
  Addresses/Telephone Numbers (MN, ND, SD, MT)
  Bankruptcy (MN, ND, SD, MT)
  Credit Information (US)
  Criminal Information (US)
  Litigation/Judgments/Tax Liens (US)
  Real Estate/Assessor (MN, ND, SD, MT)

Proprietary Products:
  Name/Desc: Pdrlog
  Info Provided: Uniform Commercial Code
  Media: Lists or Labels
  Coverage: US

Membership: NAFE, NALA, NPRRA, PRRN

Statement of Capabilities: Paragon Document Research's services include searches throughout state and county levels of Minnesota, Montana, North Dakota and South Dakota covering UCC, tax liens, bankruptcy filings, past and present litigation, searches for ownership of, and liens on DMV reports, assumed name searches, name reservations and corporate agents. There are no correspondent fees applied.

Free Web Information:
Federal and state tax lien report samples are available on their web site.

Paralegal Resource Center Inc

4 Faneuil Hall Marketplace
Boston, MA 02109-1647
Telephone: **Fax:**
617-742-1939 617-742-1417
www.go.boston.com/paralegal

Year Founded: 1976

Clientele: Legal Profession, Financial Institutions, Public Record Research Firms, Credit Reporting Agencies, Asset-Based Lenders, Equipment Leasing Companies

Applications: Litigation, Asset/Lien Searching/Verification, General Business Information, Legal Compliance, Filing/Recording Documents

Information Types:
Bankruptcy (MA)
Litigation/Judgments/Tax Liens (MA)
Uniform Commercial Code (MA)
Real Estate/Assessor (MA)
Vital Records (MA)
Legislation/Regulation (MA)

Membership: NPRRA

Statement of Capabilities: Paralegal Resource Center's president, Shelley Widoff, has over 20 years experience providing paralegal services and training legal assistants in Massachusetts. The Boston staff is within walking distance of the State House and courthouses, allowing for rush and same day service. A network of correspondents cover the state. The firm also provides teams of specialists for staffing temporary projects.

PARASEC

PO Box 160568
Sacramento, CA 95816-0568

Telephone: **Fax:**
800-533-7272 800-603-5868
916-441-1001 916-447-6091
www.parasec.com
parasec@parasec.com

Clientele: Business - General, Legal Profession, Accountants, Asset-Based Lenders

Applications: Legal Compliance, Asset/Lien Searching/Verification, Filing/Recording Documents, Lending/Leasing, Litigation

Information Types:
Corporate/Trade Name Data (US)
Uniform Commercial Code (US)
Litigation/Judgments/Tax Liens (US)
Bankruptcy (US)
Criminal Information (US)
Real Estate/Assessor (US)
Vital Records (US)
Trademarks/Patents (US)

Membership: NALV, NPRRA

Statement of Capabilities: PARASEC is a national public record filing and retrieval company. They can obtain documents from any state or county nationwide. They also provide corporate services, including registered agent services in all 50 states. They have service centers in Los Angeles and San Diego as well as Carson City, NV.

Free Web Information:
Access links to free forms and a newsletter.

Paul C Klumb, MLIS

6688 N Shawmoors Dr
Chenequa, WI 53029-9032
Telephone: **Fax:**
800-648-1844 414-966-1864
414-966-3712
www.Paul_Klumb.com
PKLUMB@hotmail.com
Parent Company: Paul C Klumb Agency
Year Founded: 1972

Clientele: Accountants, Credit Grantors, Employers (HR/Personnel Depts), Government Agencies, Legal Profession, Lending Institutions, Direct Marketers

Applications: Background Info - Individuals, Competitive Intelligence, Direct Marketing, Litigation, Real Estate Transactions

Information Types:
Addresses/Telephone Numbers (US, WI)
Driver and/or Vehicle (US, WI)
Education/Employment (US, WI)

Legislation/Regulation (US, WI)
Litigation/Judgments/Tax Liens (US, WI)
News/Current Events (US, WI)
Criminal Information (US)

Membership: ABA, ALA, SCIP, SLA, WS Bar

Statement of Capabilities: Officed between Milwaukee and Madison, WI and serving SE Wisconsin, Paul Klumb has a highly-trained staff, full networking, and offers immediate turnarounds on basic information.

Peartree Information Services
PO Box 5214
Largo, FL 33779
Telephone: **Fax:**
813-585-3225   813-585-3360
peartree@gte.net
Year Founded: 1996

Information Types:
Litigation/Judgments/Tax Liens (FL, UT, VA, AL, WA)
Criminal Information (FL, UT, VA. AL, WA)

Statement of Capabilities: Most Searches are performed and returned in 24 hours or less.

Penncorp Servicegroup Inc
PO Box 1210
Harrisburg, PA 17108-1210
Telephone: **Fax:**
800-544-9050   800-264-1137
717-234-2300   717-238-8232
Year Founded: 1987

Clientele: Credit Reporting Agencies, Financial Institutions, Insurance - General, Legal Profession, Public Record Research Firms

Applications: Legal Compliance, General Business Information, Real Estate Transactions, Lending/Leasing

Information Types:
Litigation/Judgments/Tax Liens (US, PA)
Corporate/Trade Name Data (US, PA)
Driver and/or Vehicle (US, PA)
Licenses/Registrations/Permits (US, PA)
Uniform Commercial Code (US, PA)
Vital Records (US, PA)

Membership: NPRRA

Statement of Capabilities: Penncorp Servicegroup has expanded its jurisdiction coverage from Pennsylvania state agencies to cover all US states, counties, parishes, as well

as provinces of Canada. They maintain a 24-hour turnaround time on most requests.

PeopleSearch
PO Box 873
Waukegan, IL 60085
Telephone: **Fax:**
847-360-0360   847-623-3501
Year Founded: 1995

Clientele: Apartment Owners/Managers, Legal Profession, Business - General, Employers (HR/Personnel Depts), Genealogists, Property Owners/Managers, Attorney Firms

Applications: Background Info - Business, Background Info - Individuals, Employment Screening, Genealogical Research, Locating People/Businesses

Information Types:
Addresses/Telephone Numbers (IL)
Genealogical Information (US)
Litigation/Judgments/Tax Liens (IL)

Membership: APG

Statement of Capabilities: The principal of PeopleSearch has 26 years genealogical research experience, 8 years criminal/civil background check experience, and 6 years experience in locating missing heirs/lost relatives/skip tracing. Also, the principal was trained in research at the National Archives (Institute of Historical and Genealogical Research at Samford University--Birmingham, AL) and is a confidential adoption intermediary for the State of Illinois.

PFC Information Services
6114 La Salle Ave #638
Oakland, CA 94611
Telephone: **Fax:**
510-653-5061   510-653-0842
www.pfcinformation.com
Year Founded: 1989

Clientele: Legal Profession, Public Record Research Firms, Employers (HR/Personnel Depts), Business - General, Property Owners/Managers, Credit Grantors, Attorney Firms

Applications: Litigation, Locating People/Businesses, Background Info - Individuals, Asset/Lien Searching/Verification, Employment Screening

Information Types:
Litigation/Judgments/Tax Liens (US)
Criminal Information (US)
Uniform Commercial Code (US)
Real Estate/Assessor (US)
Bankruptcy (US)
Credit Information (US)
Voter Registration (US)
Addresses/Telephone Numbers (US)

Membership: AIIP, PRRN, SCIP

Statement of Capabilities: PFC Information Services is a public records research firm serving the legal community, corporations, employers and other information companies. They have electronic access to hundreds of public record databases nationwide as well as a network of skilled local record retrievers. PFC provides all types of research, and specializes in company profiles, background information on individuals, asset/lien searching, pre-employment screening and locating missing persons. Consulting services are also available to aspiring public record researchers.

Phoenix Research Corp

PO Box 579
Commack, NY 11787
Telephone: **Fax:**
800-944-5692   800-430-3232
516-361-7272   516-361-7118
Year Founded: 1982

Clientele: Attorney Firms, Insurance - Claims, Insurance - General, Lending Institutions, Legal Profession, Real Estate Owners/Managers, Landlords

Applications: Background Info - Business, Background Info - Individuals, Employment Screening, Locating People/Businesses

Information Types:
Addresses/Telephone Numbers (US)
Bankruptcy (US)
Driver and/or Vehicle (NY)
Licenses/Registrations/Permits (NY, NJ, PA)
News/Current Events (US)
Social Security (Numbers) (US)
Uniform Commercial Code (US)

Membership: ASIS, CII, W.A.D.

Statement of Capabilities: Phoenix Research provides employment screening services to large and small corporations through a variety of sources and data banks.' Licensed in New York, New Jersey, Connecticut, & Florida, they offer investigative services to supplement research. Experienced in conducting background investigations for the New York Banking Department relative to licensing. They also perform more complicated due diligence investigations. Affidavits of due diligence are available for court services. Credit reports & litigation searches are available for insurance providers and landlords. Credit cards accepted.

Phoenix Research Inc

3181 Linwood Ave #22
Cincinnati, OH 45208
Telephone: **Fax:**
800-260-1092   800-260-3997
www.hrliability.com
Year Founded: 1994

Clientele: Apartment Owners/Managers, Employers (HR/Personnel Depts), Information - Brokers/Retrievers, Landlords, Legal Service Companies, Public Record Research Firms, Loss Prevention Specialists

Applications: Background Info - Individuals, Competitive Intelligence, Employment Screening, Litigation, Tenant Screening

Information Types:
Credit Information (US)
Criminal Information (US)
Driver and/or Vehicle (US)
Social Security (Numbers) (US)
Tenant History (US)
Workers' Compensation (US)

Membership: ASIS, ION, NAIS, PRRN, SCIP

Statement of Capabilities: Phoenix Research specializes in criminal history checks at the county level. They offer nationwide coverage with normal turnaround time in 24-72 hours. Order online, no signup fee for large daily volume. President Rick Misch has published books on background investigations, undercover investigations, and executive protection for ICS Learning Systems. Rick also hosted the radio show "The Investigators Hour" in 1997 in Cincinnati.

Pinnacle Research Inc

90 North Street #224
Park Forest, IL 60466
Telephone: **Fax:**
888-216-1434   708-283-9400
708-283-9500
Year Founded: 1995

Clientele: Asset-Based Lenders, Business - General, Private Investigators, Corporate Counsel, Attorney Firms, Investment Bankers, Lending Institutions

Applications: Competitive Intelligence, Filing/Recording Documents, Fraud Prevention/Detection, Litigation, Locating People/Businesses

Information Types:
Addresses/Telephone Numbers (US)
Corporate/Trade Name Data (US)
Credit Information (US)
Education/Employment (US)
Environmental (US)
Foreign Country Information (US, International)
Legislation/Regulation (US)
SEC/Other Financial (US)

Membership: ACFE, AFSAIRS, FIA, NALI, NAWBO, SCIP

Plat System Services Inc
12450 Wayzata Blvd #108
Minnetonka, MN 55305-1926
Telephone: **Fax:**
612-544-0012   612-544-0617
www.platsystems.com
Year Founded: 1961

Clientele: Financial Institutions, Government Agencies, Insurance - Agents/Brokers, Legal Profession, Mortgage Bankers, Property Owners/Managers

Proprietary Products:

Name/Desc: System90
Info Provided: Real Estate/Assessor
Media: Disk, Lists or labels, Direct Online and Printed Report
Coverage: MN- Minneapolis, St. Paul

Name/Desc: CompUmap
Info Provided: Addresses/Telephone Numbers and Real Estate Assessor
Media: Direct Online
Coverage: MN-Minneapolis and St Paul

Name/Desc: PID Directory
Info Provided: Real Estate/Assessor
Media: Reports, Lists or Labels, Publication and Disk
Coverage: MN-Minneapolis, St. Paul

Statement of Capabilities: Plat System Services has a variety of services available including online services updated weekly, PID

directories published annually, commercial sold reports monthly, residential sold reports monthly, custom reports updated weekly, and other monthly reports such as contract for deeds, and commercial buyers and sellers reports. They also offer mailing lists and labels, diskettes updated weekly, and PLAT books updated semi-annually. They provide computerized county plat maps.

Prime Information Brokers Inc
PO Box 3028
Boynton Beach, FL 33424-3028
Telephone: **Fax:**
800-837-7607   561-740-1644
561-740-9040
www.pimall.com/prime/prime1.html
eriarn@ix.netcom.com
Year Founded: 1995

Clientele: Legal Profession, Business - General, Financial Institutions, Corporate Counsel, Investment Bankers, Secured Lenders, Attorney Firms

Applications: Competitive Intelligence, Background Info - Business, General Business Information, Litigation, Background Info - Individuals

Information Types:
Bankruptcy (US)
Corporate/Trade Name Data (US)
Criminal Information (US)
Driver and/or Vehicle (US, FL, NY)
Litigation/Judgments/Tax Liens (US)
News/Current Events (US)
Real Estate/Assessor (US)
Social Security (Numbers) (US)

Membership: ASIS, SCIP, FALI, INTELNET

Statement of Capabilities: Prime Information Brokers provide informative and detailed answers to clients' investigative and research needs, specific to, but not limited to, the following areas: due diligence, background checks, pre-employment checks, litigation support, courthouse public record research, skip tracing, field investigations, asset and liability tracing, insurance fraud, corporate fraud, and competitive intelligence.

Pro Search Inc
91 Dora St
Stamford, CT 06902

Telephone: **Fax:**
203-348-6994   203-348-6994
Year Founded: 1988

Clientele: Attorney Firms, Lending Institutions, Corporate Counsel, Financial Institutions, Insurance - Underwriting, Legal Profession, Mortgage Bankers

Applications: Asset/Lien Searching/Verification, Lending/Leasing, Real Estate Transactions

Information Types:
Litigation/Judgments/Tax Liens (CT)
Real Estate/Assessor (CT)

Membership: ALTA

Statement of Capabilities: Pro Search specializes in full-search title reports and UCC and lien searches.

Professional Research Services Inc
7151 Metro Blvd #210
Minneapolis, MN 55439
Telephone: **Fax:**
612-941-9040   612-941-9041
Year Founded: 1990

Clientele: Business - General, Employers (HR/Personnel Depts), Insurance - General, Professionals-Other

Applications: Employment Screening
Statement of Capabilities: Professional Research Services (PRS) is a national company offering comprehensive background screening that includes verbal responses within 24-48 hours followed by documented hard copy. Client anonymity is maintained throughout the investigative process.

Professional Services Bureau
315 S College #245
Lafayette, LA 70503
Telephone: **Fax:**
800-960-2214   318-235-5318
318-234-9933

casey@casepi.com
Parent Company: Tenstar Corporation
Year Founded: 1989

Clientele: Attorney Firms, Credit Grantors, Information - Brokers/Retrievers, Legal Profession, Lending Institutions, Mortgage Bankers, Public Record Research Firms

Applications: Asset/Lien Searching/Verification, Real Estate Transactions, Filing/Recording

Documents, Lending/Leasing, Document Retrieval

Information Types:
Bankruptcy (LA,MS)
Criminal Information (LA,MS)
Driver and/or Vehicle (LA,MS)
Litigation/Judgments/Tax Liens (LA,MS)
Real Estate/Assessor (LA,MS)
Uniform Commercial Code (LA,MS)
Corporate/Trade Name Data (LA,MS)
Addresses/Telephone Numbers (LA,MS)

Proprietary Products:

Name/Desc: PSB Database
Info Provided: Addresses/Telephone Numbers, Credit Information, Social Security (Numbers), Criminal Information
Media: Online, Print, Disk, Magnetic Tape
Coverage: LA

Membership: ION, NAIS, NAPPS, PRRN, ACA, ICA

Statement of Capabilities: Professional Services Bureau is a full service agency covering Louisiana and Mississippi. They offer background, criminal, employment, insurance, financial, activity checks, fraud, and missing person investigations, also surveillance and process service. They perform courthouse research, document filing and retrieval at all municipal, state and federal courts. Other services are title abstracting, notary services and claims adjusting. Their firm has proprietary sources of background information in South Louisiana. All 64 Louisiana parishes can be researched in about 48 hours; about 72 hours for Mississippi.

Profiles International
615 Oak Street #3
Missoula, MT 59801-2460
Telephone: **Fax:**
406-543-2540   406-543-0293
Year Founded: 1994

Clientele: Employers (HR/Personnel Depts), Collection Agencies, Genealogists, Legal Profession, Public Record Research Firms, Libraries, Lending Institutions

Applications: Asset/Lien Searching/Verification, Background Info - Business, Background Info - Individuals, Collections, Employment Screening

Information Types:
Credit Information (US)
Driver and/or Vehicle (US)
Genealogical Information (MT)

Membership: NGS

Statement of Capabilities: Profiles
International also offers driver background
information for the trucking industry.

Progenitor

PO Box 345
Paradise, UT 84328
Telephone:
435-245-9386
Year Founded: 1983

Clientele: Consulting Firms, Consumers
(Individuals), Genealogists, Information -
Brokers/Retrievers, Direct Marketers,
Libraries, Product Development Managers

Applications: Locating People/Businesses,
Genealogical Research, Direct Marketing,
Competitive Intelligence, General Business
Information

Information Types:
Associations/Trade Groups (US)
Vital Records (US)
Military Svc (US)
Foreign Country Information (US,
International)

Proprietary Products:

Name/Desc: North American Surname Folder
Index
Info Provided: Genealogical Information
Media: CD-ROM, 609, Lists or labels,
Magnetic Tape, Microfilm/Microfiche and
Printed Report
Coverage: US, CD

Name/Desc: World Source Index
Info Provided: Genealogical Information
Media: CD-ROM, Lists or labels, Magnetic
Tape, Microfilm/Microfiche and Printed
Report
Coverage: US, International

Statement of Capabilities: Progenitor
specializes in surname databases, source
databases, pedigree analysis, surname surveys,
ethnic information, denominational
information, and specific record location
services. Other services include family records
located, manuscripts located, maiden names
determined, obituary locator, cemeteries
located/searched, immigration and

naturalization sources, locating ancestral
villages, contacting collateral cousins, and
burned courthouse equivalents.

Promesa Enterprises Inc

3939 Bee Caves Rd #22
Austin, TX 78746
Telephone: **Fax:**
800-474-4420   512-328-7066
512-328-7230
www.promesa.com
Year Founded: 1994

Clientele: Financial Institutions, Collection
Agencies, Employers (HR/Personnel Depts),
Legal Profession

Applications: Asset/Lien Searching/Verification,
Lending/Leasing, Employment Screening,
Background Info - Individuals, Locating
People/Businesses

Information Types:
Real Estate/Assessor (US, TX)
Litigation/Judgments/Tax Liens (US)
Bankruptcy (US)
Credit Information (US)
Criminal Information (US, TX)
Driver and/or Vehicle (US, TX)
Education/Employment (US, TX)
Corporate/Trade Name Data (TX)

Statement of Capabilities: Promesa provides
research on a nationwide basis through a well-
established network of correspondent
relationships. They specialize in the research of
individuals and corporate entities.

Property Data Center Inc

7100 E Bellevue #110
Greenwood Village, CO 80111
Telephone: **Fax:**
303-850-9586   303-850-9637
www.pdclane.net
Year Founded: 1984

Clientele: Financial Institutions, Real Estate
Owners/Managers, Insurance - General

Applications: Real Estate Transactions,
Asset/Lien Searching/Verification, Direct
Marketing, Lending/Leasing, Insurance
Underwriting

Proprietary Products:

Name/Desc: Real Property Assessments
Info Provided: Real Estate/Assessor

Media: Direct Online, Disk, Lists or labels, Magnetic Tape and Printed Report
Coverage: CO

Name/Desc: Real Property Taxes
Info Provided: Real Estate/Assessor
Media: Direct Online, Disk, Lists or labels, Magnetic Tape and Printed Report
Coverage: CO

Name/Desc: Owner Phone Numbers
Info Provided: Addresses/Telephone Numbers
Media: Online Database, Disk, Magnetic Tape, Printed Reports and Lists or Labels
Coverage: CO

Name/Desc: PDC
Info Provided: Real Estate/Assessor
Media: Online Database, Disk, Magnetic Tape, Printed Reports and Lists or Labels
Coverage: CO

Membership: NPRRA, REIPA, DMA, NAR

Statement of Capabilities: Property Data Center's PDC database includes three million real property ownership and deed transfer records for the metro Denver area, plus counties of Adams, Arapahoe, Boulder, Denver, Douglas, El Paso, Eagle, Elbert, Jefferson, Larimer, Mesa, Pitkin, Pueblo, Summit, Weld. Data is accessible by owner, location, and indicators such as property value. They specialize in lender marketing data, new owners, sold comparables, mapping data and direct mail lists.

Free Web Information:
Provides an address lookup with data that includes property ownership and characteristics.

Prosearch of Texas

5103 timber Circle
San Antonio, TX 78250
Telephone: **Fax:**
888-273-3132 888-523-1061
210-523-0061 210-523-0061
www.CENTERCOURT.com/PROSEARC HUSA

Parent Company: Affiliate of Prosearch USA
Year Founded: 1992

Clientele: Public Record Research Firms, Legal Profession, Credit Reporting Agencies, Financial Institutions, Business- General

Applications: Asset/Lien Searching/Verification, Background Info - Business, Filing/Recording

Documents, Real Estate Transactions, Background Info - Individuals

Information Types:
Uniform Commercial Code (TX)
Litigation/Judgments/Tax Liens (US)
Real Estate/Assessor (US)
Environmental (US)
Bankruptcy (TX)
Criminal Information (TX)
Wills/Probate (TX)

Membership: PRRN

Statement of Capabilities: Prosearch of Texas covers over 75 Texas counties including Bexar, Travis, Ft Worth, Dallas, Nueces, Houston. They specialize in complex real estate documents and the other instruments they research. They consult with and train others who want to set up their own research staff.

PROTEC

PO Box 54866
Cincinnati, OH 45254
Telephone: **Fax:**
800-543-7651 513-528-4402
513-528-4400

procaq007@fuse.net
Parent Company: World Search Group, Inc
Year Founded: 1964

Clientele: Asset-Based Lenders, Attorney Firms, Employers (HR/Personnel Depts), Legal Profession, Investigators - Fraud, Insurance - Claims, Equipment Leasing Companies

Applications: Asset/Lien Searching/Verification, Background Info - Business, Background Info - Individuals, Employment Screening, Fraud Prevention/Detection

Information Types:
Credit Information (US)
Criminal Information (US)
Driver and/or Vehicle (US)
Education/Employment (US)
Litigation/Judgments/Tax Liens (US)
Workers' Compensation (US)

Proprietary Products:

Name/Desc: Consta-Trac
Info Provided: Identifiers-DOB, Social Security (Numbers), Addresses/Telephone Numbers
Media: Printed Report
Coverage: US

Membership: ACFE, EPIC, ICA, NCISS, WAD

Statement of Capabilities: PROTEC has 35 years of concurrent exposure to the information highway, beginning its database system in 1979 using its own information. Since that beginning, they have remained unique in responsible information gathering, being useful in fraud detection and factual data gathering. Their newest and most successful database is "CONSTRA-TRAC" - a master compilation of over 700 record systems and special use cross-check histories from individuals, businesses, societies, and public record data.

Public Data Corporation
38 East 29th St
New York, NY 10016
Telephone: **Fax:**
212-519-3063   212-519-3065
www.pdcny.com
Year Founded: 1988

Clientele: Business - General, Insurance - General, Legal Profession, Public Record Research Firms, Professionals-Other

Applications: General Business Information, Legal Compliance, Locating People/Businesses, Asset/Lien Searching/Verification, Background Info - Business/Individuals

Information Types:
Bankruptcy (NY)
Associations/Trade Groups (NY-New York City)

Proprietary Products:
Name/Desc: Public Data
Info Provided: Real Estate Assessor, Environmental, Litigation/Judgments/Tax Liens and Uniform Commercial Code
Media: Call-in, Disk, Magnetic Tape and Online Database
Coverage: NY

Statement of Capabilities: Public Data Corporation's 24 million records database includes real estate, lien, bankruptcy, environmental and other records for the boroughs of Manhattan, Bronx, Brooklyn, Queens. Information is updated daily.

Public Information Resource Inc
PO Box 299

Monmouth, ME 04259-0299
Telephone: **Fax:**
207-933-3606   207-933-9064
Year Founded: 1983

Clientele: Financial Institutions, Employers (HR/Personnel Depts), Insurance - General, Legal Profession, Public Record Research Firms

Applications: Asset/Lien Searching/Verification, Legal Compliance, Employment Screening, Real Estate Transactions

Information Types:
Bankruptcy (ME)
Litigation/Judgments/Tax Liens (ME)
Uniform Commercial Code (ME)
Corporate/Trade Name Data

Membership: NPRRA

Statement of Capabilities: Public Information Resource specializes in UCC searches, certificates of good standing, articles of incorporation, and real estate searches and title updates in all 16 Maine counties and 18 registries. They perform searches in federal, state, and district courts, also bankruptcy and probate. Just outside Maine's capitol, they access all Maine agencies including DMV, State Police, Insurance Bureau, and Fisheries and Wildlife.

Public Record Research Library
4653 S Lakeshore #3
Tempe, AZ 85282
Telephone: **Fax:**
800-939-2811   800-929-3810
602-838-8909   602-838-8324
http://brbpub.com
brb@brbpub.com
Parent Company: BRB Publications Inc
Year Founded: 1989

Clientele: Business - General, Corporate Security, Employers (HR/Personnel Depts), Information - Brokers/Retrievers, Public Record Research Firms, Information - Brokers/Retrievers, Insurance - Underwriting

Applications: General Business Information, Government Document Retrieval, Risk Management, Locating People/Businesses, Competitive Intelligence

Proprietary Products:
Name/Desc: PRRS

Info Provided: Addresses/Telephone Numbers, Legislation/Regulations
Media: CD-ROM, Disk, Publication
Coverage: US

Membership: PRRN, AIIP, AALL, SIIA

Statement of Capabilities: The Public Record Research Library is a series of in-depth databases formatted into books, CDs and soon to be online. BRB is recognized as the nation's leading research and reference publisher of public record related information. The principals of the parent company are directors of the Public Record Retriever Network, the nation's largest organization of public record professionals. Over 26,000 government and private enterprises are analyzed in-depth regarding regulations and access of public records and public information. The Public Record Research System (PRRS) is available on CD, loose-leaf print, and as a customized database.

Free Web Information:
The web site provides an update list of government agencies that offer free access to public records. Also, timely articles dealing with critical issues (FCRA, etc.) can be downloaded.

Public Record Services

PO Box 11565
Montgomery, AL 36111
Telephone: **Fax:**
334-262-0350   334-613-0289
Year Founded: 1974

Clientele: Financial Institutions, Legal Profession, Professionals-Other, Public Record Research Firms

Applications: Asset/Lien Searching/Verification, Legal Compliance, Lending/Leasing, General Business Information

Information Types:
Bankruptcy (AL)
Litigation/Judgments/Tax Liens (AL)
Corporate/Trade Name Data (AL)
Legislation/Regulation (AL)
Trademarks/Patents (AL)
Uniform Commercial Code (AL)

Membership: NPRRA

Statement of Capabilities: Public Record Services is the oldest public record research firm in Alabama. They provide banks, lending institutions, and law firms with document

filing and retrieval services in Alabama on an expedited basis.

Public Records Research Service

PO Box 245
Azalea, OR 97410
Telephone:
541-837-3355

nharrold@mcsi.net
Year Founded: 1996

Clientele: Consumers (Individuals), Genealogists, Legal Profession, Private Investigators

Applications: Genealogical Research, Locating People/Businesses, Asset/Lien Searching/Verification, Collections

Information Types:
Addresses/Telephone Numbers (US, International)
Genealogical Information (US, International)
Vital Records (US)
Criminal Information (US)
Military Svc (US)
Licenses/Registrations/Permits (US)
Education/Employment (US)
Social Security (Numbers) (US)

Statement of Capabilities: Public Records Research Service specializes in locating missing relatives, friends, military buddies, debtors, birth parents and adoptees. They provide prompt and thorough service at reasonable rates. References are available upon request.

Quest Information Service Inc

15541 Norborne
Redford, MI 48239
Telephone: **Fax:**
888-682-8805   313-535-8862
313-537-0613
www.home.att.net/~TamaraShoe
TamaraShoe@worldnet.att.net
Clientele: Legal Profession, Collection Agencies, Information - Brokers/Retrievers,

Private Investigators, Legal Service Companies, Attorney Firms

Applications: Asset/Lien Searching/Verification, Background Info - Business, Background Info - Individuals, Collections, Employment Screening

Information Types:
Addresses/Telephone Numbers (US-Detroit, MI)
Corporate/Trade Name Data (US-Detroit, MI)
Criminal Information (US-Detroit, MI)
Education/Employment (US-Detroit, MI)
Licenses/Registrations/Permits (US-Detroit, MI)
Litigation/Judgments/Tax Liens (US-Detroit, MI)
Social Security (Numbers) (US-Detroit, MI)
Vital Records (US-Detroit, MI)

Statement of Capabilities: Quest Information Services offers a full range of services that include paralegal, research, database information, process service, and courier service. Courier service can be simple pick-up and delivery to filings and retrievals.

Quest Research

PO Box 34077
Little Rock, AR 72203
Telephone: **Fax:**
800-467-0712   501-374-3029
501-374-4712
Parent Company: RJS Business Services Inc
Year Founded: 1982

Clientele: Credit Reporting Agencies, Financial Institutions, Legal Profession, Public Record Research Firms

Applications: Asset/Lien Searching/Verification, Lending/Leasing, Litigation, Filing/Recording Documents, Real Estate Transactions

Information Types:
Bankruptcy (AR)
Litigation/Judgments/Tax Liens (AR)
Corporate/Trade Name Data (AR)
Uniform Commercial Code (AR)
Real Estate/Assessor (AR)

Membership: NPRRA, PRRN

Statement of Capabilities: Quest Research provides concise public record reports quickly from all levels of government in Arkansas. Their full-time staff of 13 is augmented by over 15 contract searchers throughout the state, providing coverage of all Arkansas counties.

Quik Check Records

PO Box 440
Willamina, OR 97396
Telephone: **Fax:**
503-876-6477   503-876-6877
Year Founded: 1996

Clientele: Employers (HR/Personnel Depts), Information - Brokers/Retrievers, Insurance - General, Private Investigators, Property Owners/Managers, Public Record Research Firms

Applications: Background Info - Business, Background Info - Individuals, Employment Screening, General Business Information, Insurance Underwriting

Information Types:
Bankruptcy (US)
Criminal Information (OR, WA)
Litigation/Judgments/Tax Liens (OR, WA)
Uniform Commercial Code (OR-Marion)

Membership: PRRN

Statement of Capabilities: Quik Check Records' turnaround time is 24-48 hours.

R

Raczak Inc

215 S Monarch #106
Aspen, CO 81611
Telephone: **Fax:**
970-925-4869   970-925-7654
raczak@vof.net
Year Founded: 1985

Clientele: Leasing Agents - Personal Property, Legal Profession, Lending Institutions, Information - Brokers/Retrievers, Real Estate Owners/Managers, Collection Agencies, Public Record Research Firms

Applications: Asset/Lien Searching/Verification, Background Info - Business, Background Info - Individuals, Litigation, Filing/Recording Documents

Information Types:
Litigation/Judgments/Tax Liens (CO)
Uniform Commercial Code (CO)

Membership: NAR, NPRRA

Statement of Capabilities: Raczak, Inc provides services for document recordation, retrieval, research and recording for UCCs, fixtures, tax liens, judgments and litigation, real estate ownership and title searches, motor vehicle and vessel lien searches, record-keeping, minutes and transactions services, also incorporation and qualification assistance and process service. They serve Pitkin, Eagle, Garfield, Rio Blanco, Moffat, Delta, Montrose and Mesa Counties, with associates in Denver and throughout the US, and some overseas. They also research public records associated with public reviews and land use applications in Pitkin, Garfield, and Eagle counties. No legal advice is rendered.

Rafael Jorge Investigations

2219 W Olive Blvd #295
Burbank, CA 91506
Telephone: **Fax:**
800-344-4754 818-846-5799
818-846-5038
Year Founded: 1988

Clientele: Public Record Research Firms, Employers (HR/Personnel Depts), Professionals-Other

Applications: Employment Screening, Background Info - Business, Background Info - Individuals

Information Types:
Criminal Information (US, CA)
Education/Employment (US)
Bankruptcy (CA)
Litigation/Judgments/Tax Liens (CA)
Uniform Commercial Code (CA)
Driver and/or Vehicle (CA)

Membership: NAIS, CALI, CIPI, PRRN

Statement of Capabilities: RJI specializes in research and retrieval of criminal and litigation records in the State of California, and they have a network of correspondents for public records in other states.

RC Information brokers

PO Box 1114
Framingham, MA 01701-0206
Telephone: **Fax:**
508-651-1126 508-657-2414

psconnor@gis.net

Clientele: Attorney Firms, Lending Institutions, Corporate Counsel, Insurance - General, Investment Bankers, Private Investigators

Applications: Background Info - Business, Background Info - Individuals, Collections, Genealogical Research, Litigation

Information Types:
Addresses/Telephone Numbers (US)
Credit Information (US)
Driver and/or Vehicle (US)
Education/Employment (US)
Genealogical Information (MA)
Litigation/Judgments/Tax Liens (MA)
Social Security (Numbers) (US)

Proprietary Products:
Name/Desc: MassData
Info Provided: Addresses/Telephone Numbers and Vital Records
Media: Disk, Call-in Only and Internet
Coverage: MA

Statement of Capabilities: RC Information Brokers provide "critical information support" to attorneys, licensed private investigators and other professionals. RCIB specializes in supporting attorneys seeking information on individuals for litigation, credit checks, internal financial investigations and background checks. Information support is also available for major financial centers outside the US, especially London. Specific proprietary databases include "MassData" compiled from various databases archived over the past 22 years on current and previous residents of Massachusetts. Turnaround time depends on specific needs and caseload. Locating Massachusetts individuals past and present including adoption cases is their specialty.

Real Estate Guide Inc, The

PO Box 338
Ravena, NY 12143
Telephone: **Fax:**
800-345-3822 800-252-0906
www.eguides.com
Year Founded: 1995

Clientele: Legal Profession, Lending Institutions, Mortgage Bankers, Public Record Research Firms

Applications: Real Estate Transactions, Lending/Leasing

Information Types:
Credit Information

Proprietary Products:

Name/Desc: Real Estate Filing Guide
Info Provided: Real Estate/Assessor
Media: Print and CD-ROM
Coverage: US

Membership: SIIA, REIPA, Joint Task Force

Statement of Capabilities: The Real Estate Filing Guide is a 4,400 page, 6 volume quarterly-updated service used by real estate documentation specialists for the purpose of accurately recording those documents in any of the 3,600 county recording offices nationwide. It is available in print and CD-ROM. Firms wishing to integrate this information with internal documentation systems may license the underlying databases.

Real Estate InfoService

Box 5178
Herndon, VA 20172

Telephone: **Fax:**
800-924-1117   800-884-8212
703-787-0506   703-787-05-9

Year Founded: 1989

Clientele: Attorney Firms, Lending Institutions, Corporate Security, Information - Brokers/Retrievers, Investigators - Fraud, Private Investigators, Public Record Research Firms

Applications: Asset/Lien Searching/Verification, Background Info - Business, Collections, Filing/Recording Documents, General Business Information

Information Types:
Real Estate/Assessor (VA)

Membership: ALTA

real-info Inc

247 Cayuga Rd
Buffalo, NY 14225

Telephone: **Fax:**
800-771-5246   716-632-3152
716-632-2800
www.real-info.com
jakirch@real-info.com

Year Founded: 1996

Clientele: Financial Institutions, Apartment Owners/Managers, Asset-Based Lenders, Business - General, Consumers (Individuals), Credit Reporting Agencies, Mortgage Bankers

Applications: Fraud Prevention/Detection, Lending/Leasing, Litigation, Locating People/Businesses, Real Estate Transactions

Information Types:
Real Estate/Assessor (NY-57 counties; not NYC)

Membership: MBAA, NAHB, NAR, REIPA, APMW

Statement of Capabilities: Real-info is a real estate information company that provides Internet searchable info on properties in New York state. James Kirchmeyer has been in the industry 15 years and formed the company due to increased need for access to reliable property info. They also offer property Record Info Sheets (realRecords), the Custom Report Generator (realReports) and Comparable Sales Finder (realComps). They also developed Q-Val, and automated valuation model system that predicts market values for a residential property.

Record Access

4134 Massachusetts Street #A
Long Beach, CA 90814

Telephone: **Fax:**
888-621-1491   562-621-0542
562-621-0143
recaxes@jps.net

Year Founded: 1996

Clientele: Accountants, Attorney Firms, Lending Institutions, Information - Brokers/Retrievers, Private Investigators, Public Record Research Firms

Applications: Asset/Lien Searching/Verification, Background Info - Business, Background Info - Individuals, Employment Screening, Litigation

Information Types:
Bankruptcy (CA)
Corporate/Trade Name Data (CA)
Licenses/Registrations/Permits (CA)
Uniform Commercial Code (CA)
Vital Records (CA)

Membership: PRRN

Statement of Capabilities: Record Access provides accurate searches and retrievals of public records throughout California. For name searches, they conduct a thorough search, reporting name variations and similar names. They are committed to providing customers with accurate background information for their research and investigative needs.

Record Finders

PO Box 3242
Brownsville, TX 78523
Telephone: **Fax:**
956-571-5378 956-350-5120
Year Founded: 1998

Clientele: Information - Brokers/Retrievers, Lending Institutions, Public Record Research Firms

Applications: Asset/Lien Searching/Verification, Employment Screening, Filing/Recording Documents, Lending/Leasing, Real Estate Transactions

Information Types:
Bankruptcy (TX-Cameron)
Corporate/Trade Name Data (TX-Cameron)
Criminal Information (TX-Cameron, Willacy)
Litigation/Judgments/Tax Liens (TX-Cameron, Willacy)
Real Estate/Assessor (TX-Cameron, Willacy)
Uniform Commercial Code (TX-Cameron)
Vital Records (TX-Cameron)

Membership: PRRN

Statement of Capabilities: Record Finders' normal turnaround time is 24-48 hours; some special projects may take longer. They specialize in current property and lien searches, chain-of-title searches, civil litigation and criminal background checks.

Record Information Services Inc

Box 1183
St Charles, IL 60174
Telephone: **Fax:**
630-365-6490 630-365-6524
http://www.public-record.com
metcalf@elnet.com
Year Founded: 1993

Clientele: Accountants, Legal Profession, Business - General, Financial Institutions, Information - Brokers/Retrievers, Mortgage Bankers, Direct Marketers

Applications: Collections, Direct Marketing, Real Estate Transactions

Information Types:
UCC (IL-DuPage, Kane, Kendall, Lake, McHenry)

Proprietary Products:

Name/Desc: Foreclosures
Info Provided: Litigation/Judgments/Tax Liens
Media: Disk, Fax-on-Demand, Internet, Lists or labels and Printed Report
Coverage: IL

Name/Desc: Bankruptcies
Info Provided: Bankruptcy
Media: Disk, Fax-on-Demand, Internet, Lists or labels and Printed Report
Coverage: IL

Name/Desc: Judgments, State & Federal Tax Liens
Info Provided: Litigation/Judgments/Tax Liens
Media: Disk, Direct Online, Fax-on-Demand, Printed Report and Software
Coverage: IL

Name/Desc: Business Licenses
Info Provided: Licenses/Registrations/Permits
Media: Disk, Direct Online, Fax-on-Demand, Printed Report and Software
Coverage: IL

Name/Desc: News Incorporations
Info Provided: Licenses/Registrations/Permits
Media: Disk, Direct Online, Fax-on-Demand, Printed Report and Software
Coverage: IL

Name/Desc: New Homeowners
Info Provided: Real Estate/Assessor
Media: Disk, Direct Online, Fax-on-Demand, Printed Report and Software
Coverage: IL

Name/Desc: Divorces
Info Provided: Vital Records
Media: Disk, Direct Online, Fax-on-Demand, Printed Report and Software
Coverage: IL

Statement of Capabilities: Record Information Services provides complete and timely public record data that is delivered through state-of-the-art technology. Custom reports are available upon request.

Record Retrieval Services Inc

PO Box 264
Allen, TX 75013-0005
Telephone: **Fax:**
888-311-5001 972-527-5266
972-527-5355
dairrs@gte.net

Year Founded: 1996

Clientele: Financial Institutions, Legal Profession, Employers (HR/Personnel Depts), Information - Brokers/Retrievers, Private Investigators, Public Record Research Firms

Applications: Asset/Lien Searching/Verification, Background Info - Business, Background Info - Individuals, Employment Screening, Filing/Recording Documents

Information Types:
Criminal Information (TX,US)
Education/Employment (US)
Litigation/Judgments/Tax Liens (TX,US)
Real Estate/Assessor (TX,US)

Membership: PRRN

Statement of Capabilities: They specialize in document retrieval in TX and have correspondents nationwide.

Record Search & Information Services

6140 Corporal Ln
Boise, ID 83704
Telephone: **Fax:**
208-375-1906   208-322-5469
Year Founded: 1991

Clientele: Legal Profession, Public Record Research Firms, Lending Institutions, Mortgage Bankers, Investigators - Fraud, Employers (HR/Personnel Depts), Attorney Firms

Applications: Background Info - Business, Background Info - Individuals, General Business Information, Real Estate Transactions, Asset/Lien Searching/Verification

Information Types:
Uniform Commercial Code (ID)
Litigation/Judgments/Tax Liens (ID)
Bankruptcy (ID)
Corporate/Trade Name Data (ID)

Membership: NPRRA, NAIS, ACFE

Statement of Capabilities: As a business information service servicing Idaho, Utah, Washington, Oregon, Montana, and Nevada, RSIS features affordable information research designed to answer routine information needs. RSIS also offers high-quality, quick response document retrieval for custom projects, and they are specialists at retrieving legal documents in public record repositories.

Records Research Inc

PO Box 19300
Sacramento, CA 95819
Telephone: **Fax:**
800-952-5766   800-870-6877
Year Founded: 1981

Clientele: Insurance - General, Legal Profession, Public Record Research Firms, Employers (HR/Personnel Depts)

Applications: Insurance Underwriting, Background Info - Business, Background Info - Individuals, Asset/Lien Searching/Verification

Information Types:
Corporate/Trade Name Data (US)
Driver and/or Vehicle (US, CA)
Real Estate/Assessor (CA)

Statement of Capabilities: Records Research (RRI) specializes in providing California motor vehicle reports (MVRs) to insurance and related industries. Driving histories and vehicle reports are available online, allowing instant response to client requests. Overnight service available. They offer a variety of searches including plate, VIN, automated name index, soundex searches, and financial responsibility reports. RRI offers MVRs from all other states with a 24-48 hour turnaround. RPI offers a wide range of other public record services including corporate and property searches. Clients must establish a commercial account with the state, which RRI will be happy to help expedite.

Redi-Info Information Services

PO Box 12145
Oklahoma City, OK 73157
Telephone: **Fax:**
800-349-7334   800-410-3299
405-946-4636   405-917-5961
www.REDI-INFO.com
customerservice@REDI-INFO.com
Year Founded: 1992

Clientele: Employers (HR/Personnel Depts), Collection Agencies, Employers (HR/Personnel Depts), Investigators - Fraud, Legal Profession, Public Record Research Firms, Real Estate Owners/Managers

Applications: Employment Screening, Background Info - Individuals, Employment

Screening, Fraud Prevention/Detection, Tenant Screening

Information Types:
Social Security (Numbers) (US)
Credit Information (US)
Bankruptcy (US)
Criminal Information (US)
Driver and/or Vehicle (US)
Litigation/Judgments/Tax Liens (US)
Workers' Compensation (US)
Credit Information (US)

Membership: ACFE, ACA

Statement of Capabilities: Redi-Info maintains an extensive list of online resources for nationwide record retrieval. Reports may be ordered by fax or online via the Internet. They accumulate search results in an in-house database for the purpose of developing reports and locating persons or businesses in the future. This is in addition to their ongoing search capabilities. Redi-Info also specializes in searching licenses of bail bondsman and providing information on FDIC insured financial institutions.

Registry Research

PO Box 448
South Egremont, MA 01258
Telephone: **Fax:**
413-528-3919 413-528-0907
Year Founded: 1988

Clientele: Genealogists, Legal Profession, Asset-Based Lenders, Public Record Research Firms, Property Owners/Managers, Attorney Firms, Lending Institutions

Applications: Genealogical Research, General Business Information, Asset/Lien Searching/Verification, Real Estate Transactions, Government Document Retrieval

Information Types:
Genealogical Information (MA-Berkshire)
Real Estate/Assessor (MA-Berkshire)

Membership: ALTA

Statement of Capabilities: Registry Research works only in Southern Berkshire County. They specialize in title work and historical/genealogical documentation.

Relyea Services Inc

PO Box 5167
Albany, NY 12205-0167
Telephone: **Fax:**
800-854-4111 800-854-4112
Year Founded: 1991

Clientele: Attorney Firms, Business - General, Corporate Security, Credit Grantors, Financial Institutions

Applications: Legal Compliance, Asset/Lien Searching/Verification, Filing/Recording Documents, Litigation

Information Types:
Litigation/Judgments/Tax Liens (NY,US)
Uniform Commercial Code (NY,US)
Corporate/Trade Name Data (NY,US)
Bankruptcy (NY,US)

Membership: PRRN

Statement of Capabilities: The principal of Relyea Services, Glenn Relyea, has more than 25 years experience in public record searching and filing. The firm has agents in every court and UCC filing office in the country.

Research & Retrieval

111 Pier Ave #111
Hermosa Beach, CA 90254
Telephone: **Fax:**
800-707-8771 310-798-8100
310-798-9394
Year Founded: 1990

Clientele: Legal Profession, Private Investigators, Financial Institutions, Libraries, Attorney Firms, Consulting Firms

Applications: Litigation, Background Info - Business, Filing/Recording Documents, Employment Screening, Background Info - Individuals

Information Types:
Bankruptcy (US, CA)
Litigation/Judgments/Tax Liens (US)
Criminal Information (US)
Uniform Commercial Code (US)
Real Estate/Assessor (US)
Corporate/Trade Name Data (US)
Vital Records (US)

Membership: PRRN

Statement of Capabilities: Research and Retrieval can retrieve any kind of public records anywhere in the US. Their services include obtaining court documents from federal and state courts, searching fictitious names, and filing documents nationwide.

Research Data Service

9030 W Sahara Ave #270
The Lakes, NV 89117
Telephone: **Fax:**
702-733-4990   702-733-1646
www.researchdatanv.com
rdsusa@msn.com
Year Founded: 1980

Clientele: Apartment Owners/Managers, Corporate Security, Employers (HR/Personnel Depts), Legal Profession, Legal Service Companies, News Media, Private Investigators

Applications: Background Info - Business, Background Info - Individuals, Employment Screening, Insurance Underwriting, Tenant Screening

Information Types:
Bankruptcy (US)
Corporate/Trade Name Data (US)
Criminal Information (US)
Credit Information (US)
Driver and/or Vehicle (US)
Real Estate/Assessor (US)
Social Security (Numbers) (US)
Voter Registration (US)

Membership: SHRM

Statement of Capabilities: Research Data Service (RDS) provides a wide range of nationwide services including employment screening, tenant rental screening, background investigations, and in-depth specialized personal and corporate dossier reports. RDS services the fortune 1000 companies, government agencies, law enforcement, the gaming industry and small to medium businesses as well. They have a correspondent network of over 5,000 professionally trained and licensed court record searchers who hand search all court requests. RDS covers all 50 states, 3,347 counties, 94 federal districts -- over 10,000 courts located in the US on a daily basis. Turnaround times range from 5 minutes to 2 days for all searches (except state agencies). Credit cards are accepted.

Free Web Information:
Free modem software provided to all customers.

Research Group, The

8348 Crystalwood Dr
Dallas, TX 75249

Telephone: **Fax:**
972-283-4319   972-296-5092
www.researchgrp.com
mcoopernap@aol.com
Parent Company: Joe & Cache Inc
Year Founded: 1996

Clientele: Legal Profession, Business - General, Consulting Firms, Employers (HR/Personnel Depts), Information - Brokers/Retrievers, Lending Institutions, Public Record Research Firms

Applications: Asset/Lien Searching/Verification, Background Info - Individuals, Employment Screening, Filing/Recording Documents, Real Estate Transactions

Information Types:
Bankruptcy (US-Dallas, Denton, Tarrant, Wichita)
Criminal Information (US-Dallas, Denton, Tarrant, Wichita)
Driver and/or Vehicle (US)
Education/Employment (US)
Licenses/Registrations/Permits (US)
Litigation/Judgments/Tax Liens (US)
Social Security (Numbers) (US)
Uniform Commercial Code (US)

Membership: ABW, PRRN

Statement of Capabilities: The Research Group offers a guaranteed 24-hour turnaround. They offer referral discounts and quality land research. They also offer monthly billing, volume discounts, personal service and quality customer service.

Research North Inc

207 Michigan St
Petoskey, MI 49770
Telephone: **Fax:**
616-347-7366   616-347-7685
crett@sunny.ncmc.cc.mi.us
Year Founded: 1981

Clientele: Attorney Firms, Business - General, Employers (HR/Personnel Depts), Insurance - Claims, Investigators - Fraud, Legal Profession, Private Investigators

Applications: Background Info - Business, Competitive Intelligence, Fraud Prevention/Detection, Litigation, Locating People/Businesses

Information Types:
Criminal Information (MI)

Driver and/or Vehicle (MI)
Litigation/Judgments/Tax Liens (MI)
Real Estate/Assessor (MI)
Uniform Commercial Code (MI)
Vital Records (MI)
Voter Registration (MI)
Workers' Compensation (MI)

Membership: ACFE, ASIS, ION, NCISS, WAD

Statement of Capabilities: Research North handles insurance defense matters, financial investigations, and business-related inquires. Five branches serve Michigan.

Research Services & Recovery LLC
PO Box 11226
Waterbury, CT 06703
Telephone: **Fax:**
203-754-7673 800-915-9809
203-754-7674 203-597-8159
www.researchsvcs.com
searches@aol.com
Year Founded: 1996

Clientele: Attorney Firms, Lending Institutions, Employers (HR/Personnel Depts), Information - Brokers/Retrievers, Private Investigators, Public Record Research Firms, Business - General

Applications: Asset/Lien Searching/Verification, Background Info - Individuals, Collections, Employment Screening, Litigation

Information Types:
Addresses/Telephone Numbers (US)
Bankruptcy (US)
Credit Information (US)
Driver and/or Vehicle (US)
Education/Employment (US)
Real Estate/Assessor (US)
Social Security (Numbers) (US)

Membership: NABEA

Statement of Capabilities: Research Services & Recovery LLC offers full service to clients, including a full line of data research, investigations, process serving, asset repossession and bail enforcement. Their data includes asset searches, skiptracing, individual searches, business records, motor vehicle records, court records, telephone searches, and a variety of other searches, most nationwide. Prices are competitive, and quick turnaround time and no-fee fax back service makes them convenient to use. Accepts major credit cards and checks by fax.

Research Specialists
PO Box 540488
Grand Prairie, TX 75054-0488
Telephone: **Fax:**
800-771-7547 888-522-3600
972-263-0500 972-263-1992
rsildallas@aol.com
Parent Company: Challenge 2010 Inc
Year Founded: 1983

Clientele: Legal Profession, Financial Institutions, Employers (HR/Personnel Depts), Insurance - Agents/Brokers, Loss Prevention Specialists, Attorney Firms

Applications: Asset/Lien Searching/Verification, Collections, Employment Screening, Litigation, Locating People/Businesses

Information Types:
Addresses/Telephone Numbers (US)
Bankruptcy (US)
Corporate/Trade Name Data (US)
Criminal Information (US)
Driver and/or Vehicle (US)
Education/Employment (US)
Social Security (Numbers) (US)
Vital Records (US)

Statement of Capabilities: Research Specialists is a full service company with associates worldwide. They dedicate themselves to the single goal of providing their clients with the "service they deserve with the results they demand."

Research World Unlimited
PO Box 111506
Houston, TX 77293
Telephone: **Fax:**
800-311-6516 713-868-3850
713-869-7300
http://member.aol.com/sonjad
ee/ResearchWorld
sonjadee@aol.com
Year Founded: 1988

Clientele: Apartment Owners/Managers, Attorney Firms, Legal Profession, Insurance - Claims, Investigators - Fraud

Applications: Background Info - Business, Background Info - Individuals, Employment

Screening, Fraud Prevention/Detection, Litigation

Information Types:
Criminal Information (TX-Harris, Ft Bend, Montgomery)
Driver and/or Vehicle (US)
Licenses/Registrations/Permits (US)
Litigation/Judgments/Tax Liens (TX-Harris, Ft Bend, Montgomery)
UCC (US)
Education/Employment (US)

Membership: NAFE

Statement of Capabilities: Research World Unlimited is a licensed private investigation company specializing in document retrieval. The staff possesses years of experience in the area of investigation and government document retrieval. Selected from former city, county, and state employees, the staff knows how to get information fast. RESEARCH is their first name and first priority.

RIBackgrounds
PO Box 173
East Greenwich, RI 02818
Telephone:　　**Fax:**
800-285-9690　　　401-397-0015
401-884-9690
www.RIBackgrounds.com
Pryeyess@aol.com
Parent Company: Eyewitness Investigations
Year Founded:　1990

Clientele: Public Record Research Firms, Employers (HR/Personnel Depts), Business - General, Information - Brokers/Retrievers

Applications: Background Info - Individuals, Employment Screening

Information Types:
Criminal Information (RI)
Litigation/Judgments/Tax Liens (RI)

Membership: PRRN, FLEOA

Statement of Capabilities: RIBackgrounds is a Rhode island information wholesaler of public records for the purpose of pre-employment screening companies. They search every county in Rhode Island. Normal turnaround time is 24-48 hours, although sameday service is available if the request is received by 10am EST. They specialize in the county level of criminal and civil record searches.

Richland County Abstract Co
POB 910
Wahpeton, ND 58074-0910
Telephone:　　**Fax:**
701-642-3781　　701-642-3852
Year Founded:　1922

Clientele: Financial Institutions, Legal Profession, Government Agencies, Public Record Research Firms

Applications: Real Estate Transactions, Filing/Recording Documents, Asset/Lien Searching/Verification

Information Types:
Real Estate/Assessor (MN, ND)
Environmental (MN, ND)
Wills/Probate (MN, ND)
Vital Records (MN, ND)

Proprietary Products:
Name/Desc: Judgment & Tax Liens
Info Provided: Litigation/Judgments/Tax Liens
Media: Disk and Printed Report
Coverage: MN, ND

Membership: ALTA, MLTA, NDLTA

Statement of Capabilities: Richland County Abstract specializes in providing real estate information for the states of Minnesota and North Dakota.

S

Sacramento Attorneys Service Inc
1005 12th St #F
Sacramento, CA 95814-3920
Telephone:　　**Fax:**
800-499-1180　　　800-499-7599
916-441-6565　　　916-441-2087
www.cwo.com/~sacatty
Year Founded:　1974

Clientele: Financial Institutions, Legal Profession

Applications: Asset/Lien Searching/Verification, Legal Compliance, General Business Information, Litigation

Information Types:
Litigation/Judgments/Tax Liens (US, CA)
Corporate/Trade Name Data (US, CA)
Uniform Commercial Code (US, CA)

Membership: NPRRA

Statement of Capabilities: Sacramento Attorneys' Service specializes in corporate and limited partnership document filing and retrieval together with UCC searches. Their online access to the state's corporate records and in-house microfilm allows them to provide fast service. County Recorder searches include examining the records for UCC financing statements, fixture filings, tax liens and abstracts of judgments. They also provide property record research, litigation searches at all court levels, and trademark searches. They maintain searching contacts nationwide and in some foreign countries.

San Diego Daily Transcript/San Diego Source

2131 Third Ave
San Diego, CA 92101
Telephone:
800-697-6397
619-232-4381
www.sddt.com

editor@sddt.com

Clientele: Business - General, Legal Profession, Real Estate Owners/Managers, Public Record Research Firms

Applications: Filing/Recording Documents, Real Estate Transactions, Background Info - Business

Proprietary Products:

Name/Desc: San Diego Source
Info Provided: Litigation/Judgments/Tax Liens and Uniform Commercial Code
Media: Internet
Coverage: CA

Name/Desc: US Bankruptcy Court Filings
Info Provided: Bankruptcy
Media: Internet
Coverage: US

Statement of Capabilities: The San Diego Source is a leading California web site for public record information and business data. Site visitors can perform customized searches on one or more than fifteen databases. Links with Transcripts Online are provided.

Free Web Information:

Info and ordering.

SEAFAX Inc

PO Box 15340
Portland, ME 04112-5340
Telephone: **Fax:**
800-777-3533 800-876-3533
207-773-3533 207-773-9564
www.seafax.com

Year Founded: 1985

Clientele: Financial Institutions, Business - General

Applications: Background Info - Business, General Business Information, Lending/Leasing

Information Types:
Legislation/Regulation (US, International)
News/Current Events (US, International)
SEC/Other Financial (US, International)
Bankruptcy (US, International)
Corporate/Trade Name Data (US, International)

Proprietary Products:

Name/Desc: Business Reports
Info Provided: Credit Information
Media: Fax-on-Demand and Internet
Coverage: US

Statement of Capabilities: Seafax is an information provider for the seafood industry, offering complete credit monitoring services, accounts receivable discounting, customized marketing data, contingent collections services, outsourcing, receivables management, and consulting services. Seafax provides one central location for the information for conducting business in the seafood industry.

Free Web Information:
All Seafax products are available online free of charge to Seafax customers.

Search Associates Inc

3100 W Layton Ave
Greenfield, WI 53221
Telephone: **Fax:**
414-325-9330 414-325-9335

saeidts@aol.com
Year Founded: 1991

Clientele: Financial Institutions, Business - General, Mortgage Bankers, Public Record

Research Firms, Savings and Loans, Lending Institutions, Business - General

Applications: Real Estate Transactions, Asset/Lien Searching/Verification, Filing/Recording Documents, Legal Compliance, Lending/Leasing

Information Types:
Real Estate/Assessor (WI)
Litigation/Judgments/Tax Liens (WI)
Criminal Information (WI)
Bankruptcy (WI)
Uniform Commercial Code (WI)

Membership: PRRN, MBA

Statement of Capabilities: Search Associates specializes in providing real estate record searches anywhere in the State of Wisconsin. They also provide closing services seven days a week.

Search Company of North Dakota LLC

1008 E Capitol Ave
Bismarck, ND 58501-1930
Telephone: **Fax:**
701-258-5375   701-258-5375
mkautzma@btigate.com
Year Founded: 1987

Clientele: Legal Profession, Financial Institutions, Insurance - General, Accountants, Public Record Research Firms, Consulting Firms, Private Investigators

Applications: Current Events, Filing/Recording Documents, Asset/Lien Searching/Verification, Background Info - Business, Employment Screening

Information Types:
Bankruptcy (ND)
Corporate/Trade Name Data (ND)
Criminal Information (ND)
Driver and/or Vehicle (ND)
Litigation/Judgments/Tax Liens (ND)
Uniform Commercial Code (ND)
Vital Records (ND)
Social Security (Numbers) (ND)

Proprietary Products:

Name/Desc: North Dakota Records
Info Provided: Addresses/Telephone Numbers, Social Security Numbers, Litigation/Judgments/Tax Liens, Licenses/Registrations/Permits, Driver and/or Vehicle, Criminal Information and Bankruptcy

Media: Printed Report, Fax-on-Demand and Lists or labels
Coverage: ND

Name/Desc: ND UCC
Info Provided: Uniform Commercial Code, Litigation/Judgments/Tax Liens
Media: Printed Report, Fax-on-Demand and Lists or labels
Coverage: ND

Membership: NPRRA, PRRN

Statement of Capabilities: Michael Kautzman, the owner of The Search Company of North Dakota, has ten years of public record searching and filing experience. He concentrates in North Dakota, including 24-48 hour access to all state agencies and to local offices in any of the 53 counties.

Search Network Ltd

Two Corporate Place #210
1501 42nd St
West Des Moines, IA 50266-1005
Telephone: **Fax:**
800-383-5050   800-383-5060
515-223-1153   515-223-2814
Year Founded: 1965

Clientele: Financial Institutions, Government Agencies, Public Record Research Firms, Equipment Leasing Companies

Applications: Lending/Leasing, Filing/Recording Documents, Asset/Lien Searching/Verification

Information Types:
Litigation/Judgments/Tax Liens (US, IA, KS)
Corporate/Trade Name Data (US, IA, KS)
Uniform Commercial Code (US, IA, KS, MO)

Proprietary Products:

Name/Desc: Search Network
Info Provided: Uniform Commercial Code
Media: Online Database, Printed Reports, Lists or Labels, Publication and Microfilm
Coverage: IA, KS

Membership: NPRRA

Statement of Capabilities: In business for over 30 years, Search Network provides full service public record search information. The company maintains an on-site UCC database for Iowa and Kansas. Same day searches and copies are available as well as personal filing service for UCC and corporate documents. Since 1980, they have offered direct online access to their databases of UCC filing/records information in Iowa and Kansas

Search One Services

6746 Axtel Drive
Canal Winchester, OH 43110
Telephone: **Fax:**
614-834-5603 614-834-5605
Year Founded: 1996

Clientele: Attorney Firms, Financial Institutions, Information - Brokers/Retrievers, Legal Service Companies, Lending Institutions, Public Record Research Firms

Applications: Asset/Lien Searching/Verification, Background Info - Business, Filing/Recording Documents

Information Types:
Bankruptcy (OH)
Legislation/Regulation (OH)
Uniform Commercial Code (OH)

Membership: PRRN, NPRRA

Statement of Capabilities: Search One Services provides same or next day service for UCC, tax lien, civil suit/judgment searches and document retrievals in Franklin County and the Ohio Secretary of State, and for searches and document retrievals at the US Bankruptcy Court and Federal District Court in Columbus. They also have correspondents that handle the Cleveland, Akron, Toledo and Cincinnati areas, and some rural counties. Promising quality, responsive customer service, they are covered with E & O insurance.

Search Resources Inc

617 Carmen Forest Ln
Manchester, MO 63021
Telephone: **Fax:**
800-863-9364 314-227-9364
314-394-0295

jwestc3590@aol.com
Year Founded: 1993

Clientele: Attorney Firms, Consumers (Individuals), Legal Profession

Applications: Locating People/Businesses, Genealogical Research, Locating Unknown/Missing Heirs

Information Types:
Genealogical Information (MO,IL,CO,US)
Social Security (Numbers) (US)
Vital Records (US)

Wills/Probate (US)
Foreign Country Information (Poland, Germany)

Membership: AICPA

Statement of Capabilities: Search Resources, Inc is a specialist in obtaining information related to identifying and locating missing/unknown heirs in and outside the US. They also handle document collection and family tree construction for court documentation. They can move probate cases forward at low or no cost to the Estate or law firm. They have researchers and extensive experience in Missouri, Illinois, Colorado, and Poland. The president is a CPA. Call for free consultation.

Search Systems

PO Box 544
Newbury Park, CA 91319-0544
Telephone: **Fax:**
800-350-2232 805-375-4042
805-375-4041
www.pac-info.com
tjkoster@pac-info.com
Parent Company: Pacific Information Resources Inc
Year Founded: 1989

Clientele: Attorney Firms, Corporate Counsel, Financial Institutions, Investment Bankers, Legal Profession, Lending Institutions, Savings and Loans

Applications: Asset/Lien Searching/Verification, Background Info - Business, Collections, Competitive Intelligence, General Business Information

Information Types:
Addresses/Telephone Numbers (US, CA)
Aviation/Vessels (US)
Bankruptcy (US)
Corporate/Trade Name Data (US)
Criminal Information (US)
Genealogical Information (US)
Litigation/Judgments/Tax Liens (US)
Uniform Commercial Code (US)

Statement of Capabilities: Search Systems specializes in four primary services; skip tracing, asset evaluations, asset recovery, and information services. They locate the right person (verify the identity and guarantee that the address is correct); analyze public record information; determine business ownership;

perform bank, employment and property searches for asset recovery; and do research and problem-solving.

Free Web Information:
Search Systems provides links to free public record databases through their web site at www.pac-info.com. Searchable databases include corporate, UCC, property, licensing, SS death benefit, marriage, and other useful databases.

Search-Net Management Corp
577 Second Ave #143
New York, NY 10015
Telephone: **Fax:**
212-447-5913   212-889-9447
www.pimall.com/searchnet
searchnet@worldnet.att.net
Year Founded: 1996

Clientele: Attorney Firms, Collection Agencies, Legal Profession, Private Investigators

Applications: Asset/Lien Searching, Collections, Legal Compliance, Locating People/Businesses

Information Types:
Addresses/Telephone Numbers (US)
Corporate/Trade Name Data (US)
Credit Information (US)
Licenses/Registrations/Permits (US)
Litigation/Judgments/Tax Liens (US)
Real Estate/Assessor (US)
Social Security (Numbers) (US)
Uniform Commercial Code (US)

Membership: ACFE, AIIP, NAFE, NAIS

Statement of Capabilities: Search-Net Management is an asset search firm specializing in judgement collections. Services include online research, Internet research, public records and financial statement analysis. They have a CFE on staff, a certified polygraphist on staff, and provide investigative services in Connecticut, New Jersey, New York and Florida.

Search/America
PO Box 20193
Tampa, FL 33622-2193
Telephone: **Fax:**
800-572-8815   813-264-5472
813-264-7603
Year Founded: 1991

Clientele: Apartment Owners/Managers, Legal Profession, Collection Agencies, Credit

Grantors, Employers (HR/Personnel Depts), Insurance - Claims, Insurance - Underwriting

Applications: Asset/Lien Searching/Verification, Background Info - Business, Background Info - Individuals, Collections, Litigation

Information Types:
Addresses/Telephone Numbers (US)
Bankruptcy (US)
Corporate/Trade Name Data (US)
Credit Information (US)
Criminal Information (US)
Litigation/Judgments/Tax Liens (US)
Real Estate/Assessor (US)
Uniform Commercial Code (US)

Statement of Capabilities: Search/America provides in-depth asset and liability searches that allow clients to determine the cost effectiveness of litigating a debt, locating attachable assets in order to enforce a court judgment, and determining the credit-worthiness of customers prior to extending credit. Each report includes the following types of information: addresses, real property, civil records, bankruptcy records, corporate records, and vehicle records.

Searching Registration Service
PO Box 15824
Sacramento, CA 95852
Telephone: **Fax:**
800-488-0238   800-488-0231
916-452-8231   916-451-2322
Year Founded: 1946

Clientele: Financial Institutions, Insurance - Agents/Brokers, Insurance - General, Legal Profession, Public Record Research Firms

Applications: Insurance Underwriting, Litigation, Lending/Leasing, Asset/Lien Searching/Verification

Information Types:
Driver and/or Vehicle (CA)
Addresses/Telephone Numbers (CA)
Licenses/Registrations/Permits (CA)
Uniform Commercial Code (CA)

Statement of Capabilities: Searching Registration Service is located close to the California Department of Motor Vehicles. They are a courier for information vendors around the country that have a need for California drivers' license or vehicle registration information. They have overnight batch processing of requests sent to their mainframe or through hardware installed at client locations. Both a monthly flat rate and per item billing are available.

SearchNY Inc

349 11th St
Brooklyn, NY 11215
Telephone: **Fax:**
718-965-1965 718-965-1911
Year Founded: 1988

Clientele: Legal Profession, Financial Institutions, Public Record Research Firms

Applications: Asset/Lien Searching/Verification, Lending/Leasing, Legal Compliance, General Business Information, Filing/Recording Documents

Information Types:
Bankruptcy (NY-New York City)
Litigation/Judgments/Tax Liens (NY-New York City)
Uniform Commercial Code (NY-New York City)
Criminal Information (NY-New York City)
Real Estate/Assessor (NY-New York City)
Vital Records (NY-New York City)
Corporate/Trade Name Data (NY-New York City)

Membership: AIIP, NPRRA, PRRN

Statement of Capabilities: SearchNY covers the 5 boroughs of New York City and surrounding counties. They provide public record searches and retrieval from courts, city and county registers, and local, state and federal agencies. They primarily service other public record search firms.

SearchTec Inc

211 N 13th St
Philadelphia, PA 19107
Telephone: **Fax:**
800-762-5018 215-851-8775
215-963-0888
Year Founded: 1990

Clientele: Financial Institutions, Legal Profession, Collection Agencies, Public Record Research Firms, Real Estate Owners/Managers

Applications: Asset/Lien Searching/Verification, Lending/Leasing, Real Estate Transactions, Background Info - Business

Information Types:
Real Estate/Assessor (DE, NJ, PA)

Bankruptcy (US, PA-Eastern Dist)
Corporate/Trade Name Data (US)
Uniform Commercial Code (US)

Membership: NPRRA

Statement of Capabilities: SearchTec is a "one-stop" source for lenders that require searches, title insurance and all types of real property appraisals. SearchTec uses automation combined with an online entry and retrieval system to track search requests from beginning to end. Most reports are issued within 24-48 hours of request. All of their packaged search products can be customized to fit particular needs and requirements.

Security Research Consultants

PO Box 18852
St Louis, MO 63118
Telephone: **Fax:**
800-464-2158 314-464-3050
314-464-3999
SRCAGENTS@aol.com
Year Founded: 1996

Clientele: Business - General, Consumers (Individuals), Employers (HR/Personnel Depts), Government Agencies, Loss Prevention Specialists, Property Owners/Managers

Applications: Background Info - Business, Background Info - Individuals, Employment Screening, Fraud Prevent/Detection, Tenant Screening

Information Types:
Addresses/Telephone Numbers (US)
Corporate/Trade Name Data (US)
Credit Information (US)
Criminal Information (US)
Driver and/or Vehicle (US)
Education/Employment (US)
Social Security (Numbers) (US)
Workers' Compensation (US)

Membership: AIIP, NAPI, NAWBO, SHRM

Statement of Capabilities: Security Research Consultants is a licensed and insured private investigations firm. They specialize in background investigations of any type--from retrieving one record to a comprehensive investigation. Services are customized to fit the client's specific needs. Volume and package pricing are available. They have a network of record retrievers across the nation and have accounts with government agencies.

Turnaround time for retrieval of most records is from same day to 3 days. Findings are compiled in a report that is typed in a professional, easy to read format.

Security Search & Abstract Co
926 Pine St
Philadelphia, PA 19107

Telephone: **Fax:**
800-345-9494   800-343-4294
215-592-0660   215-592-0998

Year Founded: 1961

Clientele: Financial Institutions, Legal Profession, Public Record Research Firms, Real Estate Owners/Managers, Credit Reporting Agencies

Applications: Real Estate Transactions, Legal Compliance, Asset/Lien Searching/Verification, Filing/Recording Documents

Information Types:
Bankruptcy (US, PA, NJ)
Litigation/Judgments/Tax Liens (US, PA, NJ)
Corporate/Trade Name Data (US, PA, NJ)
Uniform Commercial Code (US, PA, NJ)
Vital Records (US)
Wills/Probate (US)
Real Estate/Assessor (US, NJ, PA)

Proprietary Products:

Name/Desc: Security Search
Info Provided: Real Estate/Assessor
Media: Call-in
Coverage: PA

SIC Inc
986 NE 84th St
Miami, FL 33138

Telephone: **Fax:**
888-311-3342   305-758-3341
305-751-0015
www.fdn.net/sic

sicmoney@email.msn.com

Year Founded: 1984

Clientele: Attorney Firms, Corporate Counsel, Insurance Claims, Investigators - Fraud, Legal Profession, Private Investigators

Applications: Asset/Lien Searching/Verification, Background Info - Business, Background Info - Individuals, Competitive Intelligence, Litigation

Information Types:
Addresses/Telephone Numbers (US)
Aviation/Vessels (US)
Bankruptcy (US)
Corporate/Trade Name Data (US)
Credit Information (US)
Criminal Information (US)
Driver and/or Vehicle (US)
Foreign Country Information (Europe/FIX)

Membership: ASIS, ATIA, CII, SCIP

Silver Plume
4775 Walnut St #2B
Boulder, CO 80301

Telephone: **Fax:**
800-677-4442   303-449-1199
303-444-0695
www.silverplume.iix.com

Year Founded: 1989

Clientele: Insurance - Agents/Brokers, Insurance - General

Applications: Insurance Underwriting

Information Types:
SEC/Other Financial (US)

Proprietary Products:

Name/Desc: Insurance Industry Rates, Forms and Manuals
Info Provided: Legislation/Regulations
Media: CD-ROM, Magnetic Tape
Coverage: US

Statement of Capabilities: Silver Plume supplies most of the widely-used manuals in the property and casualty insurance industry in electronic format. All manuals are updated monthly and distributed to subscribing agencies and companies to provide convenient access to vital information without the hassles.

SingleSource Services Corp
2320 S Third St #7
Jacksonville Beach, FL 32250

Telephone: **Fax:**
800-713-3412   877-835-5787
904-241-1821   904-241-0601
www.SingleSourceServices.com

checkit@singlesourceServices.com

Year Founded: 1995

Clientele: Public Record Research Firms, Property Owners/Managers, Business -

General, Corporate Security, Employers (HR/Personnel Depts), Legal Profession, Lending Institutions

Applications: Background Info - Business, Background Info - Individuals, Employment Screening, General Business Information, Tenant Screening

Information Types:
Bankruptcy (US)
Criminal Information (US, AL, DE, FL, MD, NC, SC, VA)
Driver and/or Vehicle (US, FL)
Foreign Country Information (UK, Europe)
Litigation/Judgments/Tax Liens (US, FL)
Vital Records (US, FL)
Uniform Commercial Code (US, FL)
Licenses/Registrations/Permits (US, FL)

Membership: ACFE, NPRRA, PRRN

Statement of Capabilities: SingleSource Services provides public record research and full pre-employment screening nationwide, specializing in the SE states. They offer daily service to all Florida State Records in Tallahassee, Florida including Leon County and Duval County. On all other locations, they offer two business day service.

Free Web Information:
Hotlinks to relevant sites such as FCRA & FDLE Florida. Online order form.

SKLD Information Services LLC
4647 E Evans Ave
Denver, CO 80222-5111
Telephone: **Fax:**
800-727-6358   303-758-6847
303-758-6358
Year Founded: 1961

Clientele: Business - General, Financial Institutions, Public Record Research Firms, Insurance - Agents/Brokers, Direct Marketers, Attorney Firms, Government Agencies

Applications: Real Estate Transactions, Asset/Lien Searching/Verification, Direct Marketing, Filing/Recording Documents

Information Types:
Bankruptcy (CO)
Litigation/Judgments/Tax Liens (CO-Metro Denver Counties)

Proprietary Products:
Name/Desc: New Homeowners List
Info Provided: Real Estate/Assessor

Media: Disk, Magnetic Tape, Call-back, and Labels
Coverage: CO

Membership: NPRRA, DMA, National Association of Mortgage Brokers

Statement of Capabilities: SKLD Information Services maintains a complete database of public record information keyed from documents recorded in County Recorder offices since 1990. Information is available to enhance existing databases, create new homeowner mailing lists, report on real estate loan transaction information, and as mortgage marketing data. With archived county recorded documents in their in-house microfilm library, SKLD can provide quick turnaround times. Reports available include: real estate loan activity reports, warranty deed/trust deed match, trust deed report, owner carry 1 and 2 reports, notice of election and demand, and new homeowners list.

Sleuth Research
4213 N Strand Dr
Decatur, GA 30035
Telephone: **Fax:**
404-286-1107   404-289-0621
Year Founded: 1994

Information Types:
Criminal Information (GA)

Statement of Capabilities: Sleuth Research specializes in criminal background checks and in-house record retrieval. Their turnaround time is 24-72 hours.

Solons Legal Document Service Center
100 Brentwood Dr
Gadsden, AL 35902
Telephone: **Fax:**
800-732-0175   256-547-9593
Year Founded: 1990

Clientele: Legal Profession, Financial Institutions, Government Agencies

Applications: Filing/Recording Documents, Litigation

Information Types:
Bankruptcy (US)
Litigation/Judgments/Tax Liens (US)
Criminal Information (US)

Membership: ABI

Statement of Capabilities: Solons Legal Document Service provides searches and document retrieval in all US federal courts nationwide as well as in Canadian courts. They also offer medical record retrieval services.

Sorensen Information Service

5580 La Jolla Blvd #324
La Jolla, CA 92037
Telephone: **Fax:**
619-272-1672 619-272-3092

sasipi@san.rr.com

Clientele: Attorney Firms, Information -
Brokers/Retrievers, Legal Profession, Private
Investigators

Applications: Asset/Lien Searching/Verification,
Background Info - Individuals, Collections,
Employment Screening, Locating
People/Businesses

Information Types:
Addresses/Telephone Numbers (US)
Bankruptcy (US)
Litigation/Judgments/Tax Liens (US)
Real Estate/Assessor (US)
Criminal Information (US)
Driver and/or Vehicle (US)
Credit Information (US)
Social Security (Numbers) (US)

Statement of Capabilities: Sorenson
Information specializes in asset locates,
national and international money transfer paper
trails, telephone numbers research, and
employment locates.

Source Resources

PO Box 88
Cookeville, TN 38503
Telephone: **Fax:**
800-678-8774 800-537-3297
931-537-3641
www.sourceresources.com

source@multipro.com
Year Founded: 1985

Membership: ASIS

Statement of Capabilities: Source Resources
provides more than 100 types of public record
searches that users can order online or by
phone.

Free Web Information:
Order form, report descriptions, product line
descriptions.

Southwest InfoNet

2252 N 44th St #1007
Phoenix, AZ 85008-7201
Telephone: **Fax:**
800-579-1892 800-549-1925
602-286-6804 602-286-6712
www.unisearch.com

paulstr24@aol.com
Parent Company: Unisearch Inc
Year Founded: 1991

Clientele: Legal Profession, Financial
Institutions, Equipment Leasing Companies,
Public Record Research Firms, Attorney
Firms, Secured Lenders

Applications: Asset/Lien Searching/Verification,
Filing/Recording Documents, Government
Document Retrieval, Lending/Leasing,
Litigation

Information Types:
Bankruptcy (US-AZ)
Corporate/Trade Name Data (US-AZ)
Litigation/Judgments/Tax Liens (US, AZ-
Maricopa)
Trademarks/Patents (US)
Uniform Commercial Code (US, AZ-
Maricopa)

Proprietary Products:
Name/Desc: WALDO
Info Provided: Uniform Commercial Code
Media: Internet and Direct Online
Coverage: CA, IL, WA

Membership: NPRRA

Statement of Capabilities: Southwest
InfoNet's normal turnaround time is 24-48
hours. Projects are generally billed by the
number of names searched or records located.
Copy costs and disbursements are added to the
search charge. Their large microfilm library
allows immediate copy retrieval for many
states. Their web site includes news,
jurisdiction updates and online ordering.

Free Web Information:
Online ordering available.

Specialty Services

8491 Hospital Dr #151
Douglasville, GA 30134
Telephone: **Fax:**
770-942-8264 770-942-5355
Parent Company: Specialty Legal Services Inc
Year Founded: 1992

Clientele: Attorney Firms, Business - General, Employers (HR/Personnel Depts), Insurance - Claims, Legal Profession, Private Investigators, Public Record Research Firms

Applications: Asset/Lien Searching/Verification, Background Info - Business, Background Info - Individuals, Employment Screening, Litigation

Information Types:
Bankruptcy (AL, GA)
Criminal Information (AL, GA)
Education/Employment (AL, GA)
Litigation/Judgments/Tax Liens (AL, GA)
Uniform Commercial Code (GA)

Proprietary Products:
Name/Desc: Fulco
Info Provided: Criminal Information and Litigation/Judgments/Tax Liens
Media: Fax-on-Demand
Coverage: US

Membership: APS, NICA, NAPPS, NPRRA, PRRN

Statement of Capabilities: Speciality Services specializes in record retrieval from county, state and federal courts as well as criminal/civil backgrounds for pre-employment screening, litigation support, insurance fraud investigation assistance, asset reports, UCC searches, title work, etc.

Staftrack Inc
PO Box 1133
Largo, FL 33779
Telephone: **Fax:**
800-275-2966   727-581-3725
727-581-3603
www.STAFTRACK.com
STAFTRACK@aol.com

Clientele: Apartment Owners/Managers, Consulting Firms, Employers (HR/Personnel Depts), Financial Institutions, Insurance - Underwriting, Loss Prevention Specialists, Public Record Research Firms

Applications: Collections, Employment Screening, Fraud Prevention/Detection, Insurance Underwriting, Tenant Screening

Information Types:
Addresses/Telephone Numbers (US)
Bankruptcy (US)
Credit Information (US)
Criminal Information (US)
Driver and/or Vehicle (US)
Education/Employment (US)

Military Svc (US)
Voter Registration (AR)

Statement of Capabilities: Florida-based Staftrack is a leader in databased and computerized access to information vital to pre-employment screening. They offer a wide range of information to meet client's screening needs, including driver records, workers comp claims, credit info, SS searches, fraud prevention and their standard Credit Profile. Offers instant access to the Staftrack Termination and Verified Work History database. Other screening reports include work records, criminal histories, educational verifications and occupational license checks.

State Information Bureau
842 E Park Ave
Tallahassee, FL 32301
Telephone: **Fax:**
800-881-1742   850-561-3995
850-561-3990
armadillo@nxus.com
Year Founded: 1986

Clientele: Attorney Firms, Insurance - Agents/Brokers, Investigators - Fraud, Private Investigators

Applications: Background Info - Business, Background Info - Individuals, Competitive Intelligence, Fraud Prevention/Detection, Litigation

Information Types:
Addresses/Telephone Numbers (US)
Criminal Information (FL)
Driver and/or Vehicle (FL)
Licenses/Registrations/Permits (FL)
Litigation/Judgments/Tax Liens (FL)
Social Security (Numbers) (US)
Uniform Commercial Code (FL)
Workers' Compensation (FL)

Membership: ACFE, COIN, NAIS, NALI, NCISS, PRRN

Statement of Capabilities: State Information Bureau specializes in utilizing the public records of the State of Florida to conduct a variety of investigations. By utilizing licensed investigators, they conduct thorough searches. They access these records manually as well as by computer to assure complete searches. They have 3 licensed investigators on staff, each with a minimum of 10 years experience. If it is a record maintained in Florida, they specialize in getting it.

Suburban Record Research
12 Main St
Dover, MA 02030

Telephone: **Fax:**
617-536-3486   508-785-2852

Parent Company: A. Scott Broadhurst & Associates

Year Founded: 1982

Clientele: Asset-Based Lenders, Attorney Firms, Information - Brokers/Retrievers, Legal Profession, Legal Service Companies, Public Record Research Firms, Secured Lenders

Applications: Government Document Retrieval, Background Info - Business, Background Info - Individuals, Litigation, Legal Compliance

Information Types:
Bankruptcy (MA)
Corporate/Trade Name Data (MA)
Litigation/Judgments/Tax Liens (MA)
Real Estate/Assessor (MA)
Uniform Commercial Code (MA)
Vital Records (MA)
Workers' Compensation (MA)
Criminal Information (MA)

Membership: ABA, NALI, NPRRA

Statement of Capabilities: Suburban Record Research provides reliable, 24-hour turnaround time in most instances. Accessing Massachusetts Secretary of State, Superior Court, Land Court, Registry of Deeds (including recorded land), they provide UCCs at local level detail reports, rundowns, "bring downs" and most all other public record retrieval/information services for financial, legal, and general business operations.

Super Search Inc
PO Box 770
Hurst, TX 76053

Telephone: **Fax:**
800-687-5553   800-687-5554
817-268-3224   817-285-9956

ecturner@flash.net

Year Founded: 1989

Clientele: Public Record Research Firms, Legal Profession, Credit Reporting Agencies, Financial Institutions, Information - Brokers/Retrievers, Banks, Attorney Firms

Applications: Background Info - Business, Litigation, Lending/Leasing, Filing/Recording Documents, Asset/Lien Searching/Verification

Information Types:
Uniform Commercial Code (US, TX)
Litigation/Judgments/Tax Liens (US, TX)
Bankruptcy (US, TX)
Credit Information (US)
Addresses/Telephone Numbers (TX)
Real Estate/Assessor (US, TX)
Criminal Information (TX)

Membership: NAFE, NPRRA, PRRN

Statement of Capabilities: Super Search offers asset/background searching services at the state, local, and federal levels. They also specialize in obtaining case records from the National Archives at the Federal Records Center in Ft. Worth.

Superior Information Services LLC
PO Box 8787
Trenton, NJ 08650-0787

Telephone: **Fax:**
800-848-0489   800-883-0677
609-883-7000   609-883-0677

www.superiorinfo.com

Year Founded: 1987

Clientele: Financial Institutions, Insurance - General, Legal Profession, Public Record Research Firms

Applications: Litigation, Lending/Leasing, Legal Compliance, Asset/Lien Searching/Verification

Proprietary Products:

Name/Desc: Superior Online
Info Provided: Litigation/Judgments/Tax Liens and Bankruptcy
Media: Online Database
Coverage: DC, DE, MD, NC, NJ, NY, PA, VA

Name/Desc: Superior Online
Info Provided: Corporate/Trade Name Data
Media: Online Database
Coverage: NY, PA

Name/Desc: Superior Online
Info Provided: Uniform Commercial Code
Media: Online Database
Coverage: PA

Name/Desc: Superior Online
Info Provided: Real Estate/Assessor
Media: Online Database
Coverage: NY (NYC), NJ

Membership: NPRRA, ICA, AALL, SLA

Statement of Capabilities: Superior Information Services provides accuarte, reliable and comprehensive information to a wide variety of clients including attorneys, investigators, financial institutions, financial underwriters, employment agencies, insurance claims departments, leasing companies, and government agencies. Our proprietary database searches all counties in the following states: NY, NJ, PA, DE, MD, DC, VA and NC. Our search engine uncovers filings under similar/misspelled names. Superior Information Services is the leading supplier of public record information in the Mid-Atlantic region.

T

T-R Information Services

12805 SW 91 Ct, Box 10
Miami, FL 33176
Telephone: **Fax:**
305-278-2138 305-253-8334
www.fullsearch.com
sales@fullsearch.com
Parent Company: T-R Communications Inc
Year Founded: 1994

Clientele: Business - General, Legal Profession, Employers (HR/Personnel Depts), Public Record Research Firms, Consumers (Individuals), Landlords, Collection Agencies

Applications: Asset/Lien Searching/Verification, Employment Screening, Background Info - Business, Background Info - Individuals, Locating People/Businesses

Information Types:
Addresses/Telephone Numbers (US)
Real Estate/Assessor (US)
Credit Information (US)
Driver and/or Vehicle (US)
Criminal Information (US)
Litigation/Judgments/Tax Liens (US)
Bankruptcy (US)
Education/Employment (US)

Statement of Capabilities: T-R Information Services provides nationwide public record

information. They specialize in pre-employment screening and asset searches. They can provide a complete dossier on an individual or business. In addition to asset searches to locate real estate and personal property, they provide premium searches for bank accounts and bank balances. They can also provide information about stocks and other investments, IRAs and the location of safe deposit boxes.

Tax Analysts

6830 N Fairfax Dr
Arlington, VA 22213
Telephone: **Fax:**
703-533-4600 705-533-4444
www.tax.org

Year Founded: 1970

Clientele: Legal Profession, Professionals-Other

Applications: Current Events, Litigation, Legal Compliance, Background Info - Business, General Business Information

Information Types:
Associations/Trade Groups (US)

Proprietary Products:

Name/Desc: Exempt Organization Master List
Info Provided: Corporate/Trade Name Data
Media: CD-ROM and Disk
Coverage: US

Name/Desc: The Tax Directory
Info Provided: Addresses/Telephone Numbers
Media: Publication, CD-ROM and Available on DIALOG & LEXIS
Coverage: US, International

Name/Desc: The OneDisc
Info Provided: Legislation/Regulations
Media: CD-ROM
Coverage: US

Name/Desc: TAXBASE
Info Provided: Legislation/Regulations
Media: Internet
Coverage: US

Coverage: US, International
Statement of Capabilities: Tax Analysts is a nonprofit organization dedicated to providing timely, comprehensive information to tax professionals at a reasonable cost. They are the leading electronic publisher of tax information. The Exempt Organization Master List contains information about more than 1.1 million not-

for-profit organizations registered with the federal government. The Tax Directory contains information about 14,000 federal tax officials, 9000 private tax professionals and 8000 corporate tax professionals. Online databases include daily federal, state and international tax information as well as complete research libraries.

Texas Driving Record Express Service

7401 Gulf Freeway #103
Houston, TX 77017
Telephone: **Fax:**
800-671-2287   800-671-2287
713-641-5252   713-641-5252
Year Founded: 1991

Clientele: Attorney Firms, Business - General, Consumers (Individuals), Employers (HR/Personnel Depts), Insurance - Underwriting, Legal Profession, Legal Service Companies

Applications: Background Info - Individuals, Employment Screening, Insurance Underwriting, Legal Compliance

Information Types:
Driver and/or Vehicle (TX)
Licenses/Registrations/Permits (TX)

Statement of Capabilities: Texas Driving Record Express Service obtains driving records and provides them with unique turnaround time capabilities.

Texas Title Search

11555 Mulholland Dr
Stafford, TX 77477
Telephone: **Fax:**
281-568-1900   281-568-1185
Year Founded: 1988

Clientele: Insurance - Agents/Brokers, Insurance - Claims, Insurance - Underwriting, Investigators - Fraud

Applications: Asset/Lien Searching/Verification, Fraud Prevention/Detection, General Business Information, Litigation

Information Types:
Driver and/or Vehicle (TX)

Statement of Capabilities: Texas Title Search has been providing title information on Texas vehicles since 1988. Data is retrieved directly from the State, assuring current information.

Reports include make and model, license plate numbers, VIN, title issue date, license expiration date, current owner's name/address, previous owner, lienholder and vehicle history remarks. These reports help identify vehicles that may cause serious underwriting or claims problems. They offer same day turnaround and rush orders are available.

The Court System Inc

1700 Commerce #1050
Dallas, TX 75201
Telephone: **Fax:**
800-856-0585   214-744-0586
214-744-0585
Year Founded: 1989

Clientele: Financial Institutions, Legal Profession, Other Professionals, Public Record Research Firms

Information Types:
Bankruptcy (US, TX)
Litigation/Judgments/Tax Liens (US, TX)
Uniform Commercial Code (US, TX)
Corporate/Trade Name Data (US)

Membership: NAPPS, NPRRA

Statement of Capabilities: The Court System is a Dallas-based document retrieval and research service owned and operated by a paralegal with more than 20 years experience. Turnaround time is 1-2 working days on most Dallas requests, providing the information requested is readily available. Rush requests are returned within a few hours if placed before noon. Orders outside the Dallas area vary, but are normally completed within 1-3 days or can be obtained on a rush basis.

The Pettit Company

1744 Theresa Ln
Powhatan, VA 23139
Telephone: **Fax:**
800-752-6158   800-236-2859
804-379-2462   804-379-3217
www.pettitcompany.com
Year Founded: 1994

Clientele: Asset-Based Lenders, Legal Profession, Credit Grantors, Equipment Leasing Companies, Public Record Research Firms, Financial Institutions, Secured Lenders

Applications: Asset/Lien Searching/Verification, Filing/Recording Documents, Legal Compliance, Lending/Leasing, Litigation

Information Types:
Bankruptcy (US,VA)
Corporate/Trade Name Data (US,VA)
Criminal Information (VA)
Legislation/Regulation (VA)
Litigation/Judgments/Tax Liens (VA,US)
Licenses/Registrations/Permits (VA,US)
Uniform Commercial Code (US,VA)
Real Estate/Assessor (VA)

Membership: NPRRA, PRRN

Statement of Capabilities: The Pettit Company LC is a family owned and operated business, providing public record search and document retrieval services throughout the world. The principals of the company are Eddie and Carolyn, whose experience began in 1987, and Buddy and Pat, whose experience began in 1982. They don't employ a sales or marketing staff, nor do we employ "account reps." Their entire staff is experienced and understand the industry.

Free Web Information:
Virginia State Corporation and UCC information, Corporation Guide Forms, UCC Forms for all states, and Virginia court information.

The Records Reviewer Inc
PO Box 3073
Hallandale, FL 33008
Telephone: **Fax:**
800-206-2890   954-458-5300
recrev@gate.net
Year Founded: 1984

Clientele: Legal Profession, Credit Reporting Agencies, Public Record Research Firms

Applications: Asset/Lien Searching/Verification, Litigation, Background Info - Business, Background Info - Individuals, Real Estate Transactions

Information Types:
Bankruptcy (FL)
Uniform Commercial Code (FL)
Litigation/Judgments/Tax Liens (FL)
Real Estate/Assessor (FL)
Environmental (FL)
Criminal Information (FL)

Membership: PRRN

Statement of Capabilities: The Records Reviewer specializes in monitoring bankruptcy

and environmental actions, also environmental and criminal background searches.

The Search Company Inc
1410-439 University Ave
Toronto, ON M5G 1Y8
Telephone: **Fax:**
800-396-8241   800-396-8219
416-979-5858   416-979-5857
www.thesearchcompany.com
info@thesearchcompany.com
Year Founded: 1993

Clientele: Lending Institutions, Legal Profession, Financial Institutions, Insurance - Claims, Investigators - Fraud, Mortgage Bankers, Public Record Research Firms

Applications: Asset/Lien Searching/Verification, Background Info - Business, Background Info - Individuals, Government Document Retrieval, Litigation

Information Types:
Bankruptcy (CD)
Corporate/Trade Name Data (CD)
Credit Information (CD)
Driver and/or Vehicle (CD-Ontario)
Trademarks/Patents (CD)

Proprietary Products:
Name/Desc: Property Ownership & Tenant Data
Info Provided: Real Estate/Assessor
Media: Direct Online, Internet, Printed Report and Software
Coverage: CD

Statement of Capabilities: The Search Company covers 2 distinct markets: 1) Canada wide public record retrieval; 2) Litigation related asset and corporate background reporting with or without a full narrative report, with analysis and opinion regarding the advisability of litigation.

The Search Is On Inc
PO Box 120598
Nashville, TN 37212
Telephone: **Fax:**
800-324-2050   800-788-0835
615-321-2050   615-329-3343
www.tsio.com
search@tsio.com
Year Founded: 1979

Clientele: Financial Institutions, Legal Profession

Applications: Asset/Lien Searching/Verification, Legal Compliance, Background Info - Business, Background Info - Individuals

Information Types:
Uniform Commercial Code (US, TN)
Corporate/Trade Name Data (US, TN)
Driver and/or Vehicle (US, TN)
Litigation/Judgments/Tax Liens (US, TN)
Vital Records (US, TN)

Membership: NPRRA

Statement of Capabilities: The Search Is On Inc is one of the largest service companies of its kind in Tennessee.

Thomas Paralegal Services

294 Wright Ave #261
Gretna, LA 70056
Telephone:
504-263-0715
www.angelfire.com/biz/tpserv ices

Year Founded: 1983

Clientele: Legal Profession, Business - General, Consulting Firms, Attorney Firms, Legal Service Companies

Applications: Filing/Recording Documents, Legal Compliance, Litigation, Locating People/Businesses, Real Estate Transactions

Information Types:
Bankruptcy (LA-Jefferson, New Orleans)
Criminal Information (LA-Jefferson, New Orleans)
Litigation/Judgments/Tax Liens (LA-Jefferson, New Orleans)

Membership: NALA, NALI, NFPA

Statement of Capabilities: Thomas Paralegal Services is an efficient business that improves the delivery and quality of legal assistance, and strives to restore the trust in the legal system and its practitioners.

Thomson & Thomson

500 Victory Rd
North Quincy, MA 02171-3145
Telephone: **Fax:**
800-692-8833   800-543-1983
617-479-1600   617-786-8273
www.thomson-thomson.com

Parent Company: The Thomson Corporation

Year Founded: 1922

Clientele: Legal Profession, Libraries, Educational Institutions, Business - General, Corporate Counsel, Legal Service Companies, Direct Marketers

Applications: Legal Compliance, Direct Marketing, Competitive Intelligence, Background Info - Business, Background Info - Individuals

Information Types:
Litigation/Judgments/Tax Liens (US)
Corporate/Trade Name Data (US)

Proprietary Products:

Name/Desc: TRADEMARKSCAN
Info Provided: Trademarks/Patents and Foreign Country Information
Media: CD-ROM, Direct Online and Internet
Coverage: US, International

Name/Desc: Worldwide Domain
Info Provided: Foreign Country Information
Media: Internet
Coverage: US, International

Name/Desc: Site Comber
Info Provided: Trademarks/Patents
Media: Internet and Printed Report
Coverage: US

Name/Desc: US Full Trademark Search
Info Provided: Trademarks/Patents
Media: Internet and Printed Report
Coverage: US

Name/Desc: US Full Copyright Search
Info Provided: Licenses/Registrations/Permits
Media: Printed Report
Coverage: US

Name/Desc: US Title Availability Search
Info Provided: Vital Records
Media: Printed Report
Coverage: US

Name/Desc: The deForest Report for Script Clearance
Info Provided: Vital Records
Media: Fax-on-Demand
Coverage: US

Membership: INTA, SIIA, AALL

Statement of Capabilities: Thomson & Thomson is a world leader in trademark, copyright and script clearance services, with over 75 years of experience and offices in the US, Canada, Europe and Japan. Accessing trademark records from more than 200

countries, T&T analysts provide reports to help clients determine if their proposed trademarks are available for use. Clients can perform their own trademark searches via Thomson & Thomson's TRADEMARKSCAN online databases. Thomson & Thomson also provides a complete offering of equally impressive copyright, title and script clearance services-- allowing you to manage and protect your intellectual property assets.

Free Web Information:

Two free services:. West Group on SAEGIS is an online tool that provides industry information. It includes intellectual property issues ranging from litigation to corporate mergers. SAEGIS Library includes reference links, industry news, archives, domain name news and the copyright corner.

Title Court Service

205 Broadway #302
Los Angeles, CA 90012
Telephone: **Fax:**
213-626-8753 213-626-0147
www.TITLECOURT.com

Year Founded: 1978

Clientele: Public Record Research Firms, Credit Reporting Agencies, Financial Institutions, land title companies

Applications: Real Estate Transactions, Filing/Recording Documents

Information Types:
Bankruptcy (CA)
Litigation/Judgments/Tax Liens (CA)
Wills/Probate (CA)

Membership: NPRRA

Statement of Capabilities: Title Court Services is a record verification company serving primarily the land title and credit reporting industries. Their 14 offices in California's population centers are staffed with attorney-supervised employees to insure single-source professional service to clients. California Hall Service, a subsidiary, offers document recording and title searching at county offices throughout California.

TML Information Services Inc

116-55 Queens Blvd
Forest Hills, NY 11375
Telephone: **Fax:**
800-743-7891 718-544-2853

718-793-3737
www.tml.com

Year Founded: 1985

Clientele: Insurance - Agents/Brokers, Insurance - General, Public Record Research Firms, Legal Profession, Auto Rental Companies, Automotive Dealers

Applications: Insurance Underwriting, Employment Screening, Driver Screening for Auto Rental

Information Types:
Driver and/or Vehicle (US)

Proprietary Products:

Name/Desc: Auto-Search
Info Provided: Driver and/or Vehicle
Media: Online Database, Internet, Call-back, and Fax
Coverage: AL, AZ, CT, DC, FL, ID, IN, KS, KY, LA, MA, MI, MN, MS, NC, ND, NE, NH, NJ, NY, OH, SC, VA, WI, WV

Name/Desc: Title File
Info Provided: Driver and/or Vehicle
Media: Online Database, Call-back and Fax
Coverage: AL, FL, SD

Name/Desc: Driver Check
Info Provided: Driver and/or Vehicle
Media: Online Database and Automated Telephone Lookup
Coverage: AL, AZ, CA, CT, FL, ID, KS, LA, MD, MI, MN, NE, NH, NY, NC, OH, PA, SC, VA, WV

Membership: AAMVA, IIAA, NAPIA, NETS

Statement of Capabilities: TML Information Services specializes in providing access to motor vehicle information in an online, real-time environment. Their standardization format enables TML to offer several unique automated applications for instant access to multiple states' driver and vehicle information, including a touch-tone fax-on-demand service and a rule-based decision processing service for driver qualification for car rental. TML has online access to more than 200 million driver and vehicle records in more than 30 states and expects to add several more states soon.

Todd Wiegele Research Co Inc

1345 16th Ave #6
Grafton, WI 53024
Telephone: **Fax:**
800-754-7800 717-276-3395

717-276-3393
www.execpc.com/~research/

Year Founded: 1994

Clientele: Insurance - Agents/Brokers, Legal Profession, Employers (HR/Personnel Depts), Legal Service Companies, Mortgage Bankers, Savings and Loans, Financial Institutions

Applications: Real Estate Transactions, Asset/Lien Searching/Verification, Background Info - Individuals, Employment Screening, Litigation

Information Types:
Real Estate/Assessor (US)
Credit Information (US)
Litigation/Judgments/Tax Liens (US)
Uniform Commercial Code (US)
Criminal Information (US)
Bankruptcy (US)

Proprietary Products:
Name/Desc: FASTRACT
Info Provided: Real Estate/Assessor
Media: Disk, Magnetic Tape and Microfiche
Coverage: WI

Membership: PRRN, NACM

Statement of Capabilities: The Todd Wiegele Research Co specializes in Milwaukee County records, but also provides nationwide services utilizing online databases and correspondents. Records specialties include title searches, criminal background checks, asset investigations, civil background checks and database consulting. They offer a database, FASTRACT, to track real estate information in Milwaukee County, WI.

Tracers Choice
1321 Miller #208
Anaheim, CA 92806
Telephone: **Fax:**
800-444-5508   800-444-3351
714-695-0452   714-695-0455
tracerschoic@earthlink.com
Year Founded: 1989

Clientele: Attorney Firms, Collection Agencies, Government Agencies, Insurance - Claims, Legal Profession, Private Investigators

Applications: Asset/Lien Searching/Verification, Background Info - Individuals, Collections, Employment Screening, Legal Compliance

Information Types:
Addresses/Telephone Numbers (US)

Bankruptcy (US)
Criminal Information (US)
Litigation/Judgments/Tax Liens (US)
Real Estate/Assessor (US)
Uniform Commercial Code (US)
Vital Records (US)

Statement of Capabilities: Tracer's Choice service is specifically for those who do not have the resources or the computer to be able to have record access from the large commercial vendors. There is no monthly minimum.

Tracers Information Specialists Inc
39 Federal St
Greenfield, MA 01301
Telephone: **Fax:**
888-753-8848   413-772-8995
413-772-8998
www.tracersinfo.com
sales@tracersinfo.com
Year Founded: 1996

Clientele: Legal Profession, Collection Agencies, Employers (HR/Personnel Depts), Information - Brokers/Retrievers, Private Investigators

Applications: Asset/Lien Searching/Verification, Background Info - Individuals, Employment Screening, Locating People/Businesses, Tenant Screening

Information Types:
Addresses/Telephone Numbers (US)
Credit Information (US)
Criminal Information (US)
Driver and/or Vehicle (US)
Litigation/Judgments/Tax Liens (US)
Real Estate/Assessor (US)
Social Security (Numbers) (US)
Uniform Commercial Code (US)

Statement of Capabilities: Tracers Information Specialists is a full-service research firm specializing in the rapid return of accurate, up-to-date information. They operate strictly in compliance with the myriad of state and federal laws. Avoiding archived information, they acquire public records directly from states and/or counties to ensure the accuracy and timeliness of the information they deliver. Their staff is highly trained and knowledgeable about the legal uses for information. They anticipate industry trends and keep clients informed about changes that will affect them.

Trans Union

555 W Adams
Chicago, IL 60661-3601
Telephone:
800-899-7132
312-258-1717
www.transunion.com

Year Founded: 1969

Clientele: Apartment Owners/Managers, Credit Grantors, Credit Reporting Agencies, Employers (HR/Personnel Depts), Business - General, Financial Institutions, Equipment Leasing Companies

Applications: Collections, Lending/Leasing, Insurance Underwriting, Real Estate Transactions, General Business Information

Proprietary Products:

Name/Desc: CRONUS
Info Provided: Credit Information, Addresses, Litigation/Judgments/Tax Liens
Media: Online, Paper
Coverage: US

Name/Desc: Real Estate Services
Info Provided: Real Estate/Assessor
Media: Online, Printed Report, Disks
Coverage: US

Name/Desc: Business Information
Info Provided: Credit Information, Corporate/Trade Name Data
Media: Online, Printed Report
Coverage: US

Membership: SIIA

Statement of Capabilities: Trans Union, best known for its national consumer credit information file, provides a number of information services. Their TRACE product, based on Social Security Numbers, expands searching facilities to locate people who have changed names or moved without a forwarding address.

Trax

17 Joy St
Barrington, RI 02806
Telephone: **Fax:**
401-245-3004 401-245-9443
Year Founded: 1983

Clientele: Public Record Research Firms, Insurance - General, Legal Profession

Applications: Locating People/Businesses, Background Info - Business, Background Info - Individuals

Information Types:
Driver and/or Vehicle (FL, MA, ME, RI)
Litigation/Judgments/Tax Liens (RI)
Criminal Information (RI)

Statement of Capabilities: Trax specializes in same-day service for public records in the Rhode Island and the New England area. They also provide locating services.

UCC Guide Inc, The

PO Box 338
Ravena, NY 12143
Telephone: **Fax:**
800-345-3822 800-252-0906
www.equides.com

Year Founded: 1992

Clientele: Financial Institutions, Legal Profession, Public Record Research Firms

Applications: Legal Compliance, Lending/Leasing

Proprietary Products:

Name/Desc: Uniform Commercial Code Filing Guide
Info Provided: Uniform Commercial Code Filing Guide
Media: Print, Disk and CD-ROM
Coverage: US

Membership: AIIP, SIIA, NPRRA, PRRN

Statement of Capabilities: The UCC Filing Guide is a unique 5 volume, 6000 page quarterly updated service used by multi-state UCC filers to prepare UCC financing statements accurately. All 4300 UCC filing offices in the US are covered. Monthly newsletter is included with the annual subscription. The service includes UCC searching information. The disk media includes a database for automatic fee determination and address label/cover letter preparation. An affiliated company now publishes the Real Estate Recording Guide, designed to assist real estate documentation specialists.

UCC Retrievals Inc

7288-A Hanover Green Dr
Mechanicsville, VA 23111
Telephone: **Fax:**
804-559-5919   804-559-5920
Year Founded: 1988

Clientele: Financial Institutions, Legal Profession, Public Record Research Firms

Applications: Asset/Lien Searching/Verification, Legal Compliance, Litigation, Filing/Recording Documents

Information Types:
Bankruptcy (VA)
Corporate/Trade Name Data (VA)
Driver and/or Vehicle (VA)
Trademarks/Patents (US)

Proprietary Products:

Name/Desc: Federal Tax Liens and UCCs
Info Provided: Litigation/judgments/Tax Liens and Uniform Commercial Code
Media: Printed Reports, Lists or Labels and Online Database
Coverage: VA

Membership: NPRRA, PRRN

Statement of Capabilities: UCC Retrievals specializes in searching UCC and federal tax liens in Virginia. They also file motor vehicle records, do corporate filings and retrievals, and assist with pending litigation. Their turnaround time is 24-48 hours.

UCC Search Inc

PO Box 9315
Santa Fe, NM 87504
Telephone: **Fax:**
800-453-9404   800-642-6382
505-983-4228   505-983-1169
Year Founded: 1985

Clientele: Attorney Firms, Business - General, Legal Service Companies, Financial Institutions

Applications: Asset/Lien Searching/Verification, Lending/Leasing, Filing/Recording Documents

Information Types:
Uniform Commercial Code (US, NM)
Corporate/Trade Name Data (US, NM)
Litigation/Judgments/Tax Liens (US, NM)
Bankruptcy (US, NM)

Membership: NPRRA

Statement of Capabilities: UCC Search specializes in searching and filing UCC and corporate records at the Secretary of State and Corporation Commission of the state of New Mexico. They perform searches and file documents county and nationwide.

UMI Company

PO Box 1346
Ann Arbor, MI 48106-1346
Telephone: **Fax:**
734-761-4700   734-975-6486
800-521-0600
www.umi.com
business service@umi.com
Parent Company: Bell & Howell Inc.
Clientele: Business - General, Government Agencies, Financial Planners, Educational Institutions, Libraries, Real Estate Owners/Managers

Applications: General Business Information, Background Info - Business, Competitive Intelligence, Current Events

Information Types:
News/Current Events (US)

Statement of Capabilities: UMI, formerly operated DataTimes, now offers a number of useful electronic and print services with information on business, current events, technology innovations, including graphics, charts, photos. Their products are useful to libraries, researchers, scientists, schools, and competitive intelligence gathering. Products include ProQuest packages (includes newspapers) and IntellX.

Free Web Information:
Product descriptions, ordering info, UMI background

Unisearch Inc

PO Box 11940
Olympia, WA 98508-1940
Telephone: **Fax:**
800-722-0708   800-531-1717
360-956-9500   360-956-9504
www.unisearch.com
Year Founded: 1991

Clientele: Financial Institutions, Legal Profession, Public Record Research Firms

Applications: Asset/Lien Searching/Verification, Lending/Leasing, Legal Compliance, Real Estate Transactions, Corporate Registered Agent Service

Information Types:
Bankruptcy (US)
Litigation/Judgments/Tax Liens (US)
Corporate/Trade Name Data (US)
Uniform Commercial Code (AK, CA, ID, MN, OR, UT, WA, WI)

Proprietary Products:

Name/Desc: WALDO
Info Provided: Uniform Commercial Code
Media: Direct Online, Internet and Printed Report
Coverage: CA, IL, WA

Membership: NPRRA

Statement of Capabilities: Unisearch is online with over 30 states and British Columbia, providing instant access to the most current information available. They maintain a film library of UCC documents for WA, OR, AK, UT, CA, IL, MT, NV, WI, MN. In areas where computer access is not yet available, Unisearch employs a network of correspondents to provide service.

Free Web Information:
office locations, employees, services, fees and informative newsletter.

Unisyn Information Services
110 West C St #914
San Diego, CA 92101
Telephone: **Fax:**
800-869-8040   800-648-2009
619-233-7725   619-232-6426

Unisyn/4240124@MCIMail.com
Year Founded: 1980

Clientele: Financial Institutions, Collection Agencies, Legal Profession, Attorney Firms, Investigators - Fraud

Applications: Asset/Lien Searching/Verification, Background Info - Business, Background Info - Individuals, Locating People/Businesses

Information Types:
Bankruptcy (US)
Addresses/Telephone Numbers (US)
Criminal Information (US)
Social Security (Numbers) (US)

Licenses/Registrations/Permits (US)
Uniform Commercial Code (US)
Litigation/Judgments/Tax Liens (US)
Workers' Compensation (US)

US Corporate Services
200 Minnesota Bldg, 46 E Fourth St
St Paul, MN 55101
Telephone: **Fax:**
800-327-1886   800-603-0266
651-227-7575   651-225-9244
www.uscorpserv.com

info@uscorpserv.com
Parent Company: Dolan Media Co
Year Founded: 1966

Clientele: Legal Profession, Asset-Based Lenders, Equipment Leasing Companies, Financial Institutions, Public Record Research Firms, Corporate Counsel, Lending Institutions

Applications: Asset/Lien Searching/Verification, Competitive Intelligence, Filing/Recording Documents, Lending/Leasing, Real Estate Transactions

Information Types:
Bankruptcy (US)
Corporate/Trade Name Data (US)
Driver and/or Vehicle (US)
Litigation/Judgments/Tax Liens (US)
Uniform Commercial Code (US)

Proprietary Products:

Name/Desc: MN Secretary of State Records
Info Provided: Corporation/Trade Name Data
Media: Online, Print
Coverage: MN

Name/Desc: WI UCCs
Info Provided: Uniform Commerical Code
Media: Online, Print
Coverage: WI

Membership: NPRRA, PRRN

Statement of Capabilities: US Corporate Services is a full service UCC, tax lien, judgment, litigation and corporate search and filing firm. Their optical image library of Minnesota enables them to provide custom reports to their clients. They have nationwide correspondent relationships. Their turnaround time is 24-72 hours. They will invoice monthly; projects are generally billed by the number of names searched.

US Datalink Inc

6711 Bayway Dr
Baytown, TX 77520

Telephone: **Fax:**
800-527-7930   800-364-8885
281-424-7223   281-424-3415
www.usdatalink.com

Year Founded: 1986

Clientele: Employers (HR/Personnel Depts),
Public Record Research Firms, Professionals-
Other

Applications: Employment Screening,
Asset/Lien Searching/Verification, Locating
People/Businesses, General Business
Information

Information Types:
Litigation/Judgments/Tax Liens (US)
Credit Information (US)
Criminal Information (US)
Driver and/or Vehicle (US)
Workers' Compensation (US)

Membership: AIIP, NPRRA

Statement of Capabilities: US Datalink
(USDL) utilizes proprietary software for the
user to enter search requests off-line, then
transmitted in batches to USDL. With over
1500 independent searchers to fill orders across
the country, USDL offers a wide range of
searches, from motor vehicle and driving
record information to pre-employment
screening and business information. Almost
anything that is a matter of public record can
be retrieved, but their primary focus is pre-
employment screening. Most search requests
are filled within 24-48 hours and returned
electronically. Users also have the option of
accessing the service via fax and having the
results faxed back. Internet access is also
available for inputting and retrieving requests.

US Document Services Inc

PO Box 50486
Columbia, SC 29250

Telephone: **Fax:**
803-254-9193   803-771-9905
www.us-doc-services.com

info@us-doc-services.com

Year Founded: 1990

Clientele: Business - General, Financial
Institutions

Applications: Asset/Lien Searching/Verification,
Background Info - Business, Filing/Recording
Documents, Government Document Retrieval

Information Types:
Uniform Commercial Code (US, SC, NC)
Litigation/Judgments/Tax Liens (US, SC, NC)
Corporate/Trade Name Data (US, SC, NC)
Vital Records

Proprietary Products:
Name/Desc: Secretary of State
Info Provided: Corporation/Trade Name Data
Media: Printed Report
Coverage: NC, SC

Membership: NPRRA, PRRN

Statement of Capabilities: US Document
Services is a nationwide public record search
and document retrieval company specializing
in North Carolina and South Carolina. They
offer UCC, tax lien, suit and judgment,
bankruptcy and asset searches, and provide
legal, financial and commercial clients with a
wide variety of services including formation,
qualification and registrations of corporations,
etc. With an in-house South Carolina and
North Carolina microfilm and online database,
they provide up-to-date results, with 48-hour
turnarounds

US Search & Background

790 W 40 Hwy #248
Blue Springs, MO 64015

Telephone: **Fax:**
888-267-5534   816-224-8725
816-229-3463

Year Founded: 1998

Clientele: Attorney Firms, Business - General,
Genealogists, Insurance - Claims, Legal
Profession, Private Investigators

Applications: Asset/Lien Searching/Verification,
Background Info - Individuals, Employment
Screening, Genealogical Research, Insurance
Underwriting

Information Types:
Addresses/Telephone Numbers (US)
Bankruptcy (US)
Criminal Information (US)
Education/Employment (US)
Genealogical Information (US)
Litigation/Judgments/Tax Liens (US)
Social Security (Numbers) (US)

Statement of Capabilities: US Search &
Background provides address information,

criminal background searches, employment information, genealogy lists, credit information and other public information on a national basis. They are fast, efficient and reasonably priced.

Vehicle Operator Searches

PO Box 15334
Sacramento, CA 95851-1334
Telephone: **Fax:**
916-447-2814   916-447-2818
Year Founded: 1970

Clientele: Financial Institutions, Insurance - Agents/Brokers, Legal Profession, Public Record Research Firms, Lending Institutions, Insurance - Claims, Employers (HR/Personnel Depts)

Applications: Insurance Underwriting, Legal Compliance, Lending/Leasing, Employment Screening

Information Types:
Addresses/Telephone Numbers (US)
Driver and/or Vehicle (US, CA)
Real Estate/Assessor (US)
Uniform Commercial Code (CA)
Criminal Information (CA)
Aviation/Vessels (CA)

Statement of Capabilities: By accessing the 50 states and Washington DC for driver and vehicle information, Vehicle Operator Searches offers a variety of options for requesting information, including mail, phone, fax and computer. Their replies vary from 1 hour to 3 weeks depending on the search and the state.

Virginia Information Providers Network

1111 East Main Street
Richmond, VA 23219
Telephone:
804-786-4718
www.vipnet.org

webmaster@vipnet.org
Year Founded: 1996

Clientele: Attorney Firms, Insurance - Underwriting, Corporate Security, Employers (HR/Personnel Depts), Credit Reporting Agencies, Financial Institutions

Applications: Employment Screening, Litigation, Insurance Underwriting

Information Types:
Associations/Trade Groups (VA)

Proprietary Products:
Name/Desc: VIPNet
Info Provided: Driver and/or Vehicle
Media: Internet
Coverage: VA

Statement of Capabilities: The Virginia Information Providers Network was created by the state of Virginia to streamline and enhance the ways in which citizens and businesses access government information. VIPNet premium services includes access to state motor vehicle records.

Free Web Information:
The web site is an excellent sources of information links for state agencies and businesses.

VISTA Information Solutions

5060 Shoreham Place
San Diego, CA 92122
Telephone: **Fax:**
800-767-0403   619-450-6195
619-450-6100
www.vistainfo.com

Year Founded: 1989

Clientele: Asset-Based Lenders, Credit Grantors, Credit Reporting Agencies, Financial Institutions, Legal Service Companies

Applications: Risk Management, Insurance Underwriting, Legal Compliance, Lending/Leasing

Proprietary Products:
Name/Desc: VISTACheck
Info Provided: Environmental, Corporation/Trade Name Data
Media: Online, Software, Lists
Coverage: US

Membership: SIIA, ABA

Statement of Capabilities: VISTA is a premier provider of environmental risk information software and services and has exclusive endorsements by the American Bankers Association. Their myriad of products provide information to the environmental and insurance underwriting industries to assist with risk management. The VISTA environmental database includes environmental record information from more than 500 state and federal sources, and contains over 10 million records which are geo-coded.

VitalChek Network

4512 Central Pike
Hermitage, TN 37076
Telephone:
800-255-2414
www.vitalchek.com

webcomment@vitalchek.com
Clientele: Consumers (Individuals), Genealogists, Business - General

Applications: Genealogical Research, Background Info - Individuals

Information Types:
Vital Records (US)

Proprietary Products:

Name/Desc: VitalChek
Info Provided: Vital Records
Coverage: US

Statement of Capabilities: VitalChek Network has a sophisticated voice and fax network setup to help people get certified copies of birth, death and marriage certificates and other vital records. VitalChek provides a direct access gateway to participating agencies at the state and local level.
Free Web Information:
The web site is filled with information on each state and local agency regarding access and prices of vital records.

VTS Inc

PO Box 971
Elgin, IL 60121-0971
Telephone: **Fax:**
800-538-4464   847-888-4464
800-688-5742   847-888-8588
www.PIchicago.com

Year Founded: 1979

Membership: ION, NALI, NAPPS, WAD, COIN

Statement of Capabilities: With years of expertise in conducting searches in Cook County, IL, VTS has a current staff of 18 covering the Chicago Metropolitan area. Staff

includes varied backgrounds: paralegals, police, FBI, insurance, and legal.

Washington Document Service, Inc

400 7th St NW #300
Washington, DC 20004
Telephone: **Fax:**
800-728-5201   800-385-3823
202-628-5200   202-626-7628
www.wdsdocs.com

info@wddsdocs.com
Year Founded: 1978

Clientele: Legal Profession, Financial Institutions, Business - General, Corporate Counsel, Securities Industry, Accountants

Applications: Litigation, General Business Information, Asset/Lien Searching/Verification, Filing/Recording Documents, Competitive Intelligence

Information Types:
Licenses/Registrations/Permits (US)
Bankruptcy (US)
SEC/Other Financial (US)
Legislation/Regulation (US)
Trademarks/Patents (US)
Environmental (US)
Criminal Information (US)
Uniform Commercial Code (US)

Membership: AALL, SLA

Statement of Capabilities: WDS Inc provides publicly available documents from any civil, bankruptcy or criminal case filed anywhere in the US. The can obtain Supreme Court, Federal, Bankruptcy or State Court documents from anywhere in the US, usually faxed the same day of the request. In addition to the courts, WDS covers all Federal, State and local government agencies. WDS utilizes a full complement of online information sources in addition to their resident staff of experts and network of nationwide resources, to provide documents in the most efficient way possible.

West Group

620 Opperman Dr
Eagan, MN 55123
Telephone: **Fax:**
800-328-9352   612-687-7302
612-687-7000
www.westgroup.com

Year Founded: 1872

Clientele: Legal Profession

Applications: Legal Compliance, Current Events, General Business Information, Competitive Intelligence, Government Document Retrieval

Proprietary Products:

Name/Desc: West CD-ROM Libraries
Info Provided: Legislation/Regulations
Media: CD-ROM
Coverage: US

Name/Desc: Westlaw
Info Provided: Environmental, Legislation/Regulations
Media: Online Database
Coverage: US

Name/Desc: Westlaw
Info Provided: Corporate/Trade Name Data, Uniform Commercial Code
Media: Online Database
Coverage: US

Membership: SIIA

Statement of Capabilities: West Group is one of the largest providers of information to US legal professionals. West Group includes renowned names such as Barclays, Bancroft Whitney, Clark Boardman Callaghan, Counterpoint, Lawyers Cooperative Publishing, West Publishing and Westlaw. Westlaw is a computer-assisted research service consisting of more than 9,500 legal, financial and news databases, including Dow Jones News/Retrieval. West Group produces a total of more than 3,800 products including 300 CD-ROMs.

Free Web Information:

West legal Directory (WLD) is a database of attorneys and law firms. Users can find legal resources plus receive information about legal proceedings and search legal periodicals.

Western Regional Data Inc

PO Box 20520
Reno, NV 89515
Telephone: **Fax:**
702-329-9544   702-345-1652
www.wrdi.com

Year Founded: 1984

Clientele: Legal Profession, Business - General, Financial Institutions, Collection Agencies, Public Record Research Firms, Real Estate Owners/Managers, Direct Marketers

Applications: Direct Marketing, Asset/Lien Searching/Verification, Legal Compliance, Locating People/Businesses, Real Estate Transactions

Information Types:
Addresses/Telephone Numbers (NV)
Corporate/Trade Name Data (NV)
Voter Registration (NV)
Uniform Commercial Code (NV)
Legislation/Regulation (NV)

Proprietary Products:

Name/Desc: WRDI's Lead Focus
Info Provided: Real Estate Assessor and Vital Records
Media: Fax-on-Demand, Lists or labels, Disk, Internet and Microfilm/Microfiche
Coverage: NV

Membership: NPRRA

Statement of Capabilities: Western Regional Data (WDRI) gathers public record information from all 17 counties in Nevada and state agencies, making it available in one online system. The information includes property tax data, building permits, business licenses and other less well known types of public records. They have a new program called "Lead Focus" that makes available targeted mailing list data with more than 35 ways to pinpoint your market.

Wholesale Information Network Inc

703 Broadway #510
Vancouver, WA 98660
Telephone: **Fax:**
800-942-7744   888-695-7007
www.win-world.com

Year Founded: 1994

Applications: Background Info - Individuals, Asset/Lien Searching/Verification, Litigation

Information Types:
Criminal Information (US)
Driver and/or Vehicle (US)

Licenses/Registrations/Permits (US)
Litigation/Judgments/Tax Liens (US)
Uniform Commercial Code (US)
Vital Records (US)
Credit Information (US)

Statement of Capabilities: The Wholesale Information Network offers 24-72 hour turnaround time for $10 per search or less for volume orders. They specialize in criminal history retrieval nationwide. Their research is performed "hands on" at the local courthouses around the nation.

WinStar Telebase Inc

435 Devon Park Dr #600
Wayne, PA 19087
Telephone: **Fax:**
800-220-4664   610-341-9447
610-254-2420
www.telebase.com

Year Founded: 1984

Clientele: Business - General, Consumers (Individuals), Private Investigators, Property Owners/Managers

Applications: General Business Information, Background Info - Business, Direct Marketing, Competitive Intelligence, Collections

Information Types:
Addresses/Telephone Numbers (US, International)
Trademarks/Patents (US, International)
News/Current Events (US, International)
Credit Information (US, International)

Proprietary Products:

Name/Desc: Brainwave
Info Provided: SEC/Other Financial, Corporate/Trade Name Data, Trademarks/Patents
Media: Direct Online
(www.brainwave.telebase.com
Coverage: US, International

Name/Desc: Iquest
Info Provided: Corporate/Trade Name Data, Addresses/Telephone Numbers, News/Current Events, Credit Information, Trademarks/Patents, SEC/Other Financial
Media: Direct Online via CompuServe and www.request.telebase.com
Coverage: US, International

Name/Desc: LEXIS-NEXIS Caselow @AOL
Info Provided: Litigation/Judgments/Tax Liens
Media: Direct Online via America Online - Keyword: LEXIS-NEXIS
Coverage: US

Name/Desc: Dun & Bradstreet @ AOL
Info Provided: Credit Information, Addresses/Telephone Numbers
Media: Direct Online via America Online, Keyword: D&B
Coverage: US

Membership: SPA/SIIA

Statement of Capabilities: Winstar Telebase's Information Services are designed for people with little or no online searching experience and provide easy access to business information for sales prospecting, market analysis, competitive intelligence, product development, and other research. Several thousand sources, from over 450 databases, are available including credit reports, financial reports, company directories, magazines, newspapers, newswires, industry newsletters, etc. For a list of distribution partners visit www.telebase.com.

Free Web Information:
Product information and registration

National Associations

Throughout the Company Profiles section, firms indicated (by acronym) their affiliation with national organizations

Listed on the following two pages are the organizations with their full names, web sites and membership numbers.

Acronym	Organization	Web Site	Members
AALL	American Assn of Law Librarians	www.aallnet.org/index.asp	4600
AAMVA	American Assn of Motor Vehicle Administrators	www.aamva.org/	1500
AAPL	American Assn of Professional Landmen	www.landman.ord	7000
ABA	American Bar Assn	www.abanet.org/home.html	417000
ABA (2)	American Banking Assn	www.aba.com	470
ABFE	American Board of Forensic Examiners	www.acfe.com	12000
ABI	American Bankruptcy Institute	www.abiworld.org/	6500
ABW	American Business Women	www.abwahq.org/	80000
ACA	American Collectors Assn	www.collector.com/home.html	3500
ACFE	Assn of Certified Fraud Examiners	http://cfenet.com/	20000
AFIO	Assn of Former Intelligence Officers	www.his.com/afio	2500
AICPA	Assn of Certified Public Accountants	www.aicpa.org/	330000
AIIP	Assn of Independent Information Professionals	www.aiip.org/	750
AIPLA	American Intellectual Property Law Assn	www.aipla.org/	10000
ALA	American Library Assn	www.ala.org/	56800
ALTA	American Land Title Association	www.alta.org/	2400
AMA	American Management Assn	www.amanet.org/	70000
APA (2)	American Psychological Assn	www.apa.org/	155000
APG	Assn of Professional Genealogists	www.apgen.org/~apg/	1000
ASIS	American Society for Industrial Security	www.asisonline.org	40000
ASLET	American Society of Law Enforcement Trainers	www.aslet.com/	
ASSE	American Society of Safety Engineers	www.asse.org/	35000
ATA	American Truckers Assn	www.trucking.org	4100
ATLA	Assn of Trial Lawyers of America	www.atlanet.org	56000
BMC	Bureau of Missing Children Inc	http://pw2.netcom.com/ ~repoguy/missing.html	
CII	Council of Intl Investigators	www.cii2.org/	
DMA	Direct Marketing Assn	www.the-dma.org	4500
EAE	Environmental Assessment Assn	www.iami.org/eaa.html	3500
EMA	Employment Management Assn	www.shrm.org/EMA/	4200
EPIC	Evidence Photographers Intl Council	www.epic-photo.org/	1000
FBINAA	FBI Natl Academy Assn	www.fbinaa.org/	17000
IAAI	Intl Assn of Arson Investigators	www.fire-investigators.org	9000
IAHSS	Intl Assn of Healthcare Security & Safety	www.iahss.org/	
IALEIA	Intl Assn of Law Enforcement Intelligence Analysts	www.ialeia.org/	1000
ICA	Intl Credit Asssn	www.ica-credit.org	10500
IIAA	Independent Insurance Agents of America	www.iiaa.org/	300000
INA	Intl Nanny Assn	www.nanny.org/index.html	
INOA	Intl Narcotics Officers Assn	www.ineoa.org/	
INTA	Intl Trademark Assn	www.inta.org/	
ION	Investigative Open Network	www.ioninc.com/index.html	500
IREM	Institute of Real Estate Management	www.irem.org/	8600
LES	Licensing Executive Society	www.usa-canada.les.org/	4700
MBAA	Mortgage Bankers Assn of America	www.mbaa.org/	2700

Acronym	Organization	Web Site	Members
NABEA	Natl Assn of Bail Enforcement Agents	www.ranchochamber.org/ members1/v01/909-989-0505.html	
NAC	Natl Assn of Counselors	http://nac.lincoln-grad.org	500
NACM	Natl Assn of Credit Managers	www.nacm.org	35000
NAFE	Natl Assn of Female Executives	www.nafs.com	150000
NAFI	Natl Assn of Fire Investigators	www.eku.edu/fse/nafi/home.htm	5000
NAHB	Natl Assn of Home Builders	www.nahb.com/	197000
NAHRO	Natl Assn of Housing & Redvlp Officials	www.nahro.org/	8500
NAIS	Natl Assn of Investigative Specialists	www.pimall.com/nais/nais.menu.html	3000
NALA	Natl Assn of Legal Assistants	www.nala.org/	17000
NALFM	Natl Assn of Law Firm Marketers	www.legalmarketing.org	1000
NALI	Natl Assn of Legal Investigators	www.nali.com	800
NALSC	Natl Assn of Legal Search Consultants	www.nalsc.org/	130
NAMSS	Natl Assn of Medical Staff Svcs	www.namss.org/	4000
NAPIA	Natl Assn of Public Insurance Adjustors	www.napia.com/	
NAPPS	Natl Assn of Professional Process Servers	www.napps.org/	1100
NAR	Natl Assn of Realtors	www.realtor.com	805000
NAREIT	Natl Assn of Real Estate Investment Trusts	www.nareit.org/	1080
NARPM	Natl Assn of Residential Property Managers	www.nareit.org/	1400
NASA	Natl Assn of Screening Agencies	www.n-a-s-a.com/	25
NASIR	Natl Assn of Security & Investgt Regulators	www.nasir.org/	90
NAWBO	Natl Assn of Women Business Owners	www.nawbo.org/nawbo/nawbostart.nsf	3000
NCIS	Natl Council of Investigation & Security	www.ncis.com	
NCJHS	Natl Criminal Justice Honor Society	www.fiu.edu/~aps_natl/apsindex.htm	
NCRA	Natl Court Reporters Assn	www.usps.gov	23
NDIA	Natl Defender Investigator Assn	www.ncraonline.org/	32000
NFIB	Natl Federation of Independent Businesses	www.ndia-inv.org/index.htm	650
NFIP	Natl Flood Insurance Program	www.nfib.org/	600000
NFPA	Natl Federation of Paralegal Assn	www.fema.gov/nfip/	
NGS	Natl Genealogical Society	www.ngsgenealogy.org	
NHEMA	Natl Home Equity Mortgage Assn	www.nhema.org/	240
NHRA	Natl Human Resources Assn	www.humanresources.org/	1500
NICA	Natl Insurance Claims Assn	www.gonatgo.com/	
NLG	Natl Lawyers Guild	www.nlg.org/	6000
NPPRA	Natl Public Record Research Assn	www.nprra.com	450
PIHRA	Professionals in Human Resources Assn	www.pihra.org/	3500
PLA	Public Library Assn	www.pla.org	
PRRN	Public Record Retriever Network	www.brbpub.com	672
REIPA	Real Estate Information Providers Assn	www.reipa.org	
SCIP	Society of Competitive Intelligence Professionals	www.scip.org	6500
SFSA	Society of Former Special Agents of the FBI	socxfbi.org/	7800
SHRM	Society of Human Resources Management	www.shrm.org	65000
SILA	Society of Insurance License Administrators	www.slia.org	
SLA	Special Libraries Assn	www.sla.org	14000
USFN	US Foreclosure Network	www.usfn.org	
WAD	World Assn of Detectives	www.wad.net	

Useful Internet Resources

Over the last five years, the Internet has become a major source of business and government information. What follows are detailed profiles of selected web sites that are oriented toward finding information about people and businesses. They are grouped into the following categories:

♦ General Business & Competitive Intelligence

♦ Government Records

♦ Miscellaneous Recommended Sites

♦ Privacy

Remember that many of the private companies profiled in this book (in the previous section) also have excellent web sites.

The privacy section includes great sites for those interested in finding out how to minimize their "exposure."

The sites for this chapter were submitted by and used with the permission of **Alan M. Schlein**. Mr. Schlein is the author of *Find It Online* (1999, 513 pages, $19.95). This excellent book can be purchased at a local bookstore or by calling 1-800-929-3811. The book contains more than 1,200 web site profiles and is an excellent resource guide for performing online research.

General Business & Competitive Intelligence

Acxiom Direct Media

www.directmedia.com

Sells mailing lists.

Fee-Based Site

American City Business Journals

www.amcity.com

More than 35 local business publications pooled together. Includes in-depth details about companies headquartered by region. Searchable either all at once, or one by one.

American Demographics / Marketing Tools

www.demographics.com

The nationally-reknowned magazine company offers access to the magazine's archives and also its sister publication Marketing Tools.

American Real Estate Exchange, The (Amrex)

www.amrex.com

Real estate information site with extensive resources including property data

Fee-Based Site

American Society of Association Executives

www.asaenet.org

The central clearinghouse of the thousands of trade associations based in Washington, D.C. Links more than 1700 associations searchable by name of association.

Association of Independent Information Professionals (AIIP)

www.aiip.org

Source for finding professional researchers.

AT&T Business Network

www.bnet.att.com

This free site has links to more than 1000 business sites and offers reviews of several market research sites.

Bank Rate Monitor

www.bankrate.com

Banking site with international information, newsletters includes calculators for mortgage rates and other things to help you customize to your needs.

Barron's

www.barrons.com

Published weekly by Dow Jones. Provides investment information and analysis to both individuals and institutional investors.

BizWiz

www.clickit.com/touch/bizwiz.htm

A business supersite.

Briefings.com

www.briefings.com

Business newsletters and magazines.

Fees for Some Content

Business Advisor - Deloitte & Touche

www.dtonline.com/ba/ba.htm

Deloitte & Touche business adviser.

Business Wire

www.businesswire.com

PR wire for business announcements – great for locating what information a company wants the public to know.

BusinessWeek Online

www.businessweek.com

Publishes its entire text online as well as many value-added features including tables, graphics and photos, a topical article library, current stock market information and hourly market news updates in Real Audio format.

Fees for Some Content

CARL Corporation

www.carl.org

Click on Search CARL or Search UnCover. CARL provides an article delivery service with a table of contents database and an index to nearly 18,000 periodicals.

Fee-Based Site

CBS MarketWatch

www.cbsmarketwatch.com

Excellent site for breaking news on business issues.

CEO Express

www.ceoexpress.com

Collection of business news tools.

Charles Schwab & Co.

www.schwab.com

Investors' resource center for business info.

CIT Group

www.citgroup.com/insi.htm

CIT Group's resources page.

CNET's News.Com

www.news.com

CNET's news site for high tech issues.

CompaniesOnline

www.companiesonline.com

Short company capsule profiles from Dun and Bradstreet and Lycos.

Fees for Some Content

Company News On Call

www.prnewswire.com/cnoc/cnoc.html

PR Newswire's company research database, allows you to search for news or PR stories about specific companies

Corporate Information

www.corporateinformation.com

Information on private and international companies.

Corporate Watch: Researching Corporations

www.corpwatch.org/trac/resrch/resrch.html

Corporate Watch's "How to Research a Transnational Company." Contains valuable tips.

CorpTech

www.corptech.com

Background on private companies, geared to high tech companies.

Crain's New York Business

www.crainsny.com

Another good regional business site.

Daily Stocks

www.dailystocks.com

One of the best sites online for information on investing.

Derwent information

www.derwent.com

Patent and scientific information.

Fee-Based Site

DIALOG Web
www.dialog.com

Among the largest fee-based services; offers people finders, business, credit, legal, public records and other databases.

Fee-Based Site

Direct Marketing Association
www.the-dma.org

Trade association for direct marketing industry.

Disclosure SEC Site
www.disclosure-investor.com

Disclosure Inc's SEC site, loaded with resources.

Fee-Based Site

Dow Jones Interactive
www.dowjones.com

Among the largest fee-based services – offers people finders, business, credit, legal, public records and other databases.

EBN Interactive
http://gretel.econ.surrey.ac.uk/~ivan/WebDoc/ebn-inde.htm

European business resource.

EDGAR Access
http://edgar.disclosure.com/ea

Inexpensive way to track companies. Reports can be full-text EDGAR filings or short summaries.

Fee-Based Site

Edward Lowe Foundation
www.lowe.org

Extensive Small Business Resource Center.

Entrepreneur Magazine's BizSquare
www.entrepreneurmag.com

Enterpreneur Magazine and links.

European Patent Office
www.european-patent-office.org

European patent and trademark information.

Export@ll.net
www.exportall.net

Site with strong international links for export-related and country-specific info.

Family Business
www.smartbiz.com/sbs/cats/family.htm

Small Business Supersite from Smart Biz.

Fidelity
www.fidelity.com

Fidelity Investments resource center.

Financenter
www.financenter.com

Personal finance site with tools.

Financial Web
www.financialweb.com

Thorough business resource site.

FIND/SVP

www.findsvp.com

Major market research firm with their own web site. Reports can be bought through their commercial online services. Also host of excellent Information Adviser newsletter.

Fees for Some Content

First Call Corporation

www.firstcall.com

Provides corporate and industry research to the desktop via the Internet using Adobe Acrobat.

Fee-Based Site

FreeEDGAR

www.freeedgar.com

E-mail notification of SEC filings.

Frost & Sullivan

www.frost.com

International marketing, consulting and training company with their own web site. Reports must be purchased through online providers or a client. Expensive.

Fees for Some Content

Fuld & Company Inc

www.fuld.com

Competitive intelligence web site.

Fuld & Company Inc: CI Strategies & Tools

www.fuld.com/i3

Competitive intelligence tools.

Gale Group

www.gale.com

Provides easy access to brand and manufacturing information and Gale's Business Resources database, which has detailed information on more than 400,000 American and foreign companies.

Fee-Based Site

Gomez Advisors

www.gomez.com

Independent rating of top online stockbrokers.

Green Book, The

www.greenbook.org

The New York Chapter of the American Marketing Association publishes a free directory of market research firms. This is a valuable free source to identify companies in specific industries.

GT Online

www.gt.com/gtonline/ind_tc_main.html

GT Online resources page.

IAC InSite

www.iac-insite.com

An excellent collection of news related resources in an easily searchable database.

Fee-Based Site

IBM Infomarket

www.infomarket.ibm.com

A web based research service that lets you search both the Internet and private databases simultaneously. Priced on a per document basis.

Fee-Based Site

IBM Intellectual Property Network

http://patent.womplex.ibm.com

Searches US Patent and Trademark files.

IDS: The Internet Database Service

www.csa.com/ijs-desc.html

Cambridge Information Group publishes the Worldwide Directory of Market Research Reports, Studies and Surveys, which can be located on Dialog and also at Cambridge Scientific Abstracts Internet Database Service.

iMarket Inc

www.imarketinc.com

This site requires registration, features New Business Leads Online, which can help you identify business prospects and generate mailing lists.
Fees for Some Content

Inc.'s Resources for Growing Small Business

www.inc.com

Inc Magazine's online resources

Infobel: International Directories

www.infobel.be/infobel/infobelworld.html

International business resources.

Internet Public Library's Associations on the Net (AON)

www.ipl.org/ref/AON

Another great collection of association sites.

INTERNET.ORG!

www.internet.org

This site offers a lookup site for companies and domains.

IPO Central

www.ipocentral.com

Current list of initial public offerings. This site also has a comprehensive list of all US IPOs filed since mid-1996. It also provides some news and analysis on a weekly basis.

Larry Chase's Web Digest for Marketers

http://wdfm.com

Good collection of business sites from Larry Chase. Regularly updated with fresh links regularly with marketing tools.

Merrill Lynch Financial News & Research Center

www.merrill-lynch.ml.com/financial/index.html

Resource for finding analysts/brokers reports.
Fees for Some Content

Mining Company, The: Business

www.miningcompany.com/business

Gathers and packages business information for users.

Montague Institute

www.montague.com

Competitive intelligence web site.

Motley Fool

www.fool.com

A high profile business resource center.

MSN Money Center Investor

http://investor.msn.com

A business-oriented resource collection.

NASD Regulation

www.nasdr.com

This is the regulatory arm of the National Association of Securities Deadlers, the organization that separately runs the Nasdaq Stock Market. It's public disclosure program helps investors to select brokers or securities firms.

National Association for the Self Employed

www.membership.com/nase

National Association for the Self-Employed's resource list.

NetPartners Internet Solutions: Company Locator

www.netpartners.com/resources/search.html

Searches a database of web addresses from InterNIC, an organization that provides Internet registration services. The database primarily contains American companies.

Newsbytes News Network

www.nbnn.com

Telecommunications business resource from Post-Newsweek.

Fee-Based Site

NewsEdge Company Lookup

www.companylink.com

From NewsPage. It provides contact information, ticker symbol (if public) state and industry. This site also links you to press releases from the company's themselves, stock quotes, news articles and financial filings. Registration also entitles you to information about competitors.

OneSource Information Services

www.OneSource.com

Company and industry information.

Fee-Based Site

Open Source Solutions

www.oss.net

Competitive intelligence web site.

PAWWS Financial Network

www.pawws.com

Brokerage and business resources

PR Newswire

www.prnewswire.com

PR news wire for business.

Princeton University Survey Research Center

www.princeton.edu/~abelson/index.html

Links to a lot of survey and polling information, including the Gallup and Pew Research Centers.

Profound

www.profound.com

Database of over 20 million articles, reports and studies.

Fee-Based Site

Proquest Direct

www.umi.com

Extensive business-news database.

Fee-Based Site

Public Register's Annual Report Service, The (PRARS)

www.prars.com

An annual report service.

QPAT-US

www.qpat.com

Patent information.

Fee-Based Site

Responsive Database Services

www.rdsinc.com

Database of several business resources, including Table Base, a collection of graphs and charts on business resources

Fee-Based Site

Reuters Business Information

www.bizinfo.reuters.com

One of many Reuters' tailored services, this one is just business briefing resources – this one goes back 10 years with more than 2000 publications.

SBFocus.com: Small Business Information Search Engine

www.sbfocus.com

Searches through thousands of business web sites, finds resources relevant to the needs of small businesses, and indexes only those sites.

SilverPlatter

www.silverplatter.com

Proprietary site with organization and special business listings.

Fee-Based Site

Small Business Administration

www.sbaonline.sba.gov

Government clearinghouse on small business.

Small Business Journal

www.tsbj.com

Small Business Journal magazine.

Society of Competitive Intelligence Professionals

www.scip.org

Association of competitive intelligence folks

System for Electronic Document Analysis & Retrieval (SEDAR)

www.sedar.com

Searches Canada's electronic securities documentation filing system. Also in French.

The Street.Com

www.thestreet.com

A news wire for Wall Street related issues.

Thomas Register of American Manufacturers

www.thomasregister.com

Catalog of manufacturers and products covering 155,000 companies in the US, Canada and Mexico.

Thomson & Thomson

www.thomson-thomson.com

An excellent trademark site.

Trade Show Central

www2.tscentral.com

A clearinghouse of trade shows – good for finding background info on companies.

Transium Corporation

www.transium.com

An extensive database of business information.

Fees for Some Content

US Patent & Trademark Office

www.uspto.gov

The Federal Government's patent information center.

USADATA

www.usadata.com/usadata/market

Market data by community and region.

Wall Street Journal Interactive Edition

www.wsj.com

News and information services from the Dow Jones Company net.

Fees for Some Content

Washington Researchers

www.researchers.com/
freefact.html

A factsheet for competitive intelligence researchers.

WorldOpinion

www.worldopinion.com/wo

International market research, this site has all kinds of interesting links as well.

Zacks Investment Research Inc

www.zacks.com

An extensive collection of business market information.

Fees for Some Content

Government Records

Bureau of Economic Analysis in the Commerce Department

www.bea.doc.gov

Statistical analysis and information from the Commerce Department's site for business & investments.

Bureau of Justice Statistics

www.ojp.usdoj.gov/bjs

Justice Department statistics collection, includes crime numbers.

Bureau of Labor Statistics

www.bls.gov

One of the top statistical collections, from the Federal government's Labor Department.

Bureau of Transportation Statistics

www.bts.gov

US Department of Transportation stats, an extensive list.

Center for Responsive Politics

www.crp.org

Excellent advocacy site for tracking campaign information.

CIA World Factbook

www.cia.gov/cia/publications/
factbook/index.html

Reference tool for background information on countries.

CNN/Time All Politics

http://allpolitics.com/1997/
index.html

CNN/CQ's combined site – best place for political news online.

Commerce Business Daily

http://cbdnet.gpo.gov

Commerce Business Daily is the government's list of all bids and contracts and announcement awards. Essential reading for anyone wanting to do business with the government. Available free from the government or for pay on many sources.

Commonly Requested Federal Services

www.whitehouse.gov/WH/Services

Central resource for federal sites.

Congressional Quarterly

www.cq.com

News magazine covering US Congress.

Defense LINK - US Department of Defense (DOD)

www.defenselink.mil

Main Pentagon site.

Defense Technical Information Center (DTIC)

www.dtic.mil

Pentagon's thorough site for technology-related military things.

Department of Education: Topics A to Z

http://ed.gov/topicsaz.html

US Education Department's links to the best starting points on a variety of educational topics.

Documents Center

www.lib.umich.edu/libhome/
Documents.center/index.html

University of Michigan's superb document clearinghouse.

EDGAR Database

www.sec. gov/edgarhp.htm

A searchable database of publicly held companies, which are required by law to file information with the SEC.

EDGAR Online People

http://people.edgar-
online.com/people

Allows users to search the SEC filings for information about executives by name. Indexes are free, details cost money. Information is available from the last six months of proxy statements.

Fees for Some Content

EPA's Toxic Release Inventory TRI Query Form

www.epa.gov/enviro/html/
tris/tris_query_java.html

Environmental Protection Agency's database of company toxic filings.

Establishment Search in Occupational Safety & Health Administration (OSHA)

www.osha.gov/cgi-bin/est/est1

Database of health inspection reports.

FAA Office of System Safety, Safety Data

http://nasdac.faa.gov/
safety_data

Federal Aviation Administration safety data site, including "Excel" and Bureau of Transportation statistics.

FDIC (Federal Deposit Insurance Corporation) Institutions

http://www2.fdic.gov/structur/
search

US government's database of banks and other institution ownership.

Federal Election Commission (FEC)

www.fec.gov

Official site to track campaign-related information.

Federal Web Locator, The

www.law.vill.edu/
Fed-Agency/fedwebloc.html

Links to thousands of government agencies and departments.

FedLaw

http://fedlaw.gsa.gov

Resource for federal legal and regulatory research. It has more than 1600 links to legal-related information and is operated by the General Services Organization.

Fedstats

www.fedstats.gov

Central clearinghouse for government statistical sites.

FedWorld

www.fedworld.gov

Collection of 14,000 government sites, including bulletin boards so you can reach government employees with expertise on many subjects.

FindLaw

www.findlaw.com

Well-organized directory of Internet legal sites.

FindLaw: Law Crawler

www.lawcrawler.com/index.html

Search engine for legal resources.

Foreign Government Resources on the Web

www.lib.umich.edu/libhome/Documents.center/frames/forfr.html

Excellent list of foreign government resources.

Free *Congressional Quarterly* Sites: American Voter

http://voter.cq.com

Search for Congressional lawmaker's voting records.

Geneva International Forum

http://geneva.intl.ch/geneva-intl/gi/egimain/edir.htm

International resources for business.

Global Computing

www.globalcomputing.com/states.html

State-by-state resources.

Governments on the WWW

www.gksoft.com/govt

A great collection of international and local government related servers.

Healthfinder

www.healthfinder.org

Great starting point for health resources.

IGnet: Internet for Federal IG Community

www.ignet.gov

Collection of reports and information from the Inspector General of as many as 60 federal agency departments.

International Agencies & Information on the Web

www.lib.umich.edu/libhome/Documents.Center/frames/intlfr.html

International and inter-governmental web sites lists.

International Documents Task Force (IDTF)

www.library.nwu.edu/govpub/idtf/home.html

Documents from international organizations and governents, with links.

Internet Law Library

http://law.house.gov

Congressional resources for lawyers.

Inter-Parliamentary Union

www.ipu.org

Links to parliamentary web sites around the world – elections information.

Law Library of Congress

http://lcweb2.loc.gov/glin/lawhome.html

Law library of the Library of Congress.

Legal Information Institute

www.law.cornell.edu

One of the best legal libraries online. (Cornell's law school page).

Library of Congress

www.loc.gov

The main site for the Library of Congress.

Meta-Index for US Legal Research

http://gsulaw.gsu.edu/metaindex

Central clearinghouse for circuit court opinions.

Monthly Estimates of the US Population

www.census.gov/population/
estimates/nation/intfile1-1.txt

Downloadable text files of population estimate information.

NASIRE: National Association of State Information Resource Executivies (NASIRE)

www.nasire.org

State-specific information on state government innovations.

National Archives & Records Administration

www.nara.gov

Presidential libraries of all past American presidents.

National Atlas of the United States of America

www-atlas.usgs.gov

Official maps.

National Council of State Legislators

www.ncsl.org/public/
sitesleg.htm

Search for state legislation.

National Science Foundation

www.nsf.gov

This site is focused mainly on the bureaucratic structure of this government agency; but on the interior pages you'll find a wealth of scientific information. Recommended visit: the external links page to National Science Foundation-funded sites –here you'll find the research, supercomputing, and engineering centers that do the work.

National Technical Information Service (NTIS)

www.ntis.gov

Federal government reports related to technology and science.

NTSB (National Traffic Safety Board) Aviation Accident/Incident Database

http://nasdac.faa.gov/asp/
asy_ntsb.asp

Transportation Safety Board's database of aircraft accidents.

Oyez Oyez Oyez

http://oyez.nwu.edu/

Information about Supreme Court cases, including some actual proceedings in Real Audio format.

PACER - Directory of Electronic Public Access Services

www.uscourts.gov/PubAccess.html

Federal court's electronic bulletin board of docket numbers, case summaries and opinions.

Regions & Countries Information

www.ita.doc.gov/ita_home/
itacnreg.html

US Dept. of Commerce International Trade Administration's country and regional resource site, good for trade-related issues.

Social Law Library

www.socialaw.com

A great legal research site including international law sites.

State & Local Government on the 'Net

www.piperinfo.com/state/
states.html

State government resources as well as local ones.

State Court Locator, The

www.law.vill.edu/State-Ct

State court locator.

State Poverty Rates

www.census.gov/hhes/poverty/
poverty96/pv96state.html

HTML tables of US Census information.

State Web Locator, The

www.law.vill.edu/
State-Agency/index.html

State web locator.

StateLaw: State & Local Government - Executive, Legislative & Judicial Information

http://lawlib.wuacc.edu/
washlaw/uslaw/statelaw.html

State Internet resoruces, legislation, courts, statutes, etc.

Stateline.Org

www.stateline.org

The Pew Center on the States, tracking policy developments on a state-by-state basis.

StateSearch - Sponsored by NASIRE

www.nasire.org/ss

The state government search site.

Statistical Abstract of the US

www.census.gov:80/
stat_abstract.

US Government's statistical resource.

STAT-USA

www.stat-usa.gov

Comprehensive collection of federal statistics from all agencies.

Fee-Based Site

Superintendant of Documents Home Page (Government Printing Office)

www.access.gpo.gov/
su_docs/index.html

The Government Printing Office.

TaxWeb

www.taxweb.com

Consumer-oriented directory for federal and state information.

Thomas - US Congress on the Internet

http://thomas.loc.gov

Search for federal legislation.

United Nations System

www.unsystem.org

Foreign government resources.

US Census Bureau

www.census.gov

Clearinghouse for statistics, includes the current edition of the Statistical Abstracts, a great reference book. Search by city, state, ZIP Code or specific industries.

US Federal Government Agencies Directory

www.lib.lsu.edu/gov/fedgov.html

Links to hundreds of federal government Internet sites.

US Government Information

www-libraries.colorado.edu/
ps/gov/us/federal.htm

A clearinghouse of government sites

US Postal Service ZIP Code Lookup

www.usps.gov/ncsc

US Postal Services's ZIP Code lookup service.

US Securities & Exchange Commission (SEC)

www.sec.gov

One of the top government sites, let's you track information about publicly held companies.

US State Department: Regions

www.state.gov/www/regions.html

Information and news from around the world.

USADATA

www.usadata.com/usadata/market

Market data by community and region.

USGS National Mapping Information

http://mapping.usgs.gov

The federal government's site with global land information, online data, and map ordering.

Web sites on National Parliaments

www.soc.umn.edu/~sssmith/
Parliaments.html

Resource of foreign government sites.

Welcome To The White House

www.whitehouse.gov

The White House's site.

WWW Virtual Library: Law: State Government

www.law.indiana.edu/
law/v-lib/states.html

A collection of state government resources.

Miscellaneous Recommended Sites

555-1212.com
www.555-1212.com

Phone books online. Better than many others because you can search several of the other web telephone services from this site.

Ancestry.com
www.ancestry.com

Geneology company; offers SSN's death index free.

Fees for Some Content

Bigfoot
www.bigfoot.com

This e-mail search tool is one of the best. Includes e-mail listings by state and white page information by state and city.

BigYellow
www.bigyellow.com

National business listings - searchable by name and type of business. Also has a good e-mail finder and phone lookup.

Black Book Online
www.crimetime.come/online.html

Robert Scott's excellent site geared to investigators includes links to sites for reverse directories and other phone books, state and federal records online, non-profit sites, verdict and settlement sites, and some pay databases.

Black's LawPage
www.tfs.net/~dlblack/lawpage.html

A nice collection of legal-related sites.

California Sex Offenders
www.sexoffenders.net

Site that tracks sex offenders who have been released into communities.

Canada411
http://canada411.sympatico.ca

A Canadian phone book for almost all provinces and territories.

Church Family History Library
www.lds.org/en/2-Family_History/Family_History_Main.html

Good starting place for genealogical research. Find search strategies, forms, and directions to access LDS's reasonably priced Family Searcher and Personal Ancestral File databases, available from the Church or its local Family History Centers..

CompData
www.compdatagovtedi.com

EDEX data about Workers' Compensation claims.

Contacts Directory, The
www.dir.org

Phone, fax and e-mail contact information for companies and individuals.

Cyber 411
www.cyber411.com

Sixteen search engines, advanced queries, yellow pages, maps, directories, white pages and e-mail.

Dogpile
www.dogpile.com

The most complex, but easily the most thorough of all the meta-tools. It allows you to run your query in as many as 25 search engines at once. For some reason, however, it does not include Northern Light. It's customized features allows you to pick which engines and directories you want to look in.

Greg Notess'

www.imt.net/~notess

Shows how search engines rank pages.

HotBot

www.hotbot.com

HotBot is one of the more complex search engines, but that's because it offers you so many options to focus your search. It lets you do several kinds of specific research at the very beginning of your search, like narrowing for photos or images.

Information & Privacy, The Office of

www.usdoj.gov.oip

Various filtering agents and bots.

International Association of Assessing Officers (IAAO)

www.iaao.org

Education and trade arm for tax assessors worldwide; also, web site links.

Internet Sleuth, The

www.isleuth

The Internet Sleuth, or iSleuth, is a meta-tool that runs as many as six other search tools at once. It also allows Top, Reviewed, New, and Best of Web searches.

MetaCrawler

www.metacrawler.com

A meta-search tool – it allows you to search multiple Internet directories simultaneously.

Mining Company, The

www.miningcompany.com

Evaluative guides on over 500 subject areas. A top quality subject directory.

Public Interest Research Groups (PIRG)

www.pirg.org/reports/consumer

Consumer protection information, environmental concerns, dangerous toys, tobacco, etc.

Public Interest Research Groups Credit Bureaus

www.pirg.org/reports/consumer/credti

PIRG carries issues about credit bureaus.

Public Record Retriever Network

www.brbpub.com/prrn

Record retrieval companies and public record news.

SavvySearch

www.savvysearch.com/search

This meta-search tool is particularly good for looking up international sites, allowing searches in many languages. You can limit your search to people finders, reference tools and images. You can also vary the way the results are presented, getting one continuous list or separate lists, by different search engines. Leaving the integrate results box unchecked allows you to see which search engine is helping most.

Snap

www.snap.com

Sixteen major topics, plus chat, free e-mail, message boards, yellow pages, maps, classifieds, downloads, stock quotes horoscopes and searching.

Telephone Directories On the Web

www.contractjobs.com/tel

A great site for finding telephone directories for countries other than the US. Includes links to online telephone, fax and business directories from around the world.

Transactional Records Access Clearinghouse (TRAC)

http://trac.syr.edu

Amazing collection of law enforcement related information that can be localized to your region.

Ultimate White Pages

www.theultimates.com/white

The white pages online.

UT Austin Search: Searching for People

www.utexas.edu/search/
email.html

Good collection of e-mail address finders.

WebCrawler

www.webcrawler.com

Both a search directory and a search engine. Owned by the Excite company.

Yahoo!

www.yahoo.com

Categorizes subjects into 14 topics and hundreds of subtopics, one of the most thorough of the subject directories.

Yahoo! - Search Engines

www.yahoo.com/Computers_and_Int
ernet/Internet/World_Wide_Web/S
earching_the_Web/Search_Engines

A comprehensive list of search engines.

Privacy

Anonymizer

www.anonymizer.com

Tool for anonymous remailing.

Fees for Some Content

CDT | Internet Family Empowerment White Paper

www.cdt.org/speech/empower.html

A white paper on Internet Parental Empowerment Tools by the Center for Democracy and Technology.

Center for Democracy & Technology

www.cdt.org

Center for Democracy and Technology's excellent privacy site, which allows you to find out what people know about you when you visit their site.

CyberAngels.org Home Page

www.cyberangels.org

Safety and educational programing.

Electronic Privacy Information Center

www.epic.org

Privacy activist group.

HNC Software Inc.

www.hncs.com

Check fraud detection system software and other products.

Fee-Based Site

Junkbusters

www.junkbusters.com/ht/en/cookies.html

Explanation of cookie technology and privacy ramifications.

KidsCom: Play Smart, Stay Safe & Have Fun!

www.kidscom.com

Children's resources and entertainment.

National Fraud Information Center (NFIC)

www.fraud.org

Fights telemarketing fraud.

Pretty Good Privacy (PGP)

www.pgp.com/products/pgpfreeware.cgi

An encryption tool to protect your privacy.

Privacy Rights Clearinghouse

www.privacyrights.org

An activist site with excellent backgrounders on privacy issues.

Privacy Times

www.privacytimes.com

Privacy newsletter.

Fee-Based Site

Project OPEN/Protecting Your Privacy When You Go Online

www.isa.net/project-open/priv-broch.html

Privacy protection on the Internet.

QSpace Inc

www.qspace.com

An Oakland, CA company, allows you to fill out a form and within minutes you get your credit file on screen.

Fee-Based Site

Robert Brooks' Cookie Taste Test

www.geocities.com/SoHo/
4535/cookie.html

Expanation of "cookies."

The Lucent Personalized Web Assistant: Proxy Home Page

http://lpwa.com:8000

Let's you surf anonymously, protecting your privacy while you are on the Web.

Welcome to Engage Technologies | Accipiter

www.engagetech.com

A sophisticated marketing technology used by advertisers.